THE
DIVINE HOURS™

PRAYERS FOR SPRINGTIME

THE
DIVINE HOURS™

PRAYERS FOR SPRINGTIME:
A MANUAL FOR PRAYER

Compiled and with a Preface by

Phyllis Tickle

Doubleday

New York London Toronto Sydney Auckland

PUBLISHED BY DOUBLEDAY
a division of Random House, Inc.
1540 Broadway, New York, New York 10036

DOUBLEDAY and the portrayal of an anchor with a dolphin are trademarks
of Doubleday, a division of Random House, Inc.

The Divine Hours™ Tickle, Inc.

BOOK DESIGN BY RENATO STANISIC

Library of Congress Cataloging-in-Publication Data
The divine hours: prayers for springtime: a manual for prayer / compiled and
   with a preface by Phyllis Tickle.
        p.   cm.
     Includes index.
     1. Divine office—Texts.   2. Spring—Prayer-books and devotions—English.
   I. Tickle, Phyllis.
   BV199.D3 D58 2001
   264'.15—dc21   99-046531

ISBN 0-385-49758-X
Copyright © 2001 by Tickle, Incorporated

Contents

An Introduction to This Manual

Two things have from the beginning been the necessary form and mystery of Christian spirituality. Two things, even before the closing events of resurrection, ascension, and commission, wove disparate and often renegade believers into an inspirited body of the whole, connected to God and each other.

Like a double helix rendered elegant by complexity and splendid by authority, the amalgam of gospel and shared meal with the discipline of fixed-hour prayer were, and have remained, the chain of golden connection tying Christian to Christ and Christian to Christian across history, across geography, and across idiosyncrasies of faith. The former is known as the food and sustenance of the Church, the latter as its work. *The Divine Hours* is about the second part of this double strand, the work; it is a manual for the contemporary exercise of fixed-hour prayer.

Although designed primarily for private use by individuals or by small groups, *The Divine Hours* may certainly be employed by larger and/or more public communities. Likewise, though designed primarily for lay use, it can as well be employed by the ordained in either private or corporate prayer.

Those already familiar with fixed-hour prayer (variously referred to as "doing 'The Liturgy of the Hours' " or "keeping the hours" or "saying the offices") and with its tools (the breviaries of monastic worship and the Book of Hours manuals for laity that date from medieval times) will find some modifications and innovations here. They may wish to scan what follows for explication of these changes.

Others, especially those for whom keeping the hours is a new practice, may wish to read the remainder of this introduction more thoroughly.

A Brief History of Fixed-Hour Prayer

The Age of the Apostles

Fixed-hour prayer, while it is with the Eucharist the oldest surviving form of Christian spirituality, actually had its origins in the Judaism out of which Christianity came. Centuries before the birth of Jesus of Nazareth, the Hebrew psalmist wrote that "Seven times a day do I praise you." (Ps. 119:164) Although scholars do not agree on the hours of early Judaism's set prayers (they were probably adjusted and readjusted many times), we do know that by the first century a.d. the ritual of daily prayer had assumed two characteristics that would travel down the millennia to us: The prayers had been set or fixed into something very close to their present-day schedule, and they had begun to assume something very close to their present-day intention.

By the beginning of the common era, Judaism and its adherents were scattered across the Roman Empire, an empire whose efficiency and commerce depended in no small part upon the orderly and organized conduct of each business day. In the cities of the Empire, the forum bell rang the beginning of that day at six o'clock each morning (*prime* or "first" hour); noted the day's progress by striking again at nine o'clock (*terce* or third hour); sounded the lunch break at noon (*sext* or sixth hour); called citizens back to work by striking at three o'clock (*none* or ninth hour); and closed the day's markets by sounding again at six o'clock in the afternoon (vespers or evening hour). Every part of daily life within Roman culture eventually came, to some greater or lesser extent, to be ordered by the ringing of the forum bells, including Jewish prayer and, by natural extension, Christian prayer as well.

The first detailed miracle of the apostolic Church, the healing of the lame man on the Temple steps by Sts. Peter and John (Acts 3:1), occurred when and where it did because two devout Jews (who did not yet know they were Christians as such) were on their way to ninth-hour (three o'clock) prayers. Not many years later, one of the great defining events of Christianity—St. Peter's vision of the descending sheet filled with both clean and unclean animals—was to occur at noon on a rooftop because he had gone there to observe the sixth-hour prayers.

The directive Peter received during his noon devotion—i.e., to accept all that God had created as clean—was pivotal because it became the basis of the ecumenism that rapidly thereafter expanded Church fellowship beyond Jewry. Peter was on the roof, however, not by some accident of having been in that spot when the noon bell caught him, but by his own intention. In Joppa and far from Jerusalem and the Temple, Peter had sought out the solitude of his host's rooftop as a substitute site for keeping the appointed time of prayer.

Such readiness to accommodate circumstance was to become a characteristic of fixed-hour prayer. So too were some of the words Peter must have used. We know, for instance, that from its very earliest days, the Christian community incorporated the Psalms in their prayers. (Acts 4:23–30); and the Psalter has remained as the living core of the daily offices ever since. Likewise, by c. 60 a.d., the author of the first known manual of Christian practice, the *Didache*, was teaching the inclusion of the Lord's Prayer at least three times each day, a usage that was to expand quickly to include all the offices.

From the Apostles to the Early Fathers

As Christianity grew and, thanks to Peter's rooftop vision, as it spread, so too did the practice of formalized daily prayer. The process by which the fixed-hour prayers of the first century slowly recast themselves as the Divine Hours or Daily Offices of later Christians is blurred in some of its particulars, though we can attest to the approximate date and agency of many of them.

We know from their writings that by the second and third centuries the great Fathers of the Church—Clement (c. 150–215 a.d.), Origen (c. 185–254 a.d.), Tertullian (c. 160–225 a.d.), etc.—assumed as normative the observance of prayers in the morning and at night as well as for the so-called "little hours" of *terce, sext, and none* . . . or in modern parlance, nine a.m., noon, and three p.m. These daily prayers were often said or observed alone, though they could be offered by families or in small groups.

Regardless of whether or not the fixed-hour prayers were said alone or in community, however, they were never individualistic in nature. Rather, they employed the time-honored and time-polished prayers and recitations of the faith. Every Christian was to observe the prayers, none was empowered to create them.

Within the third century, the Desert Fathers, the earliest monastics of the Church, began to pursue the desideratum of living out, within their communities, St. Paul's admonition to "pray without ceasing." (I Th. 5:17) To accomplish this, they devised the stratagem of having one group of monks pass the praying of an office on seamlessly to another group of monks waiting to commence the next office. The result was the introduction into Christian thinking of the concept of a continuous cascade of prayer before the throne of God. That concept was to remain into our own time as a realized grace for many, many Christians, both monastic and lay.

Christians today, wherever they practice the discipline of fixed-hour prayer, frequently find themselves filled with a conscious awareness that they are handing their worship, at its final "Amen," on to other Christians in the next time zone. Like relay runners passing a lighted torch, those who do the work of fixed-hour prayer create thereby a continuous cascade of praise before the throne of God. To participate in such a regimen with such an awareness is to pray, as did the Desert Fathers, from within the spiritual community of shared texts as well as within the company of innumerable other Christians, unseen but present, who have preceded one across time or who, in time, will follow one.

From St. Benedict to the Middle Ages

Once the notion of unbroken and uninterrupted prayer had entered monastic practice, so too, almost by default, did much longer prayers enter there. Yet for all their lengthiness and growing complexity and cumbersomeness, the monks' fixed-hour prayers became normative for the religious in both the Eastern and the Western branches of the Church. By the fourth century, certainly, the principal characteristics of the daily offices as we know them today were plainly in place, and their organization would be more or less recognizable as such to us today.

Meanwhile for secular (i.e., nonmonastic) clergy and for the laity, the prayers appointed for the fixed hours were of necessity much, much shorter, often confined to something not unlike the brief minutes of present-day observance. There were also many public churches or basilicas that, despite their uncloistered nature, were pastored by monastic orders, and in these there was some, almost inevitable, blending of the two forms—i.e., of the cumbersome monastic and the far more economical lay practice. St. Benedict, for example, fashioned his famous Rule after the offices as they were observed by monastics in the open basilicas of Rome.

It was, of course, St. Benedict whose ordering of the prayers was to become a kind of master template against which all subsequent observance and structuring of the divine hours was to be tested. It was also Benedict who first said, *"Orare est laborare, laborare est orare."* "To pray is to work, to work is to pray." In so doing he gave form to another of the great, informing concepts of Christian spirituality—the inseparability of spiritual life from physical life. He also formalized the concept of "divine work."

"Office" as a word comes into modern usage from the Latin word *opus*, or "work." For most English speakers, it immediately connotes a place, rather than an activity. Yet those same speakers quite as naturally refer to professional functions—political ones, for example—as "offices," as in "He is running for office." Most of them readily refer to the voluntary giving up of the product of work as "offering" or "an offering." And those who govern or regulate work are routinely referred to as "officers" of a corporation or a civic unit. Thus in an earlier time that was much closer than we to the original possibilities of *opus*, it was entirely fitting that "office" should become the denominator for "the work of God."

For Benedict, as for many before him and almost all after him, fixed-hour prayer was and will always be *opus dei*, "the work of God," "the offices." As for the hours on whose striking the prayers are done, those belong to God and are, as a result, "divine." And the work is real, as fixed in its understanding of itself as it is in its timing.

Prayer is as variform as any other human activity. The Liturgy of the Hours, or the Divine Offices, is but one of those forms, yet it is the only one consistently referred to as "the work of God." The Divine Hours are prayers of praise offered as a sacrifice of thanksgiving and faith to God and as a sweet-smelling incense of the human soul before the throne of God. To offer them is to serve before that throne as part of the priesthood of all believers. It is to assume the "office" of attendant upon the Divine.

While the words and ordering of the prayers of the Divine Hours have changed and changed again over the centuries, that purpose and that characterization have remained constant. Other prayers may be petitionary or intercessory or valedictory or any number of other things, but the Liturgy of the Hours remains an act of offering . . . offering by the creature to the Creator. The fact that the creature grows strong and his or her faith more sinewy and efficacious as a result of keeping the hours is a by-product (albeit a desirable one) of that practice and not its purpose.

From the Middle Ages to Us

As the keeping of the hours grew in importance to become the organizing principle of both Christian spirituality and the Christian day, so too did the elaboration of the offices. By the eleventh century, saying an office required a veritable stack of books . . . a Psalter from which to sing the Psalms appointed for that day and hour, a lectionary from which to ascertain the appointed scripture reading, a sacred text from which to read the scripture thus discovered, a hymnal for singing, etc., etc. As the growth of small communities took the laity away from the great cathedral centers where such tools and their ordering were available, it also created a need for some kind of unification of all the pieces and parts into a more manageable and more portable form. The result was the creation of a set of mnemonics, a kind of master list or, in Latin, *breviarium*, of how the fixed-hour prayers were to be observed and of the texts to be used.

From the less cumbersome listings of the *breviarium*, it was a short leap to incorporating into a book at least the first few words (and sometimes the whole) of all the texts required by the listing. This the officiants of the Papal Chapel did in the twelfth century, and the modern breviary was born. Breviaries, or manuals of prayer for keeping the daily offices, have varied over the subsequent centuries from order to order, from church to church, and from communion to communion within Christianity. So too have the ordering and number of the offices to be observed and even, in some cases, the setting of the appointed hours themselves.

The Anglican communion, for example, as one of its first acts of defiance in the time of the Reformation, created a new prayer book to govern the thinking and the practice of Christians in the new Church of England. That manual was given the intentionally populist name of *The Book of Common Prayer*. More often referred to affectionately today simply as the BCP, the manual has gone through many updates and revisions that have adjusted its language and even its theology to changing times and sensibilities. Despite those changes, however, and perhaps as a result of them, the BCP still orders, through one edition or another, the spiritual and religious lives of millions of Christians, many of them not Anglican by profession and all save a few of them certainly not English.

As one of its more "reforming" amendments, the first and subsequent editions of the BCP reduced or collapsed the Daily Offices into only two obligatory observances—morning prayer and evensong. Almost four hundred and fifty years later, in 1979, the U.S. (or Episcopal) Church bowed to the centuries and the yearning of many remembering hearts by restoring the noon office to its rightful place in the American BCP. In doing so, the Episcopal Church in the United States also acted within another abiding consistency of fixed-hour prayer—the enduring sense that the so-called Little Hours of terce, sext, and none, even when collapsed into one noontime observance, are the core of the Offices and of daily Christian practice, be it private or public.

Episcopal practice was not the first to undergo restructuring in the closing years of the twentieth century. In 1971 Pope Paul VI issued The Liturgy of the Hours, which modified the Offices to an ordering very similar to the one the American BCP would assume eight years later. Four offices were now suggested to laity and required of monastics, secular clergy, and those under orders: a morning office called still by its Latin name of Lauds; a noon office that allows the individual Christian to choose the hour of his or her workday (either terce, sext, or none) in which to pray the Office and, as a result of that first choice, which of the three possible texts will be prayed; the early evening office of vespers; and before retiring, the simple, consoling office of compline. Under Paul VI's rubrics, there is also an obligatory Office of Readings that may be observed at any time of the believer's day as is most convenient.

Despite all the diversity that centuries and evolving doctrine have laid upon them, the Divine Hours have none the less remained absolute in their adherence to certain principles that have become their definition. The Daily Offices and the manuals that effect them are, as a result of that defining constancy, dedicated: to the exercise of praise as the work of God and the core of the Offices; to the informing concept of a cascade of prayer being lifted ceaselessly by Christians around the world; to the recognition for every observant of an exultant membership with other observants in a communion of saints across both time and space; to the centrality of the Psalms as the informing text of all the Offices (a centrality made doubly intense by the fact that theirs are the words, rhythms, and understandings that Jesus of Nazareth himself used in his own devotions while on earth); to the establishment in every breviary or manual of a fixed cycle that provides for the reading of at least some portion of all save three of the Psalms in the Hebrew/Christian Psalter (the present manual employs a six-week cycle and some portion of every Psalm); to the necessity of fixed components like the Our Father; to the formal ordering of each Office's conduct; and to the efficacy of the repetition of prayers, creeds, and sacred texts in spiritual growth and exercise. It is on these principles and within the scope of these purposes that *The Divine Hours* is built.

Notes for the Use of This Manual

The Divine Hours: Prayers for Springtime, like most variations and revisions of established forms, is born out of contemporary need. In particular the manual strives for simplicity or familiarity of wording and ease of use. Not only will such an approach reassure those Christians who have not yet begun the practice of keeping the hours, but it will also provide even the liturgically accomplished with what one observer referred to as "a welcome lack of so many ribbons." With few exceptions, the entire text for each office is printed within that office, and the rubrics or headers of each part of each office are in contemporary rather than ecclesial English. The first evidence of this approach is in the manual's title itself. *Prayers for Springtime* references the seasons of the physical, rather than the liturgical, year. In the same manner, the Daily Offices in this manual are appointed neither by the date of an individual day nor by the week of the liturgical year; rather they are dated from the Sunday of each week of the physical calendar. The Church has long assigned certain prayers, readings, and intentions to certain days of the week. Thus, Friday is normally regarded as a penitential day, Saturday as a day of preparation for corporate worship, Sunday as a sabbath. Ordering the offices by calendar dates rather than from the first Sunday of each calendar week obscures these historic rhythms.

Any system of ordering, however, including this one, must also accommodate the changing seasons of the Church's year. In *Prayers for Springtime,* this correspondence is between what common speech conceives of as a single season and calls springtime and what the Church conceives of as a period of several seasons and designates by several liturgical or religious names, principal among them being the seasons of Lent, Easter, Ascensiontide, and Pentecost.

The liturgical calendar of the Church is filled, as is the secular calendar, with observances and seasons that both acknowledge and give exercise to the rhythms of life. Almost all of these feasts and celebrations are like Christmas or the saints' days; that is, they are tied to a specific dates of the physical calendar. The liturgical seasons that fall within springtime, unfortunately, are not so easily dated, for they are all calculated from the date of Easter; and Easter is calculated by that most physical of calendars, the lunar one. Easter falls on the first Sunday after the first full moon after the vernal equinox. That is to say, Easter may come as early as March 22 or as late as April 25. Lent commences forty days and six Sundays before Easter on Ash Wednesday. Ascensiontide begins forty days after Easter, and Pentecost fifty days and seven Sundays after it.

Despite all these very real variances, there are some consistencies. The month of March, for example, falls always in large part or totally within the season of Lent. For that reason, users of this manual will find that the March offices are penitential in nature. The season of Ascension occurs most frequently in May; and the offices for May draw upon the prayers and readings the Church has for centuries assigned to that season and to Pentecost.

In order to assure the appropriately timed use of the Easter texts, however, there is a special set of offices included here for the eight days or octave of Holy Week. Commencing with Palm Sunday and concluding with compline on Easter Monday, these offices may be found on pages 320–370 of the manual.

Following current Church practice, the offices appointed for each day are four in number: morning, noon, vespers, and compline. Following the ancient principle of accommodation, there is flexibility about the hour or half hour within which each may be observed. The morning and vespers or evening prayers adhere to the general configurations of their antecedents, and the noon office is an amalgam of the Little Hours of terce, sext, and none into one whole. The fourth—compline—is frequently referred to as "the dear office." Unlike the others, compline is fixed by the individual and not by the clock, for it is observed just before retiring.

Because compline is indeed the dear office of rest and because it is freer in its timing, it is also more repetitive or fixed here in its structure. For this reason, there is only one week of compline texts for each month of the manual. Thus the compline for the first Monday in February is the compline for each Monday in February. The only variance from this pattern is, as noted, in the addition of texts specifically for the octave of Holy Week.

Each month's offices are preceded by a prefatory page that gives the page number for that month's compline texts; the physical or calendar date of saints' days and observances for the month; and the text of the Gloria and the Our Father. Most Christians are so absolutely familiar with both of these fixed prayers as to need no assistance in praying them. For that reason, they are the only parts of the daily offices not reproduced here within the texts of each office. On the other hand, new Christians or those just commencing the practice of the Offices may find it reassuring to know that these two integral components are immediately available at the head of each month.

The Feasts and saints' days of the Church are so numerous as to be only rarely incorporated *in toto* by any breviary or manual. Rather, each selects for inclusion those holy days which are the major observances of the Church as well as some of those that seem most applicable to the volume's intended communion. Although this manual lists on each month's header the exact date of observation for each selected observance, it follows the pattern of celebrating the saint or feast on the Monday of the week within which the occasion falls. This system allows the user the flexibility to choose between precise commemoration or that of the memorializing week in general.

To facilitate the Church's increasing emphasis on sacred texts, *The Divine Hours* incorporates readings into three offices—morning, noon, and compline. To make such incorporation feasible as well as possible, hymns are primary here only in the vespers office. In much the same way, some of the more repetitive practices of earlier manuals have been omitted. The list, which follows below, of the symbols and conventions used in this manual will enrich the user's understanding of some of the other particulars of *The Divine Hours* as well.

The Symbols and Conventions Used in This Manual

Except where otherwise indicated, the texts for the sacred readings in this manual are taken from *The New Jerusalem Bible*. Thus, the conventions of that translation obtain here as well. For example, the italicizing of a segment within a reading, both in the NJB and in the readings taken from it for use here, indicates that those words or phrases have also occurred elsewhere in scripture and probably constitute a direct quotation or incorporation by the current speaker.

On those few occasions when a sacred reading is from the King James Version rather than *The New Jerusalem*, that change is noted at the reading's conclusion by the notation, "KJV." The texts for all save a handful of the Psalms and Psalm hymns employed here are from the Psalter of *The Book of Common Prayer*. These departures are marked with the appropriate citing words with only one exception: Because of frequency and for aesthetic reasons, the symbol ❖ is used to indicate a medley or hymning of the canonical Psalms as assembled by Dr. Fred Bassett (c.f., Acknowledgments).

Unless otherwise indicated, the appointed prayers are taken from the BCP. Many of them have been adapted, however, for use here. Such texts are indicated by the symbol, †. Principally, the user already familiar with the BCP will note that many of the first person plural pronouns of "us, we, our" have been changed to the singular ones of "me, I, my." The sensibility informing these adaptations has been the desire to make each more immediately personal. Whether the Offices as they are produced here are said in private (as will be by far the greater use) or in public, each observant prays both as an individual and as a participant in a praying community. Where the pronominal singulars of "me, I, my" are employed, the attention should be directed toward the individual. Where the plurals are employed, attention and intention are toward the larger community of the Church.

The Psalms are poetry, albeit a poetry that does not work on a poetics familiar to most English speakers. Few translations of that great body of devotion have come so close, however, as has the Psalter of the BCP to exposing and celebrating the rhythms, images, and aesthetic force of the originals; and it is for that reason that they have been used here. The BCP Psalter, like every other, has its own conventions, and they are followed here. This is particularly obvious in the presentations of the name of God. Long a problem for translators as well as readers, the presence in the Psalms of three different terms for the divine name requires carefully chosen English wording as well as a clearly defined rationale for the application of each term chosen. This rationale, while too lengthy for inclusion here, may be found in the prefatory material to the BCP Psalter.

The Psalms as reproduced here retain as well the*, or asterisks, that indicate the poetic breaks in the original Hebrew poem. Whether one is reading or chanting the Psalm, there should be a pause at this point in order for the rhythm of the poetry to be realized fully. Many Christians will want to chant the Psalms, since that most ancient of practices still extends to the observant the greatest and purest spiritual benefit personally. For the more chary, reading aloud will offer a similar benefit, since it too involves the body as well as the intellect in the keeping of the office.

Most contemporary observants, be they lay or ordained, keep the Hours during the workday, a circumstance that means that the noon office in particular is observed within a space that is not only secular, but frequently populated. While one may withdraw to some removed space like a break-room or a car, one still is rarely sufficiently secluded to be comfortable chanting or reading aloud. By contrast, for weekend days and for the offices of morning and evening, chanting or oral reading may be both possible and desirable.

Chanting an office is a complex exercise with an equally complex and intricate history. Those who are already informed in the art will find that the asterisks here furnish the necessary pointing. For those who have not previously chanted the offices but wish to add that exercise to their spiritual discipline and for those who are new observants, a few simple principles may be sufficient for basic proficiency.

In general, Psalms are sung or chanted along one single note or tone, one that is chosen by the observant as pleasing and comfortable to maintain over the course of the text. The pacing is natural, neither hurried nor pretentiously extended. By chanting, the observant is weaving in yet another part of the bouquet of prayer that is being offered to God, and a constant remembrance of this purpose will do much to make the discipline acceptable and pleasing. Each verse of the Psalm, by and large, constitutes a poetic unit and is interrupted or pointed by an asterisk. The asterisk signals not only the poetic break in the verse but also the point at which the chanter is to raise his or her tone one note. That raising occurs on the last accented syllable nearest to the asterisk. At the end of the second half of the verse—i.e., the sequence of words after the asterisk—the chanter lowers by one note the final, accented syllable. Pronouns like "me, he, thee," etc., are never elevated or lowered. The ear and the throat will soon show the new chanter as well that many English words are trisyllabic, having their accent on the first syllable. When such a word is the last one before an asterisk or a verse end, the first unaccented syllable goes up or down a note or half note as the case may be, and the second unaccented syllable goes up or down another, similar gradation.

From such basic premises, the intrigued or impassioned chanter will discover rather quickly ways to elaborate the office to a rendering pleasing to him or her. Such elaborations, the chanter should be assured, have probably already been tried through the centuries by other Christians and may well be in full, current use by many of them. So also is there a range of options for rendering the prose or unpointed portions of each office. Readings or appointed prayers, for example, if chanted, are normally offered in a monotone with a lengthening of the final syllable of each breath-pause or sentence unit. The Our Father is frequently the exception to this principle, being offered silently by many worshipers.

The only necessary principle, in fact, is really to remember the words of St. Augustine, "Whoever sings, prays twice." In so saying, Augustine spoke to the attitude as well as the benefit of chanting the Psalms: That which deepens the observant's contemplation and that which increases the beauty of our devotion are, by definition, appropriate and good.

THE
DIVINE HOURS™

PRAYERS FOR SPRINGTIME

The Gloria

Glory be to God the Father, God the Son, and God the Holy Spirit. As it was in the beginning, so it is now and so it shall ever be, world without end. Alleluia.* *Amen.*

The Lord's Prayer

Our Father, who art in heaven, hallowed be your Name.
May your kingdom come, and your will be done, on earth as in heaven.
Give us today our daily bread.
Forgive us our sins as we forgive those who sin against us.
Lead us not into temptation, but deliver us from evil;
for yours are the kingdom and the power and the glory
forever and ever. *Amen.*

Compline Prayers for February Are Located on Page 129.

The Following Holy Days Occur in February:
The Feast of the Presentation of Our Lord Jesus Christ in the Temple/
The Feast of the Purification of the Blessed Virgin Mary: *February 2*
The Feast of St. Mathias the Apostle: *February 24*

*The Gloria is omitted during Lent by many Christian communities. "Alleluia" is always omitted from every part of the Church's worship during Lent; the use of both is restored at Easter.

February

The Morning Office To Be Observed on the Hour or Half Hour
Between 6 and 9 a.m.

The Call to Prayer

Come, let us sing to the LORD;* Let us rejoice this day in the strength of our
salvation.
Let us come into His presence with thanksgiving,* and raise a loud shout to Him
with psalms.

Psalm 95:1–2

The Request for Presence

Hear, O Shepherd of Israel, leading Joseph like a flock;* shine forth, you that are
enthroned upon the cherubim.
In the presence of Ephraim, Benjamin, and Manasseh,* stir up your strength and
come to help us,
Restore us, O God of hosts;* show the light of your countenance, and we shall be
saved.

Psalm 80:1–3

The Greeting

It is a good thing to give thanks to the LORD,* and to sing praises to your Name, O
Most High;
To tell of your loving-kindness early in the morning* and of your faithfulness in
the night season.

Psalm 92:1–2

The Refrain for the Morning Lessons

In God, whose word I praise, in God I trust and will not be afraid,* for what can
flesh do to me?

Psalm 56:4

A Reading

Jesus taught us, saying: "Treat others as you would like people to treat you. If you
love those who love you, what credit can you expect? Even sinners love those
who love them. And if you do good to those who do good to you, what credit
can you expect? For even sinners do that much. And if you lend to those from
whom you hope to get money back, what credit can you expect? Even sinners
lend to sinners to get back the same amount. Instead, love your enemies and do
good to them, and lend without any hope of return. You will have a great
reward, and you will be children of the Most High, for he himself is kind to the
ungrateful and the wicked."

Luke 6:31–35

The Refrain

In God, whose word I praise, in God I trust and will not be afraid,* for what can
flesh do to me?

The Morning Psalm   *I Will Give Attention to Your Ways*

How shall a young man cleanse his way?* By keeping to your words.

With my whole heart I seek you;* let me not stray from your commandments.

I treasure your promise in my heart,* that I may not sin against you.

Blessed are you, O LORD;* instruct me in your statutes.

With my lips will I recite* all the judgments of your mouth.

I have taken greater delight in the way of your decrees* than in all manner of riches.

I will meditate on your commandments* and give attention to your ways.

My delight is in your statutes;* I will not forget your word.

Psalm 119:9–16

The Refrain

In God, whose word I praise, in God I trust and will not be afraid,* for what can flesh do to me?

The Gloria

The Lord's Prayer

The Prayer Appointed for the Week

Set me free, O God, from the bondage of my sins, and give me the liberty of that abundant life which you have made known to me in your Son our Savior Jesus Christ; who lives and reigns with you and the Holy Spirit, one God, now and for ever. *Amen.* †

The Concluding Prayer of the Church

Lord God, almighty and everlasting Father, you have brought me in safety to this new day: Preserve me with your mighty power, that I may not fall into sin, nor be overcome by adversity; and in all I do direct me to the fulfilling of your purpose; through Jesus Christ my Lord. *Amen.* †

The Midday Office   **To Be Observed on the Hour or Half Hour**
Between 11 a.m. and 2 p.m.

The Call to Prayer

Proclaim with me the greatness of the LORD;* let us exalt his Name together.

Psalm 34:3

The Request for Presence

LORD, hear my prayer,* and let my cry come before you

Incline your ear to me;* when I call, make haste to answer me.

Psalm 102:1ff

The Greeting

Let all who seek you rejoice and be glad in you;* let those who love your salvation say for ever, "Great is the LORD!"

Psalm 70:4

The Refrain for the Midday Lessons

I will give thanks to you, O LORD, with my whole heart:* I will tell all your
marvelous works.

Psalm 9:1

A Reading

Of Jesus, the Apostle wrote: "It was fitting that God, for whom and through whom
everything exists, should, in bringing many sons to glory, make perfect
through suffering the leader of their salvation. For consecrator and consecrated
are all of the same stock; . . . For it was not the angels that he took to himself; he
took to himself *the line of Abraham.*

Hebrews 2:10ff

The Refrain

I will give thanks to you, O LORD, with my whole heart:* I will tell of all your marvelous works.

The Midday Psalm   *We Will Not Fear, Though the Earth Be Moved*

God is our refuge and strength,* a very present help in trouble.

Therefore we will not fear, though the earth be moved,* and though the mountains be toppled into the depths of the sea;

Though its waters rage and foam,* and though the mountains tremble at its tumult.

The LORD of hosts is with us;* the God of Jacob is our stronghold.

"Be still, then, and know that I am God;* I will be exalted among the nations; I will
be exalted in the earth."

The LORD of hosts is with us;* the God of Jacob is our stronghold.

Psalm 46:1–4, 11–12

The Refrain

I will give thanks to you, O LORD, with my whole heart:* I will tell of all your marvelous works.

The Gloria

The Lord's Prayer

The Prayer Appointed for the Week

Set me free, O God, from the bondage of my sins, and give me the liberty of that
abundant life which you have made known to me in your Son our Savior Jesus
Christ; who lives and reigns with you and the Holy Spirit, one God, now and
for ever. *Amen.* †

The Concluding Prayer of the Church

Lord, My God, King of heaven and of earth, for this day please direct and sanctify,
set right and govern my heart and my body, my sentiments, my words and my
actions in conformity with Your law and Your commandments. Thus I shall be
able to attain salvation and deliverance, in time and in eternity, by Your help, O
Savior of the world, who lives and reigns forever. *Amen.*

adapted from DIVINE OFFICE, II

The Vespers Office   **To Be Observed on the Hour or Half Hour**
                                          Between 5 and 8 p.m.

The Call to Prayer
Come let us bow down, and bend the knee* and kneel before the LORD our Maker.
For he is our God and we are the people of his pasture and the sheep of his hand.

Psalm 95:6–7

The Request for Presence
I call upon you, O God, for you will answer me;* incline your ear to me, and hear
   my words.

Psalm 17:6

The Greeting
You are God: I praise you;* you are the Lord: I acclaim you;
You are the eternal Father:* all creation worships you.
Throughout the world the holy Church acclaims you:* Father, of majesty
   unbounded,
your true and only Son,* worthy of all worship,
and the Holy Spirit,* advocate and guide.
As these have been from the beginning,* so they are now and evermore shall be.
   Alleluia.

based on the Te Deum *and* Gloria

The Hymn
   Hail to the Lord who comes, comes to his temple gate;
   Not with his angel host, not in his kingly state;
   No shouts proclaim him nigh, no crowds his coming wait;
   But borne upon the throne of Mary's gentle breast,
   Watched by her duteous love, in her fond arms at rest,
   Thus to his Father's house he comes, the heavenly guest.

   There Joseph at her side in reverent wonder stands;
   And, filled with holy joy, old Simeon in his hands
   Takes up the promised child, the glory of all lands.
   O Light of all the earth, your children wait for thee!
   Come to your temples here, that we, from sin set free,
   Before your Father's face may all presented be!

John Ellerton

The Refrain for the Vespers Lessons
O LORD, you are my portion and my cup;* it is you who uphold my lot.

Psalm 16:5

The Vespers Psalm   *In Your Paths My Feet Shall Not Stumble*
Hear my plea of innocence, O LORD; give heed to my cry;* listen to my prayer,
   which does not come from lying lips.
Weigh my heart, summon me by night,* melt me down; you will find no impurity
   in me.

I give no offense with my mouth as others do;* I have heeded the words of your lips.
My footsteps hold fast to the ways of your law;* in your paths my feet shall not
stumble.
I call upon you, O God, for you will answer me;* incline your ear to me and hear
my words.
Show me your marvelous loving-kindness,* O Savior of those who take refuge at
your right hand from those who rise up against them.
Keep me as the apple of your eye;* hide me under the shadow of your wings,

Psalm 17:1, 3–8

The Refrain

O LORD, you are my portion and my cup;* it is you who uphold my lot.

The Lord's Prayer

The Prayer Appointed for the Week

Set me free, O God, from the bondage of my sins, and give me the liberty of that
abundant life which you have made known to me in your Son our Savior Jesus
Christ; who lives and reigns with you and the Holy Spirit, one God, now and
for ever. *Amen.* †

Concluding Prayers of the Church

O God, who wonderfully created and yet more wonderfully restored, the dignity
of human nature: Grant that I may share the divine life of him who humbled
himself to share our humanity, your Son Jesus Christ; who lives and reigns
with you in the unity of the Holy Spirit, one God, for ever and ever. *Amen.* †

Lord Jesus, stay with me, for evening is at hand and the day is past; be my companion in the way, kindle my heart, and awaken hope, that I may know you as
you are revealed in Scripture and in the breaking of bread. Grant this for the
sake of your love toward me. *Amen.* †

The Morning Office   **To Be Observed on the Hour or Half Hour**
Between 6 and 9 a.m.

The Call to Prayer

One day in your courts is better than a thousand in my own room,* and to stand at
the threshold of the house of my God than to dwell in the tents of the wicked.

Psalm 84:9

The Request for Presence

LORD God of hosts, hear my prayer;* hearken, O God of Jacob.

Psalm 84:7

The Greeting

The LORD lives! Blessed is my Rock!* Exalted is the God of my salvation!
Therefore will I extol you among the nations, O LORD,* and sing praises to your
Name.

Psalm 18:46ff

The Refrain for the Morning Lessons
The heaven of heavens is the LORD's,* but he entrusted the earth to its peoples.

Psalm 115:16

A Reading   *On February 2, the Church observes the obedience of the Holy Family
                    to the Law. On that day, the forty-first after Christmas, the Virgin
                    entered the Temple in Jerusalem with Joseph to offer a sacrifice for
                    her purification after childbirth and to present her Son to the Temple
                    priests.*

And when the day came for them to be purified in keeping with the Law of Moses,
   they took him up to Jerusalem to present him to the Lord—observing what is
   written in the Law of the Lord: *Every first-born male must be consecrated to the
   Lord*—and also to offer in sacrifice, in accordance with what is prescribed in the
   Law of the Lord, *a pair of turtledoves, or two young pigeons.*

Luke 2:22–24

The Refrain
The heaven of heavens is the LORD's,* but he entrusted the earth to its peoples.

The Morning Psalm   *Like a Child Upon Its Mother's Breast*
O LORD, I am not proud;* I have no haughty looks.
I do not occupy myself with great matters,* or with things that are too hard for me.
But I still my soul and make it quiet, like a child upon its mother's breast;* my soul
   is quieted within me.

Psalm 131:1–3

The Refrain
The heaven of heavens is the LORD's,* but he entrusted the earth to its peoples.

The Small Verse
Show us your mercy O Lord; and grant us your salvation.
Clothe your ministers with righteousness; let your people sing with joy.
Give peace, O Lord, in all the world; for only in you can we live in safety.

The Lord's Prayer

The Prayer Appointed for the Week
Set me free, O God, from the bondage of my sins, and give me the liberty of that
   abundant life which you have made known to me in your Son our Savior Jesus
   Christ; who lives and reigns with you and the Holy Spirit, one God, now and
   for ever. *Amen.* †

Concluding Prayers of the Church
O Almighty and everlasting God, I humbly beseech Your Majesty, that as Your
   only-begotten Son was this day presented in the Temple in the substance of
   flesh, so too You would grant that I be presented to You with a purified soul.
   Through the Lord Jesus Christ. *Amen.*

adapted from THE SHORT BREVIARY

Lord God, almighty and everlasting Father, you have brought me in safety to this new day: Preserve me with your mighty power, that I may not fall into sin, nor be overcome by adversity; and in all I do direct me to the fulfilling of your purpose; through Jesus Christ my Lord. *Amen.* †

The Midday Office   **To Be Observed on the Hour or Half Hour**
Between 11 a.m. and 2 p.m.

The Call to Prayer
Sing to God, O kingdoms of the earth;* sing praises to the Lord.
He rides in the heavens, the ancient heavens;* he sends forth his voice, his mighty voice.

Psalm 68:33–34

The Request for Presence
May the glory of the LORD endure for ever;* may the LORD rejoice in all his works.

Psalm 104:32

The Greeting
Let the words of my mouth and the meditation of my heart be acceptable in your sight,* O LORD, my strength and my redeemer.

Psalm 19:14

The Refrain for the Midday Lessons
My tongue will proclaim your righteousness all day long.

Psalm 71:24

A Reading
When the period of purification is over, for either boy or girl, she will bring the priest at the entrance of the Tent of Meeting a lamb one year old for a burnt offering, and a young pigeon or turtledove as a sacrifice for sin. The priest must offer this before YAHWEH, perform the rite of expiation for her, and she will be purified from her discharge of blood. Such is the law concerning a woman who gives birth to either a boy or a girl. If she cannot afford a lamb, she must take two turtledoves or two young pigeons, one for the burnt offering and the other for the sacrifice of sin. The priest will perform the rite of expiation for her and she will be purified.

Leviticus 12:6–8

The Refrain
My tongue will proclaim your righteousness all day long.

The Midday Psalm   *My Soul Longs for the Courts of the LORD*
How dear to me is your dwelling, O LORD of hosts!* My soul has a desire and longing for the courts of the LORD; my heart and my flesh rejoice in the living God.
The sparrow has found her a house and the swallow a nest where she may lay her young;* by the side of your altars, O LORD of hosts, my King and my God.
Happy are they who dwell in your house!* they will always be praising you.

Happy are the people whose strength is in you!* whose hearts are set on the
  pilgrims' way.
Those who go through the desolate valley will find it a place of springs,* for the
  early rains have covered it with pools of water.
They will climb from height to height,* and the God of gods will reveal himself in
  Zion.
Lord God of hosts, hear my prayer;* hearken, O God of Jacob.
Behold our defender, O God;* and look upon the face of your Anointed.

Psalm 84:1–8

The Refrain
My tongue will proclaim your righteousness all day long.

The Gloria

The Lord's Prayer

The Prayer Appointed for the Week
Set me free, O God, from the bondage of my sins, and give me the liberty of that
  abundant life which you have made known to me in your Son our Savior Jesus
  Christ; who lives and reigns with you and the Holy Spirit, one God, now and
  for ever. *Amen.* †

The Concluding Prayer of the Church
Almighty and ever living God, I humbly pray that, as your only begotten Son was
  this day presented in the temple, so I may be presented to you with a pure and
  clean heart by Jesus Christ our Lord, who lives and reigns with you and the
  Holy Spirit, one God, now and for ever. *Amen.* †

The Vespers Office

To Be Observed on the Hour or Half Hour
Between 5 and 8 p.m.

The Call to Prayer
The Lord is in his holy temple.* Let all the earth keep silence before him.

based on Psalms 11:4

The Request for Presence
O Lord, I call to you; come to me quickly* hear my voice when I cry to you.
Let my prayer be set forth in your sight as incense,* the lifting up of my hands as
  the evening sacrifice.

Psalm 141:1–2

The Greeting
O Lamb of God, that takes away the sins of the world, have mercy on us.
O Lamb of God, that takes away the sins of the world, have mercy on us.
O Lamb of God, that takes away the sins of the world, grant us your peace.

The Hymn
  O Zion, open wide your gates, let symbols disappear;
  A priest and victim both in one, the Truth himself is here.

Aware of hidden deity the lowly Virgin brings
Her newborn babe, with two young doves, her humble offerings.

The aged Simeon sees at last his Lord, so long desired,
And Anna welcomes Israel's hope, with holy rapture fired.

But silent knelt the mother blessed of the yet silent Word,
And pondering all things in her heart, with speechless praise adored.

All glory to the Father be, all glory to the Son,
All glory, Holy Ghost, to Thee, while endless ages run.

Jean Baptiste de Santeuil

The Refrain for the Vespers Lessons
He who dwells in the shelter of the Most High,* abides under the shadow of the
 Almighty.
He shall say to the Lord, "You are my refuge and my stronghold,* my God in
 whom I put my trust."

Psalm 91:1–2

The Vespers Psalm   *Holiness Adorns Your House, O Lord*
The Lord is King; he has put on splendid apparel;* the Lord has put on his
 apparel and girded himself with strength.
He has made the whole world so sure* that it cannot be moved;
Ever since the world began, your throne has been established;* you are from
 everlasting.
The waters have lifted up, O Lord, the waters have lifted up their voice;* the
 waters have lifted up their pounding waves.
Mightier than the sound of many waters, mightier than the breakers of the sea,*
 mightier is the Lord who dwells on high.
Your testimonies are very sure,* and holiness adorns your house, O Lord, for ever
 and for evermore.

Psalm 93

The Refrain
He who dwells in the shelter of the Most High,* abides under the shadow of the
 Almighty.
He shall say to the Lord, "You are my refuge and my stronghold,* my God in
 whom I put my trust."

The Gloria

The Lord's Prayer

The Prayer Appointed for the Week
Set me free, O God, from the bondage of my sins, and give me the liberty of that
 abundant life which you have made known to me in your Son our Savior Jesus
 Christ; who lives and reigns with you and the Holy Spirit, one God, now and
 for ever. *Amen.* †

The Concluding Prayer of the Church
O Almighty and everlasting God, I humbly beseech Your Majesty, that as Your
only-begotten Son was this day presented in the temple in the substance of
flesh, so too You would grant that I be presented to You with a purified soul.
Through the Lord Jesus Christ. *Amen.*

adapted from THE SHORT BREVIARY

The Morning Office   **To Be Observed on the Hour or Half Hour**
Between 6 and 9 a.m.

The Call to Prayer
For the LORD God is both sun and shield;* he will give grace and glory;
No good thing will the LORD withhold* from those who walk with integrity.
O LORD of hosts,* happy are they who put their trust in you!

Psalm 84:10–12

The Request for Presence
Early in the morning I cry out to you,* for in your word is my trust.

Psalm 119:147

The Greeting
I put my trust in your mercy;* my heart is joyful because of your saving help.

Psalm 13:5

The Refrain for the Morning Lessons
Yours are the heavens, the earth is also yours;* you laid the foundations of the
world and all that is in it.

Psalm 89:11

A Reading
Now in Jerusalem there was a man named Simeon. He was an upright and devout
man; he looked forward to the restoration of Israel and the Holy Spirit rested
on him. It had been revealed to him by the Holy Spirit that he would not see
death until he had set eyes on the Christ of the Lord. Prompted by the Spirit he
came to the Temple; and when the parents brought in the child Jesus to do for
him what the Law required, he took him into his arms and blessed God; and he
said: Now, Master, you are letting your servant go in peace as you promised;
for my eyes have seen the salvation which you have made ready in the sight of
the nations; a light of revelation for the gentiles and glory for your people
Israel. As the child's father and mother were wondering at the things that were
being said about him, Simeon blessed them and said to Mary his mother,
'Look, he is destined for the fall and for the rise of many in Israel, destined to
be a sign that is opposed—and a sword will pierce your soul too—so that the
secret thoughts of many may be laid bare.'

Luke 2:25–35

The Refrain
Yours are the heavens, the earth is also yours;* you laid the foundations of the
world and all that is in it.

The Morning Psalm   *Wait Upon the* Lord
Wait upon the Lord and keep his way;* he will raise you up to possess the land,
and when the wicked are cut off, you will see it.
I have seen the wicked in their arrogance,* flourishing like a tree in full leaf.
I went by, and behold, they were not there;* I searched for them, but they could
not be found.
Mark those who are honest; observe the upright;* for there is a future for the
peaceable.
Transgressors shall be destroyed, one and all;* the future of the wicked is cut off.
But the deliverance of the righteous comes from the Lord;* he is their stronghold
in time of trouble.
The Lord will help them and rescue them;* he will rescue them from the wicked
and deliver them, because they seek refuge in him.

Psalm 37:36–42

The Refrain
Yours are the heavens, the earth is also yours;* you laid the foundations of the
world and all that is in it.

The Gloria

The Lord's Prayer

The Prayer Appointed for the Week
Set me free, O God, from the bondage of my sins, and give me the liberty of that
abundant life which you have made known to me in your Son our Savior Jesus
Christ; who lives and reigns with you and the Holy Spirit, one God, now and
for ever. *Amen.* †

The Concluding Prayer of the Church
Lord God, almighty and everlasting Father, you have brought me in safety to this
new day: Preserve me with your mighty power, that I may not fall into sin, nor
be overcome by adversity; and in all I do direct me to the fulfilling of your purpose; through Jesus Christ my Lord. *Amen.* †

The Midday Office   To Be Observed on the Hour or Half Hour
                                               Between 11 a.m. and 2 p.m.

The Call to Prayer
Sing to him, sing praise to him,* and speak of all his marvelous works.

Psalm 105:2

The Request for Presence
Let your countenance shine upon your servant* and teach me your statutes.

Psalm 119:135

The Greeting
Let all who seek you rejoice and be glad in you;* let those who love your salvation
say for ever, "Great is the LORD!"

Psalm 70:4

The Refrain for the Midday Lessons
Happy are those who act with justice* and always do right!

Psalm 106:3

A Reading
'Look, I shall send my messenger to clear a way before me. And suddenly the Lord
whom you seek will come to his Temple; yes, the angel of the covenant for
whom you long, is on his way, says Yahweh Sabaoth. Who will be able to resist
the day of his coming? Who will remain standing when he appears? For he will
be like a refiner's fire, like fuller's alkali. He will take his seat as refiner and
purifier . . .'

Malachi 3:1–3

The Refrain
Happy are those who act with justice* and always do right!

The Midday Psalm   *You Are My Refuge and My Stronghold*
He who dwells in the shelter of the Most High,* abides under the shadow of the
Almighty.
He shall say to the LORD, "You are my refuge and my stronghold,* my God in
whom I put my trust."
He shall deliver you from the snare of the hunter* and from the deadly pestilence.
He shall cover you with his pinions, and you shall find refuge under his wings;*
his faithfulness shall be a shield and buckler.
You shall not be afraid of any terror by night,* nor of the arrow that flies by day;
Of the plague that stalks in the darkness,* nor of the sickness that lays waste at
mid-day.

Psalm 91:1–6

The Refrain
Happy are those who act with justice* and always do right!

The Gloria

The Lord's Prayer

The Prayer Appointed for the Week
Set me free, O God, from the bondage of my sins, and give me the liberty of that
abundant life which you have made known to me in your Son our Savior Jesus
Christ; who lives and reigns with you and the Holy Spirit, one God, now and
for ever. *Amen.* †

The Concluding Prayer of the Church
God of mercy,
this midday moment of rest

is your welcome gift.
Bless the work we have begun,
make good its defects,
and let us finish it in a way that pleases you.
Grant this through Christ our Lord. *Amen.*

Liturgy of the Hours, Vol. III

The Vespers Office   To Be Observed on the Hour or Half Hour
Between 5 and 8 p.m.

The Call to Prayer
Let Israel rejoice in his Maker;* let the children of Zion be joyful in their King.
Let them praise his Name in the dance;* let them sing praise to him with timbrel
    and harp.
For the LORD takes pleasure in his people* and adorns the poor with victory.
Let the faithful rejoice in triumph;* let them be joyful on their beds.

Psalm 149:2–5

The Request for Presence
Show us your mercy, O LORD,* and grant us your salvation.

Psalm 85:7

The Greeting
Zion hears and is glad, and the cities of Judah rejoice,* because of your judgments,
    O LORD.

Psalm 97:8

The Hymn   *Mary, Mother Meek and Mild*
Virgin born, we bow before you:
Blessed was the womb that bore you—
Mary, Mother meek and mild—
Blessed was she in her Child.
Blessed was the breast that fed you;
Blessed was the hand that led you;
Blessed was the parent's eye
That watched about your infancy.

Blessed she by all creation,
Who brought forth the world's salvation,
And blessed they, for ever blessed,
Who love you most and serve you best.
Virgin-born, we bow before you;
Blessed was the womb that bore you;
Mary, Mother meek and mild,
Blessed was she in her child.

Reginald Heber

The Refrain for the Vespers Lessons

For one day in your courts is better than a thousand in my own room,* and to
stand at the threshold of the house of my God than to dwell in the tents of the
wicked.

Psalm 84:9

The Vespers Psalm   *I Will Sing to the* LORD

O LORD, you are my portion and my cup;* it is you who uphold my lot.

My boundaries enclose a pleasant land;* indeed, I have a goodly heritage.

I will bless the LORD who gives me counsel;* my heart teaches me, night after
night.

I have set the LORD always before me;* because he is at my right hand I shall not
fall.

My heart, therefore, is glad, and my spirit rejoices;* my body also shall rest in
hope.

For you will not abandon me to the grave,* nor let your holy one see the Pit.

You will show me the path of life;* in your presence there is fullness of joy, and in
your right hand are pleasures for evermore.

Psalm 16:5–11

The Refrain

For one day in your courts is better than a thousand in my own room,* and to
stand at the threshold of the house of my God than to dwell in the tents of the
wicked.

The Gloria

The Lord's Prayer

The Prayer Appointed for the Week

Set me free, O God, from the bondage of my sins, and give me the liberty of that
abundant life which you have made known to me in your Son our Savior Jesus
Christ; who lives and reigns with you and the Holy Spirit, one God, now and
for ever. *Amen.* †

The Concluding Prayer of the Church

Father, all-powerful and ever-living God,

we do well always and everywhere to give you thanks.

All things are of your making,

all times and seasons obey your laws,

but you chose to create us in your own image,

setting us over the whole world in all its wonder.

You made us the steward of creation,

to praise you day by day for the marvels of your wisdom and power.

THE ROMAN MISSAL

The Morning Office To Be Observed on the Hour or Half Hour
Between 6 and 9 a.m.

The Call to Prayer
Hallelujah! Give praise, you servants of the LORD;* praise the Name of the LORD.
Psalm 113:1

The Request for Presence
Test me, O LORD, and try me;* examine my heart and mind.
Psalm 26:2

The Greeting
All your works praise you, O LORD,* and your faithful servants bless you.
They make known the glory of your kingdom* and speak of your power.
Psalm 145:10–11

The Refrain for the Morning Lessons
Those who sowed with tears* will reap with songs of joy.
Those who go out weeping, carrying the seed,* will come again with joy,
    shouldering their sheaves.
Psalm 126:6–7

A Reading
There was a prophetess, too, Anna the daughter of Phanuel, of the tribe of Asher.
    She was well on in years. Her days of girlhood were over, she had been mar-
    ried for seven years before becoming a widow. She was now eighty-four years
    old and never left the Temple, serving God night and day with fasting and
    prayer. She came up just at that moment and began to praise God; and she
    spoke of the child to all who looked forward to the deliverance of Jerusalem.
    When they had done everything that the Law of the Lord required, they went
    back to Galilee, to their own town of Nazareth. And as the child grew to matu-
    rity, he was filled with wisdom; and God's favor was with him.
Luke 2:36–40

The Refrain
Those who sowed with tears* will reap with songs of joy.
Those who go out weeping, carrying the seed,* will come again with joy, shoul-
    dering their sheaves.

The Morning Psalm *Who Is Like You, O God?*
Your righteousness, O God, reaches to the heavens;* you have done great things;
    who is like you, O God?
You have showed me great troubles and adversities,* but you will restore my life
    and bring me up again from the deep places of the earth.
You strengthen me more and more;* you enfold and comfort me,
Therefore I will praise you upon the lyre for your faithfulness, O my God;* I will
    sing to you with the harp, O Holy One of Israel.
My lips will sing with joy when I play to you,* and so will my soul, which you
    have redeemed.

My tongue will proclaim your righteousness all day long,* for they are ashamed
and disgraced who sought to do me harm.

Psalm 71:19–24

The Refrain
Those who sowed with tears* will reap with songs of joy.
Those who go out weeping, carrying the seed,* will come again with joy, shoul-
dering their sheaves.

The Cry of the Church
In the evening, in the morning, and at noonday, I will complain and lament,* and
he will hear my voice.

Psalm 55:18

The Lord's Prayer

The Prayer Appointed for the Week
Set me free, O God, from the bondage of my sins, and give me the liberty of that
abundant life which you have made known to me in your Son our Savior Jesus
Christ; who lives and reigns with you and the Holy Spirit, one God, now and
for ever. *Amen.* †

The Concluding Prayer of the Church
Lord God, almighty and everlasting Father, you have brought me in safety to this
new day: Preserve me with your mighty power, that I may not fall into sin, nor
be overcome by adversity; and in all I do direct me to the fulfilling of your purpose; through Jesus Christ my Lord. *Amen.* †

The Midday Office   To Be Observed on the Hour or Half Hour
                                        Between 11 a.m. and 2 p.m.

The Call to Prayer
Praise the LORD, for the LORD is good;* sing praises to his Name, for it is lovely.

Psalm 135:3

The Request for Presence
Hear the voice of my prayer when I cry out to you,* when I lift up my hands to
your holy of holies.

Psalm 28:2

The Greeting
Who is like you, LORD God of hosts?* O mighty LORD, your faithfulness is all
around you.

Psalm 89:8

The Refrain for the Midday Lessons
But it is good for me to be near God;* I have made the Lord GOD my refuge.

Psalm 73:28

A Reading

To which of the angels, then, has God ever said: *You are my Son, today I have fathered you*, or: *I shall be a father to him and he a son to me?* Again, when he brings the First-born into the world, he says: *Let all the angels of the world pay him homage.* To the angels, he says: *appointing the winds and flames of fire his servants*, but to the Son, he says: *Your throne, God, is for ever and ever;* and: *the scepter of his kingdom is a scepter of justice; you love uprightness and detest evil. This is why God, your God, has anointed you with the oil of gladness, as none of your rivals.*

Hebrews 1:5–9

The Refrain

But it is good for me to be near God; I have made the Lord GOD my refuge.

The Midday Psalm   *I Will Thank You with an Unfeigned Heart*

Happy are they whose way is blameless,* who walk in the law of the LORD!

Happy are they who observe his decrees* and seek him with all their hearts!

Who never do any wrong,* but always walk in his ways.

You laid down your commandments,* that we should fully keep them.

Oh, that my ways were made so direct* that I might keep your statutes!

Then I should not be put to shame,* when I regard all your commandments.

I will thank you with an unfeigned heart,* when I have learned your righteous judgments.

I will keep your statutes;* do not utterly forsake me.

Psalm 119:1–8

The Refrain

But it is good for me to be near God;* I have made the Lord GOD my refuge.

The Gloria

The Lord's Prayer

The Prayer Appointed for the Week

Set me free, O God, from the bondage of my sins, and give me the liberty of that abundant life which you have made known to me in your Son our Savior Jesus Christ; who lives and reigns with you and the Holy Spirit, one God, now and for ever. *Amen.* †

The Concluding Prayer of the Church

Almighty and eternal God, ruler of all things in heaven and earth: Mercifully accept my prayers, and strengthen me to do your will; through Jesus Christ our Lord. *Amen.* †

The Vespers Office   **To Be Observed on the Hour or Half Hour**
                                         Between 5 and 8 p.m.

The Call to Prayer

Be glad, you righteous, and rejoice in the LORD;* shout for joy, all who are true of heart.

Psalm 32:12

The Request for Presence
Exalt yourself above the heavens, O God,* and your glory over all the earth.

Psalm 57:11

The Greeting
May God give us his blessing,* and may all the ends of the earth stand in awe of
him.

Psalm 67:7

The Hymn
Blessed Mother of Christ, the Son, dove of Virgins, holy maid,
Starry hosts proclaim your praises, praise the crown to virtue paid,
While our joyful hearts and voices join the anthem unafraid.

Crash of tempest, roll of thunder, lightning flash from pole to pole,
But the storm of love is stronger, brighter flashes in the soul,
While the peace of Christ the Bridegroom holds you still and keeps you whole.

Glory to the Father we sing, glory to the only Son;
To the Paraclete in glory, equal tribute be begun,
At whose pleasure made and governed, all the ages' course is run.

adapted from THE SHORT BREVIARY

The Refrain for the Vespers Lessons
Let your ways be known upon earth,* your saving health among all nations.

Psalm 67:2

The Vespers Psalm   *Summon Me by Night*
Weigh my heart, summon me by night,* melt me down; you will find no impurity
in me.
I give no offense with my mouth as others do;* I have heeded the words of your
lips.
My footsteps hold fast to the ways of your law;* in your paths my feet shall not
stumble.
I call upon you, O God, for you will answer me;* incline your ear to me and hear
my words.
Show me your marvelous loving-kindness,* O Savior of those who take refuge at
your right hand from those who rise up against them.
Keep me as the apple of your eye;* hide me under the shadow of your wings.

Psalm 17:3–8

The Refrain
Let your ways be known upon earth,* your saving health among all nations.

The Cry of the Church
In the evening, in the morning, and at noonday, I will complain and lament,* and
he will hear my voice.

Psalm 55:18

The Lord's Prayer

The Prayer Appointed for the Week
Set me free, O God, from the bondage of my sins, and give me the liberty of that
abundant life which you have made known to me in your Son our Savior Jesus
Christ; who lives and reigns with you and the Holy Spirit, one God, now and
for ever. *Amen.* †

The Concluding Prayer of the Church
Almighty and eternal God, ruler of all things in heaven and earth: Mercifully
accept the prayers of your people everywhere, and strengthen each of us to do
your will; through Jesus Christ my Lord. *Amen.* †

The Morning Office   To Be Observed on the Hour or Half Hour
Between 6 and 9 a.m.

The Call to Prayer
The LORD is King; let the people tremble;* he is enthroned upon the cherubim; let
the earth shake.

Psalm 99:1

The Request for Presence
Be seated on your lofty throne, O Most High;* O LORD, judge the nations.

Psalm 7:8

The Greeting
Save us, O LORD our God, and gather us from among the nations,* that we may
give thanks to your holy Name and glory in your praise.

Psalm 106:47

The Refrain for the Morning Lessons
Let all the earth fear the LORD;* let all who dwell in the world stand in awe of him.

Psalm 33:8

A Reading
Jesus taught us, saying: "So when you give alms, do not have it trumpeted before
you; this is what the hypocrites do in the synagogues and in the streets to win
human admiration. In truth I tell you, they have had their reward. But when
you give alms, your left hand must not know what your right is doing; your
almsgiving must be secret, and your Father who sees all that is done in secret
will reward you."

Matthew 6:2–4

The Refrain
Let all the earth fear the LORD;* let all who dwell in the world stand in awe of him.

The Morning Psalm   *The Just Shall Not Put Their Hands to Evil*
Those who trust in the LORD are like Mount Zion,* which cannot be moved, but
stands fast for ever.

The hills stand about Jerusalem;* so does the LORD stand round about his people, from this time forth for evermore.
The scepter of the wicked shall not hold sway over the land allotted to the just,* so that the just shall not put their hands to evil.

Psalm 125:1–3

The Refrain
Let all the earth fear the LORD;* let all who dwell in the world stand in awe of him.

The Small Verse
"I am the Alpha and the Omega," says the Lord God, who is, who was, and who is to come, the Almighty.

Revelation 1:8

The Lord's Prayer

The Prayer Appointed for the Week
Set me free, O God, from the bondage of my sins, and give me the liberty of that abundant life which you have made known to me in your Son our Savior Jesus Christ; who lives and reigns with you and the Holy Spirit, one God, now and for ever. *Amen.* †

The Concluding Prayer of the Church
Lord God, almighty and everlasting Father, you have brought me in safety to this new day: Preserve me with your mighty power, that I may not fall into sin, nor be overcome by adversity; and in all I do direct me to the fulfilling of your purpose; through Jesus Christ my Lord. *Amen.* †

The Midday Office
To Be Observed on the Hour or Half Hour Between 11 a.m. and 2 p.m.

The Call to Prayer
Sing to the LORD, you servants of his;* give thanks for the remembrance of his holiness.
For his wrath endures but the twinkling of an eye,* his favor for a lifetime.

Psalm 30:4–5

The Request for Presence
Look upon your covenant;* the dark places of the earth are haunts of violence.

Psalm 74:19

The Greeting
O LORD, your love endures for ever;* do not abandon the works of your hands.

Psalm 138:9

The Refrain for the Midday Lessons
He has not dealt with us according to our sins,* nor rewarded us according to our wickedness.

Psalm 103:10

A Reading

With what shall I enter YAHWEH's presence and bow down before God All-high? Shall I enter with burnt offerings, with calves one year old? Will he be pleased with rams by the thousand, with ten thousand streams of oil? Shall I offer my eldest son for my wrong-doing, the child of my own body for my sin? You have already been told what is right and what YAHWEH wants of you. Only this, to do what is right, to love loyalty and to walk humbly with your God.

Micah 6:6–8

The Refrain

He has not dealt with us according to our sins,* nor rewarded us according to our wickedness.

The Midday Psalm   *How Exalted Is Your Name*

O LORD our Governor,* how exalted is your Name in all the world!

Out of the mouths of infants and children* your majesty is praised above the heavens.

You have set up a stronghold against your adversaries,* to quell the enemy and the avenger.

When I consider your heavens, the work of your fingers,* the moon and the stars you have set in their courses,

What is man that you should be mindful of him?* the son of man that you should seek him out?

You have made him but little lower than the angels;* you adorn him with glory and honor;

You give him mastery over the works of your hands;* you put all things under his feet:

All sheep and oxen,* even the wild beasts of the field,

The birds of the air, the fish of the sea,* and whatsoever walks in the paths of the sea.

O LORD our Governor,* how exalted is your Name in all the world!

Psalm 8

The Refrain

He has not dealt with us according to our sins,* nor rewarded us according to our wickedness.

The Gloria

The Lord's Prayer

The Prayer Appointed for the Week

Set me free, O God, from the bondage of my sins, and give me the liberty of that abundant life which you have made known to me in your Son our Savior Jesus Christ; who lives and reigns with you and the Holy Spirit, one God, now and for ever. *Amen.* †

The Concluding Prayer of the Church

Almighty God, to whom our needs are known before we ask: Help me to ask only what accords with your will; and those good things which I dare not, or in my blindness cannot ask, grant for the sake of your Son Jesus Christ our Lord. *Amen.* †

The Vespers Office

To Be Observed on the Hour or Half Hour Between 5 and 8 p.m.

The Call to Prayer
Rejoice in the LORD, you righteous,* and give thanks to his holy Name.

Psalm 97:12

The Request for Presence
Send forth your strength, O God;* establish, O God, what you have wrought for us.

Psalm 68:28

The Greeting
One generation shall praise your works to another* and shall declare your power.

Psalm 145:4

The Hymn
My song is love unknown,
  my Savior's love to me,
love to the loveless shown
    that they might lovely be.
      O who am I
        that for my sake
        my Lord should take
      frail flesh, and die?

In life no house, no home
    my Lord on earth might have;
in death no friendly tomb
    but what a stranger gave.
      What may I say?
        Heaven was his home;
        but mine the tomb
      wherein he lay.

Here might I stay and sing,
    no story so divine:
never was love, dear King,
    never was grief like thine.
      This is my friend,
        in whose sweet praise
        I all my days
      could gladly spend.
          Samuel Crossman

The Refrain for the Vespers Lessons
The hills stand about Jerusalem;* so does the Lord stand round about his people,
from this time forth for evermore.

Psalm 125:2

The Vespers Psalm   *Your Love Is Ever Before My Eyes*
Test me, O Lord, and try me;* examine my heart and my mind.
For your love is before my eyes;* I have walked faithfully with you.
I have not sat with the worthless,* nor do I consort with the deceitful.
I have hated the company of evildoers;* I will not sit down with the wicked.
I will wash my hands in innocence, O Lord,* that I may go in procession round
your altar,
Singing aloud a song of thanksgiving* and recounting all your wonderful deeds.

Psalm 26:2–7

The Refrain
The hills stand about Jerusalem;* so does the Lord stand round about his people,
from this time forth for evermore.

The Small Verse
But if you will not serve the Lord, choose today whom you wish to serve, whether
the gods that your ancestors served beyond the River, or the gods of the
Amorites in whose land you are now living. As for me and my House, we will
serve Yahweh.

Joshua 24:15

The Lord's Prayer

The Prayer Appointed for the Week
Set me free, O God, from the bondage of my sins, and give me the liberty of that
abundant life which you have made known to me in your Son our Savior Jesus
Christ; who lives and reigns with you and the Holy Spirit, one God, now and
for ever. *Amen.* †

The Concluding Prayer of the Church
Lord God Almighty, you have made all the peoples of the earth for your glory, to
serve you in freedom and in peace: Give to the people of our country a zeal for
justice and the strength of forbearance, that we may use our liberty in accordance with your gracious will; through Jesus Christ our Lord, who lives and
reigns with you and the Holy Spirit, one God, for ever and ever. *Amen.* †

The Morning Office   **To Be Observed on the Hour or Half Hour**
Between 6 and 9 a.m.

The Call to Prayer
Proclaim the greatness of the Lord our God and worship him upon his holy hill;*
for the Lord our God is the Holy One.

Psalm 99:9

The Request for Presence

Be pleased, O LORD, to deliver me;* O LORD, make haste to help me.

Psalm 40:14

The Greeting

But you, O Lord my GOD, oh, deal with me according to your Name;* for your
   tender mercy's sake, deliver me.

For I am poor and needy,* and my heart is wounded within me.

Psalm 109:20–21

The Refrain for the Morning Lessons

The LORD is full of compassion and mercy,* slow to anger and of great kindness.

Psalm 103:8

A Reading

Jesus taught his disciples, saying: "And indeed, which of you here, intending to build
   a tower, would not first sit down and work out the cost to see if he had enough to
   complete it? Otherwise if he laid the foundation and then found himself unable to
   finish the work, everyone who saw it would start making fun of him and saying,
   'Here is someone who started to build and was unable to finish.' "

Luke 14:28–30

The Refrain

The LORD is full of compassion and mercy,* slow to anger and of great kindness.

The Morning Psalm   *The LORD Preserves All Those Who Love Him*

The LORD is near to those who call upon him,* to all who call upon him faithfully.

He fulfills the desire of those who fear him;* he hears their cry and helps them.

The LORD preserves all those who love him,* but he destroys all the wicked.

Psalm 145:19–21

The Refrain

The LORD is full of compassion and mercy,* slow to anger and of great kindness.

Cry of the Church

In the evening, in the morning, and at noonday, I will complain and lament,* and
   he will hear my voice.

Psalm 55:18

The Lord's Prayer

The Prayer Appointed for the Week

Set me free, O God, from the bondage of my sins, and give me the liberty of that
   abundant life which you have made known to me in your Son our Savior Jesus
   Christ; who lives and reigns with you and the Holy Spirit, one God, now and
   for ever. *Amen.* †

The Concluding Prayer of the Church

Lord God, almighty and everlasting Father, you have brought me in safety to this
   new day: Preserve me with your mighty power, that I may not fall into sin, nor

be overcome by adversity; and in all I do direct me to the fulfilling of your purpose; through Jesus Christ my Lord. *Amen.* †

The Midday Office   **To Be Observed on the Hour or Half Hour**
                                                    Between 11 a.m. and 2 p.m.

The Call to Prayer
Come, let us bow down, and bend the knee,* and kneel before the LORD our
   Maker.
For he is our God, and we are the people of his pasture and the sheep of his hand.
Psalm 95:6–7

The Request for Presence
Hear my prayer, O God;* do not hide yourself from my petition.
Listen to me and answer me.
Psalm 55:1–2

The Greeting
O God, you know my foolishness,* and my faults are not hidden from you.
Answer me, O LORD, for your love is kind;* in your great compassion, turn to me.
Psalm 69:6ff

The Refrain for the Midday Lessons
Our sins are stronger than we are,* but you will blot them out.
Psalm 65:3

A Reading
The Apostle wrote, saying: ". . . we have never failed to remember you in our
   prayers and ask that through perfect wisdom and spiritual understanding you
   should reach the fullest knowledge of his will and so be able to lead a life worthy of the Lord, a life acceptable to him in all its aspects, bearing fruit in every
   kind of good work and growing in knowledge of God."
Colossians 1:9–10

The Refrain
Our sins are stronger than we are,* but you will blot them out.

The Midday Psalm   *The LORD Is a Friend to Those Who Fear Him*
Who are they who fear the LORD?* he will teach them the way that they should
   choose.
They shall dwell in prosperity,* and their offspring shall inherit the land.
The LORD is a friend to those who fear him* and will show them his covenant.
Psalm 25:11–13

The Refrain
Our sins are stronger than we are,* but you will blot them out.

The Cry of the Church
Even so come, Lord Jesus.

The Lord's Prayer

The Prayer Appointed for the Week

Set me free, O God, from the bondage of my sins, and give me the liberty of that
abundant life which you have made known to me in your Son our Savior Jesus
Christ; who lives and reigns with you and the Holy Spirit, one God, now and
for ever. *Amen.* †

The Concluding Prayer of the Church

Almighty God, whose most dear Son went not up to joy before he first suffered
pain, and did not enter into glory before he was crucified: Mercifully grant that
I, walking in the way of the cross, may find it to be none other than the way of
life and peace; through Jesus Christ your Son my Lord. *Amen.* †

The Vespers Office　　　　　　　　　**To Be Observed on the Hour or Half Hour**
Between 5 and 8 p.m.

The Call to Prayer

I will call upon God,* and the LORD will deliver me.
In the evening, in the morning, and at the noonday, I will complain and lament,*
and he will hear my voice.
He will bring me safely back . . . God, who is enthroned of old, will hear me.

Psalm 55:17ff

The Request for Presence

Teach me your way, O LORD, and I will walk in your truth;* knit my heart to you
that I may fear your Name.

Psalm 86:11

The Greeting

To you, O LORD, I lift up my soul;* my God, I put my trust in you.

Psalm 25:1

The Hymn

Hail, O Star of ocean God's own Mother blessed,
Ever sinless Virgin gate of heavenly rest.

Show yourself a Mother, may the Word divine
Born for us your Infant hear my prayer through thine.

Keep my life all spotless, Make my way secure,
Till I find in Jesus joy that will endure.

Praise to God the Father honor to the Son,
In the Holy Spirit be the glory one.

adapted from THE SHORT BREVIARY

The Refrain for the Vespers Lessons

As far as the east is from the west,* so far has he removed our sins from us.

Psalm 103:12

The Vespers Psalm   *You Are the Holy One, Enthroned Upon the Praises of Israel*

My God, my God, why have you forsaken me?* and are so far from my cry and
   from the words of my distress?

O my God, I cry in the daytime, but you do not answer;* by night as well, but I
   find no rest.

Yet you are the Holy One,* enthroned upon the praises of Israel.

Our forefathers put their trust in you;* they trusted, and you delivered them.

They cried out to you and were delivered;* they trusted in you and were not put to
   shame.

Psalm 22:1–5

The Refrain

As far as the east is from the west,* so far has he removed our sins from us.

The Cry of the Church

O God, come to my assistance! O Lord, make haste to help me!

The Lord's Prayer

The Prayer Appointed for the Week

Set me free, O God, from the bondage of my sins, and give me the liberty of that
   abundant life which you have made known to me in your Son our Savior Jesus
   Christ; who lives and reigns with you and the Holy Spirit, one God, now and
   for ever. *Amen.* †

Concluding Prayers of the Church

Almighty God, who has promised to hear the petitions of those who ask in your
   Son's Name: I beseech you mercifully to incline your ear to me who have made
   my prayers and supplications to you; and grant that those things which I have
   faithfully asked according to your will, may effectually be obtained, to the
   relief of my necessity, and to the setting forth of your glory; through Jesus
   Christ my Lord. *Amen.* †

May the souls of the faithful departed, through the mercy of God, rest in eternal
   peace. *Amen.*

The Morning Office   **To Be Observed on the Hour or Half Hour**
                                          Between 6 and 9 a.m.

The Call to Prayer

Ascribe to the Lord the glory due his Name;* worship the Lord in the beauty of
   holiness.

Psalm 29:2

The Request for Presence

O God, you are my God; eagerly I seek you;* my soul thirsts for you, my flesh
   faints for you, as in barren and dry land where there is no water.

Psalm 63:1

The Greeting
We have heard with our ears, O God, our forefathers have told us,* the deeds you
did in their days, in the days of old.

Psalm 44:1

The Refrain for the Morning Lessons
Rescue the weak and the poor;* deliver them from the power of the wicked.

Psalm 82:4

A Reading
Jesus taught us, saying: "You have heard how it was said, *You will love your neighbor* and hate your enemy. But I say this to you, love your enemies and pray for
those who persecute you; so that you may be children of your Father in
heaven, for he causes his sun to rise on the bad as well as the good, and sends
down rain to fall on the upright and the wicked alike."

Matthew 5:43–45

The Refrain
Rescue the weak and the poor;* deliver them from the power of the wicked.

The Morning Psalm   *Whoever Is Wise Will Ponder These Things*
The LORD changed rivers into deserts,* and water-springs into thirsty ground,
A fruitful land into salt flats,* because of the wickedness of those who dwell there.
He changed deserts into pools of water* and dry land into water-springs.
He settled the hungry there,* and they founded a city to dwell in.
They sowed fields, and planted vineyards,* and brought in a fruitful harvest.
He blessed them, so that they increased greatly;* he did not let their herds decrease.
Yet when they were diminished and brought low,* through stress of adversity and
sorrow,
(He pours contempt on princes* and makes them wander in trackless wastes)
He lifted up the poor out of misery* and multiplied their families like flocks of
sheep.
The upright will see this and rejoice,* but all wickedness will shut its mouth.
Whoever is wise will ponder these things,* and consider well the mercies of the
LORD.

Psalm 107:33–43

The Refrain
Rescue the weak and the poor;* deliver them from the power of the wicked.

The Gloria

The Lord's Prayer

The Prayer Appointed for the Week
Set me free, O God, from the bondage of my sins, and give me the liberty of that
abundant life which you have made known to me in your Son our Savior Jesus
Christ; who lives and reigns with you and the Holy Spirit, one God, now and
for ever. *Amen.* †

The Concluding Prayer of the Church
Lord God, almighty and everlasting Father, you have brought me in safety to this
new day: Preserve me with your mighty power, that I may not fall into sin, nor
be overcome by adversity; and in all I do direct me to the fulfilling of your purpose; through Jesus Christ my Lord. *Amen.* †

The Midday Office **To Be Observed on the Hour or Half Hour**
Between 11 a.m. and 2 p.m.

The Call to Prayer
Bless God in the congregation;* bless the LORD, you that are of the fountain of
Israel.

Psalm 68:26

The Request for Presence
I call upon you, O God, for you will answer me;* incline your ear to me and hear
my words.

Psalm 17:6

The Greeting
You are my God, and I will thank you;* you are my God, and I will exalt you.

Psalm 118:28

The Refrain for the Midday Lessons
The LORD, the God of gods, has spoken;* he has called the earth from the rising of
the sun to its setting.

Psalm 50:1

A Reading
The Apostle wrote, saying: "I have accepted the loss of all other things, and look
on them all as filth if only I can gain Christ and be given a place in him, with
the uprightness I have gained not from the Law, but through faith in Christ, an
uprightness from God, based on faith, that I may come to know him and the
power of his resurrection."

Philippians 3:8–10

The Refrain
The LORD, the God of gods, has spoken;* he has called the earth from the rising of
the sun to its setting.

The Midday Psalm *Kingship Belongs to the LORD*
All the ends of the earth shall remember and turn to the LORD,* and all the families
of the nations shall bow before him.
For kingship belongs to the LORD;* he rules over the nations.
To him alone all who sleep in the earth bow down in worship;* who go down to
the dust fall before him.

My soul shall live for him; my descendants shall serve him;* they shall be known
   as the LORD's for ever.
They shall come and make known to a people yet unborn* the saving deeds that
   he has done.

Psalm 22:26–30

The Refrain
The LORD, the God of gods, has spoken;* he has called the earth from the rising of
   the sun to its setting.

The Gloria

The Lord's Prayer

The Prayer Appointed for the Week
Set me free, O God, from the bondage of my sins, and give me the liberty of that
   abundant life which you have made known to me in your Son our Savior Jesus
   Christ; who lives and reigns with you and the Holy Spirit, one God, now and
   for ever. *Amen.* †

The Concluding Prayer of the Church
O God, the source of eternal light: Shed forth your unending day upon all of us
   who watch for you, that our lips may praise you, our lives may bless you, and
   our worship may give you glory; through Jesus Christ our Lord. *Amen.* †

The Vespers Office   To Be Observed on the Hour or Half Hour
                                      Between 5 and 8 p.m.

The Call to Prayer
The LORD is my strength and my shield;* my heart trusts him, and I have been
   helped;
Therefore my heart dances for joy,* and in my song I will praise him.

Psalm 28:8–9

The Request for Presence
Hear, O LORD, and have mercy upon me;* O LORD, be my helper.

Psalm 30:11

The Greeting
Your righteousness, O God, reaches to the heavens;* you have done great things;
   who is like you, O God?

Psalm 71:19

The Hymn
Blessed Jesus, at Your word we are gathered all to hear You;
Let our hearts and souls be stirred now to seek and love and fear You,
      By your teachings sweet and holy,
      Drawn from earth to love You solely.

All our knowledge, sense, and sight lie in deepest darkness shrouded,
Till Your spirit breaks our night with the beams of truth unclouded.
>   You alone to God can win us;
>   You must work all good within us.

Glorious Lord, Yourself impart! Light of light, from God proceeding,
Open now our ears and heart; help is by Your spirit's pleading;
>   Hear the cry your people raises;
>   Hear, and bless our prayers and praises.

Tobias Clausnitzer

The Refrain for the Vespers Lessons

Remember me, O LORD, with the favor you have for your people,* and visit me
with your saving help.

Psalm 106:4

The Vespers Psalm   Who Can Ascend the Hill of the LORD?

The earth is the LORD's and all that is in it,* the world and all who dwell therein.
For it is he who founded it upon the seas* and made it firm upon the rivers of the
deep.
"Who can ascend the hill of the LORD?* and who can stand in his holy place?"
"Those who have clean hands and a pure heart,* who have not pledged themselves
to falsehood, nor sworn by what is a fraud.
They shall receive a blessing from the LORD* and a just reward from the God of
their salvation."
Such is the generation of those who seek him,* of those who seek your face, O God
of Jacob.

Psalm 24:1–6

The Refrain

Remember me, O LORD, with the favor you have for your people,* and visit me
with your saving help.

The Gloria

The Lord's Prayer

The Prayer Appointed for the Week

Set me free, O God, from the bondage of my sins, and give me the liberty of that
abundant life which you have made known to me in your Son our Savior Jesus
Christ; who lives and reigns with you and the Holy Spirit, one God, now and
for ever. *Amen.* †

The Concluding Prayer of the Church

Give me courage to resist, patience to endure, constancy to persevere. Grant, in
place of all consolations of the world, the most sweet unction of Thy Spirit, and
in place of carnal love, pour into me the love of Thy Name.

Thomas à Kempis

The Morning Office   To Be Observed on the Hour or Half Hour
                                                           Between 6 and 9 a.m.

The Call to Prayer
Let the peoples praise you, O God;* let all the peoples praise you.
Let the nations be glad and sing for joy,* for you judge the peoples with equity and
    guide all nations upon the earth.
Let the peoples praise you, O God;* let all the peoples praise you.

Psalm 67:3–5

The Request for Presence
Hear my voice, O Lord, according to your loving-kindness;* according to your
    judgments, give me life.

Psalm 119:149

The Greeting
Hosanna, Lord, hosanna!* Lord, send us now success.
Blessed is he who comes in the name of the Lord;* we bless you from the house of
    the Lord.

Psalm 118:25–26

The Refrain for the Morning Lessons
I was glad when they said to me,* "Let us go to the house of the Lord."

Psalm 122:1

A Reading
Jesus said: "The Sabbath was made for man, not man for the Sabbath; so the Son of
    man is master even of the Sabbath."

Mark 2:27–28

The Refrain
I was glad when they said to me,* "Let us go to the house of the Lord."

The Morning Psalm   *The Lord Has Ordained a Blessing*
Oh, how good and pleasant it is,* when brethren live together in unity!
It is like fine oil upon the head* that runs down upon the beard,
Upon the beard of Aaron,* and runs down upon the collar of his robe.
It is like the dew of Hermon* that falls upon the hills of Zion.
For there the Lord has ordained the blessing:* life for evermore.

Psalm 133

The Refrain
I was glad when they said to me,* "Let us go to the house of the Lord."

The Cry of the Church
O God, come to my assistance! O Lord, make haste to help me.

The Lord's Prayer

The Prayer Appointed for the Week
O God, the strength of all who put their trust in you: Mercifully accept my
prayers; and because in my weakness I can do nothing good without you, give
me the help of your grace, that in keeping your commandments I may please
you in both will and deed; through Jesus Christ my Lord, who lives and reigns
with you and the Holy Spirit, one God, for ever and ever. *Amen.* †

The Concluding Prayer of the Church
Lord God, almighty and everlasting Father, you have brought me in safety to this
new day: Preserve me with your mighty power, that I may not fall into sin, nor
be overcome by adversity; and in all I do direct me to the fulfilling of your purpose; through Jesus Christ my Lord. *Amen.* †

The Midday Office **To Be Observed on the Hour or Half Hour**
Between 11 a.m. and 2 p.m.

The Call to Prayer
Worship the LORD in the beauty of holiness;* let the whole earth tremble before
him.

Psalm 96:9

The Request for Presence
Hear, O Shepherd of Israel, leading Joseph like a flock;* shine forth, you that are
enthroned upon the cherubim.

Psalm 80:1

The Greeting
Yours is the day, yours also is the night;* you established the moon and the sun.
You fixed all the boundaries of the earth;* you made both summer and winter.

Psalm 74:15–16

The Refrain for the Midday Lessons
The earth, O LORD, is full of your love;* instruct me in your statutes.

Psalm 119:64

A Reading
The past is out of reach, buried deep—who can discover it? But I have reached the
point where, having learned, explored and investigated wisdom and reflection,
I recognize evil as being a form of madness, and folly as something stupid.

Ecclesiastes 7:24–25

The Refrain
The earth, O LORD, is full of your love;* instruct me in your statutes.

The Midday Psalm   *The Righteous Shall Flourish Like a Palm Tree*

LORD, how great are your works!* your thoughts are very deep.

The dullard does not know, nor does the fool understand,* that though the wicked grow like weeds, and all the workers of iniquity flourish,

They flourish only to be destroyed for ever;* but you, O LORD, are exalted for evermore.

For lo, your enemies, O LORD, lo, your enemies shall perish,* and all the workers of iniquity shall be scattered.

But my horn you have exalted like the horns of wild bulls;* I am anointed with fresh oil.

My eyes also gloat over my enemies,* and my ears rejoice to hear the doom of the wicked who rise up against me.

The righteous shall flourish like a palm tree,* and shall spread abroad like a cedar of Lebanon.

Those who are planted in the house of the LORD* shall flourish in the courts of our God;

They shall still bear fruit in old age;* they shall be green and succulent;

That they may show how upright the LORD is,* my Rock, in whom there is no fault.

Psalm 92:5–14

The Refrain

The earth, O LORD, is full of your love;* instruct me in your statutes.

The Gloria

The Lord's Prayer

The Prayer Appointed for the Week

O God, the strength of all who put their trust in you: Mercifully accept my prayers; and because in my weakness I can do nothing good without you, give me the help of your grace, that in keeping your commandments I may please you in both will and deed; through Jesus Christ my Lord, who lives and reigns with you and the Holy Spirit, one God, for ever and ever. *Amen.* †

The Concluding Prayer of the Church

O God, you make me glad with the weekly remembrance of the glorious resurrection of your Son my Lord: Give me this day such blessing through my worship of you, that the week to come may be spent in your favor; through Jesus Christ our Lord. *Amen.* †

The Vespers Office   **To Be Observed on the Hour or Half Hour**
                                                Between 5 and 8 p.m.

The Call to Prayer

Let the Name of the LORD be blessed,* from this time forth for evermore.

From the rising of the sun to its going down* let the Name of the LORD be praised.

Psalm 113:2–3

The Request for Presence
As the eyes of servants look to the hand of their masters,* and the eyes of a maid to
the hand of her mistress,
So our eyes look to you, O LORD our God.

adapted from Psalm 123:2–3

The Greeting
Blessed is the LORD!* for he has heard the voice of my prayer.

Psalm 28:7

The Hymn *Something for Thee*

Savior, Your dying love you gave to me,
Nothing should I withhold, Dear Lord, from Thee:
    In love my soul would bow,
    My heart fulfill its vow,
    Some offering bring you now,
Something for Thee.

At the blessed mercy seat, pleading for me,
My feeble faith looks up, Jesus, to Thee:
    Help me the cross to bear,
    Your wondrous love declare,
    Some song to raise, or prayer,
Something for Thee.

Give me a faithful heart, likeness to Thee,
That each departing day henceforth may see
    Some work of love begun,
    Some deed of kindness done,
    Some wanderer sought and won,
Something for Thee.

All that I am and have, Your gifts so free,
In joy, in grief, through life, Dear Lord, for Thee!
    And when your face I see,
    My ransomed soul shall be,
    Through all eternity,
Something for Thee.

Sylvanus Phelps

The Refrain for the Vespers Lessons
For you, O LORD, are good and forgiving,* and great is your love toward all who
call upon you.

Psalm 86:5

The Vespers Psalm *More Than Watchmen for the Morning*
I wait for the LORD; my soul waits for him;* in his word is my hope.
My soul waits for the LORD, more than watchmen for the morning,* more than
watchmen for the morning.

Psalm 130:4–5

The Refrain
For you, O LORD, are good and forgiving,* and great is your love toward all who
call upon you.

The Cry of the Church
Lord, have mercy on us. Christ, have mercy on us. Lord, have mercy on us.

The Lord's Prayer

The Prayer Appointed for the Week
O God, the strength of all who put their trust in you: Mercifully accept my
prayers; and because in my weakness I can do nothing good without you, give
me the help of your grace, that in keeping your commandments I may please
you in both will and deed; through Jesus Christ my Lord, who lives and reigns
with you and the Holy Spirit, one God, for ever and ever. *Amen.* †

The Concluding Prayer of the Church
In truth God has heard me;* he has attended to the voice of my prayer.
Blessed be God, who has not rejected my prayer,* nor withheld his love from me.
Psalm 66:17–18

The Morning Office   **To Be Observed on the Hour or Half Hour**
                                                  Between 6 and 9 a.m.

The Call to Prayer
The LORD is King; let the earth rejoice;* let the multitude of the isles be glad.
Psalm 97:1

The Request for Presence
I long for your salvation, O LORD,* and your law is my delight.
Psalm 119:174

The Greeting
The LORD lives! Blessed is my Rock!* Exalted is the God of my salvation!
Psalm 18:46

The Refrain for the Morning Lessons
The fool has said in his heart, "There is no God."
Psalm 14:1

A Reading
He went back again to the far side of the Jordan to the district where John had
been baptizing at first and he stayed there. Many people who came to him said,
'John gave no signs, but all he said about this man was true'; and many of them
believed in him.
John 10:40–42

The Refrain
The fool has said in his heart, "There is no God."

The Morning Psalm   *This Is My Prayer to You*

But as for me, this is my prayer to you,* at the time you have set, O LORD:

"In your great mercy, O God,* answer me with your unfailing help.

Save me from the mire; do not let me sink;* let me be rescued from those who hate
    me and out of the deep waters.

Let not the torrent of waters wash over me, neither let the deep swallow me up;*
    do not let the Pit shut its mouth upon me.

Answer me, O LORD, for your love is kind;* in your great compassion, turn to me."

                                                            Psalm 69:14–18

The Refrain

The fool has said in his heart, "There is no God."

The Cry of the Church

Even so, come Lord Jesus!

The Lord's Prayer

The Prayer Appointed for the Week

O God, the strength of all who put their trust in you: Mercifully accept my
    prayers; and because in my weakness I can do nothing good without you, give
    me the help of your grace, that in keeping your commandments I may please
    you in both will and deed; through Jesus Christ my Lord, who lives and reigns
    with you and the Holy Spirit, one God, for ever and ever. *Amen.* †

The Concluding Prayer of the Church

Lord God, almighty and everlasting Father, you have brought me in safety to this
    new day: Preserve me with your mighty power, that I may not fall into sin, nor
    be overcome by adversity; and in all I do direct me to the fulfilling of your pur-
    pose; through Jesus Christ my Lord. *Amen.* †

The Midday Office   To Be Observed on the Hour or Half Hour
                                            Between 11 a.m. and 2 p.m.

The Call to Prayer

Let us make a vow to the LORD our God and keep it;* let all around him bring gifts
    to him who is worthy to be feared.

                                            adapted from Psalm 76:11

The Request for Presence

Let the peoples praise you, O God;* let all the peoples praise you.

                                            Psalm 67:3

The Greeting

Happy are the people whose strength is in you!* whose hearts are set on the
    pilgrims' way.

                                            Psalm 84:4

The Refrain for the Midday Lessons
All the nations you have made will come and worship you, O LORD,* and glorify
your Name.

Psalm 86:9

A Reading
Who can overcome the world but the one who believes in the Son of God?

I John 5:5

The Refrain
All the nations you have made will come and worship you, O LORD,* and glorify
your Name.

The Midday Psalm   *Great Is Our* LORD
Hallelujah! How good it is to sing praises to our God!* how pleasant it is to honor
him with praise!
The LORD rebuilds Jerusalem;* he gathers the exiles of Israel.
He heals the brokenhearted* and binds up their wounds.
He counts the number of the stars* and calls them all by their names.
Great is our LORD and mighty in power;* there is no limit to his wisdom.
The LORD lifts up the lowly,* but casts the wicked to the ground.
Sing to the LORD with thanksgiving;* make music to our God upon the harp.

Psalm 147:1–7

The Refrain
All the nations you have made will come and worship you, O LORD,* and glorify
your Name.

The Small Verse
Give thanks to the LORD, for he is good,* for his mercy endures for ever.
Give thanks to the God of gods,* for his mercy endures for ever.
Give thanks to the Lord of lords,* for his mercy endures for ever.

Psalm 136:1–3

The Lord's Prayer

The Prayer Appointed for the Week
O God, the strength of all who put their trust in you: Mercifully accept my
prayers; and because in my weakness I can do nothing good without you, give
me the help of your grace, that in keeping your commandments I may please
you in both will and deed; through Jesus Christ my Lord, who lives and reigns
with you and the Holy Spirit, one God, for ever and ever. *Amen.* †

The Concluding Prayer of the Church
Let us bless the Lord God living and true! Let us always render him praise, glory,
honor, blessing, and all good things! Amen. Amen. So be it! So be it!

St. Francis of Assisi

The Vespers Office   **To Be Observed on the Hour or Half Hour**
                                                          Between 5 and 8 p.m.

The Call to Prayer
Open my lips, O Lord,* and my mouth shall proclaim your praise.
Had you desired it, I would have offered sacrifice,* but you take no delight in
    burnt-offerings.
The sacrifice of God is a troubled spirit;* and a broken and contrite heart, O God,
    you will not despise.

Psalm 51:16–18

The Request for Presence
Give ear, O LORD, to my prayer,* and attend to the voice of my supplications.

Psalm 86:6

The Greeting
I give you thanks, O God, I give you thanks,* calling upon your Name and declaring
    all your wonderful deeds.

adapted from Psalm 75:1

The Hymn
Praise the Lord through every nation;
His holy arm has brought salvation;
            Exalt him on his Father's throne.
Praise your King, you Christian legions,
Who now prepares in heavenly regions
            Unfailing mansions for his own:
With voice and minstrelsy
Extol his majesty,
            Raise your anthem now!
His praise shall sound
All nature round,
and hymns on every tongue abound.

Jesus, Lord, our captain glorious,
Over sin and death, and hell victorious,
            Wisdom and might to you belong:
We confess, proclaim, adore you;
We bow the knee, we fall before you;
            Your love henceforth will be our song.
The cross meanwhile we bear,
The crown ere long to wear;
            Raise your anthem now!
Your reign extend
World without end;
Let praise from all to you ascend.

Rhijnvis Feith

The Refrain for the Vespers Lessons
For you are my hope, O Lord GOD,* my confidence since I was young.

Psalm 71:5

The Vespers Psalm   *May All the Nations Bless Themselves*
                                       in Him and Call Him Blessed
Long may he live! and may there be given to him gold from Arabia;* may prayer
    be made for him always, and may they bless him all the day long.
May there be abundance of grain on the earth, growing thick even on the hilltops;*
    may its fruit flourish like Lebanon, and its grain like grass upon the earth.
May his Name remain for ever and be established as long as the sun endures;*
    may all the nations bless themselves in him and call him blessed.

Psalm 72:15–17

The Refrain
For you are my hope, O Lord GOD,* my confidence since I was young.

The Small Verse
The Lord is my shepherd and nothing is wanting to me. In green pastures He has
    settled me.

The Lord's Prayer

The Prayer Appointed for the Week
O God, the strength of all who put their trust in you: Mercifully accept my
    prayers; and because in my weakness I can do nothing good without you, give
    me the help of your grace, that in keeping your commandments I may please
    you in both will and deed; through Jesus Christ my Lord, who lives and reigns
    with you and the Holy Spirit, one God, for ever and ever. *Amen.* †

The Concluding Prayer of the Church
Visit, I beseech you, O Lord, this dwelling and drive far from it all the snares of the
    enemy; let Your holy angels dwell herein, who may keep us in peace, and let
    Your blessing always be upon me. Through our Lord Jesus Christ, Your Son,
    who lives and reigns with You in the unity of the Holy Spirit, God. World with-
    out end. *Amen.*

adapted from THE SHORT BREVIARY

The Morning Office   To Be Observed on the Hour or Half Hour
                                      Between 6 and 9 a.m.

The Call to Prayer
Hallelujah! Praise the Name of the LORD;* give praise, you servants of the LORD,
Praise the LORD, for the LORD is good;* sing praises to his Name, for it is lovely.
For I know that the LORD is great,* and that our Lord is above all gods.

Psalm 135:1ff

The Request for Presence
Satisfy us by your loving-kindness in the morning;* so shall we rejoice and be glad
all the days of our life.

Psalm 90:14

The Greeting
Out of Zion, perfect in its beauty,* God reveals himself in glory.
Let the heavens declare the rightness of his cause;* for God himself is judge.

Psalm 50:2, 6

The Refrain for the Morning Lessons
Wake up, my spirit; awake, lute and harp;* I myself will waken the dawn.

Psalm 108:2

A Reading
He said again to the crowds, "When you see a cloud looming up in the west you
say at once that rain is coming, and so it does. And when the wind is from the
south you say it's going to be hot, and it is. Hypocrites! You know how to inter-
pret the face of the earth and the sky. How is it you do not know how to inter-
pret these times?"

Luke 12:54–56

The Refrain
Wake up, my spirit; awake, lute and harp;* I myself will waken the dawn.

The Morning Psalm   *Praise Him, All His Host*
Praise the Lord from the earth,* you sea-monsters and all deeps;
Fire and hail, snow and fog,* tempestuous wind, doing his will;
Mountains and all hills,* fruit trees and all cedars;
Wild beasts and all cattle,* creeping things and winged birds;
Kings of the earth and all peoples,* princes and all rulers of the world;
Young men and maidens,* old and young together.
Let them praise the Name of the Lord,* for his Name only is exalted, his splendor
is over earth and heaven.
He has raised up strength for his people and praise for all his loyal servants,* the
children of Israel, a people who are near him. Hallelujah!

Psalm 148:6–14

The Refrain
Wake up, my spirit; awake, lute and harp;* I myself will waken the dawn.

The Gloria

The Lord's Prayer

The Prayer Appointed for the Week
O God, the strength of all who put their trust in you: Mercifully accept my
prayers; and because in my weakness I can do nothing good without you, give
me the help of your grace, that in keeping your commandments I may please

you in both will and deed; through Jesus Christ my Lord, who lives and reigns
with you and the Holy Spirit, one God, for ever and ever. *Amen.* †

The Concluding Prayer of the Church
Lord God, almighty and everlasting Father, you have brought me in safety to this
new day: Preserve me with your mighty power, that I may not fall into sin, nor
be overcome by adversity; and in all I do direct me to the fulfilling of your purpose; through Jesus Christ my Lord. *Amen.* †

The Midday Office   To Be Observed on the Hour or Half Hour
                                     Between 11 a.m. and 2 p.m.

The Call to Prayer
Worship the LORD in the beauty of holiness;* let the whole earth tremble before
him.
Tell it among the nations: "The LORD is King!* he has made the world so firm that
it cannot be moved; he will judge the peoples with equity."

Psalm 96:9–10

The Request for Presence
Be my strong rock, a castle to keep me safe,* for you are my crag and my stronghold; for the sake of your Name, lead me and guide me.

Psalm 31:3

The Greeting
I love you, O LORD of my strength,* O LORD my stronghold, my crag, and my
haven.
My God, my rock in whom I put my trust,* my shield, the horn of my salvation,
and my refuge; you are worthy of praise.

Psalm 18:1–2

The Refrain for the Midday Lessons
Into your hands I commend my spirit.
Psalm 31:5

A Reading
Here is a saying you can rely on: If we have died with him, then we shall live with
him. If we persevere, then we shall reign with him. If we disown him, then he
will disown us. If we are faithless, he is faithful still, for he can not disown his
own self.

2 Timothy 2:11–13

The Refrain
Into your hands I commend my spirit.

The Midday Psalm   *He Turns the Flint-stone into a Flowing Spring*
Hallelujah! When Israel came out of Egypt,* the house of Jacob from a people of
strange speech,

Judah became God's sanctuary* and Israel his dominion.
The sea beheld it and fled;* Jordan turned and went back.
The mountains skipped like rams,* and the little hills like young sheep.
What ailed you, O sea, that you fled?* O Jordan, that you turned back?
You mountains, that you skipped like rams?* you little hills like young sheep?
Tremble, O earth, at the presence of the Lord,* at the presence of the God of Jacob,
Who turned the hard rock into a pool of water* and flint-stone into a flowing
    spring.

Psalm 114

The Refrain
Into your hands I commend my spirit.

The Small Verse
I will bless the Lord at all times
And his praise shall be always in my mouth.
Glory to the Father and the Son
And the eternal Spirit.

Traditional

The Lord's Prayer

The Prayer Appointed for the Week
O God, the strength of all who put their trust in you: Mercifully accept my
    prayers; and because in my weakness I can do nothing good without you, give
    me the help of your grace, that in keeping your commandments I may please
    you in both will and deed; through Jesus Christ my Lord, who lives and reigns
    with you and the Holy Spirit, one God, for ever and ever. *Amen.* †

The Concluding Prayer of the Church
Heavenly Father, you have promised to hear what we ask in the Name of your
    Son: Accept and fulfill my petitions, I pray, not as I ask in my ignorance, nor as
    I deserve in my sinfulness, but as you know and love me in your Son Jesus
    Christ our Lord. *Amen.* †

The Vespers Office   To Be Observed on the Hour or Half Hour
                                            Between 5 and 8 p.m.

The Call to Prayer
Sing to the LORD, you servants of his;* give thanks for the remembrance of his
    holiness.
For his wrath endures but the twinkling of an eye,* his favor for a lifetime.

Psalm 30:4–5

The Request for Presence
Hear my prayer, O LORD, and give ear to my cry; . . . For I am but a sojourner with
    you,* a wayfarer, as all my forebears were.

Psalm 39:13–14

The Greeting

O God, when you went forth before your people* when you marched through the
wilderness,

The earth shook, and the skies poured down rain, at the presence of God, the God
of Sinai* at the presence of God, the God of Israel.

You sent a gracious rain, O God, upon your inheritance;* you refreshed the land
when it was weary.

The Lord gave the word;* great was the company of women who bore the tidings.

Psalm 68:7ff

The Hymn

O for a thousand tongues to sing my dear Redeemer's praise,
The glories of my God and King, the triumphs of his grace!

My gracious Master and my God, assist me to proclaim
And spread through all the earth abroad the honors of your Name.

Jesus! The Name that charms our fears and bids our sorrows cease;
'Tis music in the sinners' ears, 'tis life and health and peace.

He speaks; and, listening to his voice, new life the dead receive,
The mournful broken hearts rejoice, the humble poor believe.

Hear him, you deaf, you voiceless ones, your loosened tongues employ;
You blind, behold, your Savior comes; and leap, you lame, for joy!

Glory to God and praise and love be now and ever given
By saints below and saints above, the Church in earth and heaven.

Charles Wesley

The Refrain for the Vespers Lessons

Weeping may spend the night,* but joy comes in the morning.

Psalm 30:6

The Vespers Psalm   **Blessed Be the LORD**

Blessed be the LORD!* he has not given us over to be a prey for their teeth.

We have escaped like a bird from the snare of the fowler;* the snare is broken, and
we have escaped.

Our help is in the Name of the LORD,* the maker of heaven and earth.

Psalm 124:6-8

The Refrain

Weeping may spend the night,* but joy comes in the morning.

The Gloria

The Lord's Prayer

The Prayer Appointed for the Week

O God, the strength of all who put their trust in you: Mercifully accept my
prayers; and because in my weakness I can do nothing good without you, give

me the help of your grace, that in keeping your commandments I may please you in both will and deed; through Jesus Christ my Lord, who lives and reigns with you and the Holy Spirit, one God, for ever and ever. *Amen.* †

The Concluding Prayer of the Church
Hear, O Lord, your servants, offering evening praises to your Name. Through the silent hours of the night deign to watch over us, whom You have protected in all dangers of the day. Through Jesus Christ our Lord. *Amen.*

Anglo-Saxon, Traditional

The Morning Office   To Be Observed on the Hour or Half Hour
                                       Between 6 and 9 a.m.

The Call to Prayer
I will call upon God,* and the LORD will deliver me.
In the evening, in the morning, and at the noonday, I will complain and lament,* and he will hear my voice.
He will bring me safely back . . . God, who is enthroned of old, will hear me.

Psalm 55:17ff

The Request for Presence
Show us the light of your countenance, O God,* and come to us.

based on Psalm 67:1

The Greeting
In you, O LORD, have I taken refuge; let me never be put to shame;* deliver me in your righteousness.

Psalm 31:1

The Refrain for the Morning Lessons
The same stone that the builders rejected* has become the chief cornerstone.

Psalm 118:22

A Reading
The apostles said to the Lord, 'Increase our faith.' The Lord replied, 'If you had faith like a mustard seed you could say to this mulberry tree, "Be uprooted and planted in the sea," and it would obey you.'

Luke 17:5–6

The Refrain
The same stone that the builders rejected* has become the chief cornerstone.

The Morning Psalm   *A Canticle of the Messiah*
The LORD said to my Lord, "Sit at my right hand,* until I make your enemies your footstool."

The LORD will send the scepter of your power out of Zion,* saying, "Rule over
  your enemies round about you.
Princely state has been yours from the day of your birth;* in the beauty of holiness
  have I begotten you, like dew from the womb of the morning."
The LORD has sworn and he will not recant:* "You are a priest for ever after the
  order of Melchizedek."

Psalm 110:1–4

The Refrain
The same stone that the builders rejected* has become the chief cornerstone.

The Cry of the Church
O God, come to my assistance! O Lord, make haste to help me!

The Lord's Prayer

The Prayer Appointed for the Week
O God, the strength of all who put their trust in you: Mercifully accept my
  prayers; and because in my weakness I can do nothing good without you, give
  me the help of your grace, that in keeping your commandments I may please
  you in both will and deed; through Jesus Christ my Lord, who lives and reigns
  with you and the Holy Spirit, one God, for ever and ever. *Amen.* †

The Concluding Prayer of the Church
Lord God, almighty and everlasting Father, you have brought me in safety to this
  new day: Preserve me with your mighty power, that I may not fall into sin, nor
  be overcome by adversity; and in all I do direct me to the fulfilling of your purpose; through Jesus Christ my Lord. *Amen.* †

The Midday Office   **To Be Observed on the Hour or Half Hour**
Between 11 a.m. and 2 p.m.

The Call to Prayer
Hallelujah! Sing to the LORD a new song;* sing his praise in the congregation of the
  faithful.

Psalm 149:1

The Request for Presence
You are good and you bring forth good;* instruct me in your statutes.

Psalm 119:68

The Greeting
Be exalted, O LORD, in your might;* we will sing and praise your power.

Psalm 21:14

The Refrain for the Midday Lessons
It is better to rely on the LORD* than to put any trust in flesh.
It is better to rely on the LORD* than to put any trust in rulers.

Psalm 118:8–9

A Reading
For *all humanity is grass, and all its beauty like the wildflower's. As grass withers, the flower fades, but the Word of the Lord remains for ever.* And this Word is the Good News that has been brought to you.

I Peter 1:24–25

The Refrain
It is better to rely on the LORD* than to put any trust in flesh.
It is better to rely on the LORD* than to put any trust in rulers.

The Midday Psalm   *The Judgments of the LORD Are Sweeter Far Than Honey*
The law of the LORD is perfect and revives the soul;* the testimony of the LORD is sure and gives wisdom to the innocent.
The statutes of the LORD are just and rejoice the heart;* the commandment of the LORD is clear and gives light to the eyes.
The fear of the LORD is clean and endures for ever;* the judgments of the LORD are true and righteous altogether.
More to be desired are they than gold, more than much fine gold,* sweeter far than honey, than honey in the comb.
By them also is your servant enlightened,* and in keeping them there is great reward.

Psalm 19:7–11

The Refrain
It is better to rely on the LORD* than to put any trust in flesh.
It is better to rely on the LORD* than to put any trust in rulers.

The Gloria

The Lord's Prayer

The Prayer Appointed for the Week
O God, the strength of all who put their trust in you: Mercifully accept my prayers; and because in my weakness I can do nothing good without you, give me the help of your grace, that in keeping your commandments I may please you in both will and deed; through Jesus Christ my Lord, who lives and reigns with you and the Holy Spirit, one God, for ever and ever. *Amen.* †

The Concluding Prayer of the Church
God of justice, God of mercy, bless all those who are surprised with pain this day from suffering caused by their own weakness or that of others. Let what we suffer teach us to be merciful; let our sins teach us to forgive. This I ask through the intercession of Jesus and all who died forgiving those who oppressed them. *Amen.* †

The Vespers Office   To Be Observed on the Hour or Half Hour
                                              Between 5 and 8 p.m.

The Call to Prayer
Let us give thanks to the LORD for his mercy* and the wonders he does for his
children.

Psalm 107:8

The Request for Presence
You are good and you bring forth good;* instruct me in your statutes.

Psalm 119:68

The Greeting
You are the LORD, most high over all the earth;* you are exalted far above all gods.

Psalm 97:9

The Hymn
Creator Spirit, by whose aid
The world's foundations first were laid,
Come, visit every humble mind;
Come, pour your joys on human-kind;
From sin and sorrow set us free,
And make your temples fit for thee.

O Source of uncreated light,
The Father's promised Paraclete,
Thrice holy Fount, Thrice holy Fire,
Our hearts and heavenly love inspire;
Come and your sacred unction bring
To sanctify us while we sing.

Plenteous of grace, come from on high,
Rich in your seven-fold energy;
Make us eternal truth receive,
And practice all that we believe;
Give us yourself, that we may see
The Father and the Son by thee.

John Dryden

The Refrain for the Vespers Lessons
The LORD, the God of gods, has spoken;* he has called the earth from the rising of
the sun to its setting.

Psalm 50:1

The Vespers Psalm   *O Mighty LORD, Your Faithfulness Is All Around You*
Who is like you, LORD God of hosts?* O mighty LORD, your faithfulness is all
around you.
You rule the raging of the sea* and still the surging of its waves.

You have crushed Rahab of the deep with a deadly wound;* you have scattered
 your enemies with your mighty arm.
Yours are the heavens; the earth also is yours;* you laid the foundations of the
 world and all that is in it.
You have made the north and the south;* Tabor and Hermon rejoice in your Name.
You have a mighty arm;* strong is your hand and high is your right hand.
Righteousness and justice are the foundations of your throne;* love and truth go
 before your face.

Psalm 89:8–14

The Refrain
The LORD, the God of gods, has spoken;* he has called the earth from the rising of
 the sun to its setting.

The Gloria

The Lord's Prayer

The Prayer Appointed for the Week
O God, the strength of all who put their trust in you: Mercifully accept my
 prayers; and because in my weakness I can do nothing good without you, give
 me the help of your grace, that in keeping your commandments I may please
 you in both will and deed; through Jesus Christ my Lord, who lives and reigns
 with you and the Holy Spirit, one God, for ever and ever. *Amen.* †

The Concluding Prayer of the Church
God our Father in Heaven have mercy on us.
God the Son, Redeemer of the world have mercy on us.
God the Holy Spirit have mercy on us.
Holy Trinity, one God have mercy on us.

Traditional

The Morning Office   **To Be Observed on the Hour or Half Hour**
                               Between 6 and 9 a.m.

The Call to Prayer
Come, let us sing to the LORD; . . . For the LORD is a great God,* and a great King
 above all gods.

Psalm 95:1, 3

The Request for Presence
Gladden the soul of your servant,* for to you, O LORD, I lift up my soul.

Psalm 86:4

The Greeting
Exalt yourself above the heavens, O God,* and your glory over all the earth.

Psalm 57:6

The Refrain for the Morning Lessons
Let not those who hope in you be put to shame through me, Lord GOD of hosts;*
　　let not those who seek you be disgraced because of me.

Psalm 69:7

A Reading
Jesus taught the people, saying: "You have heard how it was said: *Eye for eye and tooth for tooth*. But I say this to you: offer no resistance to the wicked. On the contrary, if anyone hits you on the right cheek, offer him the other as well; if someone wishes to go to law with you to get your tunic, let him have your cloak as well."

Matthew 5:38–41

The Refrain
Let not those who hope in you be put to shame through me, Lord GOD of hosts;*
　　let not those who seek you be disgraced because of me.

The Morning Psalm　　　　　　　*Your Throne, O God, Endures For Ever and Ever*
My heart is stirring with a noble song; let me recite what I have fashioned for the
　　king;* my tongue shall be the pen of a skilled writer.
You are the fairest of men;* grace flows from your lips, because God has blessed
　　you for ever.
Strap your sword upon your thigh, O mighty warrior,* in your pride and in your
　　majesty.
Ride out and conquer in the cause of truth* and for the sake of justice.
Your right hand will show you marvelous things;* your arrows are very sharp, O
　　mighty warrior.
The peoples are falling at your feet,* and the king's enemies are losing heart.
Your throne, O God, endures for ever and ever,* a scepter of righteousness is the
　　scepter of your kingdom; you love righteousness and hate iniquity.
Therefore God, your God, has anointed you* with the oil of gladness above your
　　fellows.

Psalm 45:1–8

The Refrain
Let not those who hope in you be put to shame through me, Lord GOD of hosts;*
　　let not those who seek you be disgraced because of me.

The Gloria

The Lord's Prayer

The Prayer Appointed for the Week
O God, the strength of all who put their trust in you: Mercifully accept my
　　prayers; and because in my weakness I can do nothing good without you, give
　　me the help of your grace, that in keeping your commandments I may please
　　you in both will and deed; through Jesus Christ my Lord, who lives and reigns
　　with you and the Holy Spirit, one God, for ever and ever. *Amen.* †

The Concluding Prayer of the Church
Lord God, almighty and everlasting Father, you have brought me in safety to this
new day: Preserve me with your mighty power, that I may not fall into sin, nor
be overcome by adversity; and in all I do direct me to the fulfilling of your purpose; through Jesus Christ my Lord. *Amen.* †

The Midday Office   To Be Observed on the Hour or Half Hour
                                   Between 11 a.m. and 2 p.m.

The Call to Prayer
Be strong and let your heart take courage,* all you who wait for the LORD.
                                                        Psalm 31:24

The Request for Presence
Hear my cry, O God,* and listen to my prayer.
I call upon you from the ends of the earth.
                                   Psalm 61:1–2

The Greeting
I love you, O LORD my strength,* O LORD my stronghold, my crag, and my haven.
                                                        Psalm 18:1

The Refrain for the Midday Lessons
Though my father and my mother forsake me,* the LORD will sustain me.
                                                        Psalm 27:14

A Reading
Again, do not listen to all that people say, then you will not hear your servant
abusing you. For often, as you very well know, you have abused others.
                                                 Ecclesiastes 7:21–22

The Refrain
Though my father and my mother forsake me,* the LORD will sustain me.

The Midday Psalm   *The Righteous Will Be Kept in Everlasting Remembrance*
Light shines in the darkness for the upright;* the righteous are merciful and full of
compassion.
It is good for them to be generous in lending* and to manage their affairs with
justice.
For they will never be shaken;* the righteous will be kept in everlasting
remembrance.
They will not be afraid of any evil rumors;* their heart is right; they put their trust
in the Lord.
Their heart is established and will not shrink,* until they see their desire upon
their enemies.
They have given freely to the poor,* and their righteousness stands fast for ever;
they will hold up their head with honor.

The wicked will see it and be angry; they will gnash their teeth and pine away;*
  the desires of the wicked will perish.

Psalm 112:4–10

The Refrain
Though my father and my mother forsake me,* the LORD will sustain me.

The Cry of the Church
In the evening, in the morning, and at noonday, I will complain and lament,* and
  he will hear my voice.

Psalm 55:18

The Lord's Prayer

The Prayer Appointed for the Week
O God, the strength of all who put their trust in you: Mercifully accept my
  prayers; and because in my weakness I can do nothing good without you, give
  me the help of your grace, that in keeping your commandments I may please
  you in both will and deed; through Jesus Christ my Lord, who lives and reigns
  with you and the Holy Spirit, one God, for ever and ever. *Amen.* †

The Concluding Prayer of the Church
God of mercy,
this midday moment of rest
is your welcome gift.
Bless the work we have begun,
and make good its defects
and let us finish it in a way that pleases you.
Grant this through Christ our Lord.

THE LITURGY OF THE HOURS, VOL. III

The Vespers Office **To Be Observed on the Hour or Half Hour**
Between 5 and 8 p.m.

The Call to Prayer
Come, let us sing to the LORD;* let us shout for joy to the Rock of our salvation.
Let us come before his presence with thanksgiving* and raise a loud shout to him
  with psalms.
For the LORD is a great God,* and a great King above all gods.
In his hands are the caverns of the earth,* and the heights of the hills are his also.
The sea is his, for he made it,* and his hands have molded the dry land.

Psalm 95:1–5

The Request for Presence
To you I lift up my eyes,* to you enthroned in the heavens.

Psalm 123:1

The Greeting
I put my trust in your mercy;* my heart is joyful because of your saving help.

Psalm 13:5

The Hymn

O Holy Spirit, by whose breath;
Life rises vibrant out of death;
Come to create, renew, inspire;
Kindle in our hearts your fire.

You are the seeker's sure resource,
Of burning love the living source,
Protector in the midst of strife,
The giver and the Lord of life.

Flood our dull senses with your light;
In mutual love our hearts unite.
Your power the whole creation fills;
Confirm our weak, uncertain wills.

From inner strife grant us release;
Turn nations to the ways of peace.
To fuller life your people bring
That as one body we may sing:

Praise to the Father, Christ his Word,
And to the Spirit: God the Lord,
To whom all honor, glory be
Both now and for eternity.

Rabanus Maurus

The Refrain for the Vespers Lessons
For we are your people and the sheep of your pasture;* we will give you thanks
for ever and show forth your praise from age to age.

Psalm 79:13

The Vespers Psalm   *Those Who Sowed with Tears Will Reap with Songs of Joy*
When the LORD restored the fortunes of Zion,* then were we like those who
dream.
Then was our mouth filled with laughter,* and our tongue with shouts of joy.
Then they said among the nations,* "The LORD has done great things for them."
The LORD has done great things for us,* and we are glad indeed.
Restore our fortunes, O LORD,* like the watercourses of the Negev.
Those who sowed with tears* will reap with songs of joy.
Those who go out weeping, carrying the seed,* will come again with joy,
shouldering their sheaves.

Psalm 126:1–7

The Refrain
For we are your people and the sheep of your pasture;* we will give you thanks
for ever and show forth your praise from age to age.

The Cry of the Church
O God, come to my assistance! O Lord, make haste to help me!

The Lord's Prayer

The Prayer Appointed for the Week
O God, the strength of all who put their trust in you: Mercifully accept my
prayers; and because in my weakness I can do nothing good without you, give
me the help of your grace, that in keeping your commandments I may please

you in both will and deed; through Jesus Christ my Lord, who lives and reigns with you and the Holy Spirit, one God, for ever and ever. *Amen.* †

The Concluding Prayer of the Church
May God, the Lord, bless us with heavenly benediction, and make us pure and holy in his sight.
May the riches of his glory abound in us.
May He instruct us with the word of truth, inform us with the Gospel of salvation, and enrich us with his love, Through Jesus Christ, our Lord.

Gelasian Sacramentary

The Morning Office   **To Be Observed on the Hour or Half Hour Between 6 and 9 a.m.**

The Call to Prayer
I will call upon God,* and the Lord will deliver me.
God, who is enthroned of old, will hear me.

Psalm 55:17, 20

The Request for Presence
Our God will come and will not keep silence;* before him there is a consuming flame, and round about him a raging storm.

Psalm 50:3

The Greeting
For your Name's sake, O Lord,* forgive my sin, for it is great.

Psalm 25:10

The Refrain for the Morning Lessons
Help me, O Lord my God;* save me for your mercy's sake.

Psalm 109:25

A Reading
Jesus said: "If your right eye should be your downfall, tear it out and throw it away; for it will do you less harm to lose one part of yourself than to have your whole body thrown into hell. And if your right hand should be your downfall, cut it off and throw it away; for it will do you less harm to lose one part of yourself than to have your whole body thrown into hell."

Matthew 5:29–30

The Refrain
Help me, O Lord my God;* save me for your mercy's sake.

The Morning Psalm   *Let Them Offer a Sacrifice of Thanksgiving*
He sent forth his word and healed them* and saved them from the grave.
Let them give thanks to the Lord for his mercy* and the wonders he does for his children.

Let them offer a sacrifice of thanksgiving* and tell of his acts with shouts of joy.

Psalm 107:20–22

The Refrain
Help me, O LORD my God;* save me for your mercy's sake.

The Cry of the Church
O God, come to my assistance! O Lord, make haste to help me!

The Lord's Prayer

The Prayer Appointed for the Week
O God, the strength of all who put their trust in you: Mercifully accept my
    prayers; and because in my weakness I can do nothing good without you, give
    me the help of your grace, that in keeping your commandments I may please
    you in both will and deed; through Jesus Christ my Lord, who lives and reigns
    with you and the Holy Spirit, one God, for ever and ever. *Amen.* †

The Concluding Prayer of the Church
Lord God, almighty and everlasting Father, you have brought me in safety to this
    new day: Preserve me with your mighty power, that I may not fall into sin, nor
    be overcome by adversity; and in all I do direct me to the fulfilling of your pur-
    pose; through Jesus Christ my Lord. *Amen.* †

The Midday Office   **To Be Observed on the Hour or Half Hour**

Between 11 a.m. and 2 p.m.

The Call to Prayer
Worship the LORD in the beauty of holiness;* let the whole earth tremble before him.

Psalm 96:9

The Request for Presence
Remember not our past sins; let your compassion be swift to meet us.

Psalm 79:8

The Greeting
There is forgiveness with you;* therefore you shall be feared.

Psalm 130:3

The Refrain for the Midday Lessons
The LORD has pleasure in those who fear him,* in those who await his gracious
    favor.

Psalm 147:12

A Reading
Children, our love must not be just words or mere talk, but something active and
    genuine. This will be the proof that we belong to the truth, and it will convince

us in his presence, even if our own feelings condemn us, that God is greater
than our feelings and knows all things.

I John 3:18–20

The Refrain
The LORD has pleasure in those who fear him,* in those who await his gracious
favor.

The Midday Psalm   *Into Your Hands I Commend My Spirit*
In you, O LORD, have I taken refuge; let me never be put to shame;* deliver me in
your righteousness.
Incline your ear to me;* make haste to deliver me.
Be my strong rock, a castle to keep me safe, for you are my crag and my strong-
hold;* for the sake of your Name, lead me and guide me.
Into your hands I commend my spirit,* for you have redeemed me, O LORD, O
God of truth.

Psalm 31:1–3, 5

The Refrain
The LORD has pleasure in those who fear him,* in those who await his gracious
favor.

The Small Verse
Create in me a clean heart, O God,* and renew a right spirit within me.
Cast me not away from your presence* and take not your holy Spirit from me.
Give me the joy of your saving help again* and sustain me with your bountiful spirit.

Psalm 51:11–13

The Lord's Prayer

The Prayer Appointed for the Week
O God, the strength of all who put their trust in you: Mercifully accept my
prayers; and because in my weakness I can do nothing good without you, give
me the help of your grace, that in keeping your commandments I may please
you in both will and deed; through Jesus Christ my Lord, who lives and reigns
with you and the Holy Spirit, one God, for ever and ever. *Amen.* †

The Concluding Prayer of the Church
Lord Jesus Christ, by your death you took away the sting of death: Grant me to so
follow in faith where you have led the way, that I may at length fall asleep peacefully in you and wake in your likeness; for your tender mercies' sake. *Amen.* †

The Vespers Office   **To Be Observed on the Hour or Half Hour**
Between 5 and 8 p.m.

The Call to Prayer
May these words of mine please him;* I will rejoice in the LORD.

Psalm 104:35

The Request for Presence
Remember not our past sins;* let your compassion be swift to meet us; . . .
Help us, O God our Savior, for the glory of your Name;* deliver us and forgive us
    our sins, for your Name's sake.

Psalm 79:8–9

The Greeting
You are to be praised, O God, in Zion . . .
To you that hear prayer shall all flesh come,* because of their transgressions.

Psalm 65:1–2

The Hymn   *God of Our Fathers*
    God of our fathers, whose almighty hand
    Leads forth in beauty all the starry band
    Of shining worlds in splendor through the skies,
    Our grateful songs before Your throne arise.

    From war's alarms, from deadly pestilence,
    Be Your strong arm our eternal defense;
    Your true religion in our hearts increase,
    Your bounteous goodness nourish us in peace.

    Refresh Your people on their toilsome way,
    Lead us from night to never ending day;
    Fill all our lives with love and grace divine,
    And glory, laud, and praise ever be Thine.

Daniel C. Roberts

The Refrain for the Vespers Lessons
Remember not the sins of my youth and my transgressions;* remember me
    according to your love and for the sake of your goodness, O Lord.

Psalm 25:6

The Vespers Psalm   *Cleanse Me from My Secret Faults*
Who can tell how often he offends?* cleanse me from my secret faults.
Above all, keep your servant from presumptuous sins; let them not get dominion
    over me;* then shall I be whole and sound, and innocent of a great offense.

Psalm 19:12–13

The Refrain
Remember not the sins of my youth and my transgressions;* remember me
    according to your love and for the sake of your goodness, O Lord.

The Cry of the Church
Lord, have mercy on us. Christ, have mercy on us. Lord, have mercy on us.

The Lord's Prayer

The Prayer Appointed for the Week

O God, the strength of all who put their trust in you: Mercifully accept my prayers; and because in my weakness I can do nothing good without you, give me the help of your grace, that in keeping your commandments I may please you in both will and deed; through Jesus Christ my Lord, who lives and reigns with you and the Holy Spirit, one God, for ever and ever. *Amen.* †

Concluding Prayers of the Church

Almighty God, who has promised to hear the petitions of those who ask in your Son's Name: I beseech you mercifully to incline your ear to me who have made my prayers and supplications to you; and grant that those things which I have faithfully asked according to your will may effectually be obtained, to the relief of my necessity, and to the setting forth of your glory; through Jesus Christ my Lord. *Amen.* †

May the souls of the faithful departed, through the mercy of God, rest in eternal peace. Amen.

The Morning Office   **To Be Observed on the Hour or Half Hour Between 6 and 9 a.m.**

The Call to Prayer

Let us give thanks to the LORD for his mercy* and the wonders he does for his children.

For he satisfies the thirsty* and fills the hungry with good things.

based on Psalm 107:8–9

The Request for Presence

Give ear to my words, O LORD;* consider my meditation.

Psalm 5:1

The Greeting

Out of the mouths of infants and children, O LORD,* your majesty is praised above the heavens.

based on Psalm 8:2

The Refrain for the Morning Lessons

I am small and of little account* yet I do not forget your commandments.

Psalm 119:141

A Reading

As they traveled along they met a man on the road who said, 'I will follow you wherever you go.' Jesus answered, 'Foxes have holes and the birds of the air have nests, but the Son of man has nowhere to lay his head.' Another to whom he said, 'Follow me,' replied, 'Let me go and bury my father first.' But he answered, 'Leave the dead to bury their dead; your duty is to go and spread the news of the kingdom of God.'

Luke 9:57–60

The Refrain

I am small and of little account* yet I do not forget your commandments.

The Morning Psalm   *Renew a Right Spirit Within Me*

Create in me a clean heart, O God,* and renew a right spirit within me.
Cast me not away from your presence* and take not your holy Spirit from me.
Give me the joy of your saving help again* and sustain me with your bountiful Spirit.
I shall teach your ways to the wicked,* and sinners shall return to you.

Psalm 51:11–14

The Refrain

I am small and of little account* yet I do not forget your commandments.

The Cry of the Church

O Lamb of God, that takes away the sins of the world, have mercy upon me.
O Lamb of God, that takes away the sins of the world, have mercy upon me.
O Lamb of God, that takes away the sins of the world, grant me your peace.

The Lord's Prayer

The Prayer Appointed for the Week

O God, the strength of all who put their trust in you: Mercifully accept my
prayers; and because in my weakness I can do nothing good without you, give
me the help of your grace, that in keeping your commandments I may please
you in both will and deed; through Jesus Christ my Lord, who lives and reigns
with you and the Holy Spirit, one God, for ever and ever. *Amen.* †

The Concluding Prayer of the Church

Lord God, almighty and everlasting Father, you have brought me in safety to this
new day: Preserve me with your mighty power, that I may not fall into sin, nor
be overcome by adversity; and in all I do direct me to the fulfilling of your purpose; through Jesus Christ my Lord. *Amen.* †

The Midday Office   To Be Observed on the Hour or Half Hour
Between 11 a.m. and 2 p.m.

The Call to Prayer

Let the righteous be glad and rejoice before God;

Psalm 68:3

The Request for Presence

You are the Lord; do not withhold your compassion from me;* let your love and
your faithfulness keep me safe forever,

Psalm 40:12

The Greeting

Therefore I will praise you upon the lyre for your faithfulness, O my God;* I will
sing to you with the harp, O Holy One of Israel.

Psalm 71:22

The Refrain for the Midday Lessons
For the LORD God is both sun and shield;* he will give grace and glory.

Psalm 84:10

A Reading
That day, the root of Jesse, standing as a signal for all the peoples, will be sought out by the nations and its home will be glorious. When that day comes, the Lord will raise his hand a second time to ransom the remnant of his people . . .

Isaiah 11:10–11

The Refrain
For the LORD God is both sun and shield;* he will give grace and glory.

The Midday Psalm   *Your Love, O LORD, For Ever Will I Sing*
Your love, O LORD, for ever will I sing;* from age to age my mouth will proclaim your faithfulness.
For I am persuaded that your love is established for ever;* you have set your faithfulness firmly in the heavens.

Psalm 89:1–2

The Refrain
For the LORD God is both sun and shield;* he will give grace and glory.

The Gloria

The Lord's Prayer

The Prayer Appointed for the Week
O God, the strength of all who put their trust in you: Mercifully accept my prayers; and because in my weakness I can do nothing good without you, give me the help of your grace, that in keeping your commandments I may please you in both will and deed; through Jesus Christ my Lord, who lives and reigns with you and the Holy Spirit, one God, for ever and ever. *Amen.* †

The Concluding Prayer of the Church
Almighty God, who after the creation of the world rested from all works and sanctified a day of rest for all your creatures: Grant that I, putting away all earthly anxieties, may be duly prepared for the service of public worship, and grant as well that my Sabbath upon earth may be a preparation for the eternal rest promised to your people in heaven; through Jesus Christ our Lord. *Amen.* †

The Vespers Office   **To Be Observed on the Hour or Half Hour**
Between 5 and 8 p.m.

The Call to Prayer
Great is the LORD and greatly to be praised;* there is no end to his greatness.

Psalm 145:3

The Request for Presence
"Hide not your face from your servant;* be swift and answer me, . . .
Draw near to me and redeem me; . . ."

Psalm 69:19–20

The Greeting
Blessed is the LORD!* for he has heard the voice of my prayer.

Psalm 28:7

The Hymn   *Rejoice*

Rejoice, the Lord is King!   His kingdom can not fail;
Your Lord and King adore!   He rules over earth and heaven;
Mortals, give thanks and sing,   The keys of death and hell
And triumph ever more.   To Christ the Lord are given.
Lift up your heart!   Lift up your heart!
Lift up your voice!   Lift up your voice!
Rejoice! Again I say, Rejoice!   Rejoice! Again I say, Rejoice!

The Lord the Savior reigns,   Rejoice in glorious hope!
The God of truth and love: Our Lord the Judge shall come,
When he had purged our stains,   And take his servants up
He took his seat above.   To their eternal home.
Lift up your heart!   Lift up your heart!
Lift up your voice!   Lift up your voice!
Rejoice! Again I say, Rejoice!   Rejoice! Again I say, Rejoice!

Charles Wesley

The Refrain for the Vespers Lessons
Therefore I will praise you upon the lyre for your faithfulness, O my God;* I will
sing to you with the harp, O Holy One of Israel.

Psalm 71:22

The Vespers Psalm   *That Which We Have Heard and Known*
That which we have heard and known, and what our forefathers have told us,* we
will not hide from their children.
We will recount to generations to come the praiseworthy deeds and the power of
the LORD,* and the wonderful works he has done.
He gave his decrees to Jacob and established a law for Israel,* which he commanded them to teach their children;
That the generations to come might know, and the children yet unborn;* that they
in their turn might tell it to their children;
So that they might put their trust in God,* and not forget the deeds of God, but
keep his commandments;
And not be like their forefathers, a stubborn and rebellious generation,* a generation
whose heart was not steadfast, and whose spirit was not faithful to God.

Psalm 78:3–8

The Refrain
Therefore I will praise you upon the lyre for your faithfulness, O my God;* I will
  sing to you with the harp, O Holy One of Israel.

The Gloria

The Lord's Prayer

The Prayer Appointed for the Week
O God, the strength of all who put their trust in you: Mercifully accept my
  prayers; and because in my weakness I can do nothing good without you, give
  me the help of your grace, that in keeping your commandments I may please
  you in both will and deed; through Jesus Christ my Lord, who lives and reigns
  with you and the Holy Spirit, one God, for ever and ever. *Amen.* †

The Concluding Prayer of the Church
O God, the source of eternal light: Shed forth your unending day upon all of us
  who watch for you, that our lips may praise you, our lives may bless you, and
  our worship may give you glory; through Jesus Christ our Lord. *Amen.* †

The Morning Office   To Be Observed on the Hour or Half Hour
                                                 Between 6 and 9 a.m.

The Call to Prayer
Enter his gates with thanksgiving; go into his courts with praise;* give thanks to
  him and call upon his Name.

Psalm 100:3

The Request for Presence
Satisfy us by your loving-kindness in the morning* so shall we rejoice and be glad
  all the days of our life.

Psalm 90:14

The Greeting
I will give thanks to you, O Lord, with my whole heart;* I will tell of all your mar-
  velous works.
I will be glad and rejoice in you;* I will sing your Name, O Most High.

Psalm 9:1–2

The Refrain for the Morning Lessons
In God the Lord, whose word I praise, in God I trust and will not be afraid,* for
  what can mortals do to me?

Psalm 56:10

A Reading

Jesus said: "Can you not buy five sparrows for two pennies? And yet not one is forgotten in God's sight. Why, every hair on your head has been counted. There is no need to be afraid: you are worth more than many sparrows."

Luke 12:6–7

The Refrain

In God the LORD, whose word I praise, in God I trust and will not be afraid,* for what can mortals do to me?

The Morning Psalm   *The LORD Takes Pleasure in His People*

Hallelujah! Sing to the LORD a new song;* sing his praise in the congregation of the faithful.

Let Israel rejoice in his Maker;* let the children of Zion be joyful in their King.

Let them praise his Name in the dance;* let them sing praise to him with timbrel and harp.

For the LORD takes pleasure in his people* and adorns the poor with victory.

Let the faithful rejoice in triumph;* let them be joyful on their beds.

Psalm 149:1–5

The Refrain

In God the LORD, whose word I praise, in God I trust and will not be afraid,* for what can mortals do to me?

The Gloria*

The Lord's Prayer

The Prayer Appointed for the Week

O Lord, you have taught us that without love whatever we do is worth nothing: Send your Holy Spirit and pour into my heart your greatest gift, which is love, the true bond of peace and of all virtue, without which whoever lives is accounted dead before you. Grant this for the sake of your only Son Jesus Christ, who lives and reigns with you and the Holy Spirit, one God, now and for ever. *Amen.* †

The Concluding Prayer of the Church

Lord God, almighty and everlasting Father, you have brought me in safety to this new day: Preserve me with your mighty power, that I may not fall into sin, nor be overcome by adversity; and in all I do direct me to the fulfilling of your purpose; through Jesus Christ my Lord. *Amen.* †

The Midday Office   **To Be Observed on the Hour or Half Hour**
Between 11 a.m. and 2 p.m.

The Call to Prayer

Sing to the LORD and bless his Name;* proclaim the good news of his salvation from day to day.

Declare his glory among the nations* and his wonders among all peoples.

Psalm 96:2–3

The Request for Presence

Let my cry come before you, O Lord;* give me understanding, according to your
word.

Psalm 119:169

The Greeting

Lord, you have been our refuge* from one generation to another.
Before the mountains were brought forth, or the land and the earth were born,*
from age to age you are God.

Psalm 90:1–2

The Refrain for the Midday Lessons

And now, you kings, be wise;* be warned, you rulers of the earth.
Submit to the Lord with fear,* and with trembling bow before him.

Psalm 2:10–11

A Reading

I, Nebuchadnezzar, raised my eyes to heaven . . . And I blessed the Most High,
praising and glorifying him who lives for ever, for his empire is an everlasting
empire, his kingship endures, age after age. All who dwell on earth count for
nothing; as he thinks fit, he disposes the army of heaven and those who dwell
on earth. No one can arrest his hand or ask him, "What have you done?" At
that moment my reason returned and, for the honor of my royal state, my glory
and splendor returned too. My counselors and noblemen acclaimed me; I was
restored to my throne, and to my past greatness even more was added. And
now I, Nebuchadnezzar, praise, extol and glorify the King of Heaven, all of
whose deeds are true, all of whose ways are right, and who can humble those
who walk in pride.

Daniel 5:31–34

The Refrain

And now, you kings, be wise;* be warned, you rulers of the earth.
Submit to the Lord with fear,* and with trembling bow before him.

The Midday Psalm   *He Declares His Word to Jacob*

Worship the Lord, O Jerusalem;* praise your God, O Zion;
For he has strengthened the bars of your gates;* he has blessed your children
within you.
He has established peace on your borders;* he satisfies you with the finest wheat.
He sends out his command to the earth,* and his word runs very swiftly.
He gives snow like wool;* he scatters hoarfrost like ashes.
He scatters his hail like bread crumbs;* who can stand against his cold?
He sends forth his word and melts them;* he blows with his wind, and the waters
flow.
He declares his word to Jacob,* his statutes and his judgments to Israel.
He has not done so to any other nation;* to them he has not revealed his judgments.

Psalm 147:13–21

The Refrain
And now, you kings, be wise;* be warned, you rulers of the earth.
Submit to the Lord with fear,* and with trembling bow before him.

The Small Verse
Let us bless the Lord. And all that is within me, forget not his benefits.

The Lord's Prayer

The Prayer Appointed for the Week
O Lord, you have taught us that without love whatever we do is worth nothing:
Send your Holy Spirit and pour into my heart your greatest gift, which is love,
the true bond of peace and of all virtue, without which whoever lives is
accounted dead before you. Grant this for the sake of your only Son Jesus
Christ, who lives and reigns with you and the Holy Spirit, one God, now and
for ever. *Amen.* †

The Concluding Prayer of the Church
O God, you make me glad with the weekly remembrance of the glorious resurrection of your Son my Lord: Give me this day such blessing through my worship
of you, that the week to come may be spent in your favor; through Jesus Christ
our Lord. *Amen.* †

The Vespers Office   **To Be Observed on the Hour or Half Hour**
                                          Between 5 and 8 p.m.

The Call to Prayer
Hallelujah! Praise the Name of the Lord;* give praise, you servants of the Lord,
You who stand in the house of the Lord,* in the courts of the house of our God.
Praise the Lord, for the Lord is good;* sing praises to his Name, for it is lovely.

Psalm 135:1–3

The Request for Presence
Incline your ear to me;* make haste to deliver me.

Psalm 31:2

The Greeting
The Lord is in his holy temple; Let all the earth keep silence before him. *Amen.*

The Hymn   *God the Father, Heavenly Light*
  O Trinity of blessed light,   To God the Father, heavenly Light,
  O Unity of princely might,   To Christ revealed in earthly night,
  The fiery sun now goes his way;   To God the Holy Ghost we raise
  Please shed within our hearts your ray   Our equal and unceasing praise.

                                              Latin, 6th C.

  To you our morning song of praise,
  To you our evening prayer we raise;
  O grant us with your saints on high
  To praise you through eternity.

The Refrain for the Vespers Lessons
Give thanks to the LORD, for he is good,* and his mercy endures for ever.

Psalm 107:1

The Vespers Psalm   *My Soul Is Athirst for the Living God*
As the deer longs for the water-brooks,* so longs my soul for you, O God.
My soul is athirst for God, athirst for the living God;* when shall I come to appear
    before the presence of God?
My tears have been my food day and night, while all day long they say to me,*
    "Where now is your God?"
I pour out my soul when I think on these things:* how I went with the multitude
    and led them into the house of God,
With the voice of praise and thanksgiving,* among those who keep holy-day.
Why are you so full of heaviness, O my soul?* and why are you so disquieted
    within me?
Put your trust in God;* for I will yet give thanks to him, who is the help of my
    countenance, and my God.

Psalm 42:1–7

The Refrain
Give thanks to the LORD, for he is good,* and his mercy endures for ever.

*The Gloria**

The Lord's Prayer

The Prayer Appointed for the Week
O Lord, you have taught us that without love whatever we do is worth nothing:
    Send your Holy Spirit and pour into my heart your greatest gift, which is love,
    the true bond of peace and of all virtue, without which whoever lives is
    accounted dead before you. Grant this for the sake of your only Son Jesus
    Christ, who lives and reigns with you and the Holy Spirit, one God, now and
    for ever. *Amen.* †

The Concluding Prayer of the Church
Lord God, whose Son our Savior Jesus Christ, triumphed over the powers of death
    and prepares for us our place in the new Jerusalem: Grant that I, who have this
    day given thanks for the resurrection, may praise you in the City of which he is
    the light, and where he lives and reigns for ever and ever. *Amen.* †

The Morning Office   **To Be Observed on the Hour or Half Hour**
Between 6 and 9 a.m.

The Call to Prayer
Be strong and let your heart take courage,* all you who wait for the LORD.

Psalm 31:24

The Request for Presence
O LORD, watch over us* and save us from this generation for ever.

Psalm 12:7

The Greeting
Restore us, O God of hosts;* show the light of your countenance, and we shall be saved.

Psalm 80:3

The Refrain for the Morning Lessons
You strengthen me more and more;* you enfold me and comfort me.

Psalm 71:21

A Reading
He sat down opposite the treasury and watched people putting money into the treasury, and many of the rich put in a great deal. A poor widow came and put in two small coins, the equivalent of a penny. Then he called his disciples and said to them, 'In truth I tell you, this poor widow has put more in than all who have contributed to the treasury; for they have all put in money they could spare, but she in her poverty has put in everything she possessed, all she had to live on.'

Mark 12:41–44

The Refrain
You strengthen me more and more;* you enfold me and comfort me.

The Morning Psalm   *He Holds Our Souls in Life*
Bless our God, you peoples;* make the voice of his praise to be heard;
Who holds our souls in life,* and will not allow our feet to slip.
For you, O God, have proved us;* you have tried us just as silver is tried.
You brought us into the snare;* you laid heavy burdens upon our backs.
You let enemies ride over our heads; we went through fire and water;* but you brought us out into a place of refreshment.
I will enter your house with burnt-offerings and will pay you my vows,* which I promised with my lips and spoke with my mouth when I was in trouble.
If I had found evil in my heart,* the Lord would not have heard me;
But in truth God has heard me;* he has attended to the voice of my prayer.

Psalm 66:7–12, 16–17

The Refrain
You strengthen me more and more;* you enfold me and comfort me.

*The Gloria**

The Lord's Prayer

The Prayer Appointed for the Week
O Lord, you have taught us that without love whatever we do is worth nothing:
Send your Holy Spirit and pour into my heart your greatest gift, which is love,
the true bond of peace and of all virtue, without which whoever lives is

accounted dead before you. Grant this for the sake of your only Son Jesus Christ, who lives and reigns with you and the Holy Spirit, one God, now and for ever. *Amen.* †

Concluding Prayers of the Church

Heavenly Father, in you I live and have my being: I humbly pray you so to guide and govern me by your Holy Spirit, that in all the cares and occupations if my life I may not forget you, but may remember that I am ever walking in your sight; through Jesus Christ my Lord. *Amen.* †

Lord God, almighty and everlasting Father, you have brought me in safety to this new day: Preserve me with your mighty power, that I may not fall into sin, nor be overcome by adversity; and in all I do direct me to the fulfilling of your purpose; through Jesus Christ my Lord. Amen. †

The Midday Office   **To Be Observed on the Hour or Half Hour**
                                  Between 11 a.m. and 2 p.m.

The Call to Prayer

Praise the LORD, O my soul!* I will praise the LORD as long as I live; I will sing praises to God while I have my being.

Psalm 146:1

The Request for Presence

Bow your heavens, O LORD, and come down;* touch the mountains, and they shall smoke.
Hurl the lightning and scatter them;* shoot out your arrows and rout them.
Stretch out your hand from on high;* rescue me and deliver me from the great waters, from the hand of foreign peoples,
Whose mouths speak deceitfully* and whose right hand is raised in falsehood.

Psalm 144:5–8

The Greeting

To you I lift up my eyes,* to you enthroned in the heavens.
As the eyes of the servants look to the hand of their masters,* and the eyes of a maid to the hand of her mistress,
So our eyes look to the LORD our God,* until he shows us his mercy.

Psalm 123:1–3

The Refrain for the Midday Lessons

Into your hands I commend my spirit,* for you have redeemed me, O LORD, O God of truth.

Psalm 31:5

A Reading

Children, do not let anyone lead you astray. Whoever acts uprightly is upright, just as He is upright.

I John 3:7

The Refrain
Into your hands I commend my spirit,* for you have redeemed me, O LORD, O
    God of truth.

The Midday Psalm   *I Will Walk in the Presence of the LORD*
Gracious is the LORD and righteous;* our God is full of compassion.
The LORD watches over the innocent;* I was brought very low, and he helped me.
Turn again to your rest, O my soul,* for the LORD has treated you well.
For you have rescued my life from death,* my eyes from tears, and my feet from
    stumbling.
I will walk in the presence of the LORD* in the land of the living.

Psalm 116:4–8

The Refrain
Into your hands I commend my spirit,* for you have redeemed me, O LORD, O
    God of truth.

The Cry of the Church
Lord, have mercy on us. Christ, have mercy on us. Lord, have mercy on us.

The Lord's Prayer

The Prayer Appointed for the Week
O Lord, you have taught us that without love whatever we do is worth nothing:
    Send your Holy Spirit and pour into my heart your greatest gift, which is love,
    the true bond of peace and of all virtue, without which whoever lives is
    accounted dead before you. Grant this for the sake of your only Son Jesus
    Christ, who lives and reigns with you and the Holy Spirit, one God, now and
    for ever. *Amen.* †

The Concluding Prayer of the Church
Almighty and eternal God, ruler of all things in heaven and earth: Mercifully
    accept my prayers, and strengthen me to do your will; through Jesus Christ our
    Lord. *Amen.* †

The Vespers Office   To Be Observed on the Hour or Half Hour
                                                      Between 5 and 8 p.m.

The Call to Prayer
The righteous will be glad . . .
And they will say, "Surely, there is a reward for the righteous;* surely, there is a
    God who rules in the earth."

Psalm 58:10–11

The Request for Presence
Make me understand the way of your commandments,* that I may meditate on
    your marvelous works.

Psalm 119:27

The Greeting
You have made me glad by your acts, O Lord;* and I shout for joy because of the
works of your hands.

Psalm 92:4

The Hymn   *Night Is Drawing Nigh*
Now the day is over, night is drawing nigh,
Shadows of the evening steal across the sky.
Jesus, give the weary calm and sweet repose;
With your tenderest blessing may our eyelids close.
Grant to little children visions bright of thee.
Guard the sailors tossing on the sea.
Comfort every sufferer watching late in pain;
Those who plan some evil from their sin restrain.
Through the long night watches may your angels spread
Their wings above me, watching round my bed.
When the morning wakens then I may arise
Pure and fresh and sinless in your holy eyes.

Sabine Baring-Gould

The Refrain for the Vespers Lessons
My mouth shall speak of wisdom,* and my heart shall meditate on understanding.

Psalm 49:2

The Vespers Psalm   *Your Wonders Are More Than I Can Count*
Great things are they that you have done, O Lord my God! how great your
wonders and your plans for us!* there is none who can be compared with you.
Oh, that I could make them known and tell them!* but they are more than I can
count.

Psalm 40:5–6

The Refrain
My mouth shall speak of wisdom,* and my heart shall meditate on understanding.

*The Gloria**

The Lord's Prayer

The Prayer Appointed for the Week
O Lord, you have taught us that without love whatever we do is worth nothing:
Send your Holy Spirit and pour into my heart your greatest gift, which is love,
the true bond of peace and of all virtue, without which whoever lives is
accounted dead before you. Grant this for the sake of your only Son Jesus
Christ, who lives and reigns with you and the Holy Spirit, one God, now and
for ever. *Amen.* †

The Concluding Prayer of the Church
O God, the King eternal, whose light divides the day from the night and turns the
shadow of death into the morning: Drive far from me all wrong desires, incline

my heart to keep your law, and guide my feet into the way of peace; that, having done your will with cheerfulness during the day, I may, when night comes, rejoice to give you thanks; through Jesus Christ my Lord. *Amen.* †

The Morning Office   **To Be Observed on the Hour or Half Hour**
                                          Between 6 and 9 a.m.

The Call to Prayer
Be glad, you righteous, and rejoice in the LORD;* shout for joy, all who are true of heart.

Psalm 32:12

The Request for Presence
Open my eyes, that I may see* the wonders of your law.

Psalm 119:18

The Greeting
With my whole heart I seek you;* let me not stray from your commandments.

Psalm 119:10

The Refrain for the Morning Lessons
I hate those who have a divided heart,* but your law do I love.

Psalm 119:113

A Reading
Jesus said to the people: ". . . what king marching to war against another king would not first sit down and consider whether with ten thousand men he could stand up to the other who was advancing against him with twenty thousand? If not, then while the other king was still a long way off, he would send envoys to sue for peace. So in the same way, none of you can be my disciple without giving up all that he owns."

Luke 14:31–33

The Refrain
I hate those who have a divided heart,* but your law do I love.

The Morning Psalm   *He Brought Them to the Harbor They Were Bound for*
Some went down to the sea in ships* and plied their trade in deep waters;
They beheld the works of the LORD* and his wonder in the deep.
Then he spoke, and a stormy wind arose,* which tossed high the waves of the sea.
They mounted up to the heavens and fell back to the depths;* their hearts melted because of their peril.
They reeled and staggered like drunkards* and were at their wits' end.
Then they cried to the LORD in their trouble,* and he delivered them from their distress.
He stilled the storm to a whisper* and quieted the waves of the sea.
Then they were glad because of the calm,* and he brought them to the harbor they were bound for.

Let them give thanks to the LORD for his mercy* and the wonders he does for his
    children.
Let them exalt him in the congregation of the people* and praise him in the coun-
    cil of the elders.

Psalm 107:23–32

The Refrain
I hate those who have a divided heart,* but your law do I love.

The Small Verse
The Lord is my shepherd and nothing is wanting to me. In green pastures He has
    settled me.

THE SHORT BREVIARY

The Lord's Prayer

The Prayer Appointed for the Week
O Lord, you have taught us that without love whatever we do is worth nothing:
    Send your Holy Spirit and pour into my heart your greatest gift, which is love,
    the true bond of peace and of all virtue, without which whoever lives is
    accounted dead before you. Grant this for the sake of your only Son Jesus
    Christ, who lives and reigns with you and the Holy Spirit, one God, now and
    for ever. *Amen.* †

The Concluding Prayer of the Church
Lord God, almighty and everlasting Father, you have brought me in safety to this
    new day: Preserve me with your mighty power, that I may not fall into sin, nor
    be overcome by adversity; and in all I do direct me to the fulfilling of your pur-
    pose; through Jesus Christ my Lord. *Amen.* †

The Midday Office   To Be Observed on the Hour or Half Hour
Between 11 a.m. and 2 p.m.

The Call to Prayer
Know this, The LORD himself is God;* he himself made us, and we are his; we are
    his people and the sheep of his pasture.

Psalm 100:2

The Request for Presence
Open my eyes, that I may see* the wonders of your law.

Psalm 119:18

The Greeting
I restrain my feet from every evil way,* that I may keep your word.

Psalm 119:101

The Refrain for the Midday Lessons
Blessed be God, who has not rejected my prayer,* nor withheld his love from me.

Psalm 66:18

A Reading

You have not seen him, yet you love him; and still without seeing him you believe in
him and are already filled with a joy that is so glorious that it cannot be described;
and you are sure of the goal of your faith, that is, the salvation of your souls.

I Peter 1:8–9

The Refrain

Blessed be God, who has not rejected my prayer,* nor withheld his love from me.

The Midday Psalm   *We Flourish like a Flower of the Field*

Our days are like the grass;* we flourish like a flower of the field;
When the wind goes over it, it is gone,* and its place shall know it no more.
But the merciful goodness of the Lord endures for ever on those who fear him,*
and his righteousness on children's children.

Psalm 103:15–17

The Refrain

Blessed be God, who has not rejected my prayer,* nor withheld his love from me.

The Small Verse

Create in me a clean heart, O God,* and renew a right spirit within me.
Cast me not away from your presence* and take not your holy Spirit from me.
Give me the joy of your saving help again* and sustain me with your bountiful spirit.

Psalm 51:11–13

The Lord's Prayer

The Prayer Appointed for the Week

O Lord, you have taught us that without love whatever we do is worth nothing: Send
your Holy Spirit and pour into my heart your greatest gift, which is love, the true
bond of peace and of all virtue, without which whoever lives is accounted dead
before you. Grant this for the sake of your only Son Jesus Christ, who lives and
reigns with you and the Holy Spirit, one God, now and for ever. *Amen.* †

The Concluding Prayer of the Church   *The Privilege Is Ours to Share in the Loving*

Almighty God, our heavenly Father, the privilege is ours to share in the loving,
healing, reconciling mission of your Son Jesus Christ, our Lord, in this age and
wherever we are. Since without you we can do no good thing:

>   May your Spirit make us wise;
>   May your Spirit guide us;
>   May your Spirit renew us;
>   May your Spirit strengthen us;

So that we will be:

>   Strong in faith,
>   Discerning in proclamation,
>   Courageous in witness,
>   Persistent in good deeds.

This we ask through the name of the Father.

Church of the Province of the West Indies

The Vespers Office   To Be Observed on the Hour or Half Hour
                                      Between 5 and 8 p.m.

The Call to Prayer
Blessed be the LORD, the God of Israel, from everlasting and to everlasting;* and
    let all people say, "Amen!"

Psalm 106:48

The Request for Presence
Be my strong rock, a castle to keep me safe;* you are my crag and my stronghold.

Psalm 71:3

The Greeting
Your way, O God, is holy;* who is as great as our God?

Psalm 77:13

The Hymn   *Jesus, Lover of My Soul*
    Jesus, lover of my soul, let me to your bosom fly,
    While the nearer waters roll, while the tempest still is high:
    Hide, O my Savior, hide, till the storm of life is passed;
    Safe into the haven guide; O receive my soul at last.

    Other refuge have I none; hangs my helpless soul on thee;
    Leave, O leave me not alone, still support and comfort me:
    All my trust on you is laid, all my help from you I bring;
    Cover my defenseless head with the shadow of your wing.

    Plenteous grace with you is found, grace to cover all my sin;
    Let the healing streams abound; make and keep me pure within.

Charles Wesley

The Refrain for the Vespers Lessons
Truth shall spring up from the earth,* and righteousness shall look down from
    heaven.

Psalm 85:11

The Vespers Psalm   *This Is the LORD's Doing*
Open for me the gates of righteousness;* I will enter them; I will offer thanks to the
    LORD.
"This is the gate of the LORD;* he who is righteous may enter."
I will give thanks to you, for you answered me* and have become my salvation.
The same stone which the builders rejected* has become the chief cornerstone.
This is the LORD's doing,* and it is marvelous in our eyes.
On this day the LORD has acted;* we will rejoice and be glad in it.

Psalm 118:19–24

The Refrain
Truth shall spring up from the earth,* and righteousness shall look down from
    heaven.

The Cry of the Church
In the evening, in the morning, and at noonday, I will complain and lament,* and
    he will hear my voice.

Psalm 55:18

The Lord's Prayer

The Prayer Appointed for the Week
O Lord, you have taught us that without love whatever we do is worth nothing:
    Send your Holy Spirit and pour into my heart your greatest gift, which is love,
    the true bond of peace and of all virtue, without which whoever lives is
    accounted dead before you. Grant this for the sake of your only Son Jesus
    Christ, who lives and reigns with you and the Holy Spirit, one God, now and
    for ever. *Amen.* †

The Concluding Prayer of the Church
Lord Jesus, stay with me, for evening is at hand and the day is past; be my com-
    panion in the way, kindle my heart, and awaken hope, that I may know you as
    you are revealed in Scripture and in the breaking of bread. Grant this for the
    sake of your love toward me. *Amen.* †

The Morning Office

**To Be Observed on the Hour or Half Hour
Between 6 and 9 a.m.**

The Call to Prayer
Wake up, my spirit; awake lute and harp;* I myself will waken the dawn.

Psalm 57:8

The Request for Presence
O God of hosts,* show the light of your countenance, and we shall be saved.

Psalm 80:7

The Greeting
My lips will sing with joy when I play to you,* and so will my soul, which you
    have redeemed.

Psalm 71:23

The Refrain for the Morning Lessons
Send forth your strength, O God;* establish, O God, what you have wrought for us.

Psalm 68:28

A Reading
Jesus said: "In all truth I tell you, everyone who commits sin is a slave. Now a
    slave has no permanent standing in the household, but a son belongs to it for-
    ever. So if the Son sets you free, you will indeed be free."

John 8:34–36

The Refrain
Send forth your strength, O God;* establish, O God, what you have wrought for us.

The Morning Psalm   *Happy Are the People of Whom This Is So*

Rescue me from the hurtful sword* and deliver me from the hand of foreign
    peoples,
Whose mouths speak deceitfully* and whose right hand is raised in falsehood.
May our sons be like plants well nurtured from their youth,* and our daughters
    like sculptured corners of a palace.
May our barns be filled to overflowing with all manner of crops;* may the flocks
    in our pastures increase by thousands and tens of thousands; may our cattle be
    fat and sleek.
May there be no breaching of the walls, no going into exile,* no wailing in the
    public squares.
Happy are the people of whom this is so!* happy are the people whose God is the
    LORD!

Psalm 144:11–16

The Refrain
Send forth your strength, O God;* establish, O God, what you have wrought for us.

*The Gloria**

The Lord's Prayer

The Prayer Appointed for the Week
O Lord, you have taught us that without love whatever we do is worth nothing:
    Send your Holy Spirit and pour into my heart your greatest gift, which is love,
    the true bond of peace and of all virtue, without which whoever lives is
    accounted dead before you. Grant this for the sake of your only Son Jesus
    Christ, who lives and reigns with you and the Holy Spirit, one God, now and
    for ever. *Amen.* †

The Concluding Prayer of the Church
Lord God, almighty and everlasting Father, you have brought me in safety to this
    new day: Preserve me with your mighty power, that I may not fall into sin, nor
    be overcome by adversity; and in all I do direct me to the fulfilling of your pur-
    pose; through Jesus Christ my Lord. *Amen.* †

The Midday Office   **To Be Observed on the Hour or Half Hour**
Between 11 a.m. and 2 p.m.

The Call to Prayer
Sing praise to the LORD who dwells in Zion;* proclaim to the peoples the things he
    has done.

Psalm 9:11

The Request for Presence
Send out your light and your truth, that they may lead me,* and bring me to your
    holy hill and to your dwelling.

Psalm 43:3

The Greeting
How glorious you are!* more splendid than the everlasting mountains!

Psalm 76:4

The Refrain for the Midday Lessons
Away from me, you wicked!* I will keep the commandments of my God.

Psalm 119:115

A Reading
At the signal given by the voice of the Archangel and the trumpet of God, the Lord himself will come down from heaven; those who have died in Christ will be the first to rise, and only after that shall we who remain alive be taken up into the clouds, together with them, to meet the Lord in the air. This is the way we shall be with the Lord for ever. With such thoughts as these, then, you should encourage one another.

I Thessalonians 4:16–18

The Refrain
Away from me, you wicked!* I will keep the commandments of my God.

The Midday Psalm   *Give Praise, You Servants of the LORD*
Hallelujah! Give praise, you servants of the LORD;* praise the Name of the LORD.
Let the Name of the LORD be blessed,* from this time forth for evermore.
From the rising of the sun to its going down* let the Name of the LORD be praised.
The LORD is high above all nations,* and his glory above the heavens.
Who is like the LORD our God, who sits enthroned on high* but stoops to behold the heavens and the earth?
He takes up the weak out of the dust* and lifts up the poor from the ashes.
He sets them with the princes,* with the princes of his people.
He makes the woman of a childless house* to be a joyful mother of children.

Psalm 113

The Refrain
Away from me, you wicked!* I will keep the commandments of my God.

*The Gloria**

The Lord's Prayer

The Prayer Appointed for the Week
O Lord, you have taught us that without love whatever we do is worth nothing: Send your Holy Spirit and pour into my heart your greatest gift, which is love, the true bond of peace and of all virtue, without which whoever lives is accounted dead before you. Grant this for the sake of your only Son Jesus Christ, who lives and reigns with you and the Holy Spirit, one God, now and for ever. *Amen.* †

The Concluding Prayer of the Church
O Almighty God, who pours out on all who desire it the spirit of grace and of supplication: Deliver me, when I draw near to you, from coldness of heart and

wanderings of mind, that with steadfast thoughts and kindled affections we may worship you in spirit and in truth; through Jesus Christ our Lord. *Amen.* †

The Vespers Office   **To Be Observed on the Hour or Half Hour Between 5 and 8 p.m.**

The Call to Prayer
Know that the LORD does wonders for the faithful;* when I call upon the LORD, he will hear me.
Tremble, then, and do not sin;* speak to your heart in silence upon your bed.
Offer the appointed sacrifices* and put your trust in the LORD.

Psalm 4:3–5

The Request for Presence
O LORD, do not forsake me;* be not far from me, O my God.
Make haste to help me,* O Lord of my salvation.

Psalm 38:21–22

The Greeting
As the deer longs for the water-brooks,* so longs my soul for you, O God.

Psalm 42:1

The Hymn   *From Psalm 136*
Let us with a gladsome mind praise the Lord, for He is kind:
For His mercies shall endure, ever faithful, ever sure.

Let us sound His Name abroad, for of gods He is the God:
For His mercies shall endure, ever faithful, ever sure.

He, with all commanding might, filled the new-made world with light:
For His mercies shall endure, ever faithful, ever sure.

All things living He does feed; His full hand supplies their need:
℣ For His mercies shall endure, ever faithful, ever sure.

Let us then with gladsome minds praise the Lord for He is kind:
For His mercies shall endure, ever faithful, ever sure.

John Milton

The Refrain for the Vespers Lessons
Turn again to your rest, O my soul,* for the LORD has treated you well.
For you have rescued my life from death,* my eyes from tears, and my feet from stumbling.

Psalm 116:6–7

The Vespers Psalm   *One Thing I Seek*
One thing have I asked of the LORD; one thing I seek;* that I may dwell in the house of the LORD all the days of my life;
To behold the fair beauty of the LORD* and to seek him in his temple.

Psalm 27:5–6

The Refrain
Turn again to your rest, O my soul,* for the LORD has treated you well.
For you have rescued my life from death,* my eyes from tears, and my feet from
    stumbling.

The Small Verse
Lord, let your way be known upon the earth; Your saving health among all
    nations.
Let not the needy, O Lord, be forgotten; Nor the hope of the poor be taken away.
Create in me a clean heart, O God; And sustain me in your Holy Spirit.

The Lord's Prayer

The Prayer Appointed for the Week
O Lord, you have taught us that without love whatever we do is worth nothing:
    Send your Holy Spirit and pour into my heart your greatest gift, which is love,
    the true bond of peace and of all virtue, without which whoever lives is
    accounted dead before you. Grant this for the sake of your only Son Jesus
    Christ, who lives and reigns with you and the Holy Spirit, one God, now and
    for ever. *Amen.* †

The Concluding Prayer of the Church
Lord Jesus, stay with me, for evening is at hand and the day is past; be my com-
    panion in the way, kindle my heart, and awaken hope, that I may know you as
    you are revealed in Scripture and the breaking of bread. Grant this for the sake
    of your love. *Amen.* †

The Morning Office   **To Be Observed on the Hour or Half Hour**
                                                     Between 6 and 9 a.m.

The Call to Prayer
Let us bless the LORD* from this time forth for evermore.
                                        adapted from Psalm 115:18

The Request for Presence
Turn to me and have mercy upon me;* . . . and save the child of your handmaid.
                                                    Psalm 86:16

The Greeting
You are my hiding-place . . . * you surround me with shouts of deliverance.
                                                    Psalm 32:8

The Refrain for the Morning Lessons
Behold, God is my helper;* it is the Lord who sustains my life.
                                                    Psalm 54:4

A Reading
In the beginning was the Word: the Word was with God and the Word was God.
    He was with God in the beginning. Through him all things came into being,

not one thing came into being except through him. What has come into being
in him was life, life that was the light of men; and light shines in the darkness,
and darkness could not overpower it.

John 1:1–5

The Refrain
Behold, God is my helper;* it is the Lord who sustains my life.

The Morning Psalm   ***Show the Light of Your Countenance, and We Shall Be Saved***
Hear, O Shepherd of Israel, leading Joseph like a flock;* shine forth, you that are
    enthroned upon the cherubim.
In the presence of Ephraim, Benjamin, and Manasseh,* stir up your strength and
    come to help us.
Restore us, O God of hosts;* show the light of your countenance, and we shall be
    saved.

Psalm 80:1–3

The Refrain
Behold, God is my helper;* it is the Lord who sustains my life.

*The Gloria**

The Lord's Prayer

The Prayer Appointed for the Week
O Lord, you have taught us that without love whatever we do is worth nothing:
    Send your Holy Spirit and pour into my heart your greatest gift, which is love,
    the true bond of peace and of all virtue, without which whoever lives is
    accounted dead before you. Grant this for the sake of your only Son Jesus
    Christ, who lives and reigns with you and the Holy Spirit, one God, now and
    for ever. *Amen.* †

The Concluding Prayer of the Church
Lord God, almighty and everlasting Father, you have brought me in safety to this
    new day: Preserve me with your mighty power, that I may not fall into sin, nor
    be overcome by adversity; and in all I do direct me to the fulfilling of your pur-
    pose; through Jesus Christ my Lord. *Amen.* †

The Midday Office   **To Be Observed on the Hour or Half Hour**
                                     Between 11 a.m. and 2 p.m.

The Call to Prayer
Come, let us sing to the Lord;* let us shout for joy to the Rock of our salvation.

Psalm 95:1

The Request for Presence
May God be merciful to us and bless us,* show us the light of his countenance and
    come to us.

Psalm 67:1

The Greeting
Splendor and honor and kingly power are yours by right, O Lord our God, For you created everything that is, and by your will they were created and have their being.

Revelation 4:11

The Refrain for the Midday Lessons
I have been young and now I am old,* but never have I seen the righteous forsaken, or their children begging bread.

Psalm 37:26

A Reading
In the abundance of his glory may he, through the Spirit, enable you to grow firm in power with regard to your inner self, so that Christ may live in your hearts through faith, and then, planted in love and built on love, with all God's holy people you will have the strength to grasp the breadth and the length, the height and the depth; so that, knowing the love of Christ, which is beyond knowledge, you may be filled with the utter fullness of God.

Ephesians 3:16–19

The Refrain
I have been young and now I am old,* but never have I seen the righteous forsaken, or their children begging bread.

The Midday Psalm   *Happy Are They Who Consider the Poor and Needy*
Happy are they who consider the poor and needy!* the LORD will deliver them in the time of trouble.
The LORD preserves them and keeps them alive, so that they may be happy in the land;* he does not hand them over to the will of their enemies.
The LORD sustains them on their sickbed* and ministers to them in their illness.

Psalm 41:1–3

The Refrain
I have been young and now I am old,* but never have I seen the righteous forsaken, or their children begging bread.

*The Gloria**

The Lord's Prayer

The Prayer Appointed for the Week
O Lord, you have taught us that without love whatever we do is worth nothing: Send your Holy Spirit and pour into my heart your greatest gift, which is love, the true bond of peace and of all virtue, without which whoever lives is accounted dead before you. Grant this for the sake of your only Son Jesus Christ, who lives and reigns with you and the Holy Spirit, one God, now and for ever. *Amen.* †

The Concluding Prayer of the Church

You gather us together in faith, O God, as a loving mother and a gentle father.
Help us to remember that your dwelling place is built upon love and peace,
and that to bring about your reign on earth we must follow your way of peace.
We pray for all governments and legislatures that they may be mindful of the
rights of all peoples of this world to live in peace and dignity. Grant this in the
name of Jesus. *Amen.*

THE NEW COMPANION TO THE BREVIARY

The Vespers Office   **To Be Observed on the Hour or Half Hour**
Between 5 and 8 p.m.

The Call to Prayer

Bless our God, you peoples;* make the voice of his praise to be heard;
Who holds our souls in life,* and will not allow our feet to slip.

Psalm 66:7–8

The Request for Presence

Show me the light of your countenance, O God, and come to me.

adapted from Psalm 67:1

The Greeting

Whom have I in heaven but you?* and having you I desire nothing upon earth.

Psalm 73:25

The Refrain for the Vespers Lessons

I have been sustained by you ever since I was born; from my mother's womb you
have been my strength;* my praise shall be always of you.

Psalm 71:6

The Hymn

On the night before he suffered,
Seated with his chosen band,
Jesus when they all had feasted,
Faithful to the Law's command,
Far more precious food provided:
Gave himself with his own hand.

Word made flesh, true bread of heaven,
By his word made flesh to be,
From the wine his blood is taken,
Though our senses can not see,
Faith alone which is unshaken
Shows pure hearts the mystery.

Therefore we, before him falling,
This great sacrament revere;
Ancient forms are now departed,
For new acts of grace are here,
Faith our feeble senses aiding,
Makes the Savior's presence clear.

St. Thomas Aquinas

The Refrain for the Vespers Lessons

I have been sustained by you ever since I was born; from my mother's womb you
have been my strength;* my praise shall be always of you.

The Vespers Psalm　　　　　　*How Shall We Sing the Lord's Song Upon an Alien Soil*

By the waters of Babylon we sat down and wept,* when we remembered you, O
　　Zion.

As for our harps, we hung them up* on the trees in the midst of that land.

For those who led us away captive asked us for a song, and our oppressors called
　　for mirth:* "Sing us one of the songs of Zion."

How shall we sing the Lord's song* upon an alien soil.

If I forget you, O Jerusalem,* let my right hand forget its skill.

Let my tongue cleave to the roof of my mouth if I do not remember you,* if I do
　　not set Jerusalem above my highest joy.

Psalm 137:1–6

The Refrain

I have been sustained by you ever since I was born; from my mother's womb you
　　have been my strength;* my praise shall be always of you.

The Cry of the Church

O God, come to my assistance! O Lord, make haste to help me!

The Lord's Prayer

The Prayer Appointed for the Week

O Lord, you have taught us that without love whatever we do is worth nothing: Send
　　your Holy Spirit and pour into my heart your greatest gift, which is love, the true
　　bond of peace and of all virtue, without which whoever lives is accounted dead
　　before you. Grant this for the sake of your only Son Jesus Christ, who lives and
　　reigns with you and the Holy Spirit, one God, now and for ever. *Amen.* †

The Concluding Prayer of the Church

Almighty Father, you have given us strength to work throughout this day. Receive
　　our evening sacrifice of praise in thanksgiving for your countless gifts. We ask
　　this through our Lord Jesus Christ, your Son, who lives and reigns with you
　　and the Holy Spirit, one God, for ever and ever. *Amen.*

The Liturgy of the Hours, Vol. III

The Morning Office　　　　　　To Be Observed on the Hour or Half Hour
　　　　　　　　　　　　　　　　　　Between 6 and 9 a.m.

The Call to Prayer

Bless our God, you peoples;* make the voice of his praise to be heard;

Who holds our souls in life,* and will not allow our feet to slip.

Psalm 66:7–8

The Request for Presence

I call with my whole heart;* answer me, O Lord, that I may keep your statutes.

Hear my voice, O Lord, according to your loving-kindness;* according to your
　　judgments, give me life.

Psalm 119:145ff

The Greeting
I am bound by the vow I made to you, O God;* I will present to you thank-offerings;
For you have rescued my soul from death and my feet from stumbling,* that I may
    walk before God in the light of the living.

Psalm 56:11–12

The Refrain for the Morning Lessons
Keep watch over my life, for I am faithful;* save your servant whose trust is in you.

adapted from Psalm 86:2

A Reading
Jesus taught us, saying: "It is someone who is forgiven little who shows little love."

Luke 7:47

The Refrain
Keep watch over my life, for I am faithful;* save your servant whose trust is in you.

The Morning Psalm   *Happy Are the People Whose Strength Is in You*
Happy are they who dwell in your house!* they will always be praising you.
Happy are the people whose strength is in you!* whose hearts are set on the
    pilgrims' way.
Those who go through the desolate valley will find it a place of springs,* for the
    early rains have covered it with pools of water.
They will climb from height to height,* and the God of gods will reveal himself in
    Zion.
Lord God of hosts, hear my prayer;* hearken, O God of Jacob.
Behold our defender, O God;* and look upon the face of your Anointed.
For one day in your courts is better than a thousand in my own room,* and to stand
    at the threshold of the house of my God than to dwell in the tents of the wicked.

Psalm 84:3–9

The Refrain
Keep watch over my life, for I am faithful;* save your servant whose trust is in you.

The Cry of the Church
Lord, have mercy on us. Christ, have mercy on us. Lord, have mercy on us.

The Lord's Prayer

The Prayer Appointed for the Week
O Lord, you have taught us that without love whatever we do is worth nothing:
    Send your Holy Spirit and pour into my heart your greatest gift, which is love,
    the true bond of peace and of all virtue, without which whoever lives is
    accounted dead before you. Grant this for the sake of your only Son Jesus
    Christ, who lives and reigns with you and the Holy Spirit, one God, now and
    for ever. *Amen.* †

The Concluding Prayer of the Church
Lord God, almighty and everlasting Father, you have brought me in safety to this
    new day: Preserve me with your mighty power, that I may not fall into sin, nor

be overcome by adversity; and in all I do direct me to the fulfilling of your purpose; through Jesus Christ my Lord. *Amen.* †

The Midday Office

**To Be Observed on the Hour or Half Hour
Between 11 a.m. and 2 p.m.**

The Call to Prayer
"Come now, let us reason together," says the Lord.

Isaiah 1:18, KJV

The Request for Presence
O God, be not far from me;* come quickly to help me, O my God.

Psalm 71:12

The Greeting
"You are my God, and I will thank you;* you are my God and I will exalt you."

Psalm 118:28

The Refrain for the Midday Lessons
The same stone that the builders rejected* has become the chief cornerstone.
This is the LORD's doing,* and it is marvelous in our eyes.

Psalm 118:22–23

A Reading
He was marked out before the world was made, and was revealed at the final
    point of time for your sake.

I Peter 1:20

The Refrain
The same stone that the builders rejected* has become the chief cornerstone.
This is the LORD's doing,* and it is marvelous in our eyes.

The Midday Psalm   *We Are His*
Be joyful in the LORD, all you lands;* serve the LORD with gladness and come
    before his presence with a song.
Know this: The LORD himself is God;* he himself has made us, and we are his; we
    are his people and the sheep of his pasture.
Enter his gates with thanksgiving; go into his courts with praise;* give thanks to
    him and call upon his Name.
For the LORD is good; his mercy is everlasting;* and his faithfulness endures from
    age to age.

Psalm 100:1–4

The Refrain
The same stone that the builders rejected* has become the chief cornerstone.
This is the LORD's doing,* and it is marvelous in our eyes.

The Cry of the Church
Lord, have mercy on us. Christ, have mercy on us. Lord, have mercy on us.

The Lord's Prayer

The Prayer Appointed for the Week

O Lord, you have taught us that without love whatever we do is worth nothing:
Send your Holy Spirit and pour into my heart your greatest gift, which is love,
the true bond of peace and of all virtue, without which whoever lives is
accounted dead before you. Grant this for the sake of your only Son Jesus
Christ, who lives and reigns with you and the Holy Spirit, one God, now and
for ever. *Amen.* †

The Concluding Prayer of the Church

Lord Jesus Christ, by your death you took away the sting of death: Grant me to so
follow in faith where you have led the way, that I may at length fall asleep
peacefully in you and wake in your likeness; for your tender mercies sake.
Amen. †

The Vespers Office   **To Be Observed on the Hour or Half Hour**
Between 5 and 8 p.m.

The Call to Prayer

O tarry and await the LORD's pleasure; be strong, and he shall comfort your heart;*
wait patiently for the LORD.

Psalm 27:18

The Request for Presence

Out of the depths have I called to you, O LORD; LORD, hear my voice;* let your ears
consider well the voice of my supplication.

Psalm 130:1

The Greeting

For your Name's sake, O LORD,* forgive my sin, for it is great.

Psalm 25:10

The Hymn

O sacred Head, now wounded, with grief and shame weighed down,
Now scornfully surrounded with thorns, your only crown:
How pale you are with anguish, with sore abuse and scorn!
How does that visage languish which once was bright as morn!

What you, O Lord, have suffered was all for sinner's gain;
Mine, mine was the transgression, but yours the deadly pain.
Lo, here I fall, my Savior! 'Tis I deserve your place;
Look on me with your favor, vouchsafe to me your grace.

What language shall I borrow to thank you, dearest friend,
For this your dying sorrow, your pity without end?
O make me yours forever; and should I fainting be,
Lord, let me never, never outlive my love for thee.

Bernard of Clairvaux

The Refrain for the Vespers Lessons

Let not those who hope in you be put to shame through me, Lord GOD of Hosts;*
   let not those who seek you be disgraced because of me, O God of Israel.

Psalm 69:7

The Vespers Psalm   *This God Is Our God For Ever and Ever*

We have waited in silence on your loving-kindness, O God,* in the midst of your
   temple.
Your praise, like your Name, O God, reaches to the world's end;* your right hand
   is full of justice.
Let Mount Zion be glad and the cities of Judah rejoice,* because of your
   judgments.
Make the circuit of Zion; walk round about her;* count the number of her
   towers.
Consider well her bulwarks; examine her strongholds;* that you may tell those
   who come after.
This God is our God for ever and ever;* he shall be our guide for evermore.

Psalm 48:8–13

The Refrain

Let not those who hope in you be put to shame through me, Lord GOD of Hosts;*
   let not those who seek you be disgraced because of me, O God of Israel.

The Cry of the Church

Lord, have mercy on us. Christ, have mercy on us. Lord, have mercy on us.

The Lord's Prayer

The Prayer Appointed for the Week

O Lord, you have taught us that without love whatever we do is worth nothing:
   Send your Holy Spirit and pour into my heart your greatest gift, which is love,
   the true bond of peace and of all virtue, without which whoever lives is
   accounted dead before you. Grant this for the sake of your only Son Jesus
   Christ, who lives and reigns with you and the Holy Spirit, one God, now and
   for ever. *Amen.* †

Concluding Prayers of the Church

Almighty God, who has promised to hear the petitions of those who ask in your
   Son's Name: I beseech you mercifully to incline your ear to me who have made
   my prayers and supplications to you; and grant that those things which I have
   faithfully asked according to your will, may effectually be obtained, to the
   relief of my necessity, and to the setting forth of your glory; through Jesus
   Christ my Lord. *Amen.* †

May the souls of the faithful departed, through the mercy of God, rest in eternal
peace. *Amen.*

The Morning Office   To Be Observed on the Hour or Half Hour
                                                      Between 6 and 9 a.m.

The Call to Prayer
Let us come before his presence with thanksgiving* and raise a loud shout to him
     with psalms.

Psalm 95:2

The Request for Presence
Lord God of hosts, hear my prayer;* hearken, O God of Jacob.

Psalm 84:7

The Greeting
My heart is firmly fixed, O God, my heart is fixed;* I will sing and make melody.
Wake up, my spirit; awake, lute and harp;* I myself will awaken the dawn.
I will confess you among the peoples, O Lord;* I will sing praise to you among the
     nations.
For your loving-kindness is greater than the heavens,* and your faithfulness
     reaches to the clouds.
Exalt yourself above the heavens, O God,* and your glory over all the earth.

Psalm 57:7–11

The Refrain for the Morning Lessons
"I will appoint a time," says God;* "I will judge with equity . . ."

Psalm 75:2

A Reading
Jesus taught the disciples, saying: "In truth I tell you, when everything is made
     new again and the Son of man is seated on his throne of glory, you yourselves
     will sit on twelve thrones to judge the twelve tribes of Israel. And everyone
     who had left houses, brothers, sisters, father, mother, children or land for the
     sake of my name will receive a hundred times as much, and also inherit eternal
     life. Many who are first will be last, and the last, first."

Matthew 19:28–30

The Refrain
"I will appoint a time," says God;* "I will judge with equity . . ."

The Morning Psalm   *The Lord Awoke*
Then the Lord woke as though from sleep,* like a warrior refreshed with wine.
He chose instead the tribe of Judah* and Mount Zion, which he loved.
He built his sanctuary like the heights of heaven,* like the earth which he founded
     for ever.
He chose David his servant,* and took him away from the sheepfolds.
He brought him from following the ewes,* to be a shepherd over Jacob his people
     and over Israel his inheritance.
So he shepherded them with a faithful and true heart* and guided them with the
     skillfulness of his hands.

Psalm 78:65, 68–72

The Refrain
"I will appoint a time," says God;* "I will judge with equity . . ."

The Small Verse
The Lord is a great God,* and a great King above all gods.
In his hand are the caverns of the earth,* and the heights of the hills are his also.
The sea is his, for he made it,* and his hands have molded the dry land.

Psalm 95:3–5

The Lord's Prayer

The Prayer Appointed for the Week
O Lord, you have taught us that without love whatever we do is worth nothing:
Send your Holy Spirit and pour into my heart your greatest gift, which is love,
the true bond of peace and of all virtue, without which whoever lives is
accounted dead before you. Grant this for the sake of your only Son Jesus
Christ, who lives and reigns with you and the Holy Spirit, one God, now and
for ever. *Amen.* †

The Concluding Prayer of the Church
Lord God, almighty and everlasting Father, you have brought me in safety to this
new day: Preserve me with your mighty power, that I may not fall into sin, nor
be overcome by adversity; and in all I do direct me to the fulfilling of your purpose; through Jesus Christ my Lord. *Amen.* †

The Midday Office   **To Be Observed on the Hour or Half Hour**
Between 11 a.m. and 2 p.m.

The Call to Prayer
Ascribe to the Lord, you families of the peoples;* ascribe to the Lord honor and
power.
Ascribe to the Lord the honor due his Name;* bring offerings and come into his
courts.
Worship the Lord in the beauty of holiness;* let the whole earth tremble before
him.
Tell it out among the nations: "The Lord is King!"* he has made the world so firm
that it cannot be moved; he will judge the peoples with equity."

Psalm 96:7–10

The Request for Presence
Hear, O Shepherd of Israel, leading Joseph like a flock;* shine forth, you that are
enthroned upon the cherubim.
In the presence of Ephraim, Benjamin, and Manasseh,* stir up your strength and
come to help us.
Restore us, O God of hosts;* show the light of your countenance, and we shall be
saved.

Psalm 80:1–3

The Greeting

Into your hands I commend my spirit,* for you have redeemed me, O Lord, O
God of truth.

Psalm 31:5

The Refrain for the Midday Lessons

Let all the earth fear the Lord;* let all who dwell in the world stand in awe of him.

Psalm 33:8

A Reading

This alone is my conclusion: God has created man straightforward, and human
artifices are human inventions.

Ecclesiastes 7:29

The Refrain

Let all the earth fear the Lord;* let all who dwell in the world stand in awe of him.

The Midday Psalm   Come and Listen

Come and listen, all you who fear God,* and I will tell you what he has done
for me.
I called out to him with my mouth,* and his praise was on my tongue.
If I had found evil in my heart,* the Lord would not have heard me;
But in truth God has heard me;* he has attended to the voice of my prayer.
Blessed be God, who has not rejected my prayer,* nor withheld his love from me.

Psalm 66:14–18

The Refrain

Let all the earth fear the Lord;* let all who dwell in the world stand in awe of him.

The Gloria*

The Lord's Prayer

The Prayer Appointed for the Week

O Lord, you have taught us that without love whatever we do is worth nothing:
Send your Holy Spirit and pour into my heart your greatest gift, which is love,
the true bond of peace and of all virtue, without which whoever lives is
accounted dead before you. Grant this for the sake of your only Son Jesus
Christ, who lives and reigns with you and the Holy Spirit, one God, now and
for ever. *Amen.* †

The Concluding Prayer of the Church

Almighty God, who after the creation of the world rested from all your works
and sanctified a day of rest for all your creatures: Grant that I, putting away
all earthly anxieties, may be duly prepared for the service of public worship,
and grant as well that my Sabbath upon earth may be a preparation for the
eternal rest promised to your people in heaven; through Jesus Christ our
Lord. *Amen.*

The Vespers Office

To Be Observed on the Hour or Half Hour
Between 5 and 8 p.m.

The Call to Prayer
Sing with joy to God our strength* and raise a loud shout to the God of Jacob.
Raise a song and sound the timbrel,* the merry harp and the lyre.
Blow the ram's-horn at the new moon,* and at the full moon, the day of our feast.

Psalm 81:1–3

The Request for Presence
O God, do not be silent;* do not keep still nor hold your peace, O God.

Psalm 83:1

The Greeting
I will sing of mercy and justice;* to you, O LORD, will I sing praises.

Psalm 101:1

The Hymn   *O God of Truth*

O God of truth, O Lord of might,   Grant this, O Father ever one
Disposing time and change aright,   With Jesus Christ your only Son
Who clothes the splendid morning ray   And Holy Ghost, whom all adore,
And gives the heat at noon of day: Reigning and blessed for evermore.

                                                    adapted from THE SHORT BREVIARY
Extinguish every sinful fire,
And banish every ill desire;
And while you keep the body whole
Shed forth your peace upon the soul.

The Refrain for the Vespers Lessons
I will give you thanks for what you have done* and declare the goodness of your
    Name in the presence of the godly.

Psalm 52:9

The Vespers Psalm   *This Is Glory for All His Faithful People*
Let them praise his Name in the dance;* let them sing praise to him with timbrel
    and harp.
For the LORD takes pleasure in his people* and adorns the poor with victory.
Let the praises of God be in their throat* . . . this is glory for all his faithful people.

Psalm 149:4–6a, 9b

The Refrain
I will give you thanks for what you have done* and declare the goodness of your
    Name in the presence of the godly.

The Small Verse
The Lord is my shepherd and nothing is wanting to me. In green pastures He hath
    settled me.

                                                 THE SHORT BREVIARY

The Lord's Prayer

The Prayer Appointed for the Week

O Lord, you have taught us that without love whatever we do is worth nothing:
Send your Holy Spirit and pour into my heart your greatest gift, which is love,
the true bond of peace and of all virtue, without which whoever lives is
accounted dead before you. Grant this for the sake of your only Son Jesus
Christ, who lives and reigns with you and the Holy Spirit, one God, now and
for ever. *Amen.* †

The Concluding Prayer of the Church

Grant I pray, O Lord God, to me Your servant that I may evermore enjoy health of
mind and body, and by the glorious intercession of the Blessed Mary ever
Virgin be delivered from present sorrow and attain everlasting happiness.
Through our Lord Jesus Christ, Your Son, who lives and reigns with You in the
unity of the Holy Ghost, God, world without end. *Amen.*

adapted from THE SHORT BREVIARY

The Morning Office   To Be Observed on the Hour or Half Hour
                                              Between 6 and 9 a.m.

The Call to Prayer

Sing to the LORD, you servants of his;* give thanks for the remembrance of his
holiness.
For his wrath endures but the twinkling of an eye,* his favor for a lifetime.

Psalm 30:4–5

The Request for Presence

I cry out to you, O LORD;* I say, "You are my refuge, my portion in the land of the
living."

Psalm 142:5

The Greeting

Glory to God in the highest,
        and peace to his people on earth.
Lord God, heavenly King,
almighty God and Father,
        we worship you, we give you thanks,
        we praise you for your glory.
Lord Jesus Christ, only Son of the Father,
Lord God, Lamb of God,
you take away the sins of the world:
        have mercy on us;

you are seated at the right hand of the Father:
>   receive our prayer.
For you alone are the Holy One,
you alone are the Lord,
you alone are the Most High,
>   Jesus Christ,
>   with the Holy Spirit,
>   in the glory of God the Father. *Amen.*
>>   *Gloria in Excelsis*

The Refrain for the Morning Lessons

On this day the LORD has acted;* we will rejoice and be glad in it.
>   *Psalm 118:24*

A Reading

Jesus said: "I have come to bring fire to the earth, and how I wish it were blazing
>   already! There is a baptism I must still receive, and what constraint I am under
>   until it is completed!"
>>   *Luke 12:49–50*

The Refrain

On this day the LORD has acted;* we will rejoice and be glad in it.

The Morning Psalm   *So That a People Yet Unborn May Praise the LORD*

Let this be written for a future generation,* so that a people yet unborn may praise
>   the LORD.
For the LORD looked down from his holy place on high;* from the heavens he
>   beheld the earth;
That he might hear the groan of the captive* and set free those condemned to die;
That they may declare in Zion the Name of the LORD,* and his praise in Jerusalem;
When the peoples are gathered together,* and the kingdoms also, to serve the LORD.
>   *Psalm 102:18–22*

The Refrain

On this day the LORD has acted;* we will rejoice and be glad in it.

The Cry of the Church

O God, come to my assistance! O Lord, make haste to help me!

The Lord's Prayer

The Prayer Appointed for the Week

Most loving Father, whose will it is for us to give thanks for all things, to fear
>   nothing but the loss of you, and to cast all our care on you who cares for us:
>   Preserve me from faithless fears and worldly anxieties, that no clouds of this
>   mortal life may hide from me the light of that love which is immortal, and
>   which you have manifested to us in your Son Jesus Christ our Lord; who lives
>   and reigns with you, in the unity of the Holy Spirit, one God, now and for ever.
>   *Amen.* †

The Concluding Prayer of the Church

Lord God, almighty and everlasting Father, you have brought me in safety to this new day: Preserve me with your mighty power, that I may not fall into sin, nor be overcome by adversity; and in all I do direct me to the fulfilling of your purpose; through Jesus Christ my Lord. *Amen.* †

The Midday Office   To Be Observed on the Hour or Half Hour
                                          Between 11 a.m. and 2 p.m.

The Call to Prayer

Open my lips, O Lord,* and my mouth shall proclaim your praise.
Had you desired it, I would have offered sacrifice,* but you take no delight in burnt-offerings.
The sacrifice of God is a troubled spirit;* and a broken and contrite heart, O God, you will not despise.

Psalm 51:16–18

The Request for Presence

Show us the light of your countenance, O God,* and come to us.

based on Psalm 67:1

The Greeting

You, O LORD, are my lamp;* my God, you make my darkness bright.
With you I will break down an enclosure;* with the help of my God I will scale any wall.

Psalm 18:29–30

The Refrain for the Midday Lessons

Happy are those who trust in the LORD!* they do not resort to evil spirits or turn to false gods.

Psalm 40:4

A Reading

"For me it will be as in the days of Noah when I swore that Noah's waters should never flood the world again. So now I swear never to be angry with you and never to rebuke you again. For the mountains may go away and the hills may totter, but my faithful love will never leave you, my covenant of peace will never totter," says YAHWEH who takes pity on you.

Isaiah 54:9–10

The Refrain

Happy are those who trust in the LORD!* they do not resort to evil spirits or turn to false gods.

The Midday Psalm   *May They Prosper Who Love You*

I was glad when they said to me,* "Let us go to the house of the LORD."
Now our feet are standing* within your gates, O Jerusalem.
Jerusalem is built as a city* that is at unity with itself;

To which the tribes go up, the tribes of the LORD,* the assembly of Israel, to praise the Name of the LORD.
For there are the thrones of judgment,* the thrones of the house of David.
Pray for the peace of Jerusalem:* "May they prosper who love you.
Peace be within your walls* and quietness within your towers.
For my brethren and companions' sake,* I pray for your prosperity.
Because of the house of the LORD our God,* I will seek to do you good."

Psalm 122

The Refrain

Happy are those who trust in the LORD!* they do not resort to evil spirits or turn to false gods.

The Cry of the Church

Even so, come Lord Jesus!

The Lord's Prayer

The Prayer Appointed for the Week

Most loving Father, whose will it is for us to give thanks for all things, to fear nothing but the loss of you, and to cast all our care on you who cares for us: Preserve me from faithless fears and worldly anxieties, that no clouds of this mortal life may hide from me the light of that love which is immortal, and which you have manifested to us in your Son Jesus Christ our Lord; who lives and reigns with you, in the unity of the Holy Spirit, one God, now and for ever. *Amen.* †

The Concluding Prayer of the Church

O God, you make me glad with the weekly remembrance of the glorious resurrection of your Son my Lord: Give me this day such blessing through my worship of you, that the week to come may be spent in your favor; through Jesus Christ our Lord. *Amen.* †

The Vespers Office   **To Be Observed on the Hour or Half Hour**
Between 5 and 8 p.m.

The Call to Prayer

Bless the LORD, O my soul,* and all that is within me, bless his holy Name.
Bless the LORD, O my soul,* and forget not all his benefits.

Psalm 103:1-2

The Request for Presence

The LORD will hear the desire of the humble;* you will strengthen their heart and your ears shall hear.

Psalm 10:18

The Greeting

O gracious Light,
pure brightness of the everlasting Father in heaven,
O Jesus Christ, holy and blessed!

Now as we come to the setting of the sun,
and our eyes behold the vesper light,
we sing your praises O God: Father, Son and Holy Spirit.

You are worthy at all times to be praised by happy voices,
O Son of God, O giver of life,
and to be glorified through all the worlds.

Phos Hilaron

The Hymn   *Come, Pure Hearts*
Come, pure hearts, in joyful measure
sing of those who spread the treasure
          in the truth of God enshrined;
blessed tidings of salvation,
peace on earth their proclamation,
          love from God to lost mankind.

See the rivers four that gladden,
with their streams, the better Eden
          planted by our Lord most dear;
Christ the fountain, these the waters;
drink, O Zion's son and daughters,
          drink, and find salvation here.

O that we, your truth confessing,
and your holy word possessing,
          Jesus may your love adore;
unto you our voices raising,
you with all your ransomed praising,
          ever and for evermore.

Latin, 12th C.

The Refrain for the Vespers Lessons
The LORD has heard my supplication;* the LORD accepts my prayer.

Psalm 6:9

The Vespers Psalm   *I Am with Him in Trouble*
Because he is bound to me in love, therefore will I deliver him;* I will protect him,
     because he knows my Name.
He shall call upon me, and I will answer him;* I am with him in trouble; I will
     rescue him and bring him to honor.
With long life will I satisfy him,* and show him my salvation.

Psalm 91:14–16

The Refrain
The LORD has heard my supplication;* the LORD accepts my prayer.

The Small Verse
The Lord is my shepherd and nothing is wanting to me.* In green pastures He has
  settled me.

A Short Breviary

The Lord's Prayer

The Prayer Appointed for the Week
Most loving Father, whose will it is for us to give thanks for all things, to fear nothing
  but the loss of you, and to cast all our care on you who cares for us: Preserve me
  from faithless fears and worldly anxieties, that no clouds of this mortal life may
  hide from me the light of that love which is immortal, and which you have manifested to us in your Son Jesus Christ our Lord; who lives and reigns with you, in
  the unity of the Holy Spirit, one God, now and for ever. *Amen.* †

The Concluding Prayer of the Church
Heavenly Father, Shepherd of your people, thank you for your servant Matthias,
  who was faithful in the care and nurture of your flock; and I pray that, following his example, and the teaching of his holy life, I may by your grace grow
  into the stature of the fullness of our Lord and Savior Jesus Christ; who lives
  and reigns with you and the Holy Spirit, one God, for ever and ever. *Amen.* †

The Morning Office To Be Observed on the Hour or Half Hour
  Between 6 and 9 a.m.

The Call to Prayer
Bless the LORD, you angels of his, you mighty ones who do his bidding,* and
  hearken to the voice of his word.
Bless the LORD, all you his hosts,* you ministers of his who do his will.
Bless the LORD, all you works of his, in all places of his dominion;* bless the LORD,
  O my soul.

Psalm 103:20–22

The Request for Presence
Let those who seek you rejoice and be glad in you;* let those who love your
  salvation say forever, "Great is the LORD!"

Psalm 70:4

The Greeting
Therefore my heart sings to you without ceasing;* O LORD my God, I will give you
  thanks for ever.

Psalm 30:13

The Refrain for the Morning Lessons
May you be blessed by the LORD,* the maker of heaven and earth.

A Reading   *On February 24, the Church celebrates the life of*
St. Matthias who, following the betrayal and
suicide of Judas, was elected by the disciples to
assume Iscariot's place among the twelve.

One day Peter stood up to speak to the brothers—there were about a hundred and
twenty people in the congregation. 'Brothers,' he said, 'the passage of scripture
had to be fulfilled in which the Holy Spirit, speaking through David, foretells
the fate of Judas, who acted as a guide to the men who arrested Jesus—after
being one of our number and sharing our ministry . . . Now in the Book of
Psalms it says: *Reduce his encampment to ruin and leave his tent unoccupied.* And
again: *Let someone else take over his office.* Out of the men who have been with us
the whole time that the Lord Jesus was living with us, from the time when John
was baptizing until the day when he was taken up from us—one must be
appointed to serve with us as a witness to his resurrection.' Having nominated
two candidates, Joseph known as Barsabbas, whose surname was Justus, and
Matthias, they prayed, 'Lord, you can read everyone's heart: show us therefore
which of these two you have chosen to take over this ministry and apostolate,
which Judas abandoned to go to his proper place.' They then drew lots for
them, and as the lot fell to Matthias, he was listed as one of the twelve apostles.

Acts 1:15–17, 20–26

The Refrain
May you be blessed by the LORD,* the maker of heaven and earth.

The Morning Psalm   *The Fear of the LORD Is the Beginning of Wisdom*
I will give thanks to the LORD with my whole heart,* in the assembly of the
    upright, in the congregation.
Great are the deeds of the LORD!* they are studied by all who delight in them.
His work is full of majesty and splendor,* and his righteousness endures for ever.
He makes his marvelous works to be remembered;* the LORD is gracious and full
    of compassion.
The works of his hands are faithfulness and justice;* all his commandments are sure.
They stand fast for ever and ever,* because they are done in truth and equity.
He sent redemption to his people; he commanded his covenant for ever,* holy and
    awesome is his Name.

Psalm 111:1–4, 7–9

The Refrain
May you be blessed by the LORD,* the maker of heaven and earth.

The Small Verse
Open, Lord, my eyes that I may see.
Open, Lord, my ears that I may hear.
Open, Lord, my heart and my mind that I may understand.
So shall I turn to you and be healed.

Traditional

The Lord's Prayer

The Prayer Appointed for the Week
Most loving Father, whose will it is for us to give thanks for all things, to fear
nothing but the loss of you, and to cast all our care on you who cares for us:
Preserve me from faithless fears and worldly anxieties, that no clouds of this
mortal life may hide from me the light of that love which is immortal, and
which you have manifested to us in your Son Jesus Christ our Lord; who lives
and reigns with you, in the unity of the Holy Spirit, one God, now and for ever.
Amen. †

Concluding Prayers of the Church
Almighty God, who in the place of Judas chose your faithful servant Matthias to
be numbered among the Twelve: Grant that your Church, being delivered from
false apostles, may always be guided and governed by faithful and true pas-
tors; through Jesus Christ our Lord, who lives and reigns with you, in the unity
of the Holy Spirit, now and for ever. *Amen.* †

Lord God, almighty and everlasting Father, you have brought me in safety to this
new day: Preserve me with your mighty power, that I may not fall into sin, nor
be overcome by adversity; and in all I do direct me to the fulfilling of your purpose; through Jesus Christ my Lord. *Amen.*

The Midday Office   To Be Observed on the Hour or Half Hour
                                     Between 11 a.m. and 2 p.m.

The Call to Prayer
The righteous will rejoice in the LORD and put their trust in him,* and all who are
true of heart will glory.

Psalm 64:10

The Request for Presence
Show us the light of your countenance, O God,* and come to us.
based on Psalm 67:1

The Greeting
Happy are the people whose strength is in you!* whose hearts are set on the
pilgrims' way.

Psalm 84:4

The Refrain for the Midday Lessons
Happy are they who fear the LORD,* and who follow in his ways!
Psalm 128:1

A Reading
Our homeland is in heaven and it is from there that we are expecting a Savior, the
Lord Jesus Christ.

Philippians 3:20

The Refrain

Happy are they who fear the LORD,* and who follow in his ways!

The Midday Psalm   *Blessed Be God Who Has Never Withheld His Love*

Come and listen, all you who fear God,* and I will tell you what he has done for me.
I called out to him with my mouth,* and his praise was on my tongue.
If I had found evil in my heart,* the Lord would not have heard me;
But in truth God has heard me;* he has attended to the voice of my prayer.
Blessed be God, who has not rejected my prayer,* nor withheld his love from me.

Psalm 66:14–18

The Refrain

Happy are they who fear the LORD,* and who follow in his ways!

The Small Verse

Blessed be the Name of the Lord and blessed be the people who are called by it.

The Lord's Prayer

The Prayer Appointed for the Week

Most loving Father, whose will it is for us to give thanks for all things, to fear
    nothing but the loss of you, and to cast all our care on you who cares for us:
    Preserve me from faithless fears and worldly anxieties, that no clouds of this
    mortal life may hide from me the light of that love which is immortal, and
    which you have manifested to us in your Son Jesus Christ our Lord; who lives
    and reigns with you, in the unity of the Holy Spirit, one God, now and for ever.
    Amen. †

The Concluding Prayer of the Church

O God, by whose grace your servant Matthias, kindled with the flame of your
    love, became a burning and a shining light in your Church: Grant that I also
    may be aflame with the spirit of love and discipline, and walk before you as a
    child of light; through Jesus Christ our Lord, who lives and reigns with you in
    the unity of the Holy Spirit, one God, now and forever. *Amen.* †

The Vespers Office   **To Be Observed on the Hour or Half Hour**
                                          Between 5 and 8 p.m.

The Call to Prayer

It is a good thing to give thanks to the LORD* and to sing praises to your Name, O
    Most High;
To tell of your loving-kindness early in the morning* and of your faithfulness in
    the night season.

Psalm 92:1–2

The Request for Presence

Hear my prayer, O God;* give ear to the words of my mouth.

Psalm 54:2

The Greeting

I will thank you, O LORD my God, with all my heart,* and glorify your Name for
evermore.

Psalm 86:12

The Hymn

Now let the earth with joy resound
And heaven the chant re-echo round;
Nor heaven nor earth too high can raise
The great Apostles'—glorious praise!

Sickness and health your voice obey,
At your command they go or stay;
From sin's disease my soul restore,
In good confirm me more and more.

So when the world is at its end
And Christ to judgment shall descend,
May I be called those joys to see
Prepared from all eternity.

Praise to the Father, with the Son
And Paraclete for ever one:
To You, O holy Trinity
Be praise for all eternity.

adapted from THE SHORT BREVIARY

The Refrain for the Vespers Lessons

I will bless the LORD who gives me counsel;* my heart teaches me, night after night.

Psalm 16:7

The Vespers Psalm   *Show Me the Road That I Must Walk*

My spirit faints within me;* my heart within me is desolate.
I remember the time past; I muse upon all your deeds;* I consider the works of
your hands.
I spread out my hands to you;* my soul gasps to you like a thirsty land.
O LORD, make haste to answer me; my spirit fails me;* do not hide your face from
me or I shall be like those who go down to the Pit.
Let me hear of your loving-kindness in the morning, for I put my trust in you;*
show me the road that I must walk, for I lift up my soul to you.

Psalm 143:4–8

The Refrain

I will bless the LORD who gives me counsel;* my heart teaches me, night after night.

The Small Verse

Happy are the people whose strength is in you!* whose hearts are set on the
pilgrim's way,

For one day in your courts is better than a thousand in my own room,* and to stand
at the threshold of the house of my God than to dwell in the tents of the wicked.
Psalm 84:4, 9

The Lord's Prayer

The Prayer Appointed for the Week
Most loving Father, whose will it is for us to give thanks for all things, to fear nothing
but the loss of you, and to cast all our care on you who cares for us: Preserve me
from faithless fears and worldly anxieties, that no clouds of this mortal life may
hide from me the light of that love which is immortal, and which you have
manifested to us in your Son Jesus Christ our Lord; who lives and reigns with
you, in the unity of the Holy Spirit, one God, now and for ever. *Amen.* †

Concluding Prayers of the Church
Almighty God, by your Holy Spirit you have made us one with your saints in
heaven and on earth: grant that in my earthly pilgrimage I may always be
supported by this fellowship of love and prayer, and know myself to be
surrounded by their witness to your power and mercy. I ask this for the sake of
Jesus Christ, in whom all my intercessions are acceptable through the Spirit,
and who lives and reigns for ever and ever. *Amen.* †

Save me, O Lord, while I am awake, And keep me while I sleep. That I may wake
in Christ and rest in peace.
adapted from The Short Breviary

The Morning Office   To Be Observed on the Hour or Half Hour
Between 6 and 9 a.m.

The Call to Prayer
Search for the Lord and his strength;* continually seek his face.
Psalm 105:4

The Request for Presence
Show your goodness, O Lord, to those who are good* and to those who are true of
heart.
Psalm 125:4

The Greeting
You have set up a banner for those who fear you* . . .
Save us by your right hand and answer us.*
Psalm 60:4–5

The Refrain for the Morning Lessons
Our days are like the grass;* we flourish like a flower of the field;
When the wind goes over it, it is gone,* and its place shall know it no more.
Psalm 103:15–16

A Reading

John's disciples and the Pharisees were keeping a fast, when some people came to him and said to him, 'Why is it that John's disciples and the disciples of the Pharisees fast, but your disciples do not?' Jesus replied, 'Surely the bridegroom's attendants cannot fast while the bridegroom is still with them? As long as they have the bridegroom they cannot fast,. But the time will come when the bridegroom is taken away from them, and then, on that day, they will fast.'

Mark 2:18–20

The Refrain

Our days are like the grass;* we flourish like a flower of the field;

When the wind goes over it, it is gone,* and its place shall know it no more.

The Morning Psalm   *Whoever Does These Things Shall Never Be Overthrown*

LORD, who may dwell in your tabernacle?* who may abide upon your holy hill?

Whoever leads a blameless life and does what is right,* who speaks the truth from his heart.

There is no guile upon his tongue; he does no evil to his friend;* he does not heap contempt upon his neighbor.

In his sight the wicked is rejected,* but he honors those who fear the LORD.

He has sworn to do no wrong* and does not take back his word.

He does not give his money in hope of gain,* nor does he take a bribe against the innocent.

Whoever does these things* shall never be overthrown.

Psalm 15

The Refrain

Our days are like the grass;* we flourish like a flower of the field;

When the wind goes over it, it is gone,* and its place shall know it no more.

The Small Verse

Lord, have mercy; Christ, have mercy; Lord, have mercy.

The Lord's Prayer

The Prayer Appointed for the Week

Most loving Father, whose will it is for us to give thanks for all things, to fear nothing but the loss of you, and to cast all our care on you who cares for us: Preserve me from faithless fears and worldly anxieties, that no clouds of this mortal life may hide from me the light of that love which is immortal, and which you have manifested to us in your Son Jesus Christ our Lord; who lives and reigns with you, in the unity of the Holy Spirit, one God, now and for ever. Amen. †

The Concluding Prayer of the Church

Lord God, almighty and everlasting Father, you have brought me in safety to this new day: Preserve me with your mighty power, that I may not fall into sin, nor be overcome by adversity; and in all I do direct me to the fulfilling of your purpose; through Jesus Christ my Lord. *Amen.* †

The Midday Office   To Be Observed on the Hour or Half Hour
Between 11 a.m. and 2 p.m.

The Call to Prayer
Sing to the Lord and bless his Name;* proclaim the good news of his salvation
from day to day.
Declare his glory among the nations* and his wonders among all peoples.
For great is the Lord and greatly to be praised;* he is more to be feared than
all gods.

Psalm 96:2–4

The Request for Presence
I have gone astray like a sheep that is lost;* search for your servant, for I do not
forget your commandments.

Psalm 119:176

The Greeting
When your word goes forth it gives light;* it gives understanding to the simple.

Psalm 119:130

The Refrain for the Midday Lessons
He will not let your foot be moved* and he who watches over you will not
fall asleep.

Psalm 121:3

A Reading
Make sure that no one captivates you with the empty lure of a 'philosophy' of the
kind that human beings hand on, based on the principles of this world and not
on Christ.

Colossians 2:8

The Refrain
He will not let your foot be moved* and he who watches over you will not
fall asleep.

The Midday Psalm   *The Lord Will Not Abandon His People*
He that planted the ear, does he not hear?* he that formed the eye, does he not see?
He who admonishes the nations, will he not punish?* he who teaches all the
world, has he no knowledge?
The Lord knows our human thoughts;* how like a puff of wind they are.
Happy are they whom you instruct, O Lord!* whom you teach out of your law;
To give them rest in evil days,* until a pit is dug for the wicked.
For the Lord will not abandon his people,* nor will he forsake his own.
For judgment will again be just,* and all the true of heart will follow it.

Psalm 94:9–15

The Refrain
He will not let your foot be moved* and he who watches over you will not
fall asleep.

The Cry of the Church
O Lord, hear my prayer and let my cry come to you. Thanks be to God.
The Short Breviary

The Lord's Prayer

The Prayer Appointed for the Week
Most loving Father, whose will it is for us to give thanks for all things, to fear
nothing but the loss of you, and to cast all our care on you who cares for us:
Preserve me from faithless fears and worldly anxieties, that no clouds of this
mortal life may hide from me the light of that love which is immortal, and
which you have manifested to us in your Son Jesus Christ our Lord; who lives
and reigns with you, in the unity of the Holy Spirit, one God, now and for ever.
Amen. †

The Concluding Prayer of the Church
God of mystery, God of love, send your Spirit into our hearts with gifts of wisdom
and peace, fortitude and charity. We long to love and serve you. Faithful God,
make us faithful. This we ask through the intercession of all your saints. *Amen.*
The New Companion to the Breviary

The Vespers Office   **To Be Observed on the Hour or Half Hour**
Between 5 and 8 p.m.

The Call to Prayer
Worship the LORD in the beauty of holiness;* let the whole earth tremble before
him.
Psalm 31:3

The Request for Presence
Your word is a lantern to my feet* and a light upon my path.
Accept, O LORD, the willing tribute of my lips,* and teach me your judgments.
Psalm 119:105ff

The Greeting
You, O LORD, are my lamp;* my God, you make my darkness bright.
Psalm 18:29

The Hymn
> O brightness of the immortal Father's face,
> > most holy, heavenly, blessed,
> Lord Jesus Christ, in whom truth and grace
> > are visibly expressed:
> The sun is sinking now, and one by one
> > the lamps of evening shine;
> We hymn the Father eternal, and the Son,
> > and Holy Ghost Divine.

You are worthy at all times to receive
    our hallowed praises, Lord.
O Son of God, be you, in whom we live,
    through all the world adored.

Greek, 3rd C.

The Refrain for the Vespers Lessons
Your love, O LORD, for ever will I sing;* from age to age my mouth will proclaim
    your faithfulness.

Psalm 89:1

The Vespers Psalm   *A Broken and Contrite Heart, O God, You Will Not Despise*
Open my lips, O Lord,* and my mouth shall proclaim your praise.
Had you desired it, I would have offered sacrifice,* but you take no delight in
    burnt-offerings.
The sacrifice of God is a troubled spirit;* a broken and contrite heart, O God, you
    will not despise.

Psalm 51:16–18

The Refrain
Your love, O LORD, for ever will I sing;* from age to age my mouth will proclaim
    your faithfulness.

The Cry of the Church
Lord, have mercy on us. Christ, have mercy on us. Lord, have mercy on us.

The Lord's Prayer

The Prayer Appointed for the Week
Most loving Father, whose will it is for us to give thanks for all things, to fear
    nothing but the loss of you, and to cast all our care on you who cares for us:
    Preserve me from faithless fears and worldly anxieties, that no clouds of this
    mortal life may hide from me the light of that love which is immortal, and
    which you have manifested to us in your Son Jesus Christ our Lord; who lives
    and reigns with you, in the unity of the Holy Spirit, one God, now and for ever.
    Amen. †

The Concluding Prayer of the Church
Protect me, Lord, as I stay awake; watch over me as I sleep, that awake I may
    watch with Christ, and asleep, rest in his peace. *Amen.*

The Morning Office   To Be Observed on the Hour or Half Hour
Between 6 and 9 a.m.

The Call to Prayer
Love the LORD, all you who worship him;* the LORD protects the faithful, but
    repays to the full those who act haughtily.

Psalm 31:23

The Request for Presence
O Lord, I call to you; my Rock, do not be deaf to my cry;* lest, if you do not hear
    me, I become like those who go down to the Pit.

Psalm 28:1

The Greeting
Your way, O God, is holy;* who is as great as our God?

Psalm 77:13

The Refrain for the Morning Lessons
Protect my life and deliver me;* let me not be put to shame, for I have trusted in
    you.

Psalm 25:19

A Reading
. . . They made their way through Galilee; and he did not want anyone to know,
    because he was instructing his disciples; he was telling them, 'The Son of man
    will be delivered into the power of men; they will put him to death; and three
    days after he has been put to death he will rise again.' But they did not under-
    stand what he said and were afraid to ask him.

Mark 9:30–32

The Refrain
Protect my life and deliver me;* let me not be put to shame, for I have trusted in
    you.

The Morning Psalm   *In the Shadow of Your Wings Will I Take Refuge*
Be merciful to me, O God, be merciful, for I have taken refuge in you;* in the
    shadow of your wings will I take refuge until this time of trouble has gone by.
I will call upon the Most High God,* the God who maintains my cause.
He will send from heaven and save me; he will confound those who trample upon
    me;* God will send forth his love and his faithfulness.

Psalm 57:1–3

The Refrain
Protect my life and deliver me;* let me not be put to shame, for I have trusted in
    you.

The Cry of the Church
In the evening, in the morning, and at noonday, I will complain and lament, and
    he will hear my voice.

Psalm 55:18

The Lord's Prayer

The Prayer Appointed for the Week
Most loving Father, whose will it is for us to give thanks for all things, to fear
    nothing but the loss of you, and to cast all our care on you who cares for us:
    Preserve me from faithless fears and worldly anxieties, that no clouds of this
    mortal life may hide from me the light of that love which is immortal, and

which you have manifested to us in your Son Jesus Christ our Lord; who lives and reigns with you, in the unity of the Holy Spirit, one God, now and for ever. *Amen.* †

The Concluding Prayer of the Church

Lord God, almighty and everlasting Father, you have brought me in safety to this new day: Preserve me with your mighty power, that I may not fall into sin, nor be overcome by adversity; and in all I do direct me to the fulfilling of your purpose; through Jesus Christ my Lord. *Amen.* †

The Midday Office   To Be Observed on the Hour or Half Hour
Between 11 a.m. and 2 p.m.

The Call to Prayer

Sing to the LORD with thanksgiving;* make music to our God upon the harp.

Psalm 147:7

The Request for Presence

Hear the voice of my prayer when I cry out to you,* when I lift up my hands to your holy of holies.

Psalm 28:2

The Greeting

You are the LORD, most high over all the earth;* you are exalted far above all gods.

Psalm 97:9

The Refrain for the Midday Lessons

Tell it out among all the nations: "The LORD is King!* he has made the world so firm that it cannot be moved; he will judge all the peoples with equity."

Psalm 96:10

A Reading

With you is Wisdom, she who knows your works, she who was present when you made the world; she understands what is pleasing in your eyes and what agrees with your commandments. Dispatch her from the holy heavens, send her forth from your throne of glory to help me and to toil with me and teach me what is pleasing to you; since she knows and understands everything, she will guide me prudently in my actions and will protect me with her glory. Then all I do will be acceptable . . .

Wisdom 9:9–12

The Refrain

Tell it out among all the nations: "The LORD is King!* he has made the world so firm that it cannot be moved; he will judge all the peoples with equity."

The Midday Psalm   *Righteousness and Justice Are the Foundations of His Throne*

The LORD is King; let the earth rejoice;* let the multitude of the isles be glad.
Clouds and darkness are round about him,* righteousness and justice are the foundations of his throne.

A fire goes before him* and burns up his enemies on every side.
His lightnings light up the world;* the earth sees it and is afraid.
The mountains melt like wax at the presence of the LORD,* at the presence of the Lord of the whole earth.
The heavens declare his righteousness,* and all the peoples see his glory.

Psalm 97:1–6

The Refrain
Tell it out among all the nations: "The LORD is King!* he has made the world so firm that it cannot be moved; he will judge all the peoples with equity."

The Small Verse
Happy are the people whose strength is in you!* whose hearts are set on the pilgrims' way,
For one day in your courts is better than a thousand in my own room,* and to stand at the threshold of the house of my God than to dwell in the tents of the wicked.

Psalm 84:4, 9

The Lord's Prayer

The Prayer Appointed for the Week
Most loving Father, whose will it is for us to give thanks for all things, to fear nothing but the loss of you, and to cast all our care on you who cares for us: Preserve me from faithless fears and worldly anxieties, that no clouds of this mortal life may hide from me the light of that love which is immortal, and which you have manifested to us in your Son Jesus Christ our Lord; who lives and reigns with you, in the unity of the Holy Spirit, one God, now and for ever. *Amen.* †

The Concluding Prayer of the Church
Let us bless the Lord God living and true! Let us always render him praise, glory, honor, blessing, and all good things! Amen. Amen. So be it! So be it!

St. Francis of Assisi

The Vespers Office   **To Be Observed on the Hour or Half Hour**
                                          Between 5 and 8 p.m.

The Call to Prayer
Sing to God, O kingdoms of the earth;* sing praises to the Lord.
He rides in the heavens, the ancient heavens;* he sends forth his voice, his mighty voice.

Psalm 68:33–34

The Request for Presence
Protect me, O God, for I take refuge in you;* I have said to the LORD, "You are my Lord, my good above all other."

Psalm 16:1

The Greeting
Praise God from whom all blessings flow; Praise Him all creatures here below;
　　Praise Him above, you heavenly hosts; Praise Father, Son, and Holy Ghost.
　　　　　　　　　　　　　　　　　　　　　　　　　　　Doxology

The Hymn
　　Eternal Ruler of the ceaseless round
　　　　　　of circling planets singing on their way,
　　Guide of the nations from the night profound
　　　　　　into the glory of the perfect day;
　　Rule in our hearts, that we may ever be
　　　　　　guided and strengthened and upheld by thee.

　　We would be one in hatred of all wrong,
　　　　　　one in the love of all things sweet and fair,
　　One with the joy that breaks into song,
　　　　　　and with the grief that trembles into prayer;
　　One in the power that makes your children free
　　　　　　to follow truth, and thus to follow thee.
　　　　　　　　　　　　　　　　　　　John Chadwick

The Refrain for the Vespers Lessons
I will bear witness that the LORD is righteous;* I will praise the Name of the LORD
　　Most High.
　　　　　　　　　　　　　　　　　　　　　　　Psalm 7:18

The Vespers Psalm　　　　　　　　　　　*Turn Again to Your Rest, O My Soul*
The LORD watches over the innocent;* I was brought very low, and he helped me.
Turn again to your rest, O my soul,* for the LORD has treated you well.
For you have rescued my life from death,* my eyes from tears, and my feet from
　　stumbling.
I will walk in the presence of the LORD* in the land of the living.
　　　　　　　　　　　　　　　　　　　　　　　Psalm 116:5–8

The Refrain
I will bear witness that the LORD is righteous;* I will praise the Name of the LORD
　　Most High.

The Cry of the Church
Even so, come Lord Jesus!

The Lord's Prayer

The Prayer Appointed for the Week
Most loving Father, whose will it is for us to give thanks for all things, to fear
　　nothing but the loss of you, and to cast all our care on you who cares for us:
　　Preserve me from faithless fears and worldly anxieties, that no clouds of this
　　mortal life may hide from me the light of that love which is immortal, and
　　which you have manifested to us in your Son Jesus Christ our Lord; who lives

and reigns with you, in the unity of the Holy Spirit, one God, now and for ever. *Amen.* †

The Concluding Prayer of the Church

Spirit of God, promise of Jesus, come to our help at the close of this day. Come with forgiveness and healing love. Come with life and hope. Come with all that we need to continue in the way of your truth. So may we praise you in the Trinity forever. *Amen.*

THE NEW COMPANION TO THE BREVIARY

The Morning Office **To Be Observed on the Hour or Half Hour Between 6 and 9 a.m.**

The Call to Prayer

Wake up, my spirit; awake lute and harp;* I myself will waken the dawn.

Psalm 57:8

The Request for Presence

You are the LORD; do not withhold your compassion from me;* let your love and your faithfulness keep me safe for ever.

Psalm 40:12

The Greeting

My heart is firmly fixed, O God, my heart is fixed;* I will sing and make melody.

Psalm 57:7

The Refrain for the Morning Lessons

Cast your burden upon the LORD, and he will sustain you;* he will never let the righteous stumble.

Psalm 55:24

A Reading

Jesus said: "Now the hour has come for the Son of man to be glorified. In all truth I tell you, unless a wheat grain falls on earth and dies, it remains only a single grain; but if it dies, it yields a rich harvest."

John 12:23–24

The Refrain

Cast your burden upon the LORD, and he will sustain you;* he will never let the righteous stumble.

The Morning Psalm *May the LORD Strengthen You Out of Zion*

May the LORD answer you in the day of trouble,* the Name of the God of Jacob defend you;

Send you help from his holy place* and strengthen you out of Zion;

Remember all your offerings* and accept your burnt sacrifice;

Grant you your heart's desire* and prosper all your plans.

We will shout for joy at your victory and triumph in the Name of our God;* may the LORD grant all your requests.

Psalm 20:1–5

The Refrain
Cast your burden upon the LORD, and he will sustain you;* he will never let the righteous stumble.

The Small Verse
My soul thirsts for the strong, living God and all that is within me cries out to him.

The Lord's Prayer

The Prayer Appointed for the Week
Most loving Father, whose will it is for us to give thanks for all things, to fear nothing but the loss of you, and to cast all our care on you who cares for us: Preserve me from faithless fears and worldly anxieties, that no clouds of this mortal life may hide from me the light of that love which is immortal, and which you have manifested to us in your Son Jesus Christ our Lord; who lives and reigns with you, in the unity of the Holy Spirit, one God, now and for ever. Amen. †

The Concluding Prayer of the Church
Lord God, almighty and everlasting Father, you have brought me in safety to this new day: Preserve me with your mighty power, that I may not fall into sin, nor be overcome by adversity; and in all I do direct me to the fulfilling of your purpose; through Jesus Christ my Lord. Amen. †

The Midday Office
To Be Observed on the Hour or Half Hour
Between 11 a.m. and 2 p.m.

The Call to Prayer
"Come now, let us reason together," says the LORD.
Isaiah 1:18, KJV

The Request for Presence
Awake, O my God, decree justice;* let the assembly of peoples gather around you.
Let the malice of the wicked come to an end, but establish the righteous;* for you test the mind and heart, O righteous God.

Psalm 7:7, 10

The Greeting
Deliver me, O LORD, by your hand* from those whose portion in life is this world.
Psalm 17:14

The Refrain for the Midday Lessons
Righteousness shall go before him,* and peace shall be a pathway for his feet.
Psalm 85:13

A Reading

His commandment is this, that we should believe in the name of his Son Jesus Christ and that we should love each other as he commanded us. Whoever keeps his commandments remains in God, and God in him. And this is the proof that he remains in us: the Spirit that he has given us.

I John 3:23–24

The Refrain

Righteousness shall go before him,* and peace shall be a pathway for his feet.

The Midday Psalm   *You Lengthen My Stride Beneath Me*

It is God who girds me about with strength* and makes my way secure.
He makes me sure-footed like a deer* and lets me stand firm on the heights.
He trains my hands for battle* and my arms for bending even a bow of bronze.
You have given me your shield of victory;* your right hand also sustains me; your loving care makes me great.
You lengthen my stride beneath me,* and my ankles do not give way.

Psalm 18:33–37

The Refrain

Righteousness shall go before him,* and peace shall be a pathway for his feet.

The Cry of the Church

Lord, have mercy on us. Christ, have mercy on us. Lord, have mercy on us.

The Lord's Prayer

The Prayer Appointed for the Week

Most loving Father, whose will it is for us to give thanks for all things, to fear nothing but the loss of you, and to cast all our care on you who cares for us: Preserve me from faithless fears and worldly anxieties, that no clouds of this mortal life may hide from me the light of that love which is immortal, and which you have manifested to us in your Son Jesus Christ our Lord; who lives and reigns with you, in the unity of the Holy Spirit, one God, now and for ever. *Amen.* †

The Concluding Prayer of the Church

Renew in my heart, O God, the gift of your Holy Spirit, so that I may love you fully in all that I do and love all others as Christ loves me. May all that I do proclaim the good news that you are God with us. *Amen.* †

The Vespers Office   **To Be Observed on the Hour or Half Hour Between 5 and 8 p.m.**

The Call to Prayer

O tarry and await the LORD's pleasure; be strong, and he shall comfort your heart;* wait patiently for the LORD.

Psalm 27:18

The Request for Presence
Open my eyes, that I may see* the wonders of your law.
                                                    Psalm 119:18

The Greeting
Your statutes have been like songs to me* wherever I have lived as a stranger.
I remember your Name in the night, O LORD,* and dwell upon your law.
This is how it has been with me,* because I have kept your commandments.
                                                    Psalm 119:54–56

The Hymn   *Jubilate! Amen!*
     Now on land and sea descending,
     Brings the night its peace profound;
     Let our vesper hymn be blending
     With holy calm around.
               Jubilate! Jubilate!
               Jubilate! Amen!
     Let our vesper hymn be blending
     With holy calm around.

     Soon as dies the sunset glory,
     Stars of heaven shine out above,
     Telling still the ancient story,
     Their Creator's changeless love.
               Jubilate! Jubilate!
               Jubilate! Amen!
     Telling still the ancient story,
     Their Creator's changeless love.

     Now, our wants and burdens leaving
     To God's care who cares for all,
     Cease we fearing, cease we grieving;
     Touched by God our burdens fall.
               Jubilate! Jubilate!
               Jubilate! Amen!
     Cease we fearing, cease we grieving;
     Touched by God our burdens fall.

     As the darkness deepens o'er us,
     Lo! Eternal stars arise;
     Hope and faith and love rise glorious,
     Shining in the Spirit's skies.
               Jubilate! Jubilate!
               Jubilate! Amen!
     Hope and faith and love rise glorious,
     Shining in the Spirit's skies.
                    Samuel Longfellow

The Refrain for the Vespers Lessons
'I am the Alpha and the Omega,' says the Lord God, who is, who was, and who is
  to come, the Almighty.

Revelation 1:8

The Vespers Psalm   *The* LORD *Is My Shepherd*
The LORD is my shepherd;* I shall not be in want.
He makes me lie down in green pastures* and leads me beside still waters.
He revives my soul* and guides me along right pathways for his Name's sake.
Though I walk through the valley of the shadow of death, I shall fear no evil;* for
  you are with me; your rod and your staff, they comfort me.
You spread a table before me in the presence of those who trouble me;* you have
  anointed my head with oil, and my cup is running over.
Surely your goodness and mercy shall follow me all the days of my life,* and I will
  dwell in the house of the LORD for ever.

Psalm 23

The Refrain
'I am the Alpha and the Omega,' says the Lord God, who is, who was, and who is
  to come, the Almighty.

The Cry of the Church
Be, Lord, my helper and forsake me not. Do not despise me, O God, my savior.

THE SHORT BREVIARY

The Lord's Prayer

The Prayer Appointed for the Week
Most loving Father, whose will it is for us to give thanks for all things, to fear nothing
  but the loss of you, and to cast all our care on you who cares for us: Preserve me
  from faithless fears and worldly anxieties, that no clouds of this mortal life may
  hide from me the light of that love which is immortal, and which you have manifested to us in your Son Jesus Christ our Lord; who lives and reigns with you, in
  the unity of the Holy Spirit, one God, now and for ever. *Amen.* †

The Concluding Prayer of the Church
Lord Jesus Christ, you said to your apostles, "Peace I give to you; my own peace I
  leave with you." Regard not my sins, but my faith, and give to me a place in the
  peace and unity of that heavenly City, where with the Father and the Holy
  Spirit you live and reign, now and forever. *Amen.* †

The Morning Office   **To Be Observed on the Hour or Half Hour**

Between 6 and 9 a.m.

The Call to Prayer
Come now and see the works of God,* how wonderful he is in his doing toward
  all people.

Psalm 66:4

The Request for Presence
Satisfy us by your loving-kindness in the morning;* so shall we rejoice and be glad
all the days of our life.

Psalm 90:14

The Greeting
Save us, O LORD our God, and gather us from among the nations,* that we may
give thanks to your holy Name and glory in your praise.

Psalm 106:47

The Refrain for the Morning Lessons
Mercy and truth have met together;* righteousness and peace have kissed
each other.

Psalm 85:10

A Reading
Then Jesus said to his disciples, 'If anyone wants to be a follower of mine, let him
renounce himself and take up his cross and follow me. Anyone who wants to
save his life will lose it; but anyone who loses his life for my sake will find it.'

Matthew 16:24–25

The Refrain
Mercy and truth have met together;* righteousness and peace have kissed
each other.

The Morning Psalm　　　　　　　　*We Walk, O LORD, in the Light of Your Presence*
Righteousness and justice are the foundations of your throne;* love and truth go
before your face.
Happy are the people who know the festal shout!* they walk, O LORD, in the light
of your presence.
They rejoice daily in your Name;* they are jubilant in your righteousness.
For you are the glory of their strength,* and by your favor our might is exalted.
Truly, the LORD is our ruler;* the Holy One of Israel is our King.

Psalm 89:14–18

The Refrain
Mercy and truth have met together;* righteousness and peace have kissed
each other.

The Cry of the Church
Lord, have mercy on us. Christ, have mercy on us. Lord, have mercy on us.

The Lord's Prayer

The Prayer Appointed for the Week
Most loving Father, whose will it is for us to give thanks for all things, to fear
nothing but the loss of you, and to cast all our care on you who cares for us:
Preserve me from faithless fears and worldly anxieties, that no clouds of this

mortal life may hide from me the light of that love which is immortal, and which you have manifested to us in your Son Jesus Christ our Lord; who lives and reigns with you, in the unity of the Holy Spirit, one God, now and for ever. *Amen.* †

The Concluding Prayer of the Church

Lord God, almighty and everlasting Father, you have brought me in safety to this new day: Preserve me with your mighty power, that I may not fall into sin, nor be overcome by adversity; and in all I do direct me to the fulfilling of your purpose; through Jesus Christ my Lord. *Amen.* †

The Midday Office

To Be Observed on the Hour or Half Hour
Between 11 a.m. and 2 p.m.

The Call to Prayer

God is the LORD; he has shined upon us;* form a procession with branches up to the horns of the altar.

Psalm 118:27

The Request for Presence

Set watch before my mouth, O LORD, and guard the door of my lips.

Psalm 141:3

The Greeting

Remember your word to your servant,* because you have given me hope.
This is my comfort in my trouble,* that your promise gives me life.

Psalm 119:49–50

The Refrain for the Midday Lessons

For God alone my soul in silence waits;* from him comes my salvation.

Psalm 62:1

A Reading

. . . Teach each other, and advise each other, in all wisdom. With gratitude in your hearts sing psalms and hymns and inspired songs to God; and whatever you say or do, let it be in the name of the Lord Jesus, in thanksgiving to God the Father through him.

Colossians 3:16–17

The Refrain

For God alone my soul in silence waits;* from him comes my salvation.

The Midday Psalm   *With You Is the Well of Life*

Your love, O LORD, reaches to the heavens,* and your faithfulness to the clouds.
Your righteousness is like the strong mountains, your justice like the great deep;* you save both man and beast, O LORD.
How priceless is your love, O God!* your people take refuge under the shadow of your wings.

Continue your loving-kindness to those who know you,* and your favor to those
who are true of heart.

Psalm 36:5–7, 10

The Refrain
For God alone my soul in silence waits;* from him comes my salvation.

The Cry of the Church
In the evening, in the morning and at noonday, I will complain and lament,* and
he will hear my voice.

Psalm 55:18

The Lord's Prayer

The Prayer Appointed for the Week
Most loving Father, whose will it is for us to give thanks for all things, to fear
nothing but the loss of you, and to cast all our care on you who cares for us:
Preserve me from faithless fears and worldly anxieties, that no clouds of this
mortal life may hide from me the light of that love which is immortal, and
which you have manifested to us in your Son Jesus Christ our Lord; who lives
and reigns with you, in the unity of the Holy Spirit, one God, now and for ever.
Amen. †

The Concluding Prayer of the Church
Almighty God, whose most dear Son went not up to the joy before he first suffered
pain, and did not enter into glory before he was crucified: Mercifully grant that
I, walking in the way of the cross, may find it to be none other than the way of
life and peace; through Jesus Christ your Son my Lord. *Amen.* †

The Vespers Office   **To Be Observed on the Hour or Half Hour**
                                              Between 5 and 8 p.m.

The Call to Prayer
Praise the LORD, all you nations;* laud him, all you peoples.
For his loving-kindness toward us is great,* and the faithfulness of the LORD
endures for ever.

Psalm 117:1–2

The Request for Presence
Help us, O God our Savior, for the glory of your Name;* deliver us and forgive us
our sins, for your Name's sake.

Psalm 79:9

The Greeting
You are to be praised, O God, in Zion . . . To you that hear prayer shall all flesh
come,* because of their transgressions.

Psalm 65:1–2

The Hymn

> The day is past and over; all thanks, O Lord, to thee!
> I ask that offenseless now the hours of dark may be,
> O Jesus, keep me in your sight, and guard me through the coming night.
>
> The joys of day are over; I lift my heart to thee,
> and ask you that sinless now the hours of dark may be.
> O Jesus, make their darkness light, and guard me through the coming night.
>
> The toils of day are over; I raise my hymn to thee,
> and ask that free from terrors now the hours of dark may be.
> O Jesus, keep me in your sight, and guard me through the coming night.
>
> Please be my soul's preserver, O God, for you do know
> how many are the perils through which I have to go.
> Lord Jesus Christ, O hear my call, save and guard me from them all.
>
> *Greek, 6th C.*

The Refrain for the Vespers Lesson

Your love, O Lord, reaches to the heavens,* and your faithfulness to the clouds.

Psalm 36:5

The Vespers Psalm   *The Lord Shall Preserve You*

I lift up my eyes to the hills;* from where is my help to come?
My help comes from the Lord,* the maker of heaven and earth.
He will not let your foot be moved* and he who watches over you will not
  fall asleep.
Behold, he who keeps watch over Israel* shall neither slumber nor sleep;
The Lord himself watches over you;* the Lord is your shade at your right hand,
So that the sun shall not strike you by day,* nor the moon by night.
The Lord shall preserve you from all evil;* it is he who shall keep you safe.
The Lord shall watch over your going out and your coming in,* from this time
  forth for evermore.

Psalm 121

The Refrain

Your love, O Lord, reaches to the heavens,* and your faithfulness to the clouds.

The Small Verse

The people that walked in darkness have seen a great light; on the inhabitants of a
  country in shadow dark as death light has blazed forth.

Isaiah 9:1

The Lord's Prayer

The Prayer Appointed for the Week

Most loving Father, whose will it is for us to give thanks for all things, to fear nothing
  but the loss of you, and to cast all our care on you who cares for us: Preserve me
  from faithless fears and worldly anxieties, that no clouds of this mortal life may

hide from me the light of that love which is immortal, and which you have manifested to us in your Son Jesus Christ our Lord; who lives and reigns with you, in the unity of the Holy Spirit, one God, now and for ever. *Amen.* †

Concluding Prayers of the Church

Lord Jesus Christ, by your death you took away the sting of death: Grant me so to follow in faith where you have led the way, that I may at length fall asleep peacefully in you and wake up in your likeness; for your tender mercies' sake. *Amen.* †

May the souls of the faithful departed, through the mercy of God, rest in eternal peace. *Amen.*

The Morning Office   To Be Observed on the Hour or Half Hour
                        Between 6 and 9 a.m.

The Call to Prayer

I will call upon God, and the LORD will deliver me.
In the evening, in the morning, and at the noonday, he will hear my voice.
He will bring me safely back . . . God who is enthroned of old, will hear me. †

The Request for Presence

Show us your mercy, O LORD,* and grant us your salvation.
Psalm 85:7

The Greeting

Happy are those whom you choose and draw to your courts to dwell there!* they will be satisfied by the beauty of your house, by the holiness of your temple.
Psalm 65:4

The Refrain for the Morning Lessons

Happy are the people whose strength is in you!* whose hearts are set on the pilgrims' way.
Psalm 84:4

A Reading

Filled with the Holy Spirit, Jesus left the Jordan and was led by the Spirit into the desert, for forty days being put to the test by the devil. During that time he ate nothing and at the end he was hungry. Then the devil said to him, 'If you are the Son of God, tell this stone to turn into a loaf.' But Jesus replied, 'Scripture says: *Human beings live not on bread alone.*' Then leading him to a height, the devil showed him in a moment of time all the kingdoms of the world and said to him, 'I will give you all this power and their splendor, for it has been handed over to me, for me to give to anyone I choose. Do homage, then, to me and it shall all be yours.' But Jesus answered him, 'Scripture says: *You must do homage to the Lord your God, him alone you must serve.*' Then he led him to Jerusalem and set him on the parapet of the Temple. 'If you are Son of God,' he said to him, 'throw yourself down from here, for scripture says: *He has given his angels orders about you, to guard you* and again: *They will carry you in their arms in case you trip over a stone.'* But Jesus answered him, 'Scripture says: *Do not put the Lord your God to the test.'* Having exhausted every way of putting him to the test, the devil left him, until the opportune moment.

Luke 4:1–13

The Refrain
Happy are the people whose strength is in you!* whose hearts are set on the pilgrims' way.

The Morning Psalm   *To You, O My Strength, Will I Sing*
For my part, I will sing of your strength;* I will celebrate your love in the morning;
For you have become my stronghold,* a refuge in the day of my trouble.
To you, O my Strength, will I sing;* for you, O God, are my stronghold and my
    merciful God.

Psalm 59:18–20

The Refrain
Happy are the people whose strength is in you!* whose hearts are set on the pilgrims' way.

The Small Verse
My soul has a desire and longing for the courts of the LORD;* my heart and my
    flesh rejoice in the living God.

Psalm 84:1

The Lord's Prayer

The Prayer Appointed for the Week
Most loving Father, whose will it is for us to give thanks for all things, to fear nothing
    but the loss of you, and to cast all our care on you who cares for us: Preserve me
    from faithless fears and worldly anxieties, that no clouds of this mortal life may
    hide from me the light of that love which is immortal, and which you have mani-
    fested to us in your Son Jesus Christ our Lord; who lives and reigns with you, in
    the unity of the Holy Spirit, one God, now and for ever. *Amen.* †

The Concluding Prayer of the Church
Lord God, almighty and everlasting Father, you have brought me in safety to this
    new day: Preserve me with your mighty power, that I may not fall into sin, nor
    be overcome by adversity; and in all I do direct me to the fulfilling of your pur-
    pose; through Jesus Christ my Lord. *Amen.* †

The Midday Office   **To Be Observed on the Hour or Half Hour**

Between 11 a.m. and 2 p.m.

The Call to Prayer
How good it is to sing praises to our God!* how pleasant it is to honor him with
    praise!

Psalm 147:1

The Request for Presence
Remember me, O LORD, with the favor you have for your people,* and visit me
　　with your saving help;
That I may see the prosperity of your elect and be glad with the gladness of your
　　people,* that I may glory with your inheritance.

Psalm 106:4–5

The Greeting
In you, O LORD, have I taken refuge;* let me never be ashamed.

Psalm 71:1

The Refrain for the Midday Lessons
Your statutes have been like songs to me* wherever I have lived like a stranger.

Psalm 119:54

A Reading
I am coming to put you on trial and I shall be a ready witness against sorcerers,
　　adulterers, perjurers, and against those who oppress the wage-earner, the
　　widow and the orphan, and who rob the foreigner of his rights and do not
　　respect me, says Yahweh Sabaoth.

Malachi 3:5

The Refrain
Your statutes have been like songs to me* wherever I have lived like a stranger.

The Midday Psalm
The Lord loveth His foundation upon the holy mountains,* the gates of Sion more
　　than all the tents of Jacob.
Glorious things are said of thee,* O city of God!
I will number Rahab and Babylon* among those avowing Me;
Behold the Philistines and Tyre and the people of Ethiopia* are gathered there.
Shall it not be said on Sion: "This man and that is born therein,* and the Most High
　　Himself hath founded her?"
In His book the Lord recordeth nations and princes* who hail from there.
This is the joyous cry of all: "My dwelling is in thee!"

Psalm 86, THE SHORT BREVIARY

The Refrain
Your statutes have been like songs to me* wherever I have lived like a stranger.

The Cry of the Church
Lord, have mercy on us. Christ, have mercy on us. Lord, have mercy on us.

The Lord's Prayer

The Prayer Appointed for the Week
Most loving Father, whose will it is for us to give thanks for all things, to fear nothing
　　but the loss of you, and to cast all our care on you who cares for us: Preserve me

from faithless fears and worldly anxieties, that no clouds of this mortal life may hide from me the light of that love which is immortal, and which you have manifested to us in your Son Jesus Christ our Lord; who lives and reigns with you, in the unity of the Holy Spirit, one God, now and for ever. *Amen.* †

The Concluding Prayer of the Church

Almighty God, who after the creation of the world rested from all your works and sanctified a day of rest for all your creatures: Grant that I, putting away all earthly anxieties, may be duly prepared for the service of public worship, and grant as well that my Sabbath upon earth may be a preparation for the eternal rest promised to your people in heaven; through Jesus Christ our Lord. *Amen.* †

The Vespers Office   **To Be Observed on the Hour or Half Hour Between 5 and 8 p.m.**

The Call to Prayer

Let the Name of the LORD be blessed,* from this time forth for evermore.
From the rising of the sun to its going down* let the Name of the LORD be praised.

Psalm 113:2–3

The Request for Presence

Let my cry come before you, O LORD;* give me understanding, according to your word.
Let my supplication come before you;* deliver me, according to your promise.

Psalm 119:169–170

The Greeting

The Lord is in his holy temple; Let all the earth keep silence before him. *Amen.*

The Hymn   *A Story to Tell the Nations*

We've a story to tell to the nations,
That shall turn their hearts to right,
A story of truth and mercy,
A story of peace and light.
For the darkness shall turn to dawning,
And the dawning to noonday bright;
And Christ's great kingdom shall come to earth,
The kingdom of love and light.

We've a song to be sung to the nations,
That shall lift their hearts to the Lord,
A song that shall conquer evil
And shatter spear and sword.
For the darkness shall turn to dawning,
And the dawning to noonday bright;
And Christ's great kingdom shall come to earth,
The kingdom of love and light.

We've a Savior to show the nations,
Who the path of sorrow has trod,
That all of the world's peoples
Might come to the truth of God.
For the darkness shall turn to dawning,
And the dawning to noonday bright;
And Christ's great kingdom shall come to earth,
The kingdom of love and light.

H. Ernest Nichol

The Refrain for the Vespers Lessons
Turn again to your rest, O my soul,* for the LORD has treated you well.

Psalm 116:6

The Vespers Psalm   *You Will Arise and Have Compassion on Zion*
You will arise and have compassion on Zion, for it is time to have mercy upon
    her;* indeed, the appointed time has come.
For your servants love her very rubble,* and are moved to pity even for her dust.
The nations shall fear your Name, O LORD,* and all the kings of the earth your
    glory.
For the LORD will build up Zion,* and his glory will appear.
He will look with favor on the prayer of the homeless;* he will not despise their
    plea.

Psalm 102:13–17

The Refrain
Turn again to your rest, O my soul,* for the LORD has treated you well.

The Small Verse
Keep me, Lord, as the apple of your eye and carry me under the shadow of your
    wings.

The Lord's Prayer

The Prayer Appointed for the Week
Most loving Father, whose will it is for us to give thanks for all things, to fear nothing
    but the loss of you, and to cast all our care on you who cares for us: Preserve me
    from faithless fears and worldly anxieties, that no clouds of this mortal life may
    hide from me the light of that love which is immortal, and which you have mani-
    fested to us in your Son Jesus Christ our Lord; who lives and reigns with you, in
    the unity of the Holy Spirit, one God, now and for ever. *Amen.* †

The Concluding Prayer of the Church
Almighty God, who after the creation of the world rested from all your works and
    sanctified a day of rest for all your creatures: Grant that I, putting away all
    earthly anxieties, may be duly prepared for the service of public worship, and
    grant as well that my Sabbath upon the earth may be a preparation for the eternal
    rest promised to your people in heaven; through Jesus Christ our Lord. *Amen.* †

February Compline

Sunday
The Night Office To Be Observed Before Retiring

The Call to Prayer
May the Lord Almighty grant me and those I love a peaceful night and a perfect
end. *Amen.* †

The Request for Presence
Our help is in the Name of the Lord; the maker of heaven and earth.

The Greeting
Almighty God, my heavenly Father: I have sinned against you, through my own
fault, in thought, and word, and deed, in what I have done and in what I have
left undone. For the sake of your Son our Lord Jesus Christ, forgive me all my
offenses; and grant that I may serve you in newness of life, to the glory of your
Name. *Amen.* †

The Reading *Late Have I Loved Thee*
Late have I loved thee, O beauty so ancient and so new; late have I loved thee: for
behold you were within me, and I outside; and I sought you outside and in my
unloveliness fell upon those lovely things that you had made. You were with
me, and I was not with you. I was kept from you by those things, yet had they
not been in you, they would not have been at all. You called and tried to break
open my deafness: and you sent forth your beams and shone upon me and
chased away my blindness: you breathed fragrance upon me, and I drew in my
breath and I do now pant for you: I taste you, and now hunger and thirst for
you: you touched me, and I have burned for your peace.

St. Augustine

*The Gloria**

The Psalm *The Holy One of Israel Is Our King*
Your love, O LORD, for ever will I sing;* from age to age my mouth will proclaim
your faithfulness.
For I am persuaded that your love is established for ever;* you have set your
faithfulness firmly in the heavens.
"I have made a covenant with my chosen one;* I have sworn an oath to David
my servant:
'I will establish your line for ever,* and preserve your throne for all
generations.' "
Righteousness and justice are the foundations of your throne;* love and truth go
before your face.
Happy are the people who know the festal shout!* they walk, O LORD, in the light
of your presence.
They rejoice daily in your Name;* they are jubilant in your righteousness.
For you are the glory of their strength,* and by your favor our might is exalted.
Truly, the LORD is our ruler;* the Holy One of Israel is our King.

Psalm 89:1–4, 14–18

*The Gloria**

The Small Verse

Into your hands, O Lord, I commend my spirit; for you have redeemed me, O Lord, O God of truth. Keep me, O Lord, as the apple of your eye; hide me under the shadow of your wings. †

The Lord's Prayer

The Petition

Keep watch, dear Lord, with those who work, or watch, or weep this night, and give your angels charge over those who sleep. Tend the sick, Lord Christ; give rest to the weary, bless the dying, soothe the suffering, pity the afflicted, shield the joyous; and all for your love's sake. *Amen.* †

The Final Thanksgiving

Lord, you now have set your servant free to go in peace as you have promised; for these eyes of mine have seen the Savior, whom you have prepared for all the world to see: a Light to enlighten the nations, and the glory of your people Israel. Glory to the Father, and to the Son, and to the Holy Spirit: as it was in the beginning, is now, and will be for ever. *Amen.*

Monday
The Night Office   To Be Observed Before Retiring

The Call to Prayer

May the Lord Almighty grant me and those I love a peaceful night and a perfect end. *Amen.* †

The Request for Presence

Our help is in the Name of the Lord; the maker of heaven and earth.

The Greeting

Almighty God, my heavenly Father: I have sinned against you, through my own fault, in thought, and word, and deed, in what I have done and in what I have left undone. For the sake of your Son our Lord Jesus Christ, forgive me all my offenses; and grant that I may serve you in newness of life, to the glory of your Name. *Amen.* †

The Reading   *On the Exercise of Religion*

We should renew our purpose daily, and should stir up ourselves to fresh enthusiasm, as though this were the first day of our conversion, and we should say,

"Help me, Lord Jesus, that I may persevere in my good purpose and in Your holy service to my life's end. Grant that I may now, this very day, perfectly begin, for what I have done in time past is as nothing."

Thomas à Kempis

*The Gloria**

The Psalm   *You Enfold and Comfort Me*
Your righteousness, O God, reaches to the heavens;* you have done great things; who is like you, O God?
You have showed me great troubles and adversities,* but you will restore my life and bring me up again from the deep places of the earth.
You strengthen me more and more;* you enfold and comfort me,
Therefore I will praise you upon the lyre for your faithfulness, O my God;* I will sing to you with the harp, O Holy One of Israel.
My lips will sing with joy when I play to you,* and so will my soul, which you have redeemed.
My tongue will proclaim your righteousness all day long,* for they are ashamed and disgraced who sought to do me harm.

Psalm 71:19–24

*The Gloria**

The Small Verse
Into your hands, O Lord, I commend my spirit; For you have redeemed me, O Lord, O God of truth. Keep me, O Lord, as the apple of your eye; Hide me under the shadow of your wings. †

The Lord's Prayer

The Petition
Keep watch, dear Lord, with those who work, or watch, or weep this night, and give your angels charge over those who sleep. Tend the sick, Lord Christ; give rest to the weary, bless the dying, soothe the suffering, pity the afflicted, shield the joyous; and all for your love's sake. *Amen.* †

The Final Thanksgiving
Lord, you now have set your servant free to go in peace as you have promised; for these eyes of mine have seen the Savior, whom you have prepared for all the world to see: a Light to enlighten the nations, and the glory of your people Israel. Glory to the Father, and to the Son, and to the Holy Spirit: as it was in the beginning, is now, and will be for ever. *Amen.*

Tuesday
The Night Office   To Be Observed Before Retiring

The Call to Prayer
May the Lord Almighty grant me and those I love a peaceful night and a perfect
    end. *Amen.* †

The Request for Presence
Our help is in the Name of the Lord; the maker of heaven and earth.

The Greeting
Almighty God, my heavenly Father: I have sinned against you, through my own
    fault, in thought, and word, and deed, in what I have done and in what I have
    left undone. For the sake of your Son our Lord Jesus Christ, forgive me all my
    offenses; and grant that I may serve you in newness of life, to the glory of your
    Name. *Amen.* †

The Reading   *Lead Me to Calvary*
    King of my life I crown You now—
    Yours shall the glory be;
    Lest I forget your thorn-crowned brow,
    Lead me to Calvary,
    Show me the tomb where you were laid,
    Tenderly mourned and wept;
    Angels in robes of light arrayed
    Guarded You while You slept.
    Let me, like Mary, through the gloom,
    Come with a gift to Thee;
    Show to me now the empty tomb—
    Lead me to Calvary.
    May I be willing, Lord, to bear
    Daily my cross for Thee;
    Even Your cup of grief to share—
    You have borne all for me.
    Lest I forget Gethsemane.
    Lest I forget Your agony,
    Lest I forget Your love for me,
    Lead me to Calvary.
                        Jennie Hussey

*The Gloria**

The Psalm   *I Love You, O LORD My Strength*
I love you, O LORD my strength,* O LORD my stronghold, my crag, and my haven.
My God, my rock in whom I put my trust,* my shield, the horn of my salvation,
    and my refuge; you are worthy of praise.

I will call upon the LORD,* and so shall I be saved from my enemies.

The breakers of death rolled over me,* and the torrents of oblivion made me afraid.

The cords of hell entangled me,* and the snares of death were set for me.

I called upon the LORD in my distress* and cried out to my God for help.

He heard my voice from his heavenly dwelling;* my cry of anguish came to his ears.

He brought me out into an open place;* he rescued me because he delighted in me.

Psalm 18:1–7, 20

The Gloria*

The Small Verse

Into your hands, O Lord, I commend my spirit; For you have redeemed me, O Lord, O God of truth. Keep me, O Lord, as the apple of your eye; Hide me under the shadow of your wings. †

The Lord's Prayer

The Petition

Keep watch, dear Lord, with those who work, or watch, or weep this night, and give your angels charge over those who sleep. Tend the sick, Lord Christ; give rest to the weary, bless the dying, soothe the suffering, pity the afflicted, shield the joyous; and all for your love's sake. *Amen.* †

The Final Thanksgiving

Lord, you now have set your servant free to go in peace as you have promised; for these eyes of mine have seen the Savior, whom you have prepared for all the world to see: a Light to enlighten the nations, and the glory of your people Israel. Glory to the Father, and to the Son, and to the Holy Spirit: as it was in the beginning, is now, and will be for ever. *Amen.*

Wednesday
The Night Office   To Be Observed Before Retiring

The Call to Prayer

May the Lord Almighty grant me and those I love a peaceful night and a perfect end. *Amen.* †

The Request for Presence

Our help is in the Name of the Lord; the maker of heaven and earth.

The Greeting

Almighty God, my heavenly Father: I have sinned against you, through my own fault, in thought, and word, and deed, in what I have done and in what I have left undone. For the sake of your Son our Lord Jesus Christ, forgive me all my offenses; and grant that I may serve you in newness of life, to the glory of your Name. *Amen.* †

The Reading   *Seven Petitions to the Holy Cross*

Lord Jesus Christ, for the sake of Thy Holy Cross, be with me to shield me. Amen.

Lord Jesus Christ, by the memory of Thy blessed Cross, be within me to strengthen me. Amen.

Lord Jesus Christ, for Thy holy Cross, be ever round about me to protect me. Amen.

Lord Jesus Christ, for Thy glorious Cross, go before me to direct my steps. Amen.

Lord Jesus Christ, for Thy adorable Cross, come Thou after me to guard me. Amen.

Lord Jesus Christ, for Thy Cross, worthy of all praise, overshadow me to bless me. Amen.

Lord Jesus Christ, for Thy noble Cross, be Thou in me to lead me to Thy kingdom. Amen.

Ancient Anglo-Saxon

The Gloria*

The Psalm   *I Will Enter the Gates of Righteousness*

The LORD is my strength and my song,* and he has become my salvation.

There is a sound of exultation and victory* in the tents of the righteous:

"The right hand of the LORD has triumphed!* the right hand of the LORD is exalted! the right hand of the LORD has triumphed!"

I shall not die, but live,* and declare the works of the LORD.

The LORD has punished me sorely,* but he did not hand me over to death.

Open for me the gates of righteousness;* I will enter them; I will offer thanks to the LORD.

"This is the gate of the LORD;* he who is righteous may enter."

I will give thanks to you, for you answered me* and have become my salvation.

The same stone which the builders rejected* has become the chief cornerstone.

This is the LORD's doing,* and it is marvelous in our eyes.

On this day the LORD has acted;* we will rejoice and be glad in it.

Psalm 118:14–24

The Gloria*

The Small Verse

Into your hands, O Lord, I commend my spirit; For you have redeemed me, O Lord, O God of truth. Keep me, O Lord, as the apple of your eye; Hide me under the shadow of your wings. †

The Lord's Prayer

The Petition

Keep watch, dear Lord, with those who work, or watch, or weep this night, and
give your angels charge over those who sleep. Tend the sick, Lord Christ; give
rest to the weary, bless the dying, soothe the suffering, pity the afflicted, shield
the joyous; and all for your love's sake. *Amen.* †

The Final Thanksgiving

Lord, you now have set your servant free to go in peace as you have promised; for
these eyes of mine have seen the Savior, whom you have prepared for all the
world to see: a Light to enlighten the nations, and the glory of your people
Israel. Glory to the Father, and to the Son, and to the Holy Spirit: as it was in the
beginning, is now, and will be for ever. *Amen.*

Thursday
The Night Office   To Be Observed Before Retiring

The Call to Prayer

May the Lord Almighty grant me and those I love a peaceful night and a perfect
end. *Amen.* †

The Request for Presence

Our help is in the Name of the Lord; the maker of heaven and earth.

The Greeting

Almighty God, my heavenly Father: I have sinned against you, through my own
fault, in thought, and word, and deed, in what I have done and in what I have
left undone. For the sake of your Son our Lord Jesus Christ, forgive me all my
offenses; and grant that I may serve you in newness of life, to the glory of your
Name. *Amen.* †

The Reading

Exalt joy as we may—and there is surely no joy to be compared to that of the
Christian adventure—it is not to the pilgrim in quest of joy, but to the lover of
the cross, bent on sacrifice, that the secret of the Lord is revealed.

from CREATIVE PRAYER

The Gloria*

The Psalm   *You Have Set My Heart at Liberty*

My soul cleaves to the dust;* give me life according to your word.
I have confessed my ways, and you answered me;* instruct me in your statutes.

Make me understand the way of your commandments,* that I may meditate on
    your marvelous works.
My soul melts away for sorrow;* strengthen me according to your word.
Take from me the way of lying;* let me find grace through your law.
I have chosen the way of faithfulness;* I have set your judgments before me.
I hold fast to your decrees;* O LORD, let me not be put to shame.
I will run the way of your commandments,* for you have set my heart at liberty.

                                           Psalm 119:25–32

*The Gloria**

The Small Verse
Into your hands, O Lord, I commend my spirit; For you have redeemed me, O
    Lord, O God of truth. Keep me, O Lord, as the apple of your eye; Hide me
    under the shadow of your wings. †

The Lord's Prayer

The Petition
Keep watch, dear Lord, with those who work, or watch, or weep this night, and
    give your angels charge over those who sleep. Tend the sick, Lord Christ; give
    rest to the weary, bless the dying, soothe the suffering, pity the afflicted, shield
    the joyous; and all for your love's sake. *Amen.* †

The Final Thanksgiving
Lord, you now have set your servant free to go in peace as you have promised; for
    these eyes of mine have seen the Savior, whom you have prepared for all the
    world to see: a Light to enlighten the nations, and the glory of your people
    Israel. Glory to the Father, and to the Son, and to the Holy Spirit: as it was in the
    beginning, is now, and will be for ever. *Amen.*

Friday
The Night Office   To Be Observed Before Retiring

The Call to Prayer
May the Lord Almighty grant me and those I love a peaceful night and a perfect
    end. *Amen.* †

The Request for Presence
Our help is in the Name of the Lord; the maker of heaven and earth.

The Greeting
Almighty God, my heavenly Father: I have sinned against you, through my own
    fault, in thought, and word, and deed, in what I have done and in what I have

left undone. For the sake of your Son our Lord Jesus Christ, forgive me all my offenses; and grant that I may serve you in newness of life, to the glory of your Name. *Amen.* †

The Reading   *Litany of Penitence*

Most holy and merciful Father:

I confess to you and to the whole communion of saints in heaven and on earth, that I have sinned by my own fault in thought, word, and deed; by what I have done, and by what I have left undone.

I have not loved you with my whole heart, and mind, and strength. I have not loved my neighbors as myself. I have not forgiven others, as I have been forgiven.

Have mercy on me, Lord.

I have been deaf to your call to serve, as Christ served us. I have not been true to the mind of Christ. I have grieved your Holy Spirit.

Have mercy on me, Lord.

I confess to you, Lord, all my past unfaithfulness: the pride, hypocrisy, and impatience of my life.

I confess to you, Lord.

My self-indulgent appetites and ways, and my exploitation of other people, I confess to you, Lord.

My anger at my own frustration, and my envy of those more fortunate than I, I confess to you, Lord.

My intemperate love of worldly goods and comforts, and my dishonesty in daily life and work,

I confess to you, Lord.

My negligence in prayer and worship, and my failure to commend the faith that is in me,

I confess to you, Lord.

Accept my repentance, Lord, for the wrongs I have done: for my blindness to human need and suffering, and my indifference to injustice and cruelty,

Accept my repentance, Lord.

For all false judgments, for uncharitable thoughts toward my neighbors, and for my prejudice and contempt toward those who differ from me,

Accept my repentance, Lord.

For my waste and pollution of your creation, and my lack of concern for those who come after us,

Accept my repentance, Lord.

Restore me, good Lord, and let your anger depart from me,

Favorably hear me for your mercy is great.
Accomplish in me and all of your church the work of your salvation,
That I may show forth your glory in the world.

By the cross and passion of your Son our Lord,
Bring me with all your saints to the joy of his resurrection. †

The Gloria*

The Psalm   *We Shall Receive a Just Reward from the God of Our Salvation*
The earth is the LORD's and all that is in it,* the world and all who dwell therein.
For it is he who founded it upon the seas* and made it firm upon the rivers of the
    deep.
"Who can ascend the hill of the LORD?* and who can stand in his holy place?"
"Those who have clean hands and a pure heart,* who have not pledged
    themselves to falsehood, nor sworn by what is a fraud.
They shall receive a blessing from the LORD* and a just reward from the God of
    their salvation."
Such is the generation of those who seek him,* of those who seek your face, O
    God of Jacob.

Psalm 24:1–6

The Gloria*

The Small Verse
Into your hands, O Lord, I commend my spirit; for you have redeemed me, O
    Lord, O God of truth. Keep me, O Lord, as the apple of your eye; hide me
    under the shadow of your wings. †

The Lord's Prayer

The Petition
Keep watch, dear Lord, with those who work, or watch, or weep this night, and
    give your angels charge over those who sleep. Tend the sick, Lord Christ; give
    rest to the weary, bless the dying, soothe the suffering, pity the afflicted, shield
    the joyous; and all for your love's sake. *Amen.* †

The Final Thanksgiving
Lord, you now have set your servant free to go in peace as you have promised; for
    these eyes of mine have seen the Savior, whom you have prepared for all the
    world to see: a Light to enlighten the nations, and the glory of your people
    Israel. Glory to the Father, and to the Son, and to the Holy Spirit: as it was in the
    beginning, is now, and will be for ever. *Amen.*

Saturday
The Night Office   To Be Observed Before Retiring

The Call to Prayer
May the Lord Almighty grant me and those I love a peaceful night and a perfect
   end. *Amen.* †

The Request for Presence
Our help is in the Name of the Lord; the maker of heaven and earth.

The Greeting
Almighty God, my heavenly Father: I have sinned against you, through my own
   fault, in thought, and word, and deed, in what I have done and in what I have
   left undone. For the sake of your Son our Lord Jesus Christ, forgive me all my
   offenses; and grant that I may serve you in newness of life, to the glory of your
   Name. *Amen.* †

The Reading   *Christ's Mirror*
Herself a rose, who bore the Rose,
              She bore the Rose and felt its thorn,
              All Loveliness new-born
Took on her bosom its repose,
              And slept and woke there night and morn.

Lily herself, she bore the one
              Fair Lily; sweeter, whiter, far
              Than she or others are:
The Sun of Righteousness her Son,
              She was His morning star.

She gracious, He essential Grace,
              He was the fountain, she the rill:
              Her goodness to fulfill
And gladness, with proportioned pace
              He led her steps through good and ill.

Christ's mirror she of grace and love,
              Of beauty and of life and death:
              By hope and love and faith
Transfigured to His Likeness "Dove,
              Spouse, Sister, Mother," Jesus saith.
                                   Christina Rossetti

*The Gloria**

The Psalm   *The Throne of God Endures For Ever*
My heart is stirring with a noble song; let me recite what I have fashioned for the
   king;* my tongue shall be the pen of a skilled writer.

You are the fairest of men;* grace flows from your lips, because God has blessed
you for ever.
Strap your sword upon your thigh, O mighty warrior,* in your pride and in your
majesty.
Ride out and conquer in the cause of truth* and for the sake of justice.
Your right hand will show you marvelous things;* your arrows are very sharp, O
mighty warrior.
The peoples are falling at your feet,* and the king's enemies are losing heart.
Your throne, O God, endures for ever and ever,* a scepter of righteousness is the
scepter of your kingdom; you love righteousness and hate iniquity.
Therefore God, your God, has anointed you* with the oil of gladness above your
fellows.

Psalm 45:1–8

The Gloria*

The Small Verse

Into your hands, O Lord, I commend my spirit; For you have redeemed me, O
Lord, O God of truth. Keep me, O Lord, as the apple of your eye; Hide me
under the shadow of your wings. †

The Lord's Prayer

The Petition

Keep watch, dear Lord, with those who work, or watch, or weep this night, and
give your angels charge over those who sleep. Tend the sick, Lord Christ; give
rest to the weary, bless the dying, soothe the suffering, pity the afflicted, shield
the joyous; and all for your love's sake. *Amen.* †

The Final Thanksgiving

Lord, you now have set your servant free to go in peace as you have promised; for
these eyes of mine have seen the Savior, whom you have prepared for all the
world to see: a Light to enlighten the nations, and the glory of your people
Israel. Glory to the Father, and to the Son, and to the Holy Spirit: as it was in the
beginning, is now, and will be for ever. *Amen.*

The Gloria

Glory be to God the Father, God the Son, and God the Holy Spirit. As it was in the beginning, so it is now and so it shall ever be, world without end. Alleluia.* *Amen.*

The Lord's Prayer

Our Father, who art in heaven, hallowed be your Name.
May your kingdom come, and your will be done, on earth as in heaven.
Give us today our daily bread.
Forgive us our sins as we forgive those who sin against us.
Lead us not into temptation, but deliver us from evil;
for yours are the kingdom and the power and the glory
forever and ever. *Amen.*

Compline Prayers for March Are Located on Page 305.

The Following Holy Days Occur in March:
The Feast of St. Joseph: *March 19*
The Feast of the Annunciation of Our Lord Jesus Christ to the Blessed Virgin Mary: *March 25*

*The Gloria is omitted during Lent by many Christian communities. "Alleluia" is always omitted from every part of the Church's worship during Lent; the use of both is restored at Easter.

March

The Morning Office   To Be Observed on the Hour or Half Hour
Between 6 and 9 a.m.

The Call to Prayer
Ascribe to the LORD, you families of the peoples;* ascribe to the LORD honor and
    power.
Ascribe to the LORD the honor due his Name;* bring offerings and come into his
    courts.
Worship the LORD in the beauty of holiness;* let the whole world tremble before
    him.

Psalm 96:7–9

The Request for Presence
Send out your light and your truth, that they may lead me,* and bring me to your
    holy hill and to your dwelling;
That I may go to the altar of God, to the God of my joy and gladness;* and on the
    harp I will give thanks to you, O God my God.

Psalm 43:3–4

The Greeting
As the deer longs for the water-brooks,* so longs my soul for you, O God.
My soul is athirst for God, athirst for the living God.

Psalm 42:1–2

The Refrain for the Morning Lessons
For who is God, but the LORD?* who is the Rock except our God?

Psalm 18:32

A Reading
Jesus taught us, saying: "Be careful not to parade your uprightness in public to
    attract attention; otherwise you will lose all reward from your Father in
    heaven."

Matthew 6:1

The Refrain
For who is God, but the LORD?* who is the Rock except our God?

The Morning Psalm   *I Will Offer the Sacrifice of Thanksgiving*
O LORD, I am your servant;* I am your servant and the child of your handmaid;
    you have freed me from my bonds.
I will offer you the sacrifice of thanksgiving* and call upon the Name of the
    LORD.
I will fulfill my vows to the LORD* in the presence of all his people,
In the courts of the LORD's house,* in the midst of you, O Jerusalem. Hallelujah!

Psalm 116:14–17

The Refrain
For who is God, but the LORD?* who is the Rock except our God?

The Cry of the Church
Lord, have mercy on us. Christ, have mercy on us. Lord, have mercy on us.

The Lord's Prayer

The Prayer Appointed for the Week
O God, who before the passion of your only-begotten Son revealed his glory upon
the holy mountain: Grant that I, beholding by faith the light of his countenance, may be strengthened to bear my cross, and be changed into his likeness
from glory to glory; through Jesus Christ my Lord, who lives and reigns with
you and the Holy Spirit, one God, for ever and ever. *Amen.* †

The Concluding Prayer of the Church
Lord God, almighty and everlasting Father, you have brought me in safety to this
new day: Preserve me with your mighty power, that I may not fall into sin, nor
be overcome by adversity; and in all I do direct me to the fulfilling of your purpose; through Jesus Christ my Lord. *Amen.* †

The Midday Office   To Be Observed on the Hour or Half Hour
                                        Between 11 a.m. and 2 p.m.

The Call to Prayer
Let all those whom the LORD has redeemed proclaim* that he redeemed them
from the hand of the foe.
He gathered them out of the lands;* from the east and from the west, from the
north and from the south.
He put their feet on a straight path* to go to a city where they might dwell.
Let them give thanks to the LORD for his mercy* and the wonders he does for his
children.

Psalm 107:2–3, 7–8

The Request for Presence
Let all who seek you rejoice in you and be glad;* let those who love your
salvation continually say, "Great is the LORD!"
Though I am poor and afflicted,* the LORD will have regard for me.
You are my helper and my deliverer;* do not tarry, O my God.

Psalm 40:17ff

The Greeting
I love you, O LORD my strength,* O LORD my stronghold, my crag, and my haven.
My God, my rock in whom I put my trust,* my shield, the horn of my salvation,
and my refuge; you are worthy of praise.

Psalm 18:1–2

The Refrain for the Midday Lessons
I will fulfill my vows to the LORD* in the presence of all his people.

Psalm 116:16

A Reading

Let us keep our eyes fixed on Jesus, who leads us in our faith and brings it to perfection: for the sake of the joy which lay ahead of him, he endured the cross, disregarding the shame of it, and *has taken his seat at the right* of God's throne. Think of the way he persevered against such opposition from sinners and then you will not lose heart and come to grief. In the fight against sin, you have not yet had to keep fighting to the point of bloodshed.

Hebrews 12:2–4

The Refrain

I will fulfill my vows to the LORD* in the presence of all his people.

The Midday Psalm   *The Fool Has Said, "There Is No God"*

The fool has said in his heart, "There is no God."* All are corrupt and commit abominable acts; there is none who does any good.

God looks down from heaven upon us all,* to see if there is any who is wise, if there is one who seeks after God.

Every one has proved faithless; all alike have turned bad;* there is none who does good; no, not one.

Have they no knowledge, those evildoers* who eat up my people like bread and do not call upon God?

See how greatly they tremble, such trembling as never was;* for God has scattered the bones of the enemy; they are put to shame, because God has rejected them.

Oh, that Israel's deliverance would come out of Zion!* when God restores the fortunes of his people Jacob will rejoice and Israel be glad.

Psalm 53

The Refrain

I will fulfill my vows to the LORD* in the presence of all his people.

The Cry of the Church

O God, come to my assistance! O Lord, make haste to help me!

The Lord's Prayer

The Prayer Appointed for the Week

O God, who before the passion of your only-begotten Son revealed his glory upon the holy mountain: Grant that I, beholding by faith the light of his countenance, may be strengthened to bear my cross, and be changed into his likeness from glory to glory; through Jesus Christ my Lord, who lives and reigns with you and the Holy Spirit, one God, for ever and ever. *Amen.* †

The Concluding Prayer of the Church

O God, you make me and your whole church glad with the weekly remembrance of the glorious resurrection of your Son our Lord: Give me this day such blessing through my worship of you, that the week to come may be spent in your favor; through Jesus Christ our Lord. *Amen.* †

The Vespers Office   To Be Observed on the Hour or Half Hour
                                               Between 5 and 8 p.m.

The Call to Prayer
Behold now, bless the LORD, all you servants of the LORD,* you that stand by
   night in the house of the LORD.

Psalm 134:1

The Request for Presence
For God alone my soul in silence waits;* truly, my hope is in him.

Psalm 62:6

The Greeting
I remember your Name in the night, O LORD,* and dwell upon your law.

Psalm 119:55

The Hymn   *Heal Us, Emmanuel*
   Heal us, Emmanuel, Hear our prayer; we wait to feel your touch;
   deep wounded souls to you repair, and Savior, we are such.

   Our faith is feeble, we confess we faintly trust your word;
   but will you pity us the less? Be that far from you, Lord!

   Remember him who once applied with trembling for relief;
   "Lord, I believe," with tears he cried; "O help my unbelief!"

   She, too who touched you in the press and healing virtue stole,
   was answered, "Daughter, go in peace: your faith has made you whole."

   Like her, with hopes and fears we come to touch you if we may;
   O send us not despairing home; send none unhealed away.

William Cowper

The Refrain for the Vespers Lessons
Behold, he who keeps watch over Israel* shall neither slumber nor sleep.

Psalm 121:4

The Vespers Psalm   *The Just Shall See His Face*
The LORD is in his holy temple;* the LORD's throne is in heaven.
His eyes behold the inhabited world;* his piercing eye weighs our worth.
The LORD weighs the righteous as well as the wicked,* but those who delight in
   violence he abhors.
Upon the wicked he shall rain coals of fire and burning sulfur;* a scorching wind
   shall be their lot.
For the LORD is righteous; he delights in righteous deeds;* and the just shall see
   his face.

Psalm 11:4–8

The Refrain
Behold, he who keeps watch over Israel* shall neither slumber nor sleep.

The Small Verse
Keep me, Lord, as the apple of your eye
And carry me under the shadow of your wings.

The Lord's Prayer

The Prayer Appointed for the Week
O God, who before the passion of your only-begotten Son revealed his glory upon
the holy mountain: Grant that I, beholding by faith the light of his countenance, may be strengthened to bear my cross, and be changed into his likeness
from glory to glory; through Jesus Christ my Lord, who lives and reigns with
you and the Holy Spirit, one God, for ever and ever. *Amen.* †

The Concluding Prayer of the Church
Protect me, Lord, as I stay awake; watch over me as I sleep, that awake I may
watch with Christ, and asleep, rest in peace. *Amen.*

The Morning Office   **To Be Observed on the Hour or Half Hour**
                                   Between 6 and 9 a.m.

The Call to Prayer
Let my mouth be full of your praise* and your glory all the day long.
Do not cast me off in my old age;* forsake me not when my strength fails.

Psalm 71:8–9

The Request for Presence
O Lord, my God, my Savior,* by day and night I cry to you.
Let my prayer enter into your presence.

Psalm 88:1–2

The Greeting
Show me your ways, O Lord,* and teach me your paths.
Lead me in your truth and teach me,* for you are the God of my salvation; in you
have I trusted all the day long.

Psalm 25:3–4

The Refrain for the Morning Lessons
Deliverance belongs to the Lord.* Your blessing be upon your people!

Psalm 3:8

A Reading
Now it happened that he was praying alone, and his disciples came to him and he
put this question to them, 'Who do the crowds say I am?' And they answered,
'Some say John the Baptist; others Elijah; others again one of the ancient
prophets come back to life.' 'But you,' he said to them, 'who do you say I am?'
It was Peter who spoke up. 'The Christ of God,' he said. But he gave them strict
orders and charged them not to say this to anyone. He said, 'The Son of man is
destined to suffer grievously, to be rejected by the elders and chief priests and
scribes and to be put to death, and to be raised up on the third day.'

Luke 9:18–22

The Refrain
Deliverance belongs to the LORD.* Your blessing be upon your people!

The Morning Psalm   *The LORD Knows the Way of the Righteous*
Happy are they who have not walked in the counsel of the wicked,* nor lingered
    in the way of sinners, nor sat in the seats of the scornful!
Their delight is in the law of the LORD,* and they meditate on his law day
    and night.
They are like trees planted by streams of water, bearing fruit in due season, with
    leaves that do not wither;* everything they do shall prosper.
It is not so with the wicked;* they are like chaff which the wind blows away.
Therefore the wicked shall not stand upright when judgment comes,* nor the
    sinner in the council of the righteous.
For the LORD knows the way of the righteous,* but the way of the wicked is
    doomed.

Psalm 1

The Refrain
Deliverance belongs to the LORD.* Your blessing be upon your people!

The Cry of the Church
O Lamb of God, that takes away the sins of the world, have mercy on me.
O Lamb of God, that takes away the sins of the world, have mercy on me.
O Lamb of God, that takes away the sins of the world, grant me your peace.

The Lord's Prayer

The Prayer Appointed for the Week
O God, who before the passion of your only-begotten Son revealed his glory upon
    the holy mountain: Grant that I, beholding by faith the light of his counte-
    nance, may be strengthened to bear my cross, and be changed into his likeness
    from glory to glory; through Jesus Christ my Lord, who lives and reigns with
    you and the Holy Spirit, one God, for ever and ever. *Amen.* †

The Concluding Prayer of the Church
Lord God, almighty and everlasting Father, you have brought me in safety to this
    new day: Preserve me with your mighty power, that I may not fall into sin, nor
    be overcome by adversity; and in all I do direct me to the fulfilling of your pur-
    pose; through Jesus Christ my Lord. *Amen.* †

The Midday Office   **To Be Observed on the Hour or Half Hour**
                                         Between 11 a.m. and 2 p.m.

The Call to Prayer
All who take refuge in you will be glad;* they will sing out their joy forever.
You will shelter them,* so that those who love your Name may exult in you.

For you, O LORD, will bless the righteous;* you will defend them with your favor
as with a shield.

Psalm 5:13–15

The Request for Presence

You are the LORD; do not withhold your compassion from me;* let your love and
your faithfulness keep me safe for ever.

Psalm 40:12

The Greeting

O LORD, what are we that you should care for us?* mere mortals that you should
think of us?

We are like a puff of wind;* our days are passing like a shadow.

Psalm 144:3–4

The Refrain for the Midday Lessons

Protect my life and deliver me;* let me not be put to shame, for I have trusted
in you.

Let integrity and uprightness preserve me,* for my hope is in you.

Psalm 25:19–20

A Reading

All who are guided by the Spirit of God are sons of God; for what you received
was not the spirit of slavery to bring you back into fear; you received the
spirit of adoption, enabling us to cry out, 'Abba, Father!' And if we are
children, then we are heirs, heirs of God and joint-heirs with Christ, provided
that we share his suffering, so as to share his glory.

Romans 8:14–15, 17

The Refrain

Protect my life and deliver me;* let me not be put to shame, for I have trusted
in you.

Let integrity and uprightness preserve me,* for my hope is in you.

The Midday Psalm 　　　　　　　　　　*Behold, I Did Not Restrain My Lips*

I proclaimed righteousness in the great congregation;* behold, I did not restrain
my lips; and that, O LORD, you know.

Your righteousness have I not hidden in my heart; I have spoken of your
faithfulness and your deliverance;* I have not concealed your love and
faithfulness from the great congregation.

Psalm 40:10–11

The Refrain

Protect my life and deliver me;* let me not be put to shame, for I have trusted
in you.

Let integrity and uprightness preserve me,* for my hope is in you.

The Cry of the Church

O God, come to my assistance! O Lord, make haste to help me!

The Lord's Prayer

The Prayer Appointed for the Week
O God, who before the passion of your only-begotten Son revealed his glory upon
the holy mountain: Grant that I, beholding by faith the light of his countenance, may be strengthened to bear my cross, and be changed into his likeness
from glory to glory; through Jesus Christ my Lord, who lives and reigns with
you and the Holy Spirit, one God, for ever and ever. *Amen.* †

The Concluding Prayer of the Church
O God, whose blessed Son became poor that we through his poverty might be
rich: Deliver me from the inordinate love of this world, that I may serve you
with singleness of heart, and attain to the riches of the age to come; through
Jesus Christ my Lord, who lives and reigns with you and the Holy Spirit, one
God, now and for ever. *Amen.* †

The Vespers Office
To Be Observed on the Hour or Half Hour
Between 5 and 8 p.m.

The Call to Prayer
Love the LORD, all you who worship him;* the LORD protects the faithful, but
repays to the full those who act haughtily.

Psalm 31:23

The Request for Presence
Teach me your way, O LORD, and I will walk in your truth;* knit my heart to you
that I may fear your Name.

Psalm 86:11

The Greeting
Whom have I in heaven but you?* And having you I desire nothing upon earth.

Psalm 73:25

The Hymn   *Lenten Hymn*
Lord, who throughout these forty days for us did fast and pray,
Teach us with you to mourn our sins, and close by you to stay.

As You with Satan did contend and did the victory win,
O give us strength in you to fight, in you to conquer sin.

As you bore hunger and your thirst, so teach us, gracious Lord,
To die to self, and chiefly live by your most holy Word.

And through the days of penitence, and through your Passion-tide,
Yes, evermore, in life and death, Jesus! With us abide.

Abide with us, that so, this life of suffering over-past,
An Easter of unending joy we may attain at last!

Claudia Hernaman

The Refrain for the Vespers Lessons
Let Israel rejoice in his Maker;* let the children of Zion be joyful in their King.

Psalm 149:5

The Vespers Psalm　　　　　　　　　*You Yourself Created My Inmost Parts*
If I say, "Surely the darkness will cover me,* and the light around me turn to night,"
Darkness is not dark to you; the night is as bright as the day;* darkness and light to you are both alike.
For you yourself created my inmost parts;* you knit me together in my mother's womb.

Psalm 139:10–12

The Refrain
Let Israel rejoice in his Maker;* let the children of Zion be joyful in their King.

The Gloria*

The Lord's Prayer

The Prayer Appointed for the Week
O God, who before the passion of your only-begotten Son revealed his glory upon the holy mountain: Grant that I, beholding by faith the light of his countenance, may be strengthened to bear my cross, and be changed into his likeness from glory to glory; through Jesus Christ my Lord, who lives and reigns with you and the Holy Spirit, one God, for ever and ever. *Amen.* †

The Concluding Prayer of the Church
God be in my head
　　　and in my understanding.
God be in mine eyes
　　　and in my looking.
God be in my mouth
　　　and in my speaking.
God be in my heart
　　　and in my thinking.
God be at mine end
　　　and my departing.
　　　　Sarum Primer, 1527

The Morning Office　　　　　　**To Be Observed on the Hour or Half Hour**
Between 6 and 9 a.m.

The Call to Prayer
Clap your hands, all you peoples;* shout to God with a cry of joy.
For the Lord Most High is to be feared;* he is the great King over all the earth.

He subdues the peoples under us,* and the nations under our feet.
He chooses our inheritance for us,* the pride of Jacob whom he loves.

Psalm 47:1–4

The Request for Presence
Early in the morning I cry out to you,* for in your word is my trust.

Psalm 119:147

The Greeting
Not to us, O LORD, not to us, but to your Name give glory;* because of your love
and because of your faithfulness.

Psalm 115:1

The Refrain for the Morning Lessons
Those who are planted in the house of the LORD* shall flourish in the courts of
our God.

Psalm 92:12

A Reading
Then some Sadduces—who deny the Resurrection—came to him . . . Jesus said to
them, 'Surely the reason why you are wrong is that you understand neither the
scriptures nor the power of God. Now about the dead rising again, have you
ever read the book of Moses, in the passage about the bush, how God spoke to
him and said: *I am the God of Abraham, the God of Isaac and the God of Jacob?* He is
God, not of the dead, but of the living. You are very much mistaken.'

Mark 12:18a, 24, 26–27

The Refrain
Those who are planted in the house of the LORD* shall flourish in the courts of our
God.

The Morning Psalm   We Flourish Like a Flower of the Field
Our days are like the grass;* we flourish like a flower of the field;
When the wind goes over it, it is gone,* and its place shall know it no more.
But the merciful goodness of the LORD endures for ever on those who fear him,*
and his righteousness on children's children;
On those who keep his covenant* and remember his commandments and
do them.

Psalm 103:15–18

The Refrain
Those who are planted in the house of the LORD* shall flourish in the courts of our
God.

The Short Verse
'I am the Alpha and the Omega,' says the Lord God, 'who is, who was, and who is
to come, the Almighty.'

Revelation 1:8

The Lord's Prayer

The Prayer Appointed for the Week
O God, who before the passion of your only-begotten Son revealed his glory upon
the holy mountain: Grant that I, beholding by faith the light of his countenance, may be strengthened to bear my cross, and be changed into his likeness
from glory to glory; through Jesus Christ my Lord, who lives and reigns with
you and the Holy Spirit, one God, for ever and ever. *Amen.* †

The Concluding Prayer of the Church
Lord God, almighty and everlasting Father, you have brought me in safety to this
new day: Preserve me with your mighty power, that I may not fall into sin, nor
be overcome by adversity; and in all I do direct me to the fulfilling of your purpose; through Jesus Christ my Lord. *Amen.* †

The Midday Office   **To Be Observed on the Hour or Half Hour**
                                          Between 11 a.m. and 2 p.m.

The Call to Prayer
God has gone up with a shout,* the LORD with the sound of the ram's-horn.

Psalm 47:5

The Request for Presence
Accept, O LORD, the willing tribute of my lips,* and teach me your judgments.

Psalm 119:108

The Greeting
I will offer you the sacrifice of thanksgiving* and call upon the Name of the
LORD.

Psalm 116:15

The Refrain for the Midday Lessons
He shall say to the LORD, "You are my refuge and my stronghold,* my God in
whom I put my trust."

Psalm 91:2

A Reading
'But now'—declares YAHWEH—'come back to me with all your heart, fasting,
weeping, mourning.' Tear your hearts and not your clothes, and come back to
YAHWEH your God, for he is gracious and compassionate, slow to anger, rich in
faithful love . . .

Joel 2:12–13

The Refrain
He shall say to the LORD, "You are my refuge and my stronghold,* my God in
whom I put my trust."

The Midday Psalm   *He Guides the Humble in Doing Right*

Gracious and upright is the Lord;* therefore he teaches sinners in his way.

He guides the humble in doing right* and teaches his way to the lowly.

All the paths of the Lord are love and faithfulness* to those who keep his
   covenant and his testimonies.

Psalm 25:7–9

The Refrain

He shall say to the Lord, "You are my refuge and my stronghold,* my God in
   whom I put my trust."

The Cry of the Church

Lord, have mercy on us. Christ, have mercy on us. Lord, have mercy on us.

The Lord's Prayer

The Prayer Appointed for the Week

O God, who before the passion of your only-begotten Son revealed his glory upon
   the holy mountain: Grant that I, beholding by faith the light of his countenance, may be strengthened to bear my cross, and be changed into his likeness
   from glory to glory; through Jesus Christ my Lord, who lives and reigns with
   you and the Holy Spirit, one God, for ever and ever. *Amen.* †

The Concluding Prayer of the Church

Almighty and everlasting God, by whose Spirit the whole body of your faithful
   people is governed and sanctified: Receive my supplications and prayers
   which I offer before you for all members of your holy Church, that in our voca-
   tion and ministry we all may truly and godly serve you, through our Lord and
   Savior Jesus Christ. *Amen.*

The Vespers Office   **To Be Observed on the Hour or Half Hour**
                                             Between 5 and 8 p.m.

The Call to Prayer

Come, let us bow down, and bend the knee,* and kneel before the Lord our
   Maker.

For he is our God,* and we are the people of his pasture and the sheep of his hand.

Psalm 95:6–7

The Request for Presence

To you I lift up my eyes,* to you enthroned in the heavens.

Psalm 123:1

The Greeting

How priceless is your love, O God!* your people take refuge under the shadow of
   your wings.

For with you is the well of life,* and in your light we see light.

Psalm 36:7, 9

The Hymn   *Dear Lord and Father of Mankind*

Dear Lord and Father of mankind,
Forgive our foolish ways;
Reclothe us in our rightful mind;
In purer lives Your service find,
In deeper reverence praise.

Drop Your still dews of quietness,
Till all our strivings cease;
Take from our souls the strain and stress,
And let our ordered lives confess
The beauty of Your peace.

Breathe through the heats of our desire
Your coolness and Your balm;
Let sense be dumb, let flesh retire;
Speak through the earthquake, wind and fire,
O still small voice of calm!

In simple trust like theirs who heard,
Beside the Syrian sea,
The gracious calling of the Lord,
Let us, like them, without a word,
Rise up and follow Thee.

John G. Whittier

The Refrain for the Vespers Lessons
Come and listen, all you who fear God,* and I will tell you what he has done
for me.

Psalm 66:14

The Vespers Psalm   *He Strengthens Those in Whose Way He Delights*
Our steps are directed by the Lord;* he strengthens those in whose way he
delights.
If they stumble, they shall not fall headlong,* for the Lord holds them by the hand.
I have been young and now I am old,* but never have I seen the righteous forsaken,
or their children begging bread.

Psalm 37:24–26

The Refrain
Come and listen, all you who fear God,* and I will tell you what he has done for
me.

The Small Verse
Have mercy on me, Lord, have mercy.
Lord, show me your love and mercy; For I put my trust in you.
In you, Lord, is my hope; And I shall never hope in vain.

The Lord's Prayer

The Prayer Appointed for the Week
O God, who before the passion of your only-begotten Son revealed his glory upon
the holy mountain: Grant that I, beholding by faith the light of his countenance, may be strengthened to bear my cross, and be changed into his likeness
from glory to glory; through Jesus Christ my Lord, who lives and reigns with
you and the Holy Spirit, one God, for ever and ever. *Amen.* †

The Concluding Prayer of the Church
Blessed be God, who has not rejected my prayer,* nor withheld his love from me.
Psalm 66:18

The Morning Office   **To Be Observed on the Hour or Half Hour**
Between 6 and 9 a.m.

The Call to Prayer
Sing to the LORD a new song,* for he has done marvelous things.
With his right hand and his holy arm* has he won for himself the victory.
The LORD has made known his victory;* his righteousness has he openly shown in
the sight of the nations.
Psalm 98:1–3

The Request for Presence
Our soul waits for the LORD;* he is our help and our shield.
Indeed, our heart rejoices in him,* for in his holy Name we put our trust.
Let your loving-kindness, O LORD, be upon us,* as we have put our trust in you.
Psalm 33:20–22

The Greeting
How deep I find your thoughts, O God!* how great is the sum of them!
If I were to count them, they would be more in number than the sand;* to count
them all, my life span would need to be like yours.
Psalm 139:16–17

The Refrain for the Morning Lessons
I will confess you among the peoples, O LORD;* I will sing praises to you among
the nations.
Psalm 108:3

A Reading
Though they had been present when he gave so many signs, they did not believe
in him; this was to fulfill the words of the prophet Isaiah: *Lord, who has given
credence to what they have heard from us, and who has seen in it a revelation of the
Lord's arm?* Indeed, they were unable to believe because, as Isaiah says again:
*He has blinded their eyes, he has hardened their heart, to prevent them from using their
eyes to see, using their heart to understand, changing their ways and being healed by
me.* Isaiah said this because he saw his glory, and his words referred to Jesus.
And yet there were many who did believe in him, even among the leading

men, but they did not admit it, because of the Pharisees and for fear of being banned from the synagogue: they put human glory before God's glory.

John 12:27–43

The Refrain
I will confess you among the peoples, O Lord;* I will sing praises to you among the nations.

The Morning Psalm   *Those Who Act Deceitfully Shall Not Dwell in My House*
My eyes are upon the faithful in the land, that they may dwell with me,* and only those who lead a blameless life shall be my servants.
Those who act deceitfully shall not dwell in my house,* and those who tell lies shall not continue in my sight.
I will soon destroy all the wicked in the land,* that I may root out all evildoers from the city of the Lord.

Psalm 101:6–8

The Refrain
I will confess you among the peoples, O Lord;* I will sing praises to you among the nations.

The Small Verse
Today if you shall hear His voice, harden not your heart.

The Lord's Prayer

The Prayer Appointed for the Week
O God, who before the passion of your only-begotten Son revealed his glory upon the holy mountain: Grant that I, beholding by faith the light of his countenance, may be strengthened to bear my cross, and be changed into his likeness from glory to glory; through Jesus Christ my Lord, who lives and reigns with you and the Holy Spirit, one God, for ever and ever. *Amen.* †

The Concluding Prayer of the Church
Lord God, almighty and everlasting Father, you have brought me in safety to this new day: Preserve me with your mighty power, that I may not fall into sin, nor be overcome by adversity; and in all I do direct me to the fulfilling of your purpose; through Jesus Christ my Lord. *Amen.* †

The Midday Office   **To Be Observed on the Hour or Half Hour**
Between 11 a.m. and 2 p.m.

The Call to Prayer
Search for the Lord and his strength;* continually seek his face.
Remember the marvels he has done,* his wonders and the judgments of his mouth.

Psalm 105:4–5

The Request for Presence
Teach me your way, O LORD, and I will walk in your truth;* knit my heart to you
that I may fear your Name.

Psalm 86:11

The Greeting
My mouth shall recount your mighty acts and saving deeds all the day long;*
though I can not know the number of them.

Psalm 71:15

The Refrain for the Midday Lessons
The LORD has sworn an oath to David;* in truth, he will not break it:
"A son, the fruit of your body* will I set upon your throne."

Psalm 132:11–12

A Reading
Since he did not spare his own Son, but gave him up for the sake of all of us, then
can we not expect that with him he will freely give us all his gifts? Who can
bring any accusation against those that God has chosen? *When God grants saving justice who can condemn?* Are we not sure that it is Christ Jesus, who died—
yes and more, who was raised from the dead and is at God's right hand—and
who is adding his plea for us?

Romans 8:32–34

The Refrain
The LORD has sworn an oath to David;* in truth, he will not break it:
"A son, the fruit of your body* will I set upon your throne."

The Midday Psalm   *A Song of the Messiah*
O God, give to the king Your judgment,* and to the son of the king Your justice,
To judge Your people with justice,* and Your poor with judgment.
Let the mountains bring peace to the people* and the hills bring righteousness.

Psalm 72:1–7 adapted from THE SHORT BREVIARY

The Refrain
The LORD has sworn an oath to David;* in truth, he will not break it:
"A son, the fruit of your body* will I set upon your throne."

The Small Verse
The Lord is my shepherd and nothing is wanting to me.* In green pastures He has
settled me.

THE SHORT BREVIARY

The Lord's Prayer

The Prayer Appointed for the Week
O God, who before the passion of your only-begotten Son revealed his glory upon
the holy mountain: Grant that I, beholding by faith the light of his countenance, may be strengthened to bear my cross, and be changed into his likeness

from glory to glory; through Jesus Christ my Lord, who lives and reigns with you and the Holy Spirit, one God, for ever and ever. *Amen.* †

The Concluding Prayer of the Church

O Lord my God, to you and your service I devote myself, body, soul, and spirit. Fill my memory with the record of your mighty works; enlighten my understanding with the light of your Holy Spirit; and may all the desires of my heart and will center in what you would have me do. Make me an instrument of your salvation for the people entrusted to my care, and let me by my life and speaking set forth your true and living Word. Be always with me in carrying out the duties of my salvation; in praises heighten my love and gratitude; in speaking of You give me readiness of thought and expression; and grant that, by the clearness and brightness of your holy Word, all the world may be drawn to your blessed kingdom. All this I ask for the sake of your Son my Savior Jesus Christ. *Amen.* †

The Vespers Office   **To Be Observed on the Hour or Half Hour**
                                                        Between 5 and 8 p.m.

The Call to Prayer

Give thanks to the LORD, for he is good;* his mercy endures for ever.

Psalm 118:29

The Request for Presence

As the eyes of servants look to the hand of their masters,* and the eyes of a maid to the hand of her mistress,
So my eyes look to you, O Lord my God.

adapted from Psalm 123:2–3

The Greeting

You have turned my wailing into dancing;* you have put off my sack-cloth and clothed me with joy.
My heart sings to you without ceasing;* O LORD my God, I will give you thanks for ever.

Psalm 30:12–13

The Hymn   *O Love, How Deep*

O love, how deep, how broad, how high,
It fills the heart with ecstasy,
That God, the Son of God, should take
Our mortal form for mortals' sake!

For us baptized, for us he bore
His holy fast and hungered sore,
For us temptation sharp he knew;
For us the tempter overthrew.

For us he prayed; for us he taught;
For us his daily works he wrought;
By words and signs and actions thus
Still seeking not himself, but us.

For us to evil power betrayed,
Scourged, mocked, in purple robe arrayed,
He bore the shameful cross and death,
For us gave up his dying breath.

For us he rose from death again,
For us he went on high to reign;
For us he sent his Spirit here,
To guide, to strengthen, and to cheer.

All glory to our Lord and God
For love so deep, so high, so broad;
The Trinity whom we adore,
For ever and for evermore.

Latin, 15th C.

The Refrain for the Vespers Lessons

But you, O LORD, are gracious and full of compassion,* slow to anger, and full of
kindness and truth.

Psalm 86:15

The Vespers Psalm   *I Tell of Your Wonderful Works*

But I shall always wait in patience,* and shall praise you more and more.
My mouth shall recount your mighty acts and saving deeds all day long;* though I
cannot know the number of them.
I will begin with the mighty works of the Lord GOD;* I will recall your
righteousness, yours alone.
O God, you have taught me since I was young,* and to this day I tell of your
wonderful works.

Psalm 71:14–17

The Refrain

But you, O LORD, are gracious and full of compassion,* slow to anger, and full of
kindness and truth.

The Cry of the Church

In the evening, in the morning, and at noonday, I will complain and lament,* and
he will hear my voice.

Psalm 55:18

The Lord's Prayer

The Prayer Appointed for the Week

O God, who before the passion of your only-begotten Son revealed his glory upon
the holy mountain: Grant that I, beholding by faith the light of his counte-

nance, may be strengthened to bear my cross, and be changed into his likeness from glory to glory; through Jesus Christ my Lord, who lives and reigns with you and the Holy Spirit, one God, for ever and ever. *Amen.* †

The Concluding Prayer of the Church

I thank you, my God, for your care and protection this day, keeping me from physical harm and spiritual ignorance. I now place the work of the day into Your hands, trusting that You will redeem my mistakes, and transform my accomplishments into works of praise.

And now I ask that You will work within me while I sleep, using the hours of my rest to create in me a new mind and heart and soul.

May my mind, which during the day was directed to my work and activities, through the night be directed wholly to You.

Jacob Boehme

The Morning Office

**To Be Observed on the Hour or Half Hour
Between 6 and 9 a.m.**

The Call to Prayer

Wake up, my spirit; awake lute and harp;* I myself will waken the dawn.

Psalm 57:8

The Request for Presence

O God of hosts,* show the light of your countenance, and we shall be saved.

Psalm 80:7

The Greeting

My lips will sing with joy when I play to you,* and so will my soul, which you have redeemed.

Psalm 71:23

The Refrain for the Morning Lessons

Send forth your strength, O God;* establish, O God, what you have wrought for us.

Psalm 68:28

A Reading

He said to his disciples, 'A time will come when you will long to see one of the days of the Son of Man and will not see it. They will say to you, "Look, it is there!" or, "Look, it is here!" Make no move; do not set off in pursuit; for as the lightning flashing from one part of heaven lights up the other, so will be the Son of man when his Day comes. But first he is destined to suffer grievously and be rejected by this generation.'

Luke 17:22–25

The Refrain

Send forth your strength, O God;* establish, O God, what you have wrought for us.

The Morning Psalm   *What Are We That You Should Care for Us*

O LORD, what are we that you should care for us?* mere mortals that you should
    think of us?
We are like a puff of wind;* our days are like a passing shadow.
Bow your heavens, O LORD, and come down;* touch the mountains, and they shall
    smoke.
Hurl the lightning and scatter them;* shoot out your arrows and rout them.
Stretch out your hand from on high;* rescue me and deliver me from the great
    waters, from the hand of foreign peoples,
Whose mouths speak deceitfully* and whose right hand is raised in falsehood.

Psalm 144:3–8

The Refrain

Send forth your strength, O God;* establish, O God, what you have wrought for us.

The Cry of the Church

In the evening, in the morning, and at noonday, I will complain and lament,* and
    he will hear my voice.

Psalm 55:18

The Lord's Prayer

The Prayer Appointed for the Week

O God, who before the passion of your only-begotten Son revealed his glory upon
    the holy mountain: Grant that I, beholding by faith the light of his counte-
    nance, may be strengthened to bear my cross, and be changed into his likeness
    from glory to glory; through Jesus Christ my Lord, who lives and reigns with
    you and the Holy Spirit, one God, for ever and ever. *Amen.* †

The Concluding Prayer of the Church

Lord God, almighty and everlasting Father, you have brought me in safety to this
    new day: Preserve me with your mighty power, that I may not fall into sin, nor
    be overcome by adversity; and in all I do direct me to the fulfilling of your pur-
    pose; through Jesus Christ my Lord. *Amen.* †

The Midday Office   **To Be Observed on the Hour or Half Hour**
Between 11 a.m. and 2 p.m.

The Call to Prayer

"Come now, let us reason together," says the LORD.

Isaiah 1:18, KJV

The Request for Presence

Awake, O my God, decree justice;* let the assembly of peoples gather around you.
Let the malice of the wicked come to an end, but establish the righteous;* for you
    test the mind and heart, O righteous God.

Psalm 7:7, 10

The Greeting
Deliver me, O Lord, by your hand* from those whose portion in life is this
world; . . .

Psalm 17:14

The Refrain for the Midday Lessons
Righteousness shall go before him,* and peace shall be a pathway for his feet.

Psalm 85:13

A Reading
Seek out Yahweh while he is still to be found, call to him while he is still near. Let
the wicked abandon his way and the evil one his thoughts. Let him turn back
to Yahweh who will take pity on him, to our God, for he is rich in forgiveness;
for my thoughts are not your thoughts and your ways are not my ways,
declares Yahweh. For the heavens are as high above the earth as my ways are
above your ways, my thoughts above your thoughts.

Isaiah 55:6–9

The Refrain
Righteousness shall go before him,* and peace shall be a pathway for his feet.

The Midday Psalm   *You Will Save a Lowly People*
With the faithful you show yourself faithful, O God;* with the forthright you show
yourself forthright.
With the pure you show yourself pure,* but with the crooked you are wily.
You will save a lowly people,* but you will humble the haughty eyes.
You, O Lord, are my lamp;* my God, you make my darkness bright.
With you I will break down an enclosure;* with the help of my God I will scale any
wall.
As for God, his ways are perfect; the words of the Lord are tried in the fire;* he is a
shield to all who trust in him.
For who is God, but the Lord?* who is the Rock, except our God?

Psalm 18:26–32

The Refrain
Righteousness shall go before him,* and peace shall be a pathway for his feet.

The Cry of the Church
Lord, have mercy on us. Christ, have mercy on us. Lord, have mercy on us.

The Lord's Prayer

The Prayer Appointed for the Week
O God, who before the passion of your only-begotten Son revealed his glory upon
the holy mountain: Grant that I, beholding by faith the light of his countenance, may be strengthened to bear my cross, and be changed into his likeness
from glory to glory; through Jesus Christ my Lord, who lives and reigns with
you and the Holy Spirit, one God, for ever and ever. *Amen.* †

The Concluding Prayer of the Church
Renew in my heart, O God, the gift of your Holy Spirit, so that I may love you
    fully in all that I do and love all others as Christ loves me. May all that I do pro-
    claim the good news that you are God with us. *Amen.* †

The Vespers Office   **To Be Observed on the Hour or Half Hour**
                                       Between 5 and 8 p.m.

The Call to Prayer
O tarry and await the LORD's pleasure; be strong, and he shall comfort your heart;*
    wait patiently for the LORD.

Psalm 27:18

The Request for Presence
Open my eyes, that I may see* the wonders of your law.

Psalm 119:18

The Greeting
I remember your Name in the night, O LORD,* and dwell upon your law.
This is how it has been with me,* because I have kept your commandments.

Psalm 119:55–56

The Hymn

You ask what great thing I know,   This is the great thing I know;
That delights and stirs me so?   This delights and stirs me so:
What high reward I'll win?   Faith in him who died to save,
Whose the name I glory in?   Him who triumphed o'er the grave:
Jesus Christ, the crucified.   Jesus Christ, the crucified.

Johann Schwedler

Who is life in life to me?
Who the death of death will be?
Who will place me on his right,
With the countless hosts of light?
Jesus Christ, the crucified.

The Refrain for the Vespers Lessons
'I am the Alpha and the Omega,' says the Lord God, 'who is, who was, and who is
    to come, the Almighty.'

Revelation 1:8

The Vespers Psalm   *The LORD Is My Shepherd*
The LORD is my shepherd;* I shall not be in want.
He makes me lie down in green pastures* and leads me beside still waters.
He revives my soul* and guides me along right pathways for his Name's sake.
Though I walk through the valley of the shadow of death, I shall fear no evil;* for
    you are with me; your rod and your staff, they comfort me.

You spread a table before me in the presence of those who trouble me;* you have anointed my head with oil, and my cup is running over.

Surely your goodness and mercy shall follow me all the days of my life,* and I will dwell in the house of the LORD for ever.

Psalm 23

The Refrain

'I am the Alpha and the Omega,' says the Lord God, 'who is, who was, and who is to come, the Almighty.'

The Cry of the Church

O Lord, hear my prayer and let my cry come to you. Thanks be to God.

THE SHORT BREVIARY

The Lord's Prayer

The Prayer Appointed for the Week

O God, who before the passion of your only-begotten Son revealed his glory upon the holy mountain: Grant that I, beholding by faith the light of his countenance, may be strengthened to bear my cross, and be changed into his likeness from glory to glory; through Jesus Christ my Lord, who lives and reigns with you and the Holy Spirit, one God, for ever and ever. *Amen.* †

The Concluding Prayer of the Church

Lord Jesus Christ, you said to your apostles, "Peace I give to you; my own peace I leave with you:" Regard not my sins, but my faith, and give to me a place in the peace and unity of that heavenly City, where with the Father and the Holy Spirit you live and reign, now and forever. *Amen.* †

The Morning Office   **To Be Observed on the Hour or Half Hour Between 6 and 9 a.m.**

The Call to Prayer

Sing to the LORD a new song,* for he has done marvelous things.

With his right hand and his holy arm* has he won for himself the victory.

Psalm 98:1–2

The Request for Presence

Let your loving-kindness be my comfort,* as you have promised to your servant.

Let your compassion come to me, that I may live,* for your law is my delight.

Psalm 119:76–77

The Greeting

I will confess you among the peoples, O LORD;* I will sing praises to you among the nations.

For your loving-kindness is greater than the heavens,* and your faithfulness reaches to the clouds.

Psalm 108:3–4

The Refrain for the Morning Lessons
So teach us to number our days* that we may apply our hearts to wisdom.

Psalm 90:12

A Reading
Jesus said: "Do not imagine that I have come to abolish the Law or the Prophets. I have come not to abolish but to complete them. In truth I tell you, till heaven and earth disappear, not one dot, not one little stroke, is to disappear from the Law until all its purpose is achieved."

Matthew 5:17–18

The Refrain
So teach us to number our days* that we may apply our hearts to wisdom.

The Morning Psalm   *The LORD Does Not Forsake His Faithful Ones*
Turn from evil, and do good,* and dwell in the land for ever.
For the LORD loves justice;* he does not forsake his faithful ones.
They shall be kept safe for ever,* but the offspring of the wicked shall be destroyed.
The righteous shall possess the land* and dwell in it for ever.
The mouth of the righteous utters wisdom,* and their tongue speaks what is right.
The law of their God is in their heart,* and their footsteps shall not falter.

Psalm 37:28–33

The Refrain
So teach us to number our days* that we may apply our hearts to wisdom.

The Small Verse
Let me seek the Lord while he may still be found.
I will call upon his name; while he is near.

Traditional

The Lord's Prayer

The Prayer Appointed for the Week
O God, who before the passion of your only-begotten Son revealed his glory upon the holy mountain: Grant that I, beholding by faith the light of his counte-nance, may be strengthened to bear my cross, and be changed into his likeness from glory to glory; through Jesus Christ my Lord, who lives and reigns with you and the Holy Spirit, one God, for ever and ever. *Amen.* †

The Concluding Prayer of the Church
Lord God, almighty and everlasting Father, you have brought me in safety to this new day: Preserve me with your mighty power, that I may not fall into sin, nor be overcome by adversity; and in all I do direct me to the fulfilling of your pur-pose; through Jesus Christ my Lord. *Amen.* †

The Midday Office   To Be Observed on the Hour or Half Hour
                                     Between 11 a.m. and 2 p.m.

The Call to Prayer
Sing to God, O kingdoms of the earth;* sing praises to the Lord.
He rides in the heavens, the ancient heavens;* he sends forth his voice, his mighty
    voice.

Psalm 68:33–34

The Request for Presence
May God be merciful to us and bless us,* show us the light of his countenance and
    come to us.
Let your ways be known upon the earth,* your saving health among all nations.

Psalm 67:1–2

The Greeting
Exalt yourself above the heavens, O God,* and your glory all over the earth.
So that those who are dear to you may be delivered,* save with your right hand
    and answer me.

Psalm 108:5–6

The Refrain for the Midday Lessons
Righteousness and justice are the foundations of your throne;* love and truth go
    before your face.

Psalm 89:14

A Reading
Fasting like yours today will never make your voice heard on high. Is that the sort
    of fast that pleases me, a day when a person inflicts pain on himself? Hanging
    your head like a reed, spreading out sackcloth and ashes? Is that what you call
    fasting, a day acceptable to YAHWEH? Is not this the sort of fast that pleases me:
    to break unjust fetters, to undo the thongs of the yoke. To let the oppressed go
    free, and to break all yokes? Is it not sharing your food with the hungry or shel-
    tering the homeless poor; if you see someone lacking in clothes, to clothe him,
    and not to turn away from your own kin? Then your light will blaze out like
    the dawn and your wound will be quickly healed over.

Isaiah 58:4–8

The Refrain
Righteousness and justice are the foundations of your throne;* love and truth go
    before your face.

The Midday Psalm   *The LORD Will Have Regard for Me*
You are the LORD; do not withhold your compassion from me;* let your love and
    your faithfulness keep me safe for ever,
For innumerable troubles have crowded upon me; my sins have overtaken me,
    and I cannot see;* they are more in number than the hairs of my head, and my
    heart fails me.

Be pleased, O Lord, to deliver me;* O Lord, make haste to help me.
Let them be ashamed and altogether dismayed who seek after my life to destroy
    it;* let them draw back and be disgraced who take pleasure in my misfortune.
Let those who say "Aha!" and gloat over me be confounded* because they are
    ashamed.
Let all who seek you rejoice in you and be glad;* let those who love your salvation
    continually say, "Great is the Lord!"
Though I am poor and afflicted,* the Lord will have regard for me.
You are my helper and my deliverer;* do not tarry, O my God.

Psalm 40:12–19

The Refrain

Righteousness and justice are the foundations of your throne;* love and truth go
    before your face.

The Small Verse

The Son of man shall be delivered over to the Gentiles to be mocked and scourged
    and crucified.

The Lord's Prayer

The Prayer Appointed for the Week

O God, who before the passion of your only-begotten Son revealed his glory upon
    the holy mountain: Grant that I, beholding by faith the light of his counte-
    nance, may be strengthened to bear my cross, and be changed into his likeness
    from glory to glory; through Jesus Christ my Lord, who lives and reigns with
    you and the Holy Spirit, one God, for ever and ever. *Amen.* †

The Concluding Prayer of the Church

Almighty God, whose most dear Son went not up to joy before he first suffered
    pain, and did not enter into glory before he was crucified: Mercifully grant that
    I, walking in the way of the cross, may find it to be none other than the way of
    life and peace; through Jesus Christ your son my Lord. *Amen.* †

The Vespers Office To Be Observed on the Hour or Half Hour
Between 5 and 8 p.m.

The Call to Prayer

Search for the Lord and his strength;* continually seek his face.

Psalm 105:4

The Request for Presence

For God alone my soul in silence waits;* truly, my hope is in him.

Psalm 62:6

The Greeting

Out of Zion, perfect in its beauty,* God reveals himself in glory.

Psalm 50:2

The Hymn   *Hail, O Once Despised Jesus*

Hail, O once despised Jesus!   Worship, honor, power, and blessing,
Hail, O Galilean King!   You are worthy to receive;
You suffered to release us;   Loudest praises, without ceasing,
Free salvation did you bring: Right it is for us to give:
Hail, O agonizing Savior,   Help, you bright angelic spirits,
Bearer of our sin and shame!   Bring your sweetest, noblest ways;
By Your merits we find favor;   Help to sing our Savior's merits,
Life is given through Your Name.   Help to chant Immanuel's praise.

John Bakewell

Paschal Lamb, by God appointed,
All our sins on You were laid;
By almighty love anointed,
You have full atonement made:
All Your people are forgiven,
Through the virtue of Your blood;
Opened is the gate of heaven,
Made is peace 'tween man and God.

The Refrain for the Vespers Lessons
Let my mouth be full of your praise* and your glory all the day long.

Psalm 71:8

The Vespers Psalm   *The Law of the LORD Revives the Soul*
The law of the LORD is perfect and revives the soul;* the testimony of the LORD is
    sure and gives wisdom to the innocent.
The statutes of the LORD are just and rejoice the heart;* the commandment of the
    LORD is clear and gives light to the eyes.
The fear of the LORD is clean and endures for ever;* the judgments of the LORD are
    true and righteous altogether.
More to be desired are they than gold, more than much fine gold,* sweeter far than
    honey, than honey in the comb.
By them also is your servant enlightened,* and in keeping them there is great
    reward.

Psalm 19:7–11

The Refrain
Let my mouth be full of your praise* and your glory all the day long.

The Cry of the Church
Lord, have mercy upon us. Christ, have mercy upon us. Lord, have mercy upon us.

The Lord's Prayer

The Prayer Appointed for the Week
O God, who before the passion of your only-begotten Son revealed his glory upon
    the holy mountain: Grant that I, beholding by faith the light of his counte-
    nance, may be strengthened to bear my cross, and be changed into his likeness

from glory to glory; through Jesus Christ my Lord, who lives and reigns with you and the Holy Spirit, one God, for ever and ever. *Amen.* †

Concluding Prayers of the Church
Almighty God, who has promised to hear the petitions of those who ask in your Son's Name: I beseech you mercifully to incline your ear to me who have made my prayers and supplications to you; and grant that those things which I have faithfully asked according to your will, may effectually be obtained, to the relief of my necessity, and to the setting forth of your glory; through Jesus Christ my Lord. *Amen.* †

May the souls of the faithful departed, through the mercy of God, rest in eternal peace. *Amen.*

The Morning Office   To Be Observed on the Hour or Half Hour
                                           Between 6 and 9 a.m.

The Call to Prayer
Bless the LORD, you angels of his, you mighty ones who do his bidding,* and hearken to the voice of his word.
Bless the LORD, all you hosts,* you ministers of his who do his will.
Bless the LORD, all you works of his, in all places of his dominion;* bless the LORD, O my soul.

Psalm 103:20–22

The Request for Presence
Give ear to my words, O LORD;* consider my meditation.
Hearken to my cry for help, my King and my God,* for I make my prayer to you.
In the morning, LORD, you hear my voice;* early in the morning I make my appeal and watch for you.

Psalm 5:1–3

The Greeting
Let the words of my mouth and the meditation of my heart be acceptable in your sight,* O LORD, my strength and my redeemer.

Psalm 19:14

The Refrain for the Morning Lessons
The LORD's will stands fast for ever,* and the designs of his heart from age to age.

Psalm 33:11

A Reading
Jesus taught us, saying: "When the Son of Man comes in his Glory, escorted by all the angels, then he will take his seat on his throne of glory. All nations will be assembled before him and he will separate people one from another as the shepherd separates sheep from goats. He will place the sheep on his right hand and the goats on his left. Then the King will say to those on his right hand,

'Come, you whom my Father has blessed, take as your heritage the kingdom prepared for you since the foundation of the world. For I was hungry and you gave me food, I was thirsty and you gave me drink, I was a stranger and you made me welcome, lacking clothes and you clothed me, sick and you visited me.' Then the upright will say to him in reply, 'Lord, when did we see you hungry and feed you, or thirsty and give you drink? When did we see you a stranger and make you welcome, lacking clothes and clothe you? When did we see you sick or in prison and go to visit you?' And the King will answer, 'In truth I tell you, in so far as you did this to one of the least of these brothers of mine, you did it to me.' Then he will say to those on his left hand, 'Go away from me, with your curse upon you, to the eternal fire prepared for the devil and his angels. For I was hungry and you never gave me food, I was thirsty and you never gave me anything to drink, I was a stranger and you never made me welcome, lacking clothes and you never clothed me, sick and in prison and you never visited me.' Then it will be their turn to ask, 'Lord, when did we see you hungry or thirsty, a stranger or lacking clothes, sick or in prison and did not come to your help?' Then he will answer, 'In truth I tell you, in so far as you neglected to do this to one of the least of these, you neglected to do it to me.' And they will go away to eternal punishment, and the upright to eternal life."

Matthew 25:31–46

The Refrain
The Lord's will stands fast for ever,* and the designs of his heart from age to age.

The Morning Psalm   *Who May Abide Upon Your Holy Hill?*
Lord, who may dwell in your tabernacle?* who may abide upon your holy hill?
Whoever leads a blameless life and does what is right,* who speaks the truth from
  his heart.
There is no guile upon his tongue; he does no evil to his friend;* he does not heap
  contempt upon his neighbor.
In his sight the wicked is rejected,* but he honors those who fear the Lord.
He has sworn to do no wrong* and does not take back his word.
He does not give his money in hope of gain,* nor does he take a bribe against the
  innocent.
Whoever does these things* shall never be overthrown.

Psalm 15

The Refrain
The Lord's will stands fast for ever,* and the designs of his heart from age to age.

The Small Verse
The people that walked in darkness have seen a great light; on those who have
  lived in a land of deep shadow a light has shown.

Isaiah 9:1

The Lord's Prayer

The Prayer Appointed for the Week

O God, who before the passion of your only-begotten Son revealed his glory upon the holy mountain: Grant that I, beholding by faith the light of his countenance, may be strengthened to bear my cross, and be changed into his likeness from glory to glory; through Jesus Christ my Lord, who lives and reigns with you and the Holy Spirit, one God, for ever and ever. *Amen.* †

The Concluding Prayer of the Church

Lord God, almighty and everlasting Father, you have brought me in safety to this new day: Preserve me with your mighty power, that I may not fall into sin, nor be overcome by adversity; and in all I do direct me to the fulfilling of your purpose; through Jesus Christ my Lord. *Amen.* †

The Midday Office **To Be Observed on the Hour or Half Hour**
Between 11 a.m. and 2 p.m.

The Call to Prayer

Let everything that has breath* praise the LORD.

Psalm 150:6

The Request for Presence

LORD, hear my prayer, and in your faithfulness heed my supplications;* answer me in your righteousness.

Psalm 143:1

The Greeting

My eyes are fixed on you, O my Strength;* for you, O God, are my stronghold.

Psalm 59:10

The Refrain for the Midday Lessons

In righteousness shall he judge the world* and the peoples with equity.

Psalm 98:10

A Reading

YAHWEH gives death and life, brings down to Sheol and draws up; YAHWEH makes poor and rich, he humbles and also exalts. He raises the poor from the dust, he lifts the needy from the dunghill to give them a place with princes, to assign them a seat of honor; for to YAHWEH belong the pillars of the earth, on these he has poised the world.

I Samuel 2:6–10

The Refrain

In righteousness shall he judge the world* and the peoples with equity.

The Midday Psalm *Heal Me, for I Have Sinned*

Happy are they who consider the poor and needy!* the LORD will deliver them in the time of trouble.

The LORD preserves them and keeps them alive, so that they may be happy in the land;* he does not hand them over to the will of their enemies.
The LORD sustains them on their sickbed* and ministers to them in their illness.
I said, "LORD, be merciful to me;* heal me, for I have sinned against you."

Psalm 41:1–4

The Refrain
In righteousness shall he judge the world* and the peoples with equity.

The Small Verse
Today if you shall hear his voice, harden not your heart.

The Lord's Prayer

The Prayer Appointed for the Week
O God, who before the passion of your only-begotten Son revealed his glory upon the holy mountain: Grant that I, beholding by faith the light of his countenance, may be strengthened to bear my cross, and be changed into his likeness from glory to glory; through Jesus Christ my Lord, who lives and reigns with you and the Holy Spirit, one God, for ever and ever. *Amen.* †

The Concluding Prayer of the Church
O God, the source of light: Shed forth your unending day upon all of us who watch for you, that our lips may praise you, our lives may bless you, and our worship may give you glory; through Jesus Christ our Lord. *Amen.* †

The Vespers Office   To Be Observed on the Hour or Half Hour
                                      Between 5 and 8 p.m.

The Call to Prayer
We will bless the LORD,* from this time forth for evermore.

Psalm 115:18

The Request for Presence
Answer me when I call, O God, defender of my cause;* you set me free when I am hard-pressed; have mercy on me and hear my prayer.

Psalm 4:1

The Greeting
Be exalted, O LORD, in your might;* we will sing and praise your power.

Psalm 21:14

The Hymn   *O for a Thousand Tongues to Sing*
O for a thousand tongues to sing my great Redeemer's praise,
The glories of my God and King, the triumphs of his grace!

My gracious Master and my God, assist me to proclaim,
To spread through all the earth abroad the honors of your name.

Jesus! The name that charms our fears, that bids our sorrows cease;
'Tis music in the sinner's ears, 'tis life, and health, and peace.

He breaks the power of canceled sin, he sets the prisoner free;
His blood can make the foulest clean; his blood availed for me.

He speaks, and listening to his voice, new life the dead receive;
The mournful, broken hearts rejoice, the humble poor believe.

In Christ, your head, you then shall know, shall feel your sins forgiven;
Anticipate your heaven below, and own that love in heaven.

Charles Wesley

The Refrain for the Vespers Lessons
. . . I call upon you all the day long.
Psalm 86:3

The Vespers Psalm   *My Days Drift Away Like Smoke*
LORD, hear my prayer, and let my cry come before you;* hide not your face from
    me in the day of my trouble.
Incline your ear to me;* when I call, make haste to answer me,
For my days drift away like smoke,* and my bones are hot as burning coals.
My heart is smitten like grass and withered,* so that I forget to eat my bread.
Because of the voice of my groaning* I am but skin and bones.
I have become like a vulture in the wilderness,* like an owl among the ruins.
I lie awake and groan;* I am like a sparrow, lonely on a house-top.

Psalm 102:1–7

The Refrain
. . . I call upon you all the day long.

The Cry of the Church
In the evening, in the morning, and at noonday, I will complain and lament,* and
    he will hear my voice.

Psalm 55:18

The Lord's Prayer

The Prayer Appointed for the Week
O God, who before the passion of your only-begotten Son revealed his glory upon
    the holy mountain: Grant that I, beholding by faith the light of his counte-
    nance, may be strengthened to bear my cross, and be changed into his likeness
    from glory to glory; through Jesus Christ my Lord, who lives and reigns with
    you and the Holy Spirit, one God, for ever and ever. *Amen.* †

The Concluding Prayer of the Church
For an angel of peace, faithful guardian and guide of our souls and our bodies, we
    beseech thee, O Lord.

Orthodox

The Morning Office   To Be Observed on the Hour or Half Hour
Between 6 and 9 a.m.

The Call to Prayer
Praise God from whom all blessings flow; Praise Him all creatures here below;
Praise him above, you heavenly hosts; Praise Father, Son, and Holy Ghost.
Traditional Doxology

The Request for Presence
Hear, O Shepherd of Israel, leading Joseph like a flock;* shine forth, you that are
enthroned upon the cherubim.
Psalm 80:1

The Greeting
The LORD lives! Blessed is my Rock!* Exalted is the God of my salvation!
Psalm 18:46

The Refrain for the Morning Lessons
We have sinned as our forebears did;* we have done wrong and dealt wickedly.
Psalm 108:6

A Reading
Then Jesus was led by the Spirit out into the desert to be put to the test by the
devil. He fasted for forty days and forty nights, after which he was hungry, and
the tester came and said to him, 'If you are the Son of God, tell these stones to
turn into loaves.' But he replied, 'Scripture says: *Human beings live not on bread
alone but on every word that comes from the mouth of God.*' The devil then took him
to the holy city and set him upon the parapet of the Temple. 'If you are the Son
of God,' he said, 'throw yourself down; for scripture says: *He has given his
angels about you, and they will carry you in their arms in case you trip over a stone.*'
Jesus said to him, 'Scripture also says: *Do not put the Lord your God to the test.*'
Next, taking him to a very high mountain, the devil showed him all the kingdoms of the world and their splendor. And he said to him, 'I will give you all
these, if you fall at my feet and do me homage.' Then Jesus replied, 'Away with
you, Satan! For scripture says: *The Lord your God is the one to whom you must do
homage, him alone you must serve.*' Then the devil left him, and suddenly angels
appeared and looked after him.
Matthew 4:1–11

The Refrain
We have sinned as our forebears did;* we have done wrong and dealt wickedly.

The Morning Psalm   Lord, *Let My Cry Come Unto You*

Lord, hear my prayer, and let my cry come before you;* hide not your face from
    me in the day of my trouble.
Incline your ear to me;* when I call, make haste to answer me,
For my days drift away like smoke,* and my bones are hot as burning coals.
My heart is smitten like grass and withered,* so that I forget to eat my bread.
Because of the voice of my groaning* I am but skin and bones.
I have become like a vulture in the wilderness,* like an owl among the ruins.
I lie awake and groan;* I am like a sparrow, lonely on a house-top.
My enemies revile me all day long,* and those who scoff at me have taken an oath
    against me.
For I have eaten ashes for bread* and mingled my drink with weeping.
Because of your indignation and wrath* you have lifted me up and thrown me away.
My days pass away like a shadow,* and I wither like the grass.
But you, O Lord, endure for ever,* and your Name from age to age.

Psalm 102:1–12

The Refrain
We have sinned as our forebears did;* we have done wrong and dealt wickedly.

The Small Verse
The people that walked in darkness have seen a great light; on those who live in a
    land of deep shadow a light has shone.

Isaiah 9:1

The Lord's Prayer

The Prayer Appointed for the Week
Almighty God, whose blessed Son was led by the Spirit to be tempted by Satan:
    Come quickly to help us who are assaulted by many temptations; and, as you
    know the weaknesses of each of us, let each one find you mighty to save;
    through Jesus Christ your Son our Lord, who lives and reigns with you and the
    Holy Spirit, one God, now and for ever. *Amen.* †

The Concluding Prayer of the Church
Lord God, almighty and everlasting Father, you have brought me in safety to this
    new day: Preserve me with your mighty power, that I may not fall into sin, nor
    be overcome by adversity; and in all I do direct me to the fulfilling of your pur-
    pose; through Jesus Christ my Lord. *Amen.* †

The Midday Office   **To Be Observed on the Hour or Half Hour**
                                          Between 11 a.m. and 2 p.m.

The Call to Prayer
Let all those whom the Lord has redeemed proclaim* that he redeemed them from
    the hand of the foe.

Psalm 107:2

The Request for Presence
May God give us his blessing,* and may all the ends of the earth stand in awe of him.

Psalm 67:7

The Greeting
You, O Lord, are a shield about me;* you are my glory, the one who lifts up my head.
I call aloud upon the Lord,* and he answers me from his holy hill;
I lie down and go to sleep;* I wake again, because the Lord sustains me.

Psalm 3:3–5

The Refrain for the Midday Lessons
May the glory of the Lord endure for ever;* may the Lord rejoice in all his works.

Psalm 104:32

A Reading
Of Christ, the Apostle wrote: ". . . he took to himself *the line of Abraham*. It was essential that he should in this way be made completely like his brothers so that he could become a compassionate and trustworthy high priest for their relationship to God, able to expiate the sins of the people. For the suffering he himself passed through while being put to the test enables him to help others when they are being put to the test."

Hebrews 2:16–18

The Refrain
May the glory of the Lord endure for ever;* may the Lord rejoice in all his works.

The Midday Psalm   *Having You I Desire Nothing Upon Earth*
Whom have I in heaven but you?* and having you I desire nothing upon earth.
Though my flesh and my heart should waste away,* God is the strength of my heart and my portion for ever.
Truly, those who forsake you will perish;* you destroy all who are unfaithful.
But it is good for me to be near God;* I have made the Lord God my refuge.

Psalm 73:25–28

The Refrain
May the glory of the Lord endure for ever;* may the Lord rejoice in all his works.

The Cry of the Church
O God, come to my assistance! O Lord, make haste to help me!

The Lord's Prayer

The Prayer Appointed for the Week
Almighty God, whose blessed Son was led by the Spirit to be tempted by Satan: Come quickly to help us who are assaulted by many temptations; and, as you know the weaknesses of each of us, let each one find you mighty to save; through Jesus Christ your Son our Lord, who lives and reigns with you and the Holy Spirit, one God, now and for ever. *Amen.* †

The Concluding Prayer of the Church

O God, on this first day of the week, I join all creation and people of all ages in praising you. Your kindness and forgiveness flow like a river through the centuries refreshing our faith, our hope and our love. May you be forever praised throughout all the ages. *Amen.*

The Vespers Office   To Be Observed on the Hour or Half Hour
                                      Between 5 and 8 p.m.

The Call to Prayer

Bless the LORD, you angels of his, you mighty ones who do his bidding,* and hearken to the voice of his word.
Bless the LORD, all you his hosts,* you ministers of his who do his will.
Bless the LORD, all you works of his, in all places of his dominion;* bless the LORD, O my soul.

Psalm 103:20–22

The Request for Presence

Hear, O Shepherd of Israel, leading Joseph like a flock;* shine forth, you that are enthroned upon the cherubim.

Psalm 80:1

The Greeting

Praise God from whom all blessings flow;
Praise him all creatures here below;
Praise Him above, you heavenly hosts;
Praise Father, Son, and Holy Ghost.

Doxology

The Hymn   *Sing with Gladness*

Sing, you faithful, sing with gladness, wake your noblest, sweetest strain,
With the praises of your Savior let his house resound again;
Him let all your music honor, let your songs exalt his reign.

Sing how he came forth from heaven, bowed himself to Bethlehem's cave,
Stooped to wear the servant's vesture, bore the pain, the cross, the grave,
Passed within the gates of darkness, thence his banished ones to save.

So, he tasted death for mortals, he, of humankind the head,
Sinless one, among the sinful, Prince of life, among the dead;
Thus he wrought the full redemption, and the captor captive led.

Now, on high, yet ever with us, from his Father's throne the Son
Rules and guides the world he ransomed, till the appointed work be done,
Till he sees, renewed, perfected, all things gathered into one.

John Ellerton

The Refrain for the Vespers Lessons
Fight those who fight me, O Lord;* attack those who are attacking me.
. . . say to my soul, "I am your salvation."

Psalm 35:1ff

The Vespers Psalm   *Lift Up Your Heads, O Gates*
Lift up your heads, O gates; lift them high, O everlasting doors;* and the King of
   glory shall come in.
"Who is this King of glory?"* "The Lord, strong and mighty, the Lord, mighty in
   battle."
Lift up your heads, O gates; lift them high, O everlasting doors;* and the King of
   glory shall come in.
"Who is he, this King of glory?"* "The Lord of hosts, he is the King of glory."

Psalm 24:7–10

The Refrain
Fight those who fight me, O Lord;* attack those who are attacking me.
. . . say to my soul, "I am your salvation."

The Cry of the Church
Even so, come Lord Jesus!

The Lord's Prayer

The Prayer Appointed for the Week
Almighty God, whose blessed Son was led by the Spirit to be tempted by Satan:
   Come quickly to help us who are assaulted by many temptations; and, as you
   know the weaknesses of each of us, let each one find you mighty to save;
   through Jesus Christ your Son our Lord, who lives and reigns with you and the
   Holy Spirit, one God, now and for ever. *Amen.* †

The Concluding Prayer of the Church
Lord God, whose Son our Savior Jesus Christ, triumphed over the powers of death
   and prepared for us our place in the new Jerusalem: Grant that I, who have this
   day given thanks for his resurrection, may praise you in the City of which he is
   the light, and where he lives and reigns for ever and ever. *Amen.* †

The Morning Office   **To Be Observed on the Hour or Half Hour**
                                              Between 6 and 9 a.m.

The Call to Prayer
"Come now, let us reason together," says the Lord.
Isaiah 1:18, KJV

The Request for Presence
Be my strong rock, a castle to keep me safe;* you are my crag and my stronghold.
Psalm 71:3

The Greeting
The words of the LORD are pure words,* like silver refined from ore and purified
seven times in the fire.

Psalm 12:6

The Refrain for the Morning Lessons
"Because the needy are oppressed, and the poor cry out in misery,* I will rise up,"
says the LORD, "And give them the help they long for."

Psalm 12:5

A Reading
Jesus taught us, saying: "In all truth I tell you, no one can enter the kingdom of
God without being born through water and the Spirit; what is born of human
nature is human; what is born of the Spirit is spirit. Do not be surprised when I
say: You must be born from above. The wind blows where it pleases; you can
hear its sound, but you cannot tell where it comes from or where it is going. So
it is with everyone who is born of the Spirit."

John 3:5–8

The Refrain
"Because the needy are oppressed, and the poor cry out in misery,* I will rise up,"
says the LORD, "And give them the help they long for."

The Morning Psalm   *He Has Shown His People the Power of His Works*
Great are the deeds of the LORD!* they are studied by all who delight in them.
His work is full of majesty and splendor,* and his righteousness endures for ever.
He makes his marvelous works to be remembered;* the LORD is gracious and full
of compassion.
He gives food to those who fear him;* he is ever mindful of his covenant.
He has shown his people the power of his works* in giving them the lands of the
nations.
The works of his hands are faithfulness and justice;* all his commandments are
sure.
They stand fast for ever and ever,* because they are done in truth and equity.
He sent redemption to his people; he commanded his covenant for ever;* holy and
awesome is his Name.

Psalm 111:2–9

The Refrain
"Because the needy are oppressed, and the poor cry out in misery,* I will rise up,"
says the LORD, "And give them the help they long for."

The Cry of the Church
Even so, come Lord Jesus!

The Lord's Prayer

The Prayer Appointed for the Week
Almighty God, whose blessed Son was led by the Spirit to be tempted by Satan:
Come quickly to help us who are assaulted by many temptations; and, as you
know the weaknesses of each of us, let each one find you mighty to save;
through Jesus Christ your Son our Lord, who lives and reigns with you and the
Holy Spirit, one God, now and for ever. *Amen.* †

The Concluding Prayer of the Church
Lord God, almighty and everlasting Father, you have brought me in safety to this
new day: Preserve me with your mighty power, that I may not fall into sin, nor
be overcome by adversity; and in all I do direct me to the fulfilling of your purpose; through Jesus Christ my Lord. *Amen.* †

The Midday Office   To Be Observed on the Hour or Half Hour
                                        Between 11 a.m. and 2 p.m.

The Call to Prayer
Let Israel rejoice in his Maker;* let the children of Zion be joyful in their King.

Psalm 149:2

The Request for Presence
Restore us, O God of hosts;* show me the light of your countenance, and we shall
be saved.

Psalm 80:7

The Greeting
Not to us, O LORD, not to us, but to your Name give glory;* because of your love
and because of your faithfulness.

Psalm 115:1

The Refrain for the Midday Lessons
Righteousness and justice are the foundations of your throne;* love and truth go
before your face.

Psalm 89:14

A Reading
Ephraim, how could I part with you? Israel, how could I give you up? How could
I make you like Admah or treat you like Zeboiim? My heart within me is overwhelmed, fever grips my inmost being. I will not give rein to my fierce anger, I
will not destroy Ephraim again, for I am God, not man, the Holy One in your
midst, and I shall not come to you in anger.

Hosea 11:8–9

The Refrain
Righteousness and justice are the foundations of your throne;* love and truth go
before your face.

The Midday Psalm   *He Redeems Your Life from the Grave*

Bless the LORD, O my soul,* and all that is within me, bless his holy Name.

Bless the LORD, O my soul,* and forget not all his benefits.

He forgives all your sins* and heals all your infirmities;

He redeems your life from the grave* and crowns you with mercy and loving-
kindness;

He satisfies you with good things,* and your youth is renewed like an eagle's.

Psalm 103:1–5

The Refrain

Righteousness and justice are the foundations of your throne;* love and truth go
before your face.

The Cry of the Church

O God, come to my assistance! O Lord, make haste to help me!

The Lord's Prayer

The Prayer Appointed for the Week

Almighty God, whose blessed Son was led by the Spirit to be tempted by Satan:
Come quickly to help us who are assaulted by many temptations; and, as you
know the weaknesses of each of us, let each one find you mighty to save;
through Jesus Christ your Son our Lord, who lives and reigns with you and the
Holy Spirit, one God, now and for ever. *Amen.* †

The Concluding Prayer of the Church

God, you have prepared in peace the path I must follow today. Help me to walk
straight on that path. If I speak, remove lies from my lips. If I am hungry, take
away from me all complaint. If I have plenty, destroy pride in me. May I go
through the day calling on you, you, O Lord, who know no other Lord.

Ethiopian

The Vespers Office   To Be Observed on the Hour or Half Hour
                                       Between 5 and 8 p.m.

The Call to Prayer

Taste and see that the LORD is good;* happy are those who trust in him!

Psalm 34:8

The Request for Presence

LORD, hear my prayer, and let my cry come before you;* hide not your face from
me in the day of my trouble.

Psalm 102:1

The Greeting

To you, O LORD, I lift up my soul;* my God I put my trust in you; . . .

Psalm 25:1

The Hymn

God, whose almighty word
Chaos and darkness heard
　　And took their flight:
Hear us we humbly pray,
And where the gospel day
Sheds not its glorious ray
　　Let there be light.

Savior who came to bring
On your redeeming wing
　　Healing and sight—
Health to the sick in mind,
Sight to the inly blind—
O now to all mankind
　　Let there be light.

Spirit of truth and love,
Life-giving holy dove,
　　Speed on your flight;
Move on the waters' face,
Bearing the lamp of grace,
And in earth's darkest place
　　Let there be light.

Holy and blessed Three,
Glorious Trinity,
　　Wisdom, Love, Might,
Boundless as ocean-tide
Rolling in fullest pride,
Through the world, far and wide
　　Let there be light.

John Marriott

The Refrain for the Vespers Lessons

Some put their trust in chariots and some in horses,* but we will call upon the
　　Name of the LORD our God.

Psalm 20:7

The Vespers Psalm　　　　　　　　　*Glorious Things Are Spoken of You*

On the holy mountain stands the city he has founded;* the LORD loves the gates of
　　Zion more than all the dwellings of Jacob.
Glorious things are spoken of you,* O city of our God.
I count Egypt and Babylon among those who know me;* behold Philistia, Tyre,
　　and Ethiopia: in Zion were they born.
Of Zion it shall be said, "Everyone was born in her,* and the Most High himself
　　shall sustain her."
The LORD will record as he enrolls the peoples,* "These also were born there."
The singers and the dancers will say,* "All my fresh springs are in you."

Psalm 87

The Refrain

Some put their trust in chariots and some in horses,* but we will call upon the
　　Name of the LORD our God.

The Cry of the Church

Lord, have mercy on us. Christ, have mercy on us. Lord, have mercy on us.

The Lord's Prayer

The Prayer Appointed for the Week

Almighty God, whose blessed Son was led by the Spirit to be tempted by Satan:
　　Come quickly to help us who are assaulted by many temptations; and, as you
　　know the weaknesses of each of us, let each one find you mighty to save;

through Jesus Christ your Son our Lord, who lives and reigns with you and the Holy Spirit, one God, now and for ever. *Amen.* †

The Concluding Prayer of the Church
Stay, O Lord, with those who wake, or watch, or weep tonight, and give your angels and saints charge over those who sleep.

The Morning Office
To Be Observed on the Hour or Half Hour Between 6 and 9 a.m.

The Call to Prayer
Sing praise to the LORD who dwells in Zion;* proclaim to the peoples the things he has done.

Psalm 9:11

The Request for Presence
May God be merciful to us and bless us,* show us the light of his countenance and come to us.

Psalm 67:1

The Greeting
Awesome things will you show us in your righteousness, O God of our salvation,* O Hope of all the ends of the earth and of the seas that are far away.

The Refrain for the Morning Lessons
Your kingdom is an everlasting kingdom;* your dominion endures throughout all ages.

Psalm 145:13

A Reading
Jesus taught us, saying: "The sheep that belong to me listen to my voice; I know them and they follow me. I give them eternal life; they will never be lost and no one will ever steal anything from the Father's hand. The Father and I are as one."

John 10:27–30

The Refrain
Your kingdom is an everlasting kingdom;* your dominion endures throughout all ages.

The Morning Psalm *O Israel, If You Would But Listen to Me*
Hear, O my people, and I will admonish you:* O Israel, if you would but listen to me!
There shall be no strange god among you;* you shall not worship a foreign god.
I am the LORD your God, who brought you out of the land of Egypt and said,* "Open your mouth wide, and I will fill it."

Psalm 81:8–10

The Refrain
Your kingdom is an everlasting kingdom;* your dominion endures throughout
all ages.

The Cry of the Church
O God, come to my assistance! O Lord, make haste to help me!

The Lord's Prayer

The Prayer Appointed for the Week
Almighty God, whose blessed Son was led by the Spirit to be tempted by Satan:
Come quickly to help us who are assaulted by many temptations; and, as you
know the weaknesses of each of us, let each one find you mighty to save;
through Jesus Christ your Son our Lord, who lives and reigns with you and the
Holy Spirit, one God, now and for ever. *Amen.* †

The Concluding Prayer of the Church
Lord God, almighty and everlasting Father, you have brought me in safety to this
new day: Preserve me with your mighty power, that I may not fall into sin, nor
be overcome by adversity; and in all I do direct me to the fulfilling of your purpose; through Jesus Christ my Lord. *Amen.* †

The Midday Office   To Be Observed on the Hour or Half Hour
                                     Between 11 a.m. and 2 p.m.

The Call to Prayer
Let the words of my mouth and the meditation of my heart be acceptable in your
sight,* O LORD, my strength and my redeemer.

Psalm 19:14

The Request for Presence
Open my eyes, that I may see* the wonders of your law.

Psalm 119:18

The Greeting
My God, my rock in whom I put my trust,* my shield, the horn of my salvation,
and my refuge; you are worthy of praise.

Psalm 18:2

The Refrain for the Midday Lessons
When I called, you answered me;* you increased my strength within me.

Psalm 138:4

A Reading
When we were still helpless, at the appointed time, Christ died for the godless.

Romans 5:6

The Refrain
When I called, you answered me;* you increased my strength within me.

The Midday Psalm   *Give Me Life in Your Ways*

Teach me, O Lord, the way of your statutes,* and I shall keep it to the end.

Give me understanding, and I shall keep your law;* I shall keep it with all my heart.

Make me go in the path of your commandments,* for that is my desire.

Incline my heart to your decrees* and not to unjust gain.

Turn my eyes from watching what is worthless;* give me life in your ways.

Psalm 119:33–37

The Refrain

When I called, you answered me;* you increased my strength within me.

The Cry of the Church

Be, Lord, my helper and forsake me not. Do not despise me, O God, my savior.

The Short Breviary

The Lord's Prayer

The Prayer Appointed for the Week

Almighty God, whose blessed Son was led by the Spirit to be tempted by Satan: Come quickly to help us who are assaulted by many temptations; and, as you know the weaknesses of each of us, let each one find you mighty to save; through Jesus Christ your Son our Lord, who lives and reigns with you and the Holy Spirit, one God, now and for ever. *Amen.* †

The Concluding Prayer of the Church

Heavenly Father, in you I live and move and have my being: I humbly pray you so to guide and govern me by your Holy Spirit, that in all cares and occupations of my life I may not forget you, but may remember that I am ever walking in your sight; through Jesus Christ my Lord. *Amen.* †

The Vespers Office   **To Be Observed on the Hour or Half Hour**
                                                      Between 5 and 8 p.m.

The Call to Prayer

Taste and see that the Lord is good;* happy are those who trust in him!

Psalm 34:8

The Request for Presence

O Lamb of God, that takes away the sins of the world, have mercy upon me.

O Lamb of God, that takes away the sins of the world, have mercy upon me.

O Lamb of God, that takes away the sins of the world, grant me your peace.

The Greeting

Happy are those whom you choose and draw to your courts to dwell there!* they will be satisfied by the beauty of your house, by the holiness of your temple.

Psalm 65:4

The Hymn   *Throw Out the Lifeline*

Throw out the lifeline across the dark wave,
There is a sister whom someone should save;
Or somebody's brother! Oh, who then, will dare
To throw out the lifeline, his peril to share?
Throw out the lifeline!
Throw out the lifeline!
Someone's drifting away.

Throw out the lifeline with hand quick and strong:
Why do you tarry, why linger so long?
Someone is sinking; oh, hasten today,
And out with the lifeboat, away, then, away!
Throw out the lifeline!
Throw out the lifeline!
Someone's drifting away.

Throw out the lifeline to danger fraught kin,
Sinking in anguish where you've never been:
Winds of temptation and billows of woe
Will soon hurl them out where dark waters flow.
Throw out the lifeline!
Throw out the lifeline!
Someone's drifting away.

Soon will the season of rescue be o'er,
Soon will they drift to eternity's shore;
Haste then, you faithful, no time for delay,
But throw out the lifeline and save them today.
Throw out the lifeline!
Throw out the lifeline!
Someone's sinking today.

Edward Ufford

The Refrain for the Vespers Lessons
Light shines in the darkness for the upright;* the righteous are merciful and full of
    compassion.

Psalm 112:4

The Vespers Psalm   *He Gives His Beloved Sleep*
Unless the LORD builds the house,* their labor is in vain who build it.
Unless the LORD watches over the city,* in vain the watchman keeps his vigil.
It is in vain that you rise so early and go to bed so late;* vain, too, to eat the bread
    of toil, for he gives to his beloved sleep.

Psalm 127:1–3

The Refrain
Light shines in the darkness for the upright;* the righteous are merciful and full of compassion.

The Cry of the Church
In the evening, in the morning, and at noonday, I will complain and lament,* and he will hear my voice.

Psalm 55:18

The Lord's Prayer

The Prayer Appointed for the Week
Almighty God, whose blessed Son was led by the Spirit to be tempted by Satan:
Come quickly to help us who are assaulted by many temptations; and, as you know the weaknesses of each of us, let each one find you mighty to save; through Jesus Christ your Son our Lord, who lives and reigns with you and the Holy Spirit, one God, now and for ever. *Amen.* †

The Concluding Prayer of the Church
Almighty Father,
you have given me the strength
to work throughout this day.
Receive my evening sacrifice of praise
in thanksgiving for your countless gifts.
I ask this through my Lord Jesus Christ, your Son,
who lives and reigns with you and the Holy Spirit,
one God, for ever and ever.

adapted from THE LITURGY OF THE HOURS, VOL. III

The Morning Office   **To Be Observed on the Hour or Half Hour**
Between 6 and 9 a.m.

The Call to Prayer
Bless our God, you peoples;* make the voice of his praise to be heard;
Who holds our souls in life,* and will not allow our feet to slip.

Psalm 66:7–8

The Request for Presence
Come to me speedily, O God. You are my helper and my deliverer;* LORD, do not tarry.

Psalm 70:5–6

The Greeting
You are my hope, O Lord GOD,* my confidence since I was young.
I have been sustained by you ever since I was born; from my mother's womb you have been my strength;* my praise shall be always of you.

Psalm 71:5–6

The Refrain for the Morning Lessons
"Be still, then, and know that I am God;* I will be exalted among the nations; I will
be exalted in the earth."

Psalm 46:11

A Reading
Another said, 'I will follow you, sir, but first let me go and say good-bye to my
people at home.' Jesus said to him, 'Once the hand is laid on the plow, no one
who looks back is fit for the kingdom of God.'

Luke 9:61–62

The Refrain
"Be still, then, and know that I am God;* I will be exalted among the nations; I will
be exalted in the earth."

The Morning Psalm　　　　　*A Thousand Years Are Like a Watch in the Night*
Lord, you have been our refuge* from one generation to another.
Before the mountains were brought forth, or the land and the earth were born,*
from age to age you are God.
You turn us back to the dust and say,* "Go back, O child of earth."
For a thousand years in your sight are like yesterday when it is past* and like a
watch in the night.
You sweep us away like a dream;* we fade away suddenly like the grass.
In the morning it is green and flourishes;* in the evening it is dried up and
withered.
For we consume away in your displeasure;* we are afraid because of your wrathful
indignation.
Our iniquities you have set before you,* and our secret sins in the light of your
countenance.
So teach us to number our days* that we may apply our hearts to wisdom.

Psalm 90:1–8, 12

The Refrain
"Be still, then, and know that I am God;* I will be exalted among the nations; I will
be exalted in the earth."

The Small Verse
The Son of Man shall be delivered over to the Gentiles, to be mocked and scourged
and crucified.

The Lord's Prayer

The Prayer Appointed for the Week
Almighty God, whose blessed Son was led by the Spirit to be tempted by Satan:
Come quickly to help us who are assaulted by many temptations; and, as you
know the weaknesses of each of us, let each one find you mighty to save;
through Jesus Christ your Son our Lord, who lives and reigns with you and the
Holy Spirit, one God, now and for ever. *Amen.* †

The Concluding Prayer of the Church
Lord God, almighty and everlasting Father, you have brought me in safety to this
  new day: Preserve me with your mighty power, that I may not fall into sin, nor
  be overcome by adversity; and in all I do direct me to the fulfilling of your purpose; through Jesus Christ my Lord. *Amen.* †

The Midday Office   To Be Observed on the Hour or Half Hour
                                       Between 11 a.m. and 2 p.m.

The Call to Prayer
Know this: The LORD himself is God;* he himself has made us, and we are his.
                                                            Psalm 100:2

The Request for Presence
May God be merciful to us and bless us,* show us the light of his countenance and
  come to us.
                                                            Psalm 67:1

The Greeting
I will confess you among the peoples, O LORD;* I will sing praise to you among the
  nations.
For your loving-kindness is greater than the heavens,* and your faithfulness
  reaches to the clouds.
                                                            Psalm 57:9–10

The Refrain for the Midday Lessons
Whoever is wise will ponder these things,* and consider well the mercies of
  the LORD.
                                                            Psalm 107:43

A Reading
As the chosen of God, then, the holy people whom he loves, you are to be clothed
  in heartfelt compassion, in generosity and humility, gentleness and patience.
                                                            Colossians 3:12

The Refrain
Whoever is wise will ponder these things,* and consider well the mercies of
  the LORD.

The Midday Psalm   *Behold and Tend This Vine, O God of Hosts*
Restore us, O God of hosts;* show the light of your countenance, and we shall be
  saved.
You have brought a vine out of Egypt;* you cast out the nations and planted it.
You prepared the ground for it;* it took root and filled the land.
The mountains were covered by its shadow* and the towering cedar trees by its
  boughs.
You stretched out its tendrils to the Sea* and its branches to the River.
Why have you broken down its wall,* so that all who pass by pluck off its grapes?

The wild boar of the forest has ravaged it,* and the beasts of the field have grazed
   upon it.
Turn now, O God of hosts, look down from heaven; behold and tend this vine;*
   preserve what your right hand has planted.

Psalm 80:7–14

The Refrain
Whoever is wise will ponder these things,* and consider well the mercies of
   the LORD.

The Small Verse
Truth shall spring up from the earth,* and righteousness shall look down from
   heaven.

Psalm 85:11

The Lord's Prayer

The Prayer Appointed for the Week
Almighty God, whose blessed Son was led by the Spirit to be tempted by Satan:
   Come quickly to help us who are assaulted by many temptations; and, as you
   know the weaknesses of each of us, let each one find you mighty to save;
   through Jesus Christ your Son our Lord, who lives and reigns with you and the
   Holy Spirit, one God, now and for ever. *Amen.* †

The Concluding Prayer of the Church
Lord God Almighty, you have made all the peoples of the earth for your glory, to
   serve you in freedom and in peace: Give to the people of our country a zeal for
   justice and the strength of forbearance, that we may use our liberty in accordance with your gracious will; through Jesus Christ our Lord, who lives and
   reigns with you and the Holy Spirit, one God, for ever and ever. *Amen.* †

The Vespers Office

**To Be Observed on the Hour or Half Hour
Between 5 and 8 p.m.**

The Call to Prayer
Sing praises to God, sing praises;* sing praises to our King, sing praises.

Psalm 47:6

The Request for Presence
O God, be not far from me;* come quickly to help me, O my God.

Psalm 71:12

The Greeting
For you, O God, have proved us;* you have tried us just as silver is tried.
You brought us into the snare;* you laid heavy burdens upon our backs.
You let enemies ride over our heads; we went through fire and water;* but you
   brought us out into a place of refreshment.

Psalm 66:9–11

The Hymn   *On the Crucifixion*
  Behold the Savior of mankind
  Nailed to the shameful tree;
  How vast the love that him inclined
  To bleed and die for me!

  Hark how he groans! While nature shakes,
  And earth's strong pillars bend!
  The temple's veil in sunder breaks,
  The solid marbles rend.

  It's done! The precious ransom's paid!
  "Receive my soul!" he cries;
  See how he bows his sacred head!
  He bows his head and dies!

  But soon he'll break death's envious chain
  And in full glory shine.
  O Lamb of God, was ever pain,
  Was ever love, like thine?
                          Samuel Wesley

The Refrain for the Vespers Lessons
The LORD, the God of gods, has spoken;* he has called the earth from the rising of
  the sun to its setting.
                                                        Psalm 50:1

The Vespers Psalm   *So That My Ways Were Made So Direct*
Happy are they whose way is blameless,* who walk in the law of the LORD!
Happy are they who observe his decrees* and seek him with all their hearts!
Who never do any wrong,* but always walk in his ways.
You laid down your commandments,* that we should fully keep them.
Oh, that my ways were made so direct* that I might keep your statutes!
Then I should not be put to shame,* when I regard all your commandments.
I will thank you with an unfeigned heart,* when I have learned your righteous
  judgments.
I will keep your statutes;* do not utterly forsake me.
                                                        Psalm 119:1–8

The Refrain
The LORD, the God of gods, has spoken;* he has called the earth from the rising of
  the sun to its setting.

The Small Verse
Create in me a clean heart, O God,* and renew a right spirit within me.
                                                        Psalm 51:11

The Lord's Prayer

The Prayer Appointed for the Week
Almighty God, whose blessed Son was led by the Spirit to be tempted by Satan:
Come quickly to help us who are assaulted by many temptations; and, as you
know the weaknesses of each of us, let each one find you mighty to save;
through Jesus Christ your Son our Lord, who lives and reigns with you and the
Holy Spirit, one God, now and for ever. *Amen.* †

The Concluding Prayer of the Church
Protect us, Lord, as we stay awake; watch over us as we sleep, that awake we may
watch with Christ, and asleep, rest in his peace. *Amen.*

The Morning Office   **To Be Observed on the Hour or Half Hour**
                                              Between 6 and 9 a.m.

The Call to Prayer
Open my lips, O LORD,* and my mouth shall proclaim your praise.
                                                        Psalm 51:16

The Request for Presence
Send out your light and your truth, that they may lead me,* and bring me to your
holy hill and to your dwelling.
                                                        Psalm 43:3

The Greeting
Who is like you, LORD God of hosts?* O mighty LORD, your faithfulness is all
around you.
Righteousness and justice are the foundations of your throne;* love and truth go
before your face.
                                                        Psalm 89:8ff

The Refrain for the Morning Lessons
I will walk in the presence of the LORD* in the land of the living.
                                                        Psalm 116:8

A Reading
Jesus taught us, saying: "And the judgement is this: though the light has come into
the world people have preferred darkness to the light because their deeds were
evil . . . but whoever does the truth comes out into the light, so that what he is
doing may plainly appear as done in God."
                                                        John 3:19, 21

The Refrain
I will walk in the presence of the LORD* in the land of the living.

The Morning Psalm   *It Is God by Whom We Escape Death*
O God, when you went forth before your people,* when you marched through the
wilderness,
The earth shook, and the skies poured down rain at the presence of God, the God
of Sinai,* at the presence of God, the God of Israel.

You sent a gracious rain, O God, upon your inheritance;* you refreshed the land
when it was weary.
Your people found their home in it;* in your goodness, O God, you have made
provision for the poor.
The chariots of God are twenty thousand, even thousands of thousands;* the Lord
comes in holiness from Sinai.
You have gone up on high and led captivity captive; you have received gifts even
from your enemies,* that the LORD God might dwell among them.
Blessed be the Lord day by day,* the God of our salvation, who bears our burdens.
He is our God, the God of our salvation;* God is the LORD, by whom we escape
death.

Psalm 68:7–10, 17–20

The Refrain

I will walk in the presence of the LORD* in the land of the living.

The Cry of the Church

In the evening, in the morning, and at noonday, I will complain and lament,* and
he will hear my voice.

Psalm 55:18

The Lord's Prayer

The Prayer Appointed for the Week

Almighty God, whose blessed Son was led by the Spirit to be tempted by Satan:
Come quickly to help us who are assaulted by many temptations; and, as you
know the weaknesses of each of us, let each one find you mighty to save;
through Jesus Christ your Son our Lord, who lives and reigns with you and the
Holy Spirit, one God, now and for ever. *Amen.* †

The Concluding Prayer of the Church

Lord God, almighty and everlasting Father, you have brought me in safety to this
new day: Preserve me with your mighty power, that I may not fall into sin, nor
be overcome by adversity; and in all I do direct me to the fulfilling of your purpose; through Jesus Christ my Lord. *Amen.* †

The Midday Office   **To Be Observed on the Hour or Half Hour**
Between 11 a.m. and 2 p.m.

The Call to Prayer

Open my lips, O Lord,* and my mouth shall proclaim your praise.

Psalm 51:16

The Request for Presence

Bow down your ear, O LORD, and answer me . . .
Keep watch over my life, for I am faithful.

Psalm 86:1–2

The Greeting
I will offer you the sacrifice of thanksgiving* and call upon the Name of the LORD.
Psalm 116:15

The Refrain for the Midday Lessons
The angel of the LORD encompasses those who fear him,* and he will deliver them.
Psalm 34:7

A Reading
YAHWEH said: "Can a woman forget her baby at the breast, feel no pity for the child she has borne? Even if these were to forget, I shall not forget you."
Isaiah 49:15

The Refrain
The angel of the LORD encompasses those who fear him,* and he will deliver them.

The Midday Psalm   *Your Love, O LORD, Upheld Me*
If the LORD had not come to my help,* I should soon have dwelt in the land of silence.
As often as I said, "My foot has slipped,"* your love, O LORD, upheld me.
When many cares fill my mind,* your consolations cheer my soul.
Psalm 94:17–19

The Refrain
The angel of the LORD encompasses those who fear him,* and he will deliver them.

The Cry of the Church
O God, come to my assistance!* O Lord, make haste to help me!

The Lord's Prayer

The Prayer Appointed for the Week
Almighty God, whose blessed Son was led by the Spirit to be tempted by Satan: Come quickly to help us who are assaulted by many temptations; and, as you know the weaknesses of each of us, let each one find you mighty to save; through Jesus Christ your Son our Lord, who lives and reigns with you and the Holy Spirit, one God, now and for ever. *Amen.* †

The Concluding Prayer of the Church
Most gracious God and Father, you are with me as I make my journey throughout this day. Help me to look lovingly upon all people and events that come into my life today and to walk gently upon this land. Grant this through Jesus who lives and walks among us ever present at each moment. *Amen.* †

The Vespers Office   **To Be Observed on the Hour or Half Hour**
Between 5 and 8 p.m.

The Call to Prayer
Come, let us bow down, and bend the knee,* and kneel before the LORD our Maker.
Psalm 95:6

The Request for Presence
Accept, O Lord, the willing tribute of my lips,* and teach me your judgments.
Psalm 119:108

The Greeting
O Lord of hosts,* happy are they who put their trust in you!
Psalm 84:12

The Hymn   *Beneath the Cross of Jesus*
Beneath the cross of Jesus I fain would take my stand,
The shadow of a mighty rock within a weary land,
A home within the wilderness, a rest upon the way,
From the burning noontime heat and the burden of the day.

Upon the cross of Jesus my eyes at times can see
The very dying form of one who suffered there for me;
And from my smitten heart with tears two wonders I confess:
The wonders of redeeming love and my unworthiness.

I take, O cross, your shadow for my abiding place;
I ask no other sunshine than the sunshine of his face;
Content to let my pride go by, to know no gain nor loss,
My sinful self my only shame, my glory all the cross.
Elizabeth Clephane

The Refrain for the Vespers Lessons
You have been gracious to your land, O Lord,* you have restored the good fortune
of Jacob.
Psalm 85:1

The Vespers Psalm   *I Will Listen to What the Lord God Is Saying*
Show us your mercy, O Lord,* and grant us your salvation.
I will listen to what the Lord God is saying,* for he is speaking peace to his faithful
people and to those who turn their hearts to him.
Truly, his salvation is very near to those who fear him,* that his glory may dwell in
our land.
Mercy and truth have met together;* righteousness and peace have kissed each
other.
Truth shall spring up from the earth,* and righteousness shall look down from
heaven.
The Lord will indeed grant prosperity,* and our land will yield its increase.
Righteousness shall go before him,* and peace shall be a pathway for his feet.
Psalm 85:7–13

The Refrain
You have been gracious to your land, O Lord,* you have restored the good fortune
of Jacob.

The Small Verse

The Son of man shall be delivered over to the Gentiles to be mocked and scourged and crucified.

The Lord's Prayer

The Prayer Appointed for the Week

Almighty God, whose blessed Son was led by the Spirit to be tempted by Satan: Come quickly to help us who are assaulted by many temptations; and, as you know the weaknesses of each of us, let each one find you mighty to save; through Jesus Christ your Son our Lord, who lives and reigns with you and the Holy Spirit, one God, now and for ever. *Amen.* †

The Concluding Prayer of the Church

O holy God, as evening falls remain with us, Remember our good deeds and forgive our failings. Help us to reflect upon and live according to your covenant of love. Be with our lonely and elderly sisters and brothers in the evening of their lives. May all who long to see you face to face know the comfort of your presence. This we ask in union with Simeon and Anna and all who have gone before us blessing and proclaiming you by the fidelity of their lives. *Amen.*

THE NEW COMPANION TO THE BREVIARY

The Morning Office   To Be Observed on the Hour or Half Hour
                                      Between 6 and 9 a.m.

The Call to Prayer

Fear the LORD, you that are his saints,* for those who fear him lack nothing.

Psalm 34:9

The Request for Presence

Be my strong rock, a castle to keep me safe;* you are my crag and my stronghold.

Psalm 71:3

The Greeting

O LORD, I cry to you for help;* in the morning my prayer comes before you.

Psalm 88:14

The Refrain for the Morning Lessons

God is a righteous judge;* God sits in judgment every day.

Psalm 7:12

A Reading

Then, speaking to all, he said, 'If anyone wants to be a follower of mine, let him renounce himself and take up his cross everyday and follow me.'

Luke 9:23

The Refrain

God is a righteous judge;* God sits in judgment every day.

The Morning Psalm   *Teach Us to Number Our Days*

The span of our life is seventy years, perhaps in strength even eighty;* yet the sum
   of them is but labor and sorrow, for they pass away quickly and we are gone.
Who regards the power of your wrath?* who rightly fears your indignation?
So teach us to number our days* that we may apply our hearts to wisdom.

Psalm 90:10–12

The Refrain
God is a righteous judge;* God sits in judgment every day.

The Small Verse
Today if you shall hear his voice, harden not your heart.

The Lord's Prayer

The Prayer Appointed for the Week
Almighty God, whose blessed Son was led by the Spirit to be tempted by Satan:
   Come quickly to help us who are assaulted by many temptations; and, as you
   know the weaknesses of each of us, let each one find you mighty to save;
   through Jesus Christ your Son our Lord, who lives and reigns with you and the
   Holy Spirit, one God, now and for ever. *Amen.* †

The Concluding Prayer of the Church
Lord God, almighty and everlasting Father, you have brought me in safety to this
   new day: Preserve me with your mighty power, that I may not fall into sin, nor
   be overcome by adversity; and in all I do direct me to the fulfilling of your purpose; through Jesus Christ my Lord. *Amen.* †

The Midday Office   To Be Observed on the Hour or Half Hour
                                                   Between 11 a.m. and 2 p.m.

The Call to Prayer
Come now and look upon the works of the LORD,* what awesome things he has
   done on earth.

Psalm 46:9

The Request for Presence
O LORD, I call to you; come to me quickly;* hear my voice when I cry to you.

Psalm 141:1

The Greeting
When I was in trouble, I called to the LORD;* I called to the LORD, and he answered
   me.

The Refrain for the Midday Lessons
Let them be put to shame and thrown back,* all those who are enemies of Zion.

Psalm 129:5

A Reading

With so many witnesses in a great cloud all around us, we too, then, should throw
off everything that weighs us down and the sin that clings so closely and with
perseverance keep running in the race which lies ahead of us.

Hebrews 12:1

The Refrain

Let them be put to shame and thrown back,* all those who are enemies of Zion.

The Midday Psalm   *Your Word Is a Light Upon My Path*

Your word is a lantern to my feet* and a light upon my path.

I have sworn and am determined* to keep your righteous judgments.

I am deeply troubled;* preserve my life, O Lord, according to your word.

Accept, O Lord, the willing tribute of my lips,* and teach me your judgments.

My life is always in my hand,* yet I do not forget your law.

The wicked have set a trap for me,* but I have not strayed from your
commandments.

Your decrees are my inheritance for ever;* truly, they are the joy of my heart.

I have applied my heart to fulfill your statutes* for ever and to the end.

Psalm 119:105–112

The Refrain

Let them be put to shame and thrown back,* all those who are enemies of Zion.

The Small Verse

From my secret sins cleanse me, Lord. And from all strange evils deliver me.

The Lord's Prayer

The Prayer Appointed for the Week

Almighty God, whose blessed Son was led by the Spirit to be tempted by Satan:
Come quickly to help us who are assaulted by many temptations; and, as you
know the weaknesses of each of us, let each one find you mighty to save;
through Jesus Christ your Son our Lord, who lives and reigns with you and the
Holy Spirit, one God, now and for ever. *Amen.* †

The Concluding Prayer of the Church

Lord Jesus Christ, by your death you took away the sting of death: Grant me to so
follow in faith where you have led the way, that I may at length fall asleep peacefully in you and wake in your likeness; for your tender mercies' sake. *Amen.* †

The Vespers Office   **To Be Observed on the Hour or Half Hour**
                                          Between 5 and 8 p.m.

The Call to Prayer

O tarry and await the Lord's pleasure; be strong, and he shall comfort your heart;*
wait patiently for the Lord.

Psalm 27:18

The Request for Presence
I have said to the LORD, "You are my God;* listen, O LORD, to my supplication."

Psalm 140:6

The Greeting
I am bound by the vow I made to you, O God;* I will present to you thank-
offerings;
For you have rescued my soul from death and my feet from stumbling,* that I may
walk before God in the light of the living.

Psalm 56:11–12

The Hymn   *Out of My Bondage, Sorrow, and Night*
Out of my bondage, sorrow, and night,
                    Jesus, I come, Jesus, I come;
Into Your freedom, gladness, and light,
                    Jesus, I come to You;
Out of my sickness into Your health,
Out of my want and into Your wealth,
Out of my sin and into Yourself,
                    Jesus, I come to You.

Out of my shameful failure and loss,
                    Jesus, I come, Jesus, I come;
Into the glorious gain of Your cross,
                    Jesus, I come to You;
Out of earth's sorrows into Your balm,
Out of life's storm and into Your calm,
Out of distress to jubilant psalm,
                    Jesus, I come to You;

Out of unrest and arrogant pride,
                    Jesus, I come, Jesus, I come;
Into Your blessed will to abide,
                    Jesus, I come to You;
Out of myself to dwell in Your love,
Out of despair into raptures above,
Upward for ever on wings like a dove,
                    Jesus, I come to You;

Out of the fear and dread of the tomb,
                    Jesus, I come, Jesus, I come;
Into the joy and light of Your home,
                    Jesus, I come to You;
Out of the depths of ruin untold,
Into the peace of Your sheltering fold,
Ever Your glorious face to behold,
                    Jesus, I come to You;

William Sleeper

The Refrain for the Vespers Lessons

Purge me from my sin, and I shall be pure;* wash me, and I shall be clean indeed.

Psalm 51:8

The Vespers Psalm *God Reveals Himself in Glory*

The LORD, the God of gods, has spoken;* he has called the earth from the rising of the sun to its setting.

Out of Zion, perfect in its beauty,* God reveals himself in glory.

Our God will come and will not keep silence;* before him there is a consuming flame, and round about him a raging storm.

He calls the heavens and the earth from above* to witness the judgment of his people.

"Gather before me my loyal followers,* those who have made a covenant with me* and sealed it with sacrifice."

Let the heavens declare the rightness of his cause;* for God himself is judge.

Psalm 50:1–6

The Refrain

Purge me from my sin, and I shall be pure;* wash me, and I shall be clean indeed.

The Cry of the Church

Lord, have mercy on us. Christ, have mercy on us. Lord, have mercy on us.

The Lord's Prayer

The Prayer Appointed for the Week

Almighty God, whose blessed Son was led by the Spirit to be tempted by Satan: Come quickly to help us who are assaulted by many temptations; and, as you know the weaknesses of each of us, let each one find you mighty to save; through Jesus Christ your Son our Lord, who lives and reigns with you and the Holy Spirit, one God, now and for ever. *Amen.* †

Concluding Prayers of the Church

Almighty God, who has promised to hear the petitions of those who ask in your Son's Name: I beseech you mercifully to incline your ear to me who have made my prayers and supplications to you; and grant that those things which I have faithfully asked according to your will, may effectually be obtained, to the relief of my necessity, and to the setting forth of your glory; through Jesus Christ my Lord. *Amen.* †

May the souls of the faithful departed, through the mercy of God, rest in eternal peace. *Amen.*

The Morning Office **To Be Observed on the Hour or Half Hour**
Between 6 and 9 a.m.

The Call to Prayer

Praise the LORD, for the LORD is good;* sing praises to his Name for it is lovely.

Psalm 135:1

The Request for Presence
In your righteousness, deliver and set me free;* incline your ear to me and save me.
Psalm 71:2

The Greeting
O LORD I am your servant;* I am your servant and the child of your handmaid.
Psalm 116:14

The Refrain for the Morning Lessons
I was pressed so hard that I almost fell,* but the LORD came to my help.
Psalm 118:13

A Reading
Jesus said: "Jerusalem, Jerusalem, you that kill the prophets and stone those who
  are sent to you! How often have I longed to gather your children together, as a
  hen gathers her brood under her wings, and you refused! Look! Your house
  will be left to you. Yes, I promise you, you shall not see me till the time comes
  when you are saying: *Blessed is he who comes in the name of the Lord!*"
Luke 13:34–35

The Refrain
I was pressed so hard that I almost fell,* but the LORD came to my help.

The Morning Psalm   *O LORD, I Am Your Servant*
Precious in the sight of the LORD* is the death of his servants.
O LORD, I am your servant;* I am your servant and the child of your handmaid;
  you have freed me from my bonds.
I will offer you the sacrifice of thanksgiving* and call upon the Name of the LORD.
I will fulfill my vows to the LORD* in the presence of all his people,
In the courts of the LORD's house,* in the midst of you, O Jerusalem.
Psalm 116:13–17

The Refrain
I was pressed so hard that I almost fell,* but the LORD came to my help.

The Cry of the Church
O God, come to my assistance! O Lord, make haste to help me!

The Lord's Prayer

The Prayer Appointed for the Week
Almighty God, whose blessed Son was led by the Spirit to be tempted by Satan:
  Come quickly to help us who are assaulted by many temptations; and, as you
  know the weaknesses of each of us, let each one find you mighty to save;
  through Jesus Christ your Son our Lord, who lives and reigns with you and the
  Holy Spirit, one God, now and for ever. *Amen.* †

The Concluding Prayer of the Church
Lord God, almighty and everlasting Father, you have brought me in safety to this
  new day: Preserve me with your mighty power, that I may not fall into sin, nor

be overcome by adversity; and in all I do direct me to the fulfilling of your purpose; through Jesus Christ my Lord. *Amen.* †

The Midday Office   To Be Observed on the Hour or Half Hour
Between 11 a.m. and 2 p.m.

The Call to Prayer
Ascribe to the LORD the honor due his Name;* bring offerings and come into his courts.

Psalm 96:8

The Request for Presence
Accept, O LORD, the willing tribute of my lips,* and teach me your judgments.

Psalm 119:108

The Greeting
I give you thanks, O God, I give you thanks,* calling upon your Name and declaring all your wonderful deeds.

based on Psalm 75:1

The Refrain for the Midday Lessons
My tongue will proclaim your righteousness all day long.

Psalm 71:24

A Reading
'Come, let us talk this over,' says YAHWEH. 'Though your sins are like scarlet, they shall be white as snow; though they are as red as crimson, they shall be like wool. If you are willing to obey, you shall eat the good things of the earth. But if you refuse and rebel, the sword shall eat you instead—for YAHWEH's mouth has spoken.'

Isaiah 1:18–20

The Refrain
My tongue will proclaim your righteousness all day long.

The Midday Psalm   *We Will Not Let Hide What Our Forefathers Have Told Us*
Hear my teaching, O my people;* incline your ears to the words of my mouth.
I will open my mouth in a parable;* I will declare the mysteries of ancient times.
That which we have heard and known, and what our forefathers have told us,* we will not hide from their children.
We will recount to generations to come the praiseworthy deeds and the power of the LORD,* and the wonderful works he has done.
He gave his decrees to Jacob and established a law for Israel,* which he commanded them to teach their children;
That the generations to come might know, and the children yet unborn;* that they in their turn might tell it to their children;

So that they might put their trust in God,* and not forget the deeds of God, but
keep his commandments;

Psalm 78:1–7

The Refrain
My tongue will proclaim your righteousness all day long.

The Cry of the Church
O God, come to my assistance! O Lord, make haste to help me!

The Lord's Prayer

The Prayer Appointed for the Week
Almighty God, whose blessed Son was led by the Spirit to be tempted by Satan:
Come quickly to help us who are assaulted by many temptations; and, as you
know the weaknesses of each of us, let each one find you mighty to save;
through Jesus Christ your Son our Lord, who lives and reigns with you and the
Holy Spirit, one God, now and for ever. *Amen.* †

The Concluding Prayer of the Church
O God, the source of eternal light: Shed forth your unending day upon all of us
who watch for you, that our lips may praise you, our lives may bless you, and
our worship may give you glory; through Jesus Christ our Lord. *Amen.* †

The Vespers Office   **To Be Observed on the Hour or Half Hour**
Between 5 and 8 p.m.

The Call to Prayer
Proclaim with me the greatness of the LORD;* let us exalt his Name together.

Psalm 34:8

The Request for Presence
. . . Come to me speedily, O God* . . .

Psalm 70:5

The Greeting
And now that I am old and gray-headed, O God, do not forsake me,* till I make
known your strength to this generation and your power to all who are to come.
Your righteousness, O God, reaches to the heavens;*

Psalm 72:18–19

The Hymn   *Lord, I'm Coming Home*
I've wandered far away from God,
Now I'm coming home;
The paths of sin too long I've trod.
Lord, I'm coming home.
Coming home, coming home,
Nevermore to roam,
Open wide Your loving arms,
O Lord, I'm coming home.

I've wasted many precious years,
Now I'm coming home;
I now repent with bitter tears,
Lord, I'm coming home.

I've tired of sin and straying, Lord,
Now I'm coming home;
I'll trust Your love, believe Your word,
Lord, I'm coming home.

My soul is sick, my heart is sore,
Now I'm coming home;
My strength renew, my hope restore,
Lord, I'm coming home.
Now I'm coming home;
Lord, I'm coming home.
Coming home, coming home,
Nevermore to roam,
Open wide Your loving arms,
O Lord, I'm coming home.

William Kirkpatrick

The Refrain for the Vespers Lessons
Let them know that you, whose Name is YAHWEH,* you alone are the Most High
over all the earth.

Psalm 83:18

The Vespers Psalm   *I Meditate on You in the Night Watches*
O God, you are my God; eagerly I seek you;* my soul thirsts for you, my flesh
faints for you, as in a barren and dry land where there is no water.
Therefore I have gazed upon you in your holy place,* that I might behold your
power and your glory.
For your loving-kindness is better than life itself;* my lips shall give you praise.
So will I bless you as long as I live* and lift up my hands in your Name.
My soul is content, as with marrow and fatness,* and my mouth praises you with
joyful lips,
When I remember you upon my bed,* and meditate on you in the night watches.
For you have been my helper,* and under the shadow of your wings I will rejoice.
My soul clings to you;* your right hand holds me fast.

Psalm 63:1–8

The Refrain
Let them know that you, whose Name is YAHWEH,* you alone are the Most High
over all the earth.

The Small Verse
From the rising of the sun to the place of its going down, let the name of the Lord
be praised henceforth and forever more.

The Lord's Prayer

The Prayer Appointed for the Week
Almighty God, whose blessed Son was led by the Spirit to be tempted by Satan:
Come quickly to help us who are assaulted by many temptations; and, as you
know the weaknesses of each of us, let each one find you mighty to save;
through Jesus Christ your Son our Lord, who lives and reigns with you and the
Holy Spirit, one God, now and for ever. *Amen.* †

The Concluding Prayer of the Church
Glory to the Father, who has woven garments of glory for the resurrection; wor-
ship to the Son, who was clothed in them at his rising; thanksgiving to the
Spirit, who keeps them for all the Saints; one nature in three, to him be praise.

Syrian Orthodox

The Morning Office   To Be Observed on the Hour or Half Hour
                                               Between 6 and 9 a.m.

The Call to Prayer
Worship the LORD in the beauty of holiness;* let the whole earth tremble before
him.

Psalm 96:9

The Request for Presence
Return, O LORD; how long will you tarry?* be gracious to your servants.

Psalm 90:13

The Greeting
Awesome things will you show us in your righteousness, O God of our salvation,*
O Hope of all the ends of the earth and of the seas that are far away.

Psalm 65:5

The Refrain for the Morning Lessons
For he shall give his angels charge over you,* to keep you in all your ways.

Psalm 91:11

A Reading
Jesus said to his disciples: "For your part, you must have these words constantly
in your mind: The Son of man is going to be delivered into the power of men."
But they did not understand what he said; it was hidden from them so that
they should not see the meaning of it, and they were afraid to ask him about it.

Luke 9:44–45

The Refrain
For he shall give his angels charge over you,* to keep you in all your ways.

The Morning Psalm   *Teach Us to Number Our Days*
For a thousand years in your sight are like yesterday when it is past* and like a
    watch in the night.
You sweep us away like a dream;* we fade away suddenly like the grass.
In the morning it is green and flourishes;* in the evening it is dried up and withered.
For we consume away in your displeasure;* we are afraid because of your wrathful
    indignation.
Our iniquities you have set before you,* and our secret sins in the light of your
    countenance.
When you are angry, all our days are gone;* we bring our years to an end like
    a sigh.
The span of our life is seventy years, perhaps in strength even eighty;* yet the sum
    of them is but labor and sorrow, for they pass away quickly and we are gone.
Who regards the power of your wrath?* who rightly fears your indignation?
So teach us to number our days* that we may apply our hearts to wisdom.

Psalm 90:4–12

The Refrain
For he shall give his angels charge over you,* to keep you in all your ways.

The Cry of the Church
O Lord, hear my prayer and let my cry come unto you. Thanks be to God.

THE SHORT BREVIARY

The Lord's Prayer

The Prayer Appointed for the Week
O God, whose glory it is always to have mercy: Be gracious to all who have gone
    astray from your ways, and bring us again with penitent hearts and steadfast
    faith to embrace and hold fast the unchangeable truth of your Word, Jesus
    Christ your Son; who with you and the Holy Spirit lives and reigns, one God,
    for ever and ever. *Amen.* †

The Concluding Prayer of the Church
Lord God, almighty and everlasting Father, you have brought me in safety to this
    new day: Preserve me with your mighty power, that I may not fall into sin, nor
    be overcome by adversity; and in all I do direct me to the fulfilling of your pur-
    pose; through Jesus Christ my Lord. *Amen.* †

The Midday Office   **To Be Observed on the Hour or Half Hour**
                                              Between 11 a.m. and 2 p.m.

The Call to Prayer
Let the Name of the LORD be blessed,* from this time forth for evermore.

Psalm 113:2

The Request for Presence

Let the peoples praise you, O God;* let all the peoples praise you.

Psalm 67:3

The Greeting

For you alone are the Holy One, you alone are the Lord, you alone are the Most
High, Jesus Christ, with the Holy Spirit, in the glory of God the Father.

The Refrain for the Midday Lessons

Tell it out among the nations: "The LORD is King!* he has made the world so firm
that it cannot be moved; he will judge the peoples with equity."

Psalm 96:10

A Reading

He had done nothing wrong, and *had spoken no deceit*. He was insulted and did not
retaliate with insults; when he was suffering he made no threats but put his
trust in the upright judge. He was *bearing our sins* in his own body on the cross,
so that we might die to our sins and live for uprightness . . .

I Peter 2:22–24

The Refrain

Tell it out among the nations: "The LORD is King!* he has made the world so firm
that it cannot be moved; he will judge the peoples with equity."

The Midday Psalm   The LORD Most High Is to Be Feared

For the LORD Most High is to be feared;* he is the great King over all the earth.
He subdues the peoples under us,* and the nations under our feet.
He chooses our inheritance for us,* the pride of Jacob whom he loves.
God has gone up with a shout,* the LORD with the sound of the ram's-horn.
Sing praises to God, sing praises;* sing praises to our King, sing praises.
For God is King of all the earth;* sing praises with all your skill.
God reigns over the nations;* God sits upon his holy throne.
The nobles of the peoples have gathered together* with the people of the God of
Abraham.
The rulers of the earth belong to God,* and he is highly exalted.

Psalm 47:2–10

The Refrain

Tell it out among the nations: "The LORD is King!* he has made the world so firm
that it cannot be moved; he will judge the peoples with equity."

The Small Verse

The Son of man shall be delivered over to the gentiles to be mocked, scourged, and
crucified.

The Lord's Prayer

The Prayer Appointed for the Week

O God, whose glory it is always to have mercy: Be gracious to all who have gone
astray from your ways, and bring us again with penitent hearts and steadfast

faith to embrace and hold fast the unchangeable truth of your Word, Jesus Christ your Son; who with you and the Holy Spirit lives and reigns, one God, for ever and ever. *Amen.* †

The Concluding Prayer of the Church

O God, you make me glad with the weekly remembrance of the glorious resurrection of your Son my Lord: Give me this day such blessing through my worship of you, that the week to come may be spent in your favor; through Jesus Christ our Lord. *Amen.* †

The Vespers Office   **To Be Observed on the Hour or Half Hour**
Between 5 and 8 p.m.

The Call to Prayer

Praise the Lord from the heavens;* praise him in the heights.

Psalm 148:1

The Request for Presence

You are my helper and my deliverer;* O Lord, do not tarry.

Psalm 70:6

The Greeting

O Lord, I am your servant;* I am your servant and the child of your handmaid.

Psalm 116:14

The Hymn   *Come, Let Us Join Our Friends Above*

Come, let us join our friends above, who have obtained the prize,
And on eagle wings of love to joys celestial rise.
Let saints on earth unite to sing with those to glory gone,
For all the servants of our King in earth and heaven are one.

One family we dwell in him, one church above, beneath,
Though divided by the stream, the narrow stream of death;
One army of the living God, to his command we bow;
Part of his host have crossed the flood, and part are crossing now.

Ten thousand to their endless home this solemn moment fly,
And we are to the margin come, and we expect to die.
Even so by faith we join our hands with those that went before,
And greet the blood besprinkled bands on that eternal shore.

Charles Wesley

The Refrain for the Vespers Lessons

Turn again to your rest, O my soul,* for the Lord has treated you well.

Psalm 116:6

The Vespers Psalm   *My Soul Is Content*

O God, you are my God; eagerly I seek you;* my soul thirsts for you, my flesh faints for you, as in a barren and dry land where there is no water.

Therefore I have gazed upon you in your holy place,* that I might behold your
power and your glory.
For your loving-kindness is better than life itself;* my lips shall give you praise.
So will I bless you as long as I live* and lift up my hands in your Name.
My soul is content, as with marrow and fatness,* and my mouth praises you with
joyful lips,
When I remember you upon my bed,* and meditate on you in the night watches.
For you have been my helper,* and under the shadow of your wings I will rejoice.

Psalm 63:1–7

The Refrain
Turn again to your rest, O my soul,* for the LORD has treated you well.

The Cry of the Church
O Lamb of God, that takes away the sins of the world, have mercy on me.
O Lamb of God, that takes away the sins of the world, have mercy on me.
O Lamb of God, that takes away the sins of the world, grant me your peace.

The Lord's Prayer

The Prayer Appointed for the Week
O God, whose glory it is always to have mercy: Be gracious to all who have gone
astray from your ways, and bring us again with penitent hearts and steadfast
faith to embrace and hold fast the unchangeable truth of your Word, Jesus
Christ your Son; who with you and the Holy Spirit lives and reigns, one God,
for ever and ever. *Amen.* †

Concluding Prayers of the Church
O God, who in your unspeakable providence deigned to choose blessed Joseph for
your most holy Mother's spouse, grant I pray, that we who today celebrate his
place as a protector on earth may prove worthy to have him as an intercessor in
heaven.

adapted from THE SHORT BREVIARY

Lord God, whose Son our Savior Jesus Christ, triumphed over the powers of death
and prepared for us our place in the new Jerusalem: Grant that I, who have this
day given thanks for his resurrection, may praise you in the City of which he is
the light, and where he lives and reigns for ever and ever. *Amen.* †

The Morning Office   **To Be Observed on the Hour or Half Hour**
Between 6 and 9 a.m.

The Call to Prayer
Love the LORD, all you who worship him;* the LORD protects the faithful, but
repays to the full those who act haughtily.

Psalm 31:23

The Request for Presence
Be my strong rock, a castle to keep me safe, for you are my crag and my stronghold;*
    for the sake of your Name, lead me and guide me.

Psalm 31:3

The Greeting
How great is your goodness, O LORD!* which you have laid up for those who fear
    you; which you have done in the sight of all.

Psalm 31:19

The Refrain for the Morning Lessons
He multiplies the victories of his king;* he shows loving-kindness to his anointed,
    to David and his descendants for ever.

Psalm 18:50

A Reading   *On March 19, the Church celebrates the life of St. Joseph,*
a descendant of King David and earthly father of
our Lord. Joseph is honored for his obedience, his
constancy, and his protection of the Virgin and of the
boy Jesus.

Every year his parents used to go to Jerusalem for the feast of the Passover. When
    he was twelve years old, they went up for the feast as usual. When the days of
the feast were over and they set off for home, the boy Jesus stayed behind in
Jerusalem without his parents knowing it. They assumed he was somewhere in
the party, and it was only after a day's journey that they went to look for him
among their relations and acquaintances. When they failed to find him they
went back to Jerusalem looking for him everywhere. It happened that, three
days later, they found him in the Temple, sitting among the teachers, listening
to them, and asking them questions; and all those who heard him were
astounded at his intelligence and his replies. They were overcome when they
saw him, and his mother said to him, 'My child, why have you done this to us?
See how worried your father and I have been, looking for you.' He replied,
'Why were you looking for me? Did you not know that I must be in my
Father's house?' But they did not understand what he meant. He went down
with them and came to Nazareth and lived under their authority. His mother
stored up all these things in her heart. And Jesus increased in wisdom, in
stature, and in favor with God and with people.

Luke 2:41–52

The Refrain
He multiplies the victories of his king;* he shows loving-kindness to his anointed,
    to David and his descendants for ever.

The Morning Psalm   *I Have Sworn an Oath to David*
Your love, O LORD, for ever will I sing;* from age to age my mouth will proclaim
    your faithfulness.

For I am persuaded that your love is established for ever;* you have set your
faithfulness firmly in the heavens.

"I have made a covenant with my chosen one;* I have sworn an oath to David my
servant:

'I will establish your line for ever,* and preserve your throne for all generations.'"

Psalm 89:1–4

The Refrain
He multiplies the victories of his king;* he shows loving-kindness to his anointed,
to David and his descendants for ever.

The Cry of the Church
Let him be honored who is the protector of his Lord.

THE SHORT BREVIARY

The Lord's Prayer

The Prayer Appointed for the Week
O God, whose glory it is always to have mercy: Be gracious to all who have gone
astray from your ways, and bring us again with penitent hearts and steadfast
faith to embrace and hold fast the unchangeable truth of your Word, Jesus
Christ your Son; who with you and the Holy Spirit lives and reigns, one God,
for ever and ever. *Amen.* †

Concluding Prayers of the Church
O God, who from the family of your servant David raised up Joseph to be the
guardian of your incarnate Son and the spouse of his virgin mother: Give me
grace to imitate his uprightness of life and his obedience to your commands;
through Jesus Christ our Lord, who lives and reigns with you and the Holy
Spirit, one God, for ever and ever. *Amen.* †

Lord God, almighty and everlasting Father, you have brought me in safety to this
new day: Preserve me with your mighty power, that I may not fall into sin, nor
be overcome by adversity; and in all I do direct me to the fulfilling of your purpose; through Jesus Christ my Lord. *Amen.* †

The Midday Office   **To Be Observed on the Hour or Half Hour**
                                Between 11 a.m. and 2 p.m.

The Call to Prayer
Be glad, you righteous, and rejoice in the LORD;* shout for joy, all who are true of
heart.

Psalm 32:12

The Request for Presence
LORD, hear my prayer, and let my cry come before you;* hide not your face from
me in the day of my trouble.

Psalm 102:1

The Greeting
Be exalted, O LORD, in your might;* we will sing and praise your power.
Psalm 21:14

The Refrain for the Midday Lessons
My help comes from the LORD,* the maker of heaven and earth.
Psalm 121:2

A Reading
But that very night, the word of YAHWEH came to Nathan: 'Go and tell my servant
    David, "YAHWEH says this: I took you from the pasture from following the
    sheep to be leader of my people Israel; I have been with you wherever you
    went: I have got rid of all your enemies on earth. YAHWEH furthermore tells you
    that he will make you a dynasty. And when your days are over and you fall
    asleep with your ancestors, I shall appoint you an heir, your own son to suc-
    ceed you (and I shall make his sovereignty secure). I shall be a father to him
    and he a son to me. Your dynasty and your sovereignty will ever stand firm
    before me and your throne be for ever secure."' Nathan related all these words
    and his whole revelation to David.
II Samuel 7:4ff

The Refrain
My help comes from the LORD,* the maker of heaven and earth.

The Midday Psalm   *Let Everything That Has Breath Praise the LORD*
Hallelujah! Praise God in his holy temple;* praise him in the firmament of his
    power.
Praise him for his mighty acts;* praise him for his excellent greatness.
Praise him with the blast of the ram's-horn;* praise him with lyre and harp.
Praise him with timbrel and dance;* praise him with strings and pipe.
Praise him with resounding cymbals;* praise him with loud-clanging cymbals.
Let everything that has breath* praise the LORD. Hallelujah!
Psalm 150

The Refrain
My help comes from the LORD,* the maker of heaven and earth.

The Gloria*

The Lord's Prayer

The Prayer Appointed for the Week
O God, whose glory it is always to have mercy: Be gracious to all who have gone
    astray from your ways, and bring us again with penitent hearts and steadfast
    faith to embrace and hold fast the unchangeable truth of your Word, Jesus
    Christ your Son; who with you and the Holy Spirit lives and reigns, one God,
    for ever and ever. *Amen.* †

The Concluding Prayer of the Church
Almighty God, heavenly Father, you have blessed us with the joy and care of children: Give us calm strength and patient wisdom as we bring them up so that we may teach them to love whatever is just and true and good, following the example of blessed St. Joseph, through Jesus Christ our Lord. *Amen.* †

The Vespers Office   To Be Observed on the Hour or Half Hour
                                                     Between 5 and 8 p.m.

The Call to Prayer
Sing to the LORD a new song;* sing to the LORD, all the whole earth.
For great is the LORD and greatly to be praised;* he is more to be feared than all gods.

Psalm 96:1, 4

The Request for Presence
Teach me your way, O LORD, and I will walk in your truth;* knit my heart to you that I may fear your Name.

Psalm 86:11

The Greeting
Your way, O God, is holy;* who is so great a god as our God?

Psalm 77:13

The Hymn
Blessed are the pure in heart,
For they will see our God:
The secret of the Lord is theirs,
Their soul is Christ's abode.

The Lord, who left the heavens
Our life and peace to bring,
To dwell in lowliness with men,
Their pattern and their king:

Still to the lowly soul
He does himself impart,
And for his dwelling and his throne
Chooses the pure of heart.

Lord, we your presence seek;
May ours this blessing be:
That we like father Joseph meek
Providing a housing fit for thee.

J. Keble

The Refrain for the Vespers Lessons

Ascribe to the Lord, you families of the peoples;* ascribe to the Lord honor and
power.

Psalm 96:7

The Vespers Psalm   *Light Shines in Darkness for the Upright*

Light shines in the darkness for the upright;* the righteous are merciful and full of
compassion.

It is good for them to be generous in lending* and to manage their affairs with
justice.

For they will never be shaken;* the righteous will be kept in everlasting
remembrance.

They will not be afraid of any evil rumors;* their heart is right; they put their trust
in the Lord.

Their heart is established and will not shrink,* until they see their desire upon
their enemies.

They have given freely to the poor,* and their righteousness stands fast for ever;
they will hold up their head with honor.

The wicked will see it and be angry; they will gnash their teeth and pine away;*
the desires of the wicked will perish.

Psalm 112:4–10

The Refrain

Ascribe to the Lord, you families of the peoples;* ascribe to the Lord honor and
power.

The Small Verse

From the rising of the sun to the place of its going down, let the name of the Lord
be praised henceforth and forever more.

The Lord's Prayer

The Prayer Appointed for the Week

O God, whose glory it is always to have mercy: Be gracious to all who have gone
astray from your ways, and bring us again with penitent hearts and steadfast
faith to embrace and hold fast the unchangeable truth of your Word, Jesus
Christ your Son; who with you and the Holy Spirit lives and reigns, one God,
for ever and ever. *Amen.* †

The Concluding Prayer of the Church

Almighty God, our heavenly Father, who sets the solitary in families: I commend
to your continual care the homes in which your people dwell. Put far from
them, I beseech you, every root of bitterness, the desire of vainglory, and the
pride of life. Fill them like your servant St. Joseph with faith, virtue, knowledge, temperance, patience, godliness. Knit together in constant affection those
who, in holy wedlock, have been made one flesh. Turn the hearts of the parents
to the children, and the hearts of the children to the parents; and so enkindle

fervent charity among us all, that we may evermore be kindly affectioned one to another; through Jesus Christ our Lord. *Amen.* †

The Morning Office   To Be Observed on the Hour or Half Hour
                                      Between 6 and 9 a.m.

The Call to Prayer
God is King of all the earth;* sing praises with all your skill.
God reigns over the nations;* God sits upon his holy throne.

Psalm 47:7–8

The Request for Presence
Be pleased, O God, to deliver me;* O LORD, make haste to help me.

Psalm 70:1

The Greeting
Our God will come and will not keep silence;* before him there is a consuming
    flame, and round about him a raging storm.

Psalm 50:3

The Refrain for the Morning Lessons
The fool has said in his heart, "There is no God."

Psalm 14:1

A Reading
Jesus taught us, saying: "Who, then, is the wise and trustworthy servant whom
    the master placed over his household to give them their food at the proper
    time? Blessed that servant if the master's arrival finds him doing exactly that.
    In truth I tell you, he will put him in charge of everything he owns. But if the
    servant is dishonest and says to himself, 'My master is taking his time,' and
    sets about beating his fellow-servants and eating and drinking with drunk-
    ards, his master will come on a day he does not expect and at an hour he does
    not know. The master will cut him off and send him to the same fate as the hyp-
    ocrites, where there will be weeping and grinding of teeth."

Matthew 24:45–51

The Refrain
The fool has said in his heart, "There is no God."

The Morning Psalm   *The LORD Will Root Out the Remembrance of the Evil*
The eyes of the LORD are upon the righteous,* and his ears are open to their cry.
The face of the LORD is against those who do evil,* to root out the remembrance of
    them from the earth.
The righteous cry, and the LORD hears them* and delivers them from all their
    troubles.
The LORD is near to the brokenhearted* and will save those whose spirits are
    crushed.

Many are the troubles of the righteous,* but the Lord will deliver him out of
them all.
He will keep safe all his bones;* not one of them shall be broken.

Psalm 34:15–20

The Refrain
The fool has said in his heart, "There is no God."

The Cry of the Church
Lord, have mercy on us. Christ, have mercy on us. Lord, have mercy on us.

The Lord's Prayer

The Prayer Appointed for the Week
O God, whose glory it is always to have mercy: Be gracious to all who have gone
astray from your ways, and bring us again with penitent hearts and steadfast
faith to embrace and hold fast the unchangeable truth of your Word, Jesus
Christ your Son; who with you and the Holy Spirit lives and reigns, one God,
for ever and ever. *Amen.* †

The Concluding Prayer of the Church
Lord God, almighty and everlasting Father, you have brought me in safety to this
new day: Preserve me with your mighty power, that I may not fall into sin, nor
be overcome by adversity; and in all I do direct me to the fulfilling of your purpose; through Jesus Christ my Lord. *Amen.* †

The Midday Office　　　　　　　　　To Be Observed on the Hour or Half Hour
Between 11 a.m. and 2 p.m.

The Call to Prayer
I will sing to the Lord as long as I live;* I will praise my God while I have my
being.
May these words of mine please him.

Psalm 104:34–35

The Request for Presence
O God, come to my assistance! O Lord, make haste to help me!

The Greeting
I will give thanks to you, for you answered me* and have become my salvation.

Psalm 118:21

The Refrain for the Midday Lessons
I will walk in the presence of the Lord* in the land of the living.

Psalm 116:8

A Reading
Barnabas then left for Tarsus to look for Saul, and when he found him he brought
him to Antioch. And it happened that they stayed together in that church a

whole year, instructing a large number of people. It was at Antioch that the disciples were first called 'Christians.'

Acts 11:25–26

The Refrain

I will walk in the presence of the LORD* in the land of the living.

The Midday Psalm   *Let All the Earth Fear the LORD*

The LORD looks down from heaven,* and beholds all the people in the world.
From where he sits enthroned he turns his gaze* on all who dwell on the earth.
He fashions all the hearts of them* and understands all their works.
There is no king that can be saved by a mighty army;* a strong man is not
     delivered by his great strength.
The horse is a vain hope for deliverance;* for all its strength it cannot save.
Behold, the eye of the LORD is upon those who fear him,* on those who wait upon
     his love,
To pluck their lives from death,* and to feed them in time of famine.

Psalm 33:13–19

The Refrain

I will walk in the presence of the LORD* in the land of the living.

The Cry of the Church

Even so come, Lord Jesus!

The Lord's Prayer

The Prayer Appointed for the Week

O God, whose glory it is always to have mercy: Be gracious to all who have gone
     astray from your ways, and bring us again with penitent hearts and steadfast
     faith to embrace and hold fast the unchangeable truth of your Word, Jesus
     Christ your Son; who with you and the Holy Spirit lives and reigns, one God,
     for ever and ever. *Amen.* †

The Concluding Prayer of the Church

Almighty and eternal God, ruler of all things in heaven and earth: Mercifully
     accept the prayers of your people everywhere, and strengthen each of us to do
     your will; through Jesus Christ my Lord. *Amen.* †

The Vespers Office   **To Be Observed on the Hour or Half Hour**
                                              Between 5 and 8 p.m.

The Call to Prayer

Worship the LORD, O Jerusalem;* praise your God, O Zion.

Psalm 147:13

The Request for Presence

Make me understand the way of your commandments,* that I may meditate on
your marvelous works.

Psalm 119:27

The Greeting

At your rebuke, O God of Jacob,* both horse and rider lie stunned.
What terror you inspire!* who can stand before you when you are angry?

Psalm 76:6–7

The Hymn

Abroad the royal banners fly,
Now shines the Cross's mystery;
Upon it Life did death endure,
And yet by death did life procure.

O Tree of light! Whose branches shine
With purple, royal and divine!
Elect, on whose triumphal breast
Those holy limbs should find their rest.

O Cross, our one reliance, hail!
This holy Lententide avail
To give fresh merit to the saint
And pardon to the penitent.

Blessed Trinity, salvation's spring,
May every soul Your praises sing;
To those You grant conquest by
The holy Cross, rewards apply.

THE SHORT BREVIARY

The Refrain for the Vespers Lessons

Righteousness and justice are the foundations of your throne;* love and truth go
before your face.

Psalm 89:14

The Vespers Psalm   *I Will Establish His Line For Ever*

You spoke once in a vision and said to your faithful people:* "I have set the crown
upon a warrior and have exalted one chosen out of the people.
I have found David my servant;* with my holy oil have I anointed him.
My hand will hold him fast* and my arm will make him strong.
No enemy shall deceive him,* nor any wicked man bring him down.
I will crush his foes before him* and strike down those who hate him.
My faithfulness and love shall be with him,* and he shall be victorious through
my Name.
I shall make his dominion extend* from the Great Sea to the River.

He will say to me, 'You are my Father,* my God, and the rock of my salvation.'
I will make him my firstborn* and higher than the kings of the earth.
I will keep my love for him for ever,* and my covenant will stand firm for him.
I will establish his line for ever* and his throne as the days of heaven."

Psalm 89:19–29

The Refrain
Righteousness and justice are the foundations of your throne;* love and truth go
before your face.

The Small Verse
The Son of man shall be handed over to the gentiles, to be mocked, scourged, and
crucified.

The Lord's Prayer

The Prayer Appointed for the Week
O God, whose glory it is always to have mercy: Be gracious to all who have gone
astray from your ways, and bring us again with penitent hearts and steadfast
faith to embrace and hold fast the unchangeable truth of your Word, Jesus
Christ your Son; who with you and the Holy Spirit lives and reigns, one God,
for ever and ever. *Amen.* †

The Concluding Prayer of the Church
Lord Jesus Christ, you have prepared a quiet place for us in your Father's eternal
home. Watch over our welfare on this perilous journey, shade us from the
burning heat of day, and keep our lives free of evil until the end. *Amen.*

THE LITURGY OF THE HOURS, VOL. III

The Morning Office

**To Be Observed on the Hour or Half Hour
Between 6 and 9 a.m.**

The Call to Prayer
Let us make a vow to the LORD our God and keep it;* let all around him bring gifts
to him who is worthy to be feared.

Psalm 76:11

The Request for Presence
Let my cry come before you, O LORD;* give me understanding, according to your
word.
Let my supplication come before you;* deliver me, according to your promise.

Psalm 119:169–170

The Greeting
I will offer you a freewill sacrifice* and praise your Name, O LORD, for it is good.

Psalm 54:6

The Refrain for the Morning Lessons

With my whole heart I seek you;* let me not stray from your commandments.

Psalm 119:10

A Reading

He said to his disciples, 'Causes of falling are sure to come, but alas for the one through whom they occur! It would be better for him to be thrown into the sea with a millstone round the neck than to be the downfall of a single one of these little ones. Keep watch on yourselves!'

Luke 17:1–3

The Refrain

With my whole heart I seek you;* let me not stray from your commandments.

The Morning Psalm   *Only You, LORD, Make Me Dwell in Safety*

Answer me when I call, O God, defender of my cause;* you set me free when I am hard-pressed; have mercy on me and hear my prayer.

"You mortals, how long will you dishonor my glory;* how long will you worship dumb idols and run after false gods?"

Know that the LORD does wonders for the faithful;* when I call upon the LORD, he will hear me.

Tremble, then, and do not sin;* speak to your heart in silence upon your bed.

Offer the appointed sacrifices* and put your trust in the LORD.

Many are saying, "Oh, that we might see better times!"* Lift up the light of your countenance upon us, O LORD.

You have put gladness in my heart,* more than when grain and wine and oil increase.

I lie down in peace; at once I fall asleep;* for only you, LORD, make me dwell in safety.

Psalm 4

The Refrain

With my whole heart I seek you;* let me not stray from your commandments.

The Small Verse

Today if you shall hear his voice, harden not your heart.

The Lord's Prayer

The Prayer Appointed for the Week

O God, whose glory it is always to have mercy: Be gracious to all who have gone astray from your ways, and bring us again with penitent hearts and steadfast faith to embrace and hold fast the unchangeable truth of your Word, Jesus Christ your Son; who with you and the Holy Spirit lives and reigns, one God, for ever and ever. *Amen.* †

The Concluding Prayer of the Church

Lord God, almighty and everlasting Father, you have brought me in safety to this new day: Preserve me with your mighty power, that I may not fall into sin, nor

be overcome by adversity; and in all I do direct me to the fulfilling of your purpose; through Jesus Christ my Lord. *Amen.* †

The Midday Office   To Be Observed on the Hour or Half Hour
Between 11 a.m. and 2 p.m.

The Call to Prayer
Put not your trust in rulers, nor in any child of earth,* for there is no help in them.
When they breathe their last, they return to earth,* and in that day their thoughts
    perish.
Happy are they who have the God of Jacob for their help!* whose hope is in the
    LORD their God.
Psalm 146:2–4

The Request for Presence
Remember me, O LORD, with the favor you have for your people,* and visit me
    with your saving help;
That I may see the prosperity of your elect and be glad with the gladness of your
    people,* that I may glory with your inheritance.
Psalm 106:4–5

The Greeting
You are to be praised, O God, in Zion; . . .
To you that hear prayer shall all flesh come,* because of their transgressions.
Psalm 65:1–2

The Refrain for the Midday Lessons
Your statutes have been like songs to me* wherever I have lived like a stranger.
Psalm 119:54

A Reading
Israel, come back to YAHWEH your God, your guilt was the cause of your downfall.
    Provide yourself with words and come back to YAHWEH. Say to him, 'Take all
    guilt away and give us what is good, instead of bulls we will dedicate to you
    our lips.'
Hosea 14:2–3

The Refrain
Your statutes have been like songs to me* wherever I have lived like a stranger.

The Midday Psalm   *Such Knowledge Is Too Wonderful for Me*
LORD, you have searched me out and known me;* you know my sitting down and
    my rising up; you discern my thoughts from afar.
You trace my journeys and my resting-places* and are acquainted with all my
    ways.
Indeed, there is not a word on my lips,* but you, O LORD, know it altogether.
You press upon me behind and before* and lay your hand upon me.
Such knowledge is too wonderful for me;* it is so high that I cannot attain to it.

Where can I go then from your Spirit?* where can I flee from your presence?
If I climb up to heaven, you are there;* if I make the grave my bed, you are there
   also.
If I take the wings of the morning* and dwell in the uttermost parts of the sea,
Even there your hand will lead me* and your right hand hold me fast.

Psalm 139:1–9

The Refrain
Your statutes have been like songs to me* wherever I have lived like a stranger.

The Small Verse
Keep me, Lord, as the apple of your eye and carry me under the shadow of your
   wings.

Traditional

The Lord's Prayer

The Prayer Appointed for the Week
O God, whose glory it is always to have mercy: Be gracious to all who have gone
   astray from your ways, and bring us again with penitent hearts and steadfast
   faith to embrace and hold fast the unchangeable truth of your Word, Jesus
   Christ your Son; who with you and the Holy Spirit lives and reigns, one God,
   for ever and ever. *Amen.* †

The Concluding Prayer of the Church
May God himself order my days and make them acceptable in his sight. Blessed
   be the Lord always, my strength and my redeemer.

Traditional

The Vespers Office   **To Be Observed on the Hour or Half Hour**
                                          Between 5 and 8 p.m.

The Call to Prayer
Praise the LORD, all you nations;* laud him, all you peoples.
For his loving-kindness toward us is great,* and the faithfulness of the LORD
   endures for ever.

Psalm 117

The Request for Presence
Gladden the soul of your servant,* for to you, O LORD, I lift up my soul.

Psalm 86:4

The Greeting
One generation shall praise your works to another* and shall declare your power.

Psalm 145:4

The Hymn   *Jesus, Joy of Our Desiring*
 Jesus, joy of our desiring,
 Holy wisdom, love most bright;
 Drawn by you, our souls aspiring
 Soar to uncreated light.
 Word of God, our flesh that fashioned,
 With the fire of life impassioned,
 Striving still to truth unknown,
 Soaring, dying round your throne.

 Through the way where hope is guiding,
 Hark, what peaceful music rings;
 Where the flock, in you confiding,
 Drink of joy from deathless springs.
 Theirs is beauty's fairest pleasure;
 Theirs is wisdom's holiest treasure.
 You who ever lead your own
 In the love of joys unknown.
                                    Martin Janus

The Refrain for the Vespers Lessons
Happy are they all who fear the LORD,* and who follow in his ways!
                                         Psalm 128:1

The Vespers Psalm   *The LORD of Hosts Is the King of Glory*
Lift up your heads, O gates; lift them high, O everlasting doors;* and the King of
   glory shall come in.
"Who is this King of glory?"* "The LORD, strong and mighty, the LORD, mighty in
   battle."
Lift up your heads, O gates; lift them high, O everlasting doors;* and the King of
   glory shall come in.
"Who is he, this King of glory?"* "The LORD of hosts, he is the King of glory."
                                         Psalm 24:7–10

The Refrain
Happy are they all who fear the LORD,* and who follow in his ways!

The Gloria

The Lord's Prayer

The Prayer Appointed for the Week
O God, whose glory it is always to have mercy: Be gracious to all who have gone
   astray from your ways, and bring us again with penitent hearts and steadfast
   faith to embrace and hold fast the unchangeable truth of your Word, Jesus
   Christ your Son; who with you and the Holy Spirit lives and reigns, one God,
   for ever and ever. *Amen.* †

The Concluding Prayer of the Church
May Almighty God grant me a peaceful night and a perfect end. *Amen.*

The Morning Office | **To Be Observed on the Hour or Half Hour**
Between 6 and 9 a.m.

The Call to Prayer
Worship the LORD in the beauty of holiness;* let the whole earth tremble before
    him.

Psalm 96:9

The Request for Presence
Show us the light of your countenance, O God,* and come to us.

based on Psalm 67:1

The Greeting
Seven times a day do I praise you,* because of your righteous judgments.

Psalm 119:164

The Refrain for the Morning Lessons
Let integrity and uprightness preserve me,* for my hope has been in you.

Psalm 25:20

A Reading
Great crowds accompanied him on his way and he turned and spoke to them.
    'Anyone who comes to me without hating father, mother, wife, children, broth-
    ers, sisters, yes and his own life too, cannot be my disciple. No one who does
    not carry his cross and come after me can be my disciple.'

Luke 14:25–27

The Refrain
Let integrity and uprightness preserve me,* for my hope has been in you.

The Morning Psalm   *Take Delight in the* LORD
Do not fret yourself because of evildoers;* do not be jealous of those who do
    wrong.
For they shall soon wither like the grass,* and like the green grass fade away.
Put your trust in the LORD and do good;* dwell in the land and feed on its riches.
Take delight in the LORD,* and he shall give you your heart's desire.
Commit your way to the LORD and put your trust in him,* and he will bring it to
    pass.
He will make your righteousness as clear as the light* and your just dealing as the
    noonday.
Be still before the LORD* and wait patiently for him.

Psalm 37:1–7

The Refrain
Let integrity and uprightness preserve me,* for my hope has been in you.

The Cry of the Church

O Lamb of God, that takes away the sins of the world, have mercy upon me.
O Lamb of God, that takes away the sins of the world, have mercy upon me.
O Lamb of God, that takes away the sins of the world, grant me your peace.

The Lord's Prayer

The Prayer Appointed for the Week

O God, whose glory it is always to have mercy: Be gracious to all who have gone
astray from your ways, and bring us again with penitent hearts and steadfast
faith to embrace and hold fast the unchangeable truth of your Word, Jesus
Christ your Son; who with you and the Holy Spirit lives and reigns, one God,
for ever and ever. *Amen.* †

The Concluding Prayer of the Church

Lord God, almighty and everlasting Father, you have brought me in safety to this
new day: Preserve me with your mighty power, that I may not fall into sin, nor
be overcome by adversity; and in all I do direct me to the fulfilling of your purpose; through Jesus Christ my Lord. *Amen.* †

The Midday Office **To Be Observed on the Hour or Half Hour
Between 11 a.m. and 2 p.m.**

The Call to Prayer

Search for the Lord and his strength;* continually seek his face.

Psalm 105:4

The Request for Presence

You are good and you bring forth good;* instruct me in your statutes.

Psalm 119:68

The Greeting

When your word goes forth it gives light;* it gives understanding to the simple.

Psalm 119:130

The Refrain for the Midday Lessons

You strengthen me more and more; you enfold and comfort me.

Psalm 71:21

A Reading

Have you forgotten that encouraging text in which you are addressed as sons? *My
son, do not scorn correction from the Lord, do not resent his training, for the Lord
trains those he loves, and chastises every son he accepts.* Perseverance is part of your
training; God is treating you as his *sons.* Has there ever been any *son* whose
father did not *train* him?

Hebrews 12:5–8

The Refrain

You strengthen me more and more;* you enfold and comfort me.

The Midday Psalm   *The Lord Chose David His Servant*

Then the Lord woke as though from sleep,* like a warrior refreshed with wine.
He struck his enemies on the backside* and put them to perpetual shame.
He rejected the tent of Joseph* and did not choose the tribe of Ephraim;
He chose instead the tribe of Judah* and Mount Zion, which he loved.
He built his sanctuary like the heights of heaven,* like the earth which he founded
    for ever.
He chose David his servant,* and took him away from the sheepfolds.
He brought him from following the ewes,* to be a shepherd over Jacob his people
    and over Israel his inheritance.
So he shepherded them with a faithful and true heart* and guided them with the
    skillfulness of his hands.

Psalm 78:65–72

The Refrain
You strengthen me more and more;* you enfold and comfort me.

The Cry of the Church
Be, Lord, my helper and forsake me not. Do not despise me, O God, my savior.

The Short Breviary

The Lord's Prayer

The Prayer Appointed for the Week
O God, whose glory it is always to have mercy: Be gracious to all who have gone
    astray from your ways, and bring us again with penitent hearts and steadfast
    faith to embrace and hold fast the unchangeable truth of your Word, Jesus
    Christ your Son; who with you and the Holy Spirit lives and reigns, one God,
    for ever and ever. *Amen.* †

The Concluding Prayer of the Church
Lord, make me according to thy heart.
Brother Lawrence

The Vespers Office   **To Be Observed on the Hour or Half Hour
                                            Between 5 and 8 p.m.**

The Call to Prayer
Behold now, bless the Lord, all you servants of the Lord,* you that stand by night
    in the house of our Lord.

Psalm 134:1

The Request for Presence
For God alone my soul in silence waits;* from him comes my salvation.

Psalm 62:1

The Greeting
Yours is the day, yours also the night;* you established the moon and the sun.
You fixed all the boundaries of the earth;* you made both summer and winter.
Psalm 74:15–16

The Hymn   *My Soul Be on Your Guard*
My soul, be on your guard; ten thousand foes arise;
The hosts of sin are pressing hard to draw you from your prize.

O watch and fight and pray; the battle don't give over;
Renew it boldly everyday, and help from him implore.

Never think the victory won, nor lay your armor down;
Your arduous work will not be done till you obtain your crown.

Fight on, my soul, till death shall bring you to your God;
He'll take you at your parting breath, to his divine abode.
George Heath

The Refrain for the Vespers Lessons
The LORD's will stands fast for ever,* and the designs of his heart from age to age.
Psalm 33:11

The Vespers Psalm   *The LORD Shall Reign For Ever*
Put not your trust in rulers, nor in any child of earth,* for there is no help in them.
When they breathe their last, they return to earth,* and in that day their thoughts perish.
Happy are they who have the God of Jacob for their help!* whose hope is in the LORD their God;
Who made heaven and earth, the seas, and all that is in them;* who keeps his promise for ever;
Who gives justice to those who are oppressed,* and food to those who hunger.
The LORD sets the prisoners free; the LORD opens the eyes of the blind;* the LORD lifts up those who are bowed down;
The LORD loves the righteous; the LORD cares for the stranger;* he sustains the orphan and widow, but frustrates the way of the wicked.
The LORD shall reign for ever,* your God, O Zion, throughout all generations.
Psalm 146:2–9

The Refrain
The LORD's will stands fast for ever,* and the designs of his heart from age to age.

The Cry of the Church
Even so come, Lord Jesus!

The Lord's Prayer

The Prayer Appointed for the Week
O God, whose glory it is always to have mercy: Be gracious to all who have gone astray from your ways, and bring us again with penitent hearts and steadfast

faith to embrace and hold fast the unchangeable truth of your Word, Jesus
Christ your Son; who with you and the Holy Spirit lives and reigns, one God,
for ever and ever. *Amen.* †

The Concluding Prayer of the Church

May Almighty God grant me a peaceful night and a perfect end. *Amen.*

The Morning Office   **To Be Observed on the Hour or Half Hour
Between 6 and 9 a.m.**

The Call to Prayer

Come and listen, all you who fear God,* and I will tell you what he has done
for me.

Psalm 66:14

The Request for Presence

Show me your marvelous loving-kindness,* O Savior of those who take refuge at
your right hand from those who rise up against them.
Keep me as the apple of your eye;* hide me under the shadow of your wings.

Psalm 17:7–8

The Greeting

I will give thanks to you, for you answered me* and have become my salvation.

Psalm 118:21

The Refrain for the Morning Lessons

For God, who commanded the light to shine out of darkness, hath shined in our
hearts, to give the light of the knowledge of the glory of God in the face of Jesus
Christ.

II Corinthians 4:6

A Reading

Jesus taught the people, saying: "Now sentence is being passed on this world;
now the prince of the world is to be driven out. And when I am lifted up from
the earth, I shall draw all people to myself."

John 12:31–32

The Refrain

For God, who commanded the light to shine out of darkness, hath shined in our
hearts, to give the light of the knowledge of the glory of God in the face of Jesus
Christ.

The Morning Psalm   *What Is Man That You Should Be Mindful of Him?*

O LORD our Governor,* how exalted is your Name in all the world!
Out of the mouths of infants and children* your majesty is praised above the
heavens.
You have set up a stronghold against your adversaries,* to quell the enemy and
the avenger.

When I consider your heavens, the work of your fingers,* the moon and the stars
   you have set in their courses,
What is man that you should be mindful of him?* the son of man that you should
   seek him out?
You have made him but little lower than the angels;* you adorn him with glory
   and honor;
You give him mastery over the works of your hands;* you put all things under
   his feet:
All sheep and oxen,* even the wild beasts of the field,
The birds of the air, the fish of the sea,* and whatsoever walks in the paths of the sea.
O LORD our Governor,* how exalted is your Name in all the world!

Psalm 8:1–10

The Refrain
For God, who commanded the light to shine out of darkness, hath shined in our
   hearts, to give the light of the knowledge of the glory of God in the face of Jesus
   Christ.

The Small Verse
The people who have dwelt in darkness have seen a great light.

The Lord's Prayer

The Prayer Appointed for the Week
O God, whose glory it is always to have mercy: Be gracious to all who have gone
   astray from your ways, and bring us again with penitent hearts and steadfast
   faith to embrace and hold fast the unchangeable truth of your Word, Jesus
   Christ your Son; who with you and the Holy Spirit lives and reigns, one God,
   for ever and ever. *Amen.* †

The Concluding Prayer of the Church
Lord God, almighty and everlasting Father, you have brought me in safety to this
   new day: Preserve me with your mighty power, that I may not fall into sin, nor
   be overcome by adversity; and in all I do direct me to the fulfilling of your purpose; through Jesus Christ my Lord. *Amen.* †

The Midday Office   To Be Observed on the Hour or Half Hour
                                        Between 11 a.m. and 2 p.m.

The Call to Prayer
My mouth shall recount your mighty acts and saving deeds all day long;* though I
   cannot know the number of them.

Psalm 71:15

The Request for Presence
Send forth your strength, O God;* establish, O God, what you have wrought
   for us.

Psalm 68:28

The Greeting
Your way, O God, is holy;* who is so great a god as our God?

Psalm 77:13

The Refrain for the Midday Lessons
He who dwells in the shelter of the Most High,* abides under the shadow of the
   Almighty.

Psalm 91:1

A Reading
. . . *through his bruises you have been healed.* You had *gone astray like sheep* but now
   you have returned to the shepherd and guardian of your souls.

I Peter 2:24–25

The Refrain
He who dwells in the shelter of the Most High,* abides under the shadow of the
   Almighty.

The Midday Psalm   *O Israel, Trust in the LORD*
O Israel, trust in the LORD;* he is their help and their shield.
O house of Aaron, trust in the LORD;* he is their help and their shield.
You who fear the LORD, trust in the LORD;* he is their help and their shield.
The LORD has been mindful of us, and he will bless us;* he will bless the house of
   Israel; he will bless the house of Aaron;
He will bless those who fear the LORD,* both small and great together.
May the LORD increase you more and more,* you and your children after you.
May you be blessed by the LORD,* the maker of heaven and earth.
The heaven of heavens is the LORD's,* but he entrusted the earth to its peoples.
The dead do not praise the LORD,* nor all those who go down into silence;
But we will bless the LORD,* from this time forth for evermore. Hallelujah!

Psalm 115:9–18

The Refrain
He who dwells in the shelter of the Most High,* abides under the shadow of the
   Almighty.

The Cry of the Church
O Lamb of God, that takes away the sins of the world, have mercy upon me.
O Lamb of God, that takes away the sins of the world, have mercy upon me.
O Lamb of God, that takes away the sins of the world, grant me your peace.

The Lord's Prayer

The Prayer Appointed for the Week
O God, whose glory it is always to have mercy: Be gracious to all who have gone
   astray from your ways, and bring us again with penitent hearts and steadfast
   faith to embrace and hold fast the unchangeable truth of your Word, Jesus
   Christ your Son; who with you and the Holy Spirit lives and reigns, one God,
   for ever and ever. *Amen.* †

The Concluding Prayer of the Church

Lord Jesus Christ, by your death you took away the sting of death: Grant me to so follow in faith where you have led the way, that I may at length fall asleep peacefully in you and wake in your likeness; for your tender mercies' sake. *Amen.* †

The Vespers Office **To Be Observed on the Hour or Half Hour**
Between 5 and 8 p.m.

The Call to Prayer

O LORD, I call to you; my Rock, do not be deaf to my cry;* lest, if you do not hear me, I become like those who go down to the Pit.

Hear the voice of my prayer when I cry out to you,* when I lift up my hands to your holy of holies.

Psalm 28:1–2

The Request for Presence

I have gone astray like a sheep that is lost;* search for your servant, for I do not forget your commandments.

Psalm 119:176

The Greeting

How great is your goodness, O LORD! which you have laid up for those who fear you;* which you have done in the sight of all for those who put their trust in you.

Psalm 31:19

The Hymn

> Father of mercies infinite
> Ruling all things that be,
> Who shrouded in the depth and height
> Are One, and yet are Three:
>
> Accept our words, accept our tears,
> A mingled stream we pour;
> Such stream the laden bosom cheers
> To taste Your sweetness more.
>
> Most holy Father hear my cry
> Through Jesus Christ the Lord Most High,
> Who with the Holy Ghost and Thee
> Shall live and reign eternally.
>> *adapted from* THE SHORT BREVIARY

The Refrain for the Vespers Lessons

Mercy and truth have met together;* righteousness and peace have kissed each other.

Psalm 85:10

The Vespers Psalm   *He Redeems Our Life*

The LORD is full of compassion and mercy,* slow to anger and of great kindness.

He will not always accuse us,* nor will he keep his anger for ever.

He has not dealt with us according to our sins,* nor rewarded us according to our wickedness.

For as the heavens are high above the earth,* so is his mercy great upon those who fear him.

As far as the east is from the west,* so far has he removed our sins from us.

As a father cares for his children,* so does the LORD care for those who fear him.

For he himself knows whereof we are made;* he remembers that we are but dust.

Psalm 103:8–14

The Refrain

Mercy and truth have met together;* righteousness and peace have kissed each other.

The Small Verse

My help is in the Name of the Lord who made heaven and earth and all that is in them. Thanks be to God.

Traditional

The Lord's Prayer

The Prayer Appointed for the Week

O God, whose glory it is always to have mercy: Be gracious to all who have gone astray from your ways, and bring us again with penitent hearts and steadfast faith to embrace and hold fast the unchangeable truth of your Word, Jesus Christ your Son; who with you and the Holy Spirit lives and reigns, one God, for ever and ever. *Amen.* †

Concluding Prayers of the Church

Almighty God, who has promised to hear the petitions of those who ask in your Son's Name: I beseech you mercifully to incline your ear to me who have made my prayers and supplications to you; and grant that those things which I have faithfully asked according to your will, I may effectually obtain, to the relief of my necessity, and to the setting forth of your glory; through Jesus Christ my Lord. *Amen.* †

May the souls of the faithful departed, through the mercy of God, rest in eternal peace. *Amen.*

The Morning Office   To Be Observed on the Hour or Half Hour
                                            Between 6 and 9 a.m.

The Call to Prayer

Wake up, my spirit; awake, lute and harp;* I myself will waken the dawn.

Psalm 57:8

The Request for Presence
O Lamb of God, that takes away the sins of the world, have mercy upon me.
O Lamb of God, that takes away the sins of the world, have mercy upon me.
O Lamb of God, that takes away the sins of the world, grant me your peace.

Agnus Dei

The Greeting
For you alone are the Holy One, you alone are the Lord, you alone are the Most
High, Jesus Christ, with the Holy Spirit, in the Glory of God the Father.

The Refrain for the Morning Lessons
Be strong and let your heart take courage,* all you who wait for the LORD.

Psalm 31:24

A Reading
One of the rulers put this question to him, 'Good Master, what shall I do to inherit
eternal life?' Jesus said to him, 'Why do you call me good? No one is good but
God alone. You know the commandments: *You shall not commit adultery; You
shall not kill; You shall not steal; You shall not give false witness; Honor your father
and your mother.*' He replied, 'I have kept all these since my earliest days.' And
when Jesus heard this he said, 'There is still one thing you lack. Sell everything
you own and distribute the money to the poor, and you will have treasure in
heaven; then come, follow me.' But when he heard this he was overcome with
sadness, for he was very rich.

Luke 18:18–23

The Refrain
Be strong and let your heart take courage,* all you who wait for the LORD.

The Morning Psalm　　　　　　　*In the Roll of the Book It Is Written Concerning Me*
In sacrifice and offering you take no pleasure* (you have given me ears to hear
you);
Burnt-offering and sin-offering you have not required,* and so I said, "Behold, I
come.
In the roll of the book it is written concerning me:* 'I love to do your will, O my
God; your law is deep in my heart.' "

Psalm 40:7–9

The Refrain
Be strong and let your heart take courage,* all you who wait for the LORD.

The Cry of the Church
Even so come, Lord Jesus!

The Lord's Prayer

The Prayer Appointed for the Week
O God, whose glory it is always to have mercy: Be gracious to all who have gone
astray from your ways, and bring us again with penitent hearts and steadfast

faith to embrace and hold fast the unchangeable truth of your Word, Jesus Christ your Son; who with you and the Holy Spirit lives and reigns, one God, for ever and ever. *Amen.* †

The Concluding Prayer of the Church

Lord God, almighty and everlasting Father, you have brought me in safety to this new day: Preserve me with your mighty power, that I may not fall into sin, nor be overcome by adversity; and in all I do direct me to the fulfilling of your purpose; through Jesus Christ my Lord. *Amen.* †

The Midday Office   **To Be Observed on the Hour or Half Hour**
                Between 11 a.m. and 2 p.m.

The Call to Prayer

Ascribe to the LORD, you families of the peoples;* ascribe to the LORD honor and power.

Ascribe to the LORD the honor due his Name;* bring offerings and come into his courts.

Worship the LORD in the beauty of holiness . . .

Psalm 96:7–9

The Request for Presence

For God alone my soul in silence waits;* truly, my hope is in him.

Psalm 62:6

The Greeting

LORD God of hosts, hear my prayer;* hearken, O God of Jacob.

Psalm 84:7

The Refrain for the Midday Lessons

Protect me, O God, for I take refuge in you;* I have said to the LORD, "You are my Lord, my good above all other."

Psalm 16:1

A Reading

Let us keep our eyes fixed on Jesus, who leads us in our faith and brings it to perfection: for the sake of the joy which lay ahead of him, he endured the cross, disregarding the shame of it, and *has taken his seat at the right* of God's throne.

Hebrews 12:2

The Refrain

Protect me, O God, for I take refuge in you;* I have said to the LORD, "You are my Lord, my good above all other."

The Midday Psalm   ***The Righteous Shall Be Exalted***

It is God who judges;* he puts down one and lifts up another.

For in the LORD's hand there is a cup, full of spiced and foaming wine, which he pours out,* and all the wicked of the earth shall drink and drain the dregs.

But I will rejoice for ever; I will sing praises to the God of Jacob.* He shall break off all the horns of the wicked; but the horns of the righteous shall be exalted.

Psalm 75:7–10

The Refrain
Protect me, O God, for I take refuge in you;* I have said to the LORD, "You are my Lord, my good above all other."

The Small Verse
Lead me not into temptation. Deliver me from evil. Yours are the kingdom and the glory.

Traditional

The Lord's Prayer

The Prayer Appointed for the Week
O God, whose glory it is always to have mercy: Be gracious to all who have gone astray from your ways, and bring us again with penitent hearts and steadfast faith to embrace and hold fast the unchangeable truth of your Word, Jesus Christ your Son; who with you and the Holy Spirit lives and reigns, one God, for ever and ever. *Amen.* †

The Concluding Prayer of the Church
O God, the source of eternal light: Shed forth your unending day upon all of us who watch for you, that our lips may praise you, our lives may bless you, and our worship may give you glory; through Jesus Christ our Lord. *Amen.* †

The Vespers Office   **To Be Observed on the Hour or Half Hour Between 5 and 8 p.m.**

The Call to Prayer
Praise God in his holy temple;* praise him in the firmament of his power.

Psalm 150:1

The Request for Presence
O God, you are my God; eagerly I seek you;* my soul thirsts for you, my flesh faints for you, as in a barren and dry land where there is no water.
Therefore I have gazed upon you in your holy place,* that I might behold your power and your glory.

Psalm 63:1–2

The Greeting
Remember, O LORD, how the enemy scoffed,* how a foolish people despised your Name.
Do not hand over the life of your dove to wild beasts;* Never forget the lives of your poor.

Psalm 74:17–18

The Hymn
 Into the woods my Master went,
 Clean forspent, forspent;
 Into the woods my Master came,
 Forspent with love and shame.
 But the olives they were not blind to him.
 The little gray leaves were kind to him,
 The thorn tree had a mind to him,
 When into the woods he came.

 Out of the woods my Master went,
 And he was well content:
 Out of the woods my Master came,
 Content with death and shame.
 But the death and shame would woo him last,
 From under the trees they drew him last,
 'Twas on a tree they slew him last,
 When out of the woods he came.

         Sidney Lanier

The Refrain for the Vespers Lessons
The LORD is my light and my salvation; whom then shall I fear?* the LORD is the
 strength of my life; of whom then shall I be afraid?

              Psalm 27:1

The Vespers Psalm   *He Has Always Been Mindful of His Covenant*
Search for the LORD and his strength;* continually seek his face.
Remember the marvels he has done,* his wonders and the judgments of his
 mouth,
O offspring of Abraham his servant,* O children of Jacob his chosen.
He is the LORD our God;* his judgments prevail in all the world.
He has always been mindful of his covenant,* the promise he made for a thousand
 generations:
The covenant he made with Abraham,* the oath that he swore to Isaac,
Which he established as a statute for Jacob,* an everlasting covenant for Israel.

             Psalm 105:4–10

The Refrain
The LORD is my light and my salvation; whom then shall I fear?* the LORD is the
 strength of my life; of whom then shall I be afraid?

The Cry of the Church
O Lamb of God, that takes away the sins of the world, have mercy upon me.
O Lamb of God, that takes away the sins of the world, have mercy upon me.
O Lamb of God, that takes away the sins of the world, grant me your peace.

The Lord's Prayer

The Prayer Appointed for the Week

O God, whose glory it is always to have mercy: Be gracious to all who have gone
astray from your ways, and bring us again with penitent hearts and steadfast
faith to embrace and hold fast the unchangeable truth of your Word, Jesus
Christ your Son; who with you and the Holy Spirit lives and reigns, one God,
for ever and ever. *Amen.* †

The Concluding Prayer of the Church

Almighty God, who after the creation of the world rested from all your works and
sanctified a day of rest for all your creatures: Grant that I, putting away all
earthly anxieties, may be duly prepared for the service of public worship, and
grant as well that my Sabbath upon earth may be a preparation for the eternal
rest promised to your people in heaven; through Jesus Christ our Lord. *Amen.* †

The Morning Office   To Be Observed on the Hour or Half Hour
                                                    Between 6 and 9 a.m.

The Call to Prayer

The fear of the LORD is the beginning of wisdom;* those who act accordingly have
a good understanding; his praise endures for ever.

Psalm 111:10

The Request for Presence

Let them know that you, whose Name is YAHWEH,* you alone are the Most High
over all the earth.

Psalm 83:18

The Greeting

Blessed be the Lord GOD, the God of Israel,* who alone does wondrous deeds!
And blessed be his glorious Name for ever!* and may all the earth be filled with
his glory. Amen. Amen.

Psalm 72:18–19

The Refrain for the Morning Lessons

The same stone which the builders rejected* has become the chief cornerstone.

Psalm 118:22

A Reading

Now as they were eating, Jesus took bread, and when he said the blessing he
broke it and gave it to his disciples. 'Take it and eat,' he said, 'this is my body.'
Then he took a cup, and when he had given thanks he handed it to them saying, 'Drink from this, all of you, for this is my blood, the blood of the covenant,
poured out for many for the forgiveness of sins. From now on, I tell you, I shall

never again drink wine until I drink the new wine with you in the kingdom of my Father.'

Matthew 26:26–29

The Refrain

The same stone which the builders rejected* has become the chief cornerstone.

The Morning Psalm   *You Will Restore My Life*

In you, O Lord, have I taken refuge;* let me never be ashamed.

In your righteousness, deliver me and set me free;* incline your ear to me and save me.

Be my strong rock, a castle to keep me safe;* you are my crag and my stronghold.

Deliver me, my God, from the hand of the wicked,* from the clutches of the evildoer and the oppressor.

For you are my hope, O Lord God,* my confidence since I was young.

I have been sustained by you ever since I was born; from my mother's womb you have been my strength;* my praise shall be always of you.

Psalm 71:1–7

The Refrain

The same stone which the builders rejected* has become the chief cornerstone.

The Small Verse

The Son of man shall be delivered over to the gentiles, to be mocked and scourged and crucified.

The Lord's Prayer

The Prayer Appointed for the Week

Almighty God, you know that we have no power in ourselves to help ourselves: Keep me both outwardly in my body and inwardly in my soul, that I may be defended from all adversities which may happen to the body, and from all evil thoughts which may assault and hurt the soul; through Jesus Christ our Lord, who lives and reigns with you and the Holy Spirit, one God, for ever and ever. *Amen.* †

The Concluding Prayer of the Church

Lord God, almighty and everlasting Father, you have brought me in safety to this new day: Preserve me with your mighty power, that I may not fall into sin, nor be overcome by adversity; and in all I do direct me to the fulfilling of your purpose; through Jesus Christ my Lord. *Amen.* †

The Midday Office   **To Be Observed on the Hour or Half Hour**

Between 11 a.m. and 2 p.m.

The Call to Prayer

You who stand in the house of the Lord,* in the courts of the house of our God.

Praise the Lord, for the Lord is good.

Psalm 135:2–3

The Request for Presence
Let them know that you, whose Name is Yahweh,* you alone are the Most High
over all the earth.

Psalm 83:18

The Greeting
I will exalt you, O Lord, because you have lifted me up* and have not let my
enemies triumph over me.

Psalm 30:1

The Refrain for the Midday Lessons
When I called, you answered me;* you increased my strength within me.

Psalm 138:4

A Reading
Moses said: "Listen, Israel: Yahweh our God is the one, the only Yahweh. You
must love Yahweh your God with all your heart, with all your soul, with all
your strength. Let the words I enjoin on you today stay in your heart. You shall
tell them to your children, and keep telling them, when you are sitting at home,
when you are out and about, when you are lying down, when you are standing
up; you must fasten them on your hand as a sign and on your forehead as a
headband; you must write them on the doorposts of your house and on your
gates."

Deuteronomy 6:4–9

The Refrain
When I called, you answered me;* you increased my strength within me.

The Midday Psalm   *My Foot Stands on Level Ground*
Give judgment for me, O Lord, for I have lived with integrity;* I have trusted in
the Lord and have not faltered.
Test me, O Lord, and try me;* examine my heart and my mind.
For your love is before my eyes;* I have walked faithfully with you.
I have not sat with the worthless,* nor do I consort with the deceitful.
I have hated the company of evildoers;* I will not sit down with the wicked.
I will wash my hands in innocence, O Lord,* that I may go in procession round
your altar,
Singing aloud a song of thanksgiving* and recounting all your wonderful deeds.

Psalm 26:1–7

The Refrain
When I called, you answered me;* you increased my strength within me.

The Cry of the Church
Even so come, Lord Jesus!

The Lord's Prayer

The Prayer Appointed for the Week
Almighty God, you know that we have no power in ourselves to help ourselves:
Keep me both outwardly in my body and inwardly in my soul, that I may be
defended from all adversities which may happen to the body, and from all evil
thoughts which may assault and hurt the soul; through Jesus Christ our Lord,
who lives and reigns with you and the Holy Spirit, one God, for ever and ever.
Amen. †

The Concluding Prayer of the Church
O God, you make me glad with the weekly remembrance of the glorious resurrection of your Son my Lord: Give me this day such blessing through my worship
of you, that the week to come may be spent in your favor; through Jesus Christ
our Lord. *Amen.* †

The Vespers Office   **To Be Observed on the Hour or Half Hour**
Between 5 and 8 p.m.

The Call to Prayer
Let my mouth be full of your praise* and your glory all the day long.
Do not cast me off in my old age;* forsake me not when my strength fails.
Psalm 71:8–9

The Request for Presence
Let your loving-kindness, O LORD, be upon us,* as we have put our trust in you.
Psalm 33:22

The Greeting
To you I lift up my eyes,* to you enthroned in the heavens.
As the eyes of servants look to the hand of their masters,* and the eyes of a maid to
the hand of her mistress,
So my eyes look to the LORD my God,* until he shows me his mercy.
based on Psalm 123:1–3

The Hymn   *Most Highly Favored Lady*
The angel Gabriel from heaven came,
His wings as drifted snow, his eyes as flame;
"All hail," said he, "you lowly maiden Mary,
Most highly favored lady,"
Gloria!

"For know a blessed Mother you shall be,
All generations laud and honor thee,
Your Son shall be Emmanuel, by seers foretold,
Most highly favored lady,"
Gloria!

Then gentle Mary meekly bowed her head,
"To me be as it pleases God," she said,
"My soul shall laud and magnify his holy Name."
Most highly favored lady,
Gloria!

Of her, Emmanuel, the Christ, was born
In Bethlehem, all on a Christmas morn,
And Christian folk throughout the world will ever say—
"Most highly favored lady,"
Gloria!

Basque Carol

The Refrain for the Vespers Lessons
In truth God has heard me;* he has attended to the voice of my prayer.

Psalm 66:17

The Vespers Psalm   *The Lord Does Wonders for His Faithful*
Know that the Lord does wonders for the faithful;* when I call upon the Lord, he
will hear me.
Tremble, then, and do not sin;* speak to your heart in silence upon your bed.
Offer the appointed sacrifices* and put your trust in the Lord.
Many are saying, "Oh, that we might see better times!"* Lift up the light of your
countenance upon us, O Lord.
You have put gladness in my heart,* more than when grain and wine and oil
increase.
I lie down in peace; at once I fall asleep;* for only you, Lord, make me dwell in
safety.

Psalm 4:3–8

The Refrain
In truth God has heard me;* he has attended to the voice of my prayer.

Psalm 66:17

The Cry of the Church
O Lord, hear my prayer and let my cry come unto you. Thanks be to God.

The Short Breviary

The Lord's Prayer

The Prayer Appointed for the Week
Almighty God, you know that we have no power in ourselves to help ourselves:
Keep me both outwardly in my body and inwardly in my soul, that I may be
defended from all adversities which may happen to the body, and from all evil
thoughts which may assault and hurt the soul; through Jesus Christ our Lord,
who lives and reigns with you and the Holy Spirit, one God, for ever and ever.
Amen. †

Concluding Prayers of the Church

Hail Mary, full of grace, the Lord is with you. Blessed are you among women and blessed is the fruit of your womb, the Lord, Jesus Christ. Holy Mary, Mother of God, pray for us sinners now and at the hour of our death. *Amen.*

Traditional

Lord God, whose Son our Savior Jesus Christ, triumphed over the powers of death and prepared for us our place in the new Jerusalem: Grant that I, who have this day given thanks for his resurrection, may praise you in the City of which he is the light, and where he lives and reigns for ever and ever. *Amen.* †

The Morning Office **To Be Observed on the Hour or Half Hour Between 6 and 9 a.m.**

The Call to Prayer

Bless the LORD, you angels of his, you mighty ones who do his bidding,* and hearken to the voice of his word.
Bless the LORD, all you his hosts,* you ministers of his who do his will.
Bless the LORD, all you works of his, in all places of his dominion . . .

Psalm 103:20–22

The Request for Presence

Be seated on your lofty throne, O Most High;* O LORD, judge the nations.

Psalm 7:8

The Greeting

Not to us, O LORD, not to us, but to your Name give glory;* because of your love and because of your faithfulness.

Psalm 115:1

The Refrain for the Morning Lessons

On this day the LORD has acted;* we will rejoice and be glad in it.

Psalm 118:24

A Reading *On March 25, nine months before Christmas day, the Church celebrates the message of the angel Gabriel to the Virgin and her acceptance of the role of Mother to our Lord.*

My soul proclaims the greatness of the Lord,
my spirit rejoices in God my Savior;*
      for he has looked with favor on his lowly servant.
From this day all generations will call me blessed*
      the Almighty has done great things for me,
      and holy is his Name.
He has mercy on those who fear him*
      in every generation.

He has shown the strength of his arm,
>he has scattered the proud in their conceit.
He has cast down the mighty from their thrones,*
>and has lifted up the lowly.
He has filled the hungry with good things,
>and the rich he has sent away empty.
He has come to the help of his servant Israel,*
>for he has remembered the promise of mercy,
The promise he made to our fathers,*
>to Abraham and his children for ever.

Glory to the Father, and to the Son, and to the Holy Spirit:*
>as it was in the beginning, is now, and will be for ever.

The Magnificat

The Refrain

On this day the LORD has acted;* we will rejoice and be glad in it.

The Morning Psalm   *O LORD, I Am Your Servant*

O LORD, I am your servant;* I am your servant and the child of your handmaid;
>you have freed me from my bonds.
I will offer you the sacrifice of thanksgiving* and call upon the Name of the LORD.
I will fulfill my vows to the LORD* in the presence of all his people,
In the courts of the LORD's house,* in the midst of you, O Jerusalem.

Psalm 116:14–17

The Refrain

On this day the LORD has acted;* we will rejoice and be glad in it.

The Cry of the Church

Let us praise the Lord, whom the Angels are praising, whom the Cherubim and
>Seraphim proclaim: Holy, holy, holy!

THE SHORT BREVIARY

The Lord's Prayer

The Prayer Appointed for the Week

Almighty God, you know that we have no power in ourselves to help ourselves:
>Keep me both outwardly in my body and inwardly in my soul, that I may be
>defended from all adversities which may happen to the body, and from all evil
>thoughts which may assault and hurt the soul; through Jesus Christ our Lord,
>who lives and reigns with you and the Holy Spirit, one God, for ever and ever.
>*Amen.* †

Concluding Prayers of the Church

Pour your grace into my heart, O Lord, that I who have known the incarnation of
>your Son Jesus Christ, announced by an angel to the Virgin Mary, may by his
>cross and passion be brought to the glory of his resurrection; who lives and reigns
>with you, in the unity of the Holy Spirit, one God, now and for ever. *Amen.* †

Lord God, almighty and everlasting Father, you have brought me in safety to this
new day: Preserve me with your mighty power, that I may not fall into sin, nor
be overcome by adversity; and in all I do direct me to the fulfilling of your purpose; through Jesus Christ my Lord. *Amen.* †

The Midday Office

**To Be Observed on the Hour or Half Hour
Between 11 a.m. and 2 p.m.**

The Call to Prayer
Sing to the LORD a new song,* for he has done marvelous things.

Psalm 98:1

The Request for Presence
Remember me, O LORD, with the favor you have for your people,* and visit me
with your saving help;
That I may see the prosperity of your elect* and be glad with the gladness of your
people, that I may glory with your inheritance.

Psalm 106:4–5

The Greeting
Your righteousness, O God, reaches to the heavens;* you have done great things;
who is like you, O God?

Psalm 71:19

The Refrain for the Midday Lessons
I will sing to the LORD as long as I live;* I will praise my God while I have my
being.

Psalm 104:34

A Reading
YAHWEH spoke to Ahaz again and said: 'Ask YAHWEH your God for a sign, either in
the depths of Sheol or in the heights above.' But Ahaz said, 'I will not ask. I will
not put YAHWEH to the test.' He then said: 'Listen now, House of David: are you
satisfied with trying human patience that you should try my God's patience
too? The Lord will give you a sign in any case: It is this: the young woman is
with child and will give birth to a son whom she will call Immanuel.'

Isaiah 7:10–14

The Refrain
I will sing to the LORD as long as I live;* I will praise my God while I have my
being.

The Midday Psalm   *Such Is the Generation of Those Who Seek Him*
The earth is the LORD's and all that is in it,* the world and all who dwell therein.
For it is he who founded it upon the seas* and made it firm upon the rivers of the
deep.
"Who can ascend the hill of the LORD?"* and who can stand in his holy place?"

"Those who have clean hands and a pure heart,* who have not pledged themselves to falsehood, nor sworn by what is a fraud.
They shall receive a blessing from the LORD* and a just reward from the God of
   their salvation."
Such is the generation of those who seek him,* of those who seek your face, O God
   of Jacob.

Psalm 24:1–6

The Refrain
I will sing to the LORD as long as I live;* I will praise my God while I have my being.

The Cry of the Church
Even so, come Lord Jesus!

The Lord's Prayer

The Prayer Appointed for the Week
Almighty God, you know that we have no power in ourselves to help ourselves:
   Keep me both outwardly in my body and inwardly in my soul, that I may be
   defended from all adversities which may happen to the body, and from all evil
   thoughts which may assault and hurt the soul; through Jesus Christ our Lord,
   who lives and reigns with you and the Holy Spirit, one God, for ever and ever.
   Amen. †

The Concluding Prayer of the Church
O God, who so ordered the world that at the message of an Angel Your Word
   should take flesh in the womb of the Blessed Virgin Mary, grant unto us that
   we who believe her to truly be the Mother of God, may be aided by her intercession before You. Through Jesus Christ our Lord. *Amen.*

adapted from The Short Breviary

The Vespers Office   **To Be Observed on the Hour or Half Hour**
                                          Between 5 and 8 p.m.

The Call to Prayer
Be joyful in God, all you lands;* sing the glory of his Name; sing the glory of his
   praise.
Say to God, "How awesome are your deeds! . . .
All the earth bows down before you,* sings to you, sings out your Name."

Psalm 66:1–3

The Request for Presence
Let your loving-kindness, O LORD, be upon us,* as we have put our trust in you.

Psalm 33:22

The Greeting
Blessed is the LORD!* for he has heard the voice of my prayer.

Psalm 28:7

The Hymn   *Hymn of the Virgin*
The Word whom earth and sea and sky
adore and laud and magnify,
whose might they show, whose praise they tell,
in Mary's body deigned to dwell.

Blessed is the message Gabriel brought,
blessed is the work the Spirit wrought,
most blessed to bring to human birth
the long-desired of all the earth.

Lord Jesus, Virgin born, to thee
eternal praise and glory be,
whom with the Father we adore
and Holy Spirit evermore.

Latin, 7th C.

The Refrain for the Vespers Lessons
Turn again to your rest, O my soul,* for the LORD has treated you well.
For you have rescued my life from death,* my eyes from tears, and my feet from
stumbling.

Psalm 116:6–7

The Vespers Psalm   *You Are with Me*
The LORD is my shepherd;* I shall not be in want.
He makes me lie down in green pastures* and leads me beside still waters.
He revives my soul* and guides me along right pathways for his Name's sake.
Though I walk through the valley of the shadow of death, I shall fear no evil;* for
you are with me; your rod and your staff, they comfort me.
You spread a table before me in the presence of those who trouble me;* you have
anointed my head with oil, and my cup is running over.
Surely your goodness and mercy shall follow me all the days of my life,* and I will
dwell in the house of the LORD for ever.

Psalm 23

The Refrain
Turn again to your rest, O my soul,* for the LORD has treated you well.
For you have rescued my life from death,* my eyes from tears, and my feet from
stumbling.

The Cry of the Church
O Lord, hear my prayer and let my cry come unto you. Thanks be to God.

THE SHORT BREVIARY

The Lord's Prayer

The Prayer Appointed for the Week
Almighty God, you know that we have no power in ourselves to help ourselves:
Keep me both outwardly in my body and inwardly in my soul, that I may be

defended from all adversities which may happen to the body, and from all evil
thoughts which may assault and hurt the soul; through Jesus Christ our Lord,
who lives and reigns with you and the Holy Spirit, one God, for ever and ever.
Amen. †

The Concluding Prayer of the Church

Hail, holy Queen, Mother of Mercy. Hail, our life, our sweetness and our hope. To
you do we cry, poor banished children of Eve; to you do we send up our sighs,
mourning, and weeping in this vale of tears. Turn then, most gracious advocate, your eyes of mercy towards us, and after this, our exile, show us the
blessed fruit of your womb, Jesus; O clement, O loving, O sweet Virgin Mary.
Pray for us, O holy Mother of God, that we may be made worthy of the
promises of Christ, your Son. *Amen.*

Traditional

The Morning Office	To Be Observed on the Hour or Half Hour
	Between 6 and 9 a.m.

The Call to Prayer

Come and listen, all you who fear God,* and I will tell you what he has done for me.

Psalm 66:14

The Request for Presence

May God be merciful to us and bless us,* show us the light of his countenance and
come to us.
Let your ways be known upon earth,* your saving health among all nations.

Psalm 67:1–2

The Greeting

Your statutes have been like songs to me* wherever I have lived as a stranger.

Psalm 119:54

The Refrain for the Morning Lessons

Purge me from my sin, and I shall be pure;* wash me, and I shall be clean indeed.

Psalm 51:8

A Reading

James and John, the sons of Zebedee, approached him. "Master," they said to him,
"We want you to do us a favor." He said to them, "What is it you want me to do
for you?" They said to him, "Allow us to sit one at your right hand and the
other at your left in your glory." But Jesus said to them, "You do not know
what you are asking. Can you drink the cup that I shall drink, or be baptized
with the baptism with which I shall be baptized?" They replied, "We can."
Jesus then said to them, "The cup that I shall drink, you shall drink, and with
the baptism with which I shall be baptized, you shall be baptized, but as for
seats at my right hand or my left, these are not mine to grant; they belong to
those to whom they have been allotted."

Mark 10:35–40

The Refrain
Purge me from my sin, and I shall be pure;* wash me, and I shall be clean indeed.

The Morning Psalm   *You, O God, Have Heard My Vows*
Hear my cry, O God,* and listen to my prayer.
I call upon you from the ends of the earth* with heaviness in my heart; set me
    upon the rock that is higher than I.
For you have been my refuge,* a strong tower against the enemy.
I will dwell in your house for ever;* I will take refuge under the cover of your wings.
For you, O God, have heard my vows;* you have granted me the heritage of those
    who fear your Name.

Psalm 61:1–5

The Refrain
Purge me from my sin, and I shall be pure;* wash me, and I shall be clean indeed.

The Small Verse
The people that dwelt in darkness have seen a great light.

The Lord's Prayer

The Prayer Appointed for the Week
Almighty God, you know that we have no power in ourselves to help ourselves:
    Keep me both outwardly in my body and inwardly in my soul, that I may be
    defended from all adversities which may happen to the body, and from all evil
    thoughts which may assault and hurt the soul; through Jesus Christ our Lord,
    who lives and reigns with you and the Holy Spirit, one God, for ever and ever.
    Amen. †

The Concluding Prayer of the Church
Lord God, almighty and everlasting Father, you have brought me in safety to this
    new day: Preserve me with your mighty power, that I may not fall into sin, nor
    be overcome by adversity; and in all I do direct me to the fulfilling of your pur-
    pose; through Jesus Christ my Lord. Amen. †

The Midday Office   **To Be Observed on the Hour or Half Hour**
                                      Between 11 a.m. and 2 p.m.

The Call to Prayer
Give thanks to the LORD, for he is good;* his mercy endures for ever.

Psalm 118:1

The Request for Presence
You are my helper and my deliverer;* do not tarry, O my God.

Psalm 40:19

The Greeting
Had you desired it, I would have offered sacrifice,* but you take no delight in
    burnt-offerings.

The sacrifice of God is a troubled spirit;* a broken and contrite heart, O God, you will not despise.

Psalm 51:17–18

The Refrain for the Midday Lessons

Whom have I in heaven but you?* and having you I desire nothing upon earth.

Psalm 73:25

A Reading

The wage paid by sin is death; the gift freely given by God is eternal life in Christ Jesus our Lord.

Romans 6:23

The Refrain

Whom have I in heaven but you?* and having you I desire nothing upon earth.

The Midday Psalm   *Who Is Like the LORD Our God*

Who is like the LORD our God, who sits enthroned on high* but stoops to behold the heavens and the earth?
He takes up the weak out of the dust* and lifts up the poor from the ashes.
He sets them with the princes,* with the princes of his people.
He makes the woman of a childless house* to be a joyful mother of children.

Psalm 113:5–8

The Refrain

Whom have I in heaven but you?* and having you I desire nothing upon earth.

The Small Verse

My help is in the Name of the Lord who made the heavens and the earth. What then shall I fear of what shall I be afraid?

Traditional

The Lord's Prayer

The Prayer Appointed for the Week

Almighty God, you know that we have no power in ourselves to help ourselves: Keep me both outwardly in my body and inwardly in my soul, that I may be defended from all adversities which may happen to the body, and from all evil thoughts which may assault and hurt the soul; through Jesus Christ our Lord, who lives and reigns with you and the Holy Spirit, one God, for ever and ever. Amen. †

The Concluding Prayer of the Church

Direct me, O Lord, in all my doings with your most gracious favor, and further me with your continual help; that in all my work begun, continued, and ended in you, I may glorify your holy name, and finally, by your mercy, obtain everlasting life; through Jesus Christ my Lord. Amen.

The Vespers Office To Be Observed on the Hour or Half Hour
Between 5 and 8 p.m.

The Call to Prayer
Let Israel now proclaim,* "His mercy endures for ever."
Let the house of Aaron now proclaim,* "His mercy endures for ever."
Let those who fear the LORD now proclaim,* "His mercy endures for ever."

Psalm 118:2–4

The Request for Presence
Show me the light of your countenance, O God,* and come to me.

based on Psalm 67:1

The Greeting
But you, O LORD, are gracious and full of compassion,* slow to anger, and full of
kindness and truth.

Psalm 86:15

The Hymn *Have Your Own Way, Lord!*
Have Your own way, Lord! Have Your own way!
You are the potter, I am the clay;
Mold me and make me
After Your will,
While I am waiting,
Yielded and still.

Have Your own way, Lord! Have Your own way!
Search me and try me, Master today!
Whiter than snow, Lord,
Wash me just now,
As in Your presence
Humbly I bow.

Have Your own way, Lord! Have Your own way!
Wounded and weary, help me, I pray!
Power, all power
Surely is Thine!
Touch me and heal me,
Savior Divine!

Have Your own way, Lord! Have Your own way!
Hold over my being absolute sway!
Fill with Your Spirit
Till all will see
Christ only, always,
Living in me.

Adelaide Pollard

The Refrain for the Vespers Lessons
Remember me, O LORD, with the favor you have for your people,* and visit me
with your saving help.

Psalm 106:4

The Vespers Psalm   *He Will Judge the People with His Truth*
Ascribe to the LORD, you families of the peoples;* ascribe to the LORD honor and
power.
Ascribe to the LORD the honor due his Name;* bring offerings and come into his
courts.
Worship the LORD in the beauty of holiness;* let the whole earth tremble before
him.
Tell it out among the nations: "The LORD is King!* he has made the world so firm
that it cannot be moved; he will judge the peoples with equity."
Let the heavens rejoice, and let the earth be glad; let the sea thunder and all that is
in it;* let the field be joyful and all that is therein.
Then shall all the trees of the wood shout for joy before the LORD when he comes,*
when he comes to judge the earth.
He will judge the world with righteousness* and the peoples with his truth.

Psalm 96:7–13

The Refrain
Remember me, O LORD, with the favor you have for your people,* and visit me
with your saving help.

The Small Verse
The Lord is my shepherd and nothing is wanting to me. In green pastures He hath
settled me.

THE SHORT BREVIARY

The Lord's Prayer

The Prayer Appointed for the Week
Almighty God, you know that we have no power in ourselves to help ourselves:
Keep me both outwardly in my body and inwardly in my soul, that I may be
defended from all adversities which may happen to the body, and from all evil
thoughts which may assault and hurt the soul; through Jesus Christ our Lord,
who lives and reigns with you and the Holy Spirit, one God, for ever and ever.
Amen. †

The Concluding Prayer of the Church
O Lord my God, I am not worthy to have you come under my roof; yet you have
called me to stand in this house, and to serve at this work. To you and to your
service I devote myself, body, soul, and spirit. Fill my memory with the record
of your mighty works; enlighten my understanding with the light of your Holy
Spirit; and may all the desires of my heart and will center in what you would
have me do. Make me an instrument of your salvation for the people entrusted
to my care, and grant that by my life and teaching I may set forth your true and

living Word. Be always with me in carrying out the duties of my faith. In prayer, quicken my devotion; in praises, heighten my love and gratitude; in conversation give me readiness of thought and expression; and grant that, by the clearness and brightness of your holy Word, all the world may be drawn into your blessed kingdom. All this I ask for the sake of your Son our Savior Jesus Christ. *Amen.* †

The Morning Office   To Be Observed on the Hour or Half Hour
                                   Between 6 and 9 a.m.

The Call to Prayer

I will give great thanks to the LORD with my mouth;* in the midst of the multitude will I praise him;
Because he stands at the right hand of the needy,* to save his life from those who would condemn him.

Psalm 109:29–30

The Request for Presence

Send out your light and your truth, that they may lead me,* and bring me to your holy hill and to your dwelling;
That I may go to the altar of God, to the God of my joy and gladness;* and on the harp I will give thanks to you, O God my God.

Psalm 43:3–4

The Greeting

Splendor and honor and kingly power* are yours by right, O Lord our God,
For you created everything that is,* and by your will they were created and have their being.

A Song to the Lamb

The Refrain for the Morning Lessons

And yet my people did not hear my voice,* and Israel would not obey me.

Psalm 84:11

A Reading

Just at this time, some Pharisees came up. 'Go away,' they said. 'Leave this place because Herod means to kill you.' He replied, 'You may go and give that fox this message: Look! Today and tomorrow and the next day I must go on since it would not be right for a prophet to die outside Jerusalem.'

Luke 13:31–33

The Refrain

And yet my people did not hear my voice,* and Israel would not obey me.

The Morning Psalm   *Proclaim the Greatness of Our God*

Proclaim the greatness of the LORD our God and fall down before his footstool;* he is the Holy One.

Moses and Aaron among his priests, and Samuel among those who call upon his
  Name,* they called upon the LORD, and he answered them.
He spoke to them out of the pillar of cloud;* they kept his testimonies and the
  decree that he gave them.
O LORD our God, you answered them indeed;* you were a God who forgave them,
  yet punished them for their evil deeds.
Proclaim the greatness of the LORD our God and worship him upon his holy hill;*
  for the LORD our God is the Holy One.

Psalm 99:5–9

The Refrain
And yet my people did not hear my voice,* and Israel would not obey me.

The Small Verse
The people that walked in darkness have seen a great light; on those who live in a
  land of deep shadow a light has shone.

Isaiah 9:1

The Lord's Prayer

The Prayer Appointed for the Week
Almighty God, you know that we have no power in ourselves to help ourselves:
  Keep me both outwardly in my body and inwardly in my soul, that I may be
  defended from all adversities which may happen to the body, and from all evil
  thoughts which may assault and hurt the soul; through Jesus Christ our Lord,
  who lives and reigns with you and the Holy Spirit, one God, for ever and ever.
  Amen. †

The Concluding Prayer of the Church
Lord God, almighty and everlasting Father, you have brought me in safety to this
  new day: Preserve me with your mighty power, that I may not fall into sin, nor
  be overcome by adversity; and in all I do direct me to the fulfilling of your purpose; through Jesus Christ my Lord. *Amen.* †

The Midday Office To Be Observed on the Hour or Half Hour
Between 11 a.m. and 2 p.m.

The Call to Prayer
Come, let us bow down, and bend the knee,* and kneel before the LORD our
  Maker.
For he is our God, and we are the people of his pasture and the sheep of his hand.*
  Oh, that today you would hearken to his voice!

Psalm 95:6–7

The Request for Presence
Remember not our past sins;* let your compassion be swift to meet us.

Psalm 79:8

The Greeting

Zion hears and is glad, and the cities of Judah rejoice,* because of your judgments,
O LORD.

Psalm 97:8

The Refrain for the Midday Lessons

I will listen to what the LORD God is saying,* for he is speaking peace to his faithful
people and to those who turn their hearts to him.

Psalm 85:8

A Reading

Those who forsake the law sing the praises of the wicked, those who observe the
law are angered by them. The wicked do not know what justice means, those
who seek YAHWEH understand everything.

Proverbs 28:4–5

The Refrain

I will listen to what the LORD God is saying,* for he is speaking peace to his faithful
people and to those who turn their hearts to him.

The Midday Psalm   *Let Your Heart Take Courage*

How great is your goodness, O LORD! which you have laid up for those who fear
you;* which you have done in the sight of all for those who put their trust
in you.

You hide them in the covert of your presence from those who slander them;* you
keep them in your shelter from the strife of tongues.

Blessed be the LORD!* for he has shown me the wonders of his love in a besieged
city.

Love the LORD, all you who worship him;* the LORD protects the faithful, but
repays to the full those who act haughtily.

Be strong and let your heart take courage,* all you who wait for the LORD.

Psalm 31:19–21, 23–24

The Refrain

I will listen to what the LORD God is saying,* for he is speaking peace to his faithful
people and to those who turn their hearts to him.

The Cry of the Church

Even so come, Lord Jesus!

The Lord's Prayer

The Prayer Appointed for the Week

Almighty God, you know that we have no power in ourselves to help ourselves:
Keep me both outwardly in my body and inwardly in my soul, that I may be
defended from all adversities which may happen to the body, and from all evil
thoughts which may assault and hurt the soul; through Jesus Christ our Lord,
who lives and reigns with you and the Holy Spirit, one God, for ever and ever.
Amen. †

The Concluding Prayer of the Church
Direct me, O Lord, on all my doings with your most gracious favor, and further
  me with your continual help; that in all my work begun, continued, and ended
  in you, I may glorify your holy name, and finally, by your mercy, obtain everlasting life; through Jesus Christ my Lord. *Amen.* †

The Vespers Office   **To Be Observed on the Hour or Half Hour**
                                          Between 5 and 8 p.m.

The Call to Prayer
The LORD is King; let the people tremble;* he is enthroned upon the cherubim; let
  the earth shake.
The LORD is great in Zion;* he is high above all peoples.
Let them confess his Name, which is great and awesome;* he is the Holy One.
                                                          Psalm 99:1–3

The Request for Presence
May God be merciful to us and bless us,* show us the light of his countenance and
  come to us.
                                                          Psalm 67:1

The Greeting
Exalt yourself above the heavens, O God,* and your glory over all the earth.
                                                          Psalm 57:6

The Hymn   *May His Grace Rest Upon Us*
  May the grace of Christ our Savior,   Thus may we abide in union
  And the Father's boundless love,   With each other and the Lord,
  With the Holy Spirit's favor,   And possess, in sweet communion,
  Rest upon us from above.   Joys which earth cannot afford.
                                                          John Newton

The Refrain for the Vespers Lessons
Those who trust in the LORD are like Mount Zion,* which cannot be moved, but
  stands fast for ever.
                                                          Psalm 125:1

The Vespers Psalm   *The Words of the LORD Are Pure Words*
"Because the needy are oppressed, and the poor cry out in misery,* I will rise up,"
  says the LORD, "and give them the help they long for."
The words of the LORD are pure words,* like silver refined from ore and purified
  seven times in the fire.
O LORD, watch over us* and save us from this generation for ever.
The wicked prowl on every side,* and that which is worthless is highly prized by
  everyone.
                                                          Psalm 12:5–8

The Refrain
Those who trust in the LORD are like Mount Zion,* which cannot be moved, but
stands fast for ever.

The Cry of the Church
Even so come, Lord Jesus!

The Lord's Prayer

The Prayer Appointed for the Week
Almighty God, you know that we have no power in ourselves to help ourselves:
Keep me both outwardly in my body and inwardly in my soul, that I may be
defended from all adversities which may happen to the body, and from all evil
thoughts which may assault and hurt the soul; through Jesus Christ our Lord,
who lives and reigns with you and the Holy Spirit, one God, for ever and ever.
Amen. †

The Concluding Prayer of the Church
Protect us, Lord, as we stay awake; watch over us as we sleep, that awake we may
watch with Christ, and asleep, rest in peace. *Amen.*

The Morning Office   **To Be Observed on the Hour or Half Hour**
Between 6 and 9 a.m.

The Call to Prayer
Hear, O my people, and I will admonish you:* O Israel, if you would but listen to
me!
There shall be no strange god among you;* you shall not worship a foreign god.
I am the LORD your God, who brought you out of the land of Egypt and said,*
"Open your mouth wide, and I will fill it."

Psalm 81:8–10

The Request for Presence
Teach me your way, O LORD,* and I will walk in your truth; knit my heart to you
that I may fear your Name.

Psalm 86:11

The Greeting
My mouth shall recount your mighty acts and saving deeds all day long;* though I
cannot know the number of them.

Psalm 71:15

The Refrain for the Morning Lessons
The LORD has pleasure in those who fear him, in those who await his gracious
favor.

Psalm 147:12

A Reading

Then some of the scribes and Pharisees spoke up. 'Master,' they said, 'we should like to see a sign from you.' He replied, 'It is an evil and unfaithful generation that asks for a sign! The only sign it will be given is the sign of the prophet Jonah. For as Jonah *remained in the belly of the sea-monster for three days and three nights,* so will the Son of man be in the heart of the earth for three days and three nights.'

Matthew 12:38–40

The Refrain

The LORD has pleasure in those who fear him,* in those who await his gracious favor.

The Morning Psalm　　　　　　　　　　　*You Crown the Year with Your Goodness*

You visit the earth and water it abundantly; you make it very plenteous;* the river of God is full of water.

You prepare the grain,* for so you provide for the earth.

You drench the furrows and smooth out the ridges;* with heavy rain you soften the ground and bless its increase.

You crown the year with your goodness,* and your paths overflow with plenty.

May the fields of the wilderness be rich for grazing,* and the hills be clothed with joy.

May the meadows cover themselves with flocks, and the valleys cloak themselves with grain;* let them shout for joy and sing.

Psalm 65:9–14

The Refrain

The LORD has pleasure in those who fear him,* in those who await his gracious favor.

The Small Verse

Today if you shall hear His voice, harden not your heart.

The Lord's Prayer

The Prayer Appointed for the Week

Almighty God, you know that we have no power in ourselves to help ourselves: Keep me both outwardly in my body and inwardly in my soul, that I may be defended from all adversities which may happen to the body, and from all evil thoughts which may assault and hurt the soul; through Jesus Christ our Lord, who lives and reigns with you and the Holy Spirit, one God, for ever and ever. *Amen.* †

The Concluding Prayer of the Church

Lord God, almighty and everlasting Father, you have brought me in safety to this new day: Preserve me with your mighty power, that I may not fall into sin, nor be overcome by adversity; and in all I do direct me to the fulfilling of your purpose; through Jesus Christ my Lord. *Amen.* †

The Midday Office   **To Be Observed on the Hour or Half Hour**
                                           Between 11 a.m. and 2 p.m.

The Call to Prayer
Sing to God, O kingdoms of the earth;* sing praises to the Lord.
He rides in the heavens, the ancient heavens;* he sends forth his voice, his mighty
    voice.

Psalm 68:33–34

The Request for Presence
For God alone my soul in silence waits;* from him comes my salvation.

Psalm 62:1

The Greeting
Awesome things will you show us in your righteousness,* O God of our salvation,
    O Hope of all the ends of the earth . . .

Psalm 65:5

The Refrain for the Midday Lessons
Happy are they who trust in the LORD!*

Psalm 40:4

A Reading
Of those who are sleeping in the Land of Dust, many will awaken, some to ever-
    lasting life, some to shame and everlasting disgrace.

Daniel 12:2

The Refrain
Happy are they who trust in the LORD!*

The Midday Psalm   *Light Shines in the Darkness for the Upright*
Light shines in the darkness for the upright;* the righteous are merciful and full of
    compassion.
It is good for them to be generous in lending* and to manage their affairs with
    justice.
For they will never be shaken;* the righteous will be kept in everlasting
    remembrance.
They will not be afraid of any evil rumors;* their heart is right; they put their trust
    in the Lord.
Their heart is established and will not shrink,* until they see their desire upon
    their enemies.
They have given freely to the poor,* and their righteousness stands fast for ever;
    they will hold up their head with honor.
The wicked will see it and be angry; they will gnash their teeth and pine away;*
    the desires of the wicked will perish.

Psalm 112:4–10

The Refrain
Happy are they who trust in the LORD!*

The Cry of the Church
Be, Lord, my helper and forsake me not. Do not despise me, O God, my savior.

THE SHORT BREVIARY

The Lord's Prayer

The Prayer Appointed for the Week
Almighty God, you know that we have no power in ourselves to help ourselves:
Keep me both outwardly in my body and inwardly in my soul, that I may be
defended from all adversities which may happen to the body, and from all evil
thoughts which may assault and hurt the soul; through Jesus Christ our Lord,
who lives and reigns with you and the Holy Spirit, one God, for ever and ever.
Amen. †

The Concluding Prayer of the Church
May God have mercy on me, forgive me my sins and bring me to life everlasting.
In Jesus' name. *Amen.*

The Vespers Office   **To Be Observed on the Hour or Half Hour**
                                          Between 5 and 8 p.m.

The Call to Prayer
Let Israel now proclaim,* "His mercy endures for ever."
Let the house of Aaron now proclaim,* "His mercy endures for ever."
Let those who fear the LORD now proclaim,* "His mercy endures for ever."

Psalm 118:2–4

The Request for Presence
O LORD, I call to you; my Rock, do not be deaf to my cry;* lest, if you do not hear
me, I become like those who go down to the Pit.

Psalm 28:1

The Greeting
Your kingdom is an everlasting kingdom;* your dominion endures throughout
all ages.

Psalm 145:10–12

The Hymn   *Lord of All Being*
Lord of all being, throned afar,
Your glory flames from sun and star;
Center and soul of every sphere,
And yet to loving hearts how near.

Sun of life, your living ray
Sheds on our path the glow of day;
Star of our hope your gentle light
Shall ever cheer the longest night.

Lord of all life, below, above,
Whose light is truth, whose warmth is love;
Before the brilliance of your throne
We ask no luster of our own.

Give us your grace to make us true,
And kindling hearts that burn for you,
Till all your living altars claim
One holy light, one heavenly flame.

Oliver Wendell Holmes

The Refrain for the Vespers Lessons

Show your goodness, O LORD, to those who are good* and to those who are true of
heart.

Psalm 125:4

The Vespers Psalm — Let Your Ways Be Known Upon Earth

May God be merciful to us and bless us,* show us the light of his countenance and
come to us.
Let your ways be known upon earth,* your saving health among all nations.
Let the peoples praise you, O God;* let all the peoples praise you.
Let the nations be glad and sing for joy,* for you judge the peoples with equity and
guide all the nations upon earth.
Let the peoples praise you, O God;* let all the peoples praise you.

Psalm 67:1–5

The Refrain

Show your goodness, O LORD, to those who are good* and to those who are true of
heart.

The Small Verse

The earth is the Lord's and all the fullness thereof, the world and we who dwell
within. Thanks be to God.

Traditional

The Lord's Prayer

The Prayer Appointed for the Week

Almighty God, you know that we have no power in ourselves to help ourselves:
Keep me both outwardly in my body and inwardly in my soul, that I may be
defended from all adversities which may happen to the body, and from all evil
thoughts which may assault and hurt the soul; through Jesus Christ our Lord,
who lives and reigns with you and the Holy Spirit, one God, for ever and ever.
Amen. †

The Concluding Prayer of the Church

May God himself order my days and make them acceptable in his sight. Blessed is
the Lord always, my strength and my redeemer.

Traditional

The Morning Office   To Be Observed on the Hour or Half Hour
                                                              Between 6 and 9 a.m.

The Call to Prayer
Know this: The LORD himself is God;* he himself has made us, and we are his; we
  are his people and the sheep of his pasture.

Psalm 100:2

The Request for Presence
Lead me, O LORD, in your righteousness, . . . * make your way straight before me.

Psalm 5:8

The Greeting
Blessed is he who comes in the name of the Lord;* we bless you from the house of
  the LORD.

Psalm 118:26

The Refrain for the Morning Lessons
Let not those who hope in you be put to shame through me, Lord GOD of hosts;*
  let not those who seek you be disgraced because of me, O God of Israel.

Psalm 69:7

A Reading
They then said to him, 'John's disciples are always fasting and saying prayers, and
  the disciples of the Pharisees, too, but yours go on eating and drinking.' Jesus
  replied, 'Surely you cannot make the bridegroom's attendants fast while the
  bridegroom is still with them? But the time will come when the bridegroom is
  taken away from them; then, in those days, they will fast.'

Luke 5:33–35

The Refrain
Let not those who hope in you be put to shame through me, Lord GOD of hosts;*
  let not those who seek you be disgraced because of me, O God of Israel.

The Morning Psalm   *Shepherd Your Inheritance, O LORD*
O LORD, I call to you; my Rock, do not be deaf to my cry;* lest, if you do not hear
  me, I become like those who go down to the Pit.
Hear the voice of my prayer when I cry out to you,* when I lift up my hands to
  your holy of holies.
Do not snatch me away with the wicked or with the evildoers,* who speak
  peaceably with their neighbors, while strife is in their hearts.
Repay them according to their deeds,* and according to the wickedness of their
  actions.
According to the work of their hands repay them,* and give them their just
  deserts.
They have no understanding of the LORD's doings, nor of the works of his hands;*
  therefore he will break them down and not build them up.
The LORD is the strength of his people,* a safe refuge for his anointed.

Save your people and bless your inheritance;* shepherd them and carry them for ever.

Psalm 28:1–6, 10–11

The Refrain
Let not those who hope in you be put to shame through me, Lord GOD of hosts;* let not those who seek you be disgraced because of me, O God of Israel.

The Cry of the Church
O God, come to my assistance! O Lord, make haste to help me!

The Lord's Prayer

The Prayer Appointed for the Week
Almighty God, you know that we have no power in ourselves to help ourselves: Keep me both outwardly in my body and inwardly in my soul, that I may be defended from all adversities which may happen to the body, and from all evil thoughts which may assault and hurt the soul; through Jesus Christ our Lord, who lives and reigns with you and the Holy Spirit, one God, for ever and ever. *Amen.* †

The Concluding Prayer of the Church
Lord God, almighty and everlasting Father, you have brought me in safety to this new day: Preserve me with your mighty power, that I may not fall into sin, nor be overcome by adversity; and in all I do direct me to the fulfilling of your purpose; through Jesus Christ my Lord. *Amen.* †

The Midday Office   **To Be Observed on the Hour or Half Hour Between 11 a.m. and 2 p.m.**

The Call to Prayer
Worship the LORD, O Jerusalem;* praise your God, O Zion.

Psalm 147:13

The Request for Presence
Restore us, O God of hosts;* show the light of your countenance, and we shall be saved.

Psalm 80:7

The Greeting
Be merciful to me, O God, be merciful, for I have taken refuge in you;* in the shadow of your wings will I take refuge until this time of trouble has gone by.

Psalm 57:1

The Refrain for the Midday Lessons
The LORD has sworn and he will not recant:* "You are a priest for ever after the order of Melchizedek."

Psalm 110:4

A Reading
He said, 'Son of man, get to your feet; I will speak to you.' As he said these words
the spirit came into me and put me on my feet, and I heard him speaking to me.
He said, 'Son of man, I am sending you to the Israelites, to the rebels who have
rebelled against me . . . I am sending you to them, to say, "Lord YAHWEH says
this." Whether they listen or not, this tribe of rebels will know there is a
prophet among them. And you, son of man, do not be afraid of them or what
they say, though you find yourself surrounded with brambles and sitting on
scorpions. Do not be afraid of their words or alarmed by their looks . . . You are
to deliver my words to them whether they listen or not, for they are a tribe of
rebels.

Ezekiel 2:1ff

The Refrain
The LORD has sworn and he will not recant:* "You are a priest for ever after the
order of Melchizedek."

The Midday Psalm   *May All the Nations Bless Themselves in Him*
May his Name remain for ever and be established as long as the sun endures;*
     may all the nations bless themselves in him and call him blessed.
Blessed be the Lord GOD, the God of Israel,* who alone does wondrous deeds!
And blessed be his glorious Name for ever!* and may all the earth be filled with
     his glory. Amen. Amen.

Psalm 72:17–19

The Refrain
The LORD has sworn and he will not recant:* "You are a priest for ever after the
order of Melchizedek."

The Cry of the Church
Even so come, Lord Jesus!

The Lord's Prayer

The Prayer Appointed for the Week
Almighty God, you know that we have no power in ourselves to help ourselves:
     Keep me both outwardly in my body and inwardly in my soul, that I may be
     defended from all adversities which may happen to the body, and from all evil
     thoughts which may assault and hurt the soul; through Jesus Christ our Lord,
     who lives and reigns with you and the Holy Spirit, one God, for ever and ever.
     Amen. †

The Concluding Prayer of the Church
Lord Jesus Christ, by your death you took away the sting of death: Grant me to so
     follow in faith where you have led the way, that I may at length fall asleep
     peacefully in you and wake in your likeness; for your tender mercies' sake.
     Amen. †

The Vespers Office   To Be Observed on the Hour or Half Hour
                                                   Between 5 and 8 p.m.

The Call to Prayer
The LORD is my strength and my shield;* my heart trusts in him, and I have been
   helped.

Psalm 28:8

The Request for Presence
I have gone astray like a sheep that is lost;* search for your servant, for I do not
   forget your commandments.

Psalm 119:176

The Greeting
How great is your goodness, O LORD! which you have laid up for those who fear
   you;* which you have done in the sight of all for those who put their trust in you.

Psalm 31:19

The Hymn   *O Love of God, How Strong*
   O love of God, how strong and true,
   eternal and yet ever new;
   uncomprehended and unbought,
   beyond all knowledge and all thought.

   O wide embracing, wondrous Love,
   we read you in the sky above;
   we read you in the earth below,
   in seas that swell and streams that flow.

   We read you best in him who came
   to bear for us the cross of shame,
   sent by the Father from on high,
   our life to live, our death to die.

   We read your power to bless and save
   even in the darkest grave;
   still more in resurrection light
   we read the fullness of your might.

                              Horatius Bonar

The Refrain for the Vespers Lessons
Mercy and truth have met together;* righteousness and peace have kissed each
   other.

Psalm 85:10

The Vespers Psalm   *Bring Me to Your Holy Hill*
Send out your light and your truth, that they may lead me,* and bring me to your
   holy hill and to your dwelling;
That I may go to the altar of God, to the God of my joy and gladness;* and on the
   harp I will give thanks to you, O God my God.

Why are you so full of heaviness, O my soul?* and why are you so disquieted
within me?
Put your trust in God;* for I will yet give thanks to him, who is the help of my
countenance, and my God.

Psalm 43:3–6

The Refrain
Mercy and truth have met together;* righteousness and peace have kissed each
other.

The Small Verse
My help is in the Name of the Lord who made heaven and earth and all that is in
them. Thanks be to God.

Traditional

The Lord's Prayer

The Prayer Appointed for the Week
Almighty God, you know that we have no power in ourselves to help ourselves:
Keep me both outwardly in my body and inwardly in my soul, that I may be
defended from all adversities which may happen to the body, and from all evil
thoughts which may assault and hurt the soul; through Jesus Christ our Lord,
who lives and reigns with you and the Holy Spirit, one God, for ever and ever.
Amen. †

Concluding Prayers of the Church
Almighty God, who has promised to hear the petitions of those who ask in your
Son's Name: I beseech you mercifully to incline your ear to me who have made
my prayers and supplications to you; and grant that those things which I have
faithfully asked according to your will, I may effectually obtain, to the relief of
my necessity, and to the setting forth of your glory; through Jesus Christ my
Lord. *Amen.* †

May the souls of the faithful departed, through the mercy of God, rest in eternal
peace. *Amen.*

The Morning Office   **To Be Observed on the Hour or Half Hour**
Between 6 and 9 a.m.

The Call to Prayer
Wake up, my spirit; awake, lute and harp;* I myself will waken the dawn.

Psalm 57:8

The Request for Presence
O Lamb of God, that takes away the sins of the world, have mercy upon me.
O Lamb of God, that takes away the sins of the world, have mercy upon me.
O Lamb of God, that takes away the sins of the world, grant me your peace.

Agnus Dei

The Greeting

For you alone are the Holy One, you alone are the Lord, you alone are the Most
   High, Jesus Christ, with the Holy Spirit, in the Glory of God the Father.

The Refrain for the Morning Lessons

Into your hands I commend my spirit,* for you have redeemed me, O Lord, O
   God of truth.

Psalm 31:5

A Reading

Then he began to teach them that the Son of man was destined to suffer grievously,
   and to be rejected by the elders and the chief priests and the scribes, and to be
   put to death, and after three days to rise again; and he said all this quite openly.
   Then, taking him aside, Peter tried to rebuke him. But, turning and seeing his
   disciples, he rebuked Peter and said to him, 'Get behind me, Satan! You are
   thinking not as God thinks, but as human beings do.'

Mark 8:31–33

The Refrain

Into your hands I commend my spirit,* for you have redeemed me, O Lord, O
   God of truth.

The Morning Psalm   *You Are My Confidence, O Lord, Since I Was Young*

In you, O Lord, have I taken refuge;* let me never be ashamed.
In your righteousness, deliver me and set me free;* incline your ear to me and
   save me.
Be my strong rock, a castle to keep me safe;* you are my crag and my stronghold.
Deliver me, my God, from the hand of the wicked,* from the clutches of the
   evildoer and the oppressor.
For you are my hope, O Lord God,* my confidence since I was young.
I have been sustained by you ever since I was born; from my mother's womb you
   have been my strength;* my praise shall be always of you.
I have become a portent to many;* but you are my refuge and my strength.
Let my mouth be full of your praise* and your glory all the day long.
Do not cast me off in my old age;* forsake me not when my strength fails.

Psalm 71:1–9

The Refrain

Into your hands I commend my spirit,* for you have redeemed me, O Lord, O
   God of truth.

The Cry of the Church

Even so come, Lord Jesus!

The Lord's Prayer

The Prayer Appointed for the Week

Almighty God, you know that we have no power in ourselves to help ourselves:
   Keep me both outwardly in my body and inwardly in my soul, that I may be

defended from all adversities which may happen to the body, and from all evil thoughts which may assault and hurt the soul; through Jesus Christ our Lord, who lives and reigns with you and the Holy Spirit, one God, for ever and ever. *Amen.* †

The Concluding Prayer of the Church

Lord God, almighty and everlasting Father, you have brought me in safety to this new day: Preserve me with your mighty power, that I may not fall into sin, nor be overcome by adversity; and in all I do direct me to the fulfilling of your purpose; through Jesus Christ my Lord. *Amen.* †

The Midday Office   **To Be Observed on the Hour or Half Hour Between 11 a.m. and 2 p.m.**

The Call to Prayer

Make me hear of joy and gladness,* that the body you have broken may rejoice.

Psalm 51:9

The Request for Presence

Look well whether there be any wickedness in me* and lead me in the way that is everlasting.

Psalm 139:23

The Greeting

O Lord, I am your servant;* I am your servant and the child of your handmaid; you have freed me from my bonds.

Psalm 116:14

The Refrain for the Midday Lessons

Unless the Lord builds the house,* their labor is in vain who build it.

Psalm 127:1

A Reading

As he was dying, Jacob prophesied, saying: "The scepter shall not pass from Judah, nor the ruler's staff from between his feet, until tribute be brought to him and the peoples render him obedience. He tethers his donkey to the vine, to its stock the foal of his she-donkey. He washes his clothes in wine, his robes in the blood of the grape. His eyes are darkened with wine and his teeth are white with milk."

Genesis 49:10–12

The Refrain

Unless the Lord builds the house,* their labor is in vain who build it.

The Midday Psalm   *Light Has Sprung Up for the Righteous*

Zion hears and is glad, and the cities of Judah rejoice,* because of your judgments, O Lord.

For you are the LORD, most high over all the earth;* you are exalted far above all
    gods.
The LORD loves those who hate evil;* he preserves the lives of his saints and
    delivers them from the hand of the wicked.
Light has sprung up for the righteous,* and joyful gladness for those who are
    truehearted.

Psalm 97:8–12

The Refrain
Unless the LORD builds the house,* their labor is in vain who build it.

The Cry of the Church
Even so come, Lord Jesus!

The Lord's Prayer

The Prayer Appointed for the Week
Almighty God, you know that we have no power in ourselves to help ourselves:
    Keep me both outwardly in my body and inwardly in my soul, that I may be
    defended from all adversities which may happen to the body, and from all evil
    thoughts which may assault and hurt the soul; through Jesus Christ our Lord,
    who lives and reigns with you and the Holy Spirit, one God, for ever and ever.
    Amen. †

The Concluding Prayer of the Church
O God, the source of eternal light: Shed forth your unending day upon all of us
    who watch for you, that our lips may praise you, our lives may bless you, and
    our worship may give you glory; through Jesus Christ our Lord. *Amen.* †

The Vespers Office   **To Be Observed on the Hour or Half Hour**
Between 5 and 8 p.m.

The Call to Prayer
Bless our God, you peoples;* make the voice of his praise to be heard;
Who holds our souls in life,* and will not allow our feet to slip.

Psalm 66:7–8

The Request for Presence
O God of hosts;* show us the light of your countenance, and we shall be saved.

Psalm 80:7

The Greeting
As the eyes of servants look to the hand of their masters,* and the eyes of a maid to
    the hand of her mistress,
So my eyes look to you, O LORD my God.

based on Psalm 123:2–3

The Hymn   *Heralds of Christ*
Heralds of Christ, who bear the King's commands
immortal tidings in your mortal hands,
pass on and carry
swift the news you bring;
make straight, make straight the highway of the King.

Through desert ways, dark fen, and deep morass,
through jungles, sluggish seas, and mountain pass,
build now the road,
and falter not, nor stay;
prepare across the earth the King's highway.

Lord, give us faith and strength, the road to build,
To see the promise of the day fulfilled,
when war shall be no more,
and strife shall cease
upon the highway of the Prince of Peace.

Laura Copenhaver

The Refrain for the Vespers Lessons
And now, what is my hope?* O Lord, my hope is in you.

Psalm 39:8

The Vespers Psalm   *I Will Rejoice in Your Salvation*
Sing praise to the LORD who dwells in Zion;* proclaim to the peoples the things he
has done.
The Avenger of blood will remember them;* he will not forget the cry of the
afflicted.
Have pity on me, O LORD;* see the misery I suffer from those who hate me, O you
who lift me up from the gate of death;
So that I may tell of all your praises* and rejoice in your salvation in the gates of
the city of Zion.

Psalm 9:11–14

The Refrain
And now, what is my hope?* O Lord, my hope is in you.

The Cry of the Church
Even so come, Lord Jesus!

The Lord's Prayer

The Prayer Appointed for the Week
Almighty God, you know that we have no power in ourselves to help ourselves:
Keep me both outwardly in my body and inwardly in my soul, that I may be
defended from all adversities which may happen to the body, and from all evil
thoughts which may assault and hurt the soul; through Jesus Christ our Lord,

who lives and reigns with you and the Holy Spirit, one God, for ever and ever. *Amen.* †

The Concluding Prayer of the Church
Almighty God, who after the creation of the world rested from all your works
and sanctified a day of rest for all your creatures: Grant that I, putting away
all earthly anxieties, may be duly prepared for the service of public worship,
and grant as well that my Sabbath upon earth may be a preparation for the
eternal rest promised to your people in heaven; through Jesus Christ our
Lord. *Amen.* †

❧

The Morning Office   **To Be Observed on the Hour or Half Hour
Between 6 and 9 a.m.**

The Call to Prayer
Happy are they who have the God of Jacob for their help!* whose hope is in the
Lord their God.

Psalm 146:4

The Request for Presence
Set a watch before my mouth, O Lord, and guard the door of my lips;* let not my
heart incline to any evil thing.
Let me not be occupied in wickedness with evildoers,* nor eat of their choice
foods.
Let the righteous smite me in friendly rebuke;* let not the oil of the unrighteous
anoint my head.

Psalm 141:3–5

The Greeting
Not to us, O Lord, not to us, but to your Name give glory;* because of your love
and because of your faithfulness.

Psalm 115:1

The Refrain for the Morning Lessons
Let the words of my mouth and the meditation of my heart be acceptable in your
sight,* O Lord, my strength and my redeemer.

Psalm 19:14

A Reading
Then taking the twelve aside he said to them, 'Look, we are going up to Jerusalem,
and everything that is written by the prophets about the Son of man is to come

true. For he will be handed over to the gentiles and will be mocked, maltreated and spat on, and when they have scourged him they will put him to death; and on the third day he will rise again.' But they could make nothing of this; what he said was quite obscure to them, they did not understand what he was telling them.

Luke 18:31–34

The Refrain

Let the words of my mouth and the meditation of my heart be acceptable in your
  sight,* O LORD, my strength and my redeemer.

The Morning Psalm *How Long Will You Hide Your Face from Me?*

How long, O LORD? will you forget me for ever?* how long will you hide your face
  from me?
How long shall I have perplexity in my mind, and grief in my heart, day after
  day?* how long shall my enemy triumph over me?
Look upon me and answer me, O LORD my God;* give light to my eyes, lest I sleep
  in death;
Lest my enemy say, "I have prevailed over him,"* and my foes rejoice that I have
  fallen.
But I put my trust in your mercy;* my heart is joyful because of your saving help.
I will sing to the LORD, for he has dealt with me richly;* I will praise the Name of
  the Lord Most High.

Psalm 13

The Refrain

Let the words of my mouth and the meditation of my heart be acceptable in your
  sight,* O LORD, my strength and my redeemer.

The Cry of the Church

O God, come to my assistance! O Lord, make haste to help me!

The Lord's Prayer

The Prayer Appointed for the Week

Gracious Father, whose blessed Son Jesus Christ came down from heaven to be the
  true bread which gives life to the world: Evermore give me this bread, that he
  may live in me, and I in him; who lives and reigns with you and the Holy
  Spirit, one God, now and for ever. *Amen.* †

The Concluding Prayer of the Church

Lord God, almighty and everlasting Father, you have brought me in safety to this
  new day: Preserve me with your mighty power, that I may not fall into sin, nor
  be overcome by adversity; and in all I do direct me to the fulfilling of your purpose; through Jesus Christ my Lord. *Amen.* †

The Midday Office   To Be Observed on the Hour or Half Hour
                                                        Between 11 a.m. and 2 p.m.

The Call to Prayer
Ascribe to the LORD the glory due his Name;* worship the LORD in the beauty of
    holiness.

Psalm 29:2

The Request for Presence
Fight those who fight me, O LORD;* attack those who are attacking me.
. . . say to my soul, "I am your salvation."

Psalm 35:1, 3

The Greeting
Blessed be the Lord GOD, the God of Israel,* who alone does wondrous deeds!

Psalm 72:18

The Refrain for the Midday Lessons
My eyes are fixed on you, O my Strength;* for you, O God, are my stronghold.

Psalm 59:10

A Reading
The Apostle taught us, saying: ". . . our Passover has been sacrificed, that is,
    Christ; let us keep the feast, then, with none of the old yeast and no leavening
    of evil and wickedness, but only the unleavened bread of sincerity and truth."

I Corinthians 5:7–8

The Refrain
In my integrity you hold me fast,* and shall set me before your face for ever.

The Midday Psalm   *My Soul Has a Desire for the Court of the LORD*
How dear to me is your dwelling, O LORD of hosts!* My soul has a desire and
    longing for the courts of the LORD; my heart and my flesh rejoice in the living
    God.
The sparrow has found her a house and the swallow a nest where she may lay her
    young;* by the side of your altars, O LORD of hosts, my King and my God.
Happy are they who dwell in your house!* they will always be praising you.
Happy are the people whose strength is in you!* whose hearts are set on the
    pilgrims' way.
Those who go through the desolate valley will find it a place of springs,* for the
    early rains have covered it with pools of water.

Psalm 84:1–5

The Refrain
In my integrity you hold me fast,* and shall set me before your face for ever.

The Cry of the Church
Lord, have mercy on us. Christ, have mercy on us. Lord, have mercy on us.

The Lord's Prayer

The Prayer Appointed for the Week
Gracious Father, whose blessed Son Jesus Christ came down from heaven to be the true bread which gives life to the world: Evermore give me this bread, that he may live in me, and I in him; who lives and reigns with you and the Holy Spirit, one God, now and for ever. *Amen.* †

The Concluding Prayer of the Church
O God, you make me glad with the weekly remembrance of the glorious resurrection of your Son my Lord: Give me this day such blessing through my worship of you, that the week to come may be spent in your favor; through Jesus Christ our Lord. *Amen.* †

The Vespers Office   **To Be Observed on the Hour or Half Hour**
                  Between 5 and 8 p.m.

The Call to Prayer
Open my lips, O Lord,* and my mouth shall proclaim your praise.
Psalm 51:16

The Request for Presence
Hear, O LORD, and have mercy upon me;* O LORD, be my helper.
Psalm 30:11

The Greeting
Blessed be the Lord GOD, the God of Israel,* who alone does wondrous deeds!
And blessed be his glorious Name for ever!*
Psalm 72:18–19

The Hymn   *O Gladsome Light*
 O gladsome light, O grace of our Creator's face,
 The eternal splendor wearing; celestial, holy, blessed,
 Our Savior Jesus Christ, joyful in your appearing!

 As fades the day's last light we see the lamps of night,
 Our common hymn outpouring, O God of might unknown,
 You, the incarnate Son, and Spirit Blessed adoring.

 To you of right belongs all praise of holy songs,
 O Son of God, life-giver. You, therefore, O Most High,
 The world does glorify and shall exalt forever.
Ancient Greek Hymn

The Refrain for the Vespers Lessons
It is better to rely on the LORD* than to put any trust in flesh.
It is better to rely on the LORD* than to put any trust in rulers.
Psalm 118:8–9

The Vespers Psalm   *This God Is Our God For Ever*

Your praise, like your Name, O God, reaches to the world's end;* your right hand
    is full of justice.
Let Mount Zion be glad and the cities of Judah rejoice,* because of your judgments.
Make the circuit of Zion; walk round about her;* count the number of her towers.
Consider well her bulwarks; examine her strongholds;* that you may tell those
    who come after.
This God is our God for ever and ever;* he shall be our guide for evermore.

Psalm 48:9–13

The Refrain

It is better to rely on the LORD* than to put any trust in flesh.
It is better to rely on the LORD* than to put any trust in rulers.

The Small Verse

Their sound goes forth to all the earth and their speech to the end of the world.

adapted from THE SHORT BREVIARY

The Lord's Prayer

The Prayer Appointed for the Week

Gracious Father, whose blessed Son Jesus Christ came down from heaven to be the
    true bread which gives life to the world: Evermore give me this bread, that he
    may live in me, and I in him; who lives and reigns with you and the Holy
    Spirit, one God, now and for ever. *Amen.* †

The Concluding Prayer of the Church

Lord God, whose Son our Savior Jesus Christ, triumphed over the powers of death
    and prepared for us our place in the new Jerusalem: Grant that I, who have this
    day given thanks for his resurrection, may praise you in the City of which he is
    the light, and where he lives and reigns for ever and ever. *Amen.* †

The Morning Office   To Be Observed on the Hour or Half Hour
Between 6 and 9 a.m.

The Call to Prayer

Happy are they whose way is blameless,* who walk in the law of the LORD!
Happy are they who observe his decrees* and seek him with all their hearts!
Who never do any wrong,* but always walk in his ways.

Psalm 119:1–3

The Request for Presence

Give me the joy of your saving help again* and sustain me with your bountiful
    Spirit.

Psalm 51:13

The Greeting

You, O Lord, are gracious and full of compassion,* slow to anger, and full of
kindness and truth.

Psalm 86:15

The Refrain for the Morning Lessons

For who is God, but the Lord?* who is the Rock, except our God?

Psalm 18:32

A Reading

Jesus taught us, saying: "Again, the kingdom of heaven is like a dragnet that is
cast in the sea and brings in a haul of all kinds of fish. When it is full, the fisher-
men haul it ashore; then, sitting down, they collect the good ones in baskets
and throw away those that are of no use. This is how it will be at the end of
time: the angels will appear and separate the wicked from the upright, to
throw them into the blazing furnace, where there will be weeping and grinding
of teeth."

Matthew 13:47–50

The Refrain

For who is God, but the Lord?* who is the Rock, except our God?

The Morning Psalm   *He Sends Redemption to His People*

Great are the deeds of the Lord!* they are studied by all who delight in them.
The works of his hands are faithfulness and justice;* all his commandments are
sure.
They stand fast for ever and ever,* because they are done in truth and equity.
He sent redemption to his people; he commanded his covenant for ever;* holy and
awesome is his Name.
The fear of the Lord is the beginning of wisdom;* those who act accordingly have
a good understanding; his praise endures for ever.

Psalm 111:2, 7–10

The Refrain

For who is God, but the Lord?* who is the Rock, except our God?

The Cry of the Church

Even so come, Lord Jesus!

The Lord's Prayer

The Prayer Appointed for the Week

Gracious Father, whose blessed Son Jesus Christ came down from heaven to be the
true bread which gives life to the world: Evermore give me this bread, that he
may live in me, and I in him; who lives and reigns with you and the Holy
Spirit, one God, now and for ever. *Amen.* †

The Concluding Prayer of the Church
Lord God, almighty and everlasting Father, you have brought me in safety to this
new day: Preserve me with your mighty power, that I may not fall into sin, nor
be overcome by adversity; and in all I do direct me to the fulfilling of your purpose; through Jesus Christ my Lord. *Amen.* †

The Midday Office   **To Be Observed on the Hour or Half Hour**
                                    Between 11 a.m. and 2 p.m.

The Call to Prayer
Sing to the LORD with the harp,* with the harp and the voice of song.
With trumpets and the sound of the horn* shout with joy before the King, the
LORD.

Psalm 98:6–7

The Request for Presence
Show us the light of your countenance, O God,* and come to us.

based on Psalm 67:1

The Greeting
O LORD, what are we that you should care for us?* mere mortals that you should
think of us?
We are like a puff of wind;* our days are like a passing shadow.

Psalm 144:3–4

The Refrain for the Midday Lessons
Proclaim the greatness of the LORD our God and fall down before his footstool;* he
is the Holy One.

Psalm 99:5

A Reading
Youths grow tired and weary, the young stumble and fall, but those who hope in
YAHWEH will regain their strength, they will sprout wings like eagles, though
they run they will not grow weary, though they walk they will never tire.

Isaiah 40:30–31

The Refrain
Proclaim the greatness of the LORD our God and fall down before his footstool;* he
is the Holy One.

The Midday Psalm   *The Faithfulness of the LORD Endures*
Praise the LORD, all you nations;* laud him, all you peoples.
For his loving-kindness toward us is great,* and the faithfulness of the LORD
endures for ever.

Psalm 117

The Refrain
Proclaim the greatness of the LORD our God and fall down before his footstool;* he
is the Holy One.

The Cry of the Church
Be, Lord, my helper and forsake me not. Do not despise me, O God, my savior.
The Short Breviary

The Lord's Prayer

The Prayer Appointed for the Week
Gracious Father, whose blessed Son Jesus Christ came down from heaven to be the
true bread which gives life to the world: Evermore give me this bread, that he
may live in me, and I in him; who lives and reigns with you and the Holy
Spirit, one God, now and for ever. *Amen.* †

The Concluding Prayer of the Church
Almighty and everlasting God, who willed that our Savior should take upon Him
our flesh and suffer death upon the Cross, that all mankind should follow the
example of His great humility, mercifully grant that we may both follow the
example of His patience and also be made partakers of His resurrection.
Through the same Jesus Christ. *Amen.*
adapted from The Short Breviary

The Vespers Office　　　　　　　　**To Be Observed on the Hour or Half Hour**
Between 5 and 8 p.m.

The Call to Prayer
Let the Name of the Lord be blessed,* from this time forth for evermore.
From the rising of the sun to its going down* let the Name of the Lord be praised.
Psalm 113:2–3

The Request for Presence
Hear my prayer, O God;* do not hide yourself from my petition.
Listen to me and answer me; . . .
Psalm 55:1–2

The Greeting
The Lord is in his holy temple; let all the earth keep silence before him.
Traditional

The Hymn　　　　　　　　　　　　　　*Must Jesus Bear the Cross Alone*
　Must Jesus bear the cross alone, and all the world go free?
　No, there's a cross for everyone, and there's a cross for me.

　How happy are the saints above, who once went sorrowing here!
　But now they taste unmingled love, and joys without a tear.

　The consecrated cross I'll bear till death shall set me free;
　And then go home my crown to wear, for there's a crown for me.
Thomas Shepherd

The Refrain for the Vespers Lessons
Put your trust in God;* for I will yet give thanks to him, who is the help of my
countenance, and my God.

Psalm 42:7

The Vespers Psalm   *We Will Praise Your Name For Ever*
We have heard with our ears, O God, our forefathers have told us,* the deeds you
did in their days, in the days of old.
How with your hand you drove the peoples out and planted our forefathers in the
land;* how you destroyed nations and made your people flourish.
For they did not take the land by their sword, nor did their arm win the victory for
them;* but your right hand, your arm, and the light of your countenance,
because you favored them.
You are my King and my God;* you command victories for Jacob.
Through you we pushed back our adversaries;* through your Name we trampled
on those who rose up against us.
For I do not rely on my bow,* and my sword does not give me the victory.
Surely, you gave us victory over our adversaries* and put those who hate us to
shame.
Every day we gloried in God,* and we will praise your Name for ever.

Psalm 44:1–8

The Refrain
Put your trust in God;* for I will yet give thanks to him, who is the help of my
countenance, and my God.

The Cry of the Church
O God, come to my assistance! O Lord, make haste to help me!

The Lord's Prayer

The Prayer Appointed for the Week
Gracious Father, whose blessed Son Jesus Christ came down from heaven to be the
true bread which gives life to the world: Evermore give me this bread, that he
may live in me, and I in him; who lives and reigns with you and the Holy
Spirit, one God, now and for ever. *Amen.* †

The Concluding Prayer of the Church
Save me, Lord, while I am awake and keep me while I sleep, that I may wake with
Christ and rest in peace. *Amen.*

The Morning Office   **To Be Observed on the Hour or Half Hour**
Between 6 and 9 a.m.

The Call to Prayer
Open for me the gates of righteousness;* I will enter them; I will offer thanks to the
Lord.

Psalm 118:19

The Request for Presence
Return, O LORD; how long will you tarry?* be gracious to your servants.
Satisfy us by your loving-kindness in the morning;* so shall we rejoice and be glad all the days of our life.
Make us glad by the measure of the days that you afflicted us* and the years in which we suffered adversity.
Show your servants your works* and your splendor to their children.

Psalm 90:13–16

The Greeting
O LORD my God, how excellent is your greatness! you are clothed with majesty and splendor.

Psalm 104:1

The Refrain for the Midday Lessons
I will walk in the presence of the LORD* in the land of the living.

Psalm 116:8

A Reading
Jesus prayed, saying: ". . . Holy Father, keep those you have given me true to your name, so that they may be one like us. While I was with them, I kept those you had given me true to your name. I have watched over them and not one is lost except one who was destined to be lost, and this was to fulfill the scriptures. But now I am coming to you and I say these things in the world to share my joy with them to the full . . . I pray not only for these but also for those who through their teaching will come to believe in me. May they all be one, just as, Father, you are in me and I am in you, so that they also may be in us, so that the world may believe it was you who sent me. I have given them the glory you gave to me, that they may be one as we are one."

John 17:11–13, 20–22

The Refrain
I will walk in the presence of the LORD* in the land of the living.

The Morning Psalm   *In His Name We Put Our Trust*
Behold, the eye of the LORD is upon those who fear him,* on those who wait upon his love,
To pluck their lives from death,* and to feed them in time of famine.
Our soul waits for the LORD;* he is our help and our shield.
Indeed, our heart rejoices in him,* for in his holy Name we put our trust.
Let your loving-kindness, O LORD, be upon us,* as we have put our trust in you.

Psalm 33:18–22

The Refrain
I will walk in the presence of the LORD* in the land of the living.

The Cry of the Church
Even so come, Lord Jesus!

The Lord's Prayer

The Prayer Appointed for the Week

Gracious Father, whose blessed Son Jesus Christ came down from heaven to be the true bread which gives life to the world: Evermore give me this bread, that he may live in me, and I in him; who lives and reigns with you and the Holy Spirit, one God, now and for ever. *Amen.* †

The Concluding Prayer of the Church

Almighty and eternal God, ruler of all things in heaven and earth: Mercifully accept the prayers of your people everywhere, and strengthen each of us to do your will; through Jesus Christ my Lord. *Amen.* †

The Midday Office   To Be Observed on the Hour or Half Hour
                                           Between 11 a.m. and 2 p.m.

The Call to Prayer

Praise Him from whom all blessings flow; praise Him all creatures here below; praise Him you heavenly hosts; praise Father, Son and Holy Ghost.

Traditional

The Request for Presence

Be my strong rock, a castle to keep me safe, for you are my crag and my stronghold;* for the sake of your Name, lead me and guide me.

Psalm 31:3

The Greeting

To you, O LORD, I lift up my soul;* my God, I put my trust in you . . .

Psalm 25:1

The Refrain for the Midday Lessons

Happy are they all who fear the LORD,* and who follow in his ways!

Psalm 28:1

A Reading

All who belong to Christ Jesus have crucified self with all its passions and its desires.

Galatians 5:24

The Refrain

Happy are they all who fear the LORD,* and who follow in his ways!

The Midday Psalm   *Our Help Is in the Name of the LORD*

If the LORD had not been on our side,* let Israel now say.
If the LORD had not been on our side,* when enemies rose up against us;
Then would they have swallowed us up alive* in their fierce anger toward us;
Then would the waters have overwhelmed us* and the torrent gone over us;
Then would the raging waters* have gone right over us.
Blessed be the LORD!* he has not given us over to be a prey for their teeth.

We have escaped like a bird from the snare of the fowler;* the snare is broken, and
  we have escaped.
Our help is in the Name of the LORD,* the maker of heaven and earth.

Psalm 124

The Refrain
Happy are they all who fear the LORD,* and who follow in his ways!

The Small Verse
Keep me, Lord, as the apple of your eye and carry me under the shadow of your
  wings.

Traditional

The Lord's Prayer

The Prayer Appointed for the Week
Gracious Father, whose blessed Son Jesus Christ came down from heaven to be the
  true bread which gives life to the world: Evermore give me this bread, that he
  may live in me, and I in him; who lives and reigns with you and the Holy
  Spirit, one God, now and for ever. *Amen.* †

The Concluding Prayer of the Church
Come forth, O Christ, and help me. For your name's sake deliver me.

Traditional

The Vespers Office   **To Be Observed on the Hour or Half Hour**
                                          Between 5 and 8 p.m.

The Call to Prayer
Proclaim with me the greatness of the LORD;* let us exalt his Name together.

Psalm 34:3

The Request for Presence
Show your goodness, O LORD, to those who are good* and to those who are true of
  heart.

Psalm 125:4

The Greeting
O LORD our Governor,* how exalted is your Name in all the world!

Psalm 8:1

The Hymn   *Steal Away to Jesus*
  Steal away, steal away; steal away to Jesus.
  Steal away, steal away home.
  I ain't got long to stay here.
  My Lord, he calls me,
  he calls me by thunder;
  The trumpet sounds within my soul.
  I ain't got long to stay here.

Steal away, steal away; steal away to Jesus.
Steal away, steal away home.
I ain't got long to stay here.
Green trees a-bending,
poor sinners a-trembling;
The trumpet sounds within my soul.
I ain't got long to stay here.

Steal away, steal away; steal away to Jesus.
Steal away, steal away home.
I ain't got long to stay here.
My Lord he calls me,
he calls me by lightning;
The trumpet sounds within my soul.
I ain't got long to stay here.

African American Spiritual

The Refrain for the Vespers Lessons
We have heard with our ears, O God, our forefathers have told us,* the deeds you
did in their days, in the days of old.

Psalm 44:1

The Vespers Psalm   *Let the Nations Be Glad and Sing for Joy*
May God be merciful to us and bless us,* show us the light of his countenance and
come to us.
Let your ways be known upon earth,* your saving health among all nations.
Let the peoples praise you, O God;* let all the peoples praise you.
Let the nations be glad and sing for joy,* for you judge the peoples with equity and
guide all the nations upon earth.
Let the peoples praise you, O God;* let all the peoples praise you.
The earth has brought forth her increase;* may God, our own God, give us his
blessing.
May God give us his blessing,* and may all the ends of the earth stand in awe of
him.

Psalm 67

The Refrain
We have heard with our ears, O God, our forefathers have told us,* the deeds you
did in their days, in the days of old.

The Call to Prayer
Even so come, Lord Jesus!

The Lord's Prayer

The Prayer Appointed for the Week
Gracious Father, whose blessed Son Jesus Christ came down from heaven to be the
true bread which gives life to the world: Evermore give me this bread, that he

may live in me, and I in him; who lives and reigns with you and the Holy
Spirit, one God, now and for ever. *Amen.* †

The Concluding Prayer of the Church

Almighty and eternal God, ruler of all things in heaven and earth: Mercifully
accept my prayer, and strengthen me to do your will; through Jesus Christ our
Lord. *Amen.* †

The Morning Office   **To Be Observed on the Hour or Half Hour**
                                               Between 6 and 9 a.m.

The Call to Prayer

I will listen to what the Lord God is saying,* for he is speaking peace to his faithful
people and to those who turn their hearts to him.
Truly, his salvation is very near to those who fear him,* that his glory may dwell in
our land.

Psalm 85:8–9

The Request for Presence

Send out your light and your truth, that they may lead me,* and bring me to your
holy hill and to your dwelling;
That I may go to the altar of God, to the God of my joy and gladness;* and on the
harp I will give thanks to you, O God my God.

Psalm 43:3–4

The Greeting

Let all peoples know that you, whose Name is Yahweh,* you alone are the Most
High over all the earth.

Psalm 83:18

The Refrain for the Morning Lessons

The people that walked in darkness have seen a great light; on the inhabitants of a
country in shadow dark as death light has blazed forth.

Isaiah 9:1

A Reading

As he drew near and came into sight of the city he shed tears over it and said, 'If
you too had only recognized on this day the way to peace! But in fact it is hidden from your eyes! Yes, a time is coming when your enemies will raise fortifi-
cations all round you, when they will encircle you and hem you in on every
side; they will dash you and the children inside your walls to the ground; they
will leave not one stone standing on another within you, because you did not
recognize the moment of your visitation.'

Luke 19:41–44

The Refrain

The people that walked in darkness have seen a great light; on the inhabitants of a
country in shadow dark as death light has blazed forth.

The Morning Psalm   *Who Can Stand in His Holy Place?*

The earth is the LORD's and all that is in it,* the world and all who dwell therein.

For it is he who founded it upon the seas* and made it firm upon the rivers of the
deep.

"Who can ascend the hill of the LORD?* and who can stand in his holy place?"

"Those who have clean hands and a pure heart,* who have not pledged themselves
to falsehood, nor sworn by what is a fraud.

They shall receive a blessing from the LORD* and a just reward from the God of
their salvation."

Such is the generation of those who seek him,* of those who seek your face, O God
of Jacob.

Psalm 24:1–6

The Refrain

The people that walked in darkness have seen a great light; on the inhabitants of a
country in shadow dark as death light has blazed forth.

The Small Verse

Those who go through the desolate valley will find it a place of springs,* for the
early rains have covered it with pools of water.

Psalm 84:5

The Lord's Prayer

The Prayer Appointed for the Week

Gracious Father, whose blessed Son Jesus Christ came down from heaven to be the
true bread which gives life to the world: Evermore give me this bread, that he
may live in me, and I in him; who lives and reigns with you and the Holy
Spirit, one God, now and for ever. *Amen.* †

The Concluding Prayer of the Church

Lord God, almighty and everlasting Father, you have brought me in safety to this
new day: Preserve me with your mighty power, that I may not fall into sin, nor
be overcome by adversity; and in all I do direct me to the fulfilling of your purpose; through Jesus Christ my Lord. *Amen.* †

The Midday Office   **To Be Observed on the Hour or Half Hour**
Between 11 a.m. and 2 p.m.

The Call to Prayer

Sing to the LORD a new song;* sing his praise in the congregation of the faithful.

Psalm 149:1

The Request for Presence

Make me understand the way of your commandments,* that I may meditate on
your marvelous works.

Psalm 119:27

The Greeting
How deep I find your thoughts, O God!* how great is the sum of them!

Psalm 139:16

The Refrain for the Midday Lessons
I will thank you, O LORD my God, with all my heart* and glorify your Name for
evermore.

Psalm 86:12

A Reading
. . . I can only say that forgetting all that lies behind me, and straining forward to
what lies in front, I am racing towards the finishing point to win the prize of
God's heavenly call in Christ Jesus.

Philippians 3:13–14

The Refrain
I will thank you, O LORD my God, with all my heart* and glorify your Name for
evermore.

The Midday Psalm   *The LORD Himself Is God*
Know this: The LORD himself is God;* he himself has made us, and we are his; we
are his people and the sheep of his pasture.
Enter his gates with thanksgiving; go into his courts with praise;* give thanks to
him and call upon his Name.
For the LORD is good; his mercy is everlasting;* and his faithfulness endures from
age to age.

Psalm 100:2–4

The Refrain
I will thank you, O LORD my God, with all my heart* and glorify your Name for
evermore.

The Cry of the Church
Lord, have mercy on us. Christ, have mercy on us. Lord, have mercy on us.

The Lord's Prayer

The Prayer Appointed for the Week
Gracious Father, whose blessed Son Jesus Christ came down from heaven to be the
true bread which gives life to the world: Evermore give me this bread, that he
may live in me, and I in him; who lives and reigns with you and the Holy
Spirit, one God, now and for ever. *Amen.* †

The Concluding Prayer of the Church
Lord Jesus Christ, you said to your apostles, "Peace I give to you; my own peace I
leave with you:" Regard not my sins but my faith, and give to me and all your
church the peace and unity of that heavenly City, where with the Father and
the Holy Spirit you live and reign, now and for ever. *Amen.* †

The Vespers Office

**To Be Observed on the Hour or Half Hour
Between 5 and 8 p.m.**

The Call to Prayer
But I will call upon God,* and the LORD will deliver me.
In the evening, in the morning, and at noonday, I will complain and lament,* and
  he will hear my voice.
He will bring me safely back . . .
God, who is enthroned of old, will hear me.

Psalm 55:17ff

The Request for Presence
I cry out to you, O LORD;* I say, "You are my refuge, my portion in the land of the
  living."

Psalm 142:5

The Greeting
I will confess you among the peoples, O LORD;* I will sing praises to you among
  the nations.

Psalm 108:3

The Hymn   *Great Is Your Faithfulness*
    Great is your faithfulness, O God my Father;
    There is no shadow of turning with thee;
    You change not, your compassions, they fail not;
    As you have been, you forever will be.

    Summer and winter and springtime and harvest,
    Sun, moon, and stars in their courses above
    Join with all nature in manifold witness
    To your great faithfulness, mercy, and love.

    Pardon for sin and a peace that endures,
    Your own dear presence to cheer and to guide;
    Strength for today and bright hope for tomorrow,
    Blessings all mine, with ten-thousand beside!

    Great is your faithfulness! Great is your faithfulness!
    Morning by morning new mercies I see;
    All I have needed your hand has provided;
    Great is your faithfulness, Lord, unto me!
                              Thomas Chisholm

The Refrain for the Vespers Lessons
The LORD will hear the desire of the humble;* you will strengthen their heart and
  your ears shall hear;

Psalm 10:18

The Vespers Psalm   *He Has Heard the Voice of My Prayer*

Blessed is the LORD!* for he has heard the voice of my prayer.

The LORD is my strength and my shield;* my heart trusts in him, and I have been
    helped;

Therefore my heart dances for joy,* and in my song will I praise him.

The LORD is the strength of his people,* a safe refuge for his anointed.

Save your people and bless your inheritance;* shepherd them and carry them
    for ever.

Psalm 28:7–11

The Refrain

The LORD will hear the desire of the humble;* you will strengthen their heart and
    your ears shall hear;

The Small Verse

The Lord is my shepherd and nothing is wanting to me. In green pastures He hath
    settled me.

THE SHORT BREVIARY

The Lord's Prayer

The Prayer Appointed for the Week

Gracious Father, whose blessed Son Jesus Christ came down from heaven to be the
    true bread which gives life to the world: Evermore give me this bread, that he
    may live in me, and I in him; who lives and reigns with you and the Holy
    Spirit, one God, now and for ever. *Amen.* †

The Concluding Prayer of the Church

Lead me not into temptation. Deliver me from evil. Yours are the kingdom and the
    glory.

The Morning Office   **To Be Observed on the Hour or Half Hour**
                                                 Between 6 and 9 a.m.

The Call to Prayer

Come, let us bow down, and bend the knee,* and kneel before the LORD our
    Maker.

For he is our God,* and we are the people of his pasture and the sheep of his hand.

Psalm 95:6–7

The Request for Presence

So teach us to number our days* that we may apply our hearts to wisdom.

Psalm 90:12

The Greeting

My God, my rock in whom I put my trust,* my shield, the horn of my salvation,
    and my refuge; you are worthy of praise.

Psalm 18:2

The Refrain for the Morning Lessons
My eyes are upon the faithful in the land, that they may dwell with me.

Psalm 101:6

A Reading
When the time of the Jewish Passover was near Jesus went up to Jerusalem, and
in the Temple he found people selling cattle and sheep and doves, and the
money-changers sitting there. Making a whip out of cord, he drove them all
out of the Temple, sheep and cattle as well, scattered the money changers'
coins, knocked their tables over and said to the dove sellers, 'Take all this out
of here and stop using my Father's house as a market.' Then his disciples
remembered the words of scripture: *I am eaten up with zeal for your house.* The
Jews intervened and said, 'What sign can you show us that you should act
like this?' Jesus answered, 'Destroy this Temple, and in three days I will raise
it up.' The Jews replied, 'It has taken forty-six years to build this Temple: are
you going to raise it up again in three days?' But he was speaking of the
Temple that was his body, and when Jesus rose from the dead, his disciples
remembered that he had said this, and they believed the scripture and what
he had said.

John 2:13–22

The Refrain
My eyes are upon the faithful in the land, that they may dwell with me.

The Morning Psalm   *Be Seated on Your Lofty Throne, O Most High*
Awake, O my God, decree justice;* let the assembly of the peoples gather round you.
Be seated on your lofty throne, O Most High;* O LORD, judge the nations.
Let the malice of the wicked come to an end, but establish the righteous;* for you
   test the mind and heart, O righteous God.
God is my shield and defense;* he is the savior of the true in heart.
God is a righteous judge;* God sits in judgment every day.

Psalm 7:7–8, 10–12

The Refrain
My eyes are upon the faithful in the land, that they may dwell with me.

The Cry of the Church
O God, come to my assistance! O Lord, make haste to help me!

The Lord's Prayer

The Prayer Appointed for the Week
Gracious Father, whose blessed Son Jesus Christ came down from heaven to be the
   true bread which gives life to the world: Evermore give me this bread, that he
   may live in me, and I in him; who lives and reigns with you and the Holy
   Spirit, one God, now and for ever. *Amen.* †

The Concluding Prayer of the Church

Lord God, almighty and everlasting Father, you have brought me in safety to this new day: Preserve me with your mighty power, that I may not fall into sin, nor be overcome by adversity; and in all I do direct me to the fulfilling of your purpose; through Jesus Christ my Lord. *Amen.* †

The Midday Office   To Be Observed on the Hour or Half Hour
                                     Between 11 a.m. and 2 p.m.

The Call to Prayer

Praise God from whom all blessings flow; praise him, all creatures here below; praise him, you heavenly hosts; praise Father, Son and Holy Ghost.

Traditional

The Request for Presence

Hear my prayer, O Lord,* and give ear to my cry; . . .
For I am but a sojourner with you,* a wayfarer, as all my forebears were.

Psalm 39:13–14

The Greeting

With my whole heart I seek you;* let me not stray from your commandments.

Psalm 119:10

The Refrain for the Midday Lessons

The Lord loves those who hate evil; he preserves the lives of his saints* and delivers them from the hand of the wicked.

Psalm 97:10

A Reading

Do not be afraid, for I have redeemed you; I have called you by your name, you are mine. Should you pass through the waters, I shall be with you; or through rivers, they will not swallow you up. Should you walk through fire, you will not suffer, and the flame will not burn you. For I am Yahweh, your God, the Holy One of Israel, your Savior.

Isaiah 43:1–3

The Refrain

The Lord loves those who hate evil; he preserves the lives of his saints* and delivers them from the hand of the wicked.

The Midday Psalm   *When Will You Comfort Me?*

My soul has longed for your salvation;* I have put my hope in your word.
My eyes have failed from watching for your promise,* and I say, "When will you comfort me?"
I have become like a leather flask in the smoke,* but I have not forgotten your statutes.
How much longer must I wait?* when will you give judgment against those who persecute me?

The proud have dug pits for me;* they do not keep your law.
All your commandments are true;* help me, for they persecute me with lies.
They had almost made an end of me on earth,* but I have not forsaken your
    commandments.

Psalm 119:81–87

The Refrain
The LORD loves those who hate evil; he preserves the lives of his saints* and
    delivers them from the hand of the wicked.

The Cry of the Church
O God, come to my assistance! O Lord, make haste to help me!

The Lord's Prayer

The Prayer Appointed for the Week
Gracious Father, whose blessed Son Jesus Christ came down from heaven to be the
    true bread which gives life to the world: Evermore give me this bread, that he
    may live in me, and I in him; who lives and reigns with you and the Holy
    Spirit, one God, now and for ever. *Amen.* †

The Concluding Prayer of the Church
Almighty and everlasting God, by whose Spirit the whole body of your faithful is
    governed and sanctified: Receive my supplications and prayers which I offer
    before you for all members of your holy Church, that in our vocation and min-
    istry we all may truly serve you through our Lord and Savior Jesus Christ.
    Amen. †

The Vespers Office   **To Be Observed on the Hour or Half Hour**
Between 5 and 8 p.m.

The Call to Prayer
Blessed be the LORD, the God of Israel, from everlasting and to everlasting;* and
    let all the people say, "Amen!"

Psalm 106:48

The Request for Presence
Send forth your strength, O God;* establish, O God, what you have wrought
    for us.

Psalm 68:28

The Greeting
My heart is firmly fixed, O God, my heart is fixed;* I will sing and make melody.

Psalm 57:7

The Hymn

This Is My Father's World

This is my Father's world,
and to my listening ears
all nature sings,
and round me rings
the music of the spheres,
This is my Father's world:
I rest me in the thought
of rocks and trees,
of skies and seas;
his hand the wonders wrought.

This is my Father's world,
the birds their carols raise,
the morning light,
the lily white,
declare their maker's praise.
This is my Father's world:
he shines in all that's fair;
in the rustling grass
I hear him pass;
he speaks to me everywhere.

This is my Father's world.
O let me never forget
that though the wrong
seems oft so strong,
God is the ruler yet.
This is my Father's world:
why should my heart be sad?
The Lord is King;
let heavens ring!
God reigns; let earth be glad!

Maltbie Babcock

The Refrain for the Vespers Lessons
I trust in the mercy of God for ever and ever.

Psalm 52:8b

The Vespers Psalm

Let My Prayer Be as the Evening Sacrifice

O LORD, I call to you; come to me quickly;* hear my voice when I cry to you.
Let my prayer be set forth in your sight as incense,* the lifting up of my hands as
the evening sacrifice.
Set a watch before my mouth, O LORD, and guard the door of my lips;* let not my
heart incline to any evil thing.
Let me not be occupied in wickedness with evildoers,* nor eat of their choice
foods.
Let the righteous smite me in friendly rebuke;* let not the oil of the unrighteous
anoint my head; for my prayer is continually against their wicked deeds.
Let their rulers be overthrown in stony places,* that they may know my words are
true.

Psalm 141:1–6

The Refrain
I trust in the mercy of God for ever and ever.

The Cry of the Church
Even so, come Lord Jesus!

The Lord's Prayer

The Prayer Appointed for the Week

Gracious Father, whose blessed Son Jesus Christ came down from heaven to be the
true bread which gives life to the world: Evermore give me this bread, that he
may live in me, and I in him; who lives and reigns with you and the Holy
Spirit, one God, now and for ever. *Amen.* †

The Concluding Prayer of the Church

Almighty God, whose loving hand has given me all that I possess: Grant me grace
that I may honor you with my substance, and, remembering the account which
I must one day give, may be a faithful steward of your bounty, through Jesus
Christ our Lord. *Amen.* †

The Morning Office   To Be Observed on the Hour or Half Hour
                                            Between 6 and 9 a.m.

The Call to Prayer

I will call upon God,* and the Lord will deliver me.
In the evening, in the morning, and at noonday, I will complain and lament,* and
he will hear my voice.
He will bring me safely back . . . * God, who is enthroned of old, will hear me.

Psalm 55:17ff

The Request for Presence

Be pleased, O God, to deliver me;* O Lord, make haste to help me.

Psalm 70:1

The Greeting

Happy are they whom you choose and draw to your courts to dwell there!* they
will be satisfied by the beauty of your house, by the holiness of your temple.

Psalm 65:4

The Refrain for the Morning Lessons

The Lord knows our human thoughts;* how like a puff of wind they are.
Happy are they whom you instruct, O Lord!* whom you teach out of your law.

Psalm 94:11–12

A Reading

Jesus said: "As it was in Noah's day, so will it also be in the days of the Son of man.
People were eating and drinking, marrying wives and husbands, right to the
day Noah went into the ark, and the Flood came and destroyed them all. It will
be the same as it was in Lot's day: people were eating and drinking, buying,
selling, planting and building, but the day Lot left Sodom, it rained fire and
brimstone from heaven and it destroyed them all. It will be the same when the
day comes for the Son of man to be revealed."

Luke 17:26–30

The Refrain
The LORD knows our human thoughts;* how like a puff of wind they are.
Happy are they whom you instruct, O Lord!* whom you teach out of your law.

The Morning Psalm   *For God Alone My Soul in Silence Waits*
For God alone my soul in silence waits;* truly, my hope is in him.
He alone is my rock and my salvation,* my stronghold, so that I shall not be
    shaken.
In God is my safety and my honor;* God is my strong rock and my refuge.
Put your trust in him always, O people,* pour out your hearts before him, for God
    is our refuge.
Those of high degree are but a fleeting breath,* even those of low estate cannot be
    trusted.
On the scales they are lighter than a breath,* all of them together.
Put no trust in extortion; in robbery take no empty pride;* though wealth increase,
    set not your heart upon it.
God has spoken once, twice have I heard it,* that power belongs to God.
Steadfast love is yours, O Lord,* for you repay everyone according to his deeds.

Psalm 62:6–14

The Refrain
The LORD knows our human thoughts;* how like a puff of wind they are.
Happy are they whom you instruct, O Lord!* whom you teach out of your law.

The Cry of the Church
O God, come to my assistance! O Lord, make haste to help me!

The Lord's Prayer

The Prayer Appointed for the Week
Gracious Father, whose blessed Son Jesus Christ came down from heaven to be the
    true bread which gives life to the world: Evermore give me this bread, that he
    may live in me, and I in him; who lives and reigns with you and the Holy
    Spirit, one God, now and for ever. *Amen.* †

The Concluding Prayer of the Church
Lord God, almighty and everlasting Father, you have brought me in safety to this
    new day: Preserve me with your mighty power, that I may not fall into sin, nor
    be overcome by adversity; and in all I do direct me to the fulfilling of your pur-
    pose; through Jesus Christ my Lord. *Amen.* †

The Midday Office   To Be Observed on the Hour or Half Hour
                                     Between 11 a.m. and 2 p.m.

The Call to Prayer
Ascribe power to God;* his majesty is over Israel; his strength is in the skies.

Psalm 68:35

The Request for Presence
Accept, O LORD, the willing tribute of my lips,* and teach me your judgments.
Psalm 119:108

The Greeting
Let the words of my mouth and the meditation of my heart be acceptable in your
sight,* O LORD, my strength and my redeemer.
Psalm 19:14

The Refrain for the Midday Lessons
Light shines in the darkness for the upright.*
Psalm 112:4

A Reading
Of Christ, the Apostle wrote, saying: "During his life on earth, he offered up a
prayer and entreaty, with loud cries and with tears, to the one who had the
power to save him from death, and, winning a hearing by his reverence, he
learned obedience, Son though he was, through his sufferings; when he had
been perfected, he became for all who obey him the source of eternal salvation
and was acclaimed by God with the title of high *priest of the order of
Melchizedek.*"
Hebrews 5:7–10

The Refrain
Light shines in the darkness for the upright.*

The Midday Psalm   *His Name Only Is Exalted*
Praise the LORD from the earth,* you sea-monsters and all deeps;
Fire and hail, snow and fog,* tempestuous wind, doing his will;
Mountains and all hills,* fruit trees and all cedars;
Wild beasts and all cattle,* creeping things and winged birds;
Kings of the earth and all peoples,* princes and all rulers of the world;
Young men and maidens,* old and young together.
Let them praise the Name of the LORD,* for his Name only is exalted, his splendor
is over earth and heaven.
Psalm 148:7–13

The Refrain
Light shines in the darkness for the upright.*

The Cry of the Church
O Lord, hear my prayer and let my cry come unto you. Thanks be to God.
THE SHORT BREVIARY

The Lord's Prayer

The Prayer Appointed for the Week
Gracious Father, whose blessed Son Jesus Christ came down from heaven to be the
true bread which gives life to the world: Evermore give me this bread, that he

may live in me, and I in him; who lives and reigns with you and the Holy
Spirit, one God, now and for ever. *Amen.* †

The Concluding Prayer of the Church
Lord Jesus Christ, by your death you took away the sting of death: Grant me to so
follow in faith where you have led the way, that I may at length fall asleep
peacefully in you and wake in your likeness; for your tender mercies' sake.
Amen. †

The Vespers Office   **To Be Observed on the Hour or Half Hour**
                                          Between 5 and 8 p.m.

The Call to Prayer
I will call upon God,* and the Lord will deliver me.
He will bring me safely back . . . * God, who is enthroned of old, will hear me.
Psalm 55:17ff

The Request for Presence
You are the Lord; do not withhold your compassion from me;* let your love and
your faithfulness keep me safe for ever.
Psalm 40:12

The Greeting
I remember your Name in the night, O Lord,* and dwell upon your law.
Psalm 119:55

The Hymn   *Christ Is Made the Sure Foundation*
Christ is made the sure foundation,
Christ the head and cornerstone;
Chosen of the Lord and precious,
Binding all the Church in one;
Holy Zion's help forever,
And her confidence alone.

To this temple, where we call you,
Come, O Lord of Hosts, today!
With your faithful loving-kindness
Hear your people as they pray,
And your fullest benediction
Shed within its walls alway.

Here vouchsafe to all your servants
What they ask of you to gain;
What they gain from you forever
With the blessed to retain;
And hereafter in your glory,
While unending ages reign.

Laud and honor to the Father,
Laud and honor to the Son,
Laud and honor to the Spirit,
Ever three and ever one;
One in might and one in glory,
While unending ages run.

Latin, 7th C.

The Refrain for the Vespers Lessons

Unless the LORD watches over the city,* in vain the watchman keeps his vigil.

Psalm 127:2

The Vespers Psalm
The LORD Is Known by His Acts of Justice

The ungodly have fallen into the pit they dug,* and in the snare they set is their
own foot caught.

The LORD is known by his acts of justice;* the wicked are trapped in the works of
their own hands.

The wicked shall be given over to the grave,* and also all the peoples that forget
God.

For the needy shall not always be forgotten,* and the hope of the poor shall not
perish for ever.

Rise up, O LORD, let not the ungodly have the upper hand;* let them be judged
before you.

Put fear upon them, O LORD;* let the ungodly know they are but mortal.

Psalm 9:15–20

The Refrain

Unless the LORD watches over the city,* in vain the watchman keeps his vigil.

The Small Verse

Open, Lord, my eyes that I may see. Open, Lord, my ears that I may hear. Open,
Lord, my heart and my mind that I may understand. So shall I turn to you and
be healed.

Traditional

The Lord's Prayer

The Prayer Appointed for the Week

Gracious Father, whose blessed Son Jesus Christ came down from heaven to be the
true bread which gives life to the world: Evermore give me this bread, that he
may live in me, and I in him; who lives and reigns with you and the Holy
Spirit, one God, now and for ever. *Amen.* †

Concluding Prayers of the Church

Almighty God, who has promised to hear the petitions of those who ask in your
Son's Name: I beseech you mercifully to incline your ear to me who have made
my prayers and supplications to you; and grant that those things which I have
faithfully asked according to your will, I may effectually obtain, to the relief of

my necessity, and to the setting forth of your glory; through Jesus Christ my Lord. *Amen.* †

May the souls of the faithful departed, through the mercy of God, rest in eternal peace. *Amen.*

The Morning Office   To Be Observed on the Hour or Half Hour
Between 6 and 9 a.m.

The Call to Prayer
Let us bless the LORD,* from this time forth for evermore.
based on Psalm 115:18

The Request for Presence
I cry out to you, O LORD;* I say, "You are my refuge, my portion in the land of the living."
Psalm 142:5

The Greeting
Exalt yourself above the heavens, O God,* and your glory over all the earth.
Psalm 108:5

The Refrain for the Morning Lessons
For the LORD God is both sun and shield;* he will give grace and glory.
Psalm 84:10

A Reading
Jesus said: "So if anyone declares himself for me in the presence of human beings, I will declare myself for him in the presence of my Father in heaven. But the one who disowns me in the presence of human beings, I will disown in the presence of my Father in heaven."
Matthew 10:32–33

The Refrain
For the LORD God is both sun and shield;* he will give grace and glory.

The Morning Psalm   *I Am the LORD Your God*
Blow the ram's-horn at the new moon,* and at the full moon, the day of our feast.
For this is a statute for Israel,* a law of the God of Jacob.
He laid it as a solemn charge upon Joseph,* when he came out of the land of Egypt.
Hear, O my people, and I will admonish you:* O Israel, if you would but listen to me!
There shall be no strange god among you;* you shall not worship a foreign god.
I am the LORD your God, who brought you out of the land of Egypt and said,*
   "Open your mouth wide, and I will fill it."
Psalm 81:3–5, 8–10

The Refrain

For the LORD God is both sun and shield;* he will give grace and glory.

The Cry of the Church

O Lord, hear my prayer and let my cry come to you. Thanks be to God.

THE SHORT BREVIARY

The Lord's Prayer

The Prayer Appointed for the Week

Gracious Father, whose blessed Son Jesus Christ came down from heaven to be the
true bread which gives life to the world: Evermore give me this bread, that he
may live in me, and I in him; who lives and reigns with you and the Holy
Spirit, one God, now and for ever. *Amen.* †

The Concluding Prayer of the Church

Lord God, almighty and everlasting Father, you have brought me in safety to this
new day: Preserve me with your mighty power, that I may not fall into sin, nor
be overcome by adversity; and in all I do direct me to the fulfilling of your purpose; through Jesus Christ my Lord. *Amen.* †

The Midday Office **To Be Observed on the Hour or Half Hour**
Between 11 a.m. and 2 p.m.

The Call to Prayer

Be strong and let your heart take courage,* all you who wait for the LORD.

Psalm 31:24

The Request for Presence

Give ear to my words, O LORD;* consider my meditation.
Hearken to my cry for help, my King and my God,* for I make my prayer to you.

Psalm 5:1–2

The Greeting

> You are God; we praise you;
> You are the Lord: we acclaim you;
> You are the eternal Father:
> All creation worships you.
> To you all angels, all powers of heaven,
> Cherubim and Seraphim, sing in endless praise:
> > Holy, holy, holy Lord, God of power and might,
> > heaven and earth are full of your glory.

The Refrain for the Midday Lessons

Blessed be the LORD God of Israel,* from age to age. Amen. Amen.

Psalm 41:13

A Reading

YAHWEH said to Moses and Aaron in Egypt, 'This month must be the first of all the months for you, the first month of your year. Speak to the whole community of Israel and say, "On the tenth day of this month each man must take an animal from the flock for his family: one animal for each household . . . It must be an animal without blemish, a male one year old; you may choose it either from the sheep or from the goats. You must keep it till the fourteenth day of the month when the whole assembly of the community of Israel will slaughter it at twilight. Some of the blood must then be taken and put on both door-posts and the lintel of the houses where it is eaten. That night the flesh must be eaten, roasted over the fire; it must be eaten with unleavened bread and bitter herbs. You must not leave any of it over till the morning; whatever is left till morning you must burn. This is how you must eat it: With a belt around your waist, your sandals on your feet and your staff in your hand. You must eat it hurriedly: it is a Passover in YAHWEH's honor. That night I shall go through Egypt and strike down all the first-born in Egypt, man and beast alike, and shall execute justice on all the gods of Egypt, I, YAHWEH! The blood shall pass over you, and you will escape the destructive plague when I strike Egypt. This day must be commemorated by you, and you must keep it as a feast in YAHWEH's honor. You must keep it as a feast-day for all generations; this is a decree for all time.

Exodus 12:1–3, 5–8, 10–14

The Refrain

Blessed be the LORD God of Israel,* from age to age. Amen. Amen.

The Midday Psalm   *I Will Bow Down in Awe of You*

Give ear to my words, O LORD;* consider my meditation.

Hearken to my cry for help, my King and my God,* for I make my prayer to you.

In the morning, LORD, you hear my voice;* early in the morning I make my appeal and watch for you.

For you are not a God who takes pleasure in wickedness,* and evil cannot dwell with you.

Braggarts cannot stand in your sight;* you hate all those who work wickedness.

You destroy those who speak lies;* the bloodthirsty and deceitful, O LORD, you abhor.

But as for me, through the greatness of your mercy I go into your house;* I will bow down toward your holy temple in awe of you.

Psalm 5:1–7

The Refrain

Blessed be the LORD God of Israel,* from age to age. Amen. Amen.

The Cry of the Church

O Lord, hear my prayer and let my cry come unto you. Thanks be to God.

THE SHORT BREVIARY

The Lord's Prayer

The Prayer Appointed for the Week
Gracious Father, whose blessed Son Jesus Christ came down from heaven to be the
true bread which gives life to the world: Evermore give me this bread, that he
may live in me, and I in him; who lives and reigns with you and the Holy
Spirit, one God, now and for ever. *Amen.* †

The Concluding Prayer of the Church
O God, the source of eternal light: Shed forth your unending day upon all of us
who watch for you, that our lips may praise you, our lives may bless you, and
our worship may give you glory; through Jesus Christ our Lord. *Amen.* †

The Vespers Office   **To Be Observed on the Hour or Half Hour**
                                          Between 5 and 8 p.m.

The Call to Prayer
Come, let us bow down, and bend the knee,* and kneel before the LORD our
Maker.
For he is our God, and we are the people of his pasture and the sheep of his hand.*
Oh, that today you would hearken to his voice!

Psalm 95:6–7

The Request for Presence
Send out your light and your truth, that they may lead me,* and bring me to your
holy hill and to your dwelling.

Psalm 43:3

The Greeting
You, O LORD, are my lamp;* my God, you make my darkness bright.

Psalm 18:29

The Hymn   *My Jesus, I Love You*
My Jesus, I love you, I know you are mine;
For you all the follies of sin I resign.
My gracious Redeemer, my Savior are thou;
If ever I loved you, my Jesus 'tis now.

I love you because you have first loved me,
And purchased my pardon on Calvary's tree;
I love you for wearing the thorns on your brow
If ever I loved you, my Jesus 'tis now.

In mansions of glory and endless delight,
I'll ever adore you in heaven so bright;
I'll sing with the glittering crown on my brow,
If ever I loved you, my Jesus 'tis now.

William Featherstone

The Refrain for the Vespers Lessons
Seven times a day do I praise you,* because of your righteous judgments.
Great peace have they who love your law;* for them there is no stumbling block.

Psalm 119:164–165

The Vespers Psalm   *You Are My Hiding Place*
You are my hiding-place; you preserve me from trouble;* you surround me with
    shouts of deliverance.
"I will instruct you and teach you in the way that you should go;* I will guide you
    with my eye.
Do not be like horse or mule, which have no understanding;* who must be fitted
    with bit and bridle, or else they will not stay near you."
Great are the tribulations of the wicked;* but mercy embraces those who trust in
    the LORD.
Be glad, you righteous, and rejoice in the LORD;* shout for joy, all who are true of
    heart.

Psalm 32:8–12

The Refrain
Seven times a day do I praise you,* because of your righteous judgments.
Great peace have they who love your law;* for them there is no stumbling block.

The Cry of the Church
Even so come, Lord Jesus!

The Lord's Prayer

The Prayer Appointed for the Week
Gracious Father, whose blessed Son Jesus Christ came down from heaven to be the
    true bread which gives life to the world: Evermore give me this bread, that he
    may live in me, and I in him; who lives and reigns with you and the Holy
    Spirit, one God, now and for ever. *Amen.* †

The Concluding Prayer of the Church
Almighty God, who after the creation of the world rested from all your works and
    sanctified a day of rest for all your creatures: Grant that I, putting away all
    earthly anxieties, may be duly prepared for the service of public worship, and
    grant as well that my Sabbath upon earth may be a preparation for the eternal
    rest promised to your people in heaven; through Jesus Christ our Lord. *Amen.* †

March Compline

Sunday
The Night Office **To Be Observed Before Retiring**

The Call to Prayer
May the Lord Almighty grant me and those I love a peaceful night and a perfect
end. *Amen.* †

The Request for Presence
Our help is in the Name of the Lord; the maker of heaven and earth.

The Greeting
Almighty God, my heavenly Father: I have sinned against you, through my own
fault, in thought, and word, and deed, in what I have done and in what I have
left undone. For the sake of your Son our Lord Jesus Christ, forgive me all my
offenses; and grant that I may serve you in newness of life, to the glory of your
Name. *Amen.* †

The Reading
It happened some time later that God put Abraham to the test. 'Abraham,
Abraham!' he called. 'Here I am,' he replied. God said, 'Take your son, your
only son, your beloved Isaac, and go to the land of Moriah, where you are to
offer him as a burnt offering on one of the mountains which I shall point out to
you.' Early next morning Abraham saddled his donkey and took with him two
of his servants and his son Isaac. He chopped wood for the burnt offering and
started on his journey to the place which God had indicated to him. On the
third day Abraham looked up and saw the place in the distance. Then
Abraham said to his servants, 'Stay here with the donkey. The boy and I are
going over there; we shall worship and then come back to you.' Abraham took
the wood for the burnt offering, loaded it on Isaac, and carried in his own
hands the fire and the knife. Then the two of them set out together. Isaac spoke
to his father Abraham. 'Father?' he said. 'Yes my son,' he replied. 'Look,' he
said, 'here are the fire and the wood, but where is the lamb for the burnt offering?' Abraham replied, 'My son, God himself will supply the lamb for the
burnt offering.' And the two of them went on together. When they arrived at
the place which God had indicated to him, Abraham built an altar there, and
arranged the wood. Then he bound his son and put him on the altar on top of
the wood. Abraham stretched out his hand and took the knife to kill his son.
But the angel of YAHWEH called to him from heaven. 'Abraham, Abraham!' he
said. 'Here I am,' he replied. 'Do not raise your hand against the boy,' the angel
said. 'Do not harm him, for now I know you fear God. You have not refused me
your own beloved son.' Then looking up, Abraham saw a ram caught by its
horns in a bush. Abraham took the ram and offered it as a burnt offering in
place of his son. Abraham called this place 'YAHWEH provides,' and hence the
saying today: 'On the mountain YAHWEH provides.' The angel of YAHWEH
called Abraham a second time from heaven. 'I swear by my own self, YAHWEH
declares, that because you have done this, because you have not refused me
your own beloved son, I will shower blessings on you and make your descen-

dants as numerous as the stars of heaven and the grains of sand on the seashore. Your descendants will gain possession of the gate of their enemies. All nations on earth will bless themselves by your descendants, because you have obeyed my command.' Abraham went back to his servants, and together they set out for Beersheba, and Abraham settled in Beersheba.

Genesis 22:1–19

*The Gloria**

The Psalm   *I Put My Trust in You*

To you, O LORD, I lift up my soul; my God, I put my trust in you;* let me not be humiliated, nor let my enemies triumph over me.

Let none who look to you be put to shame;* let the treacherous be disappointed in their schemes.

Show me your ways, O LORD,* and teach me your paths.

Lead me in your truth and teach me,* for you are the God of my salvation; in you have I trusted all the day long.

Psalm 25:1–4

*The Gloria**

The Small Verse

Into your hands, O Lord, I commend my spirit; for you have redeemed me, O Lord, O God of truth. Keep me, O Lord, as the apple of your eye; hide me under the shadow of your wings. †

The Lord's Prayer

The Petition

Keep watch, dear Lord, with those who work, or watch, or weep this night, and give your angels charge over those who sleep. Tend the sick, Lord Christ; give rest to the weary, bless the dying, soothe the suffering, pity the afflicted, shield the joyous; and all for your love's sake. *Amen.* †

The Final Thanksgiving

Lord, you now have set your servant free to go in peace as you have promised; for these eyes of mine have seen the Savior, whom you have prepared for all the world to see: a Light to enlighten the nations, and the glory of your people Israel. Glory to the Father, and to the Son, and to the Holy Spirit: as it was in the beginning, is now, and will be for ever. *Amen.*

Monday
The Night Office   **To Be Observed Before Retiring**

The Call to Prayer
May the Lord Almighty grant me and those I love a peaceful night and a perfect
   end. *Amen.* †

The Request for Presence
Our help is in the Name of the Lord; the maker of heaven and earth.

The Greeting
Almighty God, my heavenly Father: I have sinned against you, through my own
   fault, in thought, and word, and deed, in what I have done and in what I have
   left undone. For the sake of your Son our Lord Jesus Christ, forgive me all my
   offenses; and grant that I may serve you in newness of life, to the glory of your
   Name. *Amen.* †

The Reading
The will of God be done by us;
The law of God be kept by us;
Our evil will controlled by us;
Our sharp tongue checked by us;
Quick forgiveness offered by us;
Speedy repentance made by us;
Temptation sternly shunned by us;
Blessed death welcomed by us;
Angels' music heard by us;
God's highest praises sung by us.
                    from CELTIC PRAYERS

The Gloria*

The Psalm   *Look on Him and Be Radiant*
I sought the LORD, and he answered me* and delivered me out of all my terror.
Look upon him and be radiant,* and let not your faces be ashamed.
I called in my affliction and the LORD heard me* and saved me from all my
   troubles.
The angel of the LORD encompasses those who fear him,* and he will deliver them.
Taste and see that the LORD is good;* happy are they who trust in him!
                              Psalm 34:4–8

The Gloria*

The Small Verse
Into your hands, O Lord, I commend my spirit; For you have redeemed me, O
   Lord, O God of truth. Keep me, O Lord, as the apple of your eye; Hide me
   under the shadow of your wings. †

The Lord's Prayer

The Petition

Keep watch, dear Lord, with those who work, or watch, or weep this night, and give your angels charge over those who sleep. Tend the sick, Lord Christ; give rest to the weary, bless the dying, soothe the suffering, pity the afflicted, shield the joyous; and all for your love's sake. *Amen.* †

The Final Thanksgiving

Lord, you now have set your servant free to go in peace as you have promised; for these eyes of mine have seen the Savior, whom you have prepared for all the world to see: a Light to enlighten the nations, and the glory of your people Israel. Glory to the Father, and to the Son, and to the Holy Spirit: as it was in the beginning, is now, and will be for ever. *Amen.*

Tuesday
The Night Office   To Be Observed Before Retiring

The Call to Prayer

May the Lord Almighty grant me and those I love a peaceful night and a perfect end. *Amen.* †

The Request for Presence

Our help is in the Name of the Lord; the maker of heaven and earth.

The Greeting

Almighty God, my heavenly Father: I have sinned against you, through my own fault, in thought, and word, and deed, in what I have done and in what I have left undone. For the sake of your Son our Lord Jesus Christ, forgive me all my offenses; and grant that I may serve you in newness of life, to the glory of your Name. *Amen.* †

The Reading   *To His Last Breath*

The brethren asked Abba Agathon: "Amongst all our different activities, father, which is the virtue that requires the greatest effort?" He answered: "Forgive me, but I think there is no labor greater than praying to God. For every time a man wants to pray, his enemies the demons try to prevent him; for they know that nothing obstructs them so much as prayer to God. In everything else that a man undertakes, if he perseveres, he will attain rest, but in order to pray a man must struggle to his last breath."

Sayings of the Desert Fathers

*The Gloria**

The Psalm   *You Have Granted Me the Heritage of Those Who Fear Your Name*
Hear my cry, O God,* and listen to my prayer.
I call upon you from the ends of the earth* with heaviness in my heart; set me
    upon the rock that is higher than I.
For you have been my refuge,* a strong tower against the enemy.
I will dwell in your house for ever;* I will take refuge under the cover of your
    wings.
For you, O God, have heard my vows;* you have granted me the heritage of those
    who fear your Name.

Psalm 61:1–5

The Gloria*

The Small Verse
Into your hands, O Lord, I commend my spirit; For you have redeemed me, O
    Lord, O God of truth. Keep me, O Lord, as the apple of your eye; Hide me
    under the shadow of your wings. †

The Lord's Prayer

The Petition
Keep watch, dear Lord, with those who work, or watch, or weep this night, and
    give your angels charge over those who sleep. Tend the sick, Lord Christ; give
    rest to the weary, bless the dying, soothe the suffering, pity the afflicted, shield
    the joyous; and all for your love's sake. *Amen.* †

The Final Thanksgiving
Lord, you now have set your servant free to go in peace as you have promised; for
    these eyes of mine have seen the Savior, whom you have prepared for all the
    world to see: a Light to enlighten the nations, and the glory of your people
    Israel. Glory to the Father, and to the Son, and to the Holy Spirit: as it was in the
    beginning, is now, and will be for ever. *Amen.*

❧

Wednesday
The Night Office   **To Be Observed Before Retiring**

The Call to Prayer
May the Lord Almighty grant me and those I love a peaceful night and a perfect
    end. *Amen.* †

The Request for Presence
Our help is in the Name of the Lord; the maker of heaven and earth.

The Greeting

Almighty God, my heavenly Father: I have sinned against you, through my own
fault, in thought, and word, and deed, in what I have done and in what I have
left undone. For the sake of your Son our Lord Jesus Christ, forgive me all my
offenses; and grant that I may serve you in newness of life, to the glory of your
Name. *Amen.* †

The Reading　　　　　　　　　　　　　　*O Lord, You Have Searched Me and Know Me*

O Lord, you have searched me
And know me;
You know when I sit down
And when I rise up.
You discern my thoughts
From far away,
And are acquainted with all my ways.

If I have raised my hand
Against the orphan,
Or have caused the eye
Of the widow to fail,
Be gracious to me, O Lord,
And forgive all my sins.

If I have seen anyone perish
For lack of clothing,
Or a poor person without covering,
Be gracious to me, O Lord,
And forgive all my sins.

If I have rejoiced at the ruin
Of those who hate me,
Or exulted when evil overtook them,
Be gracious to me, O Lord,
And forgive all my sins.

If I have walked with falsehood,
Or my foot has hurried to deceit,
Be gracious to me, O Lord,
And forgive all my sins.

If my step has turned aside
From the way,
Or my heart has followed
After my eye,
Be gracious to me, O Lord,
And forgive all my sins.

Answer me, O God of my right,
Hear my prayer,

And deliver me
From all my transgressions,
For my hope is in you. ❖

The Gloria*

The Psalm   *Our Hearts Rejoice in Him*
Our soul waits for the LORD;* he is our help and our shield.
Indeed, our heart rejoices in him,* for in his holy Name we put our trust.
Let your loving-kindness, O LORD, be upon us,* as we have put our trust in you.

Psalm 32:20–22

The Gloria*

The Small Verse
Into your hands, O Lord, I commend my spirit; For you have redeemed me, O
    Lord, O God of truth. Keep me, O Lord, as the apple of your eye; Hide me
    under the shadow of your wings. †

The Lord's Prayer

The Petition
Keep watch, dear Lord, with those who work, or watch, or weep this night, and
    give your angels charge over those who sleep. Tend the sick, Lord Christ; give
    rest to the weary, bless the dying, soothe the suffering, pity the afflicted, shield
    the joyous; and all for your love's sake. *Amen.* †

The Final Thanksgiving
Lord, you now have set your servant free to go in peace as you have promised; for
    these eyes of mine have seen the Savior, whom you have prepared for all the
    world to see: a Light to enlighten the nations, and the glory of your people
    Israel. Glory to the Father, and to the Son, and to the Holy Spirit: as it was in the
    beginning, is now, and will be for ever. *Amen.*

Thursday
The Night Office   **To Be Observed Before Retiring**

The Call to Prayer
May the Lord Almighty grant me and those I love a peaceful night and a perfect
    end. *Amen.* †

The Request for Presence
Our help is in the Name of the Lord; the maker of heaven and earth.

The Greeting
Almighty God, my heavenly Father: I have sinned against you, through my own fault, in thought, and word, and deed, in what I have done and in what I have left undone. For the sake of your Son our Lord Jesus Christ, forgive me all my offenses; and grant that I may serve you in newness of life, to the glory of your Name. *Amen.* †

The Reading   *Anima Christi*
Soul of Christ, sanctify me,
Body of Christ, save me,
Blood of Christ refresh me,
Water from the side of Christ, wash me,
Passion of Christ, strengthen me,
O good Jesus, hear me,
Within your wounds, hide me,
Let me never be separated from you,
From the powers of darkness, defend me,
In the hour of my death call me,
And bid me come with you,
That with your saints I may praise you
For ever and ever. Amen.

> *Brother Roger of Taize*

The Gloria*

The Psalm   *Gracious Is the LORD*
Remember, O LORD, your compassion and love,* for they are from everlasting.
Remember not the sins of my youth and my transgressions;* remember me
   according to your love and for the sake of your goodness, O LORD.
Gracious and upright is the LORD;* therefore he teaches sinners in his way.
He guides the humble in doing right* and teaches his way to the lowly.
All the paths of the LORD are love and faithfulness* to those who keep his
   covenant and his testimonies.
For your Name's sake, O LORD,* forgive my sin, for it is great.

> *Psalm 25:5–10*

The Gloria*

The Small Verse
Into your hands, O Lord, I commend my spirit; For you have redeemed me, O Lord, O God of truth. Keep me, O Lord, as the apple of your eye; Hide me under the shadow of your wings. †

The Lord's Prayer

The Petition
Keep watch, dear Lord, with those who work, or watch, or weep this night, and give your angels charge over those who sleep. Tend the sick, Lord Christ; give

rest to the weary, bless the dying, soothe the suffering, pity the afflicted, shield the joyous; and all for your love's sake. *Amen.* †

The Final Thanksgiving

Lord, you now have set your servant free to go in peace as you have promised; for these eyes of mine have seen the Savior, whom you have prepared for all the world to see: a Light to enlighten the nations, and the glory of your people Israel. Glory to the Father, and to the Son, and to the Holy Spirit: as it was in the beginning, is now, and will be for ever. *Amen.*

Friday
The Night Office   To Be Observed Before Retiring

The Call to Prayer

May the Lord Almighty grant me and those I love a peaceful night and a perfect end. *Amen.* †

The Request for Presence

Our help is in the Name of the Lord; the maker of heaven and earth.

The Greeting

Almighty God, my heavenly Father: I have sinned against you, through my own fault, in thought, and word, and deed, in what I have done and in what I have left undone. For the sake of your Son our Lord Jesus Christ, forgive me all my offenses; and grant that I may serve you in newness of life, to the glory of your Name. *Amen.* †

The Reading   *Litany of Penitence*

Most holy and merciful Father:
I confess to you and to the whole communion of saints
in heaven and on earth,
that I have sinned by my own fault
in thought, word, and deed;
by what I have done, and by what I have left undone.

I have not loved you with my whole heart, and mind, and strength. I have not loved my neighbors as myself. I have not forgiven others, as I have been forgiven.
Have mercy on me, Lord.

I have been deaf to your call to serve, as Christ served us. I have not been true to the mind of Christ. I have grieved your Holy Spirit.
Have mercy on me, Lord.

I confess to you, Lord, all my past unfaithfulness: the pride, hypocrisy, and impatience of my life.
I confess to you, Lord.

My self-indulgent appetites and ways, and my exploitation of other people,
I confess to you, Lord.

My anger at my own frustration, and my envy of those more fortunate than I,
I confess to you, Lord.

My intemperate love of worldly goods and comforts, and my dishonesty in daily life and work,
I confess to you, Lord.

My negligence in prayer and worship, and my failure to commend the faith that is in me,
I confess to you, Lord.

Accept my repentance, Lord, for the wrongs I have done: for my blindness to human need and suffering, and my indifference to injustice and cruelty,
Accept my repentance, Lord.

For all false judgments, for uncharitable thoughts toward my neighbors, and for my prejudice and contempt toward those who differ from me,
Accept my repentance, Lord.

For my waste and pollution of your creation, and my lack of concern for those who come after us,
Accept my repentance, Lord.
Restore me, good Lord, and let your anger depart from me,
Favorably hear me for your mercy is great.

Accomplish in me and all of your church the work of your salvation,
That I may show forth your glory in the world.

By the cross and passion of your Son our Lord,
Bring me with all your saints to the joy of his resurrection. †

*The Gloria**

The Psalm   *The LORD Will Deliver Me*

My heart quakes within me,* and the terrors of death have fallen upon me.
Fear and trembling have come over me,* and horror overwhelms me.
And I said, "Oh, that I had wings like a dove!* I would fly away and be at rest.
I would flee to a far-off place* and make my lodging in the wilderness.
I would hasten to escape* from the stormy wind and tempest."
But I will call upon God,* and the LORD will deliver me.
Cast your burden upon the LORD, and he will sustain you;* he will never let the righteous stumble.

Psalm 55:5–9, 17, 24

The Gloria*

The Small Verse
Into your hands, O Lord, I commend my spirit; for you have redeemed me, O
Lord, O God of truth. Keep me, O Lord, as the apple of your eye; hide me
under the shadow of your wings. †

The Lord's Prayer

The Petition
Keep watch, dear Lord, with those who work, or watch, or weep this night, and
give your angels charge over those who sleep. Tend the sick, Lord Christ; give
rest to the weary, bless the dying, soothe the suffering, pity the afflicted, shield
the joyous; and all for your love's sake. *Amen.* †

The Final Thanksgiving
Lord, you now have set your servant free to go in peace as you have promised; for
these eyes of mine have seen the Savior, whom you have prepared for all the
world to see: a Light to enlighten the nations, and the glory of your people
Israel. Glory to the Father, and to the Son, and to the Holy Spirit: as it was in the
beginning, is now, and will be for ever. *Amen.*

Saturday
The Night Office   **To Be Observed Before Retiring**

The Call to Prayer
May the Lord Almighty grant me and those I love a peaceful night and a perfect
end. *Amen.* †

The Request for Presence
Our help is in the Name of the Lord; the maker of heaven and earth.

The Greeting
Almighty God, my heavenly Father: I have sinned against you, through my own
fault, in thought, and word, and deed, in what I have done and in what I have
left undone. For the sake of your Son our Lord Jesus Christ, forgive me all my
offenses; and grant that I may serve you in newness of life, to the glory of your
Name. *Amen.* †

The Reading
May God support us all the day long,
Till the shades lengthen, and the evening comes,
And the busy world is hushed,

And the fever of life is over,
And our work is done.
Then in his mercy may he give us a safe lodging,
And a holy rest, and peace at last.

> John Henry Cardinal Newman

The Gloria*

The Psalm   *You Are My Strength*

My God, my God, why have you forsaken me?* and are so far from my cry and
   from the words of my distress?
I am poured out like water;* all my bones are out of joint; my heart within my
   breast is melting wax.
My mouth is dried out like a pot-shard; my tongue sticks to the roof of my
   mouth;* and you have laid me in the dust of the grave.
Packs of dogs close me in, and gangs of evildoers circle around me;* they pierce
   my hands and my feet; I can count all my bones.
They stare and gloat over me;* they divide my garments among them; they cast
   lots for my clothing.
Be not far away, O LORD;* you are my strength; hasten to help me.

> *Psalm 22:1, 14–18*

The Gloria*

The Small Verse

Into your hands, O Lord, I commend my spirit; For you have redeemed me, O
   Lord, O God of truth. Keep me, O Lord, as the apple of your eye; Hide me
   under the shadow of your wings. †

The Lord's Prayer

The Petition

Keep watch, dear Lord, with those who work, or watch, or weep this night, and
   give your angels charge over those who sleep. Tend the sick, Lord Christ; give
   rest to the weary, bless the dying, soothe the suffering, pity the afflicted, shield
   the joyous; and all for your love's sake. *Amen.* †

The Final Thanksgiving

Lord, you now have set your servant free to go in peace as you have promised; for
   these eyes of mine have seen the Savior, whom you have prepared for all the
   world to see: a Light to enlighten the nations, and the glory of your people
   Israel. Glory to the Father, and to the Son, and to the Holy Spirit: as it was in the
   beginning, is now, and will be for ever. *Amen.*

The Gloria

Glory be to God the Father, God the Son, and God the Holy Spirit. As it was in the beginning, so it is now and so it shall ever be, world without end. Alleluia*. *Amen.*

The Lord's Prayer

Our Father, who art in heaven, hallowed be your Name.
May your kingdom come, and your will be done, on earth as in heaven.
Give us today our daily bread.
Forgive us our sins as we forgive those who sin against us.
Lead us not into temptation, but deliver us from evil;
for yours are the kingdom and the power and the glory
forever and ever. *Amen.*

Compline Prayers for Holy Week and Easter Are Located on Page 367.

*The Gloria is omitted during Lent by many Christian communities.

"Alleluia" is always omitted from every part of the Church's worship during Lent; the use of both is restored at Easter.

Holy Week and Easter

The Morning Office

To Be Observed on the Hour or Half Hour
Between 6 and 9 a.m.

The Call to Prayer

Let the peoples praise you, O God;* let all the peoples praise you.
Let the nations be glad and sing for joy,* for you judge the peoples with equity and
   guide all nations upon the earth.
Let the peoples praise you, O God;* let all the peoples praise you.

Psalm 67:3–5

The Request for Presence

Hear my voice, O LORD, according to your loving-kindness;* according to your
   judgments, give me life.

Psalm 119:149

The Greeting

Hosanna, LORD, hosanna!* . . .
Blessed is he who comes in the name of the Lord.

Psalm 118:25a, 26a

The Refrain for the Morning Lessons

God is the LORD; he has shined upon us;* form a procession with branches up to
   the horns of the altar.

Psalm 118:27

A Reading

When they were approaching Jerusalem, at Bethphage and Bethany, close by the
   Mount of Olives, he sent two of his disciples and said to them, 'Go to the village facing you, and as you enter it you will at once find a tethered colt that no
   one has yet ridden. Untie it and bring it here. If anyone says to you, "What are
   you doing?" say, "The Master needs it and will send it back here at once." '
   They went off and found a colt tethered near a door in the open street. As they
   untied it, some men standing there said, 'What are you doing untying that
   colt?' They gave the answer that Jesus had told them, and the man let them go.
   Then they took the colt to Jesus and threw their cloaks on its back, and he
   mounted it. Many people spread their cloaks on the road, and others greenery
   which they had cut in the fields. And those who went in front and those who
   followed were all shouting, '*Hosanna! Blessed is he who is coming in the name of
   the Lord!* Blessed is the coming kingdom of David our father! *Hosanna* in the
   highest heavens!' He entered Jerusalem and went into the Temple; and when
   he had surveyed it all, as it was late by now, he went out to Bethany with the
   Twelve.

Mark 11:1–11

The Refrain

God is the LORD; he has shined upon us;* form a procession with branches up to
   the horns of the altar.

The Morning Psalm   *Open the Gates and Form a Procession with Branches*

Open for me the gates of righteousness;* I will enter them; I will offer thanks to the
      LORD.

"This is the gate of the LORD;* he who is righteous may enter."

I will give thanks to you, for you answered me* and have become my salvation.

The same stone which the builders rejected* has become the chief cornerstone.

This is the LORD's doing,* and it is marvelous in our eyes.

On this day the LORD has acted;* we will rejoice and be glad in it.

Hosanna, LORD, hosanna!* LORD, send us now success.

Blessed is he who comes in the name of the Lord;* we bless you from the house of
      the LORD.

God is the LORD; he has shined upon us;* form a procession with branches up to
      the horns of the altar.

"You are my God, and I will thank you;* you are my God, and I will exalt you."

Give thanks to the LORD, for he is good;* his mercy endures for ever.

Psalm 118:19–29

The Refrain

God is the LORD; he has shined upon us;* form a procession with branches up to
      the horns of the altar.

The Cry of the Church

Blessed is he who comes in the name of the Lord, Hosanna in the highest.

The Lord's Prayer

The Prayer Appointed for the Day

Assist me mercifully with your help, O Lord God of our salvation, that I may enter
      with joy upon the contemplation of those mighty acts, whereby you have given
      us life and immortality; through Jesus Christ our Lord. *Amen.* †

The Concluding Prayer of the Church

Almighty and everliving God, in your tender love for the human race you sent
      your Son our Savior Jesus Christ to take upon him our nature, and to suffer
      death upon the cross, giving us the example of his great humility: Mercifully
      grant that I may walk in the way of his suffering, and also share in his resurrec-
      tion; through Jesus Christ my Lord, who lives and reigns with you and the
      Holy Spirit, one God, for ever and ever. *Amen.* †

The Midday Office   To Be Observed on the Hour or Half Hour
                               Between 11 a.m. and 2 p.m.

The Call to Prayer

Come, let us sing to the LORD;* let us shout for joy to the Rock of our salvation.

Let us come before his presence with thanksgiving* and raise a loud shout to him
      with psalms.

For the LORD is a great God,* and a great King above all gods.

In his hands are the caverns of the earth,* and the heights of the hills are his also.
The sea is his, for he made it,* and his hands have molded the dry land.

Psalm 95:1–5

The Request for Presence

May God give us his blessing,* and may all the ends of the earth stand in awe of
him.

Psalm 67:7

The Greeting

You, O LORD, are a shield about me;* you are my glory, the one who lifts up my
head.

Psalm 3:3

The Refrain for the Midday Lessons

May the glory of the LORD endure for ever;* may the LORD rejoice in all his works.

Psalm 104:32

A Reading

Pass through, pass through the gates. Clear a way for my people! Level up, level
up the highway, remove the stones! Hoist a signal to the peoples! This is what
YAHWEH has proclaimed to the remotest part of the earth: Say to the daughter
of Zion, 'Look, your salvation is coming; with him comes his reward, his
achievement precedes him!' They will be called 'The Holy People,' 'YAHWEH's
Redeemed,' while you will be called 'Sought after,' 'City-not-forsaken.'

Isaiah 62:10–12

The Refrain

May the glory of the LORD endure for ever;* may the LORD rejoice in all his works.

The Midday Psalm   *The Earth Is the LORD's and All That Is in It*

The earth is the LORD's and all that is in it,* the world and all who dwell therein.
For it is he who founded it upon the seas* and made it firm upon the rivers of the
deep.
"Who can ascend the hill of the LORD?"* and who can stand in his holy place?"
"Those who have clean hands and a pure heart,* who have not pledged themselves
to falsehood, nor sworn by what is a fraud.
They shall receive a blessing from the LORD* and a just reward from the God of
their salvation."
Such is the generation of those who seek him,* of those who seek your face, O God
of Jacob.

Psalm 24:1–6

The Refrain

May the glory of the LORD endure for ever;* may the LORD rejoice in all his works.

The Cry of the Church

O God, come to my assistance! O Lord, make haste to help me!

The Lord's Prayer

The Prayer Appointed for the Day

Assist me mercifully with your help, O Lord God of our salvation, that I may enter with joy upon the contemplation of those mighty acts, whereby you have given us life and immortality; through Jesus Christ our Lord. *Amen.* †

The Concluding Prayer of the Church

Almighty and everlasting God, who willed that our Savior should take upon Him, our flesh and suffer death upon the Cross, that all mankind should follow the example of His great humility, mercifully grant that I may both follow the example of His patience and also partake of His resurrection. Through the same Jesus Christ. *Amen.*

adapted from THE SHORT BREVIARY

The Vespers Office   **To Be Observed on the Hour or Half Hour Between 5 and 8 p.m.**

The Call to Prayer

Come, let us bow down, and bend the knee,* and kneel before the LORD our Maker.
For he is our God* and we are the people of his pasture and the sheep of his hand.

Psalm 95:6–7

The Request for Presence

I call upon you, O God, for you will answer me;* incline your ear to me, and hear my words.

Psalm 17:6

The Greeting

You are God: I praise you;* you are the Lord: I acclaim you;
You are the eternal Father:* all creation worships you.
Throughout the world the holy Church acclaims you:* Father, of majesty unbounded,
your true and only Son,* worthy of all worship,
and the Holy Spirit,* advocate and guide.
As these have been from the beginning,* so they are now and evermore shall be. Amen.

based on the Te Deum and Gloria

The Hymn   *Ride On in Majesty*

Ride on! Ride on in majesty!
Hark! All the tribes hosanna cry;
Your humble beast pursues his road
With palms and scattered garments strowed.

Ride on! Ride on in majesty!
In lowly pomp ride on to die;
O Christ, your triumphs now begin
Over captive death and conquered sin.

Ride on! Ride on in majesty!
The angel armies of the sky
Look down with sad and wondering eyes
To see the approaching sacrifice.

Ride on! Ride on in majesty!
Your last and fiercest strife is nigh;
The Father on his sapphire throne
Expects his own anointed Son.

Ride on! Ride on in majesty!
In lowly pomp ride on to die;
Bow your meek head to mortal pain,
Then take, O God, your power and reign.

Henry H. Milman

The Refrain for the Vespers Lessons
Sing to the LORD, you servants of his;* give thanks for the remembrance of his
holiness.

Psalm 30:4

The Vespers Psalm   *In the Temple of the LORD All Are Crying, "Glory!"*
Ascribe to the LORD, you gods,* ascribe to the LORD glory and strength.
Ascribe to the LORD the glory due his Name;* worship the LORD in the beauty of
holiness.
The voice of the LORD is upon the waters; the God of glory thunders;* the LORD is
upon the mighty waters.
The voice of the LORD is a powerful voice;* the voice of the LORD is a voice of
splendor.
The voice of the LORD breaks the cedar trees;* the LORD breaks the cedars of
Lebanon;
He makes Lebanon skip like a calf,* and Mount Hermon like a young
wild ox.
The voice of the LORD splits the flames of fire; the voice of the LORD shakes the
wilderness;* the LORD shakes the wilderness of Kadesh.
The voice of the LORD makes the oak trees writhe* and strips the forests
bare.
And in the temple of the LORD* all are crying, "Glory!"
The LORD sits enthroned above the flood;* the LORD sits enthroned as King for
evermore.
The LORD shall give strength to his people;* the LORD shall give his people the
blessing of peace.

Psalm 29

The Refrain
Sing to the LORD, you servants of his;* give thanks for the remembrance of his
holiness.

The Lord's Prayer

The Prayer Appointed for the Day
Assist me mercifully with your help, O Lord God of our salvation, that I may enter
with joy upon the contemplation of those mighty acts, whereby you have given
us life and immortality; through Jesus Christ our Lord. *Amen.* †

The Concluding Prayer of the Church
Almighty and everliving God, in your tender love for the human race you sent
your Son our Savior Jesus Christ to take upon him our nature, and to suffer
death upon the cross, giving us the example of his great humility: Mercifully
grant that I may walk in the way of his suffering, and also share in his resurrection; through Jesus Christ my Lord, who lives and reigns with you and the
Holy Spirit, one God, for ever and ever. *Amen.* †

The Morning Office   **To Be Observed on the Hour or Half Hour**
Between 6 and 9 a.m.

The Call to Prayer
Let my mouth be full of your praise* and your glory all the day long.
Do not cast me off in my old age;* forsake me not when my strength fails.
Psalm 71:8–9

The Request for Presence
O LORD, my God, my Savior,* by day and night I cry to you.
Let my prayer enter into your presence.
Psalm 88:1–2

The Greeting
Show me your ways, O LORD,* and teach me your paths.
Lead me in your truth and teach me,* for you are the God of my salvation; in you
have I trusted all the day long.
Psalm 25:3–4

The Refrain for the Morning Lessons
Deliverance belongs to the LORD.* Your blessing be upon your people!
Psalm 3:8

A Reading
Now it happened that when he was near Bethpage and Bethany, close by the
Mount of Olives as it is called, he sent two of the disciples, saying, 'Go to the
village opposite, and as you enter it you will find a tethered colt that no one
has ever yet ridden. Untie it and bring it here. If anyone asks you, "Why are
you untying it?" you are to say this, "The Master needs it." ' The messengers
went off and found everything just as he had told them. As they were untying
the colt, its owner said, 'Why are you untying it?' and they answered, 'The
Master needs it.' So they took the colt to Jesus and throwing their cloaks upon
its back, they lifted Jesus onto it. As he moved off, they spread their cloaks in

the road, and now, as he was approaching the downward slope of the Mount of Olives, the whole group of disciples joyfully began to praise God at the top of their voices for all the miracles they had seen. They cried out: *Blessed is he who is coming* as King *in the name of the Lord!* Peace in heaven and glory in the highest heavens! Some Pharisees in the crowd said to him, 'Master, reprove your disciples,' but he answered, 'I tell you, if these keep silence, the stones will cry out.'

Luke 19:29–40

The Refrain
Deliverance belongs to the LORD.* Your blessing be upon your people!

The Morning Psalm   *Give Me the Joy of Your Saving Health*
Create in me a clean heart, O God,* and renew a right spirit within me.
Cast me not away from your presence* and take not your holy Spirit from me.
Give me the joy of your saving help again* and sustain me with your bountiful Spirit.
I shall teach your ways to the wicked,* and sinners shall return to you.

Psalm 51:11–14

The Refrain
Deliverance belongs to the LORD.* Your blessing be upon your people!

*The Gloria**

The Lord's Prayer

The Prayer Appointed for the Week
Almighty God, who through your only-begotten Son Jesus Christ overcame death and opened to us the gate of everlasting life: Grant that I, who celebrate with joy the day of the Lord's resurrection, may be raised from the death of sin by your life-giving Spirit; through Jesus Christ our Lord, who lives and reigns with you and the Holy Spirit, one God, now and for ever. *Amen.* †

The Concluding Prayer of the Church
Lord God, almighty and everlasting Father, you have brought me in safety to this new day: Preserve me with your mighty power, that I may not fall into sin, nor be overcome by adversity; and in all I do direct me to the fulfilling of your purpose; through Jesus Christ my Lord. *Amen.* †

The Midday Office   To Be Observed on the Hour or Half Hour
Between 11 a.m. and 2 p.m.

The Call to Prayer
Praise the LORD, O my soul!* I will praise the LORD as long as I live; I will sing praises to God while I have my being.

Psalm 146:1

The Request for Presence
Bow your heavens, O LORD, and come down;* touch the mountains, and they shall smoke.

Hurl the lightning and scatter them;* shoot out your arrows and rout them.
Stretch out your hand from on high;* rescue me and deliver me from the great
    waters, from the hand of foreign peoples.

Psalm 144:5–7

The Greeting

To you I lift up my eyes,* to you enthroned in the heavens.
As the eyes of the servants look to the hand of their masters,* and the eyes of a
    maid to the hand of her mistress,
So our eyes look to the LORD our God,* until he shows us his mercy.

Psalm 123:1–3

The Refrain for the Midday Lessons

Praise the LORD, you that fear him;* stand in awe of him, O offspring of Israel; all
    you of Jacob's line, give glory.

Psalm 22:22

A Reading

Let this mind be in you,
which was also in Christ Jesus:
Who, being in the form of God,
thought it not robbery to be equal with God:
But made himself of no reputation,
and took upon him the form of a servant,
and was made in the likeness of men:
And being found in fashion as a man,
he humbled himself,
became obedient unto death,
even the death of the cross.
Wherefore God also hath highly exalted him,
and given him a name which is above every name:
That at the name of Jesus every knee should bow,
of things in heaven,
and things in earth,
and things under the earth;
And that every tongue should confess that Jesus Christ is LORD,
to the glory of God the Father.

Phillipians 2:5–11, KJV

The Refrain

Praise the LORD, you that fear him;* stand in awe of him, O offspring of Israel; all
    you of Jacob's line, give glory.

The Midday Psalm   *The Sacrifice of God Is a Troubled Spirit*

Deliver me from death, O God,* and my tongue shall sing of your righteousness,
    O God of my salvation.

Open my lips, O Lord,* and my mouth shall proclaim your praise.

Had you desired it, I would have offered sacrifice,* but you take no delight in burnt-offerings.

The sacrifice of God is a troubled spirit;* a broken and contrite heart, O God, you will not despise.

Psalm 51:15–18

The Refrain

Praise the LORD, you that fear him;* stand in awe of him, O offspring of Israel; all you of Jacob's line, give glory.

The Cry of the Church

Lord, have mercy on us. Christ, have mercy on us. Lord, have mercy on us.

The Lord's Prayer

The Prayer Appointed for the Week

Almighty God, who through your only-begotten Son Jesus Christ overcame death and opened to us the gate of everlasting life: Grant that I, who celebrate with joy the day of the Lord's resurrection, may be raised from the death of sin by your life-giving Spirit; through Jesus Christ our Lord, who lives and reigns with you and the Holy Spirit, one God, now and for ever. *Amen.* †

The Concluding Prayer of the Church

Almighty and everlasting God, who willed that our Savior should take upon Him, our flesh and suffer death upon the Cross, that all mankind should follow the example of His great humility, mercifully grant that I may both follow the example of His patience and also partake of His resurrection. Through the same Jesus Christ. *Amen.*

adapted from THE SHORT BREVIARY

The Vespers Office   **To Be Observed on the Hour or Half Hour**
Between 5 and 8 p.m.

The Call to Prayer

The righteous will be glad . . .

And they will say, "Surely, there is a reward for the righteous;* surely, there is a God who rules in the earth."

Psalm 58:10–11

The Request for Presence

Deliver me from death, O God,* and my tongue shall sing of your righteousness, O God of my salvation.

Psalm 51:15

The Greeting

To you, O LORD, I lift up my soul;* my God, I put my trust in you.

Psalm 25:1

The Hymn   *Were You There*

Were you there when they crucified my Lord?
Were you there when they crucified my Lord?
Oh! Sometimes it causes me to tremble, tremble, tremble.
Were you there when they crucified my Lord?

Were you there when they nailed him to the tree?
Were you there when they nailed him to the tree?
Oh! Sometimes it causes me to tremble, tremble, tremble.
Were you there when they nailed him to the tree?

Were you there when they pierced him in the side?
Were you there when they pierced him in the side?
Oh! Sometimes it causes me to tremble, tremble, tremble.
Were you there when they pierced him in the side?

Were you there when they laid him in the tomb?
Were you there when they laid him in the tomb?
Oh! Sometimes it causes me to tremble, tremble, tremble.
Were you there when they laid him in the tomb?

African American Spiritual

The Refrain for the Vespers Lessons
Make me hear of joy and gladness,* that the body you have broken may rejoice.

Psalm 51:9

The Vespers Psalm   *Having You I Desire Nothing Upon Earth*
Whom have I in heaven but you?* and having you I desire nothing upon earth.
Though my flesh and heart should waste away,* God is the strength of my heart
    and my portion for ever.
Truly, those who forsake you will perish;* you destroy all who are unfaithful.
But it is good for me to be near God;* I have made the Lord GOD my refuge.

Psalm 73:25-28

The Refrain
Make me hear of joy and gladness,* that the body you have broken may rejoice.

*The Gloria**

The Lord's Prayer

The Prayer Appointed for the Week
Almighty God, who through your only-begotten Son Jesus Christ overcame death
    and opened to us the gate of everlasting life: Grant that I, who celebrate with
    joy the day of the Lord's resurrection, may be raised from the death of sin by
    your life-giving Spirit; through Jesus Christ our Lord, who lives and reigns
    with you and the Holy Spirit, one God, now and for ever. *Amen.* †

The Concluding Prayer of the Church

Save me, O Lord, while I am awake, and keep me while I sleep that I may wake in
Christ and rest in peace.

adapted from THE SHORT BREVIARY

The Morning Office

To Be Observed on the Hour or Half Hour
Between 6 and 9 a.m.

The Call to Prayer

God has gone up with a shout,* the LORD with the sound of the ram's-horn.
Sing praises to God, sing praises;* sing praises to our King, sing praises.
For God is King of all the earth;* sing praises with all your skill.
God reigns over the nation;* God sits upon his holy throne.

Psalm 47:5–8

The Request for Presence

Early in the morning I cry out to you,* for in your word is my trust.

Psalm 119:147

The Greeting

Not to us, O LORD, not to us, but to your Name give glory;* because of your love
and because of your faithfulness.

Psalm 115:1

The Refrain for the Morning Lessons

For lo, your enemies, O LORD, lo, your enemies shall perish,* and all the workers
of iniquity shall be scattered.

Psalm 92:8

A Reading

So they reached Jerusalem and he went into the Temple and began driving out the
men selling and buying there; he upset the tables of the money changers and
the seats of the dove sellers. Nor would he allow anyone to carry anything
through the Temple. And he taught them and said, 'Does not scripture say: *My
house will be called a house of prayer for all peoples?* But you have turned into *a bandits' den.'* This came to the ears of the chief priests and the scribes, and they
tried to find some way of doing away with him; they were afraid of him
because the people were carried away by his teaching. And when evening
came he went out of the city.

Mark 11:15–19

The Refrain

For lo, your enemies, O LORD, lo, your enemies shall perish,* and all the workers
of iniquity shall be scattered.

The Morning Psalm   *In Your Light We See Light*

Your love, O LORD, reaches to the heavens,* and your faithfulness to the clouds.
Your righteousness is like the strong mountains, your justice like the great deep;*
you save both man and beast, O LORD.

How priceless is your love, O God!* your people take refuge under the shadow of
    your wings.
They feast upon the abundance of your house;* you give them drink from the
    river of your delights.
For with you is the well of life,* and in your light we see light.
Continue your loving-kindness to those who know you,* and your favor to those
    who are true of heart.

Psalm 36:5–12

The Refrain
For lo, your enemies, O LORD, lo, your enemies shall perish,* and all the workers
    of iniquity shall be scattered.

The Short Verse
'I am the Alpha and the Omega' says the Lord God, 'who is, who was, and who is
    to come, the Almighty.'

Revelation 1:8

The Lord's Prayer

The Prayer Appointed for the Week
Almighty God, who through your only-begotten Son Jesus Christ overcame death
    and opened to us the gate of everlasting life: Grant that I, who celebrate with
    joy the day of the Lord's resurrection, may be raised from the death of sin by
    your life-giving Spirit; through Jesus Christ our Lord, who lives and reigns
    with you and the Holy Spirit, one God, now and for ever. *Amen.* †

The Concluding Prayer of the Church
Lord God, almighty and everlasting Father, you have brought me in safety to this
    new day: Preserve me with your mighty power, that I may not fall into sin, nor
    be overcome by adversity; and in all I do direct me to the fulfilling of your pur-
    pose; through Jesus Christ my Lord. *Amen.* †

The Midday Office   To Be Observed on the Hour or Half Hour
                                            Between 11 a.m. and 2 p.m.

The Call to Prayer
I will call upon God,* and the LORD will deliver me.
In the evening, in the morning, and at the noonday, I will complain and lament,*
    and he will hear my voice.
He will bring me safely back* . . .
God, who is enthroned of old, will hear me.

Psalm 55:17ff

The Request for Presence
I have gone astray like a sheep that is lost;* search for your servant, for I do not
    forget your commandments.

Psalm 119:176

The Greeting
When your word goes forth it gives light;* it gives understanding to the simple.

Psalm 119:130

The Refrain for the Midday Lessons
He will not let your foot be moved* and he who watches over you will not fall asleep.

Psalm 121:3

A Reading
We had all gone astray like sheep, each taking his own way, and YAHWEH brought the acts of rebellion of all of us to bear on him. Ill-treated and afflicted, he never opened his mouth, like a lamb led to the slaughter-house, like a sheep dumb before its shearers he never opened his mouth.

Isaiah 53:6–7

The Refrain
He will not let your foot be moved* and he who watches over you will not fall asleep.

The Midday Psalm   *The LORD Will Not Abandon His People*
How long shall the wicked, O LORD,* how long shall the wicked triumph?
They bluster in their insolence;* all evildoers are full of boasting.
They crush your people, O LORD,* and afflict your chosen nation.
They murder the widow and the stranger* and put the orphans to death.
Yet they say, "The LORD does not see,* the God of Jacob takes no notice."
Consider well, you dullards among the people;* when will you fools understand?
He that planted the ear, does he not hear?* he that formed the eye, does he not see?
He who admonishes the nations, will he not punish?* he who teaches all the world, has he no knowledge?
The LORD knows our human thoughts;* how like a puff of wind they are.
Happy are they whom you instruct, O Lord!* whom you teach out of your law;
To give them rest in evil days,* until a pit is dug for the wicked.
For the LORD will not abandon his people,* nor will he forsake his own.
For judgment will again be just,* and all the true of heart will follow it.

Psalm 94:3–15

The Refrain
He will not let your foot be moved* and he who watches over you will not fall asleep.

*The Gloria**

The Lord's Prayer

The Prayer Appointed for the Week
Almighty God, who through your only-begotten Son Jesus Christ overcame death and opened to us the gate of everlasting life: Grant that I, who celebrate with joy the day of the Lord's resurrection, may be raised from the death of sin by

your life-giving Spirit; through Jesus Christ our Lord, who lives and reigns with you and the Holy Spirit, one God, now and for ever. *Amen.* †

The Concluding Prayer of the Church

O God, by the passion of your blessed Son you made an instrument of shameful death to be for us the means of life: Grant me so to glory in the cross of Christ, that I may gladly suffer shame and loss for the sake of your Son our Savior Jesus Christ; who lives and reigns with you and the Holy Spirit, one God, for ever and ever. *Amen.* †

The Vespers Office   **To Be Observed on the Hour or Half Hour Between 5 and 8 p.m.**

The Call to Prayer

O tarry, and await the LORD's pleasure; be strong, and he shall comfort your heart;* wait patiently for the LORD.

Psalm 27:18

The Request for Presence

Show us your mercy, O LORD,* and grant us your salvation.

Psalm 85:7

The Greeting

For you are my hope, O Lord GOD,* my confidence since I was young.
I have been sustained by you ever since I was born; from my mother's womb you have been my strength;* my praise shall be always of you.

Psalm 71:5–6

The Hymn

Descend, O Spirit, purging flame,
Brand us this day with Jesus' Name!
Confirm our faith, consume our doubt;
Sign us as Christ's, within, without.

Forbid us not this second birth;
Grant unto us the greater worth!
Enlist us in your service, Lord;
Baptize all nations with your Word.

Scott F. Brenner

The Refrain for the Vespers Lessons

For one day in your courts is better than a thousand in my own room,* and to stand at the threshold of the house of my God than to dwell in the tents of the wicked.

Psalm 84:9

The Vespers Psalm   *My Eyes Have Failed from Looking for My God*

Save me, O God,* for the waters have risen up to my neck.
I am sinking in deep mire,* and there is no firm ground for my feet.

I have come into deep waters,* and the torrent washes over me.

I have grown weary with my crying; my throat is inflamed;* my eyes have failed from looking for my God.

Those who hate me without a cause are more than the hairs of my head; my lying foes who would destroy me are mighty.*

Psalm 69:1–5

The Refrain

For one day in your courts is better than a thousand in my own room,* and to stand at the threshold of the house of my God than to dwell in the tents of the wicked.

The Gloria*

The Lord's Prayer

The Prayer Appointed for the Week

Almighty God, who through your only-begotten Son Jesus Christ overcame death and opened to us the gate of everlasting life: Grant that I, who celebrate with joy the day of the Lord's resurrection, may be raised from the death of sin by your life-giving Spirit; through Jesus Christ our Lord, who lives and reigns with you and the Holy Spirit, one God, now and for ever. *Amen.* †

The Concluding Prayer of the Church

Grant me and all of your people the gift of your Spirit, that we may know Christ and make him known; and through him, at all times and in all places, may give thanks to you in all things. *Amen.* †

The Morning Office   To Be Observed on the Hour or Half Hour
                                      Between 6 and 9 a.m.

The Call to Prayer

Blessed be the LORD, the God of Israel,* from everlasting and to everlasting;* and let all the people say, "Amen!"

Psalm 106:48

The Request for Presence

O God of hosts,* show the light of your countenance, and we shall be saved.

Psalm 80:7

The Greeting

Let them know that this is your hand, that you, O LORD, have done it.

Psalm 109:26

The Refrain for the Morning Lessons

Send forth your strength, O God;* establish, O God, what you have wrought for us.

Psalm 68:28

A Reading

It was two days before the Passover and the feasts of Unleavened Bread, and the
chief priests and the scribes were looking for a way to arrest Jesus by some
trick and have him put to death. For they said, 'It must not be during the festiv-
ities, or there will be a disturbance among the people.' He was at Bethany in
the house of Simon, a man who had suffered from a virulent skin-disease; he
was at table when a woman came with an alabaster jar of very costly ointment,
pure nard. She broke the jar and poured the ointment on his head. Some who
were there said to one another indignantly, 'Why this waste of ointment?
Ointment like this could have been sold for over three hundred denarii and the
money given to the poor'; and they were angry with her. But Jesus said, 'Leave
her alone. Why are you upsetting her? What she has done for me is a good
work. You have the poor with you always, and you can be kind to them whenever you wish, but you will not always have me. She has done what she could:
she has anointed my body beforehand for its burial. In truth I tell you, wherever throughout all the world the gospel is proclaimed, what she has done will
be told as well, in remembrance of her.' Judas Iscariot, one of the Twelve,
approached the chief priests with an offer to hand Jesus over to them. They
were delighted to hear it, and promised to give him money; and he began to
look for a way of betraying him when the opportunity should occur.

Mark 14:1–11

The Refrain

Send forth your strength, O God;* establish, O God, what you have wrought
for us.

The Morning Psalm   *Your Testimonies Are Very Sure*

The waters have lifted up, O LORD, the waters have lifted up their voice;* the
waters have lifted up their pounding waves.

Mightier than the sound of many waters, mightier than the breakers of the sea,*
mightier is the LORD who dwells on high.

Your testimonies are very sure,* and holiness adorns your house, O LORD, for ever
and for evermore.

Psalm 93:4–6

The Refrain

Send forth your strength, O God;* establish, O God, what you have wrought
for us.

*The Gloria**

The Lord's Prayer

The Prayer Appointed for the Week

Almighty God, who through your only-begotten Son Jesus Christ overcame death
and opened to us the gate of everlasting life: Grant that I, who celebrate with
joy the day of the Lord's resurrection, may be raised from the death of sin by

your life-giving Spirit; through Jesus Christ our Lord, who lives and reigns with you and the Holy Spirit, one God, now and for ever. *Amen.* †

The Concluding Prayer of the Church
Lord God, almighty and everlasting Father, you have brought me in safety to this new day: Preserve me with your mighty power, that I may not fall into sin, nor be overcome by adversity; and in all I do direct me to the fulfilling of your purpose; through Jesus Christ my Lord. *Amen.* †

The Midday Office — To Be Observed on the Hour or Half Hour Between 11 a.m. and 2 p.m.

The Call to Prayer
Know this: The LORD himself is God;* he himself has made us, and we are his; we are his people and the sheep of his pasture.

Psalm 100:2

The Request for Presence
Hear the voice of my prayer when I cry out to you,* when I lift up my hands to your holy of holies.

Psalm 28:2

The Greeting
The eyes of all wait upon you, O LORD.*
Psalm 145:16

The Refrain for the Midday Lessons
Tell it out among all the nations: "The LORD is King!* he has made the world so firm that it cannot be moved; he will judge all the peoples with equity."

Psalm 96:10

A Reading
Lord YAHWEH has given me a disciple's tongue, for me to know how to give a word of comfort to the weary. Morning by morning he makes my ear alert to listen like a disciple. Lord YAHWEH has opened my ear and I have not resisted, I have not turned away. I have offered my back to those who struck me, my cheeks to those who plucked my beard; I have not turned my face away from insult and spitting. Lord YAHWEH comes to my help, this is why insult has not touched me, this is why I have my face like flint and know that I shall not be put to shame. Which of you fears YAHWEH and listens to his servant's voice? Which of you walks in darkness and sees no light? Let him trust in the name of YAHWEH and lean on his God!

Isaiah 50:3–7, 10

The Refrain
Tell it out among all the nations: "The LORD is King!* he has made the world so firm that it cannot be moved; he will judge all the peoples with equity."

The Midday Psalm   *There Is No End to His Greatness*

Great is the LORD and greatly to be praised;* there is no end to his greatness.

One generation shall praise your works to another* and shall declare your power.

I will ponder the glorious splendor of your majesty* and all your marvelous works.

They shall speak of the might of your wondrous acts,* and I will tell of your
   greatness.

They shall publish the remembrance of your great goodness;* they shall sing of
   your righteous deeds.

Psalm 145:3–7

The Refrain

Tell it out among all the nations: "The LORD is King!* he has made the world so
   firm that it cannot be moved; he will judge all the peoples with equity."

The Small Verse

Happy are the people whose strength is in you!* whose hearts are set on the
   pilgrims' way,

For one day in your courts is better than a thousand in my own room,* and to stand
   at the threshold of the house of my God than to dwell in the tents of the wicked.

Psalm 84:4, 9

The Lord's Prayer

The Prayer Appointed for the Week

Almighty God, who through your only-begotten Son Jesus Christ overcame death
   and opened to us the gate of everlasting life: Grant that I, who celebrate with
   joy the day of the Lord's resurrection, may be raised from the death of sin by
   your life-giving Spirit; through Jesus Christ our Lord, who lives and reigns
   with you and the Holy Spirit, one God, now and for ever. *Amen.* †

The Concluding Prayer of the Church

Lord God, whose blessed Son our Savior gave his body to be whipped and his face
   to be spit upon: Give me the grace to accept joyfully the sufferings of the
   present time, confident of the glory that shall be revealed; through Jesus Christ
   your Son my Lord, who lives and reigns with you and the Holy Spirit, one
   God, for ever and ever. *Amen.* †

The Vespers Office   **To Be Observed on the Hour or Half Hour**
                                          Between 5 and 8 p.m.

The Call to Prayer

The LORD is near to those who call upon him,* to all who call upon him faithfully.

Psalm 145:19

The Request for Presence

Protect me, O God, for I take refuge in you;* I have said to the LORD, "You are my
   Lord, my good above all other."

Psalm 16:1

The Greeting
How deep I find your thoughts, O God!* how great is the sum of them!

Psalm 139:16

The Hymn   *In the Cross of Christ I Glory*
In the cross of Christ I glory, towering over the wrecks of time;
All the light of sacred story gathers round its head sublime.

When the woes of life overtake me, hopes deceive, and fears annoy,
Never shall the cross forsake me. Lo! It glows with peace and joy.

When the sun of bliss is beaming light and love upon my way,
From the cross the radiance streaming adds more luster to the day.

Bane and blessing, pain and pleasure, by the cross are sanctified;
Peace is there that knows no measure, joys that through all time abide.

In the cross of Christ I glory, towering over the wrecks of time;
All the light of sacred story gathers round its head sublime.

John Bowring

The Refrain for the Vespers Lessons
I will bear witness that the LORD is righteous;* I will praise the Name of the LORD
   Most High.

Psalm 7:18

The Vespers Psalm   *They Shall Make Known to a People Yet Unborn*
All the ends of the earth shall remember and turn to the LORD,* and all the families
   of the nations shall bow before him.
For kingship belongs to the LORD;* he rules over the nations.
To him alone all who sleep in the earth bow down in worship;* all who go down to
   the dust fall before him.
My soul shall live for him; my descendants shall serve him;* they shall be known
   as the LORD's forever.
They shall come and make known to a people yet unborn* the saving deeds that
   he has done.

Psalm 22:26–30

The Refrain
I will bear witness that the LORD is righteous;* I will praise the Name of the LORD
   Most High.

The Cry of the Church
Even so, come Lord Jesus!

The Lord's Prayer

The Prayer Appointed for the Week
Almighty God, who through your only-begotten Son Jesus Christ overcame death
   and opened to us the gate of everlasting life: Grant that I, who celebrate with

joy the day of the Lord's resurrection, may be raised from the death of sin by your life-giving Spirit; through Jesus Christ our Lord, who lives and reigns with you and the Holy Spirit, one God, now and for ever. *Amen.* †

The Concluding Prayer of the Church
O God, who willed that Your Son should undergo for us the ignominy of the Cross to deliver us from the power of the enemy, grant to me Your servant, that I may obtain the grace of His resurrection. Through the same Jesus Christ. *Amen.*

adapted from The Short Breviary

The Morning Office   To Be Observed on the Hour or Half Hour
                                      Between 6 and 9 a.m.

The Call to Prayer
Those who trust in the Lord are like Mount Zion,* which cannot be moved, but stands fast for ever.
The hills stand about Jerusalem;* so does the Lord stand round about his people, from this time forth for evermore.

Psalm 125:1–2

The Request for Presence
Make me understand the way of your commandments,* that I may meditate on your marvelous works.

Psalm 119:27

The Greeting
Remember your word to your servant,* because you have given me hope.
This is my comfort in my trouble,* that your promise gives me life.

Psalm 119:49–50

The Refrain for the Morning Lessons
Do not let your hearts be troubled. You trust in God, trust also in me.

John 14:1

A Reading
Before the festival of Passover, Jesus, knowing that his hour had come to pass from this world to the Father, having loved those who were his in the world, loved them to the end. They were at supper, and the devil had already put it into the mind of Judas Iscariot, son of Simon, to betray him. Jesus knew that the Father had put everything into his hands, and that he had come from God and was returning to God, and he got up from the table, removed his outer garments, and, taking a towel, wrapped it around his waist; he poured water into a basin and began to wash the disciples' feet and to wipe them with the towel he was wearing. He came to Simon Peter, who said to him, 'Lord, are you going to wash my feet?' Jesus answered, 'At the moment you do not know what I am doing, but later you will understand.' 'Never!' said Peter, 'You shall never wash my feet.' Jesus replied, 'If I do not wash you, you can have no share with

me.' Simon Peter said, 'Well then, not only my feet, but my hands and my head as well!' Jesus said, 'No one who has had a bath needs washing, such a person is clean all over. You too are clean, though not all of you are.' He knew who was going to betray him, and that was why he said, 'though not all of you are.' When he had washed their feet and put on his outer garments again he went back to the table. 'Do you understand,' he said, 'what I have done to you? You call me Master and Lord, and rightly, so I am. If I then, the Lord and Master, have washed your feet, you must wash each other's feet. I have given you an example so that you may copy what I have done to you.'

John 13:1–15

The Refrain
Do not let your hearts be troubled. You trust in God, trust also in me.

The Morning Psalm   *That the Generation to Come Might Put Their Trust in God*
Hear my teaching, O my people;* incline your ears to the words of my mouth.
I will open my mouth in a parable;* I will declare the mysteries of ancient times.
That which we have heard and known, and what our forefathers have told us,* we
     will not hide from their children.
We will recount to generations to come the praiseworthy deeds and the power of
     the LORD,* and the wonderful works he has done.
He gave his decrees to Jacob and established a law for Israel,* which he commanded
     them to teach their children;
That the generations to come might know, and the children yet unborn;* that they
     in their turn might tell it to their children;
So that they might put their trust in God,* and not forget the deeds of God, but
     keep his commandments;
And not be like their forefathers, a stubborn and rebellious generation,* a generation
     whose heart was not steadfast, and whose spirit was not faithful to God.

Psalm 78:1–8

The Refrain
Do not let your hearts be troubled. You trust in God, trust also in me.

The Cry of the Church
In the evening, in the morning, and at noonday, I will complain and lament,* and
     he will hear my voice.

Psalm 55:18

The Lord's Prayer

The Prayer Appointed for the Week
Almighty God, who through your only-begotten Son Jesus Christ overcame death
     and opened to us the gate of everlasting life: Grant that I, who celebrate with
     joy the day of the Lord's resurrection, may be raised from the death of sin by
     your life-giving Spirit; through Jesus Christ our Lord, who lives and reigns
     with you and the Holy Spirit, one God, now and for ever. *Amen.* †

The Concluding Prayer of the Church

Look down, O Lord, I pray, on all of us, Your Family for whom our Lord Jesus
Christ was content to be betrayed and to be delivered into the hands of wicked
men, and to suffer the torment of the Cross. *Amen.*

adapted from The Short Breviary

The Midday Office **To Be Observed on the Hour or Half Hour**
Between 11 a.m. and 2 p.m.

The Call to Prayer

"Come now, let us reason together," says the Lord.

Isaiah 1:18, KJV

The Request for Presence

Awake, O my God, decree justice;* let the assembly of peoples gather around you.
Let the malice of the wicked come to an end, but establish the righteous;* for you
test the mind and heart, O righteous God.

Psalm 7:7, 10

The Greeting

Deliver me, O Lord, by your hand* from those whose portion in life is this world.

Psalm 17:14

The Refrain for the Midday Lessons

The sacrifice of God is a troubled spirit;* a broken and contrite heart, O God, you
will not despise.

Psalm 51:18

A Reading

For the tradition I received from the Lord and also handed on to you is that on the
night he was betrayed the Lord Jesus took some bread, and after he had given
thanks, he broke it, and he said, 'This is my body, which is slain for you; do this
in remembrance of me.' And in the same way, with the cup after supper, saying, 'This is the cup of the new covenant in my blood. Whenever you drink it,
do this in memorial of me.' Whenever you eat this bread, then, and drink this
cup, you are proclaiming the Lord's death until he comes. Therefore anyone
who eats the bread or drinks the cup of the Lord unworthily is answerable for
the body and blood of the Lord. Everyone is to examine himself and only then
eat of the bread or drink from the cup; because a person who eats and drinks
without recognizing the body is eating and drinking his own condemnation.

1 Corinthians 11:23–29

The Refrain

The sacrifice of God is a troubled spirit;* a broken and contrite heart, O God, you
will not despise.

The Midday Psalm *Why, O God, Have You Utterly Cast Us Off*

O God, why have you utterly cast us off?* why is your wrath so hot against the
sheep of your pasture?

Remember your congregation that you purchased long ago,* the tribe you
 redeemed to be your inheritance, and Mount Zion where you dwell.
Turn your steps toward the endless ruins;* the enemy has laid waste everything in
 your sanctuary.
Your adversaries roared in your holy place;* they set up their banners as tokens of
 victory.
They were like men coming up with axes to a grove of trees;* they broke down all
 your carved work with hatchets and hammers.
They set fire to your holy place;* they defiled the dwelling-place of your Name
 and razed it to the ground.
They said to themselves, "Let us destroy them altogether."* They burned down all
 the meeting-places of God in the land.
There are no signs for us to see; there is no prophet left;* there is not one among us
 who knows how long.
How long, O God, will the adversary scoff?* will the enemy blaspheme your
 Name for ever?
Why do you draw back your hand?* why is your right hand hidden in your bosom?

Psalm 74:1–10

The Refrain
The sacrifice of God is a troubled spirit;* a broken and contrite heart, O God, you
 will not despise.

The Cry of the Church
Lord, have mercy on us. Christ, have mercy on us. Lord, have mercy on us.

The Lord's Prayer

The Prayer Appointed for the Week
Almighty God, who through your only-begotten Son Jesus Christ overcame death
 and opened to us the gate of everlasting life: Grant that I, who celebrate with
 joy the day of the Lord's resurrection, may be raised from the death of sin by
 your life-giving Spirit; through Jesus Christ our Lord, who lives and reigns
 with you and the Holy Spirit, one God, now and for ever. *Amen.* †

The Concluding Prayer of the Church
Almighty Father, whose dear Son, on the night before he suffered, instituted the
 Sacrament of his Body and Blood: Mercifully grant that I may receive it thank-
 fully in remembrance of Jesus Christ our Lord, who in these holy mysteries
 gives us a pledge of eternal life; and who now lives and reigns with you and
 the Holy Spirit, one God, for ever and ever. *Amen.* †

The Vespers Office   **To Be Observed on the Hour or Half Hour**
                                          Between 5 and 8 p.m.

The Call to Prayer
Come and listen, all you who fear God,* and I will tell you what he has done for me.

Psalm 66:14

The Request for Presence
O God, be not far from me;* come quickly to help me, O my God.

Psalm 71:12

The Greeting
You have showed me great troubles and adversities,* but you will restore my life
and bring me up again from the deep places of the earth.

Psalm 71:20

The Hymn   Go to Dark Gethsemane
Go to dark Gethsemane, you that feel the tempter's power;
Your Redeemer's conflict see, Watch with him one bitter hour.
Turn not from his griefs away; learn of Jesus Christ to pray.

See him at the judgment hall, beaten, bound, reviled, arraigned;
O the worm-wood and the Gall! O the pangs his soul sustained!
Shun not suffering, shame, or loss; learn of Christ to bear the cross.

Calvary's mournful mountain climb; there, adoring at his feet,
Mark that miracle of time, God's own sacrifice complete.
"It is finished!" hear him cry; learn of Jesus Christ to die.

Early hasten to the tomb where they laid his breathless clay;
All is solitude and gloom. Who has taken him away?
Christ is risen! He meets our eyes; Savior, teach us so to rise.

James Montgomery

The Refrain for the Vespers Lessons
Deliver me, my God, from the hand of the wicked,* from the clutches of the evildoer and the oppressor.

Psalm 71:4

The Vespers Psalm   As for Me, I Am Poor and Needy
Be pleased, O God, to deliver me;* O LORD, make haste to help me.
Let those who seek my life be ashamed and altogether dismayed;* let those who
take pleasure in my misfortune draw back and be disgraced.
Let those who say to me "Aha!" and gloat over me turn back,* because they are
ashamed.
Let all who seek you rejoice and be glad in you;* let those who love your salvation
say for ever, "Great is the LORD!"
But as for me, I am poor and needy;* come to me speedily, O God.
You are my helper and my deliverer;* O LORD, do not tarry.

Psalm 70

The Refrain
Deliver me, my God, from the hand of the wicked,* from the clutches of the evildoer and the oppressor.

The Gloria*

The Lord's Prayer

The Prayer Appointed for the Week
Almighty God, who through your only-begotten Son Jesus Christ overcame death
and opened to us the gate of everlasting life: Grant that I, who celebrate with
joy the day of the Lord's resurrection, may be raised from the death of sin by
your life-giving Spirit; through Jesus Christ our Lord, who lives and reigns
with you and the Holy Spirit, one God, now and for ever. *Amen.* †

The Concluding Prayer of the Church
Almighty and everlasting God, grant that we may celebrate the mysteries of our
Lord's Passion in such a manner as to deserve Your pardon. Through the same
Jesus Christ. *Amen.*

adapted from The Short Breviary

The Morning Office　　　　　To Be Observed on the Hour or Half Hour
Between 6 and 9 a.m.

The Call to Prayer
I cry out to you, O Lord;* I say, "You are my refuge, my portion in the land of the
living."

Psalm 142:5

The Request for Presence
Be my strong rock, a castle to keep me safe;* you are my crag and my stronghold.

Psalm 71:3

The Greeting
O Lord, I cry to you for help;* in the morning my prayer comes before you.

Psalm 88:14

The Refrain for the Morning Lessons
My God, my God, why have you forsaken me?* and are so far from my cry and
from the words of my distress?

Psalm 22:1

A Reading
Pilate then had Jesus taken away and scourged; and after this, the soldiers twisted
some thorns into a crown and put it on his head and dressed him in a purple
robe. They kept coming up to him and saying, 'Hail, king of the Jews!' and
slapping him in the face. Pilate came outside again and said to them, 'Look, I
am going to bring him out to you to let you see that I find no case against him.
The chief priests and the guards shouted, 'Crucify him! Crucify him!' Pilate
said, 'Take him yourselves and crucify him: I find no case against him.' The
Jews replied, 'We have a Law, and according to that Law he ought to be put to
death, because he has claimed to be the Son of God.' . . . They [the soldiers]
then took charge of Jesus, and carrying his own cross he went out to the Place

of the Skull, or as it is called in Hebrew, Golgatha, where they crucified him with two others, one on either side, Jesus being in the middle . . . When the soldiers had finished crucifying Jesus they took his clothing and divided it into four shares, one for each soldier. His undergarment was seamless, woven in one piece from neck to hem; so they said to one another, 'Instead of tearing it, let's throw dice to decide who is to have it.' In this way the words of scripture were fulfilled: *They divide my garments among them and cast lots for my clothes.* That is what the soldiers did. Near the cross of Jesus stood his mother and his mother's sister, Mary the wife of Clopas, and Mary of Magdela. Seeing his mother and the disciple whom he loved standing near her, Jesus said to his mother, 'Woman, this is your son.' Then to the disciple he said, 'This is your mother.' And from that hour the disciple took her into his home. After this, Jesus knew that everything had now been completed and, so that the scripture should be completely fulfilled, he said: *I am thirsty.* A jar full of wine stood there; so putting a sponge in the wine on a hyssop stick, they held it up to his mouth. After Jesus had taken the wine, he said, 'It is fulfilled'; and bowing his head he gave up the spirit.

John 19:1ff

The Refrain

My God, my God, why have you forsaken me?* and are so far from my cry and from the words of my distress?

The Morning Psalm   *I Am Poured Out Like Water*

I am poured out like water;* all my bones are out of joint; my heart within my breast is melting wax.

My mouth is dried out like a pot-shard; my tongue sticks to the roof of my mouth;* and you have laid me in the dust of the grave.

Packs of dogs close me in, and gangs of evildoers circle around me;* they pierce my hands and my feet; I can count all my bones.

They stare and gloat over me;* they divide my garments among them; they cast lots for my clothing.

Be not far away, O LORD;* you are my strength; hasten to help me.

Save me from the sword,* my life from the power of the dog.

Save me from the lion's mouth,* my wretched body from the horns of wild bulls.

I will declare your Name to my brethren;* in the midst of the congregation I will praise you.

Psalm 22:14–21

The Refrain

My God, my God, why have you forsaken me?* and are so far from my cry and from the words of my distress?

The Cry of the Church

O God, come to my assistance! O Lord, make haste to help me!

The Lord's Prayer

The Prayer Appointed for the Week
Almighty God, who through your only-begotten Son Jesus Christ overcame death
and opened to us the gate of everlasting life: Grant that I, who celebrate with
joy the day of the Lord's resurrection, may be raised from the death of sin by
your life-giving Spirit; through Jesus Christ our Lord, who lives and reigns
with you and the Holy Spirit, one God, now and for ever. *Amen.* †

The Concluding Prayer of the Church
O God, you sent Christ Jesus to be my shepherd and the lamb of sacrifice. Help me
to embrace the mystery of salvation, the promise of life rising out of death.
Help me to hear the call of Christ and give me the courage to follow it readily
that I, too, may lead others to you. This I ask through Jesus, my shepherd and
guide.

from People's Companion to the Breviary, Vol. II

The Midday Office   To Be Observed on the Hour or Half Hour Between 11 a.m. and 2 p.m.

The Call to Prayer
The Lord will make good his purpose for me;* O Lord, your love endures for
ever; do not abandon the works of your hands.

Psalm 138:9

The Request for Presence
I spread out my hands to you;* my soul gasps to you like a thirsty land.
O Lord, make haste to answer me; my spirit fails me;* do not hide your face from
me or I shall be like those who go down to the Pit.

Psalm 143:6–7

The Greeting
Remember your word to your servant,* because you have given me hope.
This is my comfort in my trouble,* that your promise gives me life.

Psalm 119:49–50

The Refrain for the Midday Lessons
For God alone my soul in silence waits;* from him comes my salvation.

Psalm 62:1

A Reading
Forcibly, after sentence, he was taken. Which of his contemporaries was con-
cerned at his having been cut off from the land of the living, at his having been
struck dead for his people's rebellion? He was given a grave with the wicked,
and his tomb is with the rich, although he had done no violence, had spoken
no deceit. It was Yahweh's good pleasure to crush him with pain; if he gives
his life as a sin offering, he will see his offspring and prolong his life, and
through him Yahweh's good pleasure will be done. After the ordeal he has

endured, he will see the light and be content. By his knowledge, the upright one, my servant will justify many by taking their guilt on himself. Hence I shall give him a portion with the many, and he will share the body with the mighty, for having exposed himself to death and for being counted as one of the rebellious, whereas he was bearing the sin of many and interceding for the rebellious.

Isaiah 53:8–12

The Refrain
For God alone my soul in silence waits;* from him comes my salvation.

The Midday Psalm   Be Not Far from Me, for Trouble Is Near
But as for me, I am a worm and no man,* scorned by all and despised by the
    people.
All who see me laugh me to scorn;* they curl their lips and wag their heads,
    saying,
"He trusted in the LORD; let him deliver him;* let him rescue him, if he delights
    in him."
Yet you are he who took me out of the womb,* and kept me safe upon my
    mother's breast.
I have been entrusted to you ever since I was born;* you were my God when I was
    still in my mother's womb.
Be not far from me, for trouble is near,* and there is none to help.

Psalm 22:6–11

The Refrain
For God alone my soul in silence waits;* from him comes my salvation.

The Cry of the Church
Remember me, Lord, when You come into Your kingdom.

Luke 22:42

The Lord's Prayer

The Prayer Appointed for the Week
Almighty God, who through your only-begotten Son Jesus Christ overcame death
    and opened to us the gate of everlasting life: Grant that I, who celebrate with
    joy the day of the Lord's resurrection, may be raised from the death of sin by
    your life-giving Spirit; through Jesus Christ our Lord, who lives and reigns
    with you and the Holy Spirit, one God, now and for ever. *Amen.* †

The Concluding Prayer of the Church
Almighty God, I pray you graciously to behold those who are your family, for
    whom our Lord Jesus Christ was willing to be betrayed, and given into the
    hands of sinners, and to suffer death upon the cross; who now lives and reigns
    with you and the Holy Spirit, one God, for ever and ever. *Amen.*

The Vespers Office   To Be Observed on the Hour or Half Hour
                       Between 5 and 8 p.m.

The Call to Prayer
I will call upon God,* and the LORD will deliver me.
In the evening, in the morning, and at the noonday, I will complain and lament,*
    and he will hear my voice.
He will bring me safely back . . . God, who is enthroned of old, will hear me.

Psalm 55:17ff

The Request for Presence
Teach me your way, O LORD, and I will walk in your truth;* knit my heart to you
    that I may fear your Name.

Psalm 86:11

The Greeting
To you, O LORD, I lift up my soul;* my God, I put my trust in you.

Psalm 25:1

The Hymn   *When I Survey the Wondrous Cross*
    When I survey the wondrous cross on which the Prince of Glory died,
    My richest gain I count but loss, and pour contempt on all my pride.

    Forbid it, Lord, that I should boast, save in the death of Christ, my God;
    All the vain things that charm me most, I sacrifice them to his blood.

    See, from his head, his hands, his feet, sorrow and love flow mingled down.
    Did ever such love and sorrow meet, or thorns compose so rich a crown?

    Were the whole realm of nature mine, that were an offering far too small;
    Love so amazing, so divine, demands my soul, my life, my all.

Isaac Watts

The Refrain for the Vespers Lessons
And now, what is my hope?* O Lord, my hope is in you.

Psalm 39:8

The Vespers Psalm   *At the Time You Have Set, O LORD*
Surely, for your sake have I suffered reproach,* and shame has covered my face.
I have become a stranger to my own kindred,* an alien to my mother's children.
Zeal for your house has eaten me up;* the scorn of those who scorn you has fallen
    upon me.
I humbled myself with fasting,* but that was turned to my reproach.
I put on sack-cloth also,* and became a byword among them.
Those who sit at the gate murmur against me,* and the drunkards make songs
    about me.
But as for me, this is my prayer to you,* at the time you have set, O LORD:
"In your great mercy, O God,* answer me with your unfailing help.

Save me from the mire; do not let me sink;* let me be rescued from those who hate
    me and out of the deep waters.
Let not the torrent of waters wash over me, neither let the deep swallow me up;*
    do not let the Pit shut its mouth upon me.
Answer me, O LORD, for your love is kind;* in your great compassion, turn
    to me."

Psalm 69:8–18

The Refrain
And now, what is my hope?* O Lord, my hope is in you.

The Cry of the Church
O God, come to my assistance! O Lord, make haste to help me!

The Lord's Prayer

The Prayer Appointed for the Week
Almighty God, who through your only-begotten Son Jesus Christ overcame death
    and opened to us the gate of everlasting life: Grant that I, who celebrate with
    joy the day of the Lord's resurrection, may be raised from the death of sin by
    your life-giving Spirit; through Jesus Christ our Lord, who lives and reigns
    with you and the Holy Spirit, one God, now and for ever. *Amen.* †

The Concluding Prayer of the Church
Almighty and everlasting God, who willed that our Savior should take our flesh
    and suffer death upon the Cross, that all mankind should follow the example
    of His great humility, mercifully grant that I may both follow the example of
    His patience and also be made a partaker of His resurrection. Through the
    same Jesus Christ. *Amen.*

adapted from THE SHORT BREVIARY

The Morning Office   To Be Observed on the Hour or Half Hour
Between 6 and 9 a.m.

The Call to Prayer
Be strong and let your heart take courage,* all you who wait for the LORD.

Psalm 31:24

The Request for Presence
In your righteousness, deliver and set me free;* incline your ear to me and
    save me.

Psalm 71:2

The Greeting
O LORD, I am your servant;* I am your servant and the child of your handmaid;
My times are in your hand.*

Psalm 116:14, 31:15a

The Refrain for the Morning Lessons

I said in my alarm, "I have been cut off from the sight of your eyes."*
    Nevertheless, you heard the sound of my entreaty when I cried out to you.

Psalm 31:22

A Reading

It was the Day of Preparation, and to avoid the bodies' remaining on the cross
    during the Sabbath—since that Sabbath was a day of special solemnity—the
    Jews asked Pilate to have the legs broken and the bodies taken away.
    Consequently the soldiers came and broke the legs of the first man who had
    been crucified with him and then of the other. When they came to Jesus, they
    saw that he was already dead, so instead of breaking his legs, one of the sol-
    diers pierced his side with a lance; and immediately there came out blood and
    water. This is the evidence of one who saw it—true evidence, and he knows
    that what he says is true—and he gives it so that you may believe as well.
    Because all this happened to fulfill the words of scripture: *Not one bone of his
    will be broken;* and again, in another place scripture says: *They will look to the one
    whom they have pierced.* After this, Joseph of Arimathaea, who was a disciple of
    Jesus—though a secret one because he was afraid of the Jews—asked Pilate to
    let him remove the body of Jesus. Pilate gave permission, so they came and
    took it away. Nicodemus came as well—the same one who had first come to
    Jesus at night-time—and he brought a mixture of myrrh and aloes, weighing
    about a hundred pounds. They took the body of Jesus and bound it in linen
    cloths with the spices, following the Jewish burial custom. At the place where
    he had been crucified there was a garden, and in this garden a new tomb in
    which no one had yet been buried. Since it was the Jewish Day of Preparation
    and the tomb was near by, they laid Jesus there.

John 19:31–42

The Refrain

I said in my alarm, "I have been cut off from the sight of your eyes."*
    Nevertheless, you heard the sound of my entreaty when I cried out to you.

The Morning Psalm   *Into Your Hands I Commend My Spirit*

In you, O Lord, have I taken refuge; let me never be put to shame;* deliver me in
    your righteousness.
Incline your ear to me;* make haste to deliver me.
Be my strong rock, a castle to keep me safe, for you are my crag and my stronghold;*
    for the sake of your Name, lead me and guide me.
Take me out of the net that they have secretly set for me,* for you are my tower of
    strength.
Into your hands I commend my spirit,* for you have redeemed me, O Lord, O
    God of truth.

Psalm 31:1–5

The Refrain

I said in my alarm, "I have been cut off from the sight of your eyes."*
    Nevertheless, you heard the sound of my entreaty when I cried out to you.

*The Gloria**

The Lord's Prayer

The Prayer Appointed for the Week
Almighty God, who through your only-begotten Son Jesus Christ overcame death
and opened to us the gate of everlasting life: Grant that I, who celebrate with
joy the day of the Lord's resurrection, may be raised from the death of sin by
your life-giving Spirit; through Jesus Christ our Lord, who lives and reigns
with you and the Holy Spirit, one God, now and for ever. *Amen.* †

The Concluding Prayer of the Church
O God, at whose passion, according to the prophesy of Simeon, a sword of sorrow
pierced the sweet soul of the glorious Virgin and Mother Mary, grant in Your
mercy that we, when remembering her pierced soul, through the merits and
prayers of all the Saints faithfully standing by Your Cross, may obtain the
blessed result of Your Passion. Through our Lord. *Amen.*

adapted from THE SHORT BREVIARY

The Midday Office **To Be Observed on the Hour or Half Hour
Between 11 a.m. and 2 p.m.**

The Call to Prayer
My merciful God comes to meet me;* God will let me look in triumph on my
enemies.

Psalm 59:11

The Request for Presence
O LORD, give victory to the king* and answer us when we call.

Psalm 20:9

The Greeting
LORD, hear my prayer, and in your faithfulness heed my supplications;* answer
me in your righteousness.

Psalm 143:1

The Refrain for the Midday Lessons
Blessed be the LORD God of Israel,* from age to age. Amen. Amen.

Psalm 41:13

A Reading
There is always hope for a tree: when felled, it can start its life again; its shoots
continue to sprout. Its roots may have grown old in the earth, its stump rotting
in the ground, but let it scent the water and it buds, and puts out branches like
a plant newly set. But a human being? He dies, and dead he remains, breathes
his last, and then where is he? The waters of the sea will vanish, the rivers stop
flowing and run dry: a human being, once laid to rest, will never rise again, the
heavens will wear out before he wakes up, or before he is roused from his
sleep. Will no one hide me in Sheol, and shelter me there till your anger is past,

fixing a certain day for calling me to mind—can the dead come back to life?—day after day of my service, I should be waiting for my relief to come. Then you would call, and I should answer, you would want to see once more what you have made. Whereas now you count every step I take, you would then stop spying on my sin; you would seal up my crime in a bag, and put a cover over my fault. Alas! Just as, eventually, the mountain falls down, the rock moves from its place, water wears away the stones, the cloudburst erodes the soil; so you destroy whatever hope a person has. You crush him once and for all, and he is gone; first you disfigure him, then you dismiss him. His children may rise to honors—he does not know it; they may come down in the world—he does not care. He feels no pangs, except for his own body, makes no lament, except for his own self.

Job 14:7–22

The Refrain
Blessed be the LORD God of Israel,* from age to age. Amen. Amen.

The Midday Psalm   *Out of the Depths Have I Called to You*
Out of the depths have I called to you, O LORD; LORD, hear my voice;* let your ears
   consider well the voice of my supplication.
If you, LORD, were to note what is done amiss,* O Lord, who could stand?
For there is forgiveness with you;* therefore you shall be feared.
I wait for the LORD; my soul waits for him;* in his word is my hope.
My soul waits for the LORD, more than watchmen for the morning,* more than
   watchmen for the morning.
O Israel, wait for the LORD,* for with the LORD there is mercy;
With him there is plenteous redemption,* and he shall redeem Israel from all their
   sins.

Psalm 130

The Refrain
Blessed be the LORD God of Israel,* from age to age. Amen. Amen.

The Gloria*

The Lord's Prayer

The Prayer Appointed for the Week
Almighty God, who through your only-begotten Son Jesus Christ overcame death
   and opened to us the gate of everlasting life: Grant that I, who celebrate with
   joy the day of the Lord's resurrection, may be raised from the death of sin by
   your life-giving Spirit; through Jesus Christ our Lord, who lives and reigns
   with you and the Holy Spirit, one God, now and for ever. *Amen.* †

The Concluding Prayer of the Church
O God, Creator of heaven and earth: Grant that, as the crucified body of your dear
   Son was laid in the tomb and rested on this holy Sabbath, so I may await with
   him the coming of the third day, and rise with him to newness of life; who now
   lives and reigns with you and the Holy Spirit, one God, for ever and ever. *Amen.* †

The Vespers Office

To Be Observed on the Hour or Half Hour
Between 5 and 8 p.m.

The Call to Prayer
Let the Name of the LORD be blessed,* from this time forth for evermore.
From the rising of the sun to its going down* let the Name of the LORD be praised.

Psalm 113:2–3

The Request for Presence
Let my cry come before you, O LORD;* give me understanding, according to your
word.
Let my supplication come before you;* deliver me, according to your promise.

Psalm 119:169–170

The Greeting
The Lord is in his holy temple; Let all the earth keep silence before him. *Amen.*

The Hymn   *Take Up Your Cross*

Take up your cross, the Savior said,
If you would my disciple be;
Deny yourself, the world forsake,
And humbly follow after me.

Take up your cross, let not its weight
Fill your weak spirit with alarm;
His strength shall bear your spirit up,
Shall brace your heart and nerve your arm.

Take up your cross then in his strength,
And every danger calmly brave,
To guide you to a better home,
And victory over death and grave.

Take up your cross and follow Christ,
Nor think till death to lay it down;
For only he who bears the cross
May hope to wear the glorious crown.

To you, great Lord, the One in three,
All praise for evermore ascend;
O grant us here below to see
The heavenly life that knows no end.

Charles W. Everest

The Refrain for the Vespers Lessons
Those who sowed with tears* will reap with songs of joy.
Those who go out weeping, carrying the seed,* will come again with joy,
shouldering their sheaves.

Psalm 126:6–7

The Vespers Psalm   *My Help Comes from the* Lord

I lift up my eyes to the hills;* from where is my help to come?

My help comes from the Lord,* the maker of heaven and earth.

He will not let your foot be moved* and he who watches over you will not fall
    asleep.

Behold, he who keeps watch over Israel* shall neither slumber nor sleep.

Psalm 121:1–4

The Refrain

Those who sowed with tears* will reap with songs of joy.

Those who go out weeping, carrying the seed,* will come again with joy,
    shouldering their sheaves.

The Small Verse

Christ is risen. Alleluia!

The Lord's Prayer

The Prayer Appointed for the Week

Almighty God, who through your only-begotten Son Jesus Christ overcame death
    and opened to us the gate of everlasting life: Grant that I, who celebrate with
    joy the day of the Lord's resurrection, may be raised from the death of sin by
    your life-giving Spirit; through Jesus Christ our Lord, who lives and reigns
    with you and the Holy Spirit, one God, now and for ever. *Amen.* †

The Concluding Prayer of the Church

Rejoice now, heavenly hosts and choirs of angels, and let your trumpets shout
    salvation for the victory of our mighty King.

Rejoice and sing now, all the round earth, bright with a glorious splendor, for
    darkness has been vanquished by our eternal King.

Rejoice and be glad now, Mother Church, and let your holy courts, in radiant light,
    resound with the praises of your people.

The Morning Office   **To Be Observed on the Hour or Half Hour**
Between 6 and 9 a.m.

The Call to Prayer

Praise the Lord, all you nations;* laud him, all you peoples.

For his loving-kindness toward us is great,* and the faithfulness of the Lord
    endures for ever. Hallelujah!

Psalm 117

The Request for Presence
I will offer you the sacrifice of thanksgiving* and call upon the Name of the LORD.
I will fulfill my vows to the LORD* in the presence of all his people,
In the courts of the LORD's house,* in the midst of you, O Jerusalem. Hallelujah!

Psalm 116:15–17

The Greeting
Hosanna, LORD, hosanna!* LORD, send us now success.
Blessed is he who comes in the name of the Lord;* we bless you from the house of
the LORD.

Psalm 118:25–26

The Refrain for the Morning Lessons
It is better to rely on the LORD* than to put any trust in flesh.
It is better to rely on the LORD* than to put any trust in rulers.

Psalm 118:8–9

A Reading
After the Sabbath, and towards dawn on the first day of the week, Mary of
   Magdela and the other Mary went to visit the sepulchre. And suddenly there
   was a violent earthquake, for an angel of the Lord, descending from heaven,
   came and rolled away the stone and sat on it. His face was like lightning, his
   robe white as snow. The guards were so shaken by fear of him that they were
   like dead men. But the angel spoke; and he said to the women, 'There is no need
   for you to be afraid. I know you are looking for Jesus, who was crucified. He is
   not here, for he has risen, as he said he would. Come and see the place where he
   lay, then go quickly and tell his disciples, "He has risen from the dead and now
   he is going ahead of you to Galilee; that is where you will see him." Look! I have
   told you.' Filled with awe and great joy the women came quickly away from the
   tomb and ran to tell his disciples. And suddenly, coming to meet them, was
   Jesus. 'Greetings,' he said. And the women came up to him and, clasping his
   feet, they did him homage. Then Jesus said to them, 'Do not be afraid; go and
   tell my brothers that they must leave for Galilee; there they will see me.'

Matthew 28:1–10

The Refrain
It is better to rely on the LORD* than to put any trust in flesh.
It is better to rely on the LORD* than to put any trust in rulers.

The Morning Psalm   *I Shall Not Die, but Live*
There is a sound of exultation and victory* in the tents of the righteous:
"The right hand of the LORD has triumphed!* the right hand of the LORD is exalted!
   the right hand of the LORD has triumphed!"
I shall not die, but live,* and declare the works of the LORD.
The LORD has punished me sorely,* but he did not hand me over to death.
Open for me the gates of righteousness;* I will enter them; I will offer thanks to the
   LORD.

"This is the gate of the Lord;* he who is righteous may enter."
I will give thanks to you, for you answered me* and have become my salvation.
The same stone which the builders rejected* has become the chief cornerstone.
This is the Lord's doing,* and it is marvelous in our eyes.
On this day the Lord has acted;* we will rejoice and be glad in it.

Psalm 118:15-24

The Refrain
It is better to rely on the Lord* than to put any trust in flesh.
It is better to rely on the Lord* than to put any trust in rulers.

The Cry of the Church
Alleluia. Christ is risen.
The Lord is risen indeed. Alleluia.

The Lord's Prayer

The Prayer Appointed for the Week
Almighty God, who through your only-begotten Son Jesus Christ overcame death
and opened to us the gate of everlasting life: Grant that I, who celebrate with
joy the day of the Lord's resurrection, may be raised from the death of sin by
your life-giving Spirit; through Jesus Christ our Lord, who lives and reigns
with you and the Holy Spirit, one God, now and for ever. *Amen.* †

The Concluding Prayer of the Church
O God, of unchangeable power and eternal light: Look favorably on your whole
Church, that wonderful and sacred mystery; by the effectual working of your
providence, carry out in tranquility the plan of salvation; let the whole world
see and know that things which were cast down are being raised up, and
things which had grown old are being made new, and that all things are being
brought to their perfection by him through whom all things are made, your
Son Jesus Christ our Lord. *Amen.*

The Midday Office   **To Be Observed on the Hour or Half Hour**
Between 11 a.m. and 2 p.m.

The Call to Prayer
Come, let us sing to the Lord;* let us shout for joy to the Rock of our salvation.
Let us come before his presence with thanksgiving* and raise a loud shout to him
with psalms.
For the Lord is a great God,* and a great King above all gods.
In his hands are the caverns of the earth,* and the heights of the hills are his also.
The sea is his, for he made it,* and his hands have molded the dry land.

Psalm 95:1-5

The Request for Presence
May God give us his blessing,* and may all the ends of the earth stand in awe of him.

Psalm 67:7

The Greeting
You, O LORD, are a shield about me;* you are my glory, the one who lifts up my
 head.
I call aloud upon the LORD,* and he answers me from his holy hill.

Psalm 3:3–4

The Refrain for the Midday Lessons
May the glory of the LORD endure for ever;* may the LORD rejoice in all his works.

Psalm 104:32

A Reading
The apostle taught us, saying: "We believe that, if we died with Christ, then we
 shall live with him too. We know that Christ has been raised from the dead and
 will never die again. Death has no power over him any more. For by dying, he
 is dead to sin once and for all, and now the life that he lives is life with God. In
 the same way, you must see yourselves as being dead to sin, but alive for God
 in Christ Jesus."

Romans 6:8–11

The Refrain
May the glory of the LORD endure for ever;* may the LORD rejoice in all his works.

The Midday Psalm *Let Them Praise the Name of the LORD*
Praise the LORD from the earth,* you sea-monsters and deeps;
Fire and hail, snow and fog,* tempestuous wind, doing his will;
Mountains and all hills,* fruit trees and all cedars;
Wild beasts and all cattle, creeping things and wingèd birds; Kings of the earth
 and all peoples,* princes and all rulers of the world;
Young men and maidens,* old and young together.
Let them praise the Name of the LORD,* for his Name only is exalted, his splendor
 is over earth and heaven.
He raised up strength for his people and praise for all his loyal servants,* the
 children of Israel, a people who are near him. Hallelujah!

Psalm 148:7–14

The Refrain
May the glory of the LORD endure for ever;* may the LORD rejoice in all his works.

The Cry of the Church
Christ has died, Christ has risen, Christ will come again!

The Lord's Prayer

The Prayer Appointed for the Week
Almighty God, who through your only-begotten Son Jesus Christ overcame death
 and opened to us the gate of everlasting life: Grant that I, who celebrate with
 joy the day of the Lord's resurrection, may be raised from the death of sin by
 your life-giving Spirit; through Jesus Christ our Lord, who lives and reigns
 with you and the Holy Spirit, one God, now and for ever. *Amen.* †

The Concluding Prayers of the Church

O God, who wonderfully created, and yet more wonderfully restored, the dignity
of human nature: Grant that I may share the divine life of him who humbled
himself to share our humanity, your Son Jesus Christ our Lord. *Amen.* †

The Vespers Office   **To Be Observed on the Hour or Half Hour**
                                                      Between 5 and 8 p.m.

The Call to Prayer

Hallelujah! Give praise, you servants of the LORD;* praise the Name of the LORD.

Psalm 113:1

The Request for Presence

I call upon you, O God, for you will answer me;* incline your ear to me, and hear
my words.

Psalm 17:6

The Greeting

You are God: I praise you;* you are the Lord: I acclaim you;
You are the eternal Father:* all creation worships you.
Throughout the world the holy Church acclaims you:* Father, of majesty
unbounded,
your true and only Son,* worthy of all worship,
and the Holy Spirit,* advocate and guide.
As these have been from the beginning,* so they are now and evermore shall be.
Alleluia.

based on the Te Deum and Gloria

The Hymn   *Christ the Lord Is Risen Today*

Christ the Lord is risen today. Alleluia!
Earth and heaven in chorus say, Alleluia!
Raise your joys and triumphs high, Alleluia!
Sing, you heavens, and earth reply, Alleluia!

Love's redeeming work is done, Alleluia!
Fought the fight, the battle won, Alleluia!
Death in vain forbids him rise, Alleluia!
Christ has opened paradise, Alleluia!

Lives again our glorious King, Alleluia!
Where, O death, is now your sting? Alleluia!
Once he died our souls to save, Alleluia!
Where's your victory, boasting grave? Alleluia!

Soar we now where Christ has led, Alleluia!
Following our exalted Head, Alleluia!
Made like him, like him we rise, Alleluia!
Ours the cross, the grave, the skies, Alleluia!

Hail the Lord of earth and heaven, Alleluia!
Praise to you by both be given, Alleluia!
You we greet triumphant now, Alleluia!
Hail the Resurrection, thou, Alleluia!

King of glory, soul of bliss, Alleluia!
Everlasting life is this, Alleluia!
You to know, your power to prove, Alleluia!
Thus to sing, and thus to love, Alleluia!

Charles Wesley

The Refrain for the Vespers Lessons

We will bless the LORD,* from this time forth for evermore. Hallelujah!

Psalm 115:18

The Vespers Psalm   *An Evening Song*

I will bless the LORD who gives me counsel;* my heart teaches me, night after
    night.
I have set the LORD always before me;* because he is at my right hand I shall not
    fall.
My heart, therefore, is glad, and my spirit rejoices;* my body also shall rest in
    hope.
For you will not abandon me to the grave,* nor let your holy one see the Pit.
You will show me the path of life;* in your presence is fullness of joy, and in your
    right hand are pleasures for evermore.

Psalm 16:7–11

The Refrain

We will bless the LORD,* from this time forth for evermore. Hallelujah!

The Cry of the Church

Alleluia. Christ is risen.
The Lord is risen indeed. Alleluia!

The Lord's Prayer

The Prayer Appointed for the Week

Almighty God, who through your only-begotten Son Jesus Christ overcame death
    and opened to us the gate of everlasting life: Grant that I, who celebrate with
    joy the day of the Lord's resurrection, may be raised from the death of sin by
    your life-giving Spirit; through Jesus Christ our Lord, who lives and reigns
    with you and the Holy Spirit, one God, now and for ever. *Amen.* †

The Concluding Prayer of the Church

O God, who for our redemption gave your only-begotten Son to the death of the
    cross, and by this glorious resurrection delivered us from the power of our
    enemy: Grant me so to die daily in sin, that I may evermore live with him in the
    joy of his resurrection; through Jesus Christ your Son our Lord, who lives and
    reigns with you and the Holy Spirit, one God, now and for ever. *Amen.* †

The Morning Office   To Be Observed on the Hour or Half Hour
                                             Between 6 and 9 a.m.

The Call to Prayer
Rejoice in the LORD, you righteous;* it is good for the just to sing praises.
Praise the LORD with the harp;* play to him upon the psaltery and lyre.
Sing for him a new song;* sound a fanfare with all your skill upon the trumpet.
Psalm 33:1–3

The Request for Presence
Let your loving-kindness, O LORD, be upon us,* as we have put our trust in you.
Psalm 33:22

The Greeting
How great is your goodness, O LORD! which you have laid up for those who fear
    you;* which you have done in the sight of all for those who put their trust in
    you.
Psalm 31:19

The Refrain for the Morning Lessons
. . . the loving-kindness of the LORD fills the whole earth.
Psalm 33:5

A Reading
Now that very same day, two of them were on their way to a village called
    Emmaus, seven miles from Jerusalem, and they were talking together about all
    that had happened. And it happened that as they were talking together and
    discussing it, Jesus himself came up and walked by their side; but their eyes
    were prevented from recognizing him. He said to them, 'What are all these
    things that you are discussing as you walk along?' They stopped, their faces
    downcast. Then one of them, called Cleopas, answered him, 'You must be the
    only person staying in Jerusalem who does not know the things that have been
    happening there these last few days.' He asked, 'What things?' They answered,
    'All about Jesus of Nazareth, who showed himself a prophet powerful in action
    and speech before God and the whole people; and how our chief priests and
    our leaders handed him over to be sentenced to death, and had him crucified.
    Our own hope had been that he would be the one to set Israel free. And this is
    not all: two whole days have now gone by since it all happened; and some
    women from our group have astounded us: they went to the tomb in the early
    morning, and when they could not find the body, they came back to tell us they
    had seen a vision of angels who declared he was alive. Some of our friends
    went to the tomb and found everything exactly as the women reported, but of
    him they saw nothing.' Then he said to them, 'You foolish men! So slow to
    believe all that the prophets have said! Was it not necessary that the Christ
    should suffer before entering into his glory?' Then, starting with Moses and
    going through all the prophets, he explained to them the passages throughout

the scriptures that were about himself. When they drew near to the village to which they were going, he made as if to go on; but they pressed him to stay with them saying, 'It is nearly evening, and the day is almost over.' So he went in to stay with them. Now while he was with them at table, he took the bread and said the blessing; then he broke it and handed it to them. And their eyes were opened and they recognized him; but he had vanished from their sight. Then they said to each other, 'Did not our hearts burn within us as he talked to us on the road and explained the scriptures to us?' They set out that instant and returned to Jerusalem. There they found the Eleven assembled together with their companions, who said to them, 'The Lord has indeed risen and has appeared to Simon.' Then they told their story of what had happened on the road and how they had recognized him at the breaking of bread.

Luke 24:13–35

The Refrain
. . . the loving-kindness of the LORD fills the whole earth.

The Morning Psalm   *Happy the Nation Whose God Is the LORD*
Let all the earth fear the LORD;* let all who dwell in the world stand in awe of him.
For he spoke, and it came to pass;* he commanded, and it stood fast.
The LORD brings the will of the nations to naught;* he thwarts the designs of the peoples.
But the LORD's will stands fast for ever,* and the designs of his heart from age to age.
Happy is the nation whose God is the LORD!* happy the people he has chosen to be his own!

Psalm 33:8–12

The Refrain
. . . the loving-kindness of the LORD fills the whole earth.

The Cry of the Church
Christ has died. Christ has risen. Christ will come again!

The Lord's Prayer

The Prayer Appointed for the Week
Almighty God, who through your only-begotten Son Jesus Christ overcame death and opened to us the gate of everlasting life: Grant that I, who celebrate with joy the day of the Lord's resurrection, may be raised from the death of sin by your life-giving Spirit; through Jesus Christ our Lord, who lives and reigns with you and the Holy Spirit, one God, now and for ever. *Amen.* †

The Concluding Prayer of the Church
Grant, I pray, Almighty God, that we who celebrate with awe the Paschal feast may be found worthy to attain to everlasting joys; through Jesus Christ our Lord, who lives and reigns with you and the Holy Spirit, one God, now and for ever. *Amen.* †

The Midday Office   To Be Observed on the Hour or Half Hour
                                      Between 11 a.m. and 2 p.m.

The Call to Prayer
Give thanks to the LORD and call upon his Name;* make known his deeds among
    the peoples.
Sing to him, sing praises to him,* and speak of all his marvelous works.
Glory in his holy Name;* let the hearts of those who seek the LORD rejoice.

Psalm 105:1–3

The Request for Presence
Teach me your way, O LORD, and I will walk in your truth;* knit my heart to you
    that I may fear your Name.
I will thank you, O LORD my God, with all my heart,* and glorify your Name for
    evermore.

Psalm 86:11–12

The Greeting
My mouth shall recount your mighty acts and saving deeds all the day long;*
    though I can not know the number of them.

Psalm 71:15

The Refrain for the Midday Lessons
I will confess you among the peoples, O LORD;* I will sing praises to you among
    the nations.

Psalm 108:3

A Reading
I have been crucified with Christ and yet I am alive; yet it is no longer I, but Christ
    living in me. The life that I am now living, subject to the limitation of human
    nature, I am living in faith, faith in the Son of God who loved me and gave
    himself for me.

Galatians 2:20

The Refrain
I will confess you among the peoples, O LORD;* I will sing praises to you among
    the nations.

The Midday Psalm   *In Your Right Hand Are Pleasures for Evermore*
O LORD, you are my portion and my cup;* it is you who uphold my lot.
My boundaries enclose a pleasant land;* indeed, I have a goodly heritage.
I will bless the LORD who gives me counsel;* my heart teaches me, night after
    night.
I have set the LORD always before me;* because he is at my right hand I shall not
    fall.
My heart, therefore, is glad, and my spirit rejoices;* my body also shall rest in
    hope.
For you will not abandon me to the grave,* nor let your holy one see the Pit.

You will show me the path of life;* in your presence there is fullness of joy, and in your right hand are pleasures for evermore.

Psalm 16:5–11

The Refrain
I will confess you among the peoples, O LORD;* I will sing praises to you among the nations.

The Cry of the Church
Alleluia. Christ is risen.
The Lord is risen indeed. Alleluia.

The Lord's Prayer

The Prayer Appointed for the Week
Almighty God, who through your only-begotten Son Jesus Christ overcame death and opened to us the gate of everlasting life: Grant that I, who celebrate with joy the day of the Lord's resurrection, may be raised from the death of sin by your life-giving Spirit; through Jesus Christ our Lord, who lives and reigns with you and the Holy Spirit, one God, now and for ever. *Amen.* †

The Concluding Prayer of the Church
Almighty God, who for our redemption gave your only begotten Son to death on the cross, and by his glorious resurrection delivered us from the power of our enemy: Grant me so to die daily in sin that I may evermore live with him in the joy of his resurrection; through Jesus Christ our Lord, who lives and reigns with you and the Holy Spirit, one God, now and for ever. *Amen.* †

The Vespers Office **To Be Observed on the Hour or Half Hour**
Between 5 and 8 p.m.

The Call to Prayer
Open my lips, O Lord,* and my mouth shall proclaim your praise.
Had you desired it, I would have offered sacrifice,* but you take no delight in burnt-offerings.
The sacrifice of God is a troubled spirit;* and a broken and contrite heart, O God, you will not despise.

Psalm 51:16–18

The Request for Presence
Protect me, O God, for I take refuge in you;* I have said to the LORD, "You are my Lord, my good above all other."

Psalm 16:1

The Greeting
I give you thanks, O God, I give you thanks,* calling upon your Name and declaring all your wonderful deeds.

adapted from Psalm 75:1

The Hymn   *Welcome, Happy Morning*
"Welcome, happy morning!" age to age shall say:
hell today is vanquished, heaven is won today!
Lo! The dead is living, God for evermore!
Him their true Creator, all his works adore!

Earth her joy confesses, clothing her for spring,
All fresh gifts returned with her returning King:
Bloom in every meadow, leaves on every bough,
Speak his sorrow ended, hail his triumph now.

Months in due succession, days of lengthening light,
Hours and passing moments praise you in their flight,
Brightness of the morning, sky and fields and sea,
Vanquisher of darkness, bring their praise to thee.

Venantius Honorius Fortunatus

The Refrain for the Vespers Lessons
For you are my hope, O Lord GOD,* my confidence since I was young.

Psalm 71:5

The Vespers Psalm   *Turn Now, O God of Hosts*
You have brought the vine out of Egypt;* you cast out the nations and planted it.
You prepared the ground for it;* it took root and filled the land.
The mountains were covered by its shadow* and the towering cedar trees by its
  boughs.
You stretched out its tendrils to the Sea* and its branches to the River.
Why have you broken down its wall,* so that all that pass by pluck off its grapes?
The wild boar of the forest has ravaged it,* and the beasts of the field have grazed
  upon it.
Turn now, O God of hosts, look down from heaven; behold and tend your vine;*
  preserve what your right hand has planted.

Psalm 80:8–14

The Refrain
For you are my hope, O Lord GOD,* my confidence since I was young.

The Cry of the Church
Alleluia. Christ is risen.
The Lord is risen indeed. Alleluia.

The Lord's Prayer

The Prayer Appointed for the Week
Almighty God, who through your only-begotten Son Jesus Christ overcame death
  and opened to us the gate of everlasting life: Grant that I, who celebrate with
  joy the day of the Lord's resurrection, may be raised from the death of sin by
  your life-giving Spirit; through Jesus Christ our Lord, who lives and reigns
  with you and the Holy Spirit, one God, now and for ever. *Amen.* †

The Concluding Prayer of the Church

Almighty and everlasting God, who in the Paschal mystery established the new covenant of reconciliation: Grant that all who are reborn into the fellowship of Christ's Body may show forth in our lives what we profess by our faith; through Jesus Christ our Lord. *Amen.* †

Holy Week and Easter Compline

Sunday
The Night Office   To Be Observed Before Retiring

The Call to Prayer
May the Lord Almighty grant me and those I love a peaceful night and a perfect
    end. *Amen.* †

The Request for Presence
Our help is in the Name of the Lord; the maker of heaven and earth.

The Greeting
Almighty God, my heavenly Father: I have sinned against you, through my own
    fault, in thought, and word, and deed, in what I have done and in what I have
    left undone. For the sake of your Son our Lord Jesus Christ, forgive me all my
    offenses; and grant that I may serve you in newness of life, to the glory of your
    Name. *Amen.* †

The Reading
Faith is strengthened, increased and enriched by those very things that escape the
    senses; the less there is to see, the more there is to believe. To adore Jesus on the
    Mount of Transfiguration, to love the will of God in extraordinary things, does
    not show as much faith as loving the will of God in ordinary things and ador-
    ing Jesus on the cross.

Jean-Pierre de Caussade

*The Gloria**

The Psalm   *The Just Shall See His Face*
The LORD is in his holy temple;* the LORD's throne is in heaven.
His eyes behold the inhabited world;* his piercing eye weighs our worth.
The LORD weighs the righteous as well as the wicked,* but those who delight in
    violence he abhors.
For the LORD is righteous; he delights in righteous deeds;* and the just shall see his
    face.

Psalm 11:4–6, 8

*The Gloria**

The Small Verse
Into your hands, O Lord, I commend my spirit; for you have redeemed me, O
    Lord, O God of truth. Keep me, O Lord, as the apple of your eye; hide me
    under the shadow of your wings. †

The Lord's Prayer

The Petition
Keep watch, dear Lord, with those who work, or watch, or weep this night, and
    give your angels charge over those who sleep. Tend the sick, Lord Christ; give
    rest to the weary, bless the dying, soothe the suffering, pity the afflicted, shield
    the joyous; and all for your love's sake. *Amen.* †

The Final Thanksgiving
Lord, you now have set your servant free to go in peace as you have promised; for these eyes of mine have seen the Savior, whom you have prepared for all the world to see: a Light to enlighten the nations, and the glory of your people Israel. Glory to the Father, and to the Son, and to the Holy Spirit: as it was in the beginning, is now, and will be for ever. *Amen.*

◤

Monday
The Night Office   To Be Observed Before Retiring

The Call to Prayer
May the Lord Almighty grant me and those I love a peaceful night and a perfect end. *Amen.* †

The Request for Presence
Our help is in the Name of the Lord; the maker of heaven and earth.

The Greeting
Almighty God, my heavenly Father: I have sinned against you, through my own fault, in thought, and word, and deed, in what I have done and in what I have left undone. For the sake of your Son our Lord Jesus Christ, forgive me all my offenses; and grant that I may serve you in newness of life, to the glory of your Name. *Amen.* †

The Reading
O Mary, let me always remember when you comprehended that the depth of the love of the Eternal Father toward the human race was so great that in order to save them, He willed the death of His Son; and that on the other hand, the love of the Son lay in wishing to honor His Father perfectly and therefore to die for us: you, in order to conform yourself, who were always and in all things united to the will of God and to this excessive love of both the Father and the Son towards the human race, you also, with your entire will offered, and consented to the death of your Son, in order that we might be saved.

                                                        St. Bonaventure

*The Gloria**

The Psalm   *I Put My Trust in Your Mercy*
How long, O LORD? will you forget me for ever?* how long will you hide your face from me?
How long shall I have perplexity in my mind, and grief in my heart, day after day?* how long shall my enemy triumph over me?

Look upon me and answer me, O LORD my God;* give light to my eyes, lest I sleep in death;

Lest my enemy say, "I have prevailed over him,"* and my foes rejoice that I have fallen.

But I put my trust in your mercy;* my heart is joyful because of your saving help.

I will sing to the LORD, for he has dealt with me richly;* I will praise the Name of the Lord Most High.

Psalm 13

*The Gloria**

The Small Verse

Into your hands, O Lord, I commend my spirit; For you have redeemed me, O Lord, O God of truth. Keep me, O Lord, as the apple of your eye; Hide me under the shadow of your wings. †

The Lord's Prayer

The Petition

Keep watch, dear Lord, with those who work, or watch, or weep this night, and give your angels charge over those who sleep. Tend the sick, Lord Christ; give rest to the weary, bless the dying, soothe the suffering, pity the afflicted, shield the joyous; and all for your love's sake. *Amen.* †

The Final Thanksgiving

Lord, you now have set your servant free to go in peace as you have promised; for these eyes of mine have seen the Savior, whom you have prepared for all the world to see: a Light to enlighten the nations, and the glory of your people Israel. Glory to the Father, and to the Son, and to the Holy Spirit: as it was in the beginning, is now, and will be for ever. *Amen.*

Tuesday
The Night Office   **To Be Observed Before Retiring**

The Call to Prayer

May the Lord Almighty grant me and those I love a peaceful night and a perfect end. *Amen.* †

The Request for Presence

Our help is in the Name of the Lord; the maker of heaven and earth.

The Greeting

Almighty God, my heavenly Father: I have sinned against you, through my own fault, in thought, and word, and deed, in what I have done and in what I have left undone. For the sake of your Son our Lord Jesus Christ, forgive me all my offenses; and grant that I may serve you in newness of life, to the glory of your Name. *Amen.* †

The Reading

My devotion to the Holy Face, or rather all my spirituality, has been based on these words of Isaiah: "There is no beauty in him, nor comeliness: and we have seen him, and there was no sightliness [in him] . . . Despised and the most abject of men, a man of sorrows and acquainted with infirmity: and his look is as it were hidden and despised, whereupon we esteemed him not." I, too, desire to be without glory or beauty, to tread the winepress alone, unknown to any creature.

Thérèse of Lisieux

The Gloria*

The Psalm	*When I Awake, I Shall Be Satisfied, Beholding Your Likeness*

Hear my plea of innocence, O LORD; give heed to my cry;* listen to my prayer, which does not come from lying lips.

Let my vindication come forth from your presence;* let your eyes be fixed on justice.

Weigh my heart, summon me by night,* melt me down; you will find no impurity in me.

I give no offense with my mouth as others do;* I have heeded the words of your lips.

My footsteps hold fast to the ways of your law;* in your paths my feet shall not stumble.

I call upon you, O God, for you will answer me;* incline your ear to me and hear my words.

Show me your marvelous loving-kindness,* O Savior of those who take refuge at your right hand from those who rise up against them.

Keep me as the apple of your eye;* hide me under the shadow of your wings,

From the wicked who assault me,* from my deadly enemies who surround me.

They have closed their heart to pity,* and their mouth speaks proud things.

They press me hard, now they surround me,* watching how they may cast me to the ground,

Like a lion, greedy for its prey,* and like a young lion lurking in secret places.

Arise, O LORD; confront them and bring them down;* deliver me from the wicked by your sword.

Deliver me, O LORD, by your hand* from those whose portion in life is this world;

Whose bellies you fill with your treasure,* who are well supplied with children and leave their wealth to their little ones.

But at my vindication I shall see your face;* when I awake, I shall be satisfied, beholding your likeness.

Psalm 17

The Gloria*

The Small Verse

Into your hands, O Lord, I commend my spirit; For you have redeemed me, O Lord, O God of truth. Keep me, O Lord, as the apple of your eye; Hide me under the shadow of your wings. †

The Lord's Prayer

The Petition

Keep watch, dear Lord, with those who work, or watch, or weep this night, and give your angels charge over those who sleep. Tend the sick, Lord Christ; give rest to the weary, bless the dying, soothe the suffering, pity the afflicted, shield the joyous; and all for your love's sake. *Amen.* †

The Final Thanksgiving

Lord, you now have set your servant free to go in peace as you have promised; for these eyes of mine have seen the Savior, whom you have prepared for all the world to see: a Light to enlighten the nations, and the glory of your people Israel. Glory to the Father, and to the Son, and to the Holy Spirit: as it was in the beginning, is now, and will be for ever. *Amen.*

Wednesday
The Night Office   **To Be Observed Before Retiring**

The Call to Prayer

May the Lord Almighty grant me and those I love a peaceful night and a perfect end. *Amen.* †

The Request for Presence

Our help is in the Name of the Lord; the maker of heaven and earth.

The Greeting

Almighty God, my heavenly Father: I have sinned against you, through my own fault, in thought, and word, and deed, in what I have done and in what I have left undone. For the sake of your Son our Lord Jesus Christ, forgive me all my offenses; and grant that I may serve you in newness of life, to the glory of your Name. *Amen.* †

The Reading

Jesus keep me near the cross; there a precious fountain,
Free to all, a healing stream flows from Calvary's mountain.
In the cross, in the cross, be my glory ever,
Till my raptured soul shall find rest beyond the river.

Near the cross, a trembling soul, love and mercy found me;
There the bright and morning star sheds its beams around me.
Near the cross! O lamb of God, bring its scenes before me;
Help me walk from day to day with its shadow o'er me.

Near the cross I'll watch and wait, hoping, trusting ever,
Till I reach the golden strand just beyond the river.
In the cross, in the cross, be my glory ever,
Till my raptured soul shall find rest beyond the river.

Fanny Crosby

The Gloria*

The Psalm   *My Cry of Anguish Came to His Ears*
I love you, O LORD my strength,* O LORD my stronghold, my crag, and my haven.
My God, my rock in whom I put my trust,* my shield, the horn of my salvation,
    and my refuge; you are worthy of praise.
I will call upon the LORD,* and so shall I be saved from my enemies.
The breakers of death rolled over me,* and the torrents of oblivion made me
    afraid.
The cords of hell entangled me,* and the snares of death were set for me.
I called upon the LORD in my distress* and cried out to my God for help.
He heard my voice from his heavenly dwelling;* my cry of anguish came to his
    ears.

Psalm 18:1–7

The Gloria*

The Small Verse
Into your hands, O Lord, I commend my spirit; For you have redeemed me, O
    Lord, O God of truth. Keep me, O Lord, as the apple of your eye; Hide me
    under the shadow of your wings. †

The Lord's Prayer

The Petition
Keep watch, dear Lord, with those who work, or watch, or weep this night, and
    give your angels charge over those who sleep. Tend the sick, Lord Christ; give
    rest to the weary, bless the dying, soothe the suffering, pity the afflicted, shield
    the joyous; and all for your love's sake. *Amen.* †

The Final Thanksgiving
Lord, you now have set your servant free to go in peace as you have promised; for
    these eyes of mine have seen the Savior, whom you have prepared for all the
    world to see: a Light to enlighten the nations, and the glory of your people
    Israel. Glory to the Father, and to the Son, and to the Holy Spirit: as it was in the
    beginning, is now, and will be for ever. *Amen.*

✤

Thursday
The Night Office   To Be Observed Before Retiring

The Call to Prayer
May the Lord Almighty grant me and those I love a peaceful night and a perfect
    end. *Amen.* †

The Request for Presence
Our help is in the Name of the Lord; the maker of heaven and earth.

The Greeting
Almighty God, my heavenly Father: I have sinned against you, through my own
    fault, in thought, and word, and deed, in what I have done and in what I have
    left undone. For the sake of your Son our Lord Jesus Christ, forgive me all my
    offenses; and grant that I may serve you in newness of life, to the glory of your
    Name. *Amen.* †

The Reading
When the time came, he took his place at table, and the apostles with him. And he
    said to them, 'I have ardently longed to eat this Passover with you before I suf-
    fer; because I tell you, I shall not eat it until it is fulfilled in the kingdom of
    God.' Then, taking a cup, he gave thanks and said, 'Take this and share it
    among you because from now on, I tell you, I shall never again drink wine
    until the kingdom of God comes.' Then he took bread, and when he had given
    thanks, he broke it and gave it to them, saying, 'This is my body given for you;
    do this in remembrance of me.' He did the same with the cup after supper, and
    said, 'This cup is the new covenant in my blood poured out for you. But look,
    here with me on the table is the hand of the man who is betraying me. The Son
    of man is indeed on the path which was decreed, but alas for that man by
    whom he is betrayed!' And they began to ask one another which of them it
    could be who was to do this. An argument also began between them about
    who should be reckoned the greatest; but he said to them, 'Among the gentiles
    it is the kings who lord it over them, and those who have authority over them
    are given the title Benefactor. With you this must not happen. No; the greatest
    among you must behave as if he were the youngest, the leader as if he were the
    one who serves. For who is greater: the one at table or the one who serves? The
    one at table, surely? Yet here I am among you as one who serves! You are the
    men who have stood by me faithfully in my trials; and now I confer a kingdom
    on you, just as my Father conferred it on me: you will eat and drink at my table
    in my kingdom, and you will sit on thrones to judge the twelve tribes of Israel.'
                                                            Luke 22:14–30

The Gloria*

The Psalm   *The Statutes of the LORD Rejoice the Heart*
The law of the LORD is perfect and revives the soul;* the testimony of the LORD is
    sure and gives wisdom to the innocent.
The statutes of the LORD are just and rejoice the heart;* the commandment of the
    LORD is clear and gives light to the eyes.
The fear of the LORD is clean and endures for ever;* the judgments of the LORD are
    true and righteous altogether.
More to be desired are they than gold, more than much fine gold,* sweeter far than
    honey, than honey in the comb.
By them also is your servant enlightened,* and in keeping them there is great
    reward.
Psalm 19:7–11

The Gloria*

The Small Verse
Into your hands, O Lord, I commend my spirit; For you have redeemed me, O
    Lord, O God of truth. Keep me, O Lord, as the apple of your eye; Hide me
    under the shadow of your wings. †

The Lord's Prayer

The Petition
Keep watch, dear Lord, with those who work, or watch, or weep this night, and
    give your angels charge over those who sleep. Tend the sick, Lord Christ; give
    rest to the weary, bless the dying, soothe the suffering, pity the afflicted, shield
    the joyous; and all for your love's sake. *Amen.* †

The Final Thanksgiving
Lord, you now have set your servant free to go in peace as you have promised; for
    these eyes of mine have seen the Savior, whom you have prepared for all the
    world to see: a Light to enlighten the nations, and the glory of your people
    Israel. Glory to the Father, and to the Son, and to the Holy Spirit: as it was in the
    beginning, is now, and will be for ever. *Amen.*

Friday
The Night Office   **To Be Observed Before Retiring**

The Call to Prayer
May the Lord Almighty grant me and those I love a peaceful night and a perfect
    end. *Amen.* †

The Request for Presence
Our help is in the Name of the Lord; the maker of heaven and earth.

The Greeting
Almighty God, my heavenly Father: I have sinned against you, through my own
fault, in thought, and word, and deed, in what I have done and in what I have
left undone. For the sake of your Son our Lord Jesus Christ, forgive me all my
offenses; and grant that I may serve you in newness of life, to the glory of your
Name. *Amen.* †

The Reading

Lofty tree, bend down your branches
To embrace your sacred load;
O, relax the natural tension
Of your all too rigid wood.

Tree of all the one most worthy
Time's greatest Victim to sustain;
Arbor in a raging tempest
And ark that saves the world again;
Tree with sacred blood appointed;
Cross of the Lamb for sinners slain;
Gently bear the members
Of your God and dying King.

Lofty tree, bend down your branches
To embrace your sacred load;
O, relax the natural tension
Of your all too rigid wood.

Honor, blessing everlasting
To the immortal Deity:
To the Father, Son and Spirit
Equal praises ever be:
Glory through the earth and heaven
To that sacred Trinity.
Glory through the earth and heaven
To their sacred Unity.

adapted from The Short Breviary

*The Gloria**

The Psalm   *The Lord Gives Victory to His Anointed*
May the Lord answer you in the day of trouble,* the Name of the God of Jacob
defend you;
Send you help from his holy place* and strengthen you out of Zion;
Remember all your offerings* and accept your burnt sacrifice;
Grant you your heart's desire* and prosper all your plans.
We will shout for joy at your victory and triumph in the Name of our God;* may
the Lord grant all your requests.
Now I know that the Lord gives victory to his anointed;* he will answer him out
of his holy heaven, with the victorious strength of his right hand.
Some put their trust in chariots and some in horses,* but we will call upon the
Name of the Lord our God.
They collapse and fall down,* but we will arise and stand upright.
O Lord, give victory to the king* and answer us when we call.

Psalm 20

*The Gloria**

The Small Verse

Into your hands, O Lord, I commend my spirit; for you have redeemed me, O
Lord, O God of truth. Keep me, O Lord, as the apple of your eye; hide me
under the shadow of your wings. †

The Lord's Prayer

The Petition

Keep watch, dear Lord, with those who work, or watch, or weep this night, and
give your angels charge over those who sleep. Tend the sick, Lord Christ; give
rest to the weary, bless the dying, soothe the suffering, pity the afflicted, shield
the joyous; and all for your love's sake. *Amen.* †

The Final Thanksgiving

Lord, you now have set your servant free to go in peace as you have promised; for
these eyes of mine have seen the Savior, whom you have prepared for all the
world to see: a Light to enlighten the nations, and the glory of your people
Israel. Glory to the Father, and to the Son, and to the Holy Spirit: as it was in the
beginning, is now, and will be for ever. *Amen.*

Saturday
The Night Office   To Be Observed Before Retiring

The Call to Prayer

May the Lord Almighty grant me and those I love a peaceful night and a perfect
end. *Amen.* †

The Request for Presence

Our help is in the Name of the Lord; the maker of heaven and earth.

The Greeting

Almighty God, my heavenly Father: I have sinned against you, through my own
fault, in thought, and word, and deed, in what I have done and in what I have
left undone. For the sake of your Son our Lord Jesus Christ, forgive me all my
offenses; and grant that I may serve you in newness of life, to the glory of your
Name. *Amen.* †

The Reading   *I Would Not Live Forever*

Surely now, O God,
You have worn me out;
You have made desolate
All my company.

You lift me up on the wind
And toss me about
In the roar of the storm.

My eye has grown dim,
And all my members
Are like a shadow.

The night racks my bones,
And the pain that gnaws me
Takes no rest.

Is my strength
The strength of stones,
Or is my flesh bronze?

My heart throbs,
My strength fails me;
My soul is forlorn.

I would choose death
Rather than this body;
I loathe my life;
I would not live forever. ❖

*The Gloria**

The Psalm   *All the Ends of the Earth Shall Remember*
All the ends of the earth shall remember and turn to the LORD,* and all the families
    of the nations shall bow before him.
For kingship belongs to the LORD;* he rules over the nations.
To him alone all who sleep in the earth bow down in worship;* who go down to
    the dust fall before him.
My soul shall live for him; my descendants shall serve him;* they shall be known
    as the LORD's for ever.
They shall come and make known to a people yet unborn* the saving deeds that
    he has done.

Psalm 22:26–30

*The Gloria**

The Small Verse
Into your hands, O Lord, I commend my spirit; For you have redeemed me, O
    Lord, O God of truth. Keep me, O Lord, as the apple of your eye; Hide me
    under the shadow of your wings. †

The Lord's Prayer

The Petition

Keep watch, dear Lord, with those who work, or watch, or weep this night, and give your angels charge over those who sleep. Tend the sick, Lord Christ; give rest to the weary, bless the dying, soothe the suffering, pity the afflicted, shield the joyous; and all for your love's sake. *Amen.* †

The Final Thanksgiving

Lord, you now have set your servant free to go in peace as you have promised; for these eyes of mine have seen the Savior, whom you have prepared for all the world to see: a Light to enlighten the nations, and the glory of your people Israel. Glory to the Father, and to the Son, and to the Holy Spirit: as it was in the beginning, is now, and will be for ever. *Amen.*

The Gloria
Glory be to God the Father, God the Son, and God the Holy Spirit. As it was in the beginning, so it is now and so it shall ever be, world without end. Alleluia.* *Amen.*

The Lord's Prayer
Our Father, who art in heaven, hallowed be your Name.
May your kingdom come, and your will be done, on earth as in heaven.
Give us today our daily bread.
Forgive us our sins as we forgive those who sin against us.
Lead us not into temptation, but deliver us from evil;
for yours are the kingdom and the power and the glory
forever and ever. *Amen.*

Compline Prayers for April Are Located on Page 511.

The Following Holy Day Occurs in April:
The Feast of St. Mark the Evangelist: *April 25*

*The Gloria is omitted during Lent by many Christian communities. "Alleluia" is always omitted from every part of the Church's worship during Lent; the use of both is restored at Easter.

April

The Morning Office   **To Be Observed on the Hour and Half Hour**
Between 6 and 9 a.m.

The Call to Prayer
Out of Zion, perfect in its beauty,* God reveals himself in glory.
"Gather before me my loyal followers,* those who have made a covenant with me
    and sealed it with sacrifice."

Psalm 50:2, 5

The Request for Presence
May God be merciful to us and bless us,* show us the light of his countenance and
    come to us.

Psalm 67:1

The Greeting
You are my hiding-place; you preserve me from trouble;* you surround me with
    shouts of deliverance.

Psalm 32:8

The Refrain for the Morning Lessons
Let the words of my mouth and the meditation of my heart be acceptable in your
    sight,* O LORD, my strength and my redeemer.

Psalm 19:14

A Reading
He was driving out a devil and it was dumb; and it happened that when the devil
    had gone out the dumb man spoke, and the people were amazed. But some of
    them said, 'It is through Beelzebul, the prince of devils, that he drives devils
    out.' Others asked him, as a test, for a sign from heaven, but, knowing what
    they were thinking, he said to them, 'Any kingdom which is divided against
    itself is heading for ruin, and house collapses against house. So, too, with
    Satan: if he is divided against himself how can his kingdom last?—since you
    claim that it is through Beelzebul that I drive devils out. Now if it is through
    Beelzebul that I drive devils out, through whom do your own sons drive them
    out? They shall be our judges, then. But if it is through the finger of God that I
    drive devils out, then the kingdom of God has indeed caught you unawares.'

Luke 11:14–20

The Refrain
Let the words of my mouth and the meditation of my heart be acceptable in your
    sight,* O LORD, my strength and my redeemer.

The Morning Psalm   *I Have Set My King Upon My Holy Hill of Zion*
Why are the nations in an uproar?* Why do the peoples mutter empty threats?
Why do the kings of the earth rise up in revolt, and the princes plot together,*
    against the LORD and against his Anointed?
"Let us break their yoke," they say;* "let us cast off their bonds from us."
He whose throne is in heaven is laughing;* the Lord has them in derision.
Then he speaks to them in his wrath,* and his rage fills them with terror.

"I myself have set my king* upon my holy hill of Zion."

Let me announce the decree of the Lord:* he said to me, "You are my Son; this day have I begotten you.

Ask of me, and I will give you the nations for your inheritance* and the ends of the earth for your possession.

You shall crush them with an iron rod* and shatter them like a piece of pottery."

And now, you kings, be wise;* be warned, you rulers of the earth.

Submit to the Lord with fear,* and with trembling bow before him;

Lest he be angry and you perish;* for his wrath is quickly kindled.

Happy are they all* who take refuge in him!

Psalm 2

The Refrain
Let the words of my mouth and the meditation of my heart be acceptable in your sight,* O Lord, my strength and my redeemer.

The Small Verse
Blessed be the Lord God of Israel for he has visited and delivered us. Amen, amen, amen.

Traditional

The Lord's Prayer

The Prayer Appointed for the Week
O God, whose blessed Son made himself known to his disciples in the breaking of bread: Open the eyes of my faith, that I may behold him in all his redeeming work; who lives and reigns with you and the Holy Spirit, one God, now and for ever. *Amen.* †

The Concluding Prayer of the Church
Lord God, almighty and everlasting Father, you have brought me in safety to this new day: Preserve me with your mighty power, that I may not fall into sin, nor be overcome by adversity; and in all I do direct me to the fulfilling of your purpose; through Jesus Christ my Lord. *Amen.* †

The Midday Office   To Be Observed on the Hour or Half Hour
Between 11 a.m. and 2 p.m.

The Call to Prayer
Sing praises to God, sing praises;* sing praises to our King, sing praises.

For God is King of all the earth;* sing praises with all your skill.

God reigns over the nations;* God sits upon his holy throne.

Psalm 47:6–8

The Request for Presence
I call upon you, O God, for you will answer me;* incline your ear to me and hear my words.

Psalm 17:6

The Greeting

The Lord is in his holy temple; let all the earth keep silence before him. Amen.

Traditional

The Refrain for the Midday Lessons

The LORD is my strength and my song,* and he has become my salvation.

Psalm 118:14

A Reading

Then you will cry for help and YAHWEH will answer; you will call and he will say, 'I am here.' If you do away with the yoke, the clenched fist and malicious words, if you deprive yourself for the hungry and satisfy the needs of the afflicted, your light will rise in the darkness, and your darkest hour will be like noon.

Isaiah 58:9–10

The Refrain

The LORD is my strength and my song,* and he has become my salvation.

The Midday Psalm   *He Holds Our Souls in Life*

Come now and see the works of God,* how wonderful he is in his doing toward all people.

He turned the sea into dry land, so that they went through the water on foot,* and there we rejoiced in him.

In his might he rules for ever; his eyes keep watch over the nations;* let no rebel rise up against him.

Bless our God, you peoples;* make the voice of his praise to be heard;

Who holds our souls in life,* and will not allow our feet to slip.

For you, O God, have proved us;* you have tried us just as silver is tried.

You brought us into the snare;* you laid heavy burdens upon our backs.

You let enemies ride over our heads; we went through fire and water;* but you brought us out into a place of refreshment.

I will enter your house with burnt-offerings and will pay you my vows,* which I promised with my lips and spoke with my mouth when I was in trouble.

Psalm 66:4–12

The Refrain

The LORD is my strength and my song,* and he has become my salvation.

The Cry of the Church

Even so come, Lord Jesus!

The Lord's Prayer

The Prayer Appointed for the Week

O God, whose blessed Son made himself known to his disciples in the breaking of bread: Open the eyes of my faith, that I may behold him in all his redeeming work; who lives and reigns with you and the Holy Spirit, one God, now and for ever. *Amen.* †

The Concluding Prayer of the Church

O God, you make me glad with the weekly remembrance of the glorious resurrection of your Son my Lord: Give me this day such blessing through my worship of you, that the week to come may be spent in your favor; through Jesus Christ our Lord. *Amen.* †

The Vespers Office **To Be Observed on the Hour or Half Hour**
Between 5 and 8 p.m.

The Call to Prayer

Enter his gates with thanksgiving; go into his courts with praise;* give thanks to him and call upon his Name.

Psalm 100:3

The Request for Presence

May God give us his blessing,* and may all the ends of the earth stand in awe of him.

Psalm 67:7

The Greeting

We give you thanks, O God, we give you thanks,* calling upon your Name and declaring all your wonderful deeds.

Psalm 75:1

The Hymn *There Is a Green Hill Far Away*

There is a green hill far away, without a city wall,
Where the dear Lord was crucified, who died to save us all.
Oh, dearly, dearly has He loved, and we must love Him, too,
And trust in his redeeming blood, and try His works to do.

We may not know, we cannot tell, what pains He had to bear;
But we believe it was for us he hung and suffered there.
Oh, dearly, dearly has He loved, and we must love Him, too,
And trust in his redeeming blood, and try His works to do.

There was no other good enough to pay the price of sin,
He only could unlock the gate of heaven and let us in.
Oh, dearly, dearly has He loved, and we must love Him, too,
And trust in his redeeming blood, and try His works to do.

Cecil Alexander

The Refrain for the Vespers Lessons

I will fulfill my vows to the LORD* in the presence of all his people.

Psalm 116:16

The Vespers Psalm *Restore Us, O God of Hosts*

Hear, O Shepherd of Israel, leading Joseph like a flock;* shine forth, you that are enthroned upon the cherubim.
In the presence of Ephraim, Benjamin, and Manasseh,* stir up your strength and come to help us.

Restore us, O God of hosts;* show the light of your countenance, and we shall be
  saved.
O LORD God of hosts,* how long will you be angered despite the prayers of your
  people?
You have fed them with the bread of tears;* you have given them bowls of tears to
  drink.
You have made us the derision of our neighbors,* and our enemies laugh us to
  scorn.
Restore us, O God of hosts;* show the light of your countenance, and we shall be
  saved.

Psalm 80:1–7

The Refrain
I will fulfill my vows to the LORD* in the presence of all his people.

The Cry of the Church
Even so come, Lord Jesus!

The Lord's Prayer

The Prayer Appointed for the Week
O God, whose blessed Son made himself known to his disciples in the breaking of
  bread: Open the eyes of my faith, that I may behold him in all his redeeming
  work; who lives and reigns with you and the Holy Spirit, one God, now and
  for ever. *Amen.* †

The Concluding Prayer of the Church
Lord God, whose Son our Savior Jesus Christ, triumphed over the powers of death
  and prepared for us our place in the new Jerusalem: Grant that I, who have this
  day given thanks for his resurrection, may praise you in the City of which he is
  the light, and where he lives and reigns for ever and ever. *Amen.* †

The Morning Office   **To Be Observed on the Hour or Half Hour**
                                          Between 6 and 9 a.m.

The Call to Prayer
Bless the LORD, O my soul,* and all that is within me, bless his holy Name.
Bless the LORD, O my soul,* and forget not all his benefits.

Psalm 103:1–2

The Request for Presence
Protect me, O God, for I take refuge in you;* I have said to the LORD, "You are my
  Lord, my good above all other."

Psalm 16:1

The Greeting
I love you, O LORD my strength,* O LORD my stronghold, my crag, and my haven.

Psalm 18:1

The Refrain for the Morning Lessons
Purge me from my sin, and I shall be pure;* wash me, and I shall be clean indeed.

Psalm 51:8

A Reading
Jesus taught his disciples, saying: "When an unclean spirit goes out it wanders
   through waterless country looking for a place to rest, and cannot find one.
   Then it says, 'I will return to the home I came from.' But on arrival, finding it
   unoccupied, swept and tidied, it then goes off and collects seven other spirits
   more wicked than itself, and they go in and set up house there, and so that person ends up worse off than before. That is what will happen to this wicked
   generation."

Matthew 12:43–45

The Refrain
Purge me from my sin, and I shall be pure;* wash me, and I shall be clean indeed.

The Morning Psalm   *The Commandment of the LORD Is Clear*
The law of the LORD is perfect and revives the soul;* the testimony of the LORD is
   sure and gives wisdom to the innocent.
The statutes of the LORD are just and rejoice the heart;* the commandment of the
   LORD is clear and gives light to the eyes.
The fear of the LORD is clean and endures for ever;* the judgments of the LORD are
   true and righteous altogether.
More to be desired are they than gold, more than much fine gold,* sweeter far than
   honey, than honey in the comb.
By them also is your servant enlightened,* and in keeping them there is great
   reward.

Psalm 19:7–11

The Refrain
Purge me from my sin, and I shall be pure;* wash me, and I shall be clean indeed.

The Cry of the Church
O Lamb of God, that takes away the sins of the world, have mercy upon me.
O Lamb of God, that takes away the sins of the world, have mercy upon me.
O Lamb of God, that takes away the sins of the world, grant me your peace.

The Lord's Prayer

The Prayer Appointed for the Week
O God, whose blessed Son made himself known to his disciples in the breaking of
   bread: Open the eyes of my faith, that I may behold him in all his redeeming
   work; who lives and reigns with you and the Holy Spirit, one God, now and
   for ever. *Amen.* †

The Concluding Prayer of the Church
Lord God, almighty and everlasting Father, you have brought me in safety to this
   new day: Preserve me with your mighty power, that I may not fall into sin, nor

be overcome by adversity; and in all I do direct me to the fulfilling of your purpose; through Jesus Christ my Lord. *Amen.* †

The Midday Office   **To Be Observed on the Hour or Half Hour**
                                               Between 11 a.m. and 2 p.m.

The Call to Prayer
Blessed be the Lord, the God of Israel, from everlasting and to everlasting;* and
let all the people say, "Amen!"

Psalm 106:48

The Request for Presence
Turn to me and have mercy upon me;* give your strength to your servant; and
save the child of your handmaid.

Psalm 86:16

The Greeting
O Lord, your love endures for ever;* do not abandon the works of your hands.

Psalm 138:9

The Refrain for the Midday Lessons
The fear of the Lord is the beginning of wisdom;* those who act accordingly have
a good understanding; his praise endures for ever.

Psalm 111:10

A Reading
May the peace of Christ reign in your hearts, because it is for this that you were
called together in one body. Always be thankful.

Colossians 3:15

The Refrain
The fear of the Lord is the beginning of wisdom;* those who act accordingly have
a good understanding; his praise endures for ever.

The Midday Psalm   *The Lord Has Pleasure in Those Who Fear Him*
Hallelujah! How good it is to sing praises to our God!* how pleasant it is to honor
him with praise!
The Lord rebuilds Jerusalem;* he gathers the exiles of Israel.
He heals the brokenhearted* and binds up their wounds.
He counts the number of the stars* and calls them all by their names.
Great is our Lord and mighty in power;* there is no limit to his wisdom.
The Lord lifts up the lowly,* but casts the wicked to the ground.
Sing to the Lord with thanksgiving;* make music to our God upon the harp.
He is not impressed by the might of a horse;* he has no pleasure in the strength of
a man;
But the Lord has pleasure in those who fear him,* in those who await his gracious
favor.

Psalm 147:1–7, 11–12

The Refrain
The fear of the LORD is the beginning of wisdom;* those who act accordingly have
a good understanding; his praise endures for ever.

The Small Verse
The Lord is my shepherd and nothing is wanting to me. In green pastures He hath
settled me.

THE SHORT BREVIARY

The Lord's Prayer

The Prayer Appointed for the Week
O God, whose blessed Son made himself known to his disciples in the breaking of
bread: Open the eyes of my faith, that I may behold him in all his redeeming
work; who lives and reigns with you and the Holy Spirit, one God, now and
for ever. *Amen.* †

The Concluding Prayer of the Church
Heavenly Father, you have promised to hear what we ask in the Name of your
Son: Accept and fulfill my petitions, I pray, not as I ask in my ignorance, nor as
I deserve in my sinfulness, but as you know and love me in your Son Jesus
Christ our Lord. *Amen.* †

The Vespers Office   **To Be Observed on the Hour or Half Hour**
Between 5 and 8 p.m.

The Call to Prayer
Come now and look upon the works of the LORD,* what awesome things he has
done on earth.

Psalm 46:9

The Request for Presence
May God be merciful to us and bless us,* show us the light of his countenance and
come to us.
Let your ways be known upon earth,* your saving health among all nations.

Psalm 67:1–2

The Greeting
O LORD of hosts,* happy are they who put their trust in you!

Psalm 84:12

The Hymn
My God, I love thee, not because I hope for heaven thereby,
nor yet because, if I love not, I must forever die.

You, O my Jesus, upon the cross gave your embrace;
for me you bore the nails and spear and manifold disgrace.

Then why, O blessed Jesus Christ, should I not love you well?
Not for the sake of winning heaven, nor of escaping hell.

Not with the hope of gaining life, not seeking a reward,
but as you yourself did love me, O everlasting Lord.

So would I love you, dearest Lord, and in your praise will sing;
because you are my loving God and my eternal King.

Latin, 17th C.

The Refrain for the Vespers Lessons

Bless the LORD, you angels of his, you mighty ones who do his bidding,* and
hearken to the voice of his word.

Psalm 103:20

The Vespers Psalm   *Praise the LORD from the Earth*

Praise the LORD from the earth,* you sea-monsters and all deeps;
Fire and hail, snow and fog,* tempestuous wind, doing his will;
Mountains and all hills,* fruit trees and all cedars;
Wild beasts and all cattle,* creeping things and wingèd birds;
Kings of the earth and all peoples,* princes and all rulers of the world;
Young men and maidens,* old and young together.
Let them praise the Name of the LORD,* for his Name only is exalted, his splendor
is over earth and heaven.
He has raised up strength for his people and praise for all his loyal servants,* the
children of Israel, a people who are near him.

Psalm 148:7–14

The Refrain

Bless the LORD, you angels of his, you mighty ones who do his bidding,* and
hearken to the voice of his word.

The Small Verse

In the sight of the Angels I praise You. I adore at Your holy temple and give praise
to Your Name.

adapted from THE SHORT BREVIARY

The Lord's Prayer

The Prayer Appointed for the Week

O God, whose blessed Son made himself known to his disciples in the breaking of
bread: Open the eyes of my faith, that I may behold him in all his redeeming
work; who lives and reigns with you and the Holy Spirit, one God, now and
for ever. *Amen.* †

The Concluding Prayer of the Church

O God, who in Your ineffable providence have designed to send Your holy Angels
to watch over us, grant to Your suppliants always to find safety in their protection and in eternity to share their happiness. Through our Lord.

THE SHORT BREVIARY

The Morning Office   To Be Observed on the Hour or Half Hour
                                            Between 6 and 9 a.m.

The Call to Prayer
Come, let us bow down, and bend the knee,* and kneel before the LORD our
    Maker.
For he is our God, and we are the people of his pasture and the sheep of his hand.*
    Oh, that today you would hearken to his voice!

Psalm 95:6–7

The Request for Presence
Show us the light of your countenance, O God,* and come to us.

based on Psalm 67:1

The Greeting
To you I lift up my eyes,* to you enthroned in the heavens.
As the eyes of servants look to the hand of their masters,* and the eyes of a maid to
    the hand of her mistress,
So our eyes look to the LORD our God,* until he shows us his mercy.

Psalm 123:1–3

The Refrain for the Morning Lessons
I will bear witness that the LORD is righteous;* I will praise the Name of the LORD
    Most High.

Psalm 7:18

A Reading
Now it happened that as the time drew near for him to be taken up, he resolutely
    turned his face towards Jerusalem and sent messengers ahead of him. These set
    out, and they went into a Samaritan village to make preparations for him, but
    the people would not receive him because he was making for Jerusalem.
    Seeing this, the disciples James and John said, 'Lord, do you want us to call
    down fire from heaven to burn them up?' But he turned and rebuked them,
    and they went on to another village.

Luke 9:51–56

The Refrain
I will bear witness that the LORD is righteous;* I will praise the Name of the LORD
    Most High.

The Morning Psalm   *The LORD Is a Shield About Me*
LORD, how many adversaries I have!* how many there are who rise up against me!
How many there are who say of me,* "There is no help for him in his God."
But you, O LORD, are a shield about me;* you are my glory, the one who lifts up my
    head.
I call aloud upon the LORD,* and he answers me from his holy hill;
I lie down and go to sleep;* I wake again, because the LORD sustains me.

Psalm 3:1–5

The Refrain

I will bear witness that the LORD is righteous;* I will praise the Name of the LORD Most High.

The Small Verse

Keep me, Lord, as the apple of your eye and carry me under the shadow of your wings.

Traditional

The Lord's Prayer

The Prayer Appointed for the Week

O God, whose blessed Son made himself known to his disciples in the breaking of bread: Open the eyes of my faith, that I may behold him in all his redeeming work; who lives and reigns with you and the Holy Spirit, one God, now and for ever. *Amen.* †

The Concluding Prayer of the Church

Lord God, almighty and everlasting Father, you have brought me in safety to this new day: Preserve me with your mighty power, that I may not fall into sin, nor be overcome by adversity; and in all I do direct me to the fulfilling of your purpose; through Jesus Christ my Lord. *Amen.* †

The Midday Office   To Be Observed on the Hour or Half Hour
Between 11 a.m. and 2 p.m.

The Call to Prayer

Open my lips, O Lord,* and my mouth shall proclaim your praise.

Psalm 51:16

The Request for Presence

Let my cry come before you, O LORD;* give me understanding, according to your word.

Let my supplication come before you;* deliver me, according to your promise.

Psalm 119:169–170

The Greeting

How priceless is your love, O God!* your people take refuge under the shadow of your wings.

For with you is the well of life,* and in your light we see light.

Psalm 36:7, 9

The Refrain for the Midday Lessons

Mercy and truth have met together;* righteousness and peace have kissed each other.

Psalm 85:10

A Reading
YAHWEH, hope of Israel, all who abandon you will be put to shame, those who
turn from you will be registered in the underworld, since they have abandoned
YAHWEH, the fountain of living water. Heal me, YAHWEH, and I shall be healed,
save me, and I shall be saved, for you are my praise.

Jeremiah 17:13–14

The Refrain
Mercy and truth have met together;* righteousness and peace have kissed each
other.

The Midday Psalm   *Let Your Saving Health Be Known Among All Nations*
May God be merciful to us and bless us,* show us the light of his countenance and
come to us.
Let your ways be known upon earth,* your saving health among all nations.
Let the peoples praise you, O God;* let all the peoples praise you.
Let the nations be glad and sing for joy,* for you judge the peoples with equity and
guide all the nations upon earth.
Let the peoples praise you, O God;* let all the peoples praise you.

Psalm 67:1–5

The Refrain
Mercy and truth have met together;* righteousness and peace have kissed each
other.

The Small Verse
Lord, be merciful to me, a sinner. Christ, be merciful to me, a sinner. Father, be
merciful to me, a sinner. Spirit, be merciful to me, a sinner. Lord, be merciful to
me, a sinner.

Traditional

The Lord's Prayer

The Prayer Appointed for the Week
O God, whose blessed Son made himself known to his disciples in the breaking of
bread: Open the eyes of my faith, that I may behold him in all his redeeming
work; who lives and reigns with you and the Holy Spirit, one God, now and
for ever. *Amen.* †

The Concluding Prayer of the Church
Let us bless the Lord God living and true! Let us always render him praise, glory,
honor, blessing, and all good things! Amen. Amen. So be it! So be it!

St. Francis of Assisi

The Vespers Office   To Be Observed on the Hour or Half Hour
Between 5 and 8 p.m.

The Call to Prayer
Praise the LORD, all you nations;* laud him, all you peoples.
For his loving-kindness toward us is great,* and the faithfulness of the LORD
endures for ever.

Psalm 117:1–2

The Request for Presence
O LORD, do not forsake me;* be not far from me, O my God.
Make haste to help me,* O Lord of my salvation.

Psalm 38:21–22

The Greeting
You are my refuge and shield;* my hope is in your word.

Psalm 119:114

The Hymn   *We Shall Overcome*
We shall overcome, We shall overcome,
We shall overcome, someday!
Oh, deep in my heart, I do believe
We shall overcome someday!

We'll walk hand in hand, We'll walk hand in hand,
We'll walk hand, in hand, someday!
Oh, deep in my heart, I do believe
We'll walk hand in hand someday!

We shall all be free, We shall all be free,
We shall all be free, someday!
Oh, deep in my heart, I do believe
We shall all be free someday!

We shall live in peace, We shall live in peace,
We shall live in peace, someday!
Oh, deep in my heart, I do believe
We shall live in peace someday!

The Lord will see us through, The Lord will see us through.
The Lord will see us through, someday!
Oh, deep in my heart, I do believe
The Lord will see us through, someday!

African American Spiritual

The Refrain for the Vespers Lessons
. . . it is good for me to be near God;* I have made the Lord GOD my refuge.

Psalm 73:28

The Vespers Psalm   *Many Shall See and Stand in Awe*

I waited patiently upon the Lord;* he stooped to me and heard my cry.

He lifted me out of the desolate pit, out of the mire and clay;* he set my feet upon a
high cliff and made my footing sure.

He put a new song in my mouth, a song of praise to our God;* many shall see, and
stand in awe, and put their trust in the Lord.

Happy are they who trust in the Lord!* they do not resort to evil spirits or turn to
false gods.

Great things are they that you have done, O Lord my God! how great your wonders
and your plans for us!* there is none who can be compared with you.

Oh, that I could make them known and tell them!* but they are more than I can
count.

Psalm 40:1–6

The Refrain

. . . it is good for me to be near God;* I have made the Lord God my refuge.

The Cry of the Church

Lord, have mercy on us. Christ, have mercy on us. Lord, have mercy on us.

The Lord's Prayer

The Prayer Appointed for the Week

O God, whose blessed Son made himself known to his disciples in the breaking of
bread: Open the eyes of my faith, that I may behold him in all his redeeming
work; who lives and reigns with you and the Holy Spirit, one God, now and
for ever. *Amen.* †

The Concluding Prayer of the Church

Save me, O Lord, while I am awake,

And keep me while I sleep

That I may wake in Christ and rest in peace.

adapted from The Short Breviary

The Morning Office   **To Be Observed on the Hour or Half Hour**
                                                        Between 6 and 9 a.m.

The Call to Prayer

Rejoice in the Lord, you righteous,* and give thanks to his holy Name.

Psalm 97:12

The Request for Presence

Bow down your ear, O Lord, and answer me,* for I am poor and in misery.

Keep watch over my life, for I am faithful;* save your servant who puts his trust in
you.

Psalm 86:1–2

The Greeting

Blessed is the LORD!* for he has heard the voice of my prayer.

Psalm 28:7

The Refrain for the Morning Lessons

Blessed are they which do hunger and thirst after righteousness: for they shall be filled.

Matthew 5:6, KJV

A Reading

Jesus said to the people: "In truth I tell you, by himself the Son can do nothing; he can only do what he sees the Father doing: and whatever the Father does the Son does too. For the Father loves the Son and shows him everything he himself does, and he will show him even greater things than these, works that will astonish you. Thus, as the Father raises the dead and gives them life, so the Son gives life to anyone he chooses; for the Father judges no one; he has entrusted all judgement to the Son."

John 5:19–22

The Refrain

Blessed are they which do hunger and thirst after righteousness: for they shall be filled.

The Morning Psalm   *My Soul Longs for You*

As the deer longs for the water-brooks,* so longs my soul for you, O God.
My soul is athirst for God, athirst for the living God;* when shall I come to appear before the presence of God?
My tears have been my food day and night, while all day long they say to me,* "Where now is your God?"
I pour out my soul when I think on these things:* how I went with the multitude and led them into the house of God,
With the voice of praise and thanksgiving,* among those who keep holy-day.
Why are you so full of heaviness, O my soul?* and why are you so disquieted within me?
Put your trust in God;* for I will yet give thanks to him, who is the help of my countenance, and my God.

Psalm 42:1–7

The Refrain

Blessed are they which do hunger and thirst after righteousness: for they shall be filled.

The Small Verse

My soul thirsts for the strong, living God and all that is within me cries out to him.

Traditional

The Lord's Prayer

The Prayer Appointed for the Week

O God, whose blessed Son made himself known to his disciples in the breaking of
bread: Open the eyes of my faith, that I may behold him in all his redeeming
work; who lives and reigns with you and the Holy Spirit, one God, now and
for ever. *Amen.* †

The Concluding Prayer of the Church

Lord God, almighty and everlasting Father, you have brought me in safety to this
new day: Preserve me with your mighty power, that I may not fall into sin, nor
be overcome by adversity; and in all I do direct me to the fulfilling of your purpose; through Jesus Christ my Lord. *Amen.* †

The Midday Office   To Be Observed on the Hour or Half Hour
                                        Between 11 a.m. and 2 p.m.

The Call to Prayer

Bless the LORD, O my soul,* and all that is within me, bless his holy Name.

Psalm 103:1

The Request for Presence

Hearken to my voice, O LORD, when I call;* have mercy on me and answer me.
You speak in my heart and say, "Seek my face."* Your face, LORD, will I seek.
Hide not your face from me,* nor turn away your servant in displeasure.

Psalm 27:10–12

The Greeting

I restrain my feet from every evil way,* that I may keep your word.

Psalm 119:101

The Refrain for the Midday Lessons

For one day in your courts is better than a thousand in my own room,* and to
stand at the threshold of the house of my God than to dwell in the tents of the
wicked.

Psalm 84:9

A Reading

. . . this is the covenant I shall make with the House of Israel when those days have
come, YAHWEH declares. Within them I shall plant my Law, writing it on their
hearts. Then I shall be their God and they will be my people. There will be no
further need for everyone to teach neighbor or brother, saying, "Learn to know
YAHWEH!" No, they will all know me, from the least to the greatest, YAHWEH
declares, since I shall forgive their guilt and never more call their sin to mind.

Jeremiah 31:33–34

The Refrain

For one day in your courts is better than a thousand in my own room,* and to
stand at the threshold of the house of my God than to dwell in the tents of the
wicked.

The Midday Psalm   *Ascribe to the LORD the Glory Due His Name*

The voice of the LORD is a powerful voice;* the voice of the LORD is a voice of
  splendor.
The voice of the LORD breaks the cedar trees;* the LORD breaks the cedars of
  Lebanon;
He makes Lebanon skip like a calf,* and Mount Hermon like a young wild ox.
The voice of the LORD splits the flames of fire; the voice of the LORD shakes the
  wilderness;* the LORD shakes the wilderness of Kadesh.
The voice of the LORD makes the oak trees writhe* and strips the forests bare.
And in the temple of the LORD* all are crying, "Glory!"

                                                              Psalm 29:4–9

The Refrain

For one day in your courts is better than a thousand in my own room,* and to stand
  at the threshold of the house of my God than to dwell in the tents of the wicked.

The Cry of the Church

O Lamb of God, that takes away the sins of the world, have mercy upon me.
O Lamb of God, that takes away the sins of the world, have mercy upon me.
O Lamb of God, that takes away the sins of the world, grant me your peace.

The Lord's Prayer

The Prayer Appointed for the Week

O God, whose blessed Son made himself known to his disciples in the breaking of
  bread: Open the eyes of my faith, that I may behold him in all his redeeming
  work; who lives and reigns with you and the Holy Spirit, one God, now and
  for ever. *Amen.* †

The Concluding Prayer of the Church

God of justice, God of mercy, bless all those who are surprised with pain this day
  from suffering caused by their own weakness or that of others. Let what we
  suffer teach us to be merciful; let our sins teach us to forgive. This we ask
  through the intercession of Jesus and all who died forgiving those who
  oppressed them. *Amen.*

                              THE NEW COMPANION TO THE BREVIARY

The Vespers Office   **To Be Observed on the Hour or Half Hour
                                       Between 5 and 8 p.m.**

The Call to Prayer

But I will call upon God,* and the LORD will deliver me.
In the evening, in the morning, and at noonday, I will complain and lament,* and
  he will hear my voice.
He will bring me safely back . . .
God, who is enthroned of old, will hear me.

                                                              Psalm 55:17ff

The Request for Presence

I cry out to you, O Lord;* I say, "You are my refuge, my portion in the land of the living."

Psalm 142:5

The Greeting

I will confess you among the peoples, O Lord;* I will sing praises to you among the nations.

Psalm 108:3

The Hymn   *We Walk by Faith*

We walk by faith   Help then, O Lord,
And not by sight;   Our unbelief;
No gracious words we hear   And may our faith abound,
From him who spoke   To call on you
As none ever spoke;   When you are near,
But we believe him near.   And seek where you are found:

We may not touch   That, when our life
His hands and side,   Of faith is done,
Nor follow where he trod;   In realms of clearer light
But in his promise   We may behold
We rejoice; and cry,   You as You are,
"My Lord and God!"   With full and endless sight.

Henry Alford

The Refrain for the Vespers Lessons

The Lord will hear the desire of the humble;* you will strengthen their heart and your ears shall hear.

Psalm 10:18

The Vespers Psalm   *Let All Who Seek You Rejoice*

You are the Lord; do not withhold your compassion from me;* let your love and your faithfulness keep me safe for ever,

For innumerable troubles have crowded upon me; my sins have overtaken me, and I cannot see;* they are more in number than the hairs of my head, and my heart fails me.

Be pleased, O Lord, to deliver me;* O Lord, make haste to help me.

Let them be ashamed and altogether dismayed who seek after my life to destroy it;* let them draw back and be disgraced who take pleasure in my misfortune.

Let those who say "Aha!" and gloat over me be confounded* because they are ashamed.

Let all who seek you rejoice in you and be glad;* let those who love your salvation continually say, "Great is the Lord!"

Though I am poor and afflicted,* the Lord will have regard for me.

You are my helper and my deliverer,* do not tarry, O my God.

Psalm 40:12–19

The Refrain
The LORD will hear the desire of the humble;* you will strengthen their heart and
your ears shall hear.

The Small Verse
The Lord is my shepherd and nothing is wanting to me. In green pastures He hath
settled me.

THE SHORT BREVIARY

The Lord's Prayer

The Prayer Appointed for the Week
O God, whose blessed Son made himself known to his disciples in the breaking of
bread: Open the eyes of my faith, that I may behold him in all his redeeming
work; who lives and reigns with you and the Holy Spirit, one God, now and
for ever. *Amen.* †

The Concluding Prayer of the Church
Lead me not into temptation. Deliver me from evil. Yours are the kingdom and the
glory.

The Morning Office   **To Be Observed on the Hour or Half Hour**
Between 6 and 9 a.m.

The Call to Prayer
Open my lips, O Lord,* and my mouth shall proclaim your praise.

Psalm 51:16

The Request for Presence
Bow down your ear, O LORD, and answer me . . .
Keep watch over my life, for I am faithful.

Psalm 86:1–2

The Greeting
Lord, you have been our refuge* from one generation to another.
Before the mountains were brought forth, or the land and the earth were born,*
from age to age you are God.

Psalm 90:1–2

The Refrain for the Morning Lessons
Truly, his salvation is very near to those who fear him,* that his glory may dwell in
our land.

Psalm 85:9

A Reading
Jesus said: "Up to the time of John it was the Law and the Prophets; from then
onwards, the kingdom of God has been preached, and everyone is forcing their
way into it."

Luke 16:16

The Refrain
Truly, his salvation is very near to those who fear him,* that his glory may dwell in
    our land.

The Morning Psalm   **Bless Our God, You Peoples**
Come now and see the works of God,* how wonderful he is in his doing toward
    all people.
In his might he rules for ever; his eyes keep watch over the nations;* let no rebel
    rise up against him.
Bless our God, you peoples;* make the voice of his praise to be heard;
Who holds our souls in life,* and will not allow our feet to slip.

                                                             Psalm 66:4, 6–8

The Refrain
Truly, his salvation is very near to those who fear him,* that his glory may dwell in
    our land.

The Cry of the Church
Be, Lord, my helper and forsake me not. Do not despise me, O God, my savior.
                                                    THE SHORT BREVIARY

The Lord's Prayer

The Prayer Appointed for the Week
O God, whose blessed Son made himself known to his disciples in the breaking of
    bread: Open the eyes of my faith, that I may behold him in all his redeeming
    work; who lives and reigns with you and the Holy Spirit, one God, now and
    for ever. *Amen.* †

The Concluding Prayer of the Church
Lord God, almighty and everlasting Father, you have brought me in safety to this
    new day: Preserve me with your mighty power, that I may not fall into sin, nor
    be overcome by adversity; and in all I do direct me to the fulfilling of your pur-
    pose; through Jesus Christ my Lord. *Amen.* †

The Midday Office   **To Be Observed on the Hour or Half Hour**
                                     Between 11 a.m. and 2 p.m.

The Call to Prayer
Search for the LORD and his strength;* continually seek his face.
                                                          Psalm 105:4

The Request for Presence
You are good and you bring forth good;* instruct me in your statutes.
                                                          Psalm 119:68

The Greeting
When your word goes forth it gives light;* it gives understanding to the simple.
                                                          Psalm 119:130

The Refrain for the Midday Lessons
You strengthen me more and more; you enfold and comfort me.

Psalm 71:21

A Reading
YAHWEH says: "For, as the rain and the snow come down from the sky and do not return before having watered the earth, fertilizing it and making it germinate to provide seed for the sower and food to eat, so it is with the word that goes from my mouth: it will not return to me unfulfilled or before having carried out my good pleasure and having achieved what it was sent to do."

Isaiah 55:10–11

The Refrain
You strengthen me more and more;* you enfold and comfort me.

The Midday Psalm　　　　　*Hear, O Shepherd of Israel, Leading Joseph Like a Flock*
Hear, O Shepherd of Israel, leading Joseph like a flock;* shine forth, you that are enthroned upon the cherubim.
In the presence of Ephraim, Benjamin, and Manasseh,* stir up your strength and come to help us.
Restore us, O God of hosts;* show the light of your countenance, and we shall be saved.
Let your hand be upon the man of your right hand,* the son of man you have made so strong for yourself.
And so will we never turn away from you;* give us life, that we may call upon your Name.
Restore us, O LORD God of hosts;* show the light of your countenance, and we shall be saved.

Psalm 80:1–3, 16–18

The Refrain
You strengthen me more and more;* you enfold and comfort me.

The Cry of the Church
Even so come, Lord Jesus!

The Lord's Prayer

The Prayer Appointed for the Week
O God, whose blessed Son made himself known to his disciples in the breaking of bread: Open the eyes of my faith, that I may behold him in all his redeeming work; who lives and reigns with you and the Holy Spirit, one God, now and for ever. *Amen.* †

The Concluding Prayer of the Church
Lord, make me according to thy heart.

Brother Lawrence

The Vespers Office   To Be Observed on the Hour or Half Hour
                                                       Between 5 and 8 p.m.

The Call to Prayer
Behold now, bless the LORD, all you servants of the LORD,* you that stand by night
in the house of our LORD.

Psalm 134:1

The Request for Presence
For God alone my soul in silence waits;* from him comes my salvation.

Psalm 62:1

The Greeting
Yours is the day, yours also the night;* you established the moon and the sun.
You fixed all the boundaries of the earth;* you made both summer and winter.

Psalm 74:15–16

The Hymn   *The Solid Rock*
   My hope is built on nothing less
   Than Jesus' blood and righteousness
   I dare not trust the sweetest frame,
   But wholly lean on Jesus' name.
   On Christ the Solid Rock, I stand;
   All other ground is sinking sand,

   When darkness veils his lovely face
   I rest on his unchanging grace;
   In every high and stormy gale,
   My anchor holds within the vail.

   His oath, his covenant, his blood
   Support me in the rising flood;
   When all around my soul gives way.
   He then is all my hope and stay.

   When he shall come with trumpet sound
   O may I then in him be found,
   Dressed in his righteousness alone,
   Faultless to stand before the throne.
   On Christ the Solid Rock, I stand;
   All other ground is sinking sand.

Edward Mote

The Refrain for the Vespers Lessons
. . . Surely, there is a reward for the righteous; surely, there is a God who rules in
the earth.

Psalm 58:11b

The Vespers Psalm   *The LORD's Will Stands Forever*

By the word of the LORD were the heavens made,* by the breath of his mouth all
the heavenly hosts.

He gathers up the waters of the ocean as in a water-skin* and stores up the depths
of the sea.

Let all the earth fear the LORD;* let all who dwell in the world stand in awe of him.

For he spoke, and it came to pass;* he commanded, and it stood fast.

The LORD brings the will of the nations to naught;* he thwarts the designs of the
peoples.

But the LORD's will stands fast for ever,* and the designs of his heart from age to
age.

Psalm 33:6–11

The Refrain

Surely, there is a reward for the righteous; surely, there is a God who rules in the
earth.

The Cry of the Church

O God, come to my assistance! O Lord, make haste to help me!

The Lord's Prayer

The Prayer Appointed for the Week

O God, whose blessed Son made himself known to his disciples in the breaking of
bread: Open the eyes of my faith, that I may behold him in all his redeeming
work; who lives and reigns with you and the Holy Spirit, one God, now and
for ever. *Amen.* †

The Concluding Prayer of the Church

May Almighty God grant me a peaceful night and a perfect end. *Amen.*

The Morning Office   **To Be Observed on the Hour or Half Hour
Between 6 and 9 a.m.**

The Call to Prayer

Worship the LORD, O Jerusalem;* praise your God, O Zion;

For he has strengthened the bars of your gates;* he has blessed your children
within you.

Psalm 147:13–14

The Request for Presence

I have said to the LORD, "You are my God;* listen, O LORD, to my supplication.

Psalm 140:6

The Greeting

You are the LORD, most high over all the earth;* you are exalted far above all gods.

Psalm 97:9

The Refrain for the Morning Lessons

Everyone will stand in awe and declare God's deeds;* they will recognize his works.

Psalm 64:9

A Reading

As soon as Judas had taken the piece of bread he went out, It was night. When he had gone, Jesus said: . . . Little children I shall be with you only a little longer. You will look for me, and, as I told the Jews, where I am going, you cannot come. I give you a new commandment: Love one another; you must love one another just as I have loved you. It is by your love for one another, that everyone will recognize you as my disciples.

John 13:30–31, 33–35

The Refrain

Everyone will stand in awe and declare God's deeds;* they will recognize his works.

The Morning Psalm   *The Name of the LORD Endures from Age to Age*

The LORD does whatever pleases him, in heaven and on earth,* in the seas and all the deeps.

He brings up rain clouds from the ends of the earth;* he sends out lightning with the rain, and brings the winds out of his storehouse.

It was he who struck down the firstborn of Egypt,* the firstborn of man and beast.

He sent signs and wonders into the midst of you, O Egypt,* against Pharaoh and all his servants.

He overthrew many nations* and put mighty kings to death.

Sihon, king of the Amorites, and Og, the king of Bashan,* and all the kingdoms of Canaan.

He gave their land to be an inheritance,* an inheritance for Israel his people.

O LORD, your Name is everlasting;* your renown, O LORD, endures from age to age.

For the LORD gives his people justice* and shows compassion to his servants.

Psalm 135:6–14

The Refrain

Everyone will stand in awe and declare God's deeds;* they will recognize his works.

The Cry of the Church

O God, come to my assistance! O Lord, make haste to help me!

The Lord's Prayer

The Prayer Appointed for the Week

O God, whose blessed Son made himself known to his disciples in the breaking of bread: Open the eyes of my faith, that I may behold him in all his redeeming work; who lives and reigns with you and the Holy Spirit, one God, now and for ever. *Amen.* †

The Concluding Prayer of the Church
Lord God, almighty and everlasting Father, you have brought me in safety to this
new day: Preserve me with your mighty power, that I may not fall into sin, nor
be overcome by adversity; and in all I do direct me to the fulfilling of your purpose; through Jesus Christ my Lord. *Amen.* †

The Midday Office   **To Be Observed on the Hour or Half Hour**
                                         Between 11 a.m. and 2 p.m.

The Call to Prayer
Bless God in the congregation;* bless the Lord, you that are of the fountain of
Israel.

Psalm 68:26

The Request for Presence
Accept, O Lord, the willing tribute of my lips,* and teach me your judgments.

Psalm 119:108

The Greeting
Let the words of my mouth and the meditation of my heart be acceptable in your
sight,* O Lord, my strength and my redeemer.

Psalm 19:14

The Refrain for the Midday Lessons
Happy are they who fear the Lord* and have great delight in his commandments.

Psalm 112:1

A Reading
Now if Christ is proclaimed as raised from the dead, how can some of you be saying there is no resurrection from the dead? If there is no resurrection of the
dead, then Christ cannot have been raised either, and if Christ has not been
raised, then our preaching is without substance, and so is your faith.

1 Corinthians 15:12–14

The Refrain
Happy are they who fear the Lord* and have great delight in his commandments.

The Midday Psalm   *The Lord Is My Light and My Salvation*
The Lord is my light and my salvation; whom then shall I fear?* the Lord is the
strength of my life; of whom then shall I be afraid?
When evildoers came upon me to eat up my flesh,* it was they, my foes and my
adversaries, who stumbled and fell.
Though an army should encamp against me,* yet my heart shall not be afraid;
And though war should rise up against me,* yet will I put my trust in him.
One thing have I asked of the Lord; one thing I seek;* that I may dwell in the
house of the Lord all the days of my life;
To behold the fair beauty of the Lord* and to seek him in his temple.

Psalm 27:1–6

The Refrain
Happy are they who fear the Lord* and have great delight in his commandments.

The Cry of the Church
O Lord, hear my prayer and let my cry come unto you. Thanks be to God.

THE SHORT BREVIARY

The Lord's Prayer

The Prayer Appointed for the Week
O God, whose blessed Son made himself known to his disciples in the breaking of
bread: Open the eyes of my faith, that I may behold him in all his redeeming
work; who lives and reigns with you and the Holy Spirit, one God, now and
for ever. *Amen.* †

The Concluding Prayer of the Church
Lord Jesus Christ, by your death you took away the sting of death: Grant me to so
follow in faith where you have led the way, that I may at length fall asleep
peacefully in you and wake in your likeness; for your tender mercies' sake.
Amen. †

The Vespers Office **To Be Observed on the Hour or Half Hour**
Between 5 and 8 p.m.

The Call to Prayer
Behold now, bless the LORD, all you servants of the LORD,* you that stand by night
in the house of the LORD.
Lift up your hands in the holy place and bless the LORD;* the LORD who made
heaven and earth bless you out of Zion.

Psalm 134

The Request for Presence
Look upon me and answer me, O LORD my God;* give light to my eyes, lest I sleep
in death;

Psalm 13:3

The Greeting
O LORD, I am not proud;* I have no haughty looks.
I do not occupy myself with great matters,* or with things that are too hard for me.
But I still my soul and make it quiet, like a child upon its mother's breast;* my soul
is quieted within me.

Psalm 131:1–3

The Hymn *How Firm a Foundation*
How firm a foundation, you saints of the Lord,
Is laid for your faith in his excellent word!
What more can he say than to you he has said,
To you who for refuge to Jesus have fled?

"Fear not, I am with you, O be not dismayed,
For I am your God and will still give you aid;
I'll strengthen and help you, and cause you to stand
Upheld by my righteous, omnipotent hand.

"When through fiery trials your pathways shall lie,
My grace, all sufficient, shall be your supply;
The flame shall not hurt you; I only design
Your dross to consume, and your gold to refine.

"The soul that on Jesus still leans for repose,
I will not, I will not desert it to foes;
That soul, though all hell should endeavor to take,
I'll never, no, never, no, never forsake."

Rippon's Selection of Hymns, *1787*

The Refrain for the Vespers Lessons

Those who are planted in the house of the LORD* shall flourish in the courts of our
God.

Psalm 92:12

The Vespers Psalm   *Let Me Announce the Desire of the* LORD

Why are the nations in an uproar?* Why do the peoples mutter empty threats?
Why do the kings of the earth rise up in revolt, and the princes plot together,*
    against the LORD and against his Anointed?
"Let us break their yoke," they say;* "let us cast off their bonds from us."
He whose throne is in heaven is laughing;* the Lord has them in derision.
Then he speaks to them in his wrath,* and his rage fills them with terror.
"I myself have set my king* upon my holy hill of Zion."
Let me announce the decree of the LORD:* he said to me, "You are my Son; this day
    have I begotten you.
Ask of me, and I will give you the nations for your inheritance* and the ends of the
    earth for your possession.
You shall crush them with an iron rod* and shatter them like a piece of pottery."
And now, you kings, be wise;* be warned, you rulers of the earth.
Submit to the LORD with fear,* and with trembling bow before him;
Lest he be angry and you perish;* for his wrath is quickly kindled.
Happy are they all* who take refuge in him!

Psalm 2

The Refrain

Those who are planted in the house of the LORD* shall flourish in the courts of our
God.

The Small Verse

The Lord is my shepherd and nothing is wanting to me. In green pastures He has
settled me.

The Short Breviary

The Lord's Prayer

The Prayer Appointed for the Week

O God, whose blessed Son made himself known to his disciples in the breaking of bread: Open the eyes of my faith, that I may behold him in all his redeeming work; who lives and reigns with you and the Holy Spirit, one God, now and for ever. *Amen.* †

Concluding Prayers of the Church

Almighty God, who has promised to hear the petitions of those who ask in your Son's Name: I beseech you mercifully to incline your ear to me who have made my prayers and supplications to you; and grant that those things which I have faithfully asked according to your will, I may effectually obtain, to the relief of my necessity, and to the setting forth of your glory; through Jesus Christ my Lord. *Amen.* †

May the souls of the faithful departed, through the mercy of God, rest in eternal peace. *Amen.*

The Morning Office   **To Be Observed on the Hour or Half Hour Between 6 and 9 a.m.**

The Call to Prayer

Come now and look upon the works of the LORD,* what awesome things he has done on earth.

Psalm 46:9

The Request for Presence

O LORD, give victory to the king* and answer us when we call.

Psalm 20:9

The Greeting

My eyes are fixed on you, O my Strength;* for you, O God, are my stronghold.

Psalm 59:10

The Refrain for the Morning Lessons

As a father cares for his children,* so does the LORD care for those who fear him.

Psalm 103:13

A Reading

Jesus taught the people, saying: "Take notice of what you are hearing. The standard you use will be used for you—and you will receive more besides."

Mark 4:24

The Refrain

As a father cares for his children,* so does the LORD care for those who fear him.

The Morning Psalm   *Who May Abide on Your Holy Hill?*

LORD, who may dwell in your tabernacle?* who may abide upon your holy hill?
Whoever leads a blameless life and does what is right,* who speaks the truth from
    his heart.
There is no guile upon his tongue; he does no evil to his friend;* he does not heap
    contempt upon his neighbor.
In his sight the wicked is rejected,* but he honors those who fear the LORD.
He has sworn to do no wrong* and does not take back his word.
He does not give his money in hope of gain,* nor does he take a bribe against the
    innocent.
Whoever does these things* shall never be overthrown.

                                                              Psalm 15

The Refrain

As a father cares for his children,* so does the LORD care for those who fear him.

The Cry of the Church

Lord, have mercy on us. Christ, have mercy on us. Lord, have mercy on us.

The Lord's Prayer

The Prayer Appointed for the Week

O God, whose blessed Son made himself known to his disciples in the breaking of
    bread: Open the eyes of my faith, that I may behold him in all his redeeming
    work; who lives and reigns with you and the Holy Spirit, one God, now and
    for ever. *Amen.* †

The Concluding Prayer of the Church

Lord God, almighty and everlasting Father, you have brought me in safety to this
    new day: Preserve me with your mighty power, that I may not fall into sin, nor
    be overcome by adversity; and in all I do direct me to the fulfilling of your pur-
    pose; through Jesus Christ my Lord. *Amen.* †

The Midday Office   **To Be Observed on the Hour or Half Hour
                                                Between 11 a.m. and 2 p.m.**

The Call to Prayer

May these words of mine please him;* I will rejoice in the LORD.

                                                              Psalm 104:35

The Request for Presence

Set a watch before my mouth, O LORD, and guard the door of my lips;* let not my
    heart incline to any evil thing.
Let me not be occupied in wickedness with evildoers,* nor eat of their choice
    foods.
Let the righteous smite me in friendly rebuke;* let not the oil of the unrighteous
    anoint my head . . .

                                                              Psalm 141:3–5

The Greeting
I long for your salvation, O LORD,* and your law is my delight.
Let me live, and I will praise you,* and let your judgments help me.

Psalm 119:174–175

The Refrain for the Midday Lessons
O God, you have taught me since I was young,* and to this day I tell of your
wonderful works.

Psalm 71:17

A Reading
For the Lord YAHWEH says this: 'Look, I myself shall take care of my flock and look
after it. As a shepherd looks after his flock when he is with his scattered sheep,
so shall I look after my sheep . . . I myself shall pasture my sheep, I myself shall
give them rest—declares the Lord YAHWEH. I shall look for the lost one, bring
back the stray, bandage the injured and make the sick strong. I shall watch over
the fat and healthy. I shall be a true shepherd to them.'

Ezekiel 34:11–12, 15–16

The Refrain
O God, you have taught me since I was young,* and to this day I tell of your
wonderful works.

The Midday Psalm   *The LORD Does Not Forsake His Faithful Ones*
Our steps are directed by the LORD;* he strengthens those in whose way he
delights.
If they stumble, they shall not fall headlong,* for the LORD holds them by the hand.
I have been young and now I am old,*
For the LORD loves justice;* he does not forsake his faithful ones.
They shall be kept safe for ever,* but the offspring of the wicked shall be
destroyed.
The righteous shall possess the land* and dwell in it for ever.
The mouth of the righteous utters wisdom,* and their tongue speaks what is right.
The law of their God is in their heart,* and their footsteps shall not falter.

Psalm 37:24–26a, 29–33

The Refrain
O God, you have taught me since I was young,* and to this day I tell of your
wonderful works.

The Small Verse
Into your hands I commend my spirit for you have redeemed me, O God of my
life. Glory be to the Father, and to the Son and to the comforting Spirit.

Traditional

The Lord's Prayer

The Prayer Appointed for the Week
O God, whose blessed Son made himself known to his disciples in the breaking of
bread: Open the eyes of my faith, that I may behold him in all his redeeming
work; who lives and reigns with you and the Holy Spirit, one God, now and
for ever. *Amen.* †

The Concluding Prayer of the Church
O God, the source of eternal light: Shed forth your unending day upon all of us
who watch for you, that our lips may praise you, our lives may bless you, and
our worship may give you glory; through Jesus Christ our Lord. *Amen.* †

The Vespers Office   **To Be Observed on the Hour or Half Hour**
                                                    Between 5 and 8 p.m.

The Call to Prayer
Come now and look upon the works of the LORD,* what awesome things he has
done on earth.

Psalm 46:9

The Request for Presence
Hear my cry, O God,* and listen to my prayer.
I call upon you from the ends of the earth.
Psalm 61:1–2

The Greeting
O ruler of the universe, Lord God, great deeds are they that you have done,* sur-
passing human understanding.
Your ways are ways of righteousness and truth,* O King of all the ages.

The Song of the Redeemed

The Hymn   *Let the Lower Lights Be Burning*
Brightly beams our Father's mercy
From His lighthouse evermore,
But to us He gives the keeping
Of the lights along the shore.
Let the lower lights be burning!
Send a gleam across the wave!
Some poor, fainting, struggling seaman
You may rescue, you may save.

Dark the night of sin has settled,
Loud the angry billows roar,
Eager eyes are watching, longing
For the lights along the shore.
Let the lower lights be burning!
Send a gleam across the wave!
Some poor, fainting, struggling seaman
You may rescue, you may save.

Trim your feeble lamp, my brother:
Some poor sailor tempest tossed,
Trying now to make the harbor,
In the darkness may be lost.
Let the lower lights be burning!
Send a gleam across the wave!
Some poor, fainting, struggling seaman
You may rescue, you may save.

Philip Bliss

The Refrain for the Vespers Lessons
Happy are those who act with justice* and always do what is right!

Psalm 106:3

The Vespers Psalm   *The Lord Comes in Holiness*
The Lord gave the word;* great was the company of women who bore the tidings:
"Kings with their armies are fleeing away;* the women at home are dividing the
  spoils."
Though you lingered among the sheepfolds,* you shall be like a dove whose
  wings are covered with silver, whose feathers are like green gold.
When the Almighty scattered kings,* it was like snow falling in Zalmon.
O mighty mountain, O hill of Bashan!* O rugged mountain, O hill of Bashan!
Why do you look with envy, O rugged mountain, at the hill which God chose for
  his resting place?* truly, the LORD will dwell there for ever.
The chariots of God are twenty thousand, even thousands of thousands;* the Lord
  comes in holiness from Sinai.
You have gone up on high and led captivity captive; you have received gifts even
  from your enemies,* that the LORD God might dwell among them.
Blessed be the Lord day by day,* the God of our salvation, who bears our burdens.
He is our God, the God of our salvation;* God is the LORD, by whom we escape
  death.

Psalm 68:11–20

The Refrain
Happy are those who act with justice* and always do what is right!

The Cry of the Church
Even so, come Lord Jesus!

The Lord's Prayer

The Prayer Appointed for the Week
O God, whose blessed Son made himself known to his disciples in the breaking of
  bread: Open the eyes of my faith, that I may behold him in all his redeeming
  work; who lives and reigns with you and the Holy Spirit, one God, now and
  for ever. *Amen.* †

The Concluding Prayer of the Church
Almighty God, who after the creation of the world rested from all your works and
sanctified a day of rest for all your creatures: Grant that I, putting away all
earthly anxieties, may be duly prepared for the service of public worship, and
grant as well that my Sabbath upon earth may be a preparation for the eternal
rest promised to your people in heaven; through Jesus Christ our Lord. *Amen.* †

✦

The Morning Office   **To Be Observed on the Hour or Half Hour**
Between 6 and 9 a.m.

The Call to Prayer
I will sing of mercy and justice;* to you, O LORD, will I sing praises.
Psalm 101:1

The Request for Presence
But as for me, O LORD, I cry to you for help;* in the morning my prayer comes
before you.
Psalm 88:14

The Greeting
Your testimonies are very sure,* and holiness adorns your house, O LORD, for ever
and for evermore.
Psalm 93:6

The Refrain for the Morning Lessons
This is the LORD's doing,* and it is marvelous in our eyes.
Psalm 118:23

A Reading
Jesus taught us, saying: "No one lights a lamp to cover it with a bowl or to put it
under a bed. No, it is put on a lamp-stand so that people may see the light
when they come in. For nothing is hidden but it will be made clear, nothing
secret but it will be made known and brought to light. So take care how you listen; anyone who has, will be given more; anyone who has not, will be deprived
even of what he thinks he has."
Luke 8:16–18

The Refrain
This is the LORD's doing,* and it is marvelous in our eyes.

The Morning Psalm   *Sing to the* LORD *a New Song*
Sing to the LORD a new song;* sing his praise in the congregation of the faithful.
Let Israel rejoice in his Maker;* let the children of Zion be joyful in their King.

Let them praise his Name in the dance;* let them sing praise to him with timbrel
and harp.
For the LORD takes pleasure in his people* and adorns the poor with victory.
Let the faithful rejoice in triumph;* let them be joyful on their beds.
Let the praises of God be in their throat* and a two-edged sword in their hand;
To wreak vengeance on the nations* and punishment on the peoples;
To bind their kings in chains* and their nobles with links of iron;
To inflict on them the judgment decreed;* this is glory for all his faithful people.

Psalm 149

The Refrain
This is the LORD's doing,* and it is marvelous in our eyes.

The Cry of the Church
Even so come, Lord Jesus!

The Lord's Prayer

The Prayer Appointed for the Week
Almighty and everlasting God, who in the Paschal mystery established the new
covenant of reconciliation: Grant that all who have been reborn in this fellowship of Christ's Body may show forth in their lives what they profess by their
faith; through Jesus Christ our Lord, who lives and reigns with you and the
Holy Spirit, one God, for ever and ever. *Amen.* †

The Concluding Prayer of the Church
Lord God, almighty and everlasting Father, you have brought me in safety to this
new day: Preserve me with your mighty power, that I may not fall into sin, nor
be overcome by adversity; and in all I do direct me to the fulfilling of your purpose; through Jesus Christ my Lord. *Amen.* †

The Midday Office   **To Be Observed on the Hour or Half Hour**
Between 11 a.m. and 2 p.m.

The Call to Prayer
God is the LORD; he has shined upon us;* form a procession with branches up to
the horns of the altar.

Psalm 118:27

The Request for Presence
Open my lips, O Lord* and my mouth shall proclaim your praise.

Psalm 51:16

The Greeting
Let all who seek you rejoice and be glad in you;* let those who love your salvation
say for ever, "Great is the LORD!"

Psalm 70:4

The Refrain for the Midday Lessons

The words of the LORD are tried in the fire;* he is a shield to all who trust in him.

Psalm 18:31

A Reading

So the Lord YAHWEH says this, 'Now I shall lay a stone in Zion, a granite stone, a precious cornerstone, a firm foundation stone: no one who relies on it will stumble. And I will make fair judgement the measure, and uprightness the plumb-line.'

Isaiah 28:16–17

The Refrain

The words of the LORD are tried in the fire;* he is a shield to all who trust in him.

The Midday Psalm   *Pray for the Peace of Jerusalem*

I was glad when they said to me,* "Let us go to the house of the LORD."
Now our feet are standing* within your gates, O Jerusalem.
Jerusalem is built as a city* that is at unity with itself;
To which the tribes go up, the tribes of the LORD,* the assembly of Israel, to praise the Name of the LORD.
For there are the thrones of judgment,* the thrones of the house of David.
Pray for the peace of Jerusalem:* "May they prosper who love you.
Peace be within your walls* and quietness within your towers.
For my brethren and companions' sake,* I pray for your prosperity.
Because of the house of the LORD our God,* I will seek to do you good."

Psalm 122

The Refrain

The words of the LORD are tried in the fire;* he is a shield to all who trust in him.

The Small Verse

Blessed be the Lord God of Israel for he has visited and delivered us. Amen, amen.

Traditional

The Lord's Prayer

The Prayer Appointed for the Week

Almighty and everlasting God, who in the Paschal mystery established the new covenant of reconciliation: Grant that all who have been reborn in this fellowship of Christ's Body may show forth in their lives what they profess by their faith; through Jesus Christ our Lord, who lives and reigns with you and the Holy Spirit, one God, for ever and ever. *Amen.* †

The Concluding Prayer of the Church

O God, you make me glad with the weekly remembrance of the glorious resurrection of your Son my Lord: Give me this day such blessing through my worship of you, that the week to come may be spent in your favor; through Jesus Christ our Lord. *Amen.* †

The Vespers Office   To Be Observed on the Hour or Half Hour
                                                   Between 5 and 8 p.m.

The Call to Prayer
Open my lips, O Lord,* and my mouth shall proclaim your praise.
                                                        Psalm 51:16

The Request for Presence
Hear, O Lord, and have mercy upon me;* O Lord, be my helper."
                                                        Psalm 30:11

The Greeting
Blessed be the Lord God, the God of Israel,* who alone does wondrous deeds!
And blessed be his glorious Name for ever!* and may all the earth be filled with
   his glory. Amen. Amen.
                                                     Psalm 72:18–19

The Hymn
   Holy Spirit, from on high,
               bend over us a pitying eye;
   now refresh the drooping heart;
               bid the power of sin depart.

   Light up every dark recess
               of our heart's ungodliness;
   show us every devious way
               where our hearts have gone astray.

   Teach us, with repentant grief,
               humbly to implore relief;
   then the Savior's blood reveal,
               and our broken spirits heal.

   May we daily grow in grace,
               and with patience run the race,
   trained in wisdom, led by love,
               till we reach our home above.
                                             William Bathurst

The Refrain for the Vespers Lessons
It is better to rely on the Lord* than to put any trust in flesh.
It is better to rely on the Lord* than to put any trust in rulers.
                                                      Psalm 118:8–9

The Vespers Psalm   *He Does Not Forsake His Faithful Ones*
Our steps are directed by the Lord;* he strengthens those in whose way he
   delights.
If they stumble, they shall not fall headlong,* for the Lord holds them by the hand.

I have been young and now I am old,* but never have I seen the righteous forsaken, or their children begging bread.

The righteous are always generous in their lending,* and their children shall be a
blessing.

Turn from evil, and do good,* and dwell in the land for ever.

For the LORD loves justice;* he does not forsake his faithful ones.

They shall be kept safe for ever,* but the offspring of the wicked shall be
destroyed.

The righteous shall possess the land* and dwell in it for ever.

The mouth of the righteous utters wisdom,* and their tongue speaks what is right.

The law of their God is in their heart,* and their footsteps shall not falter.

Psalm 37:24–33

The Refrain
It is better to rely on the LORD* than to put any trust in flesh.
It is better to rely on the LORD* than to put any trust in rulers.

The Small Verse
Their sound goes forth to all the earth and their speech to the end of the world.

adapted from THE SHORT BREVIARY

The Lord's Prayer

The Prayer Appointed for the Week
Almighty and everlasting God, who in the Paschal mystery established the new
covenant of reconciliation: Grant that all who have been reborn in this fellowship of Christ's Body may show forth in their lives what they profess by their
faith; through Jesus Christ our Lord, who lives and reigns with you and the
Holy Spirit, one God, for ever and ever. *Amen.* †

The Concluding Prayer of the Church
Lord God, whose Son our Savior Jesus Christ, triumphed over the powers of death
and prepared for us our place in the new Jerusalem: Grant that I, who have this
day given thanks for his resurrection, may praise you in the City of which he is
the light, and where he lives and reigns for ever and ever. *Amen.* †

The Morning Office

**To Be Observed on the Hour or Half Hour
Between 6 and 9 a.m.**

The Call to Prayer
I will lift up my hands to your commandments,* and I will meditate on your
statutes.

Psalm 119:48

The Request for Presence
O God, be not far from me;* come quickly to help me, O my God.

Psalm 71:12

The Greeting
O God, you have taught me since I was young,* and to this day I tell of your wonderful works.

Psalm 71:17

The Refrain for the Morning Lessons
This is the LORD's doing,* and it is marvelous in our eyes.

Psalm 118:23

A Reading
Then he went into the Temple and began driving out those who were busy trading, saying to them, 'According to scripture, *my house shall be a house of prayer* but you have turned it into *a bandits' den.'*

Luke 19:45–46

The Refrain
This is the LORD's doing,* and it is marvelous in our eyes.

The Morning Psalm   *Early in the Morning I Make My Appeal*
Give ear to my words, O LORD;* consider my meditation.
Hearken to my cry for help, my King and my God,* for I make my prayer to you.
In the morning, LORD, you hear my voice;* early in the morning I make my appeal and watch for you.
For you are not a God who takes pleasure in wickedness,* and evil cannot dwell with you.
Braggarts cannot stand in your sight;* you hate all those who work wickedness.
You destroy those who speak lies;* the bloodthirsty and deceitful, O LORD, you abhor.
But as for me, through the greatness of your mercy I go into your house;* I will bow down toward your holy temple in awe of you.

Psalm 5:1–7

The Refrain
This is the LORD's doing,* and it is marvelous in our eyes.

The Cry of the Church
Even so come, Lord Jesus!

The Lord's Prayer

The Prayer Appointed for the Week
Almighty and everlasting God, who in the Paschal mystery established the new covenant of reconciliation: Grant that all who have been reborn in this fellowship of Christ's Body may show forth in their lives what they profess by their faith; through Jesus Christ our Lord, who lives and reigns with you and the Holy Spirit, one God, for ever and ever. *Amen.* †

The Concluding Prayer of the Church
Lord God, almighty and everlasting Father, you have brought me in safety to this new day: Preserve me with your mighty power, that I may not fall into sin, nor be overcome by adversity; and in all I do direct me to the fulfilling of your purpose; through Jesus Christ my Lord. *Amen.* †

The Midday Office **To Be Observed on the Hour or Half Hour**
Between 11 a.m. and 2 p.m.

The Call to Prayer
Sing to the Lord with the harp,* with the harp and the voice of song.
With trumpets and the sound of the horn* shout with joy before the King, the Lord.
Psalm 98:6–7

The Request for Presence
Show us the light of your countenance, O God,* and come to us.
based on Psalm 67:1

The Greeting
O Lord, what are we that you should care for us?* mere mortals that you should think of us?
We are like a puff of wind;* our days are like a passing shadow.
Psalm 144:3–4

The Refrain for the Midday Lessons
In righteousness shall he judge the world* and the peoples with equity.
Psalm 98:10

A Reading
The time has come for the judgement to begin at the household of God; and if it begins with us, what will be the end for those who refuse to believe God's gospel? *If it is hard for the upright to be saved, what will happen to the wicked and the sinners?*
1 Peter 4:17–18

The Refrain
In righteousness shall he judge the world* and the peoples with equity.

The Midday Psalm *He That Planted the Ear, Does He Not Hear?*
He that planted the ear, does he not hear?* he that formed the eye, does he not see?
He who admonishes the nations, will he not punish?* he who teaches all the world, has he no knowledge?
The Lord knows our human thoughts;* how like a puff of wind they are.
Happy are they whom you instruct, O Lord!* whom you teach out of your law;
To give them rest in evil days,* until a pit is dug for the wicked.
For the Lord will not abandon his people,* nor will he forsake his own.
For judgment will again be just,* and all the true of heart will follow it.
Psalm 94:9–15

The Refrain
In righteousness shall he judge the world* and the peoples with equity.

The Cry of the Church
Be, Lord, my helper and forsake me not. Do not despise me, O God, my savior.
THE SHORT BREVIARY

The Lord's Prayer

The Prayer Appointed for the Week
Almighty and everlasting God, who in the Paschal mystery established the new
covenant of reconciliation: Grant that all who have been reborn in this fellowship of Christ's Body may show forth in their lives what they profess by their
faith; through Jesus Christ our Lord, who lives and reigns with you and the
Holy Spirit, one God, for ever and ever. *Amen.* †

The Concluding Prayer of the Church
Almighty and everlasting God, who willed that our Savior should take upon Him
our flesh and suffer death upon the Cross, that all mankind should follow the
example of His great humility, mercifully grant that we may both follow the
example of His patience and also be made partakers of His resurrection.
Through the same Jesus Christ. *Amen.*
adapted from THE SHORT BREVIARY

The Vespers Office   **To Be Observed on the Hour or Half Hour**
                                       Between 5 and 8 p.m.

The Call to Prayer
Be joyful in God, all you lands;* sing the glory of his Name; sing the glory of his
praise.
Say to God, "How awesome are your deeds! . . .
All the earth bows down before you,* sings to you, sings out your Name."
Psalm 66:1–3

The Request for Presence
Let your loving-kindness, O LORD, be upon us,* as we have put our trust in you.
Psalm 33:22

The Greeting
Blessed is the LORD!* for he has heard the voice of my prayer.
Psalm 28:7

The Hymn   *Rise Up*
Rise up, you saints of God! Have done with lesser things.
Give heart and mind and soul and strength to serve the King of kings.

Rise up, you saints of God! The kingdom tarries long.
Bring in the day of brotherhood and end the night of wrong.

Rise up, you saints of God! The church for you does wait,
Her strength unequal to her task, rise up, and make her great!

Lift high the cross of Christ! Tread where His feet have trod.
As brothers of the Son of Man, rise up, you saints of God!

William Merrill

The Refrain for the Vespers Lessons
Turn again to your rest, O my soul,* for the LORD has treated you well.
For you have rescued my life from death,* my eyes from tears, and my feet from
stumbling.

Psalm 116:6–7

The Vespers Psalm   *I Will Declare Your Saving Deeds to a People Yet Unborn*
Praise the LORD, you that fear him;* stand in awe of him, O offspring of Israel; all
you of Jacob's line, give glory.
For he does not despise nor abhor the poor in their poverty; neither does he hide
his face from them;* but when they cry to him he hears them.
My praise is of him in the great assembly;* I will perform my vows in the presence
of those who worship him.
The poor shall eat and be satisfied,* and those who seek the LORD shall praise him:
"May your heart live for ever!"
All the ends of the earth shall remember and turn to the LORD,* and all the families
of the nations shall bow before him.
For kingship belongs to the LORD;* he rules over the nations.
To him alone all who sleep in the earth bow down in worship;* all who go down to
the dust fall before him.
My soul shall live for him; my descendants shall serve him;* they shall be known
as the LORD's for ever.
They shall come and make known to a people yet unborn* the saving deeds that
he has done.

Psalm 22:22–30

The Refrain
Turn again to your rest, O my soul,* for the LORD has treated you well.
For you have rescued my life from death,* my eyes from tears, and my feet from
stumbling.

The Cry of the Church
O Lord, hear my prayer and let my cry come unto you. Thanks be to God.

THE SHORT BREVIARY

The Lord's Prayer

The Prayer Appointed for the Week
Almighty and everlasting God, who in the Paschal mystery established the new
covenant of reconciliation: Grant that all who have been reborn in this fellowship of Christ's Body may show forth in their lives what they profess by their

faith; through Jesus Christ our Lord, who lives and reigns with you and the Holy Spirit, one God, for ever and ever. *Amen.* †

The Concluding Prayer of the Church
Almighty God, you have surrounded me with a great cloud of witnesses: Grant that I too may persevere in running the race that is set before me, until at last I may with him attain to your eternal joy; through Jesus Christ, the pioneer and perfecter of our faith, who lives and reigns with you and the Holy Spirit, one God, for ever and ever. *Amen.* †

The Morning Office | **To Be Observed on the Hour or Half Hour Between 6 and 9 a.m.**

The Call to Prayer
Let us come before his presence with thanksgiving* and raise a loud shout to him with psalms.

Psalm 95:1

The Request for Presence
Show us the light of your countenance, O God,* and come to us.

based on Psalm 67:1

The Greeting
To you I lift up my eyes,* to you enthroned in the heavens.
As the eyes of servants look to the hand of their masters,* and the eyes of a maid to the hand of her mistress,
So our eyes look to the LORD our God,* until he shows us his mercy.

Psalm 123:1–3

The Refrain for the Morning Lessons
I will bear witness that the LORD is righteous;* I will praise the Name of the LORD Most High.

Psalm 7:18

A Reading
John said to him, 'Master, we saw someone who is not one of us driving out devils in your name, and because he is not one of us we tried to stop him.' But Jesus said, 'You must not stop him; no one who works a miracle in my name could soon afterwards speak evil of me. Anyone who is not against us is for us.'

Mark 9:38–40

The Refrain
I will bear witness that the LORD is righteous;* I will praise the Name of the LORD Most High.

The Morning Psalm | *Let the Heavens Declare the Rightness of His Cause*
The LORD, the God of gods, has spoken;* he has called the earth from the rising of the sun to its setting.

Out of Zion, perfect in its beauty,* God reveals himself in glory.
Our God will come and will not keep silence;* before him there is a consuming
flame, and round about him a raging storm.
He calls the heavens and the earth from above* to witness the judgment of his
people.
"Gather before me my loyal followers,* those who have made a covenant with me
and sealed it with sacrifice."
Let the heavens declare the rightness of his cause;* for God himself is judge.

Psalm 50:1–6

The Refrain

I will bear witness that the LORD is righteous;* I will praise the Name of the LORD
Most High.

The Small Verse

Keep me, Lord, as the apple of your eye and carry me under the shadow of your
wings.

Traditional

The Lord's Prayer

The Prayer Appointed for the Week

Almighty and everlasting God, who in the Paschal mystery established the new
covenant of reconciliation: Grant that all who have been reborn in this fellowship of Christ's Body may show forth in their lives what they profess by their
faith; through Jesus Christ our Lord, who lives and reigns with you and the
Holy Spirit, one God, for ever and ever. *Amen.* †

The Concluding Prayer of the Church

Lord God, almighty and everlasting Father, you have brought me in safety to this
new day: Preserve me with your mighty power, that I may not fall into sin, nor
be overcome by adversity; and in all I do direct me to the fulfilling of your purpose; through Jesus Christ my Lord. *Amen.* †

The Midday Office   To Be Observed on the Hour or Half Hour
                                     Between 11 a.m. and 2 p.m.

The Call to Prayer

Sing to the LORD a new song;* sing his praise in the congregation of the faithful.

Psalm 149:1

The Request for Presence

Hear, O Shepherd of Israel, leading Joseph like a flock;* shine forth, you that are
enthroned upon the cherubim.

Psalm 80:1

The Greeting
O LORD, your word is everlasting;* it stands firm in the heavens.
Your faithfulness remains from one generation to another;* you established the
earth, and it abides.

Psalm 119:89–90

The Refrain for the Midday Lessons
The LORD shall watch over your going out and your coming in,* from this time
forth for evermore.

Psalm 121:8

A Reading
He has wiped out the record of our debt to the Law, which stood against us; he has
destroyed it by nailing it to the cross; and he has stripped the sovereignties and
the ruling forces, and paraded them in public, behind him in his triumphal
procession.

Colossians 2:15–16

The Refrain
The LORD shall watch over your going out and your coming in,* from this time
forth for evermore.

The Midday Psalm   *The LORD Has Cut the Cords of the Wicked*
"Greatly have they oppressed me since my youth,"* let Israel now say;
"Greatly have they oppressed me since my youth,* but they have not prevailed
against me."
The plowmen plowed upon my back* and made their furrows long.
The LORD, the Righteous One,* has cut the cords of the wicked.
Let them be put to shame and thrown back,* all those who are enemies of Zion.
Let them be like grass upon the housetops,* which withers before it can be
plucked;
Which does not fill the hand of the reaper,* nor the bosom of him who binds the
sheaves;
So that those who go by say not so much as,* "The LORD prosper you. We wish you
well in the Name of the LORD."

Psalm 129

The Refrain
The LORD shall watch over your going out and your coming in,* from this time
forth for evermore.

The Cry of the Church
Lord, have mercy on us. Christ, have mercy on us. Lord, have mercy on us.

The Lord's Prayer

The Prayer Appointed for the Week
Almighty and everlasting God, who in the Paschal mystery established the new
covenant of reconciliation: Grant that all who have been reborn in this fellow-

ship of Christ's Body may show forth in their lives what they profess by their
faith; through Jesus Christ our Lord, who lives and reigns with you and the
Holy Spirit, one God, for ever and ever. *Amen.* †

The Concluding Prayer of the Church

Let us bless the Lord God living and true! Let us always render him praise, glory,
honor, blessing, and all good things! Amen. Amen. So be it! So be it!

St. Francis of Assisi

The Vespers Office　　　　　　**To Be Observed on the Hour or Half Hour**
Between 5 and 8 p.m.

The Call to Prayer

Praise God, from whom all blessings flow; praise him, all creatures here below;
praise him above, you heavenly hosts; praise Father, Son and Holy Ghost.

Doxology

The Request for Presence

Show your goodness, O LORD, to those who are good* and to those who are true of
heart.

Psalm 125:4

The Greeting

Out of the mouths of infants and children* your majesty is praised above the
heavens.

Psalm 8:2

The Hymn　　　　　*The Spacious Firmament*

The spacious firmament on high,
　　　with all the blue ethereal sky,
and spangled heavens, a shining frame,
　　　their great Original proclaim.
The unwearied sun from day to day
　　　does his Creator's power display;
and publishes to every land
　　　the work of an almighty hand.

Soon as the evening shades prevail,
　　　the moon takes up the wondrous tale,
and nightly to the listening earth
　　　repeats the story of her birth:
while all the stars that round her burn,
　　　and all the planets in their turn,
confirm the tidings, as they roll
　　　and spread the truth from pole to pole.

What though in solemn silence all
> move round the dark terrestrial ball?

What though no real voice or sound
> amid the radiant orbs be found?

In reason's ear they all rejoice,
> and utter forth a glorious voice;

forever singing as they shine,
> "The hand that made us is divine."

> *Joseph Addison*

The Refrain for the Vespers Lessons

We have heard with our ears, O God, our forefathers have told us,* the deeds you
did in their days, in the days of old.

> *Psalm 44:1*

The Vespers Psalm God Is My King from Ancient Times

Yet God is my King from ancient times,* victorious in the midst of the earth.

You divided the sea by your might* and shattered the heads of the dragons upon
the waters;

You crushed the heads of Leviathan* and gave him to the people of the desert for
food.

You split open spring and torrent;* you dried up ever-flowing rivers.

Yours is the day, yours also the night;* you established the moon and the sun.

You fixed all the boundaries of the earth;* you made both summer and winter.

> *Psalm 74:11–16*

The Refrain

We have heard with our ears, O God, our forefathers have told us,* the deeds you
did in their days, in the days of old.

The Cry of the Church

In the evening, in the morning, and at noonday, I will complain and lament,* and
he will hear my voice.

> *Psalm 55:18*

The Lord's Prayer

The Prayer Appointed for the Week

Almighty and everlasting God, who in the Paschal mystery established the new
covenant of reconciliation: Grant that all who have been reborn in this fellowship of Christ's Body may show forth in their lives what they profess by their
faith; through Jesus Christ our Lord, who lives and reigns with you and the
Holy Spirit, one God, for ever and ever. *Amen.* †

The Concluding Prayer of the Church

Almighty and eternal God, ruler of all things in heaven and earth: Mercifully
accept my prayer, and strengthen me to do your will; through Jesus Christ our
Lord. *Amen.* †

The Morning Office

The Call to Prayer

The LORD is near to those who call upon him,* to all who call upon him faithfully.
He fulfills the desire of those who fear him;* he hears their cry and helps them.
The LORD preserves all those who love him,* but he destroys all the wicked.

Psalm 145:19–21

The Request for Presence

Not to us, O LORD, not to us,* but to your Name give glory; because of your love
and because of your faithfulness.

Psalm 115:1

The Greeting

Your love, O LORD, reaches to the heavens,* and your faithfulness to the clouds.

Psalm 36:5

The Refrain for the Morning Lessons

I will exalt you, O God my King,* and bless your Name for ever and ever.

Psalm 145:1

A Reading

Now it happened in those days that he went onto the mountain to pray; and he
spent the whole night in prayer to God. When day came he summoned his disciples and picked out twelve of them; he called them 'apostles': Simon whom
he called Peter, and his brother Andrew; James, John, Philip, Bartholomew,
Matthew, Thomas, James son of Alphaeus, Simon called the Zealot, Judas son
of James, and Judas Iscariot who became a traitor.

Luke 6:12–16

The Refrain

I will exalt you, O God my King,* and bless your Name for ever and ever.

The Morning Psalm   The LORD Will Make Good His Purposes

I will give thanks to you, O LORD, with my whole heart;* before the gods I will sing
your praise.
I will bow down toward your holy temple and praise your Name,* because of
your love and faithfulness;
For you have glorified your Name* and your word above all things.
When I called, you answered me;* you increased my strength within me.
All the kings of the earth will praise you, O LORD,* when they have heard the
words of your mouth.
They will sing of the ways of the LORD,* that great is the glory of the LORD.
Though the LORD be high, he cares for the lowly;* he perceives the haughty from
afar.
Though I walk in the midst of trouble, you keep me safe;* you stretch forth your
hand against the fury of my enemies; your right hand shall save me.

The LORD will make good his purpose for me;* O LORD, your love endures for
ever; do not abandon the works of your hands.

Psalm 138

The Refrain
I will exalt you, O God my King,* and bless your Name for ever and ever.

The Cry of the Church
O God, come to my assistance! O Lord, make haste to help me!

The Lord's Prayer

The Prayer Appointed for the Week
Almighty and everlasting God, who in the Paschal mystery established the new
covenant of reconciliation: Grant that all who have been reborn in this fellowship of Christ's Body may show forth in their lives what they profess by their
faith; through Jesus Christ our Lord, who lives and reigns with you and the
Holy Spirit, one God, for ever and ever. *Amen.* †

The Concluding Prayer of the Church
Lord God, almighty and everlasting Father, you have brought me in safety to this
new day: Preserve me with your mighty power, that I may not fall into sin, nor
be overcome by adversity; and in all I do direct me to the fulfilling of your purpose; through Jesus Christ my Lord. *Amen.* †

The Midday Office To Be Observed on the Hour or Half Hour
Between 11 a.m. and 2 p.m.

The Call to Prayer
"Come now, let us reason together," says the LORD.

Isaiah 1:18, KJV

The Request for Presence
O LORD, I call to you; come to me quickly;* hear my voice when I cry to you.

Psalm 141:1

The Greeting
In you, O LORD, have I taken refuge;* let me never be ashamed.

Psalm 71:1

The Refrain for the Midday Lessons
Happy are they all who fear the LORD,* and who follow in his ways!

Psalm 128:1

A Reading
For I, YAHWEH, your God, I grasp you by your right hand; I tell you, 'Do not be
afraid, I shall help you.'

Isaiah 41:13

The Refrain
Happy are they all who fear the LORD,* and who follow in his ways!

The Midday Psalm   *Happy Are They Who Delight in the LORD*
Happy are they who have not walked in the counsel of the wicked,* nor lingered
    in the way of sinners, nor sat in the seats of the scornful!
Their delight is in the law of the LORD,* and they meditate on his law day and
    night.
They are like trees planted by streams of water, bearing fruit in due season, with
    leaves that do not wither;* everything they do shall prosper.
It is not so with the wicked;* they are like chaff which the wind blows away.
Therefore the wicked shall not stand upright when judgment comes,* nor the
    sinner in the council of the righteous.
For the LORD knows the way of the righteous,* but the way of the wicked is
    doomed.

Psalm 1

The Refrain
Happy are they all who fear the LORD,* and who follow in his ways!

The Cry of the Church
Be, Lord, my helper and forsake me not. Do not despise me, O God, my savior.

THE SHORT BREVIARY

The Lord's Prayer

The Prayer Appointed for the Week
Almighty and everlasting God, who in the Paschal mystery established the new
    covenant of reconciliation: Grant that all who have been reborn in this fellow-
    ship of Christ's Body may show forth in their lives what they profess by their
    faith; through Jesus Christ our Lord, who lives and reigns with you and the
    Holy Spirit, one God, for ever and ever. *Amen.* †

The Concluding Prayer of the Church
Direct me, O Lord, in all my doings with your most gracious favor, and further me
    with your continual help; that in all my work begun, continued, and ended in
    you, I may glorify your holy name, and finally, by your mercy, obtain everlast-
    ing life; through Jesus Christ our Lord. *Amen.* †

The Vespers Office   To Be Observed on the Hour or Half Hour
                                      Between 5 and 8 p.m.

The Call to Prayer
Sing to the LORD, you servants of his;* give thanks for the remembrance of his
    holiness.
For his wrath endures but the twinkling of an eye,* his favor for a lifetime.

Psalm 30:4–5

The Request for Presence
Show us the light of your countenance, O God,* and come to us.

based on Psalm 67:1

The Greeting
Your statutes have been like songs to me* wherever I have lived as a stranger.
I remember your Name in the night, O LORD,* and dwell upon your law.
This is how it has been with me,* because I have kept your commandments.

Psalm 119:54–56

The Hymn   Lead Me Day by Day
Father, lead me day by day,   May I do the good I know,
Ever in Your own sweet way;   Serving gladly here below,
Teach me to be pure and true,   Then at last to you go home,
Show me what I ought to do.   Evermore to be your own.

John Hopps

When in danger, make me brave,
Make me know that You can save;
And when all alone I stand,
Shield me in Your mighty hand.

The Refrain for the Vespers Lessons
Righteousness shall go before him,* and peace shall be a pathway for his feet.

Psalm 85:13

The Vespers Psalm   God Is the Hope of All the Ends of the Earth
Awesome things will you show us in your righteousness, O God of our salvation,*
    O Hope of all the ends of the earth and of the seas that are far away.
You make fast the mountains by your power;* they are girded about with might.
You still the roaring of the seas,* the roaring of their waves, and the clamor of the
    peoples.
Those who dwell at the ends of the earth will tremble at your marvelous signs;*
    you make the dawn and the dusk to sing for joy.
You visit the earth and water it abundantly; you make it very plenteous;* the river
    of God is full of water.
You prepare the grain,* for so you provide for the earth.
You drench the furrows and smooth out the ridges;* with heavy rain you soften
    the ground and bless its increase.
You crown the year with your goodness,* and your paths overflow with plenty.
May the fields of the wilderness be rich for grazing,* and the hills be clothed with
    joy.
May the meadows cover themselves with flocks, and the valleys cloak themselves
    with grain;* let them shout for joy and sing.

Psalm 65:5–14

The Refrain
Righteousness shall go before him,* and peace shall be a pathway for his feet.

The Cry of the Church
Even so come, Lord Jesus!

The Lord's Prayer

The Prayer Appointed for the Week
Almighty and everlasting God, who in the Paschal mystery established the new
covenant of reconciliation: Grant that all who have been reborn in this fellowship of Christ's Body may show forth in their lives what they profess by their
faith; through Jesus Christ our Lord, who lives and reigns with you and the
Holy Spirit, one God, for ever and ever. *Amen.* †

The Concluding Prayer of the Church
May Almighty God grant me a peaceful night and a perfect end. *Amen.*

The Morning Office   **To Be Observed on the Hour or Half Hour**
Between 6 and 9 a.m.

The Call to Prayer
Come, let us bow down, and bend the knee,* and kneel before the LORD our Maker.
For he is our God,* and we are the people of his pasture and the sheep of his hand.
Psalm 95:6–7

The Request for Presence
So teach us to number our days* that we may apply our hearts to wisdom.
Psalm 90:12

The Greeting
My God, my rock in whom I put my trust,* my shield, the horn of my salvation,
and my refuge; you are worthy of praise.
Psalm 18:2

The Refrain for the Morning Lessons
My eyes are upon the faithful in the land, that they may dwell with me.
Psalm 101:6

A Reading
Jesus taught us, saying: "He who comes from above is above all others; he who is of
the earth is earthly himself and speaks in an earthly way. He who comes from
heaven bears witness to things he has seen and heard . . . since he whom God has
sent speaks God's own words, for God gives him the Spirit without reserve."
John 3:31ff

The Refrain
My eyes are upon the faithful in the land, that they may dwell with me.

The Morning Psalm   *The Eye of the LORD Is Upon Those Who Fear Him*
The LORD looks down from heaven,* and beholds all the people in the world.
From where he sits enthroned he turns his gaze* on all who dwell on the earth.

He fashions all the hearts of them* and understands all their works.
There is no king that can be saved by a mighty army;* a strong man is not delivered
　　by his great strength.
The horse is a vain hope for deliverance;* for all its strength it cannot save.
Behold, the eye of the LORD is upon those who fear him,* on those who wait upon
　　his love,
To pluck their lives from death,* and to feed them in time of famine.
Our soul waits for the LORD;* he is our help and our shield.
Indeed, our heart rejoices in him,* for in his holy Name we put our trust.
Let your loving-kindness, O LORD, be upon us,* as we have put our trust in you.

Psalm 33:13–22

The Refrain
My eyes are upon the faithful in the land, that they may dwell with me.

The Cry of the Church
O God, come to my assistance! O Lord, make haste to help me!

The Lord's Prayer

The Prayer Appointed for the Week
Almighty and everlasting God, who in the Paschal mystery established the new
　　covenant of reconciliation: Grant that all who have been reborn in this fellow-
　　ship of Christ's Body may show forth in their lives what they profess by their
　　faith; through Jesus Christ our Lord, who lives and reigns with you and the
　　Holy Spirit, one God, for ever and ever. *Amen.* †

The Concluding Prayer of the Church
Lord God, almighty and everlasting Father, you have brought me in safety to this
　　new day: Preserve me with your mighty power, that I may not fall into sin, nor
　　be overcome by adversity; and in all I do direct me to the fulfilling of your pur-
　　pose; through Jesus Christ my Lord. *Amen.* †

The Midday Office　　　　　　　　　**To Be Observed on the Hour or Half Hour**
　　　　　　　　　　　　　　　　　　　　Between 11 a.m. and 2 p.m.

The Call to Prayer
Glory in his holy Name;* let the hearts of those who seek the LORD rejoice.

Psalm 105:3

The Request for Presence
Let your compassion come to me, that I may live,* for your law is my delight.

Psalm 119:77

The Greeting
Your righteousness, O God, reaches to the heavens;* you have done great things;
　　who is like you, O God?

Psalm 71:19

The Refrain for the Midday Lessons

"I will instruct you and teach you in the way that you should go;* I will guide you
    with my eye.
Do not be like horse or mule, which have no understanding;* who must be fitted
    with bit and bridle, or else they will not stay near you."

Psalm 32:9–10

A Reading

Through him you now have faith in God, who raised him from the dead and gave
    him glory for this very purpose—that your faith and hope should be in God.

1 Peter 1:21

The Refrain

"I will instruct you and teach you in the way that you should go;* I will guide you
    with my eye.
Do not be like horse or mule, which have no understanding;* who must be fitted
    with bit and bridle, or else they will not stay near you."

The Midday Psalm   *Never Have I Seen the Righteous Forsaken*

Our steps are directed by the LORD;* he strengthens those in whose way he
    delights.
If they stumble, they shall not fall headlong,* for the LORD holds them by the hand.
I have been young and now I am old,* but never have I seen the righteous forsaken.

Psalm 37:24–26

The Refrain

"I will instruct you and teach you in the way that you should go;* I will guide you
    with my eye.
Do not be like horse or mule, which have no understanding;* who must be fitted
    with bit and bridle, or else they will not stay near you."

The Cry of the Church

Lord, have mercy on us. Christ, have mercy on us. Lord, have mercy on us.

The Lord's Prayer

The Prayer Appointed for the Week

Almighty and everlasting God, who in the Paschal mystery established the new
    covenant of reconciliation: Grant that all who have been reborn in this fellow-
    ship of Christ's Body may show forth in their lives what they profess by their
    faith; through Jesus Christ our Lord, who lives and reigns with you and the
    Holy Spirit, one God, for ever and ever. *Amen.* †

The Concluding Prayer of the Church

Open, Lord, my eyes that I may see.
Open, Lord, my ears that I may hear.
Open, Lord, my heart and my mind that I may understand.
So shall I turn to you and be healed.

Traditional

The Vespers Office   **To Be Observed on the Hour or Half Hour**
                                      Between 5 and 8 p.m.

The Call to Prayer
Come now and see the works of God,* how wonderful he is in his doing toward
    all people.
In his might he rules for ever; his eyes keep watch over the nations;* let no rebel
    rise up against him.

Psalm 66:4, 6

The Request for Presence
Show us your mercy, O Lord,* and grant us your salvation.

Psalm 85:7

The Greeting
Praise God from whom all blessings flow; praise Him all creatures here below;
    praise Him above, you heavenly hosts; praise Father, Son, and Holy Ghost.

Traditional Doxology

The Hymn   *I Want Jesus to Walk with Me*
I want Jesus to walk with me.
I want Jesus to walk with me.
All along my pilgrim journey,
Lord, I want Jesus to walk with me.

In my trials Lord, walk with me.
In my trials Lord, walk with me.
When my heart is almost breaking,
Lord, I want Jesus to walk with me.

When I'm troubled, Lord, walk with me.
When I'm troubled, Lord, walk with me.
When my head is bowed in sorrow,
Lord, I want Jesus to walk with me.

African American Spiritual

The Refrain for the Vespers Lessons
Our sins are stronger than we are,* but you will blot them out.

Psalm 65:3

The Vespers Psalm   *Remember the Marvels He Has Done*
Search for the Lord and his strength;* continually seek his face.
Remember the marvels he has done,* his wonders and the judgments of his mouth,
O offspring of Abraham his servant,* O children of Jacob his chosen.
He is the Lord our God;* his judgments prevail in all the world.
He has always been mindful of his covenant,* the promise he made for a thousand
    generations:
The covenant he made with Abraham,* the oath that he swore to Isaac,
Which he established as a statute for Jacob,* an everlasting covenant for Israel . . .

Psalm 105:4–10

The Refrain
Our sins are stronger than we are,* but you will blot them out.

The Small Verse
The Lord is my shepherd and nothing is wanting to me. In green pastures He hath
settled me.

The Short Breviary

The Lord's Prayer

The Prayer Appointed for the Week
Almighty and everlasting God, who in the Paschal mystery established the new
covenant of reconciliation: Grant that all who have been reborn in this fellowship of Christ's Body may show forth in their lives what they profess by their
faith; through Jesus Christ our Lord, who lives and reigns with you and the
Holy Spirit, one God, for ever and ever. *Amen.* †

The Concluding Prayer of the Church
Help each one of us, gracious Father, to live in such magnanimity and restraint
that the Head of the Church may never have cause to say to any one of us, This
is my body, broken by you.

Prayer from China

The Morning Office   **To Be Observed on the Hour or Half Hour**
Between 6 and 9 a.m.

The Call to Prayer
Hallelujah! Praise the Name of the LORD;* give praise, you servants of the LORD,
You who stand in the house of the LORD,* in the courts of the house of our God.
Praise the LORD, for the LORD is good;* sing praises to his Name, for it is lovely.

Psalm 135:1–3

The Request for Presence
I have said to the LORD, "You are my God;* listen, O LORD, to my supplication.

Psalm 140:6

The Greeting
You are the LORD, most high over all the earth;* you are exalted far above all gods.

Psalm 97:9

The Refrain for the Morning Lessons
The human mind and heart are a mystery; but God will loose an arrow at them,*
and suddenly they will be wounded.

Psalm 64:7

A Reading
He was still speaking to the crowds when suddenly his mother and his brothers
were standing outside and were anxious to have a word with him. But to the
man who told him this Jesus replied, 'Who is my mother? Who are my broth-

ers? Anyone who does the will of my Father in heaven is my brother and sister and mother.'

Matthew 12:46–50

The Refrain

The human mind and heart are a mystery; but God will loose an arrow at them,*
and suddenly they will be wounded.

The Morning Psalm   *My Heart Shall Meditate on Understanding*

Hear this, all you peoples; hearken, all you who dwell in the world,* you of high
degree and low, rich and poor together.

My mouth shall speak of wisdom,* and my heart shall meditate on understanding.

I will incline my ear to a proverb* and set forth my riddle upon the harp.

Why should I be afraid in evil days,* when the wickedness of those at my heels
surrounds me,

The wickedness of those who put their trust in their goods,* and boast of their
great riches?

We can never ransom ourselves,* or deliver to God the price of our life;

For the ransom of our life is so great,* that we should never have enough to pay it,

Psalm 49:1–10

The Refrain

The human mind and heart are a mystery; but God will loose an arrow at them,*
and suddenly they will be wounded.

The Cry of the Church

O God, come to my assistance! O Lord, make haste to help me!

The Lord's Prayer

The Prayer Appointed for the Week

Almighty and everlasting God, who in the Paschal mystery established the new
covenant of reconciliation: Grant that all who have been reborn in this fellowship of Christ's Body may show forth in their lives what they profess by their
faith; through Jesus Christ our Lord, who lives and reigns with you and the
Holy Spirit, one God, for ever and ever. *Amen.* †

The Concluding Prayer of the Church

Lord God, almighty and everlasting Father, you have brought me in safety to this
new day: Preserve me with your mighty power, that I may not fall into sin, nor
be overcome by adversity; and in all I do direct me to the fulfilling of your purpose; through Jesus Christ my Lord. *Amen.* †

The Midday Office   **To Be Observed on the Hour or Half Hour**

Between 11 a.m. and 2 p.m.

The Call to Prayer

Ascribe to the LORD the honor due his Name;* bring offerings and come into his
courts.

Psalm 96:8

The Request for Presence
Let your countenance shine upon your servant* and teach me your statutes.

Psalm 119:135

The Greeting
I will give thanks to you, O LORD, with my whole heart;* I will tell of all your
marvelous works.

Psalm 9:1

The Refrain for the Midday Lessons
Among the gods there is none like you, O LORD,* nor anything like your works.

Psalm 86:8

A Reading
For the love of Christ overwhelms us when we consider that if one man died for
all, then all have died; his purpose in dying for all humanity was that those
who live should live not any more for themselves, but for him who died and
was raised to life for them.

2 Corinthians 5:14–15

The Refrain
Among the gods there is none like you, O LORD,* nor anything like your works.

The Midday Psalm　　　　　　　　*You Have Declared Your Power Among the Peoples*
I will remember the works of the LORD,* and call to mind your wonders of old time.
I will meditate on all your acts* and ponder your mighty deeds.
Your way, O God, is holy;* who is so great a god as our God?
You are the God who works wonders* and have declared your power among the
peoples.

Psalm 77:11–14

The Refrain
Among the gods there is none like you, O LORD,* nor anything like your works.

The Cry of the Church
Even so come, Lord Jesus!

The Lord's Prayer

The Prayer Appointed for the Week
Almighty and everlasting God, who in the Paschal mystery established the new
covenant of reconciliation: Grant that all who have been reborn in this fellowship of Christ's Body may show forth in their lives what they profess by their
faith; through Jesus Christ our Lord, who lives and reigns with you and the
Holy Spirit, one God, for ever and ever. *Amen.* †

The Concluding Prayer of the Church
Lord Jesus Christ, by your death you took away the sting of death: Grant me to so
follow in faith where you have led the way, that I may at length fall asleep

peacefully in you and wake in your likeness; for your tender mercies' sake.
Amen. †

The Vespers Office   **To Be Observed on the Hour or Half Hour**
Between 5 and 8 p.m.

The Call to Prayer
I will glory in the LORD;* let the humble hear and rejoice.

Psalm 34:2

The Request for Presence
Turn to me and have pity on me . . .*
The sorrows of my heart have increased . . .*
Look upon my adversity and misery* and forgive me all my sin.

Psalm 25:15–17

The Greeting
LORD, how great are your works!* your thoughts are very deep.
The dullard does not know, nor does the fool understand,* that though the wicked
    grow like weeds, and all the workers of iniquity flourish,
They flourish only to be destroyed for ever;* but you, O LORD, are exalted for
    evermore.

Psalm 92:5–7

The Hymn   *What Have You Given Me?*

  I gave my life for thee,
      My precious blood I shed,
  That you might ransomed be,
      And quickened from the dead;
  I gave, I gave My life for thee,
      What have you given Me?

  My Father's house of light,
      My glory circled throne,
  I left for earthly night,
      For wanderings sad and lone;
  I left, I left it all for thee,
      Have you left aught for Me?

  I suffered much for thee,
      More than your tongue can tell,
  Of bitterest agony,
      To rescue you from hell;
  I've borne, I've borne it all for thee,
      What have you borne for Me?

And I have brought to thee,
> Down from my home above,
Salvation full and free,
> My pardon and My love;
I bring, I bring rich gifts for thee,
> What have you brought to Me?
>> *Frances Havergal*

The Refrain for the Vespers Lessons
When I was in trouble, I called to the Lord;* I called to the Lord, and he answered
me.

> *Psalm 120:1*

The Vespers Psalm   *In You, O Lord, Have I Taken Refuge*
In you, O Lord, have I taken refuge; let me never be put to shame;* deliver me in
your righteousness.
Incline your ear to me;* make haste to deliver me.
Be my strong rock, a castle to keep me safe, for you are my crag and my stronghold;*
for the sake of your Name, lead me and guide me.
Take me out of the net that they have secretly set for me,* for you are my tower of
strength.
Into your hands I commend my spirit,* for you have redeemed me, O Lord, O
God of truth.

> *Psalm 31:1–5*

The Refrain
When I was in trouble, I called to the Lord;* I called to the Lord, and he answered
me.

The Cry of the Church
Be, Lord, my helper and forsake me not. Do not despise me, O God, my savior.
> *The Short Breviary*

The Lord's Prayer

The Prayer Appointed for the Week
Almighty and everlasting God, who in the Paschal mystery established the new
covenant of reconciliation: Grant that all who have been reborn in this fellowship of Christ's Body may show forth in their lives what they profess by their
faith; through Jesus Christ our Lord, who lives and reigns with you and the
Holy Spirit, one God, for ever and ever. *Amen.* †

Concluding Prayers of the Church
Almighty God, who has promised to hear the petitions of those who ask in your
Son's Name: I beseech you mercifully to incline your ear to me who have made
my prayers and supplications to you; and grant that those things which I have
faithfully asked according to your will, I may effectually obtain, to the relief of
my necessity, and to the setting forth of your glory; through Jesus Christ my
Lord. *Amen.* †

May the souls of the faithful departed, through the mercy of God, rest in eternal peace. *Amen.*

The Morning Office   **To Be Observed on the Hour or Half Hour**
                                      Between 6 and 9 a.m.

The Call to Prayer
Bless the Lord, you angels of his, you mighty ones who do his bidding,* and hearken to the voice of his word.
Bless the Lord, all you his hosts,* you ministers of his who do his will.
Bless the Lord, all you works of his, in all places of his dominion;* bless the Lord, O my soul.

Psalm 103:20–22

The Request for Presence
Show me the light of your countenance, O God,* and come to me.

based on Psalm 67:1

The Greeting
As the deer longs for the water-brooks,* so longs my soul for you, O God.

Psalm 42:1

The Refrain for the Morning Lessons
The same stone which the builders rejected* has become the chief cornerstone.
This is the Lord's doing,* and it is marvelous in our eyes.

Psalm 118:22–23

A Reading
People even brought babies to him, for him to touch them; but when the disciples saw this they scolded them. But Jesus called the children to him and said, 'Let the little children come to me, and do not stop them; for it is to such as these that the kingdom of God belongs. In truth I tell you, anyone who does not welcome the kingdom of God like a little child will never enter it.'

Luke 18:15–17

The Refrain
The same stone which the builders rejected* has become the chief cornerstone.
This is the Lord's doing,* and it is marvelous in our eyes.

The Morning Psalm   *In a Little While the Wicked Shall Be No More*
In a little while the wicked shall be no more;* you shall search out their place, but they will not be there.
But the lowly shall possess the land;* they will delight in abundance of peace.
The wicked plot against the righteous* and gnash at them with their teeth.
The Lord laughs at the wicked,* because he sees that their day will come.
The wicked draw their sword and bend their bow to strike down the poor and needy,* to slaughter those who are upright in their ways.
Their sword shall go through their own heart,* and their bow shall be broken.

The little that the righteous has* is better than great riches of the wicked.
For the power of the wicked shall be broken,* but the LORD upholds the righteous.

Psalm 37:11–18

The Refrain
The same stone which the builders rejected* has become the chief cornerstone.
This is the LORD's doing,* and it is marvelous in our eyes.

The Cry of the Church
Even so come, Lord Jesus!

The Lord's Prayer

The Prayer Appointed for the Week
Almighty and everlasting God, who in the Paschal mystery established the new
covenant of reconciliation: Grant that all who have been reborn in this fellowship of Christ's Body may show forth in their lives what they profess by their
faith; through Jesus Christ our Lord, who lives and reigns with you and the
Holy Spirit, one God, for ever and ever. *Amen.* †

The Concluding Prayer of the Church
Lord God, almighty and everlasting Father, you have brought me in safety to this
new day: Preserve me with your mighty power, that I may not fall into sin, nor
be overcome by adversity; and in all I do direct me to the fulfilling of your purpose; through Jesus Christ my Lord. *Amen.* †

The Midday Office   **To Be Observed on the Hour or Half Hour
Between 11 a.m. and 2 p.m.**

The Call to Prayer
'Come, we will go up to YAHWEH's mountain, to the Temple of the God of Jacob so
that he may teach us his ways and we may walk in his paths.

Micah 4:2

The Request for Presence
Hear, O Shepherd of Israel, leading Joseph like a flock;* shine forth, you that are
enthroned upon the cherubim.

Psalm 80:1

The Greeting
The LORD lives! Blessed is my Rock!* Exalted is the God of my salvation!

Psalm 18:46

The Refrain for the Midday Lessons
"I will appoint a time," says God;* "I will judge with equity."

Psalm 75:2

A Reading
I exult for joy in YAHWEH, my soul rejoices in God, for he has clothed me in the garments of salvation, he has wrapped me in garments of salvation, he has

wrapped me in a cloak of saving justice, like a bridegroom wearing his garland, like a bride adorned in her jewels. For as the earth sends up its shoots and a garden makes seeds sprout, so Lord YAHWEH makes saving justice and praise spring up in the sight of all nations.

Isaiah 61:10–11

The Refrain
"I will appoint a time," says God;* "I will judge with equity."

The Midday Psalm   *Your Dominion Endures Throughout the Ages*
I will exalt you, O God my King,* and bless your Name for ever and ever.
Every day will I bless you* and praise your Name for ever and ever.
Great is the LORD and greatly to be praised;* there is no end to his greatness.
One generation shall praise your works to another* and shall declare your power.
I will ponder the glorious splendor of your majesty* and all your marvelous
   works.
They shall speak of the might of your wondrous acts,* and I will tell of your
   greatness.
They shall publish the remembrance of your great goodness;* they shall sing of
   your righteous deeds.
The LORD is gracious and full of compassion,* slow to anger and of great kindness.
The LORD is loving to everyone* and his compassion is over all his works.
All your works praise you, O LORD,* and your faithful servants bless you.
They make known the glory of your kingdom* and speak of your power;
That the peoples may know of your power* and the glorious splendor of your
   kingdom.
Your kingdom is an everlasting kingdom;* your dominion endures throughout all
   ages.

Psalm 145:1–13

The Refrain
"I will appoint a time," says God;* "I will judge with equity."

The Cry of the Church
Even so come, Lord Jesus!

The Lord's Prayer

The Prayer Appointed for the Week
Almighty and everlasting God, who in the Paschal mystery established the new
   covenant of reconciliation: Grant that all who have been reborn in this fellowship of Christ's Body may show forth in their lives what they profess by their
   faith; through Jesus Christ our Lord, who lives and reigns with you and the
   Holy Spirit, one God, for ever and ever. *Amen.* †

The Concluding Prayer of the Church
O God, the source of eternal light: Shed forth your unending day upon all of us
   who watch for you, that our lips may praise you, our lives may bless you, and
   our worship may give you glory; through Jesus Christ our Lord. *Amen.* †

The Vespers Office   **To Be Observed on the Hour or Half Hour**
Between 5 and 8 p.m.

The Call to Prayer
Give thanks to the Lord, for he is good,* and his mercy endures for ever.

Psalm 107:1

The Request for Presence
So teach us to number our days* that we may apply our hearts to wisdom.

Psalm 90:12

The Greeting
Remember not the sins of my youth and my transgressions;* remember me
according to your love and for the sake of your goodness, O Lord.

Psalm 25:6

The Hymn   *How Majestic Is Your Name*
O Lord, my Sovereign,
how majestic is your name
in all the earth!

When I look at your heavens,
the work of your fingers,
the moon and stars
that you have established—
What are human beings
that you are mindful of us;
what are mortals
that you care for us?

You have made us
a little lower than angels,
and crowned us
with glory and honor.
You have given us dominion
over the works of your hands;
you have put all things
under our feet,
all sheep and oxen,
and also the beasts of the field,
the birds of the air,
and the fish of the sea,
whatever passes along
the paths of the seas.

O Lord, my Sovereign,
how majestic is your name
in all the earth! ❖

The Refrain for the Vespers Lessons
Behold, God is my helper;* it is the Lord who sustains my life.

Psalm 54:4

The Vespers Psalm   *Come Now and Look Upon the Works of the* LORD
Come now and look upon the works of the LORD,* what awesome things he has
    done on earth.
"Be still, then, and know that I am God;* I will be exalted among the nations; I will
    be exalted in the earth."
The LORD of hosts is with us;* the God of Jacob is our stronghold.

Psalm 46:9, 11–12

The Refrain
Behold, God is my helper;* it is the Lord who sustains my life.

The Small Verse
The Lord is my shepherd and nothing is wanting to me. In green pastures He has
    settled me.

THE SHORT BREVIARY

The Lord's Prayer

The Prayer Appointed for the Week
Almighty and everlasting God, who in the Paschal mystery established the new
    covenant of reconciliation: Grant that all who have been reborn in this fellow-
    ship of Christ's Body may show forth in their lives what they profess by their
    faith; through Jesus Christ our Lord, who lives and reigns with you and the
    Holy Spirit, one God, for ever and ever. *Amen.* †

The Concluding Prayer of the Church
Almighty God, who after the creation of the world rested from all your works and
    sanctified a day of rest for all your creatures: Grant that I, putting away all
    earthly anxieties, may be duly prepared for the service of public worship, and
    grant as well that my Sabbath upon earth may be a preparation for the eternal
    rest promised to your people in heaven; through Jesus Christ our Lord. *Amen.* †

The Morning Office   **To Be Observed on the Hour or Half Hour**
Between 6 and 9 a.m.

The Call to Prayer
Sing to the LORD and bless his Name;* proclaim the good news of his salvation
    from day to day.

Declare his glory among the nations* and his wonders among all peoples.
For great is the LORD and greatly to be praised;* he is more to be feared than all
    gods.

Psalm 96:2–4

The Request for Presence

Satisfy us by your loving-kindness in the morning;* so shall we rejoice and be glad
    all the days of our life.

Psalm 90:14

The Greeting

Awesome things will you show us in your righteousness, O God of our salvation,*
    O Hope of all the ends of the earth and of the seas that are far away.

Psalm 65:5

The Refrain for the Morning Lessons

For he shall give his angels charge over you,* to keep you in all your ways.

Psalm 91:11

A Reading

Then some of his disciples said to one another, 'What does he mean, "In a short
    time you will no longer see me, and a short time later you will see me again."
    and, "I am going to the Father"? What is this "short time"? We don't know
    what he means.' Jesus knew that they wanted to question him, so he said, 'You
    are asking one another what I meant by saying, "In a short time you will no
    longer see me, and a short time later you will see me again." In all truth I tell
    you, you will be weeping and wailing while the world will rejoice; you will be
    sorrowful, but your sorrow will turn to joy. A woman in childbirth suffers,
    because her time has come; but when she has given birth to the child she for-
    gets the suffering in her joy that a human being has been born into the world.
    So it is with you: you are sad now, but I shall see you again, and your hearts
    will be full of joy, and that joy no one shall take from you. When the day comes,
    you will not ask me any questions. In truth I tell you, anything you ask from
    the Father he will grant in my name.

John 16:17–23

The Refrain

For he shall give his angels charge over you,* to keep you in all your ways.

The Morning Psalm   *There Are the Thrones of the House of David*

I was glad when they said to me,* "Let us go to the house of the LORD."
Now our feet are standing* within your gates, O Jerusalem.
Jerusalem is built as a city* that is at unity with itself;
To which the tribes go up, the tribes of the LORD,* the assembly of Israel, to praise
    the Name of the LORD.
For there are the thrones of judgment,* the thrones of the house of David.

Psalm 122:1–5

The Refrain

For he shall give his angels charge over you,* to keep you in all your ways.

The Cry of the Church

O Lord, hear my prayer and let my cry come unto you. Thanks be to God.

THE SHORT BREVIARY

The Lord's Prayer

The Prayer Appointed for the Week

O God, who by the glorious resurrection of your Son Jesus Christ destroyed death
   and brought life and immortality to light: Grant that I, who have been raised
   with him, may abide in his presence and rejoice in the hope of eternal glory;
   through Jesus Christ my Lord, to whom, with you and the Holy Spirit, be
   dominion and praise for ever and ever. *Amen.* †

The Concluding Prayer of the Church

Lord God, almighty and everlasting Father, you have brought me in safety to this
   new day: Preserve me with your mighty power, that I may not fall into sin, nor
   be overcome by adversity; and in all I do direct me to the fulfilling of your purpose; through Jesus Christ my Lord. *Amen.* †

The Midday Office

**To Be Observed on the Hour or Half Hour
Between 11 a.m. and 2 p.m.**

The Call to Prayer

God has gone up with a shout,* the LORD with the sound of the ram's-horn.
Sing praises to God, sing praises;* sing praises to our King, sing praises.
For God is King of all the earth;* sing praises with all your skill.
God reigns over the nations;* God sits upon his holy throne.

Psalm 47:5–8

The Request for Presence

Let the peoples praise you, O God;* let all the peoples praise you.

Psalm 67:3

The Greeting

For you alone are the Holy One, you alone are the Lord, you alone are the Most
   High, Jesus Christ, with the Holy Spirit, in the glory of God the Father.

The Refrain for the Midday Lessons

Tell it out among the nations: "The LORD is King!*

Psalm 96:10

A Reading

Since you have been raised up to be with Christ, you must look for the things that
   are above, where Christ is, sitting at God's right hand. Let your thoughts be on
   things above, not on things that are on the earth, because you have died and

now the life you have is hidden with Christ in God. But when Christ is revealed—and he is your life—you, too, will be revealed with him in glory.

Colossians 3:1–4

The Refrain
Tell it out among the nations: "The LORD is King!*

The Midday Psalm
Great Are the Deeds of the LORD

I will give thanks to the LORD with my whole heart,* in the assembly of the upright, in the congregation.

Great are the deeds of the LORD!* they are studied by all who delight in them.

His work is full of majesty and splendor,* and his righteousness endures for ever.

He makes his marvelous works to be remembered;* the LORD is gracious and full of compassion.

He gives food to those who fear him;* he is ever mindful of his covenant.

He has shown his people the power of his works* in giving them the lands of the nations.

The works of his hands are faithfulness and justice;* all his commandments are sure.

They stand fast for ever and ever,* because they are done in truth and equity.

He sent redemption to his people; he commanded his covenant for ever;* holy and awesome is his Name.

The fear of the LORD is the beginning of wisdom;* those who act accordingly have a good understanding; his praise endures for ever.

Psalm 111

The Refrain
Tell it out among the nations: "The LORD is King!*

The Cry of the Church
Even so come, Lord Jesus!

The Lord's Prayer

The Prayer Appointed for the Week
O God, who by the glorious resurrection of your Son Jesus Christ destroyed death and brought life and immortality to light: Grant that I, who have been raised with him, may abide in his presence and rejoice in the hope of eternal glory; through Jesus Christ my Lord, to whom, with you and the Holy Spirit, be dominion and praise for ever and ever. *Amen.* †

The Concluding Prayer of the Church
O God, you make me glad with the weekly remembrance of the glorious resurrection of your Son my Lord: Give me this day such blessing through my worship of you, that the week to come may be spent in your favor; through Jesus Christ our Lord. *Amen.* †

The Vespers Office **To Be Observed on the Hour or Half Hour Between 5 and 8 p.m.**

The Call to Prayer
Open my lips, O Lord,* and my mouth shall proclaim your praise.
Psalm 51:16

The Request for Presence
Be my strong rock, a castle to keep me safe,* for you are my crag and my stronghold.
Psalm 31:3

The Greeting
O gracious Light, pure brightness of the everlasting Father in heaven, O Jesus Christ, holy and blessed! Now as we come to the setting of the sun, and our eyes behold the vesper light, we sing your praises O God: Father, Son and Holy Spirit. You are worthy at all times to be praised by happy voices, O Son of God, O giver of life, and to be glorified through all the worlds.
Phos Hilaron

The Hymn *Praise the Savior's Glory*

I shall praise the Savior's glory,
Of his flesh the mystery sing,
And the blood, all price excelling,
Shed by our immortal King:
God made man for our salvation,
Who from Virgin pure did spring.

Born for us and for us given,
Born a man like us below,
Christ as man with man residing,
Lived the seed of truth to sow,
Suffered bitter death unflinching,
And immortal love did show.

To the everlasting Father
And his Son who reigns on high,
With the Holy Ghost proceeding
Forth from each eternally,
Be all honor, glory, blessing,
Power and endless majesty.
St. Thomas Aquinas

The Refrain for the Vespers Lessons
In God the LORD, whose word I praise, in God I trust and will not be afraid,* for what can mortals do to me?
Psalm 56:10

The Vespers Psalm *Tremble at the Presence of the LORD*
When Israel came out of Egypt,* the house of Jacob from a people of strange speech,
Judah became God's sanctuary* and Israel his dominion.
The sea beheld it and fled;* Jordan turned and went back.
The mountains skipped like rams,* and the little hills like young sheep.
What ailed you, O sea, that you fled?* O Jordan, that you turned back?
You mountains, that you skipped like rams?* you little hills like young sheep?

Tremble, O earth, at the presence of the Lord,* at the presence of the God of Jacob,
Who turned the hard rock into a pool of water* and flint-stone into a flowing
  spring.

Psalm 114

The Refrain

In God the Lord, whose word I praise, in God I trust and will not be afraid,* for
  what can mortals do to me?

The Small Verse

Into your hands I commend my spirit for you have redeemed me, O God of my
  life. Glory be to the Father, and to the Son and to the comforting Spirit.

Traditional

The Lord's Prayer

The Prayer Appointed for the Week

O God, who by the glorious resurrection of your Son Jesus Christ destroyed death
  and brought life and immortality to light: Grant that I, who have been raised
  with him, may abide in his presence and rejoice in the hope of eternal glory;
  through Jesus Christ my Lord, to whom, with you and the Holy Spirit, be
  dominion and praise for ever and ever. *Amen.* †

Concluding Prayers of the Church

Almighty and everlasting God, who kindled the flame of your love in the heart of
  your holy martyr Mark: Grant to me, your humble servant, a like faith and
  power of love, that I who rejoice in his triumph may profit by his example;
  through Jesus Christ our Lord, who lives and reigns with you and the holy
  Spirit, one God, for ever and ever. *Amen.* †

O God, you have brought me near to an innumerable company of angels, and to
  the spirits of just men made perfect: Grant me during my earthly pilgrimage to
  abide in their fellowship, and in your heavenly country to become partakers of
  their joy; through Jesus Christ our Lord, who lives and reigns with you and the
  Holy Spirit, one God, now and for ever. *Amen.* †

The Morning Office

**To Be Observed on the Hour or Half Hour
Between 6 and 9 a.m.**

The Call to Prayer

Be strong and let your heart take courage,* all you who wait for the Lord.

Psalm 31:24

The Request for Presence

For the sake of your Name, lead me and guide me.

Psalm 31:3

The Greeting

Have mercy on me, O LORD, for I am in trouble,* my eye is consumed with sorrow, and also my throat and my belly.

Psalm 31:9

The Refrain for the Morning Lessons

Those who sowed with tears* will reap with songs of joy.

Those who go out weeping, carrying the seed,* will come again with joy, shouldering their sheaves.

Psalm 126:6–7

A Reading   *On April 25, the Church celebrates the life of St. Mark. Also known as John Mark he, according to tradition, was the author of the second gospel, the companion of both Peter and Paul, and the founder of the Alexandrian Church in Egypt. His mother, Mary, was a follower of Jesus, and the "upper room" of the Last Supper was said to have been in their home. Mark was martyred in Egypt.*

He said to them, 'Go out to the whole world; proclaim the gospel to all creation. Whoever believes and is baptized will be saved; whoever does not believe will be condemned. These are the signs that will be associated with believers: in my name they will cast out devils; they will have the gift of tongues; they will pick up snakes in their hands and be unharmed should they drink deadly poison; they will lay their hands on the sick, who will recover.' And so the Lord Jesus after he had spoken to them, was taken up into heaven; there at the right hand of God he took his place, while they going out, preached everywhere, the Lord working with them and confirming the word by the signs that accompanied it.

Mark 16:15–20

The Refrain

Those who sowed with tears* will reap with songs of joy.

Those who go out weeping, carrying the seed,* will come again with joy, shouldering their sheaves.

The Morning Psalm

Why are the nations in an uproar?* Why do the peoples mutter empty threats?

Why do the kings of the earth rise up in revolt, and the princes plot together,* against the LORD and against his Anointed?

"Let us break their yoke," they say;* "let us cast off their bonds from us."

He whose throne is in heaven is laughing;* the Lord has them in derision.

Then he speaks to them in his wrath,* and his rage fills them with terror.

"I myself have set my king* upon my holy hill of Zion."

Let me announce the decree of the LORD:* he said to me, "You are my Son; this day have I begotten you.

Ask of me, and I will give you the nations for your inheritance* and the ends of the earth for your possession.

You shall crush them with an iron rod* and shatter them like a piece of pottery."

And now, you kings, be wise;* be warned, you rulers of the earth.
Submit to the LORD with fear,* and with trembling bow before him;
Lest he be angry and you perish;* for his wrath is quickly kindled.
Happy are they all* who take refuge in him!

Psalm 2

The Refrain
Those who sowed with tears* will reap with songs of joy.
Those who go out weeping, carrying the seed,* will come again with joy,
    shouldering their sheaves.

The Cry of the Church
In the evening, in the morning, and at noonday, I will complain and lament,* and
    he will hear my voice.

Psalm 55:18

The Lord's Prayer

The Prayer Appointed for the Week
O God, who by the glorious resurrection of your Son Jesus Christ destroyed death
    and brought life and immortality to light: Grant that I, who have been raised
    with him, may abide in his presence and rejoice in the hope of eternal glory;
    through Jesus Christ my Lord, to whom, with you and the Holy Spirit, be
    dominion and praise for ever and ever. *Amen.* †

Concluding Prayers of the Church
Almighty God, by the hand of Mark the evangelist you have given to your Church
    the Gospel of Jesus Christ the Son of God: I thank you for this witness, and
    pray that I may be firmly grounded in its truth; through Jesus Christ our Lord,
    who lives and reigns with you and the Holy Spirit, one God, now and for ever.
    Amen. †

Lord God, almighty and everlasting Father, you have brought me in safety to this
    new day: Preserve me with your mighty power, that I may not fall into sin, nor
    be overcome by adversity; and in all I do direct me to the fulfilling of your pur-
    pose; through Jesus Christ my Lord. *Amen.* †

The Midday Office   To Be Observed on the Hour or Half Hour
                                              Between 11 a.m. and 2 p.m.

The Call to Prayer
Bless the LORD, you angels of his, you mighty ones who do his bidding,* and
    hearken to the voice of his word.
Bless the LORD, all you his hosts,* you ministers of his who do his will.
Bless the LORD, all you works of his, in all places of his dominion;* bless the LORD,
    O my soul.

Psalm 103:20–22

The Request for Presence
I am a stranger here on earth;* do not hide your commandments from me.

Psalm 119:19

The Greeting
I am bound by the vow I made to you, O God;* I will present to you thank-
offerings;
For you have rescued my soul from death and my feet from stumbling,* that I may
walk before God in the light of the living.

Psalm 56:11–12

The Refrain for the Midday Lessons
Glory be to him whose power, working in us, can do infinitely more than we can
ask or imagine; glory be to him from generation to generation in the Church
and in Christ Jesus for ever and ever. Amen.

Ephesians 3:20–21

A Reading
How beautiful on the mountains are the feet of the messenger announcing peace,
of the messenger of good news, who proclaims salvation and says to Zion,
'Your God is king!' The voices of your watchmen! Now they raise their voices,
shouting for joy together, for with their own eyes they have seen YAHWEH
returning to Zion. Break into shouts together, shouts of joy, you ruins of
Jerusalem; for YAHWEH has consoled his people, he has redeemed Jerusalem.
YAHWEH has bared his holy arm for all the nations to see, and all the ends of the
earth have seen the salvation of our God.

Isaiah 52:7–10

The Refrain
Glory be to him whose power, working in us, can do infinitely more than we can
ask or imagine; glory be to him from generation to generation in the Church
and in Christ Jesus for ever and ever. Amen.

The Midday Psalm   *He Has Made the Whole World So Sure It Cannot Be Moved*
The LORD is King; he has put on splendid apparel;* the LORD has put on his
apparel and girded himself with strength.
He has made the whole world so sure* that it cannot be moved;
Ever since the world began, your throne has been established;* you are from
everlasting.
The waters have lifted up, O LORD, the waters have lifted up their voice;* the
waters have lifted up their pounding waves.
Mightier than the sound of many waters, mightier than the breakers of the sea,*
mightier is the LORD who dwells on high.
Your testimonies are very sure,* and holiness adorns your house, O LORD, for ever
and for evermore.

Psalm 93

The Refrain
Glory be to him whose power, working in us, can do infinitely more than we can ask or imagine; glory be to him from generation to generation in the Church and in Christ Jesus for ever and ever. Amen.

The Cry of the Church
Even so come, Lord Jesus!

The Lord's Prayer

The Prayer Appointed for the Week
O God, who by the glorious resurrection of your Son Jesus Christ destroyed death and brought life and immortality to light: Grant that I, who have been raised with him, may abide in his presence and rejoice in the hope of eternal glory; through Jesus Christ my Lord, to whom, with you and the Holy Spirit, be dominion and praise for ever and ever. *Amen.* †

Concluding Prayers of the Church
O God, who by your grace raised up blessed Mark your Evangelist to be a preacher of the Gospel, grant, I pray, that we ever may profit by his teaching and be defended by his prayers. Through our Lord. *Amen.*

adapted from THE SHORT BREVIARY

O God, the King eternal, whose light divides the day from the night and turns the shadow of death into the morning: Drive from me all wrong desires, incline my heart to keep your law, and guide my feet into the way of peace; that, having done your will with cheerfulness during the day, I may, when night comes, rejoice to give you thanks; through Jesus Christ my Lord. *Amen.* †

The Vespers Office   **To Be Observed on the Hour or Half Hour Between 5 and 8 p.m.**

The Call to Prayer
Praise God, from whom all blessings flow; praise him, all creatures here below; praise him above, you heavenly hosts; praise Father, Son and Holy Ghost.

Doxology

The Request for Presence
Show your goodness, O LORD, to those who are good* and to those who are true of heart.

Psalm 125:4

The Greeting
Out of the mouths of infants and children* your majesty is praised above the heavens.

Psalm 8:2

The Hymn   *Hymn of Martyrs*
   Blessed feasts of blessed martyrs,
   holy women, holy men,
   with affection's recollections
   greet we your return again.
   Worthy deeds they wrought, and wonders,
   worthy of the Name they bore;
   we with meetest praise and sweetest,
   honor them for evermore.

   Faith prevailing, hope unfailing,
   loving Christ with single heart,
   thus they, glorious and victorious,
   bravely bore the martyr's part,
   by contempt of every anguish,
   by unyielding battle done;
   victors at the last, they triumph,
   with the host of angels one.

   Therefore, you that reign in glory,
   fellow-heirs with Christ on high,
   join to ours your supplication
   when before him we draw nigh,
   praying that, this life completed,
   all its fleeting moments past,
   by his grace we may be worthy
   of eternal bliss at last.

                              Latin, 12th C.

The Refrain for the Vespers Lessons
We have heard with our ears, O God, our forefathers have told us,* the deeds you
   did in their days, in the days of old.

                                             Psalm 44:1

The Vespers Psalm   *Let the Nations Be Glad and Sing for Joy*
May God be merciful to us and bless us,* show us the light of his countenance and
   come to us.
Let your ways be known upon earth,* your saving health among all nations.
Let the peoples praise you, O God;* let all the peoples praise you.
Let the nations be glad and sing for joy,* for you judge the peoples with equity and
   guide all the nations upon earth.
Let the peoples praise you, O God;* let all the peoples praise you.
The earth has brought forth her increase;* may God, our own God, give us his
   blessing.

May God give us his blessing,* and may all the ends of the earth stand in awe of
   him.

Psalm 67

The Refrain
We have heard with our ears, O God, our forefathers have told us,* the deeds you
   did in their days, in the days of old.

The Call to Prayer
Even so come, Lord Jesus!

The Lord's Prayer

The Prayer Appointed for the Week
O God, who by the glorious resurrection of your Son Jesus Christ destroyed death
   and brought life and immortality to light: Grant that I, who have been raised
   with him, may abide in his presence and rejoice in the hope of eternal glory;
   through Jesus Christ my Lord, to whom, with you and the Holy Spirit, be
   dominion and praise for ever and ever. *Amen.* †

The Concluding Prayer of the Church
Almighty God, you have surrounded me with a great cloud of witnesses: Grant
   that I, encouraged by the good example of your servant Mark, may persevere
   in running the race that is set before me, until at last I may with him attain to
   your eternal joy; through Jesus Christ, the pioneer and perfecter of our faith,
   who lives and reigns with you and the Holy Spirit, one God, for ever and ever.
   Amen. †

The Morning Office   To Be Observed on the Hour or Half Hour
                                              Between 6 and 9 a.m.

The Call to Prayer
Come and listen, all you who fear God,* and I will tell you what he has done for
   me.

Psalm 66:14

The Request for Presence
May God be merciful to us and bless us,* show us the light of his countenance and
   come to us.
Let your ways be known upon earth,* your saving health among all nations.

Psalm 67:1–2

The Greeting
Your statutes have been like songs to me* wherever I have lived as a stranger.

Psalm 119:54

The Refrain for the Morning Lessons
Purge me from my sin, and I shall be pure; wash me, and I shall be clean indeed.

Psalm 51:8

A Reading
It happened that as he was speaking, a woman in the crowd raised her voice and
    said, 'Blessed be the womb that bore you and the breasts that fed you!' But he
    replied, 'More blessed still are those who hear the word of God and keep it!'

Luke 11:27–28

The Refrain
Purge me from my sin, and I shall be pure;* wash me, and I shall be clean indeed.

The Morning Psalm   *Show Me the Road I Must Walk*
LORD, hear my prayer, and in your faithfulness heed my supplications;* answer
    me in your righteousness.
My spirit faints within me;* my heart within me is desolate.
I remember the time past; I muse upon all your deeds;* I consider the works of
    your hands.
I spread out my hands to you;* my soul gasps to you like a thirsty land.
O LORD, make haste to answer me; my spirit fails me;* do not hide your face from
    me or I shall be like those who go down to the Pit.
Let me hear of your loving-kindness in the morning, for I put my trust in you;*
    show me the road that I must walk, for I lift up my soul to you.

Psalm 143:1, 4–8

The Refrain
Purge me from my sin, and I shall be pure;* wash me, and I shall be clean indeed.

The Cry of the Church
Even so come, Lord Jesus!

The Lord's Prayer

The Prayer Appointed for the Week
O God, who by the glorious resurrection of your Son Jesus Christ destroyed death
    and brought life and immortality to light: Grant that I, who have been raised
    with him, may abide in his presence and rejoice in the hope of eternal glory;
    through Jesus Christ my Lord, to whom, with you and the Holy Spirit, be
    dominion and praise for ever and ever. *Amen.* †

The Concluding Prayer of the Church
Lord God, almighty and everlasting Father, you have brought me in safety to this
    new day: Preserve me with your mighty power, that I may not fall into sin, nor
    be overcome by adversity; and in all I do direct me to the fulfilling of your pur-
    pose; through Jesus Christ my Lord. *Amen.* †

The Midday Office

**To Be Observed on the Hour or Half Hour
Between 11 a.m. and 2 p.m.**

The Call to Prayer
Praise Him from whom all blessings flow; praise Him all creatures here below;
   praise Him you heavenly hosts; praise Father, Son and Holy Ghost.

Traditional Doxology

The Request for Presence
Be my strong rock, a castle to keep me safe, for you are my crag and my stronghold;*
   for the sake of your Name, lead me and guide me.

Psalm 31:3

The Greeting
To you, O LORD, I lift up my soul;* my God, I put my trust in you.

Psalm 25:1

The Refrain for the Midday Lessons
Happy are they all who fear the LORD,* and who follow in his ways!

Psalm 28:1

A Reading
Yahweh Sabaoth, the God of Israel, says this, ". . . My one command to them was
   this: Listen to my voice, then I will be your God and you shall be my people. In
   everything, follow the way that I mark out for you, and you shall prosper."

Jeremiah 7:21, 23

The Refrain
Happy are they all who fear the LORD,* and who follow in his ways!

The Midday Psalm   *The LORD Will Bless Both Small and Great Who Trust Him*
Not to us, O LORD, not to us,* but to your Name give glory; because of your love
   and because of your faithfulness.
Why should the heathen say,* "Where then is their God?"
Our God is in heaven;* whatever he wills to do he does.
Their idols are silver and gold,* the work of human hands.
They have mouths, but they cannot speak;* eyes have they, but they cannot see;
They have ears, but they cannot hear;* noses, but they cannot smell;
They have hands, but they cannot feel; feet, but they cannot walk;* they make no
   sound with their throat.
Those who make them are like them,* and so are all who put their trust in them.
O Israel, trust in the LORD;* he is their help and their shield.
O house of Aaron, trust in the LORD;* he is their help and their shield.
You who fear the LORD, trust in the LORD;* he is their help and their shield.

The LORD has been mindful of us, and he will bless us;* he will bless the house of
  Israel; he will bless the house of Aaron;
He will bless those who fear the LORD,* both small and great together.

Psalm 115:1–13

The Refrain
Happy are they all who fear the LORD,* and who follow in his ways!

The Small Verse
The Lord is king. He has put on glorious apparel. Let all the nations praise him.
  Let those of every tongue bow before him.

Traditional

The Lord's Prayer

The Prayer Appointed for the Week
O God, who by the glorious resurrection of your Son Jesus Christ destroyed death
  and brought life and immortality to light: Grant that I, who have been raised
  with him, may abide in his presence and rejoice in the hope of eternal glory;
  through Jesus Christ my Lord, to whom, with you and the Holy Spirit, be
  dominion and praise for ever and ever. *Amen.* †

The Concluding Prayer of the Church
Come forth, O Christ, and help me. For your name's sake deliver me.

Traditional

The Vespers Office	To Be Observed on the Hour or Half Hour
	Between 5 and 8 p.m.

The Call to Prayer
Open my lips, O Lord,* and my mouth shall proclaim your praise.
Had you desired it, I would have offered sacrifice,* but you take no delight in
  burnt-offerings.
The sacrifice of God is a troubled spirit;* a broken and contrite heart, O God, you
  will not despise.

Psalm 51:16–18

The Request for Presence
Out of the depths have I called to you, O LORD; LORD, hear my voice;* let your ears
  consider well the voice of my supplication.

Psalm 130:1

The Greeting
I lie down in peace; at once I fall asleep;* for only you, LORD, make me dwell in
  safety.

Psalm 4:8

The Hymn   *Son of Man and Son of God*

How bright appears the Morning Star,
With mercy beaming from afar;
The host of heaven rejoices;
  O righteous Branch, O Jesse's Rod!
  You Son of Man and Son of God!
We, too, will lift our voices:
Jesus! Jesus! Holy, holy, yet most lowly,
Please draw near us, Emmanuel, come and hear us.

Though circled by the hosts on high,
He deigned to cast a pitying eye
Upon his helpless creature;
  The whole creation's Head and Lord,
  By highest seraphim adored,
Assumed our very nature;
Jesus, grant us, through your merit, to inherit
Your salvation; hear, O hear, our supplication.

Rejoice, you heavens; O earth, reply;
With praise, you sinners, fill the sky,
For this his Incarnation.
  Incarnate God, put forth your power,
  Ride on, ride on, great Conqueror,
Till all shall know your salvation.
Let us cry, "Bless the Lord", and again, "Bless the Lord"
Praise be given evermore, by earth and heaven.

          William Mercer

The Refrain for the Vespers Lessons

The LORD has sworn an oath to David;* in truth, he will not break it:
"A son, the fruit of your body* will I set upon your throne.

        Psalm 132:11–12

The Vespers Psalm   *My Body Also Shall Rest in Hope*

I will bless the LORD who gives me counsel;* my heart teaches me, night after
  night.
I have set the LORD always before me;* because he is at my right hand I shall not
  fall.
My heart, therefore, is glad, and my spirit rejoices;* my body also shall rest in
  hope.
For you will not abandon me to the grave,* nor let your holy one see the Pit.
You will show me the path of life;* in your presence there is fullness of joy, and in
  your right hand are pleasures for evermore.

        Psalm 16:7–11

The Refrain
The LORD has sworn an oath to David;* in truth, he will not break it:
"A son, the fruit of your body* will I set upon your throne.

The Cry of the Church
Even so come, Lord Jesus!

The Lord's Prayer

The Prayer Appointed for the Week
O God, who by the glorious resurrection of your Son Jesus Christ destroyed death
and brought life and immortality to light: Grant that I, who have been raised
with him, may abide in his presence and rejoice in the hope of eternal glory;
through Jesus Christ my Lord, to whom, with you and the Holy Spirit, be
dominion and praise for ever and ever. *Amen.* †

The Concluding Prayer of the Church
Stir up Your power, we beseech You, O Lord, and come, that by Your protection
we may deserve to be rescued from the threatening dangers of our sins and
saved by Your deliverance. Who lives and reigns with God the Father in the
unity of the Holy Ghost, God, world without end. *Amen.*

adapted from THE SHORT BREVIARY

The Morning Office　　　　　　　**To Be Observed on the Hour or Half Hour**
Between 6 and 9 a.m.

The Call to Prayer
Fear the LORD, you that are his saints,* for those who fear him lack nothing.
The young lions lack and suffer hunger,* but those who seek the LORD lack
nothing that is good.

Psalm 34:9–10

The Request for Presence
Be merciful to me, O LORD, for you are my God;* I call upon you all the day long.

Psalm 86:3

The Greeting
With my whole heart I seek you;* let me not stray from your commandments.

Psalm 119:10

The Refrain for the Morning Lessons
I will bear witness that the LORD is righteous;* I will praise the Name of the LORD
Most High.

Psalm 7:18

A Reading
Jesus said to the disciples: "In truth I tell you, when everything is made new again
and the Son of man is seated on his throne of glory, you yourselves will sit on

twelve thrones to judge the twelve tribes of Israel. And everyone who has left houses, brothers, sisters, father, mother, children or land for the sake of my name will receive a hundred times as much, and also inherit eternal life. Many who are first will be last, and the last, first."

Matthew 19:28–30

The Refrain
I will bear witness that the LORD is righteous;* I will praise the Name of the LORD Most High.

The Morning Psalm   *I Will Exalt You, O LORD*
I will exalt you, O LORD, because you have lifted me up* and have not let my enemies triumph over me.
O LORD my God, I cried out to you,* and you restored me to health.
You brought me up, O LORD, from the dead;* you restored my life as I was going down to the grave.
Sing to the LORD, you servants of his;* give thanks for the remembrance of his holiness.
For his wrath endures but the twinkling of an eye,* his favor for a lifetime.

Psalm 30:1–5

The Refrain
I will bear witness that the LORD is righteous;* I will praise the Name of the LORD Most High.

The Small Verse
Let me seek the Lord while he may still be found. I will call upon his name while he is near.

Traditional

The Lord's Prayer

The Prayer Appointed for the Week
O God, who by the glorious resurrection of your Son Jesus Christ destroyed death and brought life and immortality to light: Grant that I, who have been raised with him, may abide in his presence and rejoice in the hope of eternal glory; through Jesus Christ my Lord, to whom, with you and the Holy Spirit, be dominion and praise for ever and ever. *Amen.* †

The Concluding Prayer of the Church
Lord God, almighty and everlasting Father, you have brought me in safety to this new day: Preserve me with your mighty power, that I may not fall into sin, nor be overcome by adversity; and in all I do direct me to the fulfilling of your purpose; through Jesus Christ my Lord. *Amen.* †

The Midday Office   To Be Observed on the Hour or Half Hour
                                              Between 11 a.m. and 2 p.m.

The Call to Prayer
O Israel, wait for the LORD,* for with the LORD there is mercy;
With him there is plenteous redemption,* and he shall redeem Israel from all their ·
    sins.

Psalm 130:6–7

The Request for Presence
Remember me, O LORD, with the favor you have for your people,* and visit me
    with your saving help;
That I may see the prosperity of your elect and be glad with the gladness of your
    people,* that I may glory with your inheritance.

Psalm 106:4–5

The Greeting
You are to be praised, O God, in Zion; . . .
To you that hear prayer shall all flesh come,* because of their transgressions.

Psalm 65:1–2

The Refrain for the Midday Lessons
Happy are they who have the God of Jacob for their help!* whose hope is in the
    LORD their God.

Psalm 146:4

A Reading
Woe to those who burrow down to conceal their plans from YAHWEH, who scheme
    in the dark and say, 'Who can see us? Who knows who we are?' How perverse
    you are! Is the potter no better than the clay? Something that was made, can it
    say of its maker, 'He did not make me'? Or a pot say of a potter, 'He does not
    know his job'?

Isaiah 29:15–16

The Refrain
Happy are they who have the God of Jacob for their help!* whose hope is in the
    LORD their God.

The Midday Psalm   *In His Holy Name We Put Our Trust*
Behold, the eye of the LORD is upon those who fear him,* on those who wait upon
    his love,
To pluck their lives from death,* and to feed them in time of famine.
Our soul waits for the LORD;* he is our help and our shield.
Indeed, our heart rejoices in him,* for in his holy Name we put our trust.
Let your loving-kindness, O LORD, be upon us,* as we have put our trust in you.

Psalm 33:18–22

The Refrain
Happy are they who have the God of Jacob for their help!* whose hope is in the
LORD their God.

The Small Verse
·Keep me, Lord, as the apple of your eye and carry me under the shadow of your
wings.

Traditional

The Lord's Prayer

The Prayer Appointed for the Week
O God, who by the glorious resurrection of your Son Jesus Christ destroyed death
and brought life and immortality to light: Grant that I, who have been raised
with him, may abide in his presence and rejoice in the hope of eternal glory;
through Jesus Christ my Lord, to whom, with you and the Holy Spirit, be
dominion and praise for ever and ever. *Amen.* †

The Concluding Prayer of the Church
May God himself order my days and make them acceptable in his sight. Blessed
be the Lord always, my strength and my redeemer.

Traditional

The Vespers Office   To Be Observed on the Hour or Half Hour
                                                    Between 5 and 8 p.m.

The Call to Prayer
Come, let us sing to the LORD;* let us shout for joy to the Rock of our salvation.

Psalm 95:1

The Request for Presence
May the glory of the LORD endure for ever;* may the LORD rejoice in all his works.

Psalm 104:32

The Greeting
How great is your goodness, O LORD! which you have laid up for those who fear
you;* which you have done in the sight of all for those who put their trust in
you.

Psalm 31:19

The Hymn   *I Love to Tell the Story*
    I love to tell the story of unseen things above,
    Of Jesus and his glory, of Jesus and his love.
    I love to tell the story, because I know it's true;
    It satisfies my longings as nothing else can do.
    I love to tell the story, will be my theme in glory,
    To tell the old, old story of Jesus and his love.

I love to tell the story; more wonderful it seems
Than all the golden fancies of all our golden dreams.
I love to tell the story, it did so much for me;
And that is just the reason I tell it now to thee.
I love to tell the story, will be my theme in glory,
To tell the old, old story of Jesus and his love.

I love to tell the story, for those who know it best
Seem hungering and thirsting to hear it like the rest.
And when in scenes of glory, I sing the new, new song,
Will be the old, old story that I have loved so long.
I love to tell the story, will be my theme in glory,
To tell the old, old story of Jesus and his love.

Katherine Hankey

The Refrain for the Vespers Lessons
I am small and of little account,* yet I do not forget your commandments.

Psalm 119:141

The Vespers Psalm   *How Priceless Is Your Love, O* LORD
Your love, O LORD, reaches to the heavens,* and your faithfulness to the clouds.
Your righteousness is like the strong mountains, your justice like the great deep;*
    you save both man and beast, O LORD.
How priceless is your love, O God!* your people take refuge under the shadow of
    your wings.
They feast upon the abundance of your house;* you give them drink from the
    river of your delights.
For with you is the well of life,* and in your light we see light.
Continue your loving-kindness to those who know you,* and your favor to those
    who are true of heart.

Psalm 36:5–10

The Refrain
I am small and of little account,* yet I do not forget your commandments.

The Small Verse
Those who sowed with tears* will reap with songs of joy.
Those who go out weeping, carrying the seed,* will come again with joy,
    shouldering their sheaves.

Psalm 126:6–7

The Lord's Prayer

The Prayer Appointed for the Week
O God, who by the glorious resurrection of your Son Jesus Christ destroyed death
    and brought life and immortality to light: Grant that I, who have been raised
    with him, may abide in his presence and rejoice in the hope of eternal glory;

through Jesus Christ my Lord, to whom, with you and the Holy Spirit, be
dominion and praise for ever and ever. *Amen.* †

The Concluding Prayer of the Church

Almighty God, to whom our needs are known before we even ask, help me to ask
only what accords with your will; and those good things which I dare not, or in
my blindness I cannot ask, grant for the sake of your Son Jesus Christ our Lord.
Amen. †

The Morning Office · To Be Observed on the Hour or Half Hour Between 6 and 9 a.m.

The Call to Prayer

Know this: The LORD himself is God;* he himself has made us, and we are his; we
are his people and the sheep of his pasture.

Psalm 100:2

The Request for Presence

For God alone my soul in silence waits;* truly, my hope is in him.

Psalm 62:6

The Greeting

Your testimonies are very sure,* and holiness adorns your house, O LORD, for ever
and for evermore.

Psalm 93:6

The Refrain for the Morning Lessons

Blessed is he who comes in the name of the Lord;* we bless you from the house of
the LORD.

Psalm 118:26

A Reading

Jesus said: "Do not suppose that I have come to bring peace to earth: it is not peace
I have come to bring, but a sword. For I have come to set son against father,
daughter against mother, daughter-in-law against mother-in-law; a person's
enemies will be the members of his own household."

Matthew 10:34–36

The Refrain

Blessed is he who comes in the name of the Lord;* we bless you from the house of
the LORD.

The Morning Psalm · Our Eyes Look to the LORD

To you I lift up my eyes,* to you enthroned in the heavens.
As the eyes of servants look to the hand of their masters,* and the eyes of a maid to
the hand of her mistress,
So our eyes look to the LORD our God,* until he shows us his mercy.

Have mercy upon us, O Lord, have mercy,* for we have had more than enough of
   contempt,
Too much of the scorn of the indolent rich,* and of the derision of the proud.

Psalm 123

The Refrain
Blessed is he who comes in the name of the Lord;* we bless you from the house of
the Lord.

The Cry of the Church
O God, come to my assistance! O Lord, make haste to help me!

The Lord's Prayer

The Prayer Appointed for the Week
O God, who by the glorious resurrection of your Son Jesus Christ destroyed death
   and brought life and immortality to light: Grant that I, who have been raised
   with him, may abide in his presence and rejoice in the hope of eternal glory;
   through Jesus Christ my Lord, to whom, with you and the Holy Spirit, be
   dominion and praise for ever and ever. *Amen.* †

The Concluding Prayer of the Church
Lord God, almighty and everlasting Father, you have brought me in safety to this
   new day: Preserve me with your mighty power, that I may not fall into sin, nor
   be overcome by adversity; and in all I do direct me to the fulfilling of your purpose; through Jesus Christ my Lord. *Amen.* †

The Midday Office   **To Be Observed on the Hour or Half Hour**
                                    Between 11 a.m. and 2 p.m.

The Call to Prayer
Let us come before his presence with thanksgiving* and raise a loud shout to him
   with psalms.
For the Lord is a great God,* and a great King above all gods.

Psalm 95:2–3

The Request for Presence
Let the peoples praise you, O God;* let all the peoples praise you.

Psalm 67:3

The Greeting
Lord, how great are your works!* your thoughts are very deep.

Psalm 92:5

The Refrain for Midday Lessons
Yours are the heavens; the earth also is yours;* you laid the foundations of the
   world and all that is in it.

Psalm 89:11

A Reading

Then YAHWEH answered me and said, 'Write this vision down, inscribe it on
tablets to be easily read. For the vision is for its appointed time, it hastens
towards its end and it will not lie; although it may take some time, wait for it,
for come it certainly will before too long. You see, anyone whose heart is not
upright will succumb, but the upright will live through faithfulness.'

Habakkuk 2:2–4

The Refrain

Yours are the heavens; the earth also is yours; * you laid the foundations of the
world and all that is in it.

The Midday Psalm   *His Mercy Endures For Ever*

Give thanks to the LORD, for he is good,* for his mercy endures for ever.
Give thanks to the God of gods,* for his mercy endures for ever.
Give thanks to the Lord of lords,* for his mercy endures for ever.
Who only does great wonders,* for his mercy endures for ever;
Who by wisdom made the heavens,* for his mercy endures for ever;
Who spread out the earth upon the waters,* for his mercy endures for ever;
Who created great lights,* for his mercy endures for ever;
The sun to rule the day,* for his mercy endures for ever;
The moon and the stars to govern the night,* for his mercy endures for ever.

Psalm 136: 1–9

The Refrain

Yours are the heavens; the earth also is yours;* you laid the foundations of the
world and all that is in it.

The Cry of the Church

Be, Lord, my helper and forsake me not. Do not despise me, O God, my savior.

THE SHORT BREVIARY

The Lord's Prayer

The Prayer Appointed for the Week

O God, who by the glorious resurrection of your Son Jesus Christ destroyed death
and brought life and immortality to light: Grant that I, who have been raised
with him, may abide in his presence and rejoice in the hope of eternal glory;
through Jesus Christ my Lord, to whom, with you and the Holy Spirit, be
dominion and praise for ever and ever. *Amen.* †

The Concluding Prayer of the Church

Let us bless the Lord God living and true! Let us always render him praise, glory,
honor, blessing, and all good things! Amen. Amen. So be it! So be it!

St. Francis of Assisi

The Vespers Office   To Be Observed on the Hour or Half Hour
                                      Between 5 and 8 p.m.

The Call to Prayer
Come, let us bow down, and bend the knee,* and kneel before the LORD our
    Maker.
For he is our God, and we are the people of his pasture and the sheep of his hand.*
    Oh, that today you would hearken to his voice!

Psalm 95:6–7

The Request for Presence
You are the LORD;* do not withhold your compassion from me; let your love and
    your faithfulness keep me safe for ever.

Psalm 40:12

The Greeting
Exalt yourself above the heavens, O God,* and your glory over all the earth.

Psalm 57:11

The Hymn   *I Would Be True*
    I would be true, for there are those who trust me;
    I would be pure, for there are those who care;
    I would be strong, for there is much to suffer;
    I would be brave, for there is much to dare.

    I would be friend of all—the foe, the friendless;
    I would be giving and forget the gift;
    I would be humble for I know my weakness;
    I would look up, and laugh, and love, and lift.

    I would be prayerful through each busy moment;
    I would be constantly in touch with God;
    I would be tuned to hear the slightest whisper;
    I would have faith to keep the path Christ trod.
                                      Howard Walter

The Refrain for the Vespers Lessons
. . . when the LORD restores the fortunes of his people, Jacob will rejoice and Israel
    be glad.

Psalm 14:7b

The Vespers Psalm   *The Eyes of All Wait Upon You, O LORD*
The LORD is faithful in all his words* and merciful in all his deeds.
The LORD upholds all those who fall;* he lifts up those who are bowed down.
The eyes of all wait upon you, O LORD,* and you give them their food in due season.
You open wide your hand* and satisfy the needs of every living creature.
The LORD is righteous in all his ways* and loving in all his works.

Psalm 145:14–18

The Refrain
. . . when the LORD restores the fortunes of his people, Jacob will rejoice and Israel
be glad.

The Cry of the Church
Even so come, Lord Jesus!

The Lord's Prayer

The Prayer Appointed for the Week
O God, who by the glorious resurrection of your Son Jesus Christ destroyed death
and brought life and immortality to light: Grant that I, who have been raised
with him, may abide in his presence and rejoice in the hope of eternal glory;
through Jesus Christ my Lord, to whom, with you and the Holy Spirit, be
dominion and praise for ever and ever. *Amen.* †

The Concluding Prayer of the Church
Blessed by the Lord God of Israel for he has visited and delivered us. Amen, amen,
amen.

Traditional

The Morning Office   **To Be Observed on the Hour or Half Hour**
                                              Between 6 and 9 a.m.

The Call to Prayer
Search for the LORD and his strength;* continually seek his face.
Psalm 105:4

The Request for Presence
O Lamb of God, that takes away the sins of the world, have mercy upon me.
O Lamb of God, that takes away the sins of the world, have mercy upon me.
O Lamb of God, that takes away the sins of the world, grant me your peace.

The Greeting
O God, you know my foolishness,* and my faults are not hidden from you.
Psalm 69:6

The Refrain for the Morning Lessons
Our sins are stronger than we are,* but you will blot them out.
Psalm 65:3

A Reading
It was just about this time that some people arrived and told him about the
Galileans whose blood Pilate had mingled with that of their sacrifices. At this
he said to them, 'Do you suppose that these Galileans were worse sinners than
any others, that this should happen to them? They were not, I tell you. No; but
unless you repent you will all perish as they did. Or those eighteen on whom
the tower of Siloam fell, killing them all? Do you suppose that they were more

guilty than all the other people living in Jerusalem? They were not, I tell you. No; but unless you repent you will all perish as they did.'

Luke 13:1–5

The Refrain

Our sins are stronger than we are,* but you will blot them out.

The Morning Psalm
Teach Us to Number Our Days

Our iniquities you have set before you,* and our secret sins in the light of your countenance.

When you are angry, all our days are gone;* we bring our years to an end like a sigh.

The span of our life is seventy years, perhaps in strength even eighty;* yet the sum of them is but labor and sorrow, for they pass away quickly and we are gone.

Who regards the power of your wrath?* who rightly fears your indignation?

So teach us to number our days* that we may apply our hearts to wisdom.

Psalm 90:8–12

The Refrain

Our sins are stronger than we are,* but you will blot them out.

The Cry of the Church

O God, come to my assistance! O Lord, make haste to help me!

The Lord's Prayer

The Prayer Appointed for the Week

O God, who by the glorious resurrection of your Son Jesus Christ destroyed death and brought life and immortality to light: Grant that I, who have been raised with him, may abide in his presence and rejoice in the hope of eternal glory; through Jesus Christ my Lord, to whom, with you and the Holy Spirit, be dominion and praise for ever and ever. *Amen.* †

The Concluding Prayer of the Church

Lord God, almighty and everlasting Father, you have brought me in safety to this new day: Preserve me with your mighty power, that I may not fall into sin, nor be overcome by adversity; and in all I do direct me to the fulfilling of your purpose; through Jesus Christ my Lord. *Amen.* †

The Midday Office
To Be Observed on the Hour or Half Hour
Between 11 a.m. and 2 p.m.

The Call to Prayer

Give thanks to the LORD, for he is good;* his mercy endures for ever.

Psalm 118:29

The Request for Presence

Remember not our past sins; let your compassion be swift to meet us;* for we have been brought very low.

Help us, O God our Savior, for the glory of your Name;* deliver us and forgive us
our sins, for your Name's sake.

Psalm 79:8–9

The Greeting
There is forgiveness with you;* therefore you shall be feared.

Psalm 130:3

The Refrain for the Midday Lessons
For you, O Lord, are good and forgiving,* and great is your love toward all who
call upon you.

Psalm 86:5

A Reading
You have been buried with him by your baptism; by which, too, you have been
raised up with him through your belief in the power of God who raised him
from the dead. You were dead, because you were sinners and uncircumcised in
body: he has brought you to life with him, he has forgiven every one of our sins.

Colossians 2:12–13

The Refrain
For you, O Lord, are good and forgiving,* and great is your love toward all who
call upon you.

The Midday Psalm   We Will Call Upon the Name of the Lord Our God
May the Lord answer you in the day of trouble,* the Name of the God of Jacob
defend you;
Send you help from his holy place* and strengthen you out of Zion;
Remember all your offerings* and accept your burnt sacrifice;
Grant you your heart's desire* and prosper all your plans.
We will shout for joy at your victory and triumph in the Name of our God;* may
the Lord grant all your requests.
Now I know that the Lord gives victory to his anointed;* he will answer him out
of his holy heaven, with the victorious strength of his right hand.
Some put their trust in chariots and some in horses,* but we will call upon the
Name of the Lord our God.
They collapse and fall down,* but we will arise and stand upright.
O Lord, give victory to the king* and answer us when we call.

Psalm 20

The Refrain
For you, O Lord, are good and forgiving,* and great is your love toward all who
call upon you.

The Cry of the Church
In the evening, in the morning, and at noonday, I will complain and lament,* and
he will hear my voice.

Psalm 55:18

The Lord's Prayer

The Prayer Appointed for the Week

O God, who by the glorious resurrection of your Son Jesus Christ destroyed death
and brought life and immortality to light: Grant that I, who have been raised
with him, may abide in his presence and rejoice in the hope of eternal glory;
through Jesus Christ my Lord, to whom, with you and the Holy Spirit, be
dominion and praise for ever and ever. *Amen.* †

The Concluding Prayer of the Church

Lord Jesus Christ, by your death you took away the sting of death: Grant me to so
follow in faith where you have led the way, that I may at length fall asleep
peacefully in you and wake in your likeness; for your tender mercies' sake.
Amen. †

The Vespers Office   **To Be Observed on the Hour or Half Hour**
                                                    Between 5 and 8 p.m.

The Call to Prayer

I will call upon the LORD,* and so shall I be saved from my enemies.

Psalm 18:3

The Request for Presence

I have said to the LORD, "You are my God;* Listen, O LORD, to my supplication."

Psalm 140:6

The Greeting

But you, O Lord my GOD, oh, deal with me according to your Name;* for your
tender mercy's sake, deliver me.
For I am poor and needy,* and my heart is wounded within me.

Psalm 109:20–21

The Hymn

Trials must and will befall:
        But with humble faith to see
Love inscribed upon them all:
        This is happiness to me.

Trials make the promise sweet;
        Trials give new life to prayer;
Trials bring me to his feet,
        Lay me low, and keep me there.

Did I meet no trials here,
        No chastisement by the way,
Might I not with reason fear
        I should be a castaway?

Unknown

The Refrain for the Vespers Lessons
For the Lord has heard the sound of my weeping. The Lord has heard my
supplication;* the Lord accepts my prayer.

Psalm 6:8–9

The Vespers Psalm   *The God of Gods Will Reveal Himself in Zion*
How dear to me is your dwelling, O Lord of hosts!* My soul has a desire and
longing for the courts of the Lord; my heart and my flesh rejoice in the living
God.
The sparrow has found her a house and the swallow a nest where she may lay her
young;* by the side of your altars, O Lord of hosts, my King and my God.
Happy are they who dwell in your house!* they will always be praising you.
Happy are the people whose strength is in you!* whose hearts are set on the
pilgrims' way.
Those who go through the desolate valley will find it a place of springs,* for the
early rains have covered it with pools of water.
They will climb from height to height,* and the God of gods will reveal himself in
Zion.

Psalm 84:1–6

The Refrain
For the Lord has heard the sound of my weeping. The Lord has heard my
supplication;* the Lord accepts my prayer.

The Cry of the Church
Be, Lord, my helper and forsake me not. Do not despise me, O God, my savior.

THE SHORT BREVIARY

The Lord's Prayer

The Prayer Appointed for the Week
O God, who by the glorious resurrection of your Son Jesus Christ destroyed death
and brought life and immortality to light: Grant that I, who have been raised
with him, may abide in his presence and rejoice in the hope of eternal glory;
through Jesus Christ my Lord, to whom, with you and the Holy Spirit, be
dominion and praise for ever and ever. *Amen.* †

Concluding Prayers of the Church
Almighty God, who has promised to hear the petitions of those who ask in your
Son's Name: I beseech you mercifully to incline your ear to me who have made
my prayers and supplications to you; and grant that those things which I have
faithfully asked according to your will, I may effectually obtain, to the relief of
my necessity, and to the setting forth of your glory; through Jesus Christ my
Lord. *Amen.* †

May the souls of the faithful departed, through the mercy of God, rest in eternal
peace. *Amen.*

The Morning Office   To Be Observed on the Hour or Half Hour
                                                      Between 6 and 9 a.m.

The Call to Prayer
Proclaim with me the greatness of the LORD;* let us exalt his Name together.
                                                                    Psalm 34:3

The Request for Presence
Open my eyes, that I may see* the wonders of your law.
                                                                    Psalm 119:18

The Greeting
I will confess you among the peoples, O LORD;* I will sing praise to you among the
    nations.
For your loving-kindness is greater than the heavens,* and your faithfulness
    reaches to the clouds.
                                                                    Psalm 57:9–10

The Refrain for the Morning Lessons
Help us, O God our Savior, for the glory of your Name;* deliver us and forgive us
    our sins, for your Name's sake.
                                                                    Psalm 79:9

A Reading
Jesus looked at him and said, 'How hard it is for those who have riches to make
    their way into the kingdom of God! Yes, it is easier for a camel to pass through
    the eye of a needle than for someone rich to enter the kingdom of God.' Those
    who were listening said, 'In that case, who can be saved?' He replied, 'Things
    that are impossible by human resources, are possible for God.'
                                                                    Luke 18:24–27

The Refrain
Help us, O God our Savior, for the glory of your Name;* deliver us and forgive us
    our sins, for your Name's sake.

The Morning Psalm   *Arise, O God, and Rule the Earth*
God takes his stand in the council of heaven;* he gives judgment in the midst of
    the gods:
"How long will you judge unjustly,* and show favor to the wicked?
Save the weak and the orphan;* defend the humble and needy;
Rescue the weak and the poor;* deliver them from the power of the wicked.
They do not know, neither do they understand;* they go about in darkness; all the
    foundations of the earth are shaken.
Now I say to you, 'You are gods,* and all of you children of the Most High;
Nevertheless, you shall die like mortals,* and fall like any prince.' "
Arise, O God, and rule the earth,* for you shall take all nations for your own.
                                                                    Psalm 82

The Refrain
Help us, O God our Savior, for the glory of your Name;* deliver us and forgive us
  our sins, for your Name's sake.

The Cry of the Church
Even so come, Lord Jesus!

The Lord's Prayer

The Prayer Appointed for the Week
O God, who by the glorious resurrection of your Son Jesus Christ destroyed death
  and brought life and immortality to light: Grant that I, who have been raised
  with him, may abide in his presence and rejoice in the hope of eternal glory;
  through Jesus Christ my Lord, to whom, with you and the Holy Spirit, be
  dominion and praise for ever and ever. *Amen.* †

The Concluding Prayer of the Church
Lord God, almighty and everlasting Father, you have brought me in safety to this
  new day: Preserve me with your mighty power, that I may not fall into sin, nor
  be overcome by adversity; and in all I do direct me to the fulfilling of your purpose; through Jesus Christ my Lord. *Amen.* †

The Midday Office   **To Be Observed on the Hour or Half Hour**
                                                    Between 11 a.m. and 2 p.m.

The Call to Prayer
Ascribe to the LORD, you families of the peoples;* ascribe to the LORD honor and
  power.
Ascribe to the LORD the honor due his Name;* bring offerings and come into his
  courts.
Worship the LORD in the beauty of holiness.

Psalm 96:7–9

The Request for Presence
For God alone my soul in silence waits;* truly, my hope is in him.

Psalm 62:6

The Greeting
Happy are the people whose strength is in you!* whose hearts are set on the pilgrims' way.

Psalm 84:4

The Refrain for the Midday Lessons
My heart, therefore, is glad, and my spirit rejoices;* my body also shall rest in
  hope.

Psalm 16:9

A Reading

The spirit is poured out on us from above, and the desert becomes productive
ground, so productive you might take it for a forest. Fair judgement will fix its
home in the desert, and uprightness live in the productive ground, and the
product of uprightness will be peace, the effect of uprightness being quiet and
security for ever. My people will live in a peaceful home, in peaceful houses,
tranquil dwellings. And should the forest be totally destroyed and the city
gravely humiliated, you will be happy to sow wherever there is water and to
let the ox and the donkey roam free.

Isaiah 32:15–20

The Refrain

My heart, therefore, is glad, and my spirit rejoices;* my body also shall rest in
hope.

The Midday Psalm   *The LORD of Hosts Is with Us*

There is a river whose streams make glad the city of God,* the holy habitation of
the Most High.

God is in the midst of her; she shall not be overthrown;* God shall help her at the
break of day.

The nations make much ado, and the kingdoms are shaken;* God has spoken, and
the earth shall melt away.

The LORD of hosts is with us;* the God of Jacob is our stronghold.

Psalm 46:5–8

The Refrain

My heart, therefore, is glad, and my spirit rejoices;* my body also shall rest in
hope.

The Small Verse

'I am the Alpha and the Omega' says the Lord God, 'who is, who was, and who is
to come, the Almighty.'

Revelation 1:8

The Lord's Prayer

The Prayer Appointed for the Week

O God, who by the glorious resurrection of your Son Jesus Christ destroyed death
and brought life and immortality to light: Grant that I, who have been raised
with him, may abide in his presence and rejoice in the hope of eternal glory;
through Jesus Christ my Lord, to whom, with you and the Holy Spirit, be
dominion and praise for ever and ever. *Amen.* †

The Concluding Prayer of the Church

O God, the source of eternal light: Shed forth your unending day upon all of us
who watch for you, that our lips may praise you, our lives may bless you, and
our worship may give you glory; through Jesus Christ our Lord. *Amen.* †

The Vespers Office

To Be Observed on the Hour or Half Hour
Between 5 and 8 p.m.

The Call to Prayer
Give thanks to the LORD, for he is good,* and his mercy endures for ever.

Psalm 107:1

The Request for Presence
So teach us to number our days* that we may apply our hearts to wisdom.

Psalm 90:12

The Greeting
Remember not the sins of my youth and my transgressions;* remember me
according to your love and for the sake of your goodness, O LORD.

Psalm 25:6

The Hymn   *Bread of the World*
Bread of the world, in mercy broken,
Wine of the soul, in mercy shed,
By whom the words of life were spoken,
And in whose death our sins are dead.

Look on the heart by sorrow broken,
Look on the tears by sinners shed;
And be Your feast to us the token
That by Your grace our souls are fed.

Reginald Heber

The Refrain for the Vespers Lessons
Behold, God is my helper;* it is the Lord who sustains my life.

Psalm 54:4

The Vespers Psalm   *The LORD Has Ordained a Blessing*
Oh, how good and pleasant it is,* when brethren live together in unity!
It is like fine oil upon the head* that runs down upon the beard,
Upon the beard of Aaron,* and runs down upon the collar of his robe.
It is like the dew of Hermon* that falls upon the hills of Zion.
For there the LORD has ordained the blessing:* life for evermore.

Psalm 133

The Refrain
Behold, God is my helper;* it is the Lord who sustains my life.

The Small Verse
The Lord is my shepherd and nothing is wanting to me. In green pastures He has
settled me.

THE SHORT BREVIARY

The Lord's Prayer

The Prayer Appointed for the Week

O God, who by the glorious resurrection of your Son Jesus Christ destroyed death and brought life and immortality to light: Grant that I, who have been raised with him, may abide in his presence and rejoice in the hope of eternal glory; through Jesus Christ my Lord, to whom, with you and the Holy Spirit, be dominion and praise for ever and ever. *Amen.* †

The Concluding Prayer of the Church

Almighty God, who after the creation of the world rested from all your works and sanctified a day of rest for all your creatures: Grant that I, putting away all earthly anxieties, may be duly prepared for the service of public worship, and grant as well that my Sabbath upon earth may be a preparation for the eternal rest promised to your people in heaven; through Jesus Christ our Lord. *Amen.* †

The Morning Office   To Be Observed on the Hour or Half Hour
Between 6 and 9 a.m.

The Call to Prayer

I will sing of mercy and justice;* to you, O LORD, will I sing praises.

Psalm 101:1

The Request for Presence

Your testimonies are very sure,* and holiness adorns your house, O LORD, for ever and for evermore.

Psalm 93:6

The Greeting

We give you thanks, O God, we give you thanks,* calling upon your Name and declaring all your wonderful deeds.

Psalm 75:1

The Refrain for the Morning Lessons

Your statutes have been like songs to me.*

Psalm 119:54

A Reading

That evening they brought him many who were possessed by devils. He drove out the spirits with a command and cured all who were sick. This was to fulfill what was spoken by the prophet Isaiah: *He himself bore our sickness away and carried our diseases.*

Matthew 8:16–17

The Refrain
Your statutes have been like songs to me.*

The Morning Psalm   *This Is the Gate of the* LORD
Open for me the gates of righteousness;* I will enter them; I will offer thanks to the
   LORD.
"This is the gate of the LORD;* he who is righteous may enter."
I will give thanks to you, for you answered me* and have become my salvation.
The same stone which the builders rejected* has become the chief cornerstone.
This is the LORD's doing,* and it is marvelous in our eyes.
On this day the LORD has acted;* we will rejoice and be glad in it.

Psalm 118:19–24

The Refrain
Your statutes have been like songs to me.*

The Gloria

The Lord's Prayer

The Prayer Appointed for the Week
I thank you, heavenly Father, that you have delivered me from the dominion of sin
   and death and brought me into the kingdom of your Son; and I pray that, as by
   his death he has recalled me to life, so by his love he may raise me to eternal
   joys; who lives and reigns with you, in the unity of the Holy Spirit, one God,
   now and for ever. *Amen.* †

The Concluding Prayer of the Church
Lord God, almighty and everlasting Father, you have brought me in safety to this
   new day: Preserve me with your mighty power, that I may not fall into sin, nor
   be overcome by adversity; and in all I do direct me to the fulfilling of your purpose; through Jesus Christ my Lord. *Amen.* †

The Midday Office   **To Be Observed on the Hour or Half Hour**
                                          Between 11 a.m. and 2 p.m.

The Call to Prayer
God has gone up with a shout,* the LORD with the sound of the ram's-horn.
Sing praises to God, sing praises;* sing praises to our King, sing praises.
For God is King of all the earth;* sing praises with all your skill.
God reigns over the nations;* God sits upon his holy throne.

Psalm 47:5–8

The Request for Presence
Let the peoples praise you, O God;* let all the peoples praise you.

Psalm 67:3

The Greeting

For you alone are the Holy One, you alone are the Lord, you alone are the Most
High, Jesus Christ, with the Holy Spirit, in the glory of God the Father.

The Refrain for the Midday Lessons

Tell it out among the nations: "The LORD is King!*

Psalm 96:10

A Reading

My love is fresh and ruddy, to be known among ten thousand. His head is golden,
purest gold, his locks are palm fronds and black as the raven. His eyes are like
doves beside the water-courses, bathing themselves in milk, perching on a
fountain rim. His cheeks are beds of spices, banks sweetly scented. His lips are
lilies, distilling pure myrrh. His hands are golden, rounded, set with jewels of
Tarshish. His belly a block of ivory covered with sapphires. His legs are
alabaster columns set in sockets of pure gold. His appearance is that of
Lebanon, unrivaled as the cedars. His conversation is sweetness itself, he is
altogether lovable. Such is my love, such is my friend, O daughters of
Jerusalem.

The Song of Songs 5:10–16

The Refrain

Tell it out among the nations: "The LORD is King!*

The Midday Psalm   *Great Are the Deeds of the LORD*

Hallelujah! I will give thanks to the LORD with my whole heart,* in the assembly of
the upright, in the congregation.

Great are the deeds of the LORD!* they are studied by all who delight in them.

His work is full of majesty and splendor,* and his righteousness endures for ever.

He makes his marvelous works to be remembered;* the LORD is gracious and full
of compassion.

He gives food to those who fear him;* he is ever mindful of his covenant.

He has shown his people the power of his works* in giving them the lands of the
nations.

The works of his hands are faithfulness and justice;* all his commandments are
sure.

They stand fast for ever and ever,* because they are done in truth and equity.

He sent redemption to his people; he commanded his covenant for ever;* holy and
awesome is his Name.

The fear of the LORD is the beginning of wisdom;* those who act accordingly have
a good understanding; his praise endures for ever.

Psalm 111

The Refrain

Tell it out among the nations: "The LORD is King!*

The Cry of the Church

Christ has died, Christ is risen, Christ will come again.

The Lord's Prayer

The Prayer Appointed for the Week

I thank you, heavenly Father, that you have delivered me from the dominion of sin and death and brought me into the kingdom of your Son; and I pray that, as by his death he has recalled me to life, so by his love he may raise me to eternal joys; who lives and reigns with you, in the unity of the Holy Spirit, one God, now and for ever. *Amen.* †

The Concluding Prayer of the Church

O God, you make me glad with the weekly remembrance of the glorious resurrection of your Son my Lord: Give me this day such blessing through my worship of you, that the week to come may be spent in your favor; through Jesus Christ our Lord. *Amen.* †

The Vespers Office   **To Be Observed on the Hour or Half Hour**
                               Between 5 and 8 p.m.

The Call to Prayer

Enter his gates with thanksgiving; go into his courts with praise;* give thanks to him and call upon his Name.

Psalm 100:3

The Request for Presence

May God give us his blessing,* and may all the ends of the earth stand in awe of him.

Psalm 67:7

The Greeting

O LORD, my God, my Savior,* by day and night I cry to you.

Psalm 88:1

The Hymn   *Fairest Lord Jesus*

Fairest Lord Jesus, ruler of all nature,
O you of God and man the Son,
You will I cherish,
You will I honor,
You, my soul's glory, joy, and crown.

Fair are the meadows, fairer still the woodlands,
Robed in blooming garb of spring;
Jesus is fairer,
Jesus is purer,
Who makes the woeful heart to sing.

Fair is the sunshine, fairer still the moonlight,
And all the twinkling starry host:
Jesus shines brighter,
Jesus shines purer
Than all the angels heaven can boast.

Beautiful Savior! Lord of all the nations!
Son of God and Son of Man!
Glory and honor,
Praise, adoration,
Now and for evermore be thine.

from Münster Gesangbuch

The Refrain for the Vespers Lessons

I will fulfill my vows to the LORD* in the presence of all his people.

Psalm 116:16

The Vespers Psalm   *The LORD Will Make Good His Purpose for Me*

I will give thanks to you, O LORD, with my whole heart;* before the gods I will sing
your praise.

I will bow down toward your holy temple and praise your Name,* because of
your love and faithfulness;

For you have glorified your Name* and your word above all things.

When I called, you answered me;* you increased my strength within me.

All the kings of the earth will praise you, O LORD,* when they have heard the
words of your mouth.

They will sing of the ways of the LORD,* that great is the glory of the LORD.

Though the LORD be high, he cares for the lowly;* he perceives the haughty from
afar.

Though I walk in the midst of trouble, you keep me safe;* you stretch forth your
hand against the fury of my enemies; your right hand shall save me.

The LORD will make good his purpose for me;* O LORD, your love endures for
ever; do not abandon the works of your hands.

Psalm 138

The Refrain

I will fulfill my vows to the LORD* in the presence of all his people.

The Gloria

The Lord's Prayer

The Prayer Appointed for the Week

I thank you, heavenly Father, that you have delivered me from the dominion of sin
and death and brought me into the kingdom of your Son; and I pray that, as by
his death he has recalled me to life, so by his love he may raise me to eternal

joys; who lives and reigns with you, in the unity of the Holy Spirit, one God, now and for ever. *Amen.* †

The Concluding Prayer of the Church

Pour upon me and all who have fed on Your Paschal mysteries, O Lord, the Spirit of Your love and grant that by Your gracious mercy we may come to be of one mind in Your service. I pray this in the name of Jesus, my Lord, who with You and the Holy Spirit reigns one God world without end. *Amen.*

adapted from THE SHORT BREVIARY

The Morning Office	To Be Observed on the Hour or Half Hour Between 6 and 9 a.m.

The Call to Prayer

Sing to the LORD a new song,* for he has done marvelous things.
With his right hand and his holy arm* has he won for himself the victory.
The LORD has made known his victory;* his righteousness has he openly shown in the sight of the nations.

Psalm 98:1–3

The Request for Presence

Be my strong rock, a castle to keep me safe, for you are my crag and my stronghold;* for the sake of your Name, lead me and guide me.

Psalm 31:3

The Greeting

How great is your goodness, O LORD!* which you have laid up for those who fear you; which you have done in the sight of all.

Psalm 31:19

The Refrain for the Morning Lessons

Be strong and let your heart take courage,* all you who wait for the LORD.

Psalm 31:24

A Reading

Jesus said to us: ". . . Everything now covered up will be uncovered, and everything now hidden will be made clear. What I say in the dark, tell in the daylight; what you hear in whispers, proclaim from the housetops."

Matthew 10:26–27

The Refrain

Be strong and let your heart take courage,* all you who wait for the LORD.

The Morning Psalm   *Those Who Sowed with Tears Will Reap with Songs of Joy*

When the LORD restored the fortunes of Zion,* then were we like those who dream.
Then was our mouth filled with laughter,* and our tongue with shouts of joy.

Then they said among the nations,* "The LORD has done great things for them."
The LORD has done great things for us,* and we are glad indeed.
Restore our fortunes, O LORD,* like the watercourses of the Negev.
Those who sowed with tears* will reap with songs of joy.
Those who go out weeping, carrying the seed,* will come again with joy,
    shouldering their sheaves.

Psalm 126

The Refrain
Be strong and let your heart take courage,* all you who wait for the LORD.

The Cry of the Church
In the evening, in the morning, and at noonday, I will complain and lament,* and
    he will hear my voice.

Psalm 55:18

The Lord's Prayer

The Prayer Appointed for the Week
I thank you, heavenly Father, that you have delivered me from the dominion of sin
    and death and brought me into the kingdom of your Son; and I pray that, as by
    his death he has recalled me to life, so by his love he may raise me to eternal
    joys; who lives and reigns with you, in the unity of the Holy Spirit, one God,
    now and for ever. *Amen.* †

The Concluding Prayers of the Church
Lord God, almighty and everlasting Father, you have brought me in safety to this
    new day: Preserve me with your mighty power, that I may not fall into sin, nor
    be overcome by adversity; and in all I do direct me to the fulfilling of your pur-
    pose; through Jesus Christ my Lord. *Amen.* †

The Midday Office   **To Be Observed on the Hour or Half Hour
Between 11 a.m. and 2 p.m.**

The Call to Prayer
Blessed be the LORD, the God of Israel, from everlasting and to everlasting;* and
    let all the people say, "Amen!" Hallelujah!

Psalm 106:48

The Request for Presence
Be merciful to me, O LORD, for you are my God;* I call upon you all the day long.

Psalm 86:3

The Greeting
I will give thanks to you, O LORD, with my whole heart;* before the gods I will sing
    your praise.

Psalm 138:1

The Refrain for the Midday Lessons

The fear of the LORD is the beginning of wisdom;* those who act accordingly have a good understanding; his praise endures for ever.

Psalm 111:10

A Reading

On this mountain, he has destroyed the veil which used to veil all peoples, the pall enveloping all nations; he has destroyed death for ever. Lord YAHWEH has wiped away the tears from every cheek; he has taken his people's shame away everywhere on earth, for YAHWEH has spoken. And on that day it will be said, 'Look, this is our God, in him we put our hope that he should save us, this is YAHWEH, we put our hope in him. Let us exult and rejoice since he has saved us.' For YAHWEH'S hand will rest on his mountain . . .

Isaiah 25:7–10

The Refrain

The fear of the LORD is the beginning of wisdom;* those who act accordingly have a good understanding; his praise endures for ever.

The Midday Psalm   *I Have Prepared a Lamp for My Anointed*

For the LORD has chosen Zion;* he has desired her for his habitation:
"This shall be my resting-place for ever;* here will I dwell, for I delight in her.
I will surely bless her provisions,* and satisfy her poor with bread.
I will clothe her priests with salvation,* and her faithful people will rejoice and sing.
There will I make the horn of David flourish;* I have prepared a lamp for my Anointed.

Psalm 132:14–18

The Refrain

The fear of the LORD is the beginning of wisdom;* those who act accordingly have a good understanding; his praise endures for ever.

The Gloria

The Lord's Prayer

The Prayer Appointed for the Week

I thank you, heavenly Father, that you have delivered me from the dominion of sin and death and brought me into the kingdom of your Son; and I pray that, as by his death he has recalled me to life, so by his love he may raise me to eternal joys; who lives and reigns with you, in the unity of the Holy Spirit, one God, now and for ever. *Amen.* †

The Concluding Prayer of the Church

Heavenly Father, you have promised to hear what we ask in the Name of your Son: Accept and fulfill my petitions, I pray, not as I ask in my ignorance, nor as I deserve in my sinfulness, but as you know and love me in your Son Jesus Christ our Lord. *Amen.* †

The Vespers Office   To Be Observed on the Hour or Half Hour
                                    Between 5 and 8 p.m.

The Call to Prayer
Sing to the LORD and bless his Name;* proclaim the good news of his salvation
    from day to day.
Declare his glory among the nations* and his wonders among all peoples.

Psalm 96:2–3

The Request for Presence
Save us, O LORD our God, and gather us from among the nations,* that we may
    give thanks to your holy Name and glory in your praise.

Psalm 106:47

The Greeting
I will give you thanks for what you have done* and declare the goodness of your
    Name in the presence of the godly.

The Hymn   *He Is Risen!*

He is risen, he is risen!   He is risen, he is risen!
Tell it out with joyful voice: He has opened heaven's gate:
He has burst his three days' prison;   We are free from sin's dark prison,
Let the whole wide earth rejoice: Risen to a holier state;
Death is conquered, we are free,   And a brighter, sweeter beam
Christ has won the victory.   On our longing eyes shall stream.

                                                      Joachim Neander

Come, you sad and fearful hearted,
With glad smile and radiant brow!
Death's long shadows have departed;
Jesus' woes are over now,
And the passion that he bore—
Sin and pain can vex no more.

The Refrain for the Vespers Lessons
Let the faithful rejoice in triumph;* let them be joyful on their beds.

Psalm 149:5

The Vespers Psalm   *He Has Shown His Righteousness Openly*
Sing to the LORD a new song,* for he has done marvelous things.
With his right hand and his holy arm* has he won for himself the victory.
The LORD has made known his victory;* his righteousness has he openly shown in
    the sight of the nations.
He remembers his mercy and faithfulness to the house of Israel,* and all the ends
    of the earth have seen the victory of our God.
Shout with joy to the LORD, all you lands;* lift up your voice, rejoice, and sing.
Sing to the LORD with the harp,* with the harp and the voice of song.
With trumpets and the sound of the horn* shout with joy before the King, the
    LORD.

Psalm 98:1–7

The Refrain
Let the faithful rejoice in triumph;* let them be joyful on their beds.

The Cry of the Church
O Lord, hear my prayer and let my cry come unto you. Thanks be to God.
THE SHORT BREVIARY

The Lord's Prayer

The Prayer Appointed for the Week
I thank you, heavenly Father, that you have delivered me from the dominion of sin
and death and brought me into the kingdom of your Son; and I pray that, as by
his death he has recalled me to life, so by his love he may raise me to eternal
joys; who lives and reigns with you, in the unity of the Holy Spirit, one God,
now and for ever. *Amen.* †

The Concluding Prayer of the Church
Almighty God, by your Holy Spirit you have made us one with your faithful in
heaven and on earth: Grant that in my earthly pilgrimage I may always be supported by this fellowship of love and prayer, and know myself to be surrounded by their witness to your power and mercy. I ask this for the sake of
Jesus Christ, in whom all my intercessions are acceptable through the Spirit,
and who lives and reigns for ever and ever. *Amen.* †

The Morning Office　　　　　　To Be Observed on the Hour or Half Hour
Between 6 and 9 a.m.

The Call to Prayer
God has gone up with a shout,* the LORD with the sound of the ram's-horn.
Sing praises to God, sing praises;* sing praises to our King, sing praises.
For God is King of all the earth;* sing praises with all your skill.
God reigns over the nations;* God sits upon his holy throne.
Psalm 47:5–8

The Request for Presence
Let all who seek you rejoice and be glad in you;* let those who love your salvation
say for ever, "Great is the LORD!"
Psalm 70:4

The Greeting
Out of Zion, perfect in its beauty,* God reveals himself in glory.
Psalm 50:2

The Refrain for the Morning Lessons
When the LORD restores the fortunes of his people, Jacob will rejoice and Israel be
glad.
Psalm 14:7b

A Reading
Jesus said: "In all truth I tell you, whoever welcomes the one I send, welcomes me, and whoever welcomes me, welcomes the one who sent me."

John 13:20

The Refrain
When the LORD restores the fortunes of his people, Jacob will rejoice and Israel be glad.

The Morning Psalm   *He Has Dealt with Me Richly*
Look upon me and answer me, O LORD my God;* give light to my eyes, lest I sleep in death;
Lest my enemy say, "I have prevailed over him,"* and my foes rejoice that I have fallen.
But I put my trust in your mercy;* my heart is joyful because of your saving help.
I will sing to the LORD, for he has dealt with me richly;* I will praise the Name of the Lord Most High.

Psalm 13:3–6

The Refrain
When the LORD restores the fortunes of his people, Jacob will rejoice and Israel be glad.

The Gloria

The Lord's Prayer

The Prayer Appointed for the Week
I thank you, heavenly Father, that you have delivered me from the dominion of sin and death and brought me into the kingdom of your Son; and I pray that, as by his death he has recalled me to life, so by his love he may raise me to eternal joys; who lives and reigns with you, in the unity of the Holy Spirit, one God, now and for ever. *Amen.* †

The Concluding Prayer of the Church
Lord God, almighty and everlasting Father, you have brought me in safety to this new day: Preserve me with your mighty power, that I may not fall into sin, nor be overcome by adversity; and in all I do direct me to the fulfilling of your purpose; through Jesus Christ my Lord. *Amen.* †

The Midday Office   **To Be Observed on the Hour or Half Hour**
Between 11 a.m. and 2 p.m.

The Call to Prayer
Open my lips, O LORD,* and my mouth shall proclaim your praise.

Psalm 51:16

The Request for Presence
Blessed are you, O Lord;* instruct me in your statutes.

Psalm 119:12

The Greeting
How priceless is your love, O God!* your people take refuge under the shadow of your wings.
They feast upon the abundance of your house;* you give them drink from the river of your delights.
For with you is the well of life,* and in your light we see light.

Psalm 36:7–9

The Refrain for the Midday Lessons
Mercy and truth have met together;* righteousness and peace have kissed each other.

Psalm 85:10

A Reading
Anyone who listens to the Word and takes no action is like someone who looks at his own features in a mirror and, once he has seen what he looks like, goes off and immediately forgets it. But anyone who looks steadily at the perfect law of freedom and keeps to it—not listening and forgetting, but putting it to practice—will be blessed in every undertaking.

James 1:23–25

The Refrain
Mercy and truth have met together;* righteousness and peace have kissed each other.

The Midday Psalm   *Sing to the Lord a New Song*
Sing to the Lord a new song;* sing to the Lord, all the whole earth.
Sing to the Lord and bless his Name;* proclaim the good news of his salvation from day to day.
Declare his glory among the nations* and his wonders among all peoples.
For great is the Lord and greatly to be praised;* he is more to be feared than all gods.
As for all the gods of the nations, they are but idols;* but it is the Lord who made the heavens.
Oh, the majesty and magnificence of his presence!* Oh, the power and the splendor of his sanctuary!

Psalm 96:1–6

The Refrain
Mercy and truth have met together;* righteousness and peace have kissed each other.

The Cry of the Church
Christ has died, Christ is risen, Christ will come again.

The Lord's Prayer

The Prayer Appointed for the Week
I thank you, heavenly Father, that you have delivered me from the dominion of sin
and death and brought me into the kingdom of your Son; and I pray that, as by
his death he has recalled me to life, so by his love he may raise me to eternal
joys; who lives and reigns with you, in the unity of the Holy Spirit, one God,
now and for ever. *Amen.* †

The Concluding Prayer of the Church
Let us bless the Lord God living and true! Let us always render him praise, glory,
honor, blessing, and all good things! Amen. Amen. So be it! So be it!
St. Francis of Assisi

The Vespers Office   To Be Observed on the Hour or Half Hour
Between 5 and 8 p.m.

The Call to Prayer
Open my lips, O LORD,* and my mouth shall proclaim your praise.
Psalm 51:16

The Request for Presence
My soul waits for the LORD, more than watchmen for the morning,* more than
watchmen for the morning.
Psalm 130:5

The Greeting
You have put gladness in my heart,* more than when grain and wine and oil
increase.
I lie down in peace; at once I fall asleep;* for only you, LORD, make me dwell in
safety.
Psalm 4:7–8

The Hymn   *Love's Redeeming Work Is Done*
Love's redeeming work is done,   Soar we now where Christ has led,
Fought the fight, the battle won.   Following our exalted Head;
Death in vain forbids him rise;   Made like him, like him we rise,
Christ has opened paradise.   Ours the cross, the grave, the skies.
Charles Wesley

Lives again our glorious King;
Where, O death, is now your sting?
Once he died our souls to save,
Where your victory, O grave?

The Refrain for the Vespers Lessons
The LORD has sworn an oath to David;* in truth, he will not break it:
"A son, the fruit of your body* will I set upon your throne.
Psalm 132:11–12

The Vespers Psalm   *Our Eyes Look to the LORD Our God*
To you I lift up my eyes,* to you enthroned in the heavens.
As the eyes of servants look to the hand of their masters,* and the eyes of a maid to
    the hand of her mistress,
So our eyes look to the LORD our God,* until he shows us his mercy.
Have mercy upon us, O LORD, have mercy,* for we have had more than enough of
    contempt,
Too much of the scorn of the indolent rich,* and of the derision of the proud.

                                                              Psalm 123

The Refrain
The LORD has sworn an oath to David;* in truth, he will not break it:
"A son, the fruit of your body* will I set upon your throne."

The Gloria

The Lord's Prayer

The Prayer Appointed for the Week
I thank you, heavenly Father, that you have delivered me from the dominion of sin
    and death and brought me into the kingdom of your Son; and I pray that, as by
    his death he has recalled me to life, so by his love he may raise me to eternal
    joys; who lives and reigns with you, in the unity of the Holy Spirit, one God,
    now and for ever. *Amen.* †

The Concluding Prayer of the Church
Grant, Lord God, to all who have been baptized into the death and resurrection of
    your Son Jesus Christ, that, as we have put away the old life of sin, so we may
    be renewed in the spirit of our minds, and live in righteousness and true holi-
    ness; through Jesus Christ our Lord, who lives and reigns with you, in the
    unity of the Holy Spirit, one God, now and for ever. *Amen.* †

The Morning Office   **To Be Observed on the Hour or Half Hour**
                                                    Between 6 and 9 a.m.

The Call to Prayer
Cast your burden upon the LORD, and he will sustain you;* he will never let the
    righteous stumble.

                                                              Psalm 55:24

The Request for Presence
O LORD, I am your servant;* I am your servant and the child of your handmaid;
    you have freed me from my bonds.
I will offer you the sacrifice of thanksgiving* and call upon the Name of the LORD.
I will fulfill my vows to the LORD* in the presence of all his people.

                                                              Psalm 116:14–16

The Greeting
I will offer you a freewill sacrifice* and praise your Name, O Lord, for it is good.
For you have rescued me from every trouble,* and my eye has seen the ruin of my
    foes.

Psalm 54:6–7

The Refrain for the Morning Lessons
The Lord is near to those who call upon him,* to all who call upon him faithfully.

Psalm 145:19

A Reading
Jesus taught his disciples, saying: "You foolish men! So slow to believe all that the
    prophets have said! Was it not necessary that the Christ should suffer before
    entering into his glory?" Then, starting with Moses and going through all the
    prophets, he explained to them all the passages throughout the scriptures that
    were about himself.

Luke 24:25–27

The Refrain
The Lord is near to those who call upon him,* to all who call upon him faithfully.

The Morning Psalm   *Teach Me Your Way, O Lord*
Teach me your way, O Lord, and I will walk in your truth;* knit my heart to you
    that I may fear your Name.
I will thank you, O Lord my God, with all my heart,* and glorify your Name for
    evermore.
For great is your love toward me;* you have delivered me from the nethermost Pit.
The arrogant rise up against me, O God, and a band of violent men seeks my life;*
    they have not set you before their eyes.
But you, O Lord, are gracious and full of compassion,* slow to anger, and full of
    kindness and truth.
Turn to me and have mercy upon me;* give your strength to your servant; and
    save the child of your handmaid.
Show me a sign of your favor, so that those who hate me may see it and be
    ashamed;* because you, O Lord, have helped me and comforted me.

Psalm 86:11–17

The Refrain
The Lord is near to those who call upon him,* to all who call upon him faithfully.

The Cry of the Church
O Lord, hear my prayer and let my cry come unto you. Thanks be to God.

The Short Breviary

The Lord's Prayer

The Prayer Appointed for the Week
I thank you, heavenly Father, that you have delivered me from the dominion of sin
    and death and brought me into the kingdom of your Son; and I pray that, as by

his death he has recalled me to life, so by his love he may raise me to eternal joys; who lives and reigns with you, in the unity of the Holy Spirit, one God, now and for ever. *Amen.* †

The Concluding Prayer of the Church
Lord God, almighty and everlasting Father, you have brought me in safety to this new day: Preserve me with your mighty power, that I may not fall into sin, nor be overcome by adversity; and in all I do direct me to the fulfilling of your purpose; through Jesus Christ my Lord. *Amen.* †

The Midday Office   To Be Observed on the Hour or Half Hour
Between 11 a.m. and 2 p.m.

The Call to Prayer
Hallelujah! Praise the LORD, O my soul!* I will praise the LORD as long as I live; I will sing praises to my God while I have my being.

Psalm 146:1

The Request for Presence
Remember me, O LORD, with the favor you have for your people,* and visit me with your saving help;
That I may see the prosperity of your elect and be glad with the gladness of your people,* that I may glory with your inheritance.

Psalm 106:4–5

The Greeting
You are to be praised, O God, in Zion; . . .
To you that hear prayer shall all flesh come,* because of their transgressions.

Psalm 65:1–2

The Refrain for the Midday Lessons
Your statutes have been like songs to me* wherever I have lived like a stranger.

Psalm 119:54

A Reading
We want you to be quite certain, brothers, about those who have fallen asleep, to make sure that you do not grieve for them, as others do who have no hope. We believe that Jesus died and rose again, and that in the same way God will bring with him those who have fallen asleep in Jesus.

1 Thessalonians 4:13–14

The Refrain
Your statutes have been like songs to me* wherever I have lived like a stranger.

The Midday Psalm   *Such Knowledge Is Too Wonderful for Me*
LORD, you have searched me out and known me;* you know my sitting down and my rising up; you discern my thoughts from afar.

You trace my journeys and my resting-places* and are acquainted with all my
ways.
Indeed, there is not a word on my lips,* but you, O LORD, know it altogether.
You press upon me behind and before* and lay your hand upon me.
Such knowledge is too wonderful for me;* it is so high that I cannot attain to it.
Where can I go then from your Spirit?* where can I flee from your presence?
If I climb up to heaven, you are there;* if I make the grave my bed, you are there
also.
If I take the wings of the morning* and dwell in the uttermost parts of the sea,
Even there your hand will lead me* and your right hand hold me fast.

Psalm 139:1–9

The Refrain
Your statutes have been like songs to me* wherever I have lived like a stranger.

The Cry of the Church
Christ has died. Christ is risen. Christ will come again.

The Lord's Prayer

The Prayer Appointed for the Week
I thank you, heavenly Father, that you have delivered me from the dominion of sin
and death and brought me into the kingdom of your Son; and I pray that, as by
his death he has recalled me to life, so by his love he may raise me to eternal
joys; who lives and reigns with you, in the unity of the Holy Spirit, one God,
now and for ever. *Amen.* †

The Concluding Prayer of the Church
May God himself order my days and make them acceptable in his sight. Blessed
be the Lord always, my strength and my redeemer.

Traditional

The Vespers Office **To Be Observed on the Hour or Half Hour**
Between 5 and 8 p.m.

The Call to Prayer
Come, let us sing to the LORD;* let us shout for joy to the Rock of our salvation.

Psalm 95:1

The Request for Presence
May the glory of the LORD endure for ever,* may the LORD rejoice in all his works.

Psalm 104:32

The Greeting
How great is your goodness, O LORD! which you have laid up for those who fear
you;* which you have done in the sight of all for those who put their trust in you.

Psalm 31:19

The Hymn   *Lift Your Voice Rejoicing*

Lift your voice rejoicing, Mary,
Christ has risen from the tomb;
On the cross a suffering victim,
Now as victor he is come.
Whom your tears in death were mourning,
Welcome with your smiles returning.
Let your alleluias rise!

Raise your weary eyelids, Mary,
See him living evermore;
See his countenance, how gracious,
See the wounds for you he bore.
All the glory of the morning
Pales before those wounds redeeming.
Let your alleluias rise!

Life is yours for ever, Mary,
For your light is come once more
And the strength of death is broken;
Now your songs of joy outpour.
Ended now the night of sorrow,
Love has brought the blessed morrow.
Let your alleluias rise!

Latin, Unknown

The Refrain for the Vespers Lessons
I am small and of little account,* yet I do not forget your commandments.

Psalm 119:141

The Vespers Psalm   *He Shall Cover Me with His Pinions*
He who dwells in the shelter of the Most High,* abides under the shadow of the
    Almighty.
He shall say to the LORD, "You are my refuge and my stronghold,* my God in
    whom I put my trust."
He shall deliver you from the snare of the hunter* and from the deadly pestilence.
He shall cover you with his pinions, and you shall find refuge under his wings;*
    his faithfulness shall be a shield and buckler.
You shall not be afraid of any terror by night,* nor of the arrow that flies by day;
Of the plague that stalks in the darkness,* nor of the sickness that lays waste at
    mid-day.
A thousand shall fall at your side and ten thousand at your right hand,* but it shall
    not come near you.

Psalm 91:1-7

The Refrain
I am small and of little account,* yet I do not forget your commandments.

The Small Verse

Those who sowed with tears* will reap with songs of joy.
Those who go out weeping, carrying the seed,* will come again with joy,
    shouldering their sheaves.

Psalm 126:6–7

The Lord's Prayer

The Prayer Appointed for the Week

I thank you, heavenly Father, that you have delivered me from the dominion of sin
    and death and brought me into the kingdom of your Son; and I pray that, as by
    his death he has recalled me to life, so by his love he may raise me to eternal
    joys; who lives and reigns with you, in the unity of the Holy Spirit, one God,
    now and for ever. *Amen.* †

The Concluding Prayer of the Church

Almighty God, to whom our needs are known before we even ask, Help me to ask
    only what accords with your will; and those good things which I dare not, or in
    my blindness I cannot ask, grant for the sake of your Son Jesus Christ our Lord.
    Amen. †

The Morning Office   **To Be Observed on the Hour or Half Hour**
                                                              Between 6 and 9 a.m.

The Call to Prayer

Know this: The LORD himself is God;* he himself has made us, and we are his; we
    are his people and the sheep of his pasture.

Psalm 100:2

The Request for Presence

For God alone my soul in silence waits;* truly, my hope is in him.

Psalm 62:6

The Greeting

Your testimonies are very sure,* and holiness adorns your house, O LORD, for ever
    and for evermore.

Psalm 93:6

The Refrain for the Morning Lessons

Blessed is he who comes in the name of the Lord;* we bless you from the house of
    the LORD.

Psalm 118:26

A Reading

There were many other signs that Jesus worked in the sight of the disciples, but
    they are not recorded in this book. These are recorded so that you may believe
    that Jesus is the Christ, the Son of God, and that believing this you may have
    life through his name.

John 20:30–31

The Refrain
Blessed is he who comes in the name of the Lord;* we bless you from the house of the LORD.

The Morning Psalm   *Bless the LORD, All You Who Do His Bidding*
The merciful goodness of the LORD endures for ever on those who fear him,* and
    his righteousness on children's children;
On those who keep his covenant* and remember his commandments and do
    them.
The LORD has set his throne in heaven,* and his kingship has dominion over all.
Bless the LORD, you angels of his, you mighty ones who do his bidding,* and
    hearken to the voice of his word.
Bless the LORD, all you his hosts,* you ministers of his who do his will.
Bless the LORD, all you works of his, in all places of his dominion;* bless the LORD,
    O my soul.

                                        Psalm 103:17–22

The Refrain
Blessed is he who comes in the name of the Lord;* we bless you from the house of
    the LORD.

The Cry of the Church
Christ has died. Christ is risen. Christ will come again.

The Lord's Prayer

The Prayer Appointed for the Week
I thank you, heavenly Father, that you have delivered me from the dominion of sin
    and death and brought me into the kingdom of your Son; and I pray that, as by
    his death he has recalled me to life, so by his love he may raise me to eternal
    joys; who lives and reigns with you, in the unity of the Holy Spirit, one God,
    now and for ever. *Amen.* †

The Concluding Prayer of the Church
Lord God, almighty and everlasting Father, you have brought me in safety to this
    new day: Preserve me with your mighty power, that I may not fall into sin, nor
    be overcome by adversity; and in all I do direct me to the fulfilling of your pur-
    pose; through Jesus Christ my Lord. *Amen.* †

The Midday Office   **To Be Observed on the Hour or Half Hour**
                                        Between 11 a.m. and 2 p.m.

The Call to Prayer
Search for the LORD and his strength;* continually seek his face.

                                        Psalm 105:4

The Request for Presence
You are good and you bring forth good;* instruct me in your statutes.

                                        Psalm 119:68

The Greeting
When your word goes forth it gives light;* it gives understanding to the simple.
Psalm 119:130

The Refrain for the Midday Lessons
You strengthen me more and more;* you enfold and comfort me.
Psalm 71:21

A Reading
When that day comes, YAHWEH will start his threshing from the course of the River to the Torrent of Egypt, and you will be gathered one by one, Israelites! When that day comes, the great ram's-horn will be sounded, and those lost in Assyria will come, and those banished to Egypt, and they will worship YAHWEH on the holy mountain, in Jerusalem.
Isaiah 27:12–13

The Refrain
You strengthen me more and more;* you enfold and comfort me.

The Midday Psalm   *Hear, O Shepherd of Israel, Leading Joseph Like a Flock*
Hear, O Shepherd of Israel, leading Joseph like a flock;* shine forth, you that are enthroned upon the cherubim.
In the presence of Ephraim, Benjamin, and Manasseh,* stir up your strength and come to help us.
Restore us, O God of hosts;* show the light of your countenance, and we shall be saved.
Let your hand be upon the man of your right hand,* the son of man you have made so strong for yourself.
And so will we never turn away from you;* give us life, that we may call upon your Name.
Restore us, O LORD God of hosts;* show the light of your countenance, and we shall be saved.
Psalm 80:1–3, 16–18

The Refrain
You strengthen me more and more;* you enfold and comfort me.

The Gloria

The Lord's Prayer

The Prayer Appointed for the Week
I thank you, heavenly Father, that you have delivered me from the dominion of sin and death and brought me into the kingdom of your Son; and I pray that, as by his death he has recalled me to life, so by his love he may raise me to eternal joys; who lives and reigns with you, in the unity of the Holy Spirit, one God, now and for ever. *Amen.* †

The Concluding Prayer of the Church
Lord, make me according to thy heart.

> *Brother Lawrence*

The Vespers Office   **To Be Observed on the Hour or Half Hour**
                                          Between 5 and 8 p.m.

The Call to Prayer
God is the LORD; he has shined upon us;* form a procession with branches up to
   the horns of the altar.

> *Psalm 118:27*

The Request for Presence
Hear the voice of my prayer when I cry out to you,* when I lift up my hands to
   your holy of holies.

> *Psalm 28:2*

The Greeting
All your works praise you, O LORD,* and your faithful servants bless you.
They make known the glory of your kingdom and speak of your power . . .* and
   the glorious splendor of your kingdom.

> *Psalm 145:10–12*

The Hymn   *A Hymn of Praise*
   Alleluia, alleluia! Hearts and voices heavenward raise:
   Sing to God a hymn of gladness, sing to God a hymn of praise.
   He, who on the cross a victim, for the world's salvation bled,
   Jesus Christ, the King of glory, now is risen from the dead.

   Christ is risen, we are risen! Shed upon us heavenly grace,
   Rain and dew and gleams of glory from the brightness of your face;
   That, with hearts in heaven dwelling, we on earth may fruitful be,
   And by angel hands be gathered, and be ever, Lord, with thee.

   Alleluia, alleluia! Glory be to God on high;
   Alleluia! To the Savior who has won the victory;
   Alleluia! To the Spirit, fount of love and sanctity:
   Alleluia, alleluia! To the Triune Majesty.

> *Christopher Wordsworth*

The Refrain for the Vespers Lessons
Those who trust in the LORD are like Mount Zion,* which cannot be moved, but
   stands fast for ever.

> *Psalm 125:1*

The Vespers Psalm   *You Have Dealt Graciously with Your Servant*
O LORD, you have dealt graciously with your servant,* according to your word.
Teach me discernment and knowledge,* for I have believed in your commandments.
Before I was afflicted I went astray,* but now I keep your word.

You are good and you bring forth good;* instruct me in your statutes.
The proud have smeared me with lies,* but I will keep your commandments with
my whole heart.
Their heart is gross and fat,* but my delight is in your law.
It is good for me that I have been afflicted,* that I might learn your statutes.
The law of your mouth is dearer to me* than thousands in gold and silver.

Psalm 119:65–72

The Refrain
Those who trust in the LORD are like Mount Zion,* which cannot be moved, but
stands fast for ever.

The Small Verse
The earth is the Lord's and all the fullness thereof, the world and we who dwell
within. Thanks be to God.

Traditional

The Lord's Prayer

The Prayer Appointed for the Week
I thank you, heavenly Father, that you have delivered me from the dominion of sin
and death and brought me into the kingdom of your Son; and I pray that, as by
his death he has recalled me to life, so by his love he may raise me to eternal
joys; who lives and reigns with you, in the unity of the Holy Spirit, one God,
now and for ever. *Amen.* †

The Concluding Prayer of the Church
May God himself order my days and make them acceptable in his sight. Blessed is
the Lord always, my strength and my redeemer.

Traditional

The Morning Office   **To Be Observed on the Hour or Half Hour**
                                Between 6 and 9 a.m.

The Call to Prayer
Sing to the LORD a new song;* sing to the LORD, all the whole earth.

Psalm 96:1

The Request for Presence
I call with my whole heart;* answer me, O LORD, that I may keep your statutes.

Psalm 119:145

The Greeting   *Te Deum*
Glory to you, Lord God of our fathers; you are worthy of praise; glory to you.
Glory to you for the radiance of your holy Name; we will praise you and
highly exalt you for ever. Glory to you in the splendor of your temple; on the
throne of your majesty, glory to you. Glory to you, seated between the
Cherubim; we will praise you and highly exalt you for ever. Glory to you,

beholding the depths; in the high vault of heaven, glory to you. Glory to you, Father, Son, and Holy Spirit; we will praise you and highly exalt you for ever.

The Refrain for the Morning Lessons
Righteousness shall go before him,* and peace shall be a pathway for his feet.

Psalm 85:13

A Reading
Jesus taught us, saying: "In truth I tell you, no one can see the kingdom of God without being born from above."

John 3:3

The Refrain
Righteousness shall go before him,* and peace shall be a pathway for his feet.

The Morning Psalm   *The LORD Will Bless Those Who Fear Him*
O Israel, trust in the LORD;* he is their help and their shield.
O house of Aaron, trust in the LORD;* he is their help and their shield.
You who fear the LORD, trust in the LORD;* he is their help and their shield.
The LORD has been mindful of us, and he will bless us;* he will bless the house of Israel; he will bless the house of Aaron;
He will bless those who fear the LORD,* both small and great together.

Psalm 115:9–13

The Refrain
Righteousness shall go before him,* and peace shall be a pathway for his feet.

The Gloria

The Lord's Prayer

The Prayer Appointed for the Week
I thank you, heavenly Father, that you have delivered me from the dominion of sin and death and brought me into the kingdom of your Son; and I pray that, as by his death he has recalled me to life, so by his love he may raise me to eternal joys; who lives and reigns with you, in the unity of the Holy Spirit, one God, now and for ever. *Amen.* †

The Concluding Prayer of the Church
Lord God, almighty and everlasting Father, you have brought me in safety to this new day: Preserve me with your mighty power, that I may not fall into sin, nor be overcome by adversity; and in all I do direct me to the fulfilling of your purpose; through Jesus Christ my Lord. *Amen.* †

The Midday Office   **To Be Observed on the Hour or Half Hour**
Between 11 a.m. and 2 p.m.

The Call to Prayer
Give thanks to the LORD, for he is good;* his mercy endures for ever.

Psalm 118:29

The Request for Presence
You are the LORD;* do not withhold your compassion from me; let your love and
your faithfulness keep me safe for ever,

Psalm 40:12

The Greeting
There is forgiveness with you;* therefore you shall be feared.

Psalm 130:3

The Refrain for the Midday Lessons
Keep watch over my life, for I am faithful;* save your servant who puts his trust in
you.

Psalm 86:2

A Reading
So then, as you received Jesus as Lord and Christ, now live your lives in him, be
rooted in him and built up on him, held firm by the faith you have been taught,
and overflowing with thanksgiving.

Colossians 2:6–7

The Refrain
Keep watch over my life, for I am faithful;* save your servant who puts his trust in
you.

The Midday Psalm   *Israel Would I Satisfy with Honey from the Rock*
Hear, O my people, and I will admonish you:* O Israel, if you would but listen to
me!
There shall be no strange god among you;* you shall not worship a foreign god.
I am the LORD your God, who brought you out of the land of Egypt and said,*
"Open your mouth wide, and I will fill it."
And yet my people did not hear my voice,* and Israel would not obey me.
So I gave them over to the stubbornness of their hearts,* to follow their own
devices.
Oh, that my people would listen to me!* that Israel would walk in my ways!
I should soon subdue their enemies* and turn my hand against their foes.
Those who hate the LORD would cringe before him,* and their punishment would
last for ever.
But Israel would I feed with the finest wheat* and satisfy him with honey from the
rock.

Psalm 81:8–16

The Refrain
Keep watch over my life, for I am faithful;* save your servant who puts his trust in
you.

The Cry of the Church
In the evening, in the morning, and at noonday, I will complain and lament,* and
he will hear my voice.

Psalm 55:18

The Lord's Prayer

The Prayer Appointed for the Week
I thank you, heavenly Father, that you have delivered me from the dominion of sin
and death and brought me into the kingdom of your Son; and I pray that, as by
his death he has recalled me to life, so by his love he may raise me to eternal
joys; who lives and reigns with you, in the unity of the Holy Spirit, one God,
now and for ever. *Amen.* †

The Concluding Prayer of the Church
Lord Jesus Christ, by your death you took away the sting of death: Grant me to so
follow in faith where you have led the way, that I may at length fall asleep peacefully in you and wake in your likeness; for your tender mercies' sake. *Amen.* †

The Vespers Office   **To Be Observed on the Hour or Half Hour**
                               Between 5 and 8 p.m.

The Call to Prayer
Behold now, bless the LORD, all you servants of the LORD,* you that stand by night
in the house of the LORD.

Psalm 134:1

The Request for Presence
My soul waits for the LORD, more than watchmen for the morning,* more than
watchmen for the morning.

Psalm 130:5

The Greeting
You, O LORD, are my lamp;* my God, you make my darkness bright.
With you I will break down an enclosure;* with the help of my God I will scale any
wall.

Psalm 18:29–30

The Hymn   *Song of Triumph*
The strife is over, the battle done,
The victory of life is won;
The song of triumph has begun.
Alleluia! Alleluia, alleluia, alleluia!

The powers of death have done their worst,
But Christ their legions has dispersed:
Let shout of holy joy outburst.
Alleluia! Alleluia, alleluia, alleluia!

Lord! By the stripes which wounded thee,
From death's dread sting your servants free,
That we may live and sing to thee.
Alleluia! Alleluia, alleluia, alleluia!

Latin, 17th C.

The Refrain for the Vespers Lessons
I lie down and go to sleep;* I wake again, because the LORD sustains me.

Psalm 3:5

The Vespers Psalm　　　　　　　　*For God Alone My Soul in Silence Waits*
For God alone my soul in silence waits;* truly, my hope is in him.
He alone is my rock and my salvation,* my stronghold, so that I shall not be
　shaken.
In God is my safety and my honor;* God is my strong rock and my refuge.
Put your trust in him always, O people,* pour out your hearts before him, for God
　is our refuge.

Psalm 62:6–9

The Refrain
I lie down and go to sleep;* I wake again, because the LORD sustains me.

The Cry of the Church
O Lamb of God, that takes away the sins of the world, have mercy upon me.
O Lamb of God, that takes away the sins of the world, have mercy upon me.
O Lamb of God, that takes away the sins of the world, grant me your peace.

The Lord's Prayer

The Prayer Appointed for the Week
I thank you, heavenly Father, that you have delivered me from the dominion of sin
　and death and brought me into the kingdom of your Son; and I pray that, as by
　his death he has recalled me to life, so by his love he may raise me to eternal
　joys; who lives and reigns with you, in the unity of the Holy Spirit, one God,
　now and for ever. *Amen.* †

The Concluding Prayer of the Church
Almighty and eternal God, so draw my heart to you, so guide my mind, so fill my
　imagination, so control my will, that I may be wholly yours, utterly dedicated
　to you; and then use me, I pray you, as you will, and always to your glory and
　the welfare of your people; through my Lord and Savior Jesus Christ. *Amen.* †

The Morning Office　　　　　　**To Be Observed on the Hour or Half Hour**
Between 6 and 9 a.m.

The Call to Prayer
Be glad, you righteous, and rejoice in the LORD;* shout for joy, all who are true of
　heart.

Psalm 32:12

The Request for Presence
Let the peoples praise you, O God;* let all the peoples praise you.
Let the nations be glad and sing for joy,* for you judge the peoples with equity and
　guide all the nations upon earth.
Let the peoples praise you, O God;* let all the peoples praise you.

Psalm 37:3–5

The Greeting

. . . * O Lord my God, I will give you thanks for ever.

Psalm 30:13

The Refrain for the Morning Lessons

Great things are they that you have done, O Lord my God! how great your wonders
and your plans for us!* there is none who can be compared with you.

Oh, that I could make them known and tell them!* but they are more than I can
count.

Psalm 40:5–6

A Reading

Jesus taught us, saying: "To you my friends I say: Do not be afraid of those who
kill the body and after this can do no more. I will tell you whom to fear: fear
him who, after he has killed, has the power to cast into hell. Yes, I tell you, he is
the one to fear."

Luke 12:4–5

The Refrain

Great things are they that you have done, O Lord my God! how great your wonders
and your plans for us!* there is none who can be compared with you.

Oh, that I could make them known and tell them!* but they are more than I can
count.

The Morning Psalm   *Shout with Joy to the Lord*

With his right hand and his holy arm* has he won for himself the victory.

The Lord has made known his victory;* his righteousness has he openly shown in
the sight of the nations.

He remembers his mercy and faithfulness to the house of Israel,* and all the ends
of the earth have seen the victory of our God.

Shout with joy to the Lord, all you lands;* lift up your voice, rejoice, and sing.

Sing to the Lord with the harp,* with the harp and the voice of song.

With trumpets and the sound of the horn* shout with joy before the King, the Lord.

Let the sea make a noise and all that is in it,* the lands and those who dwell
therein.

Let the rivers clap their hands,* and let the hills ring out with joy before the Lord,
when he comes to judge the earth.

In righteousness shall he judge the world* and the peoples with equity.

Psalm 98:2–10

The Refrain

Great things are they that you have done, O Lord my God! how great your wonders
and your plans for us!* there is none who can be compared with you.

Oh, that I could make them known and tell them!* but they are more than I can
count.

The Gloria

The Lord's Prayer

The Prayer Appointed for the Week

I thank you, heavenly Father, that you have delivered me from the dominion of sin
and death and brought me into the kingdom of your Son; and I pray that, as by
his death he has recalled me to life, so by his love he may raise me to eternal
joys; who lives and reigns with you, in the unity of the Holy Spirit, one God,
now and for ever. *Amen.* †

The Concluding Prayer of the Church

O God, you have caused the holy night to shine with the brightness of the true
Light: Grant that I, who have known the mystery of that Light on earth, may
also enjoin him perfectly in heaven; where with you and the Holy Spirit he
lives and reigns, one God, in glory everlasting. *Amen.* †

The Midday Office   **To Be Observed on the Hour or Half Hour**
                                       Between 11 a.m. and 2 p.m.

The Call to Prayer

Bless God in the congregation;* bless the LORD, you that are of the fountain of
Israel.

Psalm 68:26

The Request for Presence

I call upon you, O God, for you will answer me;* incline your ear to me and hear
my words.

Psalm 17:6

The Greeting

You are my God, and I will thank you;* you are my God, and I will exalt you.

Psalm 118:28

The Refrain for the Midday Lessons

The LORD, the God of gods, has spoken;* he has called the earth from the rising of
the sun to its setting.

Psalm 50:1

A Reading

This is the proof of love, that he laid down his life for us, and we too ought to lay
down our lives for our brothers. If anyone is well off in worldly possessions
and sees his brother in need but closes his heart to him, how can the love of
God remain in him?

1 John 3:16–17

The Refrain

The LORD, the God of gods, has spoken;* he has called the earth from the rising of
the sun to its setting.

The Midday Psalm   *Kingship Belongs to the LORD*

All the ends of the earth shall remember and turn to the LORD,* and all the families
of the nations shall bow before him.

For kingship belongs to the LORD;* he rules over the nations.
To him alone all who sleep in the earth bow down in worship;* who go down to the dust fall before him.
My soul shall live for him; my descendants shall serve him;* they shall be known as the LORD's for ever.
They shall come and make known to a people yet unborn* the saving deeds that he has done.

Psalm 22:26–30

The Refrain

The LORD, the God of gods, has spoken;* he has called the earth from the rising of the sun to its setting.

The Cry of the Church

Christ has died. Christ is risen. Christ will come again.

The Lord's Prayer

The Prayer Appointed for the Week

I thank you, heavenly Father, that you have delivered me from the dominion of sin and death and brought me into the kingdom of your Son; and I pray that, as by his death he has recalled me to life, so by his love he may raise me to eternal joys; who lives and reigns with you, in the unity of the Holy Spirit, one God, now and for ever. *Amen.* †

The Concluding Prayer of the Church

O God, the source of eternal light: Shed forth your unending day upon all of us who watch for you, that our lips may praise you, our lives may bless you, and our worship may give you glory; through Jesus Christ our Lord. *Amen.* †

The Vespers Office　　　　　　**To Be Observed on the Hour or Half Hour Between 5 and 8 p.m.**

The Call to Prayer

Let everything that has breath* praise the LORD. Hallelujah!

Psalm 150:6

The Request for Presence

O God, you are my God; eagerly I seek you;* my soul thirsts for you, my flesh faints for you, as in a barren and dry land where there is no water.
Therefore I have gazed upon you in your holy place,* that I might behold your power and your glory.

Psalm 63:1–2

The Greeting

Your loving-kindness is better than life itself;* my lips shall give you praise.
So will I bless you as long as I live* and lift up my hands in your Name.

Psalm 63:3–4

The Hymn   *God of Light*

Holy Spirit, God of light,   Give to every faithful soul
Fill us with your radiance bright;   Gifts of grace to make us whole;
Gentle father of the poor,   Help us when we come to die,
Make us, by your help secure;   So that we may live on high;
Come, your boundless grace impart,   Ever let your love descend,
Bring your love to every heart.   Give us joys that never end.

                                                        Stephen Langton

Lord of consolation, come,
Warm us when our hearts are numb;
Great consoler, come and heal,
To our souls your strength reveal;
Cool, refreshing comfort pour,
And our peace of mind restore.

The Refrain for the Vespers Lessons
The LORD is my light and my salvation; whom then shall I fear?* the LORD is the
    strength of my life; of whom then shall I be afraid?

                                                        Psalm 27:1

The Vespers Psalm   *With the Faithful, You Show Yourself Faithful, O LORD*
With the faithful you show yourself faithful, O God;* with the forthright you show
    yourself forthright.
With the pure you show yourself pure,* but with the crooked you are wily.
You will save a lowly people,* but you will humble the haughty eyes.
You, O LORD, are my lamp;* my God, you make my darkness bright.
With you I will break down an enclosure;* with the help of my God I will scale any
    wall.
As for God, his ways are perfect; the words of the LORD are tried in the fire;* he is a
    shield to all who trust in him.

                                                        Psalm 18:26–31

The Refrain
The LORD is my light and my salvation; whom then shall I fear?* the LORD is the
    strength of my life; of whom then shall I be afraid?

The Cry of the Church
O Lamb of God, that takes away the sins of the world, have mercy upon me.
O Lamb of God, that takes away the sins of the world, have mercy upon me.
O Lamb of God, that takes away the sins of the world, grant me your peace.

The Lord's Prayer

The Prayer Appointed for the Week
I thank you, heavenly Father, that you have delivered me from the dominion of sin
    and death and brought me into the kingdom of your Son; and I pray that, as by
    his death he has recalled me to life, so by his love he may raise me to eternal
    joys; who lives and reigns with you, in the unity of the Holy Spirit, one God,
    now and for ever. *Amen.* †

The Concluding Prayer of the Church
Almighty God, who after the creation of the world rested from all your works and
sanctified a day of rest for all your creatures: Grant that I, putting away all
earthly anxieties, may be duly prepared for the service of public worship, and
grant as well that my Sabbath upon earth may be a preparation for the eternal
rest promised to your people in heaven; through Jesus Christ our Lord. *Amen.* †

April Compline

Sunday
The Night Office   **To Be Observed Before Retiring**

The Call to Prayer
May the Lord Almighty grant me and those I love a peaceful night and a perfect
   end. *Amen.* †

The Request for Presence
Our help is in the Name of the Lord; the maker of heaven and earth.

The Greeting
Almighty God, my heavenly Father: I have sinned against you, through my own
   fault, in thought, and word, and deed, in what I have done and in what I have
   left undone. For the sake of your Son our Lord Jesus Christ, forgive me all my
   offenses; and grant that I may serve you in newness of life, to the glory of your
   Name. *Amen.* †

The Reading
The hand of YAHWEH was on me; he carried me away by the spirit of YAHWEH and
   set me down in the middle of the valley, a valley full of bones. He made me
   walk up and down and all around among them. There were vast quantities of
   these bones on the floor of the valley; and they were completely dry. He said to
   me, 'Son of man, can these bones live?' I said, 'You know, Lord YAHWEH.' He
   said, 'Prophesy over these bones, Say, "Dry bones, hear the word of YAHWEH.
   The Lord YAHWEH said to these bones I am now going to make breath enter
   you, and you will live. I shall put sinews on you, I shall make flesh grow on
   you, I shall cover you with skin and give you breath, and you will live; and you
   will know that I am YAHWEH." ' I prophesied as I had been ordered. While I
   was prophesying, there was a noise, a clattering sound; it was the bones coming together. And as I looked, they were covered with sinews; flesh was growing on them and skin was covering them, yet there was no breath in them. He
   said to me, 'Prophesy to the breath, prophesy, son of man. Say to the breath,
   "The Lord YAHWEH says this: Come four winds, breathe; breathe on these dead,
   so that they will come to life!" ' I prophesied as he had ordered me, and the
   breath entered them; they came to life and stood up on their feet, a great, and
   immense army. Then he said, 'Son of man, these bones are the whole House of
   Israel. They keep saying, "Our bones are dry, our hope has gone; we are done
   for." So, prophesy. Say to them, "The Lord YAHWEH says this: I am now going
   to open your graves; I shall raise you from your graves, my people, and lead
   you back to the soil of Israel. And you will know that I am YAHWEH, when I
   open your graves and raise you from your graves, my people, and put my
   spirit in you, and you revive, and I resettle you in your own soil. Then you will
   know that I, YAHWEH, have spoken and done this—declares the Lord
   YAHWEH." '

Ezekiel 37:1–14

The Gloria*

The Psalm   *He Commanded and They Were Created*

Praise the LORD from the heavens;* praise him in the heights.

Praise him, all you angels of his;* praise him, all his host.

Praise him, sun and moon;* praise him, all you shining stars.

Praise him, heaven of heavens,* and you waters above the heavens.

Let them praise the Name of the LORD;* for he commanded, and they were created.

He made them stand fast for ever and ever;* he gave them a law which shall not
     pass away.

Praise the LORD from the earth,* you sea-monsters and all deeps;

Fire and hail, snow and fog,* tempestuous wind, doing his will;

Mountains and all hills,* fruit trees and all cedars;

Wild beasts and all cattle,* creeping things and wingèd birds;

Kings of the earth and all peoples,* princes and all rulers of the world;

Young men and maidens,* old and young together.

Let them praise the Name of the LORD,* for his Name only is exalted, his splendor
     is over earth and heaven.

He has raised up strength for his people and praise for all his loyal servants,* the
     children of Israel, a people who are near him.

Psalm 148

*The Gloria**

The Small Verse

Into your hands, O Lord, I commend my spirit; for you have redeemed me, O
     Lord, O God of truth. Keep me, O Lord, as the apple of your eye; hide me
     under the shadow of your wings. †

The Lord's Prayer

The Petition

Keep watch, dear Lord, with those who work, or watch, or weep this night, and
     give your angels charge over those who sleep. Tend the sick, Lord Christ; give
     rest to the weary, bless the dying, soothe the suffering, pity the afflicted, shield
     the joyous; and all for your love's sake. *Amen.* †

The Final Thanksgiving

Lord, you now have set your servant free to go in peace as you have promised; for
     these eyes of mine have seen the Savior, whom you have prepared for all the
     world to see: a Light to enlighten the nations, and the glory of your people
     Israel. Glory to the Father, and to the Son, and to the Holy Spirit: as it was in the
     beginning, is now, and will be for ever. *Amen.*

Monday
The Night Office

To Be Observed Before Retiring

The Call to Prayer

May the Lord Almighty grant me and those I love a peaceful night and a perfect end. *Amen.* †

The Request for Presence

Our help is in the Name of the Lord; the maker of heaven and earth.

The Greeting

Almighty God, my heavenly Father: I have sinned against you, through my own fault, in thought, and word, and deed, in what I have done and in what I have left undone. For the sake of your Son our Lord Jesus Christ, forgive me all my offenses; and grant that I may serve you in newness of life, to the glory of your Name. *Amen.* †

The Reading   *From a Homily of St. John Chrysostom*

Although all the solemnities which are celebrated for God's honor in our churches are holy and venerable, most dearly beloved, nevertheless the day of the Lord's resurrection has a special festivity. And that because all other feasts are days of joy for the living only, but Easter's feast is one of happiness also for the dead. This solemnity is shared by those awaiting Him in hell as also by those still living, because rising from the dead, He wrought joy both there where He conquered death and there whither He returned as Victor. In that dreadful place of night where He tarried for three days, He retained inviolate the splendor of His majesty and shone with the glory of His eternal nature. Light was not overcome by darkness, but darkness was overcome by Light. Let us therefore rejoice, most dearly beloved, and be glad in the Lord; for on Easter the Light of salvation is given to us by the Lord according to that which the psalmist has written: God is the Lord, and He has illumined us.

adapted from THE SHORT BREVIARY

The Gloria*

The Psalm   *Restore Us, O God of Hosts*

Restore us, O God of hosts;* show the light of your countenance, and we shall be saved.

Let your hand be upon the man of your right hand,* the son of man you have made so strong for yourself.

And so will we never turn away from you;* give us life, that we may call upon your Name.

Restore us, O LORD God of hosts;* show the light of your countenance, and we shall be saved.

Psalm 80:7, 16–18

The Gloria*

The Small Verse

Into your hands, O Lord, I commend my spirit; For you have redeemed me, O
Lord, O God of truth. Keep me, O Lord, as the apple of your eye; Hide me
under the shadow of your wings. †

The Lord's Prayer

The Petition

Keep watch, dear Lord, with those who work, or watch, or weep this night, and
give your angels charge over those who sleep. Tend the sick, Lord Christ; give
rest to the weary, bless the dying, soothe the suffering, pity the afflicted, shield
the joyous; and all for your love's sake. *Amen.* †

The Final Thanksgiving

Lord, you now have set your servant free to go in peace as you have promised; for
these eyes of mine have seen the Savior, whom you have prepared for all the
world to see: a Light to enlighten the nations, and the glory of your people
Israel. Glory to the Father, and to the Son, and to the Holy Spirit: as it was in the
beginning, is now, and will be for ever. *Amen.*

Tuesday
The Night Office   To Be Observed Before Retiring

The Call to Prayer

May the Lord Almighty grant me and those I love a peaceful night and a perfect
end. *Amen.* †

The Request for Presence

Our help is in the Name of the Lord; the maker of heaven and earth.

The Greeting

Almighty God, my heavenly Father: I have sinned against you, through my own
fault, in thought, and word, and deed, in what I have done and in what I have
left undone. For the sake of your Son our Lord Jesus Christ, forgive me all my
offenses; and grant that I may serve you in newness of life, to the glory of your
Name. *Amen.* †

The Reading

To do religious exercises without their essential meaning is a dangerous
thing . . . Playing at religion has always been one of its subtle temptations. It
can offer a false sense of peace and righteousness, covering up an untapped

corruption of the human heart. The words of the prophets could not be clearer. Such religion is an abomination before God!

Fr. Hal M. Helms

The Gloria*

The Psalm   *We Shall Receive a Blessing from the* Lord

"Those who have clean hands and a pure heart,* who have not pledged themselves to falsehood, nor sworn by what is a fraud.

They shall receive a blessing from the Lord* and a just reward from the God of their salvation."

Such is the generation of those who seek him,* of those who seek your face, O God of Jacob.

Psalm 24:4–6

The Gloria*

The Small Verse

Into your hands, O Lord, I commend my spirit; For you have redeemed me, O Lord, O God of truth. Keep me, O Lord, as the apple of your eye; Hide me under the shadow of your wings. †

The Lord's Prayer

The Petition

Keep watch, dear Lord, with those who work, or watch, or weep this night, and give your angels charge over those who sleep. Tend the sick, Lord Christ; give rest to the weary, bless the dying, soothe the suffering, pity the afflicted, shield the joyous; and all for your love's sake. *Amen.* †

The Final Thanksgiving

Lord, you now have set your servant free to go in peace as you have promised; for these eyes of mine have seen the Savior, whom you have prepared for all the world to see: a Light to enlighten the nations, and the glory of your people Israel. Glory to the Father, and to the Son, and to the Holy Spirit: as it was in the beginning, is now, and will be for ever. *Amen.*

Wednesday
The Night Office   To Be Observed Before Retiring

The Call to Prayer

May the Lord Almighty grant me and those I love a peaceful night and a perfect end. *Amen.* †

The Request for Presence
Our help is in the Name of the Lord; the maker of heaven and earth.

The Greeting
Almighty God, my heavenly Father: I have sinned against you, through my own
    fault, in thought, and word, and deed, in what I have done and in what I have
    left undone. For the sake of your Son our Lord Jesus Christ, forgive me all my
    offenses; and grant that I may serve you in newness of life, to the glory of your
    Name. *Amen.* †

The Reading
For we are the rind and the leaf.
The great death, that each of us carries inside, is the fruit.
Everything enfolds it.

Ranier Rilke

*The Gloria**

The Psalm   *He Revives My Soul*
The LORD is my shepherd;* I shall not be in want.
He makes me lie down in green pastures* and leads me beside still waters.
He revives my soul* and guides me along right pathways for his Name's sake.
Though I walk through the valley of the shadow of death, I shall fear no evil;* for
    you are with me; your rod and your staff, they comfort me.
You spread a table before me in the presence of those who trouble me;* you have
    anointed my head with oil, and my cup is running over.
Surely your goodness and mercy shall follow me all the days of my life,* and I will
    dwell in the house of the LORD for ever.

Psalm 23

*The Gloria**

The Small Verse
Into your hands, O Lord, I commend my spirit; For you have redeemed me, O
    Lord, O God of truth. Keep me, O Lord, as the apple of your eye; Hide me
    under the shadow of your wings. †

The Lord's Prayer

The Petition
Keep watch, dear Lord, with those who work, or watch, or weep this night, and
    give your angels charge over those who sleep. Tend the sick, Lord Christ; give
    rest to the weary, bless the dying, soothe the suffering, pity the afflicted, shield
    the joyous; and all for your love's sake. *Amen.* †

The Final Thanksgiving
Lord, you now have set your servant free to go in peace as you have promised; for
    these eyes of mine have seen the Savior, whom you have prepared for all the
    world to see: a Light to enlighten the nations, and the glory of your people

Israel. Glory to the Father, and to the Son, and to the Holy Spirit: as it was in the beginning, is now, and will be for ever. *Amen.*

❧

Thursday
The Night Office   To Be Observed Before Retiring

The Call to Prayer

May the Lord Almighty grant me and those I love a peaceful night and a perfect
    end. *Amen.* †

The Request for Presence

Our help is in the Name of the Lord; the maker of heaven and earth.

The Greeting

Almighty God, my heavenly Father: I have sinned against you, through my own
    fault, in thought, and word, and deed, in what I have done and in what I have
    left undone. For the sake of your Son our Lord Jesus Christ, forgive me all my
    offenses; and grant that I may serve you in newness of life, to the glory of your
    Name. *Amen.* †

The Reading

Surely I know the spring that swiftly flows
Even during the night.

The eternal spring is deeply hidden,
But surely I know the place where it begins
Even during the night.

I don't know its source because it has none
But know that all beginnings come from this one,
Even during the night.

I do know that nothing can equal its beauty
And that from it both heaven and earth drink
Even during the night.

I know there is no limit to its depth
And that no one can wade across its breadth,
Even during the night.

Its brightness is never clouded over,
And I know that from it all light flows,
Even during the night.

I know its current is so forceful
That it floods the nations, heaven, and hell,
Even during the night.

The current that is born of this stream,
I know, is powerful and strong,
Even during the night.

The living stream that I so desire,
I see it in this bread of life,
Even during the night.

> *St. John of the Cross*

The Gloria*

The Psalm   *Bless the LORD*
Behold now, bless the LORD, all you servants of the LORD,* you that stand by night
   in the house of the LORD.
Lift up your hands in the holy place and bless the LORD;* the LORD who made
   heaven and earth bless you out of Zion.

> *Psalm 134*

The Gloria*

The Small Verse
Into your hands, O Lord, I commend my spirit; For you have redeemed me, O
   Lord, O God of truth. Keep me, O Lord, as the apple of your eye; Hide me
   under the shadow of your wings. †

The Lord's Prayer

The Petition
Keep watch, dear Lord, with those who work, or watch, or weep this night, and
   give your angels charge over those who sleep. Tend the sick, Lord Christ; give
   rest to the weary, bless the dying, soothe the suffering, pity the afflicted, shield
   the joyous; and all for your love's sake. *Amen.* †

The Final Thanksgiving
Lord, you now have set your servant free to go in peace as you have promised; for
   these eyes of mine have seen the Savior, whom you have prepared for all the
   world to see: a Light to enlighten the nations, and the glory of your people
   Israel. Glory to the Father, and to the Son, and to the Holy Spirit: as it was in the
   beginning, is now, and will be for ever. *Amen.*

Friday
The Night Office   **To Be Observed Before Retiring**

The Call to Prayer
May the Lord Almighty grant me and those I love a peaceful night and a perfect
     end. *Amen.* †

The Request for Presence
Our help is in the Name of the Lord; the maker of heaven and earth.

The Greeting
Almighty God, my heavenly Father: I have sinned against you, through my own
     fault, in thought, and word, and deed, in what I have done and in what I have
     left undone. For the sake of your Son our Lord Jesus Christ, forgive me all my
     offenses; and grant that I may serve you in newness of life, to the glory of your
     Name. *Amen.* †

A Reading   *Litany of Penitence*
Most holy and merciful Father:
I confess to you and to the whole communion of saints
in heaven and on earth,
that I have sinned by my own fault
in thought, word, and deed;
by what I have done, and by what I have left undone.

I have not loved you with my whole heart, and mind, and strength. I have not
     loved my neighbors
as myself. I have not forgiven others, as I have been forgiven.
Have mercy on me, Lord.

I have been deaf to your call to serve, as Christ served us. I have not been true to
     the mind of
Christ. I have grieved your Holy Spirit.
Have mercy on me, Lord.

I confess to you, Lord, all my past unfaithfulness: the pride, hypocrisy, and impa-
     tience of my life.
I confess to you, Lord.

My self-indulgent appetites and ways, and my exploitation of other people,
I confess to you, Lord.

My anger at my own frustration, and my envy of those more fortunate than I,
I confess to you, Lord.

My intemperate love of worldly goods and comforts, and my dishonesty in daily
     life and work,
I confess to you, Lord.

My negligence in prayer and worship, and my failure to commend the faith that is
   in me,
I confess to you, Lord.

Accept my repentance, Lord, for the wrongs I have done: for my blindness to
   human need and
suffering, and my indifference to injustice and cruelty,
Accept my repentance, Lord.

For all false judgments, for uncharitable thoughts toward my neighbors, and for
   my prejudice and
contempt toward those who differ from me,
Accept my repentance, Lord.

For my waste and pollution of your creation, and my lack of concern for those
   who come after us,
Accept my repentance, Lord.
Restore me, good Lord, and let your anger depart from me,
Favorably hear me for your mercy is great.

Accomplish in me and all of your church the work of your salvation,
That I may show forth your glory in the world.

By the cross and passion of your Son our Lord,
Bring me with all your saints to the joy of his resurrection. †

The Gloria*

The Psalm   *I Shall Keep Your Law*
Teach me, O LORD, the way of your statutes,* and I shall keep it to the end.
Give me understanding, and I shall keep your law;* I shall keep it with all my
   heart.

                                                              Psalm 119:33–34

The Gloria*

The Small Verse
Into your hands, O Lord, I commend my spirit; for you have redeemed me, O
   Lord, O God of truth. Keep me, O Lord, as the apple of your eye; hide me
   under the shadow of your wings. †

The Lord's Prayer

The Petition
Keep watch, dear Lord, with those who work, or watch, or weep this night, and
   give your angels charge over those who sleep. Tend the sick, Lord Christ; give
   rest to the weary, bless the dying, soothe the suffering, pity the afflicted, shield
   the joyous; and all for your love's sake. *Amen.* †

The Final Thanksgiving

Lord, you now have set your servant free to go in peace as you have promised; for these eyes of mine have seen the Savior, whom you have prepared for all the world to see: a Light to enlighten the nations, and the glory of your people Israel. Glory to the Father, and to the Son, and to the Holy Spirit: as it was in the beginning, is now, and will be for ever. *Amen.*

Saturday

The Night Office   **To Be Observed Before Retiring**

The Call to Prayer

May the Lord Almighty grant me and those I love a peaceful night and a perfect end. *Amen.* †

The Request for Presence

Our help is in the Name of the Lord; the maker of heaven and earth.

The Greeting

Almighty God, my heavenly Father: I have sinned against you, through my own fault, in thought, and word, and deed, in what I have done and in what I have left undone. For the sake of your Son our Lord Jesus Christ, forgive me all my offenses; and grant that I may serve you in newness of life, to the glory of your Name. *Amen.* †

The Reading

Rejoice, O Queen of heaven.
> For he whom you were worthy to bear
> Will arise as he promised.
> Pray for us to the Father.

Rejoice and be glad, O Virgin Mary.
> Rejoice and be glad.

O God,
Who by the resurrection of your Son, our Lord Jesus Christ,
Gave joy to the world,
Grant that through his Mother, the Virgin Mary,
We may obtain the joys of everlasting life;
Through the same Christ our Lord.
Amen.

Clasp the feet of Christ
>And pray through the Mother of God and all the saints,
>And all will be well.

>>*adapted from Avvakum the Archpriest*

The Gloria*

The Psalm   *The Sacrifice of God Is a Troubled Spirit*
Create in me a clean heart, O God,* and renew a right spirit within me.

Cast me not away from your presence* and take not your holy Spirit from me.

Give me the joy of your saving help again* and sustain me with your bountiful
>Spirit.

I shall teach your ways to the wicked,* and sinners shall return to you.

Deliver me from death, O God,* and my tongue shall sing of your righteousness,
>O God of my salvation.

Open my lips, O Lord,* and my mouth shall proclaim your praise.

Had you desired it, I would have offered sacrifice,* but you take no delight in
>burnt-offerings.

The sacrifice of God is a troubled spirit;* a broken and contrite heart, O God, you
>will not despise.

>>*Psalm 51:11–18*

The Gloria*

The Small Verse
Into your hands, O Lord, I commend my spirit; For you have redeemed me, O
>Lord, O God of truth. Keep me, O Lord, as the apple of your eye; Hide me
>under the shadow of your wings. †

The Lord's Prayer

The Petition
Keep watch, dear Lord, with those who work, or watch, or weep this night, and
>give your angels charge over those who sleep. Tend the sick, Lord Christ; give
>rest to the weary, bless the dying, soothe the suffering, pity the afflicted, shield
>the joyous; and all for your love's sake. *Amen.* †

The Final Thanksgiving
Lord, you now have set your servant free to go in peace as you have promised; for
>these eyes of mine have seen the Savior, whom you have prepared for all the
>world to see: a Light to enlighten the nations, and the glory of your people
>Israel. Glory to the Father, and to the Son, and to the Holy Spirit: as it was in the
>beginning, is now, and will be for ever. *Amen.*

The Gloria
Glory be to God the Father, God the Son, and God the Holy Spirit. As it was
in the beginning, so it is now and so it shall ever be, world without end.
Alleluia.* *Amen.*

The Lord's Prayer
Our Father, who art in heaven, hallowed be your Name.
May your kingdom come, and your will be done, on earth as in heaven.
Give us today our daily bread.
Forgive us our sins as we forgive those who sin against us.
Lead us not into temptation, but deliver us from evil;
for yours are the kingdom and the power and the glory
forever and ever. *Amen.*

Compline Prayers for May Are Located on Page 651.

The Following Holy Days Occur in May:
The Feast of St. Phillip and St. James, Apostles: *May 1*
The Feast of the Visitation of the Blessed Virgin Mary: *May 31*

*The Gloria is omitted during Lent by many Christian communities. "Alleluia" is
always omitted from every part of the Church's worship during Lent;
the use of both is restored at Easter.

May

The Morning Office   To Be Observed on the Hour or Half Hour
                                                  Between 6 and 9 a.m.

The Call to Prayer

Be glad, you righteous, and rejoice in the LORD;* shout for joy, all who are true of
    heart.

Psalm 32:12

The Request for Presence

May God be merciful to us and bless us,* show us the light of his countenance and
    come to us.

Psalm 67:1

The Greeting

Out of Zion, perfect in its beauty,* God reveals himself in glory.

Psalm 50:2

The Refrain for the Morning Lessons

Let the words of my mouth and the meditation of my heart be acceptable in your
    sight,* O LORD, my strength and my redeemer.

Psalm 19:14

A Reading

He now went up the mountain and summoned those he wanted. So they came to
    him and he appointed twelve; they were to be his companions and to be sent
    out to proclaim the message, with the power to drive out devils. And so he
    appointed the Twelve, Simon to whom he gave the name Peter, James the son
    of Zebedee and John the brother of James, to whom he gave the name
    Boangeres or 'Sons of Thunder'; Andrew, Philip, Bartholomew, Matthew,
    Thomas, James the son of Alphaeus, Thaddeus, Simon the Zealot and Judas
    Iscariot, the man who was to betray him.

Mark 3:13–19

The Refrain

Let the words of my mouth and the meditation of my heart be acceptable in your
    sight,* O LORD, my strength and my redeemer.

The Morning Psalm   *I Will Establish Your Line For Ever*

"I have made a covenant with my chosen one;* I have sworn an oath to David my
    servant:
'I will establish your line for ever,* and preserve your throne for all generations.' "
The heavens bear witness to your wonders, O LORD,* and to your faithfulness in
    the assembly of the holy ones;
For who in the skies can be compared to the LORD?* who is like the LORD among
    the gods?
God is much to be feared in the council of the holy ones,* great and terrible to all
    those round about him.

Who is like you, Lord God of hosts?* O mighty Lord, your faithfulness is all
around you.

Psalm 89:3–8

The Refrain
Let the words of my mouth and the meditation of my heart be acceptable in your
sight,* O Lord, my strength and my redeemer.

The Small Verse
Blessed be the Lord God of Israel for he has visited and delivered us. Amen, amen,
amen.

Traditional

The Lord's Prayer

The Prayer Appointed for the Week
Almighty Father who gave your only Son to die for our sins and to rise for our justification: Give me grace so to put away the leaven of malice and wickedness,
that I may always serve you in pureness of living and truth; through Jesus
Christ your Son my Lord, who lives and reigns with you and the Holy Spirit,
one God, now and for ever. *Amen.* †

The Concluding Prayer of the Church
Lord God, almighty and everlasting Father, you have brought me in safety to this
new day: Preserve me with your mighty power, that I may not fall into sin, nor
be overcome by adversity; and in all I do direct me to the fulfilling of your purpose; through Jesus Christ my Lord. *Amen.* †

The Midday Office	To Be Observed on the Hour or Half Hour
	Between 11 a.m. and 2 p.m.

The Call to Prayer
Blessed be the Lord for evermore!* Amen, I say, Amen.

Psalm 89:52

The Request for Presence
May the graciousness of the Lord our God be upon us;* prosper the work of our
hands; prosper our handiwork.

Psalm 90:17

The Greeting
Whom have I in heaven but you?* and having you I desire nothing upon earth.

Psalm 73:25

The Refrain for the Midday Lessons
"I will instruct you and teach you in the way that you should go;* I will guide you
with my eye.

Do not be like horse or mule, which have no understanding;* who must be fitted
with bit and bridle, or else they will not stay near you."

Psalm 32:9–10

A Reading

How then are they to call on him if they have not come to believe in him? And
how can they believe in him if they have never heard of him? And how will
they hear of him unless there is a preacher for them? And how will there be
preachers if they are not sent? As scripture says: *How beautiful are the feet of the
messenger of good news.*

Romans 10:14–15

The Refrain

"I will instruct you and teach you in the way that you should go;* I will guide you
with my eye.
Do not be like horse or mule, which have no understanding;* who must be fitted
with bit and bridle, or else they will not stay near you."

The Midday Psalm   *In the Temple of the Lord All Are Crying, "Glory!"*

Ascribe to the Lord, you gods,* ascribe to the Lord glory and strength.
Ascribe to the Lord the glory due his Name;* worship the Lord in the beauty of
holiness.
The voice of the Lord is upon the waters; the God of glory thunders;* the Lord is
upon the mighty waters.
The voice of the Lord is a powerful voice;* the voice of the Lord is a voice of
splendor.
The voice of the Lord breaks the cedar trees;* the Lord breaks the cedars of
Lebanon;
He makes Lebanon skip like a calf,* and Mount Hermon like a young wild ox.
The voice of the Lord splits the flames of fire; the voice of the Lord shakes the
wilderness;* the Lord shakes the wilderness of Kadesh.
The voice of the Lord makes the oak trees writhe* and strips the forests bare.
And in the temple of the Lord* all are crying, "Glory!"
The Lord sits enthroned above the flood;* the Lord sits enthroned as King for
evermore.
The Lord shall give strength to his people;* the Lord shall give his people the
blessing of peace.

Psalm 29

The Refrain

"I will instruct you and teach you in the way that you should go;* I will guide you
with my eye.
Do not be like horse or mule, which have no understanding;* who must be fitted
with bit and bridle, or else they will not stay near you."

The Small Verse
My help is in the name of the Lord who made heaven and earth and all that is in them. Thanks be to God.

Traditional

The Lord's Prayer

The Prayer Appointed for the Week
Almighty Father who gave your only Son to die for our sins and to rise for our justification: Give me grace so to put away the leaven of malice and wickedness, that I may always serve you in pureness of living and truth; through Jesus Christ your Son my Lord, who lives and reigns with you and the Holy Spirit, one God, now and for ever. *Amen.* †

The Concluding Prayer of the Church
O God, you make me glad with the weekly remembrance of the glorious resurrection of your Son my Lord: Give me this day such blessing through my worship of you, that the week to come may be spent in your favor; through Jesus Christ our Lord. *Amen.* †

The Vespers Office   **To Be Observed on the Hour or Half Hour Between 5 and 8 p.m.**

The Call to Prayer
Open my lips, O Lord,* and my mouth shall proclaim your praise.

Psalm 51:16

The Request for Presence
Hear, O Lord, and have mercy upon me;* O Lord, be my helper."

Psalm 30:11

The Greeting
Blessed be the Lord God, the God of Israel,* who alone does wondrous deeds! And blessed be his glorious Name for ever!* and may all the earth be filled with his glory. Amen. Amen.

Psalm 72:18–19

The Hymn
Come sing, you choirs exultant, those messengers of God
Through whom the living message came sounding all abroad!
Whose voices proclaimed salvation that poured upon the night,
And drove away the shadows, and filled the world with light.

In one harmonious witness the chosen twelve combine,
While each his own commission fulfills in every line;
As, in the prophets' vision from out the amber flame
In mystic form and image as evangels they came.

Full-square on this foundation the Church of Christ remains,
A house to stand unshaken by floods or winds or rains.
How blessed this habitation of gospel liberty,
Where with a holy people God dwells in Unity.

Latin, 12th C.

The Refrain for the Vespers Lessons

It is better to rely on the LORD* than to put any trust in flesh.
It is better to rely on the LORD* than to put any trust in rulers.

Psalm 118:8–9

The Vespers Psalm   *This God Is Our God For Ever*

Your praise, like your Name, O God, reaches to the world's end;* your right hand
    is full of justice.
Let Mount Zion be glad and the cities of Judah rejoice,* because of your judgments.
Make the circuit of Zion; walk round about her;* count the number of her towers.
Consider well her bulwarks; examine her strongholds;* that you may tell those
    who come after.
This God is our God for ever and ever;* he shall be our guide for evermore.

Psalm 48:9–13

The Refrain

It is better to rely on the LORD* than to put any trust in flesh.
It is better to rely on the LORD* than to put any trust in rulers.

The Small Verse

Their sound goes forth to all the earth and their speech to the end of the world.

adapted from THE SHORT BREVIARY

The Lord's Prayer

The Prayer Appointed for the Week

Almighty Father who gave your only Son to die for our sins and to rise for our jus-
    tification: Give me grace so to put away the leaven of malice and wickedness,
    that I may always serve you in pureness of living and truth; through Jesus
    Christ your Son my Lord, who lives and reigns with you and the Holy Spirit,
    one God, now and for ever. *Amen.* †

The Concluding Prayer of the Church

O God, who makes me glad by the yearly festival of Your apostles Philip and James,
    I ask that all who rejoice in their merits may be taught by their example. *Amen.*

adapted from THE SHORT BREVIARY

The Morning Office   **To Be Observed on the Hour or Half Hour**
Between 6 and 9 a.m.

The Call to Prayer

Bless God in the congregation;* bless the LORD, you that are of the fountain of Israel.

Psalm 68:26

The Request for Presence
Arise, O God, maintain your cause.*
Psalm 74:21

The Greeting
Deliver me, O LORD, by your hand* from those whose portion in life is this world.
Psalm 17:14

The Refrain for the Morning Lessons
God looks down from heaven upon us all,* to see if there is any who is wise, if there is one who seeks after God.
Psalm 53:2

A Reading   *The Church celebrates on May 1 the lives of St. Philip and St. James, both members of the original circle of twelve disciples. James, (known as "James the Less" and as "the son of Alphaeus") and Philip remained fairly obscure during their lives, preferring apparently to further the Church and not their own fame.*

Thomas said, 'Lord, we do not know where you are going, so how can we know the way?' Jesus said: 'I am the Way; I am Truth and Life. No one can come to the Father except through me. If you know me, you will know my Father too. From this moment you know him and have seen him.' Philip said, 'Lord, show us the Father and then we shall be satisfied.' Jesus said to him, 'Have I been with you all this time, Philip, and you still do not know me? Anyone who has seen me has seen the Father . . .'
John 14:5–9

The Refrain
God looks down from heaven upon us all,* to see if there is any who is wise, if there is one who seeks after God.

The Morning Psalm   *Your Commandments Are My Desire*
Teach me, O LORD, the way of your statutes,* and I shall keep it to the end.
Give me understanding, and I shall keep your law;* I shall keep it with all my heart.
Make me go in the path of your commandments,* for that is my desire.
Incline my heart to your decrees* and not to unjust gain.
Turn my eyes from watching what is worthless;* give me life in your ways.
Fulfill your promise to your servant,* which you make to those who fear you.
Turn away the reproach which I dread,* because your judgments are good.
Behold, I long for your commandments;* in your righteousness preserve my life.
Psalm 119:33–40

The Refrain
God looks down from heaven upon us all,* to see if there is any who is wise, if there is one who seeks after God.

The Cry of the Church
Bless the Lord, O my soul, and forget not all his benefits.

The Lord's Prayer

The Prayer Appointed for the Week
Almighty Father who gave your only Son to die for our sins and to rise for our justification: Give me grace so to put away the leaven of malice and wickedness,
that I may always serve you in pureness of living and truth; through Jesus
Christ your Son my Lord, who lives and reigns with you and the Holy Spirit,
one God, now and for ever. *Amen.* †

The Concluding Prayer of the Church
Almighty God, who gave to your apostles Philip and James grace and strength to
bear witness to the truth: Grant that I, being mindful of their victory of faith,
may glorify in life and death the Name of my Lord Jesus Christ; who lives and
reigns with you and the Holy Spirit, one God, now and for ever. *Amen.* †

The Midday Office **To Be Observed on the Hour or Half Hour**
Between 11 a.m. and 2 p.m.

The Call to Prayer
Sing to the LORD a new song,* for he has done marvelous things.

Psalm 98:1

The Request for Presence
Remember me, O LORD, with the favor you have for your people,* and visit me
with your saving help;
That I may see the prosperity of your elect* and be glad with the gladness of your
people, that I may glory with your inheritance.

Psalm 106:4–5

The Greeting
Your righteousness, O God, reaches to the heavens;* you have done great things;
who is like you, O God?

Psalm 71:19

The Refrain for the Midday Lessons
I will sing to the LORD as long as I live;* I will praise my God while I have my
being.

Psalm 104:34

A Reading
So from the Mount of Olives, as it was called, they went back to Jerusalem, a short
distance away, no more than a Sabbath walk; and when they reached the city
they went to the upper room where they were staying; there were Peter and
John, James and Andrew, Philip and Thomas, Bartholomew and Matthew,
James son of Alphaeus and Simon the Zealot, and Jude son of James. With one

heart all these joined constantly in prayer, together with some women, including Mary the mother of Jesus, and with his brothers.

Acts 1:12–14

The Refrain
I will sing to the LORD as long as I live;* I will praise my God while I have my being.

The Midday Psalm
Come, Let Us Shout for Joy

Come, let us sing to the LORD;* let us shout for joy to the Rock of our salvation.
Let us come before his presence with thanksgiving* and raise a loud shout to him with psalms.
For the LORD is a great God,* and a great King above all gods.
In his hand are the caverns of the earth,* and the heights of the hills are his also.
The sea is his, for he made it,* and his hands have molded the dry land.

Psalm 95:1–5

The Refrain
I will sing to the LORD as long as I live;* I will praise my God while I have my being.

The Cry of the Church
Even so come, Lord Jesus!

The Lord's Prayer

The Prayer Appointed for the Week
Almighty Father who gave your only Son to die for our sins and to rise for our justification: Give me grace so to put away the leaven of malice and wickedness, that I may always serve you in pureness of living and truth; through Jesus Christ your Son my Lord, who lives and reigns with you and the Holy Spirit, one God, now and for ever. *Amen.* †

The Concluding Prayer of the Church
O God, by your Holy Spirit you give to some the word of wisdom, to others the word of knowledge, and to others the word of faith: I praise your Name for the gifts of grace manifested in your servants Philip and James, and pray that your Church may never be destitute of such gifts; through Jesus Christ my Lord, who with you and the Holy Spirit lives and reigns, one God, for ever and ever. *Amen.* †

The Vespers Office **To Be Observed on the Hour or Half Hour Between 5 and 8 p.m.**

The Call to Prayer
Be joyful in God, all you lands;* sing the glory of his Name; sing the glory of his praise.
Say to God, "How awesome are your deeds! . . .
All the earth bows down before you,* sings to you, sings out your Name."

Psalm 66:1–3

The Request for Presence
Be not far away, O Lord;* you are my strength; hasten to help me.

Psalm 22:18

The Greeting
Blessed is the Lord!* for he has heard the voice of my prayer.

Psalm 28:7

The Hymn   *For All the Saints*

For all the saints, who from their labors rest,
Who you by faith before the world confessed,
Your name, O Jesus, be forever blessed.

You were their rock, their fortress, and their might;
You, Lord, their captain in the well-fought fight;
You, in the darkness drear, their one true light.

O blessed communion, fellowship divine!
We feebly struggle, they in glory shine;
Yet all are one in you, for all are thine.

And when strife is fierce, the warfare long,
Steals on the ear the distant triumph song,
And hearts are brave again, and arms are strong.

From earth's wide bounds, from ocean's farthest coast,
Through gates of pearl come forth the countless host,
Singing to the Father, Son, and Holy Ghost:
Alleluia! Alleluia!

William How

The Refrain for the Vespers Lessons
Turn again to your rest, O my soul,* for the Lord has treated you well.
For you have rescued my life from death,* my eyes from tears, and my feet from
   stumbling.

Psalm 116:6–7

The Vespers Psalm   *All the Lord's Works Are Sure*
Rejoice in the Lord, you righteous;* it is good for the just to sing praises.
Praise the Lord with the harp;* play to him upon the psaltery and lyre.
Sing for him a new song;* sound a fanfare with all your skill upon the trumpet.
For the word of the Lord is right,* and all his works are sure.
He loves righteousness and justice;* the loving-kindness of the Lord fills the
   whole earth.

Psalm 33:1–5

The Refrain
Turn again to your rest, O my soul,* for the Lord has treated you well.
For you have rescued my life from death,* my eyes from tears, and my feet from
   stumbling.

The Cry of the Church
O Lord, hear my prayer and let my cry come unto you. Thanks be to God.
THE SHORT BREVIARY

The Lord's Prayer

The Prayer Appointed for the Week
Almighty Father who gave your only Son to die for our sins and to rise for our justification: Give me grace so to put away the leaven of malice and wickedness,
that I may always serve you in pureness of living and truth; through Jesus
Christ your Son my Lord, who lives and reigns with you and the Holy Spirit,
one God, now and for ever. *Amen.* †

The Concluding Prayer of the Church
Almighty God, you gave your servants Philip and James special gifts of grace to
understand and teach the truth as it is in Christ Jesus: Grant that by this teaching I may know you, the one true God, and Jesus Christ whom you have sent;
who lives and reigns with you and the Holy Spirit, one God, for ever and ever.
Amen. †

The Morning Office   **To Be Observed on the Hour or Half Hour**
                                Between 6 and 9 a.m.

The Call to Prayer
Come and listen, all you who fear God,* and I will tell you what he has done
for me.
Psalm 66:14

The Request for Presence
May God be merciful to us and bless us,* show us the light of his countenance and
come to us.
Let your ways be known upon earth,* your saving health among all nations.
Psalm 67:1–2

The Greeting
. . . you, O God, have heard my vows;* you have granted me the heritage of those
who fear your Name.
Psalm 61:5

The Refrain for the Morning Lessons
Create in me a clean heart, O God,* and renew a right spirit within me.
Psalm 51:11

A Reading
Jesus raised his eyes to heaven and said: "Father, the hour has come . . . I have glorified you on earth by finishing the work that you gave me to do. Now, Father,
glorify me with that glory I had with you before ever the world existed."
John 17:1, 4–5

The Refrain
Create in me a clean heart, O God,* and renew a right spirit within me.

The Morning Psalm   *Your Promise Gives Me Life*
Remember your word to your servant,* because you have given me hope.
This is my comfort in my trouble,* that your promise gives me life.
The proud have derided me cruelly,* but I have not turned from your law.
When I remember your judgments of old,* LORD, I take great comfort.
I am filled with a burning rage,* because of the wicked who forsake your law.
Your statutes have been like songs to me* wherever I have lived as a stranger.
I remember your Name in the night, O LORD,* and dwell upon your law.
This is how it has been with me,* because I have kept your commandments.

Psalm 119:49–56

The Refrain
Create in me a clean heart, O God,* and renew a right spirit within me.

The Cry of the Church
Even so come, Lord Jesus!

The Lord's Prayer

The Prayer Appointed for the Week
Almighty Father who gave your only Son to die for our sins and to rise for our jus-
    tification: Give me grace so to put away the leaven of malice and wickedness,
    that I may always serve you in pureness of living and truth; through Jesus
    Christ your Son my Lord, who lives and reigns with you and the Holy Spirit,
    one God, now and for ever. *Amen.* †

The Concluding Prayer of the Church
Lord God, almighty and everlasting Father, you have brought me in safety to this
    new day: Preserve me with your mighty power, that I may not fall into sin, nor
    be overcome by adversity; and in all I do direct me to the fulfilling of your pur-
    pose; through Jesus Christ my Lord. *Amen.* †

The Midday Office   **To Be Observed on the Hour or Half Hour**
                                         Between 11 a.m. and 2 p.m.

The Call to Prayer
Hallelujah! Give praise, you servants of the LORD;* praise the Name of the LORD.

Psalm 113:1

The Request for Presence
Hear my voice, O LORD, according to your loving-kindness;* according to your
    judgments, give me life.

Psalm 119:149

The Greeting
O Lᴏʀᴅ of hosts,* happy are they who put their trust in you!
Psalm 84:12

The Refrain for the Midday Lessons
With the faithful you show yourself faithful, O God;* with the forthright you show
yourself forthright.
With the pure you show yourself pure,* but with the crooked you are wily.
Psalm 18:26–27

A Reading
It is not ourselves that we are proclaiming, but Christ Jesus as the Lord, and ourselves as your servants for Jesus' sake. It is God who said, 'Let light shine out of
darkness,' that has shone into our hearts to enlighten them with the knowledge
of God's glory, the glory on the face of Christ.
2 Corinthians 4:5–6

The Refrain
With the faithful you show yourself faithful, O God;* with the forthright you show
yourself forthright.
With the pure you show yourself pure,* but with the crooked you are wily.

The Midday Psalm　　*The Eye of the Lᴏʀᴅ Is Upon Those Who Wait Upon His Name*
Happy is the nation whose God is the Lᴏʀᴅ!* happy the people he has chosen to be
his own!
The Lᴏʀᴅ looks down from heaven,* and beholds all the people in the world.
From where he sits enthroned he turns his gaze* on all who dwell on the earth.
He fashions all the hearts of them* and understands all their works.
There is no king that can be saved by a mighty army;* a strong man is not deliv-
ered by his great strength.
The horse is a vain hope for deliverance;* for all its strength it cannot save.
Behold, the eye of the Lᴏʀᴅ is upon those who fear him,* on those who wait upon
his love,
To pluck their lives from death,* and to feed them in time of famine.
Psalm 33:12–19

The Refrain
With the faithful you show yourself faithful, O God;* with the forthright you show
yourself forthright.
With the pure you show yourself pure,* but with the crooked you are wily.

The Cry of the Church
O God, come to my assistance! O Lord, make haste to help me!

The Lord's Prayer

The Prayer Appointed for the Week
Almighty Father who gave your only Son to die for our sins and to rise for our justification: Give me grace so to put away the leaven of malice and wickedness,

that I may always serve you in pureness of living and truth; through Jesus Christ your Son my Lord, who lives and reigns with you and the Holy Spirit, one God, now and for ever. *Amen.* †

The Concluding Prayer of the Church

O Lord, my God, accept the fervent prayers of all of us your people; in the multitude of your mercies, look with compassion upon me and all who turn to you for help; for you are gracious, O lover of souls, and to you we give glory, Father, Son, and Holy Spirit, now and forever. *Amen.* †

The Vespers Office
To Be Observed on the Hour or Half Hour Between 5 and 8 p.m.

The Call to Prayer

Give thanks to the LORD, for he is good;* his mercy endures for ever.
Let Israel now proclaim,* "His mercy endures for ever."
Let the house of Aaron now proclaim,* "His mercy endures for ever."
Let those who fear the LORD now proclaim,* "His mercy endures for ever."

Psalm 118:1–4

The Request for Presence

Show me the light of your countenance, O God,* and come to me.

based on Psalm 67:1

The Greeting

But you, O LORD, are gracious and full of compassion,* slow to anger, and full of kindness and truth.

Psalm 86:15

The Hymn   *It Was Poor Little Jesus*

It was poor little Jesus, yes, yes;
he was born on Christmas, yes, yes;
and laid in a manger, yes, yes;
wasn't that a pity and a shame, Lord, Lord,
wasn't that a pity and a shame?

It was poor little Jesus, yes, yes;
child of Mary, yes, yes;
didn't have a cradle, yes, yes;
wasn't that a pity and a shame, Lord, Lord,
wasn't that a pity and a shame?

It was poor little Jesus, yes, yes;
they nailed him to the cross, yes, yes;
they hung him with a robber, yes, yes;
wasn't that a pity and a shame, Lord, Lord,
wasn't that a pity and a shame?

It was poor little Jesus, yes, yes;
he's risen from the darkness, yes, yes;
he's ascended into glory, yes, yes;
no more a pity and a shame, Lord, Lord,
no more a pity and a shame.

African American Spiritual

The Refrain for the Vespers Lessons

Remember me, O LORD, with the favor you have for your people,* and visit me
with your saving help.

Psalm 106:4

The Vespers Psalm   *You Have Clothed Me with Joy*

While I felt secure, I said, "I shall never be disturbed.* You, LORD, with your favor,
made me as strong as the mountains."
Then you hid your face,* and I was filled with fear.
I cried to you, O LORD;* I pleaded with the Lord, saying,
"What profit is there in my blood, if I go down to the Pit?* will the dust praise you
or declare your faithfulness?
Hear, O LORD, and have mercy upon me;* O LORD, be my helper."
You have turned my wailing into dancing;* you have put off my sack-cloth and
clothed me with joy.
Therefore my heart sings to you without ceasing;* O LORD my God, I will give you
thanks for ever.

Psalm 30:7–13

The Refrain

Remember me, O LORD, with the favor you have for your people,* and visit me
with your saving help.

The Small Verse

The Lord is my shepherd and nothing is wanting to me. In green pastures He hath
settled me.

THE SHORT BREVIARY

The Lord's Prayer

The Prayer Appointed for the Week

Almighty Father who gave your only Son to die for our sins and to rise for our justification: Give me grace so to put away the leaven of malice and wickedness,
that I may always serve you in pureness of living and truth; through Jesus
Christ your Son my Lord, who lives and reigns with you and the Holy Spirit,
one God, now and for ever. *Amen.* †

The Concluding Prayer of the Church

O Lord my God, to you and to your service I devote myself, body, soul, and spirit.
Fill my memory with the record of your mighty works; enlighten my understanding with the light of your Holy Spirit; and may all the desires of my heart

and will center in what you would have me do. Make me an instrument of your salvation for the people entrusted to my care, and grant that by my life and teaching I may set forth your true and living Word. Be always with me in carrying out the duties of my faith. In prayer, quicken my devotion; in praises, heighten my love and gratitude; in conversation give me readiness of thought and expression; and grant that, by the clearness and brightness of your holy Word, all the world may be drawn into your blessed kingdom. All this I ask for the sake of your Son our Savior Jesus Christ. *Amen.* †

The Morning Office

To Be Observed on the Hour or Half Hour Between 6 and 9 a.m.

The Call to Prayer

Praise God from whom all blessings flow; praise him, all creatures here below; praise him above, you heavenly hosts; praise Father, Son and Holy Ghost.

Traditional Doxology

The Request for Presence

Send out your light and your truth, that they may lead me,* and bring me to your holy hill and to your dwelling;

That I may go to the altar of God, to the God of my joy and gladness;* and on the harp I will give thanks to you, O God my God.

Psalm 43:3–4

The Greeting

Splendor and honor and kingly power* are yours by right, O Lord our God,

For you created everything that is,* and by your will they were created and have their being.

A Song to the Lamb

The Refrain for the Morning Lessons

For one day in your courts is better than a thousand in my own room,* and to stand at the threshold of the house of my God than to dwell in the tents of the wicked.

Psalm 84:9

A Reading

Jesus taught us, saying: "Everything now covered up will be uncovered, and everything now hidden will be made clear. For this reason, whatever you have said in the dark will be heard in the daylight, and what you have whispered in hidden places will be proclaimed from the housetops."

Luke 12:2–3

The Refrain

For one day in your courts is better than a thousand in my own room,* and to stand at the threshold of the house of my God than to dwell in the tents of the wicked.

The Morning Psalm   *Who Can Stand in His Holy Place?*

The earth is the LORD's and all that is in it,* the world and all who dwell therein.

For it is he who founded it upon the seas* and made it firm upon the rivers of the
deep.

"Who can ascend the hill of the LORD?"* and who can stand in his holy place?"

"Those who have clean hands and a pure heart,* who have not pledged themselves to falsehood, nor sworn by what is a fraud.

They shall receive a blessing from the LORD* and a just reward from the God of
their salvation."

Such is the generation of those who seek him,* of those who seek your face, O God
of Jacob.

Psalm 24:1–6

The Refrain

For one day in your courts is better than a thousand in my own room,* and to
stand at the threshold of the house of my God than to dwell in the tents of the
wicked.

The Small Verse

The people that walked in darkness have seen a great light; on those who live in a
land of deep shadow a light has shone.

Isaiah 9:1

The Lord's Prayer

The Prayer Appointed for the Week

Almighty Father who gave your only Son to die for our sins and to rise for our justification: Give me grace so to put away the leaven of malice and wickedness,
that I may always serve you in pureness of living and truth; through Jesus
Christ your Son my Lord, who lives and reigns with you and the Holy Spirit,
one God, now and for ever. *Amen.* †

The Concluding Prayer of the Church

Lord God, almighty and everlasting Father, you have brought me in safety to this
new day: Preserve me with your mighty power, that I may not fall into sin, nor
be overcome by adversity; and in all I do direct me to the fulfilling of your purpose; through Jesus Christ my Lord. *Amen.* †

The Midday Office   **To Be Observed on the Hour or Half Hour**
                                                Between 11 a.m. and 2 p.m.

The Call to Prayer

"Come now, let us reason together," says the LORD.

Isaiah 1:18, KJV

The Request for Presence

O LORD, I call to you; come to me quickly;* hear my voice when I cry to you.

Psalm 141:1

The Greeting
In you, O LORD, have I taken refuge;* let me never be ashamed.

Psalm 71:1

The Refrain for the Midday Lessons
Happy are they all who fear the LORD,* and who follow in his ways!

Psalm 128:1

A Reading
The Apostle said: "The time is sure to come when people will not accept sound
teaching, but their ears will be itching for anything new and they will collect
themselves a whole series of teachers according to their own tastes; and then
they will shut their ears to the truth and will turn to myths.

2 Timothy 4:3–4

The Refrain
Happy are they all who fear the LORD,* and who follow in his ways!

The Midday Psalm   *I Will Lift Up My Hands to Your Commandments*
Let your loving-kindness come to me, O LORD,* and your salvation, according to
your promise.
Then shall I have a word for those who taunt me,* because I trust in your words.
Do not take the word of truth out of my mouth,* for my hope is in your judg-
ments.
I shall continue to keep your law;* I shall keep it for ever and ever.
I will walk at liberty,* because I study your commandments.
I will tell of your decrees before kings* and will not be ashamed.
I delight in your commandments,* which I have always loved.
I will lift up my hands to your commandments,* and I will meditate on your
statutes.

Psalm 119:41–48

The Refrain
Happy are they all who fear the LORD,* and who follow in his ways!

The Cry of the Church
Be, Lord, my helper and forsake me not. Do not despise me, O God, my savior.

THE SHORT BREVIARY

The Lord's Prayer

The Prayer Appointed for the Week
Almighty Father who gave your only Son to die for our sins and to rise for our justification: Give me grace so to put away the leaven of malice and wickedness,
that I may always serve you in pureness of living and truth; through Jesus
Christ your Son my Lord, who lives and reigns with you and the Holy Spirit,
one God, now and for ever. *Amen.* †

The Concluding Prayer of the Church

Direct me, O Lord, in all my doings with your most gracious favor, and further me
with your continual help; that in all my work begun, continued, and ended in
you, I may glorify your holy name, and finally, by your mercy, obtain everlasting life; through Jesus Christ our Lord. *Amen.* †

The Vespers Office   **To Be Observed on the Hour or Half Hour**
                                          Between 5 and 8 p.m.

The Call to Prayer

Bless the LORD, you angels of his, you mighty ones who do his bidding,* and hear-
ken to the voice of his word.
Bless the LORD, all you his hosts,* you ministers of his who do his will.
Bless the LORD, all you works of his,* in all places of his dominion.

Psalm 103:20–22

The Request for Presence

LORD God of hosts, hear my prayer;* hearken, O God of Jacob.

Psalm 84:7

The Greeting

Show me your ways, O LORD,* and teach me your paths.
Lead me in your truth and teach me,* for you are the God of my salvation; in you
have I trusted all the day long.

Psalm 25:3–4

The Hymn

The head that once was crowned with thorns is crowned with glory now;
a royal diadem adorns the mighty victor's brow.
The highest place that heaven affords is his, is his by right,
the King of kings, and Lord of lords, and heaven's eternal Light;
the joy of all who dwell above, the joy of all below,
to whom he manifests his love and grants his Name to know.
To them the cross with all its shame, with all its grace is given;
their name, an everlasting name; their joy, the joy of heaven.
They suffer with their Lord below, they reign with him above,
their profit and their joy to know the mystery of his love.
The cross he bore is life and health, though shame and death to him:
his people's hope, his people's wealth, their everlasting theme.

Thomas Kelly

The Refrain for the Vespers Lessons

But it is good for me to be near God;* I have made the Lord GOD my refuge.

Psalm 73:28

The Vespers Psalm   *You Alone Are God*

Be merciful to me, O LORD, for you are my God;* I call upon you all the day long.
Gladden the soul of your servant,* for to you, O LORD, I lift up my soul.
For you, O LORD, are good and forgiving,* and great is your love toward all who
    call upon you.
Give ear, O LORD, to my prayer,* and attend to the voice of my supplications.
In the time of my trouble I will call upon you,* for you will answer me.
Among the gods there is none like you, O LORD,* nor anything like your works.
All nations you have made will come and worship you, O LORD,* and glorify your
    Name.
For you are great; you do wondrous things;* and you alone are God.

Psalm 86:3–10

The Refrain

But it is good for me to be near God;* I have made the Lord GOD my refuge.

The Small Verse

Keep me, Lord, as the apple of your eye and carry me under the shadow of your
    wings.

Traditional

The Lord's Prayer

The Prayer Appointed for the Week

Almighty Father who gave your only Son to die for our sins and to rise for our jus-
    tification: Give me grace so to put away the leaven of malice and wickedness,
    that I may always serve you in pureness of living and truth; through Jesus
    Christ your Son my Lord, who lives and reigns with you and the Holy Spirit,
    one God, now and for ever. *Amen.* †

The Concluding Prayer of the Church

Protect me, Lord, as I stay awake; watch over me as I sleep, that awake I may
    watch with Christ, and asleep, rest in his peace. *Amen.*

The Morning Office   **To Be Observed on the Hour or Half Hour**
                                                      Between 6 and 9 a.m.

The Call to Prayer

Sing to God, O kingdoms of the earth;* sing praises to the Lord.
He rides in the heavens, the ancient heavens;* he sends forth his voice, his mighty
    voice.
Ascribe power to God;* his majesty is over Israel; his strength is in the skies.

Psalm 68:33–35

The Request for Presence

Teach me your way, O LORD,* and I will walk in your truth; knit my heart to you
    that I may fear your Name.

Psalm 86:11

The Greeting

My mouth shall recount your mighty acts* and saving deeds all day long;* though
I cannot know the number of them.

Psalm 71:15

The Refrain for the Morning Lessons

And they will say,* "Surely, there is a reward for the righteous; surely, there is a
God who rules in the earth."

Psalm 58:11

A Reading

Jesus taught us, saying: "Can you not buy two sparrows for a penny? And yet not
one falls to the ground without your Father knowing. Why, every hair on your
head has been counted. So there is no need to be afraid; you are worth more
than many sparrows."

Matthew 10:29–31

The Refrain

And they will say, "Surely, there is a reward for the righteous;* surely, there is a
God who rules in the earth."

The Morning Psalm   *If You Would but Listen*

You called on me in trouble, and I saved you;* I answered you from the secret
place of thunder and tested you at the waters of Meribah.
Hear, O my people, and I will admonish you:* O Israel, if you would but listen to
me!
There shall be no strange god among you;* you shall not worship a foreign god.
I am the LORD your God, who brought you out of the land of Egypt and said,*
"Open your mouth wide, and I will fill it."

Psalm 81:7–10

The Refrain

And they will say, "Surely, there is a reward for the righteous;* surely, there is a
God who rules in the earth."

The Gloria

The Lord's Prayer

The Prayer Appointed for the Week

Almighty Father who gave your only Son to die for our sins and to rise for our justification: Give me grace so to put away the leaven of malice and wickedness,
that I may always serve you in pureness of living and truth; through Jesus
Christ your Son my Lord, who lives and reigns with you and the Holy Spirit,
one God, now and for ever. *Amen.* †

The Concluding Prayer of the Church

Lord God, almighty and everlasting Father, you have brought me in safety to this
new day: Preserve me with your mighty power, that I may not fall into sin, nor

be overcome by adversity; and in all I do direct me to the fulfilling of your purpose; through Jesus Christ my Lord. *Amen.* †

The Midday Office   **To Be Observed on the Hour or Half Hour**
                                              Between 11 a.m. and 2 p.m.

The Call to Prayer
Glory in his holy Name;* let the hearts of those who seek the LORD rejoice.
Psalm 105:3

The Request for Presence
Let your compassion come to me, that I may live,* for your law is my delight.
Psalm 119:77

The Greeting
Your righteousness, O God, reaches to the heavens;* you have done great things;
who is like you, O God?

Psalm 71:19

The Refrain for the Midday Lessons
Happy are they whose transgressions are forgiven,* and whose sin is put away!
Psalm 32:1

A Reading   *Canticle of Judith*
I will sing a new song to my God.
Lord, you are great, you are glorious,
Wonderfully strong, unconquerable.
May your whole creation serve you!
For you spoke and things came into being,
You sent your breath and they were put together,
And no one can resist your voice.

Should mountains topple
To mingle with waves,
Should rocks melt
Like wax before your face,
To those who fear you,
You would still be merciful.

Judith 16:13ff

The Refrain
Happy are they whose transgressions are forgiven,* and whose sin is put away!

The Midday Psalm   *I Will Extol You Among the Nations*
The LORD lives! Blessed is my Rock!* Exalted is the God of my salvation!
He is the God who gave me victory* and cast down the peoples beneath me.
You rescued me from the fury of my enemies; you exalted me above those who
rose against me;* you saved me from my deadly foe.

Therefore will I extol you among the nations, O LORD,* and sing praises to your
    Name.
He multiplies the victories of his king;* he shows loving-kindness to his anointed,
    to David and his descendants for ever.

Psalm 18:46–50

The Refrain
Happy are they whose transgressions are forgiven,* and whose sin is put away!

The Cry of the Church
Lord, have mercy on us. Christ, have mercy on us. Lord, have mercy on us.

The Lord's Prayer

The Prayer Appointed for the Week
Almighty Father who gave your only Son to die for our sins and to rise for our jus-
    tification: Give me grace so to put away the leaven of malice and wickedness,
    that I may always serve you in pureness of living and truth; through Jesus
    Christ your Son my Lord, who lives and reigns with you and the Holy Spirit,
    one God, now and for ever. *Amen.* †

The Concluding Prayer of the Church
Open, Lord, my eyes that I may see.
Open, Lord, my ears that I may hear.
Open, Lord, my heart and my mind that I may understand.
So shall I turn to you and be healed.

Traditional

The Vespers Office   **To Be Observed on the Hour or Half Hour**
Between 5 and 8 p.m.

The Call to Prayer
Come now and see the works of God,* how wonderful he is in his doing toward
    all people.
In his might he rules for ever; his eyes keep watch over the nations;* let no rebel
    rise up against him.

Psalm 66:4, 6

The Request for Presence
Show us your mercy, O LORD,* and grant us your salvation.

Psalm 85:7

The Greeting
Praise God from whom all blessings flow; praise Him all creatures here below;
    praise Him above, you heavenly hosts; praise Father, Son, and Holy Ghost.

Traditional Doxology

The Hymn   *Firmly I Believe and Truly*

Firmly I believe and truly
God is three and God is one;
And I next acknowledge duly
Manhood taken by the Son.

And I trust and hope most fully
In that manhood crucified;
And I love supremely, solely
Christ who for my sins has died.

And I hold in veneration,
For the love of him alone,
Holy Church as his creation,
And her teachings as his own.

Praise and thanks be ever given
With and through the angel host,
To the God of earth and heaven,
Father, Son, and Holy Ghost.

William Boyce

The Refrain for the Vespers Lessons

You crown the year with your goodness,* and your paths overflow with plenty.

Psalm 65:12

The Vespers Psalm   *Sing the Glory of Our God*

Be joyful in God, all you lands;* sing the glory of his Name; sing the glory of his praise.

Say to God, "How awesome are your deeds!* because of your great strength your enemies cringe before you.

All the earth bows down before you,* sings to you, sings out your Name."

Psalm 66:1–3

The Refrain

You crown the year with your goodness,* and your paths overflow with plenty.

The Small Verse

The Lord is my shepherd and nothing is wanting to me. In green pastures He has settled me.

THE SHORT BREVIARY

The Lord's Prayer

The Prayer Appointed for the Week

Almighty Father who gave your only Son to die for our sins and to rise for our justification: Give me grace so to put away the leaven of malice and wickedness, that I may always serve you in pureness of living and truth; through Jesus Christ your Son my Lord, who lives and reigns with you and the Holy Spirit, one God, now and for ever. *Amen.* †

The Concluding Prayer of the Church

Help each one of us, gracious Father, to live in such magnanimity and restraint that the Head of the Church may never have cause to say to any one of us, This is my body, broken by you.

Prayer from China

The Morning Office   To Be Observed on the Hour or Half Hour
                                                        Between 6 and 9 a.m.

The Call to Prayer
Bless our God, you peoples;* make the voice of his praise to be heard;
Who holds our souls in life,* and will not allow our feet to slip.
Psalm 66:7–8

The Request for Presence
Show me your marvelous loving-kindness,* O Savior of those who take refuge at
    your right hand from those who rise up against them.
Keep me as the apple of your eye;* hide me under the shadow of your wings.
Psalm 17:7–8

The Greeting
Hosanna, LORD, hosanna!* . . .
Blessed is he who comes in the name of the LORD;* we bless you from the house of
    the LORD.
Psalm 118:25–26

The Refrain for the Morning Lessons
For God, who commanded the light to shine out of darkness, hath shined in our
    hearts, to give the light of the knowledge of the glory of God in the face of Jesus
    Christ.
2 Corinthians 4:6

A Reading
Jesus taught us, saying: "But alas for you who are rich: you are having your conso-
    lation now. Alas for you who have plenty to eat now: you shall go hungry. Alas
    for you who are laughing now: you shall mourn and weep."
Luke 6:24–25

The Refrain
For God, who commanded the light to shine out of darkness, hath shined in our
    hearts, to give the light of the knowledge of the glory of God in the face of Jesus
    Christ.

The Morning Psalm   *What Are We That You Should Care for Us?*
Blessed be the LORD my rock!* who trains my hands to fight and my fingers to
    battle;
My help and my fortress, my stronghold and my deliverer,* my shield in whom I
    trust, who subdues the peoples under me.
O LORD, what are we that you should care for us?* mere mortals that you should
    think of us?
We are like a puff of wind;* our days are like a passing shadow.
Bow your heavens, O LORD, and come down;* touch the mountains, and they shall
    smoke.
Hurl the lightning and scatter them;* shoot out your arrows and rout them.

Stretch out your hand from on high;* rescue me and deliver me from the great
waters.

Psalm 144:1–7

The Refrain

For God, who commanded the light to shine out of darkness, hath shined in our
hearts, to give the light of the knowledge of the glory of God in the face of Jesus
Christ.

The Gloria

The Lord's Prayer

The Prayer Appointed for the Week

Almighty Father who gave your only Son to die for our sins and to rise for our justification: Give me grace so to put away the leaven of malice and wickedness,
that I may always serve you in pureness of living and truth; through Jesus
Christ your Son my Lord, who lives and reigns with you and the Holy Spirit,
one God, now and for ever. *Amen.* †

The Concluding Prayer of the Church

Lord God, almighty and everlasting Father, you have brought me in safety to this
new day: Preserve me with your mighty power, that I may not fall into sin, nor
be overcome by adversity; and in all I do direct me to the fulfilling of your purpose; through Jesus Christ my Lord. *Amen.* †

The Midday Office   To Be Observed on the Hour or Half Hour
                                            Between 11 a.m. and 2 p.m.

The Call to Prayer

Bless our God, you peoples;* make the voice of his praise to be heard;
Who holds our souls in life,* and will not allow our feet to slip.

Psalm 66:7–8

The Request for Presence

Let your ways be known upon earth,* your saving health among all nations.

Psalm 67:2

The Greeting

How great is your goodness, O Lord! which you have laid up for those who fear
you.

Psalm 31:19

The Refrain for the Midday Lessons

Your love, O Lord, reaches to the heavens,* and your faithfulness to the clouds.

Psalm 36:5

A Reading
The Apostle said: "If our hope in Christ has been for this life only, we are of all
people the most pitiable."

1 Corinthians 15:19

The Refrain
Your love, O LORD, reaches to the heavens,* and your faithfulness to the clouds.

The Midday Psalm   *Our Soul Waits for the LORD*
Behold, the eye of the LORD is upon those who fear him,* on those who wait upon
his love,
To pluck their lives from death,* and to feed them in time of famine.
Our soul waits for the LORD;* he is our help and our shield.
Indeed, our heart rejoices in him,* for in his holy Name we put our trust.
Let your loving-kindness, O LORD, be upon us,* as we have put our trust in you.

Psalm 33:18–22

The Refrain
Your love, O LORD, reaches to the heavens,* and your faithfulness to the clouds.

The Small Verse
My help is in the name of the Lord who made heaven and earth and all that is in
them. Thanks be to God.

Traditional

The Lord's Prayer

The Prayer Appointed for the Week
Almighty Father who gave your only Son to die for our sins and to rise for our justification: Give me grace so to put away the leaven of malice and wickedness,
that I may always serve you in pureness of living and truth; through Jesus
Christ your Son my Lord, who lives and reigns with you and the Holy Spirit,
one God, now and for ever. *Amen.* †

The Concluding Prayer of the Church
O God, the source of eternal light: Shed forth your unending day upon all of us
who watch for you, that our lips may praise you, our lives may bless you, and
our worship may give you glory; through Jesus Christ our Lord. *Amen.* †

The Vespers Office   **To Be Observed on the Hour or Half Hour**
Between 5 and 8 p.m.

The Call to Prayer
The LORD is my strength and my shield;* my heart trusts in him, and I have been
helped;
Therefore my heart dances for joy,* and in my song will I praise him.

Psalm 28:8–9

The Request for Presence

I have gone astray like a sheep that is lost;* search for your servant, for I do not
    forget your commandments.

                        Psalm 119:176

The Greeting

How great is your goodness, O Lord!* which you have done in the sight of all for
    those who put their trust in you.

                        Psalm 31:19

The Hymn

Lord, dismiss us with your blessing;
Fill our hearts with joy and peace;
Let us each, your love possessing,
Triumph in redeeming grace.
O refresh us, O refresh us,
Travelling through this wilderness.

Thanks we give and adoration
For your gospel's joyful sound.
May the fruits of your salvation
In our hearts and lives abound;
Ever faithful, ever faithful
To the truth may we be found.

                        John Fawcett

The Refrain for the Vespers Lessons

Mercy and truth have met together;* righteousness and peace have kissed each
    other.

                        Psalm 85:10

The Vespers Psalm   *He Redeems Our Life*

Bless the Lord, O my soul,* and all that is within me, bless his holy Name.

Bless the Lord, O my soul,* and forget not all his benefits.

He forgives all your sins* and heals all your infirmities;

He redeems your life from the grave* and crowns you with mercy and loving-
    kindness;

He satisfies you with good things,* and your youth is renewed like an eagle's.

The Lord executes righteousness* and judgment for all who are oppressed.

He made his ways known to Moses* and his works to the children of Israel.

The Lord is full of compassion and mercy,* slow to anger and of great kindness.

He will not always accuse us,* nor will he keep his anger for ever.

He has not dealt with us according to our sins,* nor rewarded us according to our
    wickedness.

For as the heavens are high above the earth,* so is his mercy great upon those who
    fear him.

As far as the east is from the west,* so far has he removed our sins from us.

As a father cares for his children,* so does the Lord care for those who fear him.

For he himself knows whereof we are made;* he remembers that we are but dust.

                        Psalm 103:1–14

The Refrain

Mercy and truth have met together;* righteousness and peace have kissed each
    other.

The Small Verse
My help is in the Name of the Lord who made heaven and earth and all that is in
them. Thanks be to God.

Traditional

The Lord's Prayer

The Prayer Appointed for the Week
Almighty Father who gave your only Son to die for our sins and to rise for our justification: Give me grace so to put away the leaven of malice and wickedness,
that I may always serve you in pureness of living and truth; through Jesus
Christ your Son my Lord, who lives and reigns with you and the Holy Spirit,
one God, now and for ever. *Amen.* †

Concluding Prayers of the Church
Almighty God, who has promised to hear the petitions of those who ask in your
Son's Name: I beseech you mercifully to incline your ear to me who have made
my prayers and supplications to you; and grant that those things which I have
faithfully asked according to your will, I may effectually obtain, to the relief of
my necessity, and to the setting forth of your glory; through Jesus Christ my
Lord. *Amen.* †

May the souls of the faithful departed, through the mercy of God, rest in eternal
peace. *Amen.*

The Morning Office   To Be Observed on the Hour or Half Hour
                                       Between 6 and 9 a.m.

The Call to Prayer
Ascribe to the LORD the glory due his Name;* worship the LORD in the beauty of
holiness.

Psalm 29:2

The Request for Presence
O God, you are my God; eagerly I seek you;* my soul thirsts for you, my flesh
faints for you, as in barren and dry land where there is no water.

Psalm 63:1

The Greeting
We have heard with our ears, O God, our forefathers have told us,* the deeds you
did in their days, in the days of old.

Psalm 44:1

The Refrain for the Morning Lessons
Rescue the weak and the poor;* deliver them from the power of the wicked.

Psalm 82:4

A Reading

Jesus said to the disciples: "I have been telling you these things in veiled language. The hour is coming when I shall no longer speak to you in veiled language but tell you about the Father in plain words. When that day comes you will ask in my name; and I do not say that I shall pray to the Father for you, because the Father himself loves you for loving me and believing that I came from God. I came from the Father and have come into the world and now I am leaving the world to go to the Father."

John 16:25–28

The Refrain

Rescue the weak and the poor;* deliver them from the power of the wicked.

The Morning Psalm   *Whoever Is Wise Will Ponder These Things*

The LORD changed rivers into deserts,* and water-springs into thirsty ground,
A fruitful land into salt flats,* because of the wickedness of those who dwell there.
He changed deserts into pools of water* and dry land into water-springs.
He settled the hungry there,* and they founded a city to dwell in.
They sowed fields, and planted vineyards,* and brought in a fruitful harvest.
He blessed them, so that they increased greatly;* he did not let their herds decrease.
Yet when they were diminished and brought low,* through stress of adversity and sorrow,
(He pours contempt on princes* and makes them wander in trackless wastes)
He lifted up the poor out of misery* and multiplied their families like flocks of sheep.
The upright will see this and rejoice,* but all wickedness will shut its mouth.
Whoever is wise will ponder these things,* and consider well the mercies of the LORD.

Psalm 107:33–43

The Refrain

Rescue the weak and the poor;* deliver them from the power of the wicked.

The Gloria

The Lord's Prayer

The Prayer Appointed for the Week

Almighty Father who gave your only Son to die for our sins and to rise for our justification: Give me grace so to put away the leaven of malice and wickedness, that I may always serve you in pureness of living and truth; through Jesus Christ your Son my Lord, who lives and reigns with you and the Holy Spirit, one God, now and for ever. *Amen.* †

The Concluding Prayer of the Church

Lord God, almighty and everlasting Father, you have brought me in safety to this new day: Preserve me with your mighty power, that I may not fall into sin, nor be overcome by adversity, and in all I do direct me to the fulfilling of your purpose; through Jesus Christ my Lord. *Amen.* †

The Midday Office   To Be Observed on the Hour or Half Hour
                                        Between 11 a.m. and 2 p.m.

The Call to Prayer
Open my lips, O LORD* and my mouth shall proclaim your praise.
                                        Psalm 51:16

The Request for Presence
Look well whether there be any wickedness in me* and lead me in the way that is
    everlasting.
                                        Psalm 139:23

The Greeting
O LORD, I am your servant;* I am your servant and the child of your handmaid;
    you have freed me from my bonds.
                                        Psalm 116:14

The Refrain for the Midday Lessons
Unless the LORD builds the house,* their labor is in vain who build it.
                                        Psalm 127:1

A Reading
The hope of the godless is like chaff carried on the wind, like fine spray driven by
    the storm; it disperses like smoke before the wind, goes away like the memory
    of a one-day guest. But the upright live for ever, their recompense is with the
    Lord, and the Most High takes care of them. So they will receive a glorious
    crown and the diadem of beauty from the Lord's hand; for he will shelter them
    with his right hand and with his arm he will shield them.
                                        Wisdom 5:14–16

The Refrain
Unless the LORD builds the house,* their labor is in vain who build it.

The Midday Psalm   *In the Full Assembly, I Will Bless the LORD*
Do not sweep me away with sinners,* nor my life with those who thirst for blood,
Whose hands are full of evil plots,* and their right hand full of bribes.
As for me, I will live with integrity;* redeem me, O LORD, and have pity on me.
My foot stands on level ground;* in the full assembly I will bless the LORD
                                        Psalm 26:8–12

The Refrain
Unless the LORD builds the house,* their labor is in vain who build it.

The Cry of the Church
Even so come, Lord Jesus!

The Lord's Prayer

The Prayer Appointed for the Week
Almighty Father who gave your only Son to die for our sins and to rise for our jus-
    tification: Give me grace so to put away the leaven of malice and wickedness,

that I may always serve you in pureness of living and truth; through Jesus Christ your Son my Lord, who lives and reigns with you and the Holy Spirit, one God, now and for ever. *Amen.* †

The Concluding Prayer of the Church
O God, the source of eternal light: Shed forth your unending day upon all of us who watch for you, that our lips may praise you, our lives may bless you, and our worship may give you glory; through Jesus Christ our Lord. *Amen.* †

The Vespers Office
To Be Observed on the Hour or Half Hour Between 5 and 8 p.m.

The Call to Prayer
Behold now, bless the LORD, all you servants of the LORD,* you that stand by night in the house of the LORD.

Psalm 134:1–2

The Request for Presence
My soul waits for the LORD, more than watchmen for the morning,* more than watchmen for the morning.

Psalm 130:6

The Greeting
You, O LORD, are my lamp;* my God, you make my darkness bright.
With you I will break down an enclosure;* with the help of my God I will scale any wall.

Psalm 18:29–30

The Hymn
Eternal Monarch, King Most High,
Whose Blood has brought redemption night,
By whom the death of death was wrought
And conquering grace's battle fought.

Yes, Angels tremble when they see
How changed is our humanity.
That Flesh has purged what flesh has stained
And God, the flesh of God, has reigned.

All glory, Lord, to You we pay
Hymning over the starry ways,
All glory, as is ever meet,
To Father and to Paraclete.

adapted from THE SHORT BREVIARY

The Refrain for the Vespers Lessons
I lie down and go to sleep;* I wake again, because the LORD sustains me.

Psalm 3:5

The Vespers Psalm
It is a good thing to give thanks to the Lord,* and to sing praises to your Name, O
  Most High;
To tell of your loving-kindness early in the morning* and of your faithfulness in
  the night season,
On the psaltery, and on the lyre,* and to the melody of the harp.
For you have made me glad by your acts, O Lord;* and I shout for joy because of
  the works of your hands.

Psalm 92:1–4

The Refrain
I lie down and go to sleep;* I wake again, because the Lord sustains me.

The Cry of the Church
O Lamb of God, that takes away the sins of the world, have mercy upon me.
O Lamb of God, that takes away the sins of the world, have mercy upon me.
O Lamb of God, that takes away the sins of the world, grant me your peace.

The Lord's Prayer

The Prayer Appointed for the Week
Almighty Father who gave your only Son to die for our sins and to rise for our justification: Give me grace so to put away the leaven of malice and wickedness,
  that I may always serve you in pureness of living and truth; through Jesus
  Christ your Son my Lord, who lives and reigns with you and the Holy Spirit,
  one God, now and for ever. *Amen.* †

The Concluding Prayer of the Church
Almighty God, who after the creation of the world rested from all your works
  and sanctified a day of rest for all your creatures: Grant that I, putting away
  all earthly anxieties, may be duly prepared for the service of public worship,
  and grant as well that my Sabbath upon earth may be a preparation for the
  eternal rest promised to your people in heaven; through Jesus Christ our
  Lord. *Amen.* †

The Morning Office 　　　　　　　　**To Be Observed on the Hour or Half Hour**
Between 6 and 9 a.m.

The Call to Prayer
Hallelujah! I will give thanks to the Lord with my whole heart,* in the assembly of
  the upright, in the congregation.

Psalm 111:1

The Request for Presence
Let them know that you, whose Name is Yahweh,* you alone are the Most High
over all the earth.

Psalm 83:18

The Greeting
I shall always wait in patience,* and shall praise you more and more.

Psalm 71:14

The Refrain for the Morning Lessons
The same stone which the builders rejected* has become the chief cornerstone.

Psalm 118:22

A Reading
Then he took them as far as the outskirts of Bethany, and raising his hands he
blessed them. Now as he blessed them, he withdrew from them and was carried up to heaven. They worshipped him and then went back to Jerusalem full
of joy; and they were continually in the Temple praising God.

Luke 24:50–53

The Refrain
The same stone which the builders rejected* has become the chief cornerstone.

The Morning Psalm   *God Is King of All the Earth*
Clap your hands, all you peoples;* shout to God with a cry of joy.
For the Lord Most High is to be feared;* he is the great King over all the earth.
He subdues the peoples under us,* and the nations under our feet.
He chooses our inheritance for us,* the pride of Jacob whom he loves.
God has gone up with a shout,* the Lord with the sound of the ram's-horn.
Sing praises to God, sing praises;* sing praises to our King, sing praises.
For God is King of all the earth;* sing praises with all your skill.
God reigns over the nations;* God sits upon his holy throne.
The nobles of the peoples have gathered together* with the people of the God of
Abraham.
The rulers of the earth belong to God,* and he is highly exalted.

Psalm 47

The Refrain
The same stone which the builders rejected* has become the chief cornerstone.

The Gloria

The Lord's Prayer

The Prayer Appointed for the Week
Remember, O Lord, what you have wrought in us and not what we deserve; and,
as you have called me to your service, make me worthy of your calling;
through Jesus Christ our Lord, who lives and reigns with you and the Holy
Spirit, one God, now and for ever. *Amen.* †

The Concluding Prayer of the Church
O God, you make me glad with the weekly remembrance of the glorious resurrection of your Son my Lord: Give me this day such blessing through my worship of you, that the week to come may be spent in your favor; through Jesus Christ our Lord. *Amen.* †

The Midday Office　　　　　　　　**To Be Observed on the Hour or Half Hour**
Between 11 a.m. and 2 p.m.

The Call to Prayer
In the temple of the LORD* all are crying, "Glory!"
Psalm 29:9

The Request for Presence
Fight those who fight me, O LORD;* attack those who are attacking me.
. . . say to my soul, "I am your salvation."
Psalm 35:1, 3

The Greeting
Blessed be the Lord GOD, the God of Israel,* who alone does wondrous deeds!
And blessed be his glorious Name for ever!* and may all the earth be filled with his glory. Amen. Amen.
Psalm 72:18–19

The Refrain for the Midday Lessons
Blessed be the LORD God of Israel,* from age to age. Amen. Amen.
Psalm 41:13

A Reading
Of his vision, the prophet Daniel said: "While I was watching, thrones were set in place and one most venerable took his seat. His robe was white as snow, the hair of his head was pure as wool.
His throne was a blaze of flames, its wheels were a burning fire. A stream of fire poured out, issuing from his presence. A thousand thousand waited on him, ten thousand times ten thousand stood before him. The court was in session and the books lay open."
Daniel 7:9–10

The Refrain
Blessed be the LORD God of Israel,* from age to age. Amen. Amen.

The Midday Psalm　　　　　　　*I Will Confess You Among the Peoples, O LORD*
My heart is firmly fixed, O God, my heart is fixed;* I will sing and make melody.
Wake up, my spirit; awake, lute and harp;* I myself will waken the dawn.
I will confess you among the peoples, O LORD;* I will sing praises to you among the nations.
For your loving-kindness is greater than the heavens,* and your faithfulness reaches to the clouds.

Exalt yourself above the heavens, O God,* and your glory over all the earth.
So that those who are dear to you may be delivered,* save with your right hand
and answer me.

Psalm 108:1–6

The Refrain
Blessed be the LORD God of Israel,* from age to age. Amen. Amen.

The Cry of the Church
Lord, have mercy on us. Christ, have mercy on us. Lord, have mercy on us.

The Lord's Prayer

The Prayer Appointed for the Week
Remember, O Lord, what you have wrought in us and not what we deserve; and,
as you have called me to your service, make me worthy of your calling;
through Jesus Christ our Lord, who lives and reigns with you and the Holy
Spirit, one God, now and for ever. *Amen.* †

The Concluding Prayer of the Church
Grant, I pray, Almighty God, that as I believe your only-begotten Son our Lord
Jesus Christ to have ascended into heaven, so I may also in heart and mind
there ascend, and with him continually dwell; who lives and reigns with you
and the Holy Spirit, one God, for ever and ever. *Amen.* †

The Vespers Office   **To Be Observed on the Hour or Half Hour**
Between 5 and 8 p.m.

The Call to Prayer
Open my lips, O Lord,* and my mouth shall proclaim your praise.

Psalm 51:16

The Request for Presence
Be my strong rock, a castle to keep me safe,* for you are my crag and my stronghold;
for the sake of your Name, lead me and guide me.

Psalm 31:3

The Greeting
O gracious Light, pure brightness of the everlasting Father in heaven, O Jesus
Christ, holy and blessed! Now as we come to the setting of the sun, and our
eyes behold the vesper light, we sing your praises O God: Father, Son and Holy
Spirit. You are worthy at all times to be praised by happy voices, O Son of God,
O giver of life, and to be glorified through all the worlds.

Phos Hilaron

The Hymn
Spirit of mercy, truth and love, O shed your influence from above;
And still from age to age convey the wonders of this sacred day.

In every clime, by every tongue, be God's amazing glory sung:
Let all the listening earth be taught the deeds our great Redeemer wrought.

Unfailing Comfort, heavenly Guide, still over your holy Church preside;
O shed your influence from above, Spirit of mercy, truth, and love.

Anonymous

The Refrain for the Vespers Lessons
In God the LORD, whose word I praise, in God I trust and will not be afraid.*

Psalm 56:10

The Vespers Psalm   *You Are My God*
But as for me, I have trusted in you, O LORD.* I have said, "You are my God.
My times are in your hand;* rescue me from the hand of my enemies, and from
. those who persecute me.
Make your face to shine upon your servant,* and in your loving-kindness save
me."
LORD, let me not be ashamed for having called upon you;* . . .

Psalm 31:14–17

The Refrain
In God the LORD, whose word I praise, in God I trust and will not be afraid.*

The Small Verse
Into your hands I commend my spirit for you have redeemed me, O God of my
life. Glory be to the Father, and to the Son and to the comforting Spirit.

Traditional

The Lord's Prayer

The Prayer Appointed for the Week
Remember, O Lord, what you have wrought in us and not what we deserve; and,
as you have called me to your service, make me worthy of your calling;
through Jesus Christ our Lord, who lives and reigns with you and the Holy
Spirit, one God, now and for ever. *Amen.* †

The Concluding Prayer of the Church
O God, you have brought me near to an innumerable company of angels, and to
the spirits of just men made perfect: Grant me during my earthly pilgrimage to
abide in their fellowship, and in your heavenly country to become partakers of
their joy; through Jesus Christ our Lord, who lives and reigns with you and the
Holy Spirit, one God, now and for ever. *Amen.* †

The Morning Office   **To Be Observed on the Hour or Half Hour**
Between 6 and 9 a.m.

The Call to Prayer
Let my mouth be full of your praise* and your glory all the day long.

Psalm 71:8

The Request for Presence
Your word is a lantern to my feet* and a light upon my path.

Psalm 119:105

The Greeting
O God, you have taught me since I was young,* and to this day I tell of your
  wonderful works.

Psalm 71:17

The Refrain for the Morning Lessons
This is the LORD's doing,* and it is marvelous in our eyes.

Psalm 118:23

A Reading
Jesus said to the disciples: "When the Paraclete comes, whom I shall send to you
  from the Father, the Spirit of truth who issues from the Father, he will be my
  witness. And you too will be my witnesses, because you have been with me
  from the beginning."

John 15:26–27

The Refrain
This is the LORD's doing,* and it is marvelous in our eyes.

The Morning Psalm   *Let the Nations Be Glad and Sing for Joy*
May God be merciful to us and bless us,* show us the light of his countenance and
  come to us.
Let your ways be known upon earth,* your saving health among all nations.
Let the peoples praise you, O God;* let all the peoples praise you.
Let the nations be glad and sing for joy,* for you judge the peoples with equity and
  guide all the nations upon earth.
Let the peoples praise you, O God;* let all the peoples praise you.
The earth has brought forth her increase;* may God, our own God, give us his
  blessing.
May God give us his blessing,* and may all the ends of the earth stand in awe
  of him.

Psalm 67

The Refrain
This is the LORD's doing,* and it is marvelous in our eyes.

The Gloria

The Lord's Prayer

The Prayer Appointed for the Week
Remember, O Lord, what you have wrought in us and not what we deserve; and,
  as you have called me to your service, make me worthy of your calling;
  through Jesus Christ our Lord, who lives and reigns with you and the Holy
  Spirit, one God, now and for ever. *Amen.* †

The Concluding Prayer of the Church
Lord God, almighty and everlasting Father, you have brought me in safety to this
new day: Preserve me with your mighty power, that I may not fall into sin, nor
be overcome by adversity; and in all I do direct me to the fulfilling of your purpose; through Jesus Christ my Lord. *Amen.* †

The Midday Office   To Be Observed on the Hour or Half Hour
                                      Between 11 a.m. and 2 p.m.

The Call to Prayer
Sing to the LORD with the harp,* with the harp and the voice of song.
With trumpets and the sound of the horn* shout with joy before the King, the
LORD.

Psalm 98:6–7

The Request for Presence
Show us the light of your countenance, O God,* and come to us.

based on Psalm 67:1

The Greeting
O LORD, what are we that you should care for us?* mere mortals that you should
think of us?
We are like a puff of wind;* our days are like a passing shadow.

Psalm 144:3–4

The Refrain for the Midday Lessons
Shout with joy to the LORD, all you lands;* lift up your voice, rejoice, and sing.

Psalm 98:5

A Reading
May the God of our Lord Jesus Christ, the Father of glory, give you a spirit of wisdom and perception of what is revealed, to bring you to full knowledge of him.
May he enlighten the eyes of your mind so that you can see what hope his call
holds for you, how rich is the glory of the heritage that he offers among his
holy people, and how extraordinarily great is the power that he has exercised
for us believers; this accords with the strength of his power at work in Christ,
the power which he exercised in raising him from the dead and enthroning
him at his right hand, in heaven, far above every principality, ruling force,
power or sovereignty, or any other name that can be named, not only in this
age but also in the age to come. *He has put all things under his feet,* and made
him, as he is above all things, the head of the Church; which is his Body, the
fullness of him who is filled, all in all.

Ephesians 1:17–23

The Refrain
Shout with joy to the LORD, all you lands;* lift up your voice, rejoice, and sing.

The Midday Psalm   *The Faithfulness of the* Lord *Endures*

Praise the Lord, all you nations;* laud him, all you peoples.

For his loving-kindness toward us is great,* and the faithfulness of the Lord
  endures for ever. Hallelujah!

               Psalm 117

The Refrain

Shout with joy to the Lord, all you lands;* lift up your voice, rejoice, and sing.

The Cry of the Church

Even so come, Lord Jesus!

The Lord's Prayer

The Prayer Appointed for the Week

Remember, O Lord, what you have wrought in us and not what we deserve; and,
  as you have called me to your service, make me worthy of your calling;
  through Jesus Christ our Lord, who lives and reigns with you and the Holy
  Spirit, one God, now and for ever. *Amen.* †

The Concluding Prayer of the Church

Almighty God, whose blessed Son my Savior Jesus Christ ascended far above all
  heavens that he might fill all things: Mercifully give me faith to perceive that,
  according to his promise, he abides with his church on earth, even to the end of
  the ages; though Jesus Christ my Lord, who lives and reigns with you and the
  Holy Spirit, one God, in glory everlasting. *Amen.* †

The Vespers Office   **To Be Observed on the Hour or Half Hour**
               Between 5 and 8 p.m.

The Call to Prayer

Come now and look upon the works of the Lord,* what awesome things he has
  done on earth.

              Psalm 46:9

The Request for Presence

May God be merciful to us and bless us,* show us the light of his countenance and
  come to us.

Let your ways be known upon earth,* your saving health among all nations.

             Psalm 67:1–2

The Greeting

O Lord of hosts,* happy are they who put their trust in you!

             Psalm 84:12

The Hymn

Hail the day that sees him rise, Alleluia!
Glorious to his native skies; Alleluia!
Christ a while to mortals given, Alleluia!
Enters now the highest heaven! Alleluia!

There the glorious triumph waits; Alleluia!
Lift your heads, eternal gates! Alleluia!
Wide unfold the radiant scene; Alleluia!
Take the King of glory in! Alleluia!

Lord beyond our mortal sight, Alleluia!
Raise our hearts to reach your height, Alleluia!
There your face unclouded see, Alleluia!
Find our heaven of heavens in thee. Alleluia!

Charles Wesley

The Refrain for the Vespers Lessons

Bless the LORD, you angels of his, you mighty ones who do his bidding,* and
hearken to the voice of his word.

Psalm 103:20

The Vespers Psalm

Where Can I Go Then from Your Spirit?

LORD, you have searched me out and known me;* you know my sitting down and
my rising up; you discern my thoughts from afar.
You trace my journeys and my resting-places* and are acquainted with all my
ways.
Indeed, there is not a word on my lips,* but you, O LORD, know it altogether.
You press upon me behind and before* and lay your hand upon me.
Such knowledge is too wonderful for me;* it is so high that I cannot attain to it.

Psalm 139:1–5

The Refrain

Bless the LORD, you angels of his, you mighty ones who do his bidding,* and
hearken to the voice of his word.

The Small Verse

In the sight of the Angels I praise You. I adore at Your holy temple and give praise
to Your Name.

adapted from THE SHORT BREVIARY

The Lord's Prayer

The Prayer Appointed for the Week

Remember, O Lord, what you have wrought in us and not what we deserve; and,
as you have called me to your service, make me worthy of your calling;
through Jesus Christ our Lord, who lives and reigns with you and the Holy
Spirit, one God, now and for ever. *Amen.* †

The Concluding Prayer of the Church
Blessed be God, who has not rejected my prayer, nor withheld his love from me.

Psalm 66:18

The Morning Office   To Be Observed on the Hour or Half Hour
                                      Between 6 and 9 a.m.

The Call to Prayer
Come, let us sing to the LORD;* let us shout for joy to the Rock of our salvation.
Let us come before his presence with thanksgiving* and raise a loud shout to him
    with psalms.

Psalm 95:1–2

The Request for Presence
Show us the light of your countenance, O God,* and come to us.
based on Psalm 67:1

The Greeting
To you I lift up my eyes,* to you enthroned in the heavens.
As the eyes of servants look to the hand of their masters,* and the eyes of a maid to
    the hand of her mistress,
So our eyes look to the LORD our God,* until he shows us his mercy.

Psalm 123:1–3

The Refrain for the Morning Lessons
I will bear witness that the LORD is righteous;* I will praise the Name of the LORD
    Most High.

Psalm 7:18

A Reading
In my earlier work, Theophilus, I dealt with everything Jesus had done and taught
    from the beginning until the day he gave his instructions to the apostles he had
    chosen through the Holy Spirit, and was taken up to heaven. He had shown
    himself alive to them after his Passion by many demonstrations: for forty days
    he had continued to appear to them and tell them about the kingdom of God.
    While at table with them, he had told them not to leave Jerusalem, but to wait
    there for what the Father had promised. 'It is,' he had said, 'what you have
    heard me speak about: John baptized with water but, not many days from now,
    you are going to be baptized with the Holy Spirit.'

Acts 1:1–5

The Refrain
I will bear witness that the LORD is righteous;* I will praise the Name of the LORD
    Most High.

The Morning Psalm   *The LORD Will Not Break His Oath to David*
Arise, O LORD, into your resting-place,* you and the ark of your strength.
Let your priests be clothed with righteousness;* let your faithful people sing with
    joy.

For your servant David's sake,* do not turn away the face of your Anointed.
The LORD has sworn an oath to David;* in truth, he will not break it:
"A son, the fruit of your body* will I set upon your throne.
If your children keep my covenant and my testimonies that I shall teach them,*
  their children will sit upon your throne for evermore."

Psalm 132:8–13

The Refrain
I will bear witness that the LORD is righteous;* I will praise the Name of the LORD
  Most High.

The Small Verse
Keep me, Lord, as the apple of your eye and carry me under the shadow of your
  wings.

Traditional

The Lord's Prayer

The Prayer Appointed for the Week
Remember, O Lord, what you have wrought in us and not what we deserve; and,
  as you have called me to your service, make me worthy of your calling;
  through Jesus Christ our Lord, who lives and reigns with you and the Holy
  Spirit, one God, now and for ever. *Amen.* †

The Concluding Prayer of the Church
Lord God, almighty and everlasting Father, you have brought me in safety to this
  new day: Preserve me with your mighty power, that I may not fall into sin, nor
  be overcome by adversity; and in all I do direct me to the fulfilling of your purpose; through Jesus Christ my Lord. *Amen.* †

The Midday Office
**To Be Observed on the Hour or Half Hour
Between 11 a.m. and 2 p.m.**

The Call to Prayer
Praise Him from whom all blessings flow; praise Him all creatures here below;
  praise Him you heavenly hosts; praise Father, Son and Holy Ghost

Traditional Doxology

The Request for Presence
Be my strong rock, a castle to keep me safe, for you are my crag and my stronghold;* for the sake of your Name, lead me and guide me.

Psalm 31:3

The Greeting
To you, O LORD, I lift up my soul;* my God, I put my trust in you.

Psalm 25:1

The Refrain for the Midday Lessons
Happy are they all who fear the LORD,* and who follow in his ways!

Psalm 128:1

A Reading
A vision of the prophet Daniel: "I was gazing into the visions of the night, when I saw, coming on the clouds of heaven, as it were a son of man. He came to the One most venerable and was led into his presence. On him was conferred rule, honor and kingship, and all peoples, nations and languages became his servants. His rule is an everlasting rule which will never pass away, and his kingship will never come to an end."

Daniel 7:13–14

The Refrain
Happy are they all who fear the LORD,* and who follow in his ways!

The Midday Psalm   *The LORD Will Bless Both Small and Great Who Trust Him*
Not to us, O LORD, not to us,* but to your Name give glory; because of your love and because of your faithfulness.
Why should the heathen say,* "Where then is their God?"
Our God is in heaven;* whatever he wills to do he does.
Their idols are silver and gold,* the work of human hands.
They have mouths, but they cannot speak;* eyes have they, but they cannot see;
They have ears, but they cannot hear,* noses, but they cannot smell;
They have hands, but they cannot feel; feet, but they cannot walk;* they make no sound with their throat.
Those who make them are like them,* and so are all who put their trust in them.
O Israel, trust in the LORD;* he is their help and their shield.
O house of Aaron, trust in the LORD;* he is their help and their shield.
You who fear the LORD, trust in the LORD;* he is their help and their shield.
The LORD has been mindful of us, and he will bless us;* he will bless the house of Israel; he will bless the house of Aaron;
He will bless those who fear the LORD,* both small and great together.

Psalm 115:1–13

The Refrain
Happy are they all who fear the LORD,* and who follow in his ways!

The Small Verse
The Lord is king. He has put on glorious apparel. Let all the nations praise him. Let those of every tongue bow before him. Alleluia, alleluia, alleluia.

Traditional

The Lord's Prayer

The Prayer Appointed for the Week
Remember, O Lord, what you have wrought in us and not what we deserve; and, as you have called me to your service, make me worthy of your calling; through Jesus Christ our Lord, who lives and reigns with you and the Holy Spirit, one God, now and for ever. *Amen.* †

The Concluding Prayer of the Church

Grant, I pray, Almighty God, that I who believe in Your only-begotten Son our
Redeemer to have ascended into heaven, may myself dwell in spirit amid
heavenly things. Through Jesus Christ my Lord. *Amen.*

adapted from The Short Breviary

The Vespers Office

**To Be Observed on the Hour or Half Hour
Between 5 and 8 p.m.**

The Call to Prayer

Come, let us bow down, and bend the knee,* and kneel before the LORD our
Maker.
For he is our God,* and we are the people of his pasture and the sheep of his hand.

Psalm 95:6–7

The Request for Presence

O LORD, watch over us* and save us from this generation for ever.
The wicked prowl on every side,* and that which is worthless is highly prized by
everyone.

Psalm 12:7–8

The Greeting

How glorious you are!* more splendid than the everlasting mountains!

Psalm 76:4

The Hymn

See the Conqueror mounts in triumph;
See the King in royal state,
Riding on the clouds, his chariot,
To his heavenly palace gate!
Hark! The choirs of angel voices
Joyful alleluias sing,
And the portals high are lifted
To receive their heavenly King.

He who on the cross did suffer,
He who from the grave arose,
He has vanquished sin and Satan;
He by death has spoiled his foes.
While he lifts his hands in blessing,
He is parted from his friends;
While their eager eyes behold him,
He upon the clouds ascends.

He Has Vanquished Sin and Satan

You have raised our human nature
On the clouds to God's right hand:
There we sit in heavenly places,
There with you in glory stand.
Jesus reigns, adored by angels;
Man with God is on the throne;
Mighty Lord, in your ascension,
We by faith behold our own.

Christopher Wordsworth

The Refrain for the Vespers Lessons

Tell it among the nations: "The LORD is King!"

Psalm 96:10

The Vespers Psalm   *He Shall Keep Me Safe*

One thing have I asked of the LORD; one thing I seek;* that I may dwell in the
    house of the LORD all the days of my life;
To behold the fair beauty of the LORD* and to seek him in his temple.
For in the day of trouble he shall keep me safe in his shelter;* he shall hide me in
    the secrecy of his dwelling and set me high upon a rock.
Even now he lifts up my head* above my enemies round about me.
Therefore I will offer in his dwelling an oblation with sounds of great gladness;* I
    will sing and make music to the LORD.

Psalm 27:5–9

The Refrain

Tell it among the nations: "The LORD is King!"

The Gloria

The Lord's Prayer

The Prayer Appointed for the Week

Remember, O Lord, what you have wrought in us and not what we deserve; and,
    as you have called me to your service, make me worthy of your calling;
    through Jesus Christ our Lord, who lives and reigns with you and the Holy
    Spirit, one God, now and for ever. *Amen.* †

The Concluding Prayer of the Church

Blessed be God, who has not rejected my prayer,* nor withheld his love from me.

Psalm 66:18

The Morning Office   **To Be Observed on the Hour or Half Hour**
Between 6 and 9 a.m.

The Call to Prayer

Taste and see that the LORD is good;* happy are they who trust in him!

Psalm 34:8

The Request for Presence

Gladden the soul of your servant,* for to you, O LORD, I lift up my soul.

Psalm 86:4

The Greeting

With my whole heart I seek you;* let me not stray from your commandments.

Psalm 119:10

The Refrain for the Morning Lessons

I will bear witness that the LORD is righteous;* I will praise the Name of the LORD
    Most High.

Psalm 7:18

A Reading

Now having met together, they asked him, 'Lord, has the time come for you to restore the kingdom of Israel?' He replied, 'It is not for you to know times or dates that the Father has decided by his own authority, but you will receive the power of the Holy Spirit which will come on you, and then you will be my witnesses not only in Jerusalem but throughout Judaea and Samaria, and indeed to earth's remotest end.' As he said this he was lifted up while they looked on, and a cloud took him from their sight. They were still staring into the sky as he went when suddenly two men in white were standing beside them and they said, 'Why are you Galileans standing here looking into the sky? This Jesus who has been taken up from you into heaven will come back the same way as you have seen him go to heaven.'

Acts 1:6–11

The Refrain

I will bear witness that the LORD is righteous;* I will praise the Name of the LORD Most High.

The Morning Psalm   *I Will Not Forget Your Word*

It is better to rely on the LORD* than to put any trust in rulers.

All the ungodly encompass me;* in the name of the LORD I will repel them.

They hem me in, they hem me in on every side;* in the name of the LORD I will repel them.

They swarm about me like bees; they blaze like a fire of thorns;* in the name of the LORD I will repel them.

I was pressed so hard that I almost fell,* but the LORD came to my help.

The LORD is my strength and my song,* and he has become my salvation.

There is a sound of exultation and victory* in the tents of the righteous:

"The right hand of the LORD has triumphed!* the right hand of the LORD is exalted! the right hand of the LORD has triumphed!"

Psalm 118:9–16

The Refrain

I will bear witness that the LORD is righteous;* I will praise the Name of the LORD Most High.

The Small Verse

Let me seek the Lord while he may still be found. I will call upon his name while he is near.

Traditional

The Lord's Prayer

The Prayer Appointed for the Week

Remember, O Lord, what you have wrought in us and not what we deserve; and, as you have called me to your service, make me worthy of your calling; through Jesus Christ our Lord, who lives and reigns with you and the Holy Spirit, one God, now and for ever. *Amen.* †

The Concluding Prayer of the Church

Lord God, almighty and everlasting Father, you have brought me in safety to this new day: Preserve me with your mighty power, that I may not fall into sin, nor be overcome by adversity; and in all I do direct me to the fulfilling of your purpose; through Jesus Christ my Lord. *Amen.* †

The Midday Office

To Be Observed on the Hour or Half Hour
Between 11 a.m. and 2 p.m.

The Call to Prayer

Come, let us sing to the LORD;* let us shout for joy to the Rock of our salvation.
Let us come before his presence with thanksgiving* and raise a loud shout to him with psalms.
For the LORD is a great God,* and a great King above all gods.
In his hand are the caverns of the earth,* and the heights of the hills are his also.
The sea is his, for he made it,* and his hands have molded the dry land.

Psalm 95:1–5

The Request for Presence

Remember not our past sins;* let your compassion be swift to meet us.

Psalm 79:8

The Greeting

Zion hears and is glad, and the cities of Judah rejoice,* because of your judgments, O LORD.

Psalm 97:8

The Refrain for the Midday Lessons

I will listen to what the LORD God is saying,* for he is speaking peace to his faithful people and to those who turn their hearts to him.

Psalm 85:8

A Reading

Further, the former priests were many in number, because death put an end to each one of them; but this one, because he remains *for ever,* has a perpetual priesthood. It follows, then, that his power to save those who come to God through him is absolute, since he lives for ever to intercede for them.

Hebrews 7:23–25

The Refrain

I will listen to what the LORD God is saying,* for he is speaking peace to his faithful people and to those who turn their hearts to him.

The Midday Psalm   *Sing to the LORD a New Song*

Hallelujah! Sing to the LORD a new song;* sing his praise in the congregation of the faithful.
Let Israel rejoice in his Maker;* let the children of Zion be joyful in their King.

Let them praise his Name in the dance;* let them sing praise to him with timbrel and harp.

For the Lord takes pleasure in his people* and adorns the poor with victory.

Psalm 149:1–4

The Refrain

I will listen to what the Lord God is saying,* for he is speaking peace to his faithful people and to those who turn their hearts to him.

The Gloria

The Lord's Prayer

The Prayer Appointed for the Week

Remember, O Lord, what you have wrought in us and not what we deserve; and, as you have called me to your service, make me worthy of your calling; through Jesus Christ our Lord, who lives and reigns with you and the Holy Spirit, one God, now and for ever. *Amen.* †

The Concluding Prayer of the Church

Direct me, O Lord, on all my doings with your most gracious favor, and further me with your continual help; that in all my work begun, continued, and ended in you, I may glorify your holy name, and finally, by your mercy, obtain everlasting life; through Jesus Christ my Lord. *Amen.* †

The Vespers Office   **To Be Observed on the Hour or Half Hour**
Between 5 and 8 p.m.

The Call to Prayer

But I will call upon God,* and the Lord will deliver me.

In the evening, in the morning, and at noonday, I will complain and lament,* and he will hear my voice.

He will bring me safely back . . .

God, who is enthroned of old, will hear me.

Psalm 55:17ff

The Request for Presence

I cry out to you, O Lord;* I say, "You are my refuge, my portion in the land of the living."

Psalm 142:5

The Greeting

I will confess you among the peoples, O Lord;* I will sing praises to you among the nations.

Psalm 108:3

The Hymn

A hymn of glory let us sing,
new hymns throughout the world shall ring;
by a new way none ever trod
Christ takes his place—the throne of God!

You are a present joy, O Lord;
you will be ever our reward;
and great the light in you we see
to guide us to eternity.

O risen Christ, ascended Lord,
all praise to you let earth accord,
who are, while endless ages run,
with Father and with Spirit, One.

The Venerable Bede

The Refrain for the Vespers Lessons

The LORD will hear the desire of the humble;* you will strengthen their heart and
your ears shall hear.

Psalm 10:18

The Vespers Psalm   *Let All Who Seek You Rejoice*

You are the LORD; do not withhold your compassion from me;* let your love and
your faithfulness keep me safe for ever,
For innumerable troubles have crowded upon me; my sins have overtaken me,
and I cannot see;* they are more in number than the hairs of my head, and my
heart fails me.
Be pleased, O LORD, to deliver me;* O LORD, make haste to help me.
Let them be ashamed and altogether dismayed who seek after my life to destroy
it;* let them draw back and be disgraced who take pleasure in my misfortune.
Let those who say "Aha!" and gloat over me be confounded* because they are
ashamed.
Let all who seek you rejoice in you and be glad;* let those who love your salvation
continually say, "Great is the LORD!"
Though I am poor and afflicted,* the Lord will have regard for me.
You are my helper and my deliverer,* do not tarry, O my God.

Psalm 40:12–19

The Refrain

The LORD will hear the desire of the humble;* you will strengthen their heart and
your ears shall hear.

The Small Verse

The Lord is my shepherd and nothing is wanting to me. In green pastures He has
settled me.

THE SHORT BREVIARY

The Lord's Prayer

The Prayer Appointed for the Week
Remember, O Lord, what you have wrought in us and not what we deserve; and,
as you have called me to your service, make me worthy of your calling;
through Jesus Christ our Lord, who lives and reigns with you and the Holy
Spirit, one God, now and for ever. *Amen.* †

The Concluding Prayer of the Church
Lead me not into temptation. Deliver me from evil. Yours are the kingdom and the
glory.

The Morning Office **To Be Observed on the Hour or Half Hour**
Between 6 and 9 a.m.

The Call to Prayer
Come, let us bow down, and bend the knee,* and kneel before the LORD our
Maker.
For he is our God,* and we are the people of his pasture and the sheep of his hand.
Psalm 95:6–7

The Request for Presence
So teach us to number our days* that we may apply our hearts to wisdom.
Psalm 90:12

The Greeting
My God, my rock in whom I put my trust,* my shield, the horn of my salvation,
and my refuge; you are worthy of praise.
Psalm 18:2

The Refrain for the Morning Lessons
My eyes are upon the faithful in the land, that they may dwell with me.
Psalm 101:6

A Reading
Jesus said: "Anyone who welcomes a prophet because he is a prophet will have a
prophet's reward; and anyone who welcomes an upright person because he is
upright will have the reward of an upright person. If anyone gives so much as
a cup of cold water to one of these little ones because he is a disciple, then in all
truth I tell you, he will most certainly not go without his reward."
Matthew 10:41–42

The Refrain
My eyes are upon the faithful in the land, that they may dwell with me.

The Morning Psalm *The Eye of the LORD Is Upon Those Who Fear Him*
The LORD looks down from heaven,* and beholds all the people in the world.
From where he sits enthroned he turns his gaze* on all who dwell on the earth.
He fashions all the hearts of them* and understands all their works.

There is no king that can be saved by a mighty army;* a strong man is not delivered
by his great strength.

The horse is a vain hope for deliverance;* for all its strength it cannot save.

Behold, the eye of the LORD is upon those who fear him,* on those who wait upon
his love,

To pluck their lives from death,* and to feed them in time of famine.

Our soul waits for the LORD;* he is our help and our shield.

Indeed, our heart rejoices in him,* for in his holy Name we put our trust.

Let your loving-kindness, O LORD, be upon us,* as we have put our trust in you.

Psalm 33:13–22

The Refrain

My eyes are upon the faithful in the land, that they may dwell with me.

The Cry of the Church

O God, come to my assistance! O Lord, make haste to help me!

The Lord's Prayer

The Prayer Appointed for the Week

Remember, O Lord, what you have wrought in us and not what we deserve; and,
as you have called me to your service, make me worthy of your calling;
through Jesus Christ our Lord, who lives and reigns with you and the Holy
Spirit, one God, now and for ever. *Amen.* †

The Concluding Prayer of the Church

Lord God, almighty and everlasting Father, you have brought me in safety to this
new day: Preserve me with your mighty power, that I may not fall into sin, nor
be overcome by adversity; and in all I do direct me to the fulfilling of your purpose; through Jesus Christ my Lord. *Amen.* †

The Midday Office

**To Be Observed on the Hour or Half Hour
Between 11 a.m. and 2 p.m.**

The Call to Prayer

God has gone up with a shout,* the LORD with the sound of the ram's-horn.

Sing praises to God, sing praises;* sing praises to our King, sing praises.

For God is King of all the earth;* sing praises with all your skill.

God reigns over the nations;* God sits upon his holy throne.

Psalm 47:5–8

The Request for Presence

Answer me when I call, O God, defender of my cause;* you set me free when I am
hard-pressed; have mercy on me and hear my prayer.

Psalm 4:1

The Greeting

Deliver me, my God, from the hand of the wicked,* from the clutches of the evildoer and the oppressor.

For you are my hope, O Lord GOD,* my confidence since I was young.

I have been sustained by you ever since I was born;* from my mother's womb you have been my strength; my praise shall be always of you.

Psalm 71:4–6

The Refrain for the Midday Lessons

Your love, O LORD, for ever will I sing;* from age to age my mouth will proclaim your faithfulness.

Psalm 89:1

A Reading

But now Christ has come, as the high priest of all the blessings which were to come. He has passed through the greater, the more perfect tent, not made by human hands, that is, not of this created order; and he has entered the sanctuary once and for all, taking with him not the blood of goats and bull calves, but his own blood, having won an eternal redemption.

Hebrews 9:11–12

The Refrain

Your love, O LORD, for ever will I sing;* from age to age my mouth will proclaim your faithfulness.

The Midday Psalm   *We Shall Be Glad All the Days of Our Life*

Satisfy us by your loving-kindness in the morning;* so shall we rejoice and be glad all the days of our life.

Make us glad by the measure of the days that you afflicted us* and the years in which we suffered adversity.

Show your servants your works* and your splendor to their children.

May the graciousness of the LORD our God be upon us;* prosper the work of our hands; prosper our handiwork.

Psalm 90:14–17

The Refrain

Your love, O LORD, for ever will I sing;* from age to age my mouth will proclaim your faithfulness.

The Gloria

The Lord's Prayer

The Prayer Appointed for the Week

Remember, O Lord, what you have wrought in us and not what we deserve; and, as you have called me to your service, make me worthy of your calling; through Jesus Christ our Lord, who lives and reigns with you and the Holy Spirit, one God, now and for ever. *Amen.* †

The Concluding Prayer of the Church

In truth God has heard me; he has attended the voice of my prayer. Thanks be to God. *Amen.*

based on Psalm 66:17

The Vespers Office

To Be Observed on the Hour or Half Hour Between 5 and 8 p.m.

The Call to Prayer

Blessed be the LORD, the God of Israel, from everlasting and to everlasting;* and let all the people say, "Amen!" Hallelujah!

Psalm 106:48

The Request for Presence

Send forth your strength, O God;* establish, O God, what you have wrought for us.

Psalm 68:28

The Greeting

My heart is firmly fixed, O God, my heart is fixed;* I will sing and make melody.

Psalm 57:7

The Hymn

O Lord Most High, eternal King,
By you redeemed, your praise we sing.
The bonds of death are burst by thee,
And grace has won the victory.

You are our joy, O mighty Lord,
As you will be our great reward;
Let all our glory be in thee
Both now and through eternity.

Ascending to the Father's throne
You claim the kingdom as your own;
And angels wonder when they see
How changed is our humanity.

O risen Christ, ascended Lord,
All praise to you let earth accord,
Who are while endless ages run,
With Father and with Spirit, One.

Latin, Unknown

The Refrain for the Vespers Lessons

I trust in the mercy of God for ever and ever.
I will give you thanks for what you have done* and declare the goodness of your Name in the presence of the godly.

Psalm 52:8–9

The Vespers Psalm

I Would Make Known to This Generation Your Power and Your Strength

O God, you have taught me since I was young,* and to this day I tell of your wonderful works.
And now that I am old and gray-headed, O God, do not forsake me,* till I make known your strength to this generation and your power to all who are to come.
Your righteousness, O God, reaches to the heavens;* you have done great things; who is like you, O God?

You have showed me great troubles and adversities,* but you will restore my life
and bring me up again from the deep places of the earth.
Psalm 71:17–20

The Refrain
I trust in the mercy of God for ever and ever.
I will give you thanks for what you have done* and declare the goodness of your
Name in the presence of the godly.

The Cry of the Church
Even so, come Lord Jesus!

The Lord's Prayer

The Prayer Appointed for the Week
Remember, O Lord, what you have wrought in us and not what we deserve; and,
as you have called me to your service, make me worthy of your calling;
through Jesus Christ our Lord, who lives and reigns with you and the Holy
Spirit, one God, now and for ever. *Amen.* †

The Concluding Prayer of the Church
Almighty God, whose loving hand has given me all that I possess: Grant me grace
that I may honor you with my substance, and, remembering the account which
I must one day give, may be a faithful steward of your bounty, through Jesus
Christ our Lord. *Amen.* †

The Morning Office　　　　　　　　**To Be Observed on the Hour or Half Hour
Between 6 and 9 a.m.**

The Call to Prayer
Sing to the LORD a new song;* sing to the LORD, all the whole earth.
Psalm 96:1

The Request for Presence
I call with my whole heart;* answer me, O LORD, that I may keep your statutes.
Psalm 119:145

The Greeting
Glory to you, Lord God of our fathers; you are worthy of praise; glory to you.
Glory to you for the radiance of your holy Name; we will praise you and
highly exalt you for ever. Glory to you in the splendor of your temple; on the
throne of your majesty, glory to you. Glory to you, seated between the
Cherubim; we will praise you and highly exalt you for ever. Glory to you,
beholding the depths; in the high vault of heaven, glory to you. Glory to you,
Father, Son, and Holy Spirit; we will praise you and highly exalt you for ever.
Te Deum

The Refrain for the Morning Lessons
Righteousness shall go before him,* and peace shall be a pathway for his feet.

Psalm 85:13

A Reading
Then he told them a parable about the need to pray continually and never lose heart. 'There was a judge in a certain town,' he said, 'who had neither fear of God nor respect for anyone. In the same town there was also a widow who kept coming to him and saying, "I want justice from you against my enemy!" For a long time he refused, but at last he said to himself, "Even though I have neither fear of God nor respect for any human person, I must give this widow her just rights since she keeps pestering me, or she will come and slap me in the face." ' And the Lord said, 'You notice what the unjust judge has to say? Now, will not God see justice done to his elect if they keep calling him day and night even though he delays to help them? I promise you, he will see justice done to them, and done speedily.'

Luke 18:1–8

The Refrain
Righteousness shall go before him,* and peace shall be a pathway for his feet.

The Morning Psalm   *He Has Shown Me the Wonders of His Love*
How great is your goodness, O Lord! which you have laid up for those who fear you;* which you have done in the sight of all for those who put their trust in you.
You hide them in the covert of your presence from those who slander them;* you keep them in your shelter from the strife of tongues.
Blessed be the Lord!* for he has shown me the wonders of his love in a besieged city.

Psalm 31:19–21

The Refrain
Righteousness shall go before him,* and peace shall be a pathway for his feet.

The Gloria

The Lord's Prayer

The Prayer Appointed for the Week
Remember, O Lord, what you have wrought in us and not what we deserve; and, as you have called me to your service, make me worthy of your calling; through Jesus Christ our Lord, who lives and reigns with you and the Holy Spirit, one God, now and for ever. *Amen.* †

The Concluding Prayer of the Church
Lord God, almighty and everlasting Father, you have brought me in safety to this new day: Preserve me with your mighty power, that I may not fall into sin, nor be overcome by adversity; and in all I do direct me to the fulfilling of your purpose; through Jesus Christ my Lord. *Amen.* †

| The Midday Office | To Be Observed on the Hour or Half Hour Between 11 a.m. and 2 p.m. |

The Call to Prayer
Let us bless the LORD, from this time forth for evermore. Hallelujah!
based on Psalm 115:18

The Request for Presence
Send forth your strength, O God;* establish, O God, what you have wrought for us.
Psalm 68:28

The Greeting
I will thank you, O LORD my God, with all my heart,* and glorify your Name for
    evermore.

Psalm 86:12

The Refrain for the Midday Lessons
This is the LORD's doing,* and it is marvelous in our eyes.
Psalm 118:23

A Reading
The prophet Isaiah said: "So the Lord YAHWEH says this, 'Now I shall lay a stone in
    Zion, a granite stone, a precious corner-stone, a firm foundation-stone: No one
    who relies on this will stumble.
And I will make fair judgement the measure, and uprightness the plumb-line.' "
Isaiah 28:16–17

The Refrain
This is the LORD's doing,* and it is marvelous in our eyes.

The Midday Psalm   *He Saves for His Name's Sake*
We have sinned as our forebears did;* we have done wrong and dealt wickedly.
In Egypt they did not consider your marvelous works, nor remember the abun-
    dance of your love;* they defied the Most High at the Red Sea.
But he saved them for his Name's sake,* to make his power known.
He rebuked the Red Sea, and it dried up,* and he led them through the deep as
    through a desert.
He saved them from the hand of those who hated them* and redeemed them from
    the hand of the enemy.
The waters covered their oppressors;* not one of them was left.
Then they believed his words* and sang him songs of praise.
Psalm 106:6–12

The Refrain
This is the LORD's doing,* and it is marvelous in our eyes.

The Cry of the Church
O Lord, hear my prayer and let my cry come unto you. Thanks be to God.
THE SHORT BREVIARY

The Lord's Prayer

The Prayer Appointed for the Week
Remember, O Lord, what you have wrought in us and not what we deserve; and,
as you have called me to your service, make me worthy of your calling;
through Jesus Christ our Lord, who lives and reigns with you and the Holy
Spirit, one God, now and for ever. *Amen.* †

The Concluding Prayer of the Church
Lord Jesus Christ, by your death you took away the sting of death: Grant me to so
follow in faith where you have led the way, that I may at length fall asleep
peacefully in you and wake in your likeness; for your tender mercies' sake.
Amen. †

The Vespers Office   To Be Observed on the Hour or Half Hour
                                              Between 5 and 8 p.m.

The Call to Prayer
I will call upon God,* and the LORD will deliver me.
In the evening, in the morning, and at noonday, I will complain and lament,* and
he will hear my voice.
He will bring me safely back . . .* God, who is enthroned of old, will hear me.

Psalm 55:17ff

The Request for Presence
You are the LORD; do not withhold your compassion from me;* let your love and
your faithfulness keep me safe for ever.

Psalm 40:12

The Greeting
I remember your Name in the night, O LORD,* and dwell upon your law.

Psalm 119:55

The Hymn
> As pants the hart for cooling streams
> When heated in the chase,
> So longs my soul, O God for You,
> And Your refreshing grace.
>
> For You, my God, the living God,
> My thirsty soul does pine;
> O when shall I behold Your face,
> Your Majesty divine!
>
> Why restless, why cast down, my soul?
> Trust God; and He'll employ
> His aid for you, and change these sighs
> To thankful hymns of joy.

Why restless, why cast down, my soul?
Hope still; and you will sing
The praise of Him who is your God,
Your health's eternal spring.

> *Psalm 42; Tate and Brady's*
> *New Version, 1696*

The Refrain for the Vespers Lessons
. . . he gives to his beloved sleep.

> *Psalm 127:3*

The Vespers Psalm   The Lord Sustains Me
But you, O Lord, are a shield about me;* you are my glory, the one who lifts up my
head.
I call aloud upon the Lord,* and he answers me from his holy hill;
I lie down and go to sleep;* I wake again, because the Lord sustains me.
Deliverance belongs to the Lord.* Your blessing be upon your people!

> *Psalm 3:3–5, 8*

The Refrain
. . . he gives to his beloved sleep.

The Small Verse
Open, Lord, my eyes that I may see. Open, Lord, my ears that I may hear. Open,
Lord, my heart and my mind that I may understand. So shall I turn to you and
be healed.

> *Traditional*

The Lord's Prayer

The Prayer Appointed for the Week
Remember, O Lord, what you have wrought in us and not what we deserve; and,
as you have called me to your service, make me worthy of your calling;
through Jesus Christ our Lord, who lives and reigns with you and the Holy
Spirit, one God, now and for ever. *Amen.* †

Concluding Prayers of the Church
Lord Jesus Christ, by your death you took away the sting of death: Grant me to so
follow in faith where you have led the way, that I may at length fall asleep
peacefully in you and wake in your likeness; for your tender mercies' sake.
Amen. †

May the souls of the faithful departed, through the mercy of God, rest in eternal
peace. *Amen.*

The Morning Office   **To Be Observed on the Hour or Half Hour
Between 6 and 9 a.m.**

The Call to Prayer
Let us bless the Lord,* from this time forth for evermore. Hallelujah!
based on Psalm 115:18

The Request for Presence
I cry out to you, O Lord;* I say, "You are my refuge, my portion in the land of the
living."
Psalm 142:5

The Greeting
I will confess you among the peoples, O Lord;* I will sing praises to you among
the nations.
For your loving-kindness is greater than the heavens,* and your faithfulness
reaches to the clouds.
Psalm 108:3–4

The Refrain for the Morning Lessons
For the Lord God is both sun and shield;* he will give grace and glory.
Psalm 84:10

A Reading
Jesus taught us, saying: "When they take you before synagogues and magistrates
and authorities, do not worry about how to defend yourselves or what to say,
because when the time comes, the Holy Spirit will teach you what you should
say."
Luke 12:11–12

The Refrain
For the Lord God is both sun and shield;* he will give grace and glory.

The Morning Psalm   *You Are the God of My Salvation*
To you, O Lord, I lift up my soul; my God, I put my trust in you;* let me not be
humiliated, nor let my enemies triumph over me.
Let none who look to you be put to shame;* let the treacherous be disappointed in
their schemes.
Show me your ways, O Lord,* and teach me your paths.
Lead me in your truth and teach me,* for you are the God of my salvation; in you
have I trusted all the day long.
Psalm 25:1–4

The Refrain
For the Lord God is both sun and shield;* he will give grace and glory.

The Gloria

The Lord's Prayer

The Prayer Appointed for the Week
Remember, O Lord, what you have wrought in us and not what we deserve; and,
as you have called me to your service, make me worthy of your calling;
through Jesus Christ our Lord, who lives and reigns with you and the Holy
Spirit, one God, now and for ever. *Amen.* †

The Concluding Prayer of the Church
Lord God, almighty and everlasting Father, you have brought me in safety to this
new day: Preserve me with your mighty power, that I may not fall into sin, nor
be overcome by adversity; and in all I do direct me to the fulfilling of your purpose; through Jesus Christ my Lord. *Amen.* †

The Midday Office   To Be Observed on the Hour or Half Hour
                                                Between 11 a.m. and 2 p.m.

The Call to Prayer
Bless our God, you peoples;* make the voice of his praise to be heard;
Who holds our souls in life,* and will not allow our feet to slip.
Psalm 66:7–8

The Request for Presence
Let your ways be known upon earth,* your saving health among all nations.
Psalm 67:2

The Greeting
How great is your goodness, O LORD! which you have laid up for those who fear
you;* which you have done in the sight of all for those who put their trust in
you.
Psalm 31:19

The Refrain for the Midday Lessons
Your love, O LORD, reaches to the heavens,* and your faithfulness to the clouds.
Psalm 36:5

A Reading
Before God and before Christ Jesus who is to be judge of the living and the dead, I
charge you, in the name of his appearing and of his kingdom: proclaim the
message and, welcome or unwelcome, insist on it. Refute falsehood, correct
error, give encouragement—but do all with patience and with care to instruct.
2 Timothy 4:1–2

The Refrain
Your love, O LORD, reaches to the heavens,* and your faithfulness to the clouds.

The Midday Psalm   *Princely State Is Yours*
The LORD said to my Lord, "Sit at my right hand,* until I make your enemies your
footstool."

The LORD will send the scepter of your power out of Zion,* saying, "Rule over
  your enemies round about you.
Princely state has been yours from the day of your birth;* in the beauty of holiness
  have I begotten you, like dew from the womb of the morning."
The LORD has sworn and he will not recant:* "You are a priest for ever after the
  order of Melchizedek."
The Lord who is at your right hand will smite kings in the day of his wrath;* he
  will rule over the nations.

Psalm 110:1–5

The Refrain
Your love, O LORD, reaches to the heavens,* and your faithfulness to the clouds.

The Small Verse
My help is in the name of the Lord who made heaven and earth and all that is in
  them. Thanks be to God.

Traditional

The Lord's Prayer

The Prayer Appointed for the Week
Remember, O Lord, what you have wrought in us and not what we deserve; and,
  as you have called me to your service, make me worthy of your calling;
  through Jesus Christ our Lord, who lives and reigns with you and the Holy
  Spirit, one God, now and for ever. *Amen.* †

The Concluding Prayer of the Church
O God, the source of eternal light: Shed forth your unending day upon all of us
  who watch for you, that our lips may praise you, our lives may bless you, and
  our worship may give you glory; through Jesus Christ our Lord. *Amen.* †

The Vespers Office　　　　　　　**To Be Observed on the Hour or Half Hour**
　　　　　　　　　　　　　　　　　　　　Between 5 and 8 p.m.

The Call to Prayer
Bless our God, you peoples;* make the voice of his praise to be heard;
Who holds our souls in life,* and will not allow our feet to slip.

Psalm 66:7–8

The Request for Presence
O God of hosts;* show us the light of your countenance, and we shall be saved.

Psalm 80:7

The Greeting
As the eyes of servants look to the hand of their masters,* and the eyes of a maid to
  the hand of her mistress,
So my eyes look to you, O LORD my God.

based on Psalm 123:2–3

The Hymn   *This Little Light of Mine*
    This little light of mine, I'm gonna let it shine,
    This little light of mine, I'm gonna let it shine,
    This little light of mine, I'm gonna let it shine,
    Let it shine, let it shine, let it shine,

    Everywhere I go, I'm gonna let it shine,
    Everywhere I go, I'm gonna let it shine,
    Everywhere I go, I'm gonna let it shine,
    Let it shine, let it shine, let it shine,

    All through the night, I'm gonna let it shine,
    All through the night, I'm gonna let it shine,
    All through the night, I'm gonna let it shine,
    Let it shine, let it shine, let it shine.
                    African American Spiritual

The Refrain for the Vespers Lessons
For I am but a sojourner with you,* a wayfarer, as all my forebears were.
                                    Psalm 39:14

The Vespers Psalm   *Having You I Desire Nothing on Earth*
When my mind became embittered,* I was sorely wounded in my heart.
I was stupid and had no understanding;* I was like a brute beast in your presence.
Yet I am always with you;* you hold me by my right hand.
You will guide me by your counsel,* and afterwards receive me with glory.
Whom have I in heaven but you?* and having you I desire nothing upon earth.
Though my flesh and my heart should waste away, God is the strength of my
    heart and my portion for ever.
Truly, those who forsake you will perish;* you destroy all who are unfaithful.
But it is good for me to be near God;* I have made the Lord GOD my refuge.
I will speak of all your works* in the gates of the city of Zion.
                                    Psalm 73:21–29

The Refrain
For I am but a sojourner with you,* a wayfarer, as all my forebears were.

The Cry of the Church
Even so come, Lord Jesus!

The Lord's Prayer

The Prayer Appointed for the Week
Remember, O Lord, what you have wrought in us and not what we deserve; and,
    as you have called me to your service, make me worthy of your calling;
    through Jesus Christ our Lord, who lives and reigns with you and the Holy
    Spirit, one God, now and for ever. *Amen.* †

The Concluding Prayer of the Church
Almighty God, who after the creation of the world rested from all your works and sanctified a day of rest for all your creatures: Grant that I, putting away all earthly anxieties, may be duly prepared for the service of public worship, and grant as well that my Sabbath upon earth may be a preparation for the eternal rest promised to your people in heaven; through Jesus Christ our Lord. *Amen.* †

੭ৡৡৡ

The Morning Office   **To Be Observed on the Hour or Half Hour**
Between 6 and 9 a.m.

The Call to Prayer
Sing to the Lord and bless his Name;* proclaim the good news of his salvation from day to day.
Declare his glory among the nations* and his wonders among all peoples.
For great is the Lord and greatly to be praised;* he is more to be feared than all gods.

Psalm 96:2–4

The Request for Presence
Satisfy us by your loving-kindness in the morning;* so shall we rejoice and be glad all the days of our life.

Psalm 90:14

The Greeting
Awesome things will you show us in your righteousness, O God of our salvation,* O Hope of all the ends of the earth and of the seas that are far away.

Psalm 65:5

The Refrain for the Morning Lessons
You shall not be afraid of any terror by night,* nor of the arrow that flies by day.

Psalm 91:5

A Reading
Jesus said: "Now I am going to the one who sent me. Not one of you asks, 'Where are you going?' yet you are sad at heart because I have told you this. Still, I am telling you the truth: it is for your own good that I am going, because unless I go, the Paraclete will not come to you; but if I go, I will send him to you. And when he comes, he will show the world how wrong it was, about sin, and about who was in the right, and about judgement: about sin: in that they refuse to believe in me; about who was in the right: in that I am going to the Father and you will see me no more; about judgement: in that the prince of this world is already condemned."

John 16:5–11

The Refrain
You shall not be afraid of any terror by night,* nor of the arrow that flies by day.

The Morning Psalm   *Let the Name of the LORD Be Blessed*
Hallelujah! Give praise, you servants of the LORD;* praise the Name of the LORD.
Let the Name of the LORD be blessed,* from this time forth for evermore.
From the rising of the sun to its going down* let the Name of the LORD be praised.
The LORD is high above all nations,* and his glory above the heavens.
Who is like the LORD our God, who sits enthroned on high* but stoops to behold
    the heavens and the earth?
He takes up the weak out of the dust* and lifts up the poor from the ashes.
He sets them with the princes,* with the princes of his people.
He makes the woman of a childless house* to be a joyful mother of children.
                                                            Psalm 113

The Refrain
You shall not be afraid of any terror by night,* nor of the arrow that flies by day.

The Cry of the Church
O Lord, hear my prayer and let my cry come unto you. Thanks be to God.
                                        THE SHORT BREVIARY

The Lord's Prayer

The Prayer Appointed for the Week
Almighty and merciful God, in your goodness keep me, I pray, from all things that
    may hurt me, that I, being ready both in mind and body, may accomplish with
    a free heart those things which belong to your purpose; through Jesus Christ
    my Lord, who lives and reigns with you and the Holy Spirit, one God, now and
    for ever. *Amen.* †

The Concluding Prayer of the Church
Lord God, almighty and everlasting Father, you have brought me in safety to this
    new day: Preserve me with your mighty power, that I may not fall into sin, nor
    be overcome by adversity; and in all I do direct me to the fulfilling of your pur-
    pose; through Jesus Christ my Lord. *Amen.* †

The Midday Office   **To Be Observed on the Hour or Half Hour**
                                   Between 11 a.m. and 2 p.m.

The Call to Prayer
God is the LORD; he has shined upon us;* form a procession with branches up to
    the horns of the altar.
                                                        Psalm 118:27

The Request for Presence
Open my lips, O Lord,* and my mouth shall proclaim your praise.
                                                        Psalm 51:16

The Greeting
Let all who seek you rejoice and be glad in you;* let those who love your salvation
say for ever, "Great is the LORD!"

Psalm 70:4

The Refrain for the Midday Lessons
The words of the LORD are tried in the fire;* he is a shield to all who trust in him.

Psalm 18:31

A Reading
You were dead, because you were sinners and uncircumcised in body: he has
brought you to life with him, he has forgiven us every one of our sins. He has
wiped out the record of our debt to the Law which stood against us; he has
destroyed it by nailing it to the cross; and he has stripped the sovereignties and
the ruling forces and paraded them in public, behind him in triumphal procession.

Colossians 2:13–15

The Refrain
The words of the LORD are tried in the fire;* he is a shield to all who trust in him.

The Midday Psalm   The LORD Is Faithful in All His Works
The LORD is gracious and full of compassion,* slow to anger and of great kindness.
The LORD is loving to everyone* and his compassion is over all his works.
All your works praise you, O LORD,* and your faithful servants bless you.
They make known the glory of your kingdom* and speak of your power;
That the peoples may know of your power* and the glorious splendor of your
kingdom.
Your kingdom is an everlasting kingdom;* your dominion endures throughout all
ages.

Psalm 145:8–13

The Refrain
The words of the LORD are tried in the fire;* he is a shield to all who trust in him.

The Small Verse
Blessed be the Lord God of Israel for he has visited and delivered us. Alleluia,
alleluia, alleluia.

Traditional

The Lord's Prayer

The Prayer Appointed for the Week
Almighty and merciful God, in your goodness keep me, I pray, from all things that
may hurt me, that I, being ready both in mind and body, may accomplish with
a free heart those things which belong to your purpose; through Jesus Christ
my Lord, who lives and reigns with you and the Holy Spirit, one God, now and
for ever. *Amen.* †

The Concluding Prayer of the Church

O God, you make me glad with the weekly remembrance of the glorious resurrection of your Son my Lord: Give me this day such blessing through my worship of you, that the week to come may be spent in your favor; through Jesus Christ our Lord. *Amen.* †

The Vespers Office

To Be Observed on the Hour or Half Hour Between 5 and 8 p.m.

The Call to Prayer

Sing praise to the LORD who dwells in Zion;* proclaim to the peoples the things he has done.

Psalm 9:11

The Request for Presence

To you I lift up my eyes,* to you enthroned in the heavens.

Psalm 123:1

The Greeting

I put my trust in your mercy;* my heart is joyful because of your saving help.

Psalm 13:5

The Hymn

O Trinity of Blessed Light

O Trinity of blessed light
O Unity of princely might,
The fiery sun now goes his way;
Shed within our hearts Your ray.

To You our morning song of praise
To You our evening prayer we raise;
Your glory suppliant we adore
For ever and for evermore.

All praise to God the Father be,
All thanks, eternal Son, to Thee;
All glory as is ever meet,
To God the Holy Paraclete.

adapted from THE SHORT BREVIARY

The Refrain for the Vespers Lessons

The angel of the LORD encompasses those who fear him,* and he will deliver them.

Psalm 34:7

The Vespers Psalm   *Those Who Lie in Wait for My Life Are Taking Counsel Together*

For my enemies are talking against me,* and those who lie in wait for my life take counsel together.

They say, "God has forsaken him; go after him and seize him;* because there is none who will save."

O God, be not far from me;* come quickly to help me, O my God.

Let those who set themselves against me be put to shame and be disgraced;* let those who seek to do me evil be covered with scorn and reproach.

But I shall always wait in patience,* and shall praise you more and more.

My mouth shall recount your mighty acts and saving deeds all day long;* though I cannot know the number of them.

I will begin with the mighty works of the Lord GOD;* I will recall your
 righteousness, yours alone.
O God, you have taught me since I was young,* and to this day I tell of your
 wonderful works.

Psalm 71:10–17

The Refrain
The angel of the LORD encompasses those who fear him,* and he will deliver them.

The Cry of the Church
Lord, have mercy on us. Christ, have mercy on us. Lord, have mercy on us.

The Lord's Prayer

The Prayer Appointed for the Week
Almighty and merciful God, in your goodness keep me, I pray, from all things that
 may hurt me, that I, being ready both in mind and body, may accomplish with
 a free heart those things which belong to your purpose; through Jesus Christ
 my Lord, who lives and reigns with you and the Holy Spirit, one God, now and
 for ever. *Amen.* †

The Concluding Prayer of the Church
Almighty God, you have surrounded me with a great cloud of witnesses: Grant
 that I, encouraged by their good example; may persevere in running the race
 that is set before me, until at last I may with them attain to your eternal joy;
 through Jesus Christ, the pioneer and perfecter of our faith, who lives and
 reigns with you and the Holy Spirit, one God, for ever and ever. *Amen.* †

The Morning Office   **To Be Observed on the Hour or Half Hour**
Between 6 and 9 a.m.

The Call to Prayer
Bless the LORD, O my soul,* and all that is within me, bless his holy Name.
Bless the LORD, O my soul,* and forget not all his benefits.

Psalm 103:1–2

The Request for Presence
Protect me, O God, for I take refuge in you;* I have said to the LORD, "You are my
 Lord, my good above all other."

Psalm 16:1

The Greeting
I love you, O LORD my strength,* O LORD my stronghold, my crag, and my haven.

Psalm 18:1

The Refrain for the Morning Lessons
Purge me from my sin, and I shall be pure;* wash me, and I shall be clean indeed.

Psalm 51:8

A Reading
Jesus taught us, saying: "No one sews a piece of unshrunken cloth to an old cloak; otherwise, the patch pulls away from it, the new from the old, and the tear gets worse. And nobody puts new wine into old wineskins; otherwise, the wine will burst the skins, and the wine is lost and the skins too. No! New wine into fresh skins!"

Mark 2:21–22

The Refrain
Purge me from my sin, and I shall be pure;* wash me, and I shall be clean indeed.

The Morning Psalm   *Awesome Things Will You Show Us*
You are to be praised, O God, in Zion;* to you shall vows be performed in Jerusalem.
To you that hear prayer shall all flesh come,* because of their transgressions.
Our sins are stronger than we are,* but you will blot them out.
Happy are they whom you choose and draw to your courts to dwell there!* they will be satisfied by the beauty of your house, by the holiness of your temple.
Awesome things will you show us in your righteousness, O God of our salvation,* O Hope of all the ends of the earth and of the seas that are far away.

Psalm 65:1–5

The Refrain
Purge me from my sin, and I shall be pure;* wash me, and I shall be clean indeed.

The Cry of the Church
O Lamb of God, that takes away the sins of the world, have mercy upon me.
O Lamb of God, that takes away the sins of the world, have mercy upon me.
O Lamb of God, that takes away the sins of the world, grant me your peace.

The Lord's Prayer

The Prayer Appointed for the Week
Almighty and merciful God, in your goodness keep me, I pray, from all things that may hurt me, that I, being ready both in mind and body, may accomplish with a free heart those things which belong to your purpose; through Jesus Christ my Lord, who lives and reigns with you and the Holy Spirit, one God, now and for ever. *Amen.* †

The Concluding Prayer of the Church
Lord God, almighty and everlasting Father, you have brought me in safety to this new day: Preserve me with your mighty power, that I may not fall into sin, nor be overcome by adversity; and in all I do direct me to the fulfilling of your purpose; through Jesus Christ my Lord. *Amen.* †

The Midday Office · To Be Observed on the Hour or Half Hour
Between 11 a.m. and 2 p.m.

The Call to Prayer
Sing to the LORD a new song;* sing to the LORD, all the whole earth.
For great is the LORD and greatly to be praised;* he is more to be feared than all gods.

Psalm 96:1, 4

The Request for Presence
In your righteousness, deliver me and set me free;* incline your ear to me and save me.

Psalm 71:2

The Greeting
Exalt yourself above the heavens, O God,* and your glory over all the earth.

Psalm 108:5

The Refrain for the Midday Lessons
"Be still, then, and know that I am God;* I will be exalted among the nations; I will be exalted in the earth."

Psalm 46:11

A Reading
You may be quite sure that in the last days there will be some difficult times. People will be self-centered and avaricious, boastful, arrogant and rude; disobedient to their parents, ungrateful; heartless and intractable; they will be slanderers, profligates, savages and enemies of everything that is good; they will be treacherous and reckless and demented by pride, preferring their own pleasure to God. They will keep up outward appearance of religion but will have rejected the inner power of it. Keep away from people like that.

2 Timothy 3:1–5

The Refrain
"Be still, then, and know that I am God;* I will be exalted among the nations; I will be exalted in the earth."

The Midday Psalm · *God Is the Rock of My Trust*
As often as I said, "My foot has slipped,"* your love, O LORD, upheld me.
When many cares fill my mind,* your consolations cheer my soul.
Can a corrupt tribunal have any part with you,* one which frames evil into law?
They conspire against the life of the just* and condemn the innocent to death.
But the LORD has become my stronghold,* and my God the rock of my trust.
He will turn their wickedness back upon them and destroy them in their own malice* the LORD our God will destroy them.

Psalm 94:18–23

The Refrain
"Be still, then, and know that I am God;* I will be exalted among the nations; I will
be exalted in the earth."

The Cry of the Church
Even so, come Lord Jesus!

The Lord's Prayer

The Prayer Appointed for the Week
Almighty and merciful God, in your goodness keep me, I pray, from all things that
may hurt me, that I, being ready both in mind and body, may accomplish with
a free heart those things which belong to your purpose; through Jesus Christ
my Lord, who lives and reigns with you and the Holy Spirit, one God, now and
for ever. *Amen.* †

The Concluding Prayer of the Church
Almighty and most merciful God, grant, I beseech you, that by the indwelling of
your Holy Spirit I may be enlightened and strengthened for your service;
through Jesus Christ our Lord, who lives and reigns with you in the unity of
the Holy Spirit, one God, world without end. *Amen.* †

The Vespers Office   **To Be Observed on the Hour or Half Hour**
                                              Between 5 and 8 p.m.

The Call to Prayer
Tremble, then, and do not sin;* speak to your heart in silence upon your bed.
Offer the appointed sacrifices* and put your trust in the LORD.

Psalm 4:4–5

The Request for Presence
Give ear, O LORD, to my prayer,* and attend to the voice of my supplications.

Psalm 86:6

The Greeting
Your way, O God, is holy;* who is so great a god as our God?

Psalm 77:13

The Hymn

Lord, your word abiding,
And our footsteps guiding,
Gives us joy forever,
Shall desert us never.

Who can tell the pleasure,
Who recount the treasure,
By your word imparted
To the simple-hearted?

Word of mercy giving
Succor to the living;
Word of life supplying
Comfort to the dying.

O that we, discerning
Its most holy learning,
Lord, may love and fear you,
Evermore be near you.

Henry W. Baker

The Refrain for the Vespers Lessons
He will judge the world with righteousness* and the peoples with his truth.

Psalm 96:13

The Vespers Psalm *Bless the LORD, All You Servants of the LORD*
Behold now, bless the LORD, all you servants of the LORD,* you that stand by night
in the house of the LORD.
Lift up your hands in the holy place and bless the LORD;* the LORD who made
heaven and earth bless you out of Zion.

Psalm 134

The Refrain
He will judge the world with righteousness* and the peoples with his truth.

The Gloria

The Lord's Prayer

The Prayer Appointed for the Week
Almighty and merciful God, in your goodness keep me, I pray, from all things that
may hurt me, that I, being ready both in mind and body, may accomplish with
a free heart those things which belong to your purpose; through Jesus Christ
my Lord, who lives and reigns with you and the Holy Spirit, one God, now and
for ever. *Amen.* †

The Concluding Prayer of the Church
Almighty God, whose beloved Son willingly endured the agony and shame of the
cross for our redemption: Give me courage to take up my cross and follow him;
who lives and reigns with you and the Holy Spirit, one God, now and for ever.
Amen. †

The Morning Office **To Be Observed on the Hour or Half Hour
Between 6 and 9 a.m.**

The Call to Prayer
Love the LORD, all you who worship him;* the LORD protects the faithful, but
repays to the full those who act haughtily.

Psalm 31:23

The Request for Presence
Early in the morning I cry out to you,* for in your word is my trust.

Psalm 119:147

The Greeting
You are my God, and I will thank you;* you are my God, and I will exalt you.

Psalm 118:28

The Refrain for the Morning Lessons
I hate those who have a divided heart,* but your law do I love.

Psalm 119:113

A Reading
Jesus said: "Everyone who says a word against the Son of man will be forgiven, but no one who blasphemes against the Holy Spirit will be forgiven."

Luke 12:10

The Refrain
I hate those who have a divided heart,* but your law do I love.

The Morning Psalm   *In His Holy Name We Put Our Trust*
Rejoice in the LORD, you righteous;* it is good for the just to sing praises.
For the word of the LORD is right,* and all his works are sure.
Behold, the eye of the LORD is upon those who fear him,* on those who wait upon his love.
Our soul waits for the LORD;* he is our help and our shield.
Indeed, our heart rejoices in him,* for in his holy Name we put our trust.
Let your loving-kindness, O LORD, be upon us,* as we have put our trust in you.

Psalm 33:1, 4, 18–22

The Refrain
I hate those who have a divided heart,* but your law do I love.

The Cry of the Church
Lord, have mercy on us. Christ, have mercy on us. Lord, have mercy on us.

The Lord's Prayer

The Prayer Appointed for the Week
Almighty and merciful God, in your goodness keep me, I pray, from all things that may hurt me, that I, being ready both in mind and body, may accomplish with a free heart those things which belong to your purpose; through Jesus Christ my Lord, who lives and reigns with you and the Holy Spirit, one God, now and for ever. *Amen.* †

The Concluding Prayer of the Church
Lord God, almighty and everlasting Father, you have brought me in safety to this new day: Preserve me with your mighty power, that I may not fall into sin, nor be overcome by adversity; and in all I do direct me to the fulfilling of your purpose; through Jesus Christ my Lord. *Amen.* †

The Midday Office   To Be Observed on the Hour or Half Hour
Between 11 a.m. and 2 p.m.

The Call to Prayer
Open my lips, O Lord,* and my mouth shall proclaim your praise.

Psalm 51:16

The Request for Presence
You are my helper and my deliverer;* do not tarry, O my God.

Psalm 40:19

The Greeting
Hosanna, Lord, hosanna!* Lord, send us now success.
Blessed is he who comes in the name of the Lord;* we bless you from the house of
the Lord.

Psalm 118:25–26

The Refrain for the Midday Lessons
. . . You hold me by my right hand.
You will guide me by your counsel,* and afterwards receive me with glory.

Psalm 73:23–24

A Reading
It is by grace that you have been saved, through faith; not by anything of your
own, but by a gift from God; not by anything that you have done, so that
nobody can claim the credit. We are God's work of art, created in Christ Jesus
for the good works which God has already designated to make up our way of
life.

Ephesians 2:8–10

The Refrain
. . . You hold me by my right hand.
You will guide me by your counsel,* and afterwards receive me with glory.

The Midday Psalm   *How Sweet Are Your Words to My Taste*
Oh, how I love your law!* all the day long it is in my mind.
Your commandment has made me wiser than my enemies,* and it is always with
me.
I have more understanding than all my teachers,* for your decrees are my study.
I am wiser than the elders,* because I observe your commandments.
I restrain my feet from every evil way,* that I may keep your word.
I do not shrink from your judgments,* because you yourself have taught me.
How sweet are your words to my taste!* they are sweeter than honey to my
mouth.
Through your commandments I gain understanding;* therefore I hate every lying
way.

Psalm 119:97–104

The Refrain
. . . You hold me by my right hand.
You will guide me by your counsel,* and afterwards receive me with glory.

The Small Verse
My help is in the Name of the Lord who made the heavens and the earth. What
then shall I fear of what shall I be afraid?

Traditional

The Lord's Prayer

The Prayer Appointed for the Week
Almighty and merciful God, in your goodness keep me, I pray, from all things that
may hurt me, that I, being ready both in mind and body, may accomplish with
a free heart those things which belong to your purpose; through Jesus Christ
my Lord, who lives and reigns with you and the Holy Spirit, one God, now and
for ever. *Amen.* †

The Concluding Prayer of the Church
Direct me, O Lord, in all my doings with your most gracious favor, and further me
with your continual help; that in all my work begun, continued, and ended in
you, I may glorify your holy name, and finally, by your mercy, obtain everlasting life; through Jesus Christ my Lord. *Amen.*

The Vespers Office   **To Be Observed on the Hour or Half Hour**
                                          Between 5 and 8 p.m.

The Call to Prayer
Sing to the LORD with thanksgiving,* make music to our God upon the harp.
                                                         Psalm 147:7

The Request for Presence
Let your countenance shine upon your servant* and teach me your statutes.
                                                         Psalm 119:135

The Greeting
How glorious you are!* more splendid than the everlasting mountains!
                                                         Psalm 76:4

The Hymn
> Most ancient of all mysteries,
> Before your throne we lie;
> Have mercy now, most merciful,
> Most holy Trinity.
>
> When heaven and earth were still unmade,
> When time was yet unknown,
> You in your radiant majesty
> Did live and love alone.
>
> You were not born, there was no source
> From which your Being flowed;
> There is no end which you can reach,
> For you are simply God.
>
> How wonderful creation is,
> The work which you did bless;
> What then must you be like, dear God,
> Eternal loveliness!

Most ancient of all mysteries,
Before your throne we lie,
Have mercy now and evermore,
Most holy Trinity.

Fredrick Faber

The Refrain for the Vespers Lessons

Your love, O LORD, for ever will I sing;* from age to age my mouth will proclaim
your faithfulness.

Psalm 89:1

The Vespers Psalm   *You Make the Darkness That It May Be Night*

The trees of the LORD are full of sap,* the cedars of Lebanon which he planted,
In which the birds build their nests,* and in whose tops the stork makes his
    dwelling.
The high hills are a refuge for the mountain goats,* and the stony cliffs for the rock
    badgers.
You appointed the moon to mark the seasons,* and the sun knows the time of its
    setting.
You make darkness that it may be night,* in which all the beasts of the forest
    prowl.
The lions roar after their prey* and seek their food from God.
The sun rises, and they slip away* and lay themselves down in their dens.
Man goes forth to his work* and to his labor until the evening.

Psalm 104:17–24

The Refrain

Your love, O LORD, for ever will I sing;* from age to age my mouth will proclaim
your faithfulness.

The Gloria

The Lord's Prayer

The Prayer Appointed for the Week

Almighty and merciful God, in your goodness keep me, I pray, from all things that
may hurt me, that I, being ready both in mind and body, may accomplish with
a free heart those things which belong to your purpose; through Jesus Christ
my Lord, who lives and reigns with you and the Holy Spirit, one God, now and
for ever. *Amen.* †

The Concluding Prayer of the Church

Lord Jesus Christ, you have prepared a quiet place for us in your Father's eternal
home. Watch over our welfare on this perilous journey, shade us from the
burning heat of day, and keep our lives free of evil until the end. *Amen.*

THE LITURGY OF THE HOURS, VOL. III

The Morning Office   To Be Observed on the Hour or Half Hour
                                      Between 6 and 9 a.m.

The Call to Prayer
Let us make a vow to the LORD our God and keep it;* let all around him bring gifts
to him who is worthy to be feared.

Psalm 76:11

The Request for Presence
Let my cry come before you, O LORD;* give me understanding, according to your
word.
Let my supplication come before you;* deliver me, according to your promise.

Psalm 119:169–170

The Greeting
I will offer you a freewill sacrifice* and praise your Name, O LORD, for it is good.

Psalm 54:6

The Refrain for the Morning Lessons
How sweet are your words to my taste!* they are sweeter than honey to my
mouth.

Psalm 119:103

A Reading
Jesus taught us, saying: "So always treat others as you like them to treat you; that
is the Law and the Prophets."

Matthew 7:12

The Refrain
How sweet are your words to my taste!* they are sweeter than honey to my
mouth.

The Morning Psalm   *Happy Are Those Who Always Do What Is Right*
Hallelujah! Give thanks to the LORD, for he is good,* for his mercy endures for
ever.
Who can declare the mighty acts of the LORD* or show forth all his praise?
Happy are those who act with justice* and always do what is right!
Remember me, O LORD, with the favor you have for your people,* and visit me
with your saving help;
That I may see the prosperity of your elect and be glad with the gladness of your
people,* that I may glory with your inheritance.

Psalm 106:1–5

The Refrain
How sweet are your words to my taste!* they are sweeter than honey to my
mouth.

The Cry of the Church
O God, come to my assistance! O Lord, make haste to help me!

The Lord's Prayer

The Prayer Appointed for the Week
Almighty and merciful God, in your goodness keep me, I pray, from all things that may hurt me, that I, being ready both in mind and body, may accomplish with a free heart those things which belong to your purpose; through Jesus Christ my Lord, who lives and reigns with you and the Holy Spirit, one God, now and for ever. *Amen.* †

The Concluding Prayer of the Church
Lord God, almighty and everlasting Father, you have brought me in safety to this new day: Preserve me with your mighty power, that I may not fall into sin, nor be overcome by adversity; and in all I do direct me to the fulfilling of your purpose; through Jesus Christ my Lord. *Amen.* †

The Midday Office   **To Be Observed on the Hour or Half Hour**
                                         Between 11 a.m. and 2 p.m.

The Call to Prayer
Let Israel rejoice in his Maker;* let the children of Zion be joyful in their King.
                                                             Psalm 149:2

The Request for Presence
Make me understand the way of your commandments,* that I may meditate on your marvelous works.
                                                             Psalm 119:27

The Greeting
How deep I find your thoughts, O God!* how great is the sum of them!
                                                             Psalm 139:16

The Refrain for the Midday Lessons
Keep watch over my life, for I am faithful;* save your servant whose trust is in you.
                                                             based on Psalm 86:2

A Reading
Take courage, my children, call on God: he will deliver you from tyranny, from the clutches of your enemies; for I look to the Eternal for your rescue, and joy has come to me from the Holy One at the mercy soon to reach you from your Savior, the Eternal.
                                                             Baruch 4:21–22

The Refrain
Keep watch over my life, for I am faithful;* save your servant whose trust is in you.

The Midday Psalm   *You Are My Helper and My Deliverer*
Be pleased, O God, to deliver me;* O Lord, make haste to help me.
Let all who seek you rejoice and be glad in you;* let those who love your salvation say for ever, "Great is the Lord!"

But as for me, I am poor and needy;* come to me speedily, O God.
You are my helper and my deliverer;* O LORD, do not tarry.

Psalm 70:1, 4–6

The Refrain
Keep watch over my life, for I am faithful;* save your servant whose trust is in you.

The Cry of the Church
Lord, have mercy on us. Christ, have mercy on us. Lord, have mercy on us.

The Lord's Prayer

The Prayer Appointed for the Week
Almighty and merciful God, in your goodness keep me, I pray, from all things that
may hurt me, that I, being ready both in mind and body, may accomplish with
a free heart those things which belong to your purpose; through Jesus Christ
my Lord, who lives and reigns with you and the Holy Spirit, one God, now and
for ever. *Amen.* †

The Concluding Prayer of the Church
Lord Jesus Christ, you have prepared a quiet place for us in your Father's eternal
home. Watch over our welfare on this perilous journey, shade us from the
burning heat of day, and keep our lives free of evil until the end. *Amen.*

THE LITURGY OF THE HOURS, VOL. III

The Vespers Office **To Be Observed on the Hour or Half Hour**
Between 5 and 8 p.m.

The Call to Prayer
Bless God in the congregation;* bless the LORD, you that are the fountain of Israel.

Psalm 68:26

The Request for Presence
May God be merciful to us and bless us,* show us the light of his countenance and
come to us.

Psalm 67:1

The Greeting
Exalt yourself above the heavens, O God,* and your glory over all the earth.

Psalm 57:6

The Hymn   *Grace Greater Than Our Sin*
Marvelous grace of our loving Lord,
Grace that exceeds our sin and guilt,
Yonder on Calvary's mount out-poured,
There where the blood of the Lamb was spilt.
Grace, grace, God's grace,
Grace that will pardon and cleanse within;
Grace, grace, God's grace,
Grace that is greater than all our sin.

Marvelous, infinite, matchless grace,
Freely bestowed on all who believe;
You that are longing to see His face,
Will you this moment his grace receive?
Marvelous grace, infinite grace,
Grace that will pardon and cleanse within;
Marvelous grace, infinite grace,
Grace that is greater than all our sin.

Julia H. Johnston

The Refrain for the Vespers Lessons

Those who trust in the Lord are like Mount Zion,* which cannot be moved, but
stands fast for ever.

Psalm 125:1

The Vespers Psalm

His Mercy Endures For Ever

Give thanks to the Lord, for he is good,* for his mercy endures for ever.
Give thanks to the God of gods,* for his mercy endures for ever.
Give thanks to the Lord of lords,* for his mercy endures for ever.
Who only does great wonders,* for his mercy endures for ever;
Who struck down the firstborn of Egypt,* for his mercy endures for ever;
And brought out Israel from among them,* for his mercy endures for ever;
Who led his people through the wilderness,* for his mercy endures for ever.
Who remembered us in our low estate,* for his mercy endures for ever;
And delivered us from our enemies,* for his mercy endures for ever;
Who gives food to all creatures,* for his mercy endures for ever.
Give thanks to the God of heaven,* for his mercy endures for ever.

Psalm 136:1–4, 10–11, 16, 23–26

The Refrain

Those who trust in the Lord are like Mount Zion,* which cannot be moved, but
stands fast for ever.

The Gloria

The Lord's Prayer

The Prayer Appointed for the Week

Almighty and merciful God, in your goodness keep me, I pray, from all things that
may hurt me, that I, being ready both in mind and body, may accomplish with
a free heart those things which belong to your purpose; through Jesus Christ
my Lord, who lives and reigns with you and the Holy Spirit, one God, now and
for ever. *Amen.* †

The Concluding Prayer of the Church

Protect us, Lord, as we stay awake; watch over us as we sleep, that awake we may
watch with Christ, and asleep, rest in peace. *Amen.*

The Morning Office

To Be Observed on the Hour or Half Hour
Between 6 and 9 a.m.

The Call to Prayer
Rejoice in the LORD, you righteous,* and give thanks to his holy Name.

Psalm 97:12

The Request for Presence
Bow down your ear, O LORD, and answer me,* for I am poor and in misery.
Keep watch over my life, for I am faithful;* save your servant who puts his trust in
you.

Psalm 86:1–2

The Greeting
Blessed is the LORD!* for he has heard the voice of my prayer.

Psalm 28:7

The Refrain for the Morning Lessons
Blessed are they who do hunger and thirst after righteousness: for they shall be
filled.

Matthew 5:6, KJV

A Reading
Jesus taught us, saying: "So I say to you: Ask, and it will be given to you; search,
and you will find; knock, and the door will be opened to you. For everyone who
asks receives; everyone who searches finds; everyone who knocks will have the
door opened. What father among you, if his son asked for a fish, would hand
him a snake? Or if he asked for an egg, hand him a scorpion? If you then, evil as
you are, know how to give your children what is good, how much more will the
heavenly Father give the Holy Spirit to those who ask him!"

Luke 11:9–13

The Refrain
Blessed are they who do hunger and thirst after righteousness: for they shall be
filled.

The Morning Psalm   *Teach Me Discernment*
O LORD, you have dealt graciously with your servant,* according to your word.
Teach me discernment and knowledge,* for I have believed in your
commandments.
Before I was afflicted I went astray,* but now I keep your word.
You are good and you bring forth good;* instruct me in your statutes.
The proud have smeared me with lies,* but I will keep your commandments with
my whole heart.
Their heart is gross and fat,* but my delight is in your law.
It is good for me that I have been afflicted,* that I might learn your statutes.
The law of your mouth is dearer to me* than thousands in gold and silver.

Psalm 119:65–72

The Refrain
Blessed are they who do hunger and thirst after righteousness: for they shall be
filled.

The Small Verse
My soul thirsts for the strong, living God and all that is within me cries out to him.

Traditional

The Lord's Prayer

The Prayer Appointed for the Week
Almighty and merciful God, in your goodness keep me, I pray, from all things that
may hurt me, that I, being ready both in mind and body, may accomplish with
a free heart those things which belong to your purpose; through Jesus Christ
my Lord, who lives and reigns with you and the Holy Spirit, one God, now and
for ever. *Amen.* †

The Concluding Prayer of the Church
Lord God, almighty and everlasting Father, you have brought me in safety to this
new day: Preserve me with your mighty power, that I may not fall into sin, nor
be overcome by adversity; and in all I do direct me to the fulfilling of your purpose; through Jesus Christ my Lord. *Amen.* †

The Midday Office   **To Be Observed on the Hour or Half Hour**
Between 11 a.m. and 2 p.m.

The Call to Prayer
Come, let us sing to the LORD;* let us shout for joy to the Rock of our salvation.
Let us come before his presence with thanksgiving* and raise a loud shout to him
with psalms.
For the LORD is a great God,* and a great King above all gods.

Psalm 95:1–3

The Request for Presence
Let the peoples praise you, O God;* let all the peoples praise you.

Psalm 67:3

The Greeting
You have made me glad by your acts, O LORD;* and I shout for joy because of the
works of your hands.

Psalm 92:4

The Refrain for the Midday Lessons
Yours are the heavens; the earth also is yours;* you laid the foundations of the
world and all that is in it.

Psalm 89:11

A Reading

And let us never slacken in doing good; for if we do not give up, we shall have our harvest in due time. So then, as long as we have the opportunity let all our actions be for the good of everybody, and especially of those who belong to the household of the faith.

Galatians 6:9–10

The Refrain

Yours are the heavens; the earth also is yours;* you laid the foundations of the world and all that is in it.

The Midday Psalm *I Shall See the Goodness of the Lord in the Land of the Living!*

Hearken to my voice, O Lord, when I call;* have mercy on me and answer me.

You speak in my heart and say, "Seek my face."* Your face, Lord, will I seek.

Hide not your face from me,* nor turn away your servant in displeasure.

You have been my helper; cast me not away;* do not forsake me, O God of my salvation.

Though my father and my mother forsake me,* the Lord will sustain me.

Show me your way, O Lord;* lead me on a level path, because of my enemies.

Deliver me not into the hand of my adversaries,* for false witnesses have risen up against me, and also those who speak malice.

What if I had not believed that I should see the goodness of the Lord* in the land of the living!

Psalm 27:10–17

The Refrain

Yours are the heavens; the earth also is yours;* you laid the foundations of the world and all that is in it.

The Gloria

The Lord's Prayer

The Prayer Appointed for the Week

Almighty and merciful God, in your goodness keep me, I pray, from all things that may hurt me, that I, being ready both in mind and body, may accomplish with a free heart those things which belong to your purpose; through Jesus Christ my Lord, who lives and reigns with you and the Holy Spirit, one God, now and for ever. *Amen.* †

The Concluding Prayer of the Church

Let us bless the Lord God living and true! Let us always render him praise, glory, honor, blessing, and all good things! Amen. Amen. So be it! So be it!

St. Francis of Assisi

The Vespers Office   To Be Observed on the Hour or Half Hour
                                      Between 5 and 8 p.m.

The Call to Prayer
Behold now, bless the LORD, all you servants of the LORD,* you that stand by night
   in the house of our LORD.

Psalm 134:1

The Request for Presence
For God alone my soul in silence waits;* from him comes my salvation.

Psalm 62:1

The Greeting
Yours is the day, yours also the night;* you established the moon and the sun.
You fixed all the boundaries of the earth;* you made both summer and winter.

Psalm 74:15–16

The Hymn   *Jam Sol Recedit Igneus*
   The setting sun now dies away,
   And darkness comes at close of day;
   Your brightest beams, dear Lord, impart,
   And let them shine within our hearts.

   We praise your name with joy this night:
   Please watch and guide us till the light;
   Joining the music of the blessed,
   O Lord, we sing ourselves to rest.

   To God the Father, God the Son,
   And Holy Spirit, Three in one,
   Trinity blessed, whom we adore.
   Be praise and glory evermore.

Latin

The Refrain for the Vespers Lessons
The LORD's will stands fast for ever,* and the designs of his heart from age to age.

Psalm 33:11

The Vespers Psalm   *The LORD Shall Reign For Ever*
Hallelujah! Praise the LORD, O my soul!* I will praise the LORD as long as I live; I
   will sing praises to my God while I have my being.
Put not your trust in rulers, nor in any child of earth,* for there is no help in them.
When they breathe their last, they return to earth,* and in that day their thoughts
   perish.
Happy are they who have the God of Jacob for their help!* whose hope is in the
   LORD their God;
Who made heaven and earth, the seas, and all that is in them;* who keeps his
   promise for ever;
Who gives justice to those who are oppressed,* and food to those who hunger.

The LORD sets the prisoners free; the LORD opens the eyes of the blind;* the LORD
 lifts up those who are bowed down;
The LORD loves the righteous; the LORD cares for the stranger;* he sustains the
 orphan and widow, but frustrates the way of the wicked.
The LORD shall reign for ever,* your God, O Zion, throughout all generations.
 Hallelujah!

Psalm 146

The Refrain
The LORD's will stands fast for ever,* and the designs of his heart from age to age.

The Cry of the Church
Even so come, Lord Jesus!

The Lord's Prayer

The Prayer Appointed for the Week
Almighty and merciful God, in your goodness keep me, I pray, from all things that
 may hurt me, that I, being ready both in mind and body, may accomplish with
 a free heart those things which belong to your purpose; through Jesus Christ
 my Lord, who lives and reigns with you and the Holy Spirit, one God, now and
 for ever. *Amen.* †

The Concluding Prayer of the Church
May Almighty God grant me a peaceful night and a perfect end. *Amen.*

The Morning Office   To Be Observed on the Hour or Half Hour
                                          Between 6 and 9 a.m.

The Call to Prayer
Search for the LORD and his strength;* continually seek his face.

Psalm 105:4

The Request for Presence
O Lamb of God, that takes away the sins of the world, have mercy upon me.
O Lamb of God, that takes away the sins of the world, have mercy upon me.
O Lamb of God, that takes away the sins of the world, grant me your peace.

The Greeting
O God, you know my foolishness,* and my faults are not hidden from you.

Psalm 69:6

The Refrain for the Morning Lessons
Our sins are stronger than we are,* but you will blot them out.

Psalm 65:3

A Reading
Jesus taught us, saying: "The lamp of the body is the eye. It follows that if your eye
 is clear, your whole body will be filled with light. But if your eye is diseased,

your whole body will be darkness. If then, the light inside you is darkened, what darkness that will be!

Matthew 6:22–23

The Refrain
Our sins are stronger than we are,* but you will blot them out.

The Morning Psalm   *Forgive My Sin for Your Name's Sake*
Remember, O Lord, your compassion and love,* for they are from everlasting.
Remember not the sins of my youth and my transgressions;* remember me
    according to your love and for the sake of your goodness, O Lord.
Gracious and upright is the Lord;* therefore he teaches sinners in his way.
For your Name's sake, O Lord,* forgive my sin, for it is great.

Psalm 25:5–7, 10

The Refrain
Our sins are stronger than we are,* but you will blot them out.

The Cry of the Church
O God, come to my assistance! O Lord, make haste to help me!

The Lord's Prayer

The Prayer Appointed for the Week
Almighty and merciful God, in your goodness keep me, I pray, from all things that
    may hurt me, that I, being ready both in mind and body, may accomplish with
    a free heart those things which belong to your purpose; through Jesus Christ
    my Lord, who lives and reigns with you and the Holy Spirit, one God, now and
    for ever. *Amen.* †

The Concluding Prayer of the Church
Lord God, almighty and everlasting Father, you have brought me in safety to this
    new day: Preserve me with your mighty power, that I may not fall into sin, nor
    be overcome by adversity; and in all I do direct me to the fulfilling of your pur-
    pose; through Jesus Christ my Lord. *Amen.* †

The Midday Office   **To Be Observed on the Hour or Half Hour**
                                                      Between 11 a.m. and 2 p.m.

The Call to Prayer
Bless God in the congregation;* bless the Lord, you that are of the fountain of
    Israel.

Psalm 68:26

The Request for Presence
Accept, O Lord, the willing tribute of my lips,* and teach me your judgments.

Psalm 119:108

The Greeting
Let the words of my mouth and the meditation of my heart be acceptable in your
   sight,* O LORD, my strength and my redeemer.

Psalm 19:14

The Refrain for the Midday Lessons
Hallelujah! Happy are they who fear the Lord* and have great delight in his
   commandments.

Psalm 112:1

A Reading
Let us examine our path, let us ponder it and return to YAHWEH. Let us raise our
   hearts and hands to God in heaven. We are the ones who have sinned, who
   have rebelled.

Lamentations 40–42

The Refrain
Hallelujah! Happy are they who fear the Lord* and have great delight in his
   commandments.

The Midday Psalm   *He Has Raised Up Strength for His People*
Praise the LORD from the earth,* you sea-monsters and all deeps;
Fire and hail, snow and fog,* tempestuous wind, doing his will;
Mountains and all hills,* fruit trees and all cedars;
Wild beasts and all cattle,* creeping things and wingèd birds;
Kings of the earth and all peoples,* princes and all rulers of the world;
Young men and maidens,* old and young together.
Let them praise the Name of the LORD,* for his Name only is exalted, his splendor
   is over earth and heaven.
He has raised up strength for his people and praise for all his loyal servants,* the
   children of Israel, a people who are near him. Hallelujah!

Psalm 148:7–14

The Refrain
Hallelujah! Happy are they who fear the Lord* and have great delight in his
   commandments.

The Cry of the Church
O Lord, hear my prayer and let my cry come unto you. Thanks be to God.

THE SHORT BREVIARY

The Lord's Prayer

The Prayer Appointed for the Week
Almighty and merciful God, in your goodness keep me, I pray, from all things that
   may hurt me, that I, being ready both in mind and body, may accomplish with
   a free heart those things which belong to your purpose; through Jesus Christ
   my Lord, who lives and reigns with you and the Holy Spirit, one God, now and
   for ever. *Amen.* †

The Concluding Prayer of the Church
Lord Jesus Christ, by your death you took away the sting of death: Grant me to so
follow in faith where you have led the way, that I may at length fall asleep
peacefully in you and wake in your likeness; for your tender mercies' sake.
Amen. †

The Vespers Office   To Be Observed on the Hour or Half Hour
                                                      Between 5 and 8 p.m.

The Call to Prayer
Glory in his holy Name;* let the hearts of those who seek the LORD rejoice.
Psalm 105:3

The Request for Presence
Send forth your strength, O God;* establish, O God, what you have wrought
for us.
Psalm 68:28

The Greeting
The LORD is my strength and my song,* and he has become my salvation.
Psalm 118:14

The Hymn   *Out of the Depths I Cry to You*
Out of the depths I cry to you; O Lord, now hear me calling.
Incline your ear to my distress in spite of my rebelling.
Do not regard my sinful deeds. Send me the grace my spirit needs;
                                        Without it I am nothing.

All things you send are full of grace; you crown our lives with favor.
All our good works are done in vain without the Lord our Savior.
We praise the God who gives us faith and saves us from the grip of death;
                                        Our lives are in God's keeping.

It is in God that we shall hope, and not in our own merit;
We rest our fears in God's good Word and trust the Holy Spirit,
Whose promise keeps us strong and sure; we trust the holy signature
                                        Inscribed upon our temples.

My soul is waiting for the Lord as one who longs for morning;
No watcher waits with greater hope than I for Christ's returning.
I hope as Israel in the Lord, who sends redemption through the Word.
                                        Praise God for endless mercy.
                                             Martin Luther

The Refrain for the Vespers Lessons
Keep watch over my life, for I am faithful;* save your servant whose trust is in
you.
based on Psalm 86:2

The Vespers Psalm   *We Shall Be Saved*

Restore us, O God of hosts;* show the light of your countenance, and we shall be
    saved.

Let your hand be upon the man of your right hand,* the son of man you have
    made so strong for yourself.

And so will we never turn away from you;* give us life, that we may call upon
    your Name.

Restore us, O LORD God of hosts;* show the light of your countenance, and we
    shall be saved.

Psalm 80:7, 16–18

The Refrain

Keep watch over my life, for I am faithful;* save your servant whose trust is in
    you.

The Small Verse

My help is in the Name of the Lord who made the heavens and the earth. What
    then shall I fear, of what shall I be afraid?

Traditional

The Lord's Prayer

The Prayer Appointed for the Week

Almighty and merciful God, in your goodness keep me, I pray, from all things that
    may hurt me, that I, being ready both in mind and body, may accomplish with
    a free heart those things which belong to your purpose; through Jesus Christ
    my Lord, who lives and reigns with you and the Holy Spirit, one God, now and
    for ever. *Amen.* †

Concluding Prayers of the Church

Almighty God, who has promised to hear the petitions of those who ask in your
    Son's Name: I beseech you mercifully to incline your ear to me who have made
    my prayers and supplications to you; and grant that those things which I have
    faithfully asked according to your will, I may effectually obtain, to the relief of
    my necessity, and to the setting forth of your glory; through Jesus Christ my
    Lord. *Amen.*

May the souls of the faithful departed, through the mercy of God, rest in eternal
    peace. *Amen.*

The Morning Office   **To Be Observed on the Hour or Half Hour**
Between 6 and 9 a.m.

The Call to Prayer

Search for the LORD and his strength;* continually seek his face.

Psalm 105:4

The Request for Presence
Hearken to my voice, O Lord, when I call;* have mercy on me and answer me.
You speak in my heart and say, "Seek my face."* Your face, Lord, will I seek.
Hide not your face from me,* nor turn away your servant in displeasure.

Psalm 27:10–12

The Greeting
What terror you inspire!* who can stand before you when you are angry?

Psalm 76:7

The Refrain for the Morning Lessons
I sought the Lord, and he answered me* and delivered me out of all my terror.

Psalm 34:4

A Reading
Then he told them, 'This is what I meant when I said, while I was still with you,
that everything written about me in the Law of Moses, in the Prophets and in
the Psalms, was destined to be fulfilled.' He then opened their minds to understand the scriptures, and he said to them, 'So it is written that the Christ would
suffer and on the third day, rise from the dead, and that, in his name, repentance for the forgiveness of sins would be preached to all nations, beginning
from Jerusalem. You are witnesses to this. And now I am sending upon you
what the Father has promised. Stay in the city, then, until you are clothed with
the power from on high.'

Luke 24:44–49

The Refrain
I sought the Lord, and he answered me* and delivered me out of all my terror.

The Morning Psalm   *No Evil Shall Happen to You*
Your eyes have only to behold* to see the reward of the wicked.
Because you have made the Lord your refuge,* and the Most High your habita-
tion,
There shall no evil happen to you,* neither shall any plague come near your
dwelling.
For he shall give his angels charge over you,* to keep you in all your ways.
They shall bear you in their hands,* lest you dash your foot against a stone.
You shall tread upon the lion and adder;* you shall trample the young lion and the
serpent under your feet.

Psalm 91:8–13

The Refrain
I sought the Lord, and he answered me* and delivered me out of all my terror.

The Cry of the Church
Lord, have mercy on us. Christ, have mercy on us. Lord, have mercy on us.

The Lord's Prayer

The Prayer Appointed for the Week
Almighty and merciful God, in your goodness keep me, I pray, from all things that
may hurt me, that I, being ready both in mind and body, may accomplish with
a free heart those things which belong to your purpose; through Jesus Christ
my Lord, who lives and reigns with you and the Holy Spirit, one God, now and
for ever. *Amen.* †

The Concluding Prayer of the Church
Lord God, almighty and everlasting Father, you have brought me in safety to this
new day: Preserve me with your mighty power, that I may not fall into sin, nor
be overcome by adversity; and in all I do direct me to the fulfilling of your purpose; through Jesus Christ my Lord. *Amen.* †

The Midday Office **To Be Observed on the Hour or Half Hour**
Between 11 a.m. and 2 p.m.

The Call to Prayer
Be strong and let your heart take courage,* all you who wait for the LORD.

Psalm 31:24

The Request for Presence
Give ear to my words, O LORD;* consider my meditation.
Hearken to my cry for help, my King and my God,* for I make my prayer to you.

Psalm 5:1–2

The Greeting
You are God; we praise you;
You are the Lord: we acclaim you;
You are the eternal Father:
All creation worships you.
To you all angels, all powers of heaven,
Cherubim and Seraphim, sing in endless praise:
Holy, holy, holy Lord, God of power and might,
heaven and earth are full of your glory.

TE DEUM

The Refrain for the Midday Lessons
Great peace have they who love your law;* for them there is no stumbling block.

Psalm 119:165

A Reading
For this was how YAHWEH spoke to me when his hand seized hold of me and he
taught me not to follow the path of this people, saying, 'Do not call conspiracy
all that this people calls conspiracy; do not dread what they dread, have no fear
of that. Yahweh Sabaoth is the one you will proclaim holy, him you will dread,
him you will fear. He will be a sanctuary, a stumbling-stone, . . .'

Isaiah 8:11–14

The Refrain
Great peace have they who love your law;* for them there is no stumbling block.

The Midday Psalm   *How Wonderful Is God in His Holy Places*
Sing to God, O kingdoms of the earth;* sing praises to the Lord.
He rides in the heavens, the ancient heavens;* he sends forth his voice, his mighty
    voice.
Ascribe power to God;* his majesty is over Israel; his strength is in the skies.
How wonderful is God in his holy places!* the God of Israel giving strength and
    power to his people! Blessed be God!

Psalm 68:33–36

The Refrain
Great peace have they who love your law;* for them there is no stumbling block.

The Cry of the Church
O Lord, hear my prayer and let my cry come unto you. Thanks be to God.

THE SHORT BREVIARY

The Lord's Prayer

The Prayer Appointed for the Week
Almighty and merciful God, in your goodness keep me, I pray, from all things that
    may hurt me, that I, being ready both in mind and body, may accomplish with
    a free heart those things which belong to your purpose; through Jesus Christ
    my Lord, who lives and reigns with you and the Holy Spirit, one God, now and
    for ever. *Amen.* †

The Concluding Prayer of the Church
O God, the source of eternal light: Shed forth your unending day upon all of us
    who watch for you, that our lips may praise you, our lives may bless you, and
    our worship may give you glory; through Jesus Christ our Lord. *Amen.* †

The Vespers Office   To Be Observed on the Hour or Half Hour
                                                    Between 5 and 8 p.m.

The Call to Prayer
Sing to the LORD a new song;* sing to the LORD, all the whole earth.
Sing to the LORD and bless his Name;* proclaim the good news of his salvation
    from day to day.
Declare his glory among the nations* and his wonders among all peoples.

Psalm 96:1–3

The Request for Presence
Exalt yourself above the heavens, O God,* and your glory over all the earth.

Psalm 57:6

The Greeting
I will offer you a freewill sacrifice* and praise your Name, O Lord, for it is good.
For you have rescued me from every trouble.*

Psalm 54:6–7

The Hymn   *Your Holy Wings*
Your holy wings, O Savior, spread gently over me,
And let me rest securely through good and ill in thee.
O be my strength and portion, my rock and hiding place,
And let my every moment be lived within your grace.

O wash me in the water's of Noah's cleansing flood;
Give me a willing spirit, a heart both clean and good.
And take into your keeping your children great and small,
And while we sweetly slumber, enfold us one and all.

Caroline Sandell-Berg

The Refrain for the Vespers Lessons
I lie down and go to sleep;* I wake again, because the Lord sustains me.

Psalm 3:5

The Vespers Psalm   *My Body Shall Rest in Peace*
O Lord, you are my portion and my cup;* it is you who uphold my lot.
My boundaries enclose a pleasant land;* indeed, I have a goodly heritage.
I will bless the Lord who gives me counsel;* my heart teaches me, night after
    night.
I have set the Lord always before me;* because he is at my right hand I shall not
    fall.
My heart, therefore, is glad, and my spirit rejoices;* my body also shall rest in
    hope.
For you will not abandon me to the grave,* nor let your holy one see the Pit.
You will show me the path of life;* in your presence there is fullness of joy, and in
    your right hand are pleasures for evermore.

Psalm 16:5–11

The Refrain
I lie down and go to sleep;* I wake again, because the Lord sustains me.

The Gloria

The Lord's Prayer

The Prayer Appointed for the Week
Almighty and merciful God, in your goodness keep me, I pray, from all things that
    may hurt me, that I, being ready both in mind and body, may accomplish with
    a free heart those things which belong to your purpose; through Jesus Christ
    my Lord, who lives and reigns with you and the Holy Spirit, one God, now and
    for ever. *Amen.* †

The Concluding Prayer of the Church
O God, you have caused the holy night to shine with the brightness of the true
Light: Grant that I, who have known the mystery of that Light on earth, may
also enjoy him perfectly in heaven; where with you and the Holy Spirit he lives
and reigns, one God, in glory everlasting. *Amen.* †

✦

The Morning Office　　　　　　　**To Be Observed on the Hour or Half Hour**
Between 6 and 9 a.m.

The Call to Prayer
Sing to the LORD a new song,* for he has done marvelous things.
Psalm 98:1

The Request for Presence
Create in me a clean heart, O God,* and renew a right spirit within me.
Psalm 51:11

The Greeting
I am small and of little account,* yet I do not forget your commandments.
Psalm 119:141

The Refrain for the Morning Lessons
Let my mouth be full of your praise* and your glory all the day long.
Psalm 71:8

A Reading
A man came, sent by God. His name was John. He came as a witness, to bear witness to the light, so that everyone might believe through him. He was not the
light, he was to bear witness to the light. The Word was the real light that gives
light to everyone; he was coming into the world.
John 1:6–9

The Refrain
Let my mouth be full of your praise* and your glory all the day long.

The Morning Psalm　　　　　　*May the* LORD *Rejoice in All His Work*
May the glory of the LORD endure for ever;* may the LORD rejoice in all his works.
He looks at the earth and it trembles;* he touches the mountains and they smoke.
I will sing to the LORD as long as I live;* I will praise my God while I have my
being.
May these words of mine please him;* I will rejoice in the LORD.

Let sinners be consumed out of the earth,* and the wicked be no more.
Bless the LORD, O my soul.* Hallelujah!

Psalm 104:32–37

The Refrain
Let my mouth be full of your praise* and your glory all the day long.

The Cry of the Church
O Lord, hear my prayer and let my cry come unto you. Thanks be to God.

THE SHORT BREVIARY

The Lord's Prayer

The Prayer Appointed for the Week
Grant, O Lord, that the course of this world may be peaceably governed by your
   providence; and that your Church may joyfully serve you in confidence and
   serenity; through Jesus Christ our Lord who lives and reigns with you and the
   Holy Spirit, one God, for ever and ever. *Amen.* †

The Concluding Prayer of the Church
Lord God, almighty and everlasting Father, you have brought me in safety to this
   new day: Preserve me with your mighty power, that I may not fall into sin, nor
   be overcome by adversity; and in all I do direct me to the fulfilling of your purpose; through Jesus Christ my Lord. *Amen.* †

The Midday Office   To Be Observed on the Hour or Half Hour
                                         Between 11 a.m. and 2 p.m.

The Call to Prayer
Hallelujah! Praise the Name of the LORD;* give praise, you servants of the LORD,
You who stand in the house of the LORD,* in the courts of the house of our God.
Praise the LORD, for the LORD is good;* sing praises to his Name, for it is lovely.

Psalm 135:1–3

The Request for Presence
Let them know that you, whose Name is YAHWEH,* you alone are the Most High
   over all the earth.

Psalm 83:18

The Greeting
. . . My heart sings to you without ceasing;* O LORD my God, I will give you
   thanks for ever.

Psalm 30:13

The Refrain for the Midday Lessons
The LORD will make good his purpose for me;* O LORD, your love endures for
   ever; do not abandon the works of your hands.

Psalm 138:9

A Reading   *The First Song of Isaiah*
Seek the Lord while he wills to be found;* call upon him when he draws near.
Let the wicked forsake their ways* and the evil ones their thoughts;
And let them turn to the Lord, and he will have compassion,* and to our God, for
    he will richly pardon.
For my thoughts are not your thoughts,* nor your ways my ways, says the Lord.
For as the heavens are higher than the earth,* so are my ways higher than your
    ways, and my thoughts than your thoughts.
For as rain and snow fall from the heavens* and return not again, but water the
    earth,
Bringing forth life and giving growth,* seed for sowing and bread for eating,
So is my word that goes forth from my mouth;* it will not return empty;
But it will accomplish that which I have purposed,* and prosper in that for which I
    sent it.
Glory to the Father, and to the Son, and to the Holy Spirit:* as it was in the begin-
    ning, is now, and will be for ever. *Amen.*

                                                              Isaiah 55:6–11, BCP

The Refrain
The Lord will make good his purpose for me;* O Lord, your love endures for
    ever; do not abandon the works of your hands.

The Midday Psalm   *Open My Eyes That I May See*
Deal bountifully with your servant,* that I may live and keep your word.
Open my eyes, that I may see* the wonders of your law.
I am a stranger here on earth;* do not hide your commandments from me.
My soul is consumed at all times* with longing for your judgments.
You have rebuked the insolent;* cursed are they who stray from your
    commandments!
Turn from me shame and rebuke,* for I have kept your decrees.
Even though rulers sit and plot against me,* I will meditate on your statutes.
For your decrees are my delight,* and they are my counselors.

                                                              Psalm 119:17–24

The Refrain
The Lord will make good his purpose for me;* O Lord, your love endures for
    ever; do not abandon the works of your hands.

The Gloria

The Lord's Prayer

The Prayer Appointed for the Week
Grant, O Lord, that the course of this world may be peaceably governed by your
    providence; and that your Church may joyfully serve you in confidence and
    serenity; through Jesus Christ our Lord who lives and reigns with you and the
    Holy Spirit, one God, for ever and ever. *Amen.* †

The Concluding Prayer of the Church
O God, you make me glad with the weekly remembrance of the glorious resurrection of your Son my Lord: Give me this day such blessing through my worship of you, that the week to come may be spent in your favor; through Jesus Christ our Lord. *Amen.* †

The Vespers Office   To Be Observed on the Hour or Half Hour
                                           Between 5 and 8 p.m.

The Call to Prayer
Let my mouth be full of your praise* and your glory all the day long.
Do not cast me off in my old age;* forsake me not when my strength fails.

Psalm 71:8–9

The Request for Presence
Let your loving-kindness, O LORD, be upon us,* as we have put our trust in you.

Psalm 33:22

The Greeting
To you I lift up my eyes,* to you enthroned in the heavens.
As the eyes of servants look to the hand of their masters,* and the eyes of a maid to the hand of her mistress.
So my eyes look to the LORD my God,* until he shows me his mercy.

based on Psalm 123:1–3

The Hymn
> You who claim the faith of Jesus, sing the wonders that were done
> When the love of God the Father over sin the victory won,
> When he made the Virgin Mary mother of his only Son.
>> Hail Mary, full of grace.
>
> Blessed were the chosen people out of whom the Lord did come;
> Blessed was the land of promise fashioned for his earthly home;
> But more blessed far the mother, she who bore him in her womb.
>> Hail Mary, full of grace.
>
> Therefore let all faithful people sing the honor of her name;
> Let the Church, in her foreshadowed, part in her thanksgiving claim;
> What Christ's mother sang in gladness let Christ's people sing the same.
>> Hail Mary, full of grace.

Vincent Coles

The Refrain for the Vespers Lessons
In truth God has heard me;* he has attended to the voice of my prayer.

Psalm 66:17

The Vespers Psalm   *Look Upon Him and Be Radiant*
I will bless the LORD at all times;* his praise shall ever be in my mouth.
I will glory in the LORD;* let the humble hear and rejoice.

Proclaim with me the greatness of the LORD;* let us exalt his Name together.
I sought the LORD, and he answered me* and delivered me out of all my terror.
Look upon him and be radiant,* and let not your faces be ashamed.
I called in my affliction and the LORD heard me* and saved me from all my
    troubles.
The angel of the LORD encompasses those who fear him,* and he will deliver them.
Taste and see that the LORD is good;* happy are they who trust in him!

Psalm 34:1–8

The Refrain
In truth God has heard me;* he has attended to the voice of my prayer.

Psalm 66:17

The Cry of the Church
O Lord, hear my prayer and let my cry come unto you. Thanks be to God.

THE SHORT BREVIARY

The Lord's Prayer

The Prayer Appointed for the Week
Grant, O Lord, that the course of this world may be peaceably governed by your
    providence; and that your Church may joyfully serve you in confidence and
    serenity; through Jesus Christ our Lord who lives and reigns with you and the
    Holy Spirit, one God, for ever and ever. *Amen.* †

The Concluding Prayer of the Church
Grant, I pray, O Lord God, to me Your servant that I may evermore enjoy health of
    mind and body, and by the glorious intercession of Blessed Mary ever Virgin
    be delivered from present sorrow and attain everlasting happiness. Through
    our Lord Jesus Christ, Your Son, who lives and reigns with you in the Unity of
    the Holy Spirit, world without end.

adapted from THE SHORT BREVIARY

The Morning Office
**To Be Observed on the Hour or Half Hour
Between 6 and 9 a.m.**

The Call to Prayer
Sing to the LORD and bless his Name;* proclaim the good news of his salvation
    from day to day.
Declare his glory among the nations* and his wonders among all peoples.

Psalm 96:2–3

The Request for Presence
In the morning, LORD, you hear my voice;* early in the morning I make my appeal
    and watch for you.

Psalm 5:3

The Greeting
Be exalted, O LORD, in your might;* we will sing and praise your power.

Psalm 21:14

The Refrain for the Morning Lessons
Then shall all the trees of the wood shout for joy before the LORD when he comes,*
when he comes to judge the earth.

Psalm 96:12

A Reading
On May 31 the Church rejoices in the visit by the Virgin Mary
to her cousin Elizabeth, the mother of John the Baptizer.
Elizabeth is the first human being to see in Mary the mother
of God, and it is to Elizabeth that the Virgin speaks the
words of the Magnificat.

Mary set out at that time and went as quickly as she could into the hill country to a
town in Judah. She went into Zechariah's house and greeted Elizabeth. Now it
happened that as soon as Elizabeth heard Mary's greeting, the child leapt in
her womb and Elizabeth was filled with the Holy Spirit. She gave a loud cry
and said, 'Of all women you are the most blessed, and blessed is the fruit of
your womb. Why should I be honored with a visit from the mother of my
Lord? Look, the moment your greeting reached my ears, the child in my womb
leapt for joy. Yes, blessed is she who believed that the promise made her by the
Lord would be fulfilled.'

Luke 1:39–45

The Refrain
Then shall all the trees of the wood shout for joy before the LORD when he comes,*
when he comes to judge the earth.

The Morning Psalm   *The LORD Has Pleasure in Those Who Court His Favor*
Sing to the LORD with thanksgiving;* make music to our God upon the harp.
He covers the heavens with clouds* and prepares rain for the earth;
He makes grass to grow upon the mountains* and green plants to serve mankind.
He provides food for flocks and herds* and for the young ravens when they cry.
He is not impressed by the might of a horse;* he has no pleasure in the strength of
a man;
But the LORD has pleasure in those who fear him,* in those who await his gracious
favor.

Psalm 147:7–12

The Refrain
Then shall all the trees of the wood shout for joy before the LORD when he comes,*
when he comes to judge the earth.

The Cry of the Church
Even so come, Lord Jesus!

The Lord's Prayer

The Prayer Appointed for the Week
Grant, O Lord, that the course of this world may be peaceably governed by your
providence; and that your Church may joyfully serve you in confidence and
serenity; through Jesus Christ our Lord who lives and reigns with you and the
Holy Spirit, one God, for ever and ever. *Amen.* †

The Concluding Prayer of the Church
Father in heaven, by your grace the virgin mother of your incarnate Son was
blessed in bearing him, but still more blessed in keeping your word: Grant all
of us who honor the exaltation of her lowliness to follow the example of her
devotion to your will; through Jesus Christ my Lord, who lives and reigns with
you and the Holy Spirit, one God, for ever and ever. *Amen.* †

The Midday Office   To Be Observed on the Hour or Half Hour
                                           Between 11 a.m. and 2 p.m.

The Call to Prayer
Be glad, you righteous, and rejoice in the LORD;* shout for joy, all who are true of
heart.

Psalm 32:12

The Request for Presence
LORD, hear my prayer, and let my cry come before you;* hide not your face from
me in the day of my trouble.

Psalm 102:1

The Greeting
Into your hands I commend my spirit,* for you have redeemed me, O LORD, O
God of truth.

Psalm 31:5

The Refrain for the Midday Lessons
My help comes from the LORD,* the maker of heaven and earth.

Psalm 121:2

A Reading
Shout for joy, daughter of Zion, Israel, shout aloud! Rejoice, exult with all your
heart, daughter of Jerusalem! YAHWEH has repealed your sentence; he has
turned your enemy away. YAHWEH is king among you, Israel, you have nothing
more to fear. When that Day comes, the message for Jerusalem will be: Zion
have no fear, do not let your hands fall limp. YAHWEH your God is there with
you, the warrior-Savior. He will rejoice over you with happy song, he will
renew you by his love, he will dance with shouts of joy for you, as on a day of
festival.

Zephaniah 3:14–17

The Refrain
My help comes from the LORD,* the maker of heaven and earth.

The Midday Psalm   *Let My Heart Be Sound in Your Statutes*
Your hands have made me and fashioned me;* give me understanding, that I may
    learn your commandments.
Those who fear you will be glad when they see me,* because I trust in your word.
I know, O LORD, that your judgments are right* and that in faithfulness you have
    afflicted me.
Let your loving-kindness be my comfort,* as you have promised to your servant.
Let your compassion come to me, that I may live,* for your law is my delight.
Let the arrogant be put to shame, for they wrong me with lies;* but I will meditate
    on your commandments.
Let those who fear you turn to me,* and also those who know your decrees.
Let my heart be sound in your statutes,* that I may not be put to shame.

Psalm 119:73–80

The Refrain
My help comes from the LORD,* the maker of heaven and earth.

The Small Verse
Hail Mary, full of grace! The Lord is with you. Blessed are you among women and
    blessed is the fruit of your womb, the Lord Jesus Christ. Pray for us, sinners,
    now and at the hour of our death.

The Lord's Prayer

The Prayer Appointed for the Week
Grant, O Lord, that the course of this world may be peaceably governed by your
    providence; and that your Church may joyfully serve you in confidence and
    serenity; through Jesus Christ our Lord who lives and reigns with you and the
    Holy Spirit, one God, for ever and ever. *Amen.* †

The Concluding Prayer of the Church
O God, you have taken to yourself the blessed Virgin Mary, mother of your incar-
    nate Son: Grant that all your people, redeemed by his blood, may share with
    her the glory of your eternal kingdom; through Jesus Christ our Lord, who
    lives and reigns with you, in the unity of the Holy Spirit, one God, now and for
    ever. *Amen.* †

The Vespers Office   **To Be Observed on the Hour or Half Hour**
                                          Between 5 and 8 p.m.

The Call to Prayer
Tell it out among the nations: "The LORD is King!* he has made the world so firm
    that it cannot be moved; he will judge the peoples with equity."

Psalm 96:10

The Request for Presence
Restore our fortunes, O LORD,* like the watercourses of the Negev.

Psalm 126:5

The Greeting
Whom have I in heaven but you?* and having you I desire nothing upon earth.

Psalm 73:25

The Hymn *The Magnificat*
And Mary said:
> My soul proclaims the greatness of the Lord
> And my spirit *rejoices in God my Savior;*
> Because *he has looked upon the humiliation of his servant.*
> Yes, from now onwards all generations will call me blessed,
> For the Almighty has done great things for me.
> *Holy is his name,*
> And *his faithful love extends age after age to those who fear him.*
> He has used the power of his arm,
> He has routed the arrogant heart.
> *He has pulled down princes* from their thrones *and raised high the lowly.*
> *He has filled the starving with good things,* sent the rich away empty.
> *He has come to the help of Israel his servant, mindful of his faithful love*
> —according to the promise he made to our ancestors—
> of his mercy to Abraham and to his descendants for ever.

Luke 1:46–56

The Refrain for the Vespers Lessons
Those who sowed with tears* will reap with songs of joy.
Those who go out weeping, carrying the seed,* will come again with joy,
    shouldering their sheaves.

Psalm 126:6–7

The Vespers Psalm *Let Them Give Thanks for the Wonders He Does*
Give thanks to the LORD, for he is good,* and his mercy endures for ever.
Let all those whom the LORD has redeemed proclaim* that he redeemed them from
    the hand of the foe.
He gathered them out of the lands;* from the east and from the west, from the
    north and from the south.
He sent forth his word and healed them* and saved them from the grave.
Let them give thanks to the LORD for his mercy* and the wonders he does for his
    children.
Let them offer a sacrifice of thanksgiving* and tell of his acts with shouts of joy.

Psalm 107:1–3, 20–22

The Refrain
Those who sowed with tears* will reap with songs of joy.
Those who go out weeping, carrying the seed,* will come again with joy,
    shouldering their sheaves.

The Cry of the Church
Be, Lord, my helper and forsake me not. Do not despise me, O God, my savior.

THE SHORT BREVIARY

The Lord's Prayer

The Prayer Appointed for the Week
Grant, O Lord, that the course of this world may be peaceably governed by your
   providence; and that your Church may joyfully serve you in confidence and
   serenity; through Jesus Christ our Lord who lives and reigns with you and the
   Holy Spirit, one God, for ever and ever. *Amen.* †

The Concluding Prayer of the Church
Pour your grace into my heart, O Lord, that I who have known the incarnation of
   your Son Jesus Christ, announced by an angel to the Virgin Mary, may by his
   cross and passion be brought to the glory of his resurrection; who lives and
   reigns with you, in the unity of the Holy Spirit, one God, now and for ever.
   Amen. †

The Morning Office   **To Be Observed on the Hour or Half Hour**
                                 Between 6 and 9 a.m.

The Call to Prayer
Open my lips, O Lord,* and my mouth shall proclaim your praise.

Psalm 51:16

The Request for Presence
Open my eyes, that I may see* the wonders of your law.

Psalm 119:18

The Greeting
I will thank you, O LORD my God, with all my heart,* and glorify your Name for
   evermore.

Psalm 86:12

The Refrain for the Morning Lessons
For who is God, but the LORD?* who is the Rock, except our God?

Psalm 18:32

A Reading
Jesus taught us, saying: "Beware of false prophets who come to you disguised as
   sheep but underneath are ravenous wolves. You will be able to tell them by
   their fruits. Can people pick grapes from thorns, or figs from thistles? In the
   same way, a sound tree produces good fruit but a rotten tree bad fruit. A sound
   tree cannot bear bad fruit, nor a rotten tree bear good fruit. Any tree that does
   not produce good fruit is cut down and thrown on the fire. I repeat, you will be
   able to tell them by their fruits."

Matthew 7:15–20

The Refrain
For who is God, but the LORD?* who is the Rock, except our God?

The Morning Psalm   *Your Servant Holds Your Word to Be Dear*
You are righteous, O LORD,* and upright are your judgments.
You have issued your decrees* with justice and in perfect faithfulness.
My indignation has consumed me,* because my enemies forget your words.
Your word has been tested to the uttermost,* and your servant holds it dear.
I am small and of little account,* yet I do not forget your commandments.
Your justice is an everlasting justice* and your law is the truth.
Trouble and distress have come upon me,* yet your commandments are my
    delight.
The righteousness of your decrees is everlasting;* grant me understanding, that I
    may live.

Psalm 119:137–144

The Refrain
For who is God, but the LORD?* who is the Rock, except our God?

The Small Verse
O Lamb of God, that takes away the sins of the world, have mercy upon me.
O Lamb of God, that takes away the sins of the world, have mercy upon me.
O Lamb of God, that takes away the sins of the world, grant me your peace.

Agnus Dei

The Lord's Prayer

The Prayer Appointed for the Week
Grant, O Lord, that the course of this world may be peaceably governed by your
    providence; and that your Church may joyfully serve you in confidence and
    serenity; through Jesus Christ our Lord who lives and reigns with you and the
    Holy Spirit, one God, for ever and ever. *Amen.* †

The Concluding Prayer of the Church
Lord God, almighty and everlasting Father, you have brought me in safety to this
    new day: Preserve me with your mighty power, that I may not fall into sin, nor
    be overcome by adversity; and in all I do direct me to the fulfilling of your pur-
    pose; through Jesus Christ my Lord. *Amen.* †

The Midday Office   **To Be Observed on the Hour or Half Hour**
                                         Between 11 a.m. and 2 p.m.

The Call to Prayer
Hallelujah! Sing to the LORD a new song;* sing his praise in the congregation of the
    faithful.

Psalm 149:1

The Request for Presence
Hear, O Shepherd of Israel, leading Joseph like a flock;* shine forth, you that are
enthroned upon the cherubim.

Psalm 80:1

The Greeting
The Lord is in his holy temple; let all the earth keep silence before him. Amen.

Traditional

The Refrain for the Midday Lessons
The LORD shall watch over your going out and your coming in* from this time
forth for evermore.

Psalm 121:8

A Reading
In view of this we also pray continually that our God will make you worthy of this
call, and by his power fulfill all your desires for goodness, and complete all
you have been doing through faith; so that the name of our Lord Jesus Christ
may be glorified in you and you in him, by the grace of our God and the Lord
Jesus Christ.

2 Thessalonians 1:11–12

The Refrain
The LORD shall watch over your going out and your coming in,* from this time
forth for evermore.

The Midday Psalm *I Will Perform My Vows*
Praise the LORD, you that fear him;* stand in awe of him, O offspring of Israel; all
you of Jacob's line, give glory.
For he does not despise nor abhor the poor in their poverty; neither does he hide
his face from them;* when they cry to him he hears them.
My praise is of him in the great assembly;* I will perform my vows in the presence
of those who worship him.
The poor shall eat and be satisfied,* and those who seek the LORD shall praise him:
"May your heart live for ever!"
All the ends of the earth shall remember and turn to the LORD,* and all the families
of the nations shall bow before him.
For kingship belongs to the LORD;* he rules over the nations.

Psalm 22:22–27

The Refrain
The LORD shall watch over your going out and your coming in,* from this time
forth for evermore.

The Gloria

The Lord's Prayer

The Prayer Appointed for the Week

Grant, O Lord, that the course of this world may be peaceably governed by your providence; and that your Church may joyfully serve you in confidence and serenity; through Jesus Christ our Lord who lives and reigns with you and the Holy Spirit, one God, for ever and ever. *Amen.* †

The Concluding Prayer of the Church

Let us bless the Lord God living and true! Let us always render him praise, glory, honor, blessing, and all good things! Amen. Amen. So be it! So be it!

St. Francis of Assisi

The Vespers Office

To Be Observed on the Hour or Half Hour Between 5 and 8 p.m.

The Call to Prayer

Praise God, from whom all blessings flow; praise him, all creatures here below; praise him above, you heavenly hosts; praise Father, Son and Holy Ghost.

Traditional Doxology

The Request for Presence

Show your goodness, O LORD, to those who are good* and to those who are true of heart.

Psalm 125:4

The Greeting

Out of the mouths of infants and children* your majesty is praised above the heavens.

Psalm 8:2

The Hymn   *Breathe on Me, Breath of God*

Breathe on me, breath of God, fill me with life anew,
That I may love what you do love, and do what you would do.

Breathe on me, breath of God, until my heart is pure,
Until with you I will one will, to do and to endure.

Breathe on me, breath of God, till I am wholly thine,
Till all this earthly part of me glows with your fire divine.

Breathe on me, breath of God, so shall I never die,
But live with you the perfect life of your eternity.

Edwin Hatch

The Refrain for the Vespers Lessons

We have heard with our ears, O God, our forefathers have told us,* the deeds you did in their days, in the days of old.

Psalm 44:1

The Vespers Psalm   *Let the Nations Be Glad and Sing for Joy*

May God be merciful to us and bless us,* show us the light of his countenance and
come to us.

Let your ways be known upon earth,* your saving health among all nations.

Let the peoples praise you, O God;* let all the peoples praise you.

Let the nations be glad and sing for joy,* for you judge the peoples with equity and
guide all the nations upon earth.

Let the peoples praise you, O God;* let all the peoples praise you.

The earth has brought forth her increase;* may God, our own God, give us his
blessing.

May God give us his blessing,* and may all the ends of the earth stand in awe of
him.

Psalm 67

The Refrain

We have heard with our ears, O God, our forefathers have told us,* the deeds you
did in their days, in the days of old.

The Call to Prayer

Even so come, Lord Jesus!

The Lord's Prayer

The Prayer Appointed for the Week

Grant, O Lord, that the course of this world may be peaceably governed by your
providence; and that your Church may joyfully serve you in confidence and
serenity; through Jesus Christ our Lord who lives and reigns with you and the
Holy Spirit, one God, for ever and ever. *Amen.* †

The Concluding Prayer of the Church

Almighty and eternal God, ruler of all things in heaven and earth: Mercifully
accept my prayer, and strengthen me to do your will; through Jesus Christ our
Lord. *Amen.* †

The Morning Office   **To Be Observed on the Hour or Half Hour**
Between 6 and 9 a.m.

The Call to Prayer

Worship the LORD in the beauty of holiness;* let the whole earth tremble before him.

Psalm 96:9

The Request for Presence

Show us the light of your countenance, O God,* and come to us.

based on Psalm 67:1

The Greeting

Seven times a day do I praise you,* because of your righteous judgments.

Psalm 119:164

The Refrain for the Morning Lessons

Gracious and upright is the LORD;* therefore he teaches sinners in his way.

Psalm 25:7

A Reading

On the last day, the great day of the festival, Jesus stood and cried out: 'Let anyone who is thirsty come to me! Let anyone who believes in me come and drink! As scripture says, "From his heart shall flow streams of living water." ' He was speaking of the Spirit which those who believed in him were to receive; for there was no Spirit as yet because Jesus had not yet been glorified.

John 7:37–39

The Refrain

Gracious and upright is the LORD;* therefore he teaches sinners in his way.

The Morning Psalm   *His Loving-Kindness Toward Us Is Great*

Praise the LORD, all you nations;* laud him, all you peoples.
For his loving-kindness toward us is great,* and the faithfulness of the LORD endures for ever. Hallelujah!

Psalm 117

The Refrain

Gracious and upright is the LORD;* therefore he teaches sinners in his way.

The Cry of the Church

O Lamb of God, that takes away the sins of the world, have mercy upon me.
O Lamb of God, that takes away the sins of the world, have mercy upon me.
O Lamb of God, that takes away the sins of the world, grant me your peace.

The Lord's Prayer

The Prayer Appointed for the Week

Grant, O Lord, that the course of this world may be peaceably governed by your providence; and that your Church may joyfully serve you in confidence and serenity; through Jesus Christ our Lord who lives and reigns with you and the Holy Spirit, one God, for ever and ever. *Amen.* †

The Concluding Prayer of the Church

Lord God, almighty and everlasting Father, you have brought me in safety to this new day: Preserve me with your mighty power, that I may not fall into sin, nor be overcome by adversity; and in all I do direct me to the fulfilling of your purpose; through Jesus Christ my Lord. *Amen.* †

The Midday Office   **To Be Observed on the Hour or Half Hour**
Between 11 a.m. and 2 p.m.

The Call to Prayer

Open my lips, O Lord,* and my mouth shall proclaim your praise.
Had you desired it, I would have offered sacrifice,* but you take no delight in burnt-offerings.

The sacrifice of God is a troubled spirit;* a broken and contrite heart, O God, you will not despise.

Psalm 51:16–18

The Request for Presence
Let your ways be known upon earth,* your saving health among all nations.

Psalm 67:2

The Greeting
I hate those who have a divided heart,* but your law do I love.

Psalm 119:113

The Refrain for the Midday Lessons
I will listen to what the LORD God is saying,* for he is speaking peace to his faithful people and to those who turn their hearts to him.

Psalm 85:8

A Reading
YAHWEH then said to Moses, 'Look, I shall come to you in a dense cloud so that the people will hear when I speak to you and believe you ever after.' Moses then told YAHWEH what the people had said. YAHWEH then said to Moses, 'Go to the people and tell them to sanctify themselves today and tomorrow. They must wash their clothes and be ready for the day after tomorrow; for the day after tomorrow, in the sight of all the people, YAHWEH will descend on Mount Sinai. You will mark out the limits of the mountain and say, "Take care not to go up the mountain or to touch the edge of it. Anyone who touches the mountain will be put to death. No one may lay a hand on him: he must be stoned or shot by arrow; whether man or beast, he shall not live." When the ram's horn sounds a long blast, they must go up the mountain.' So Moses came down from the mountain to the people; he made the people sanctify themselves and they washed their clothes.

Exodus 19:9–14

The Refrain
I will listen to what the LORD God is saying,* for he is speaking peace to his faithful people and to those who turn their hearts to him.

The Midday Psalm   *The Hearts of Those Who Seek God Shall Live*
I will praise the Name of God in song;* I will proclaim his greatness with thanksgiving.
This will please the LORD more than an offering of oxen,* more than bullocks with horns and hoofs.
The afflicted shall see and be glad;* you who seek God, your heart shall live.
For the LORD listens to the needy,* and his prisoners he does not despise.
Let the heavens and the earth praise him,* the seas and all that moves in them;
For God will save Zion and rebuild the cities of Judah;* they shall live there and have it in possession.
The children of his servants will inherit it,* and those who love his Name will dwell therein.

Psalm 69:32–38

The Refrain
I will listen to what the LORD God is saying,* for he is speaking peace to his faithful
people and to those who turn their hearts to him.

The Cry of the Church
Lord, have mercy on us. Christ, have mercy on us. Lord, have mercy on us.

The Lord's Prayer

The Prayer Appointed for the Week
Grant, O Lord, that the course of this world may be peaceably governed by your
providence; and that your Church may joyfully serve you in confidence and
serenity; through Jesus Christ our Lord who lives and reigns with you and the
Holy Spirit, one God, for ever and ever. *Amen.* †

The Concluding Prayer of the Church
Heavenly, Father, in you I live and move and have my being: I humbly pray you
so to guide and govern me by your Holy Spirit, that in all the cares and occupations of my life I may not forget you, but may remember that I am ever walking
in your sight; through Jesus Christ my Lord. *Amen.* †

The Vespers Office   **To Be Observed on the Hour or Half Hour**
                                    Between 5 and 8 p.m.

The Call to Prayer
Sing to the LORD, you servants of his;* give thanks for the remembrance of his
holiness.
For his wrath endures but the twinkling of an eye,* his favor for a lifetime.
                                                        Psalm 30:4–5

The Request for Presence
Show us the light of your countenance, O God,* and come to us.
                                                based on Psalm 67:1

The Greeting
Your statutes have been like songs to me* wherever I have lived as a stranger.
I remember your Name in the night, O LORD,* and dwell upon your law.
This is how it has been with me,* because I have kept your commandments.
                                                Psalm 119:54–56

The Hymn   *Sunshine in My Soul*
    There is sunshine in my soul today,
    More glorious and bright
    Than glows in any earthly sky,
    For Jesus is the light.

    There is music in my soul today,
    A carol to my King,
    And Jesus, listening, can hear
    The songs I cannot sing.

There is music in my soul today,
For when the Lord is near,
The dove of peace sings in my heart,
The flowers of grace appear.

O there is sunshine, blessed sunshine,
When the peaceful, happy moments roll;
When Jesus shows his smiling face,
There is sunshine in my soul.

Eliza Hewitt

The Refrain for the Vespers Lessons
Righteousness shall go before him,* and peace shall be a pathway for his feet.

Psalm 85:13

The Vespers Psalm   *Cast Your Burden Upon the LORD*
But I will call upon God,* and the LORD will deliver me.
In the evening, in the morning, and at noonday, I will complain and lament,* and
     he will hear my voice.
He will bring me safely back from the battle waged against me;* for there are
     many who fight me.
God, who is enthroned of old, will hear . . .
Cast your burden upon the LORD, and he will sustain you;* he will never let the
     righteous stumble.

Psalm 55:17–20, 24

The Refrain
Righteousness shall go before him,* and peace shall be a pathway for his feet.

The Cry of the Church
O God, come to my assistance!
O Lord, make haste to help me!

The Lord's Prayer

The Prayer Appointed for the Week
Grant, O Lord, that the course of this world may be peaceably governed by your
     providence; and that your Church may joyfully serve you in confidence and
     serenity; through Jesus Christ our Lord who lives and reigns with you and the
     Holy Spirit, one God, for ever and ever. *Amen.* †

The Concluding Prayer of the Church
May Almighty God grant me a peaceful night and a perfect end. *Amen.*

The Morning Office   **To Be Observed on the Hour or Half Hour**
                                                    Between 6 and 9 a.m.

The Call to Prayer
Sing to the LORD and bless his Name;* proclaim the good news of his salvation
     from day to day.

Declare his glory among the nations* and his wonders among all peoples.
For great is the LORD and greatly to be praised;* he is more to be feared than all
  gods.

Psalm 96:2–4

The Request for Presence
"In your great mercy, O God,* answer me with your unfailing help."

Psalm 69:15

The Greeting
The LORD lives! Blessed is my Rock!* Exalted is the God of my salvation!

Psalm 18:46

The Refrain for the Morning Lessons
He looks at the earth and it trembles;* he touches the mountains and they smoke.

Psalm 104:33

A Reading
When Pentecost day came round, they had all met together, when suddenly there
  came from heaven a sound as of a violent wind which filled the entire house in
  which they were sitting; and there appeared to them tongues as of fire; these
  separated and came to rest on the head of each of them.

Acts 2:1–3

The Refrain
He looks at the earth and it trembles;* he touches the mountains and they smoke.

The Morning Psalm   *My Heart Rejoices in the LORD*
The LORD looks down from heaven,* and beholds all the people in the world.
From where he sits enthroned he turns his gaze* on all who dwell on the earth.
He fashions all the hearts of them* and understands all their works.
There is no king that can be saved by a mighty army;* a strong man is not delivered
  by his great strength.
The horse is a vain hope for deliverance;* for all its strength it cannot save.
Behold, the eye of the LORD is upon those who fear him,* on those who wait upon
  his love,
To pluck their lives from death,* and to feed them in time of famine.
Our soul waits for the LORD;* he is our help and our shield.
Indeed, our heart rejoices in him,* for in his holy Name we put our trust.
Let your loving-kindness, O LORD, be upon us,* as we have put our trust in you.

Psalm 33:13–22

The Refrain
He looks at the earth and it trembles;* he touches the mountains and they smoke.

The Cry of the Church
O God, come to my assistance! O Lord, make haste to help me!

The Lord's Prayer

The Prayer Appointed for the Week
Grant, O Lord, that the course of this world may be peaceably governed by your
    providence; and that your Church may joyfully serve you in confidence and
    serenity; through Jesus Christ our Lord who lives and reigns with you and the
    Holy Spirit, one God, for ever and ever. *Amen.* †

The Concluding Prayer of the Church
Lord God, almighty and everlasting Father, you have brought me in safety to this
    new day: Preserve me with your mighty power, that I may not fall into sin, nor
    be overcome by adversity; and in all I do direct me to the fulfilling of your pur-
    pose; through Jesus Christ my Lord. *Amen.* †

The Midday Office   To Be Observed on the Hour or Half Hour
                                                    Between 11 a.m. and 2 p.m.

The Call to Prayer
Praise God from whom all blessings flow; praise him, all creatures here below;
    praise him, you heavenly hosts; praise Father, Son and Holy Ghost.
                                                    Traditional Doxology

The Request for Presence
Hear my prayer, O LORD,* and give ear to my cry . . .
For I am but a sojourner with you,* a wayfarer, as all my forebears were.
                                                    Psalm 39:13–14

The Greeting
My spirit shakes with terror,* how long, O LORD, how long?
                                                    Psalm 6:3

The Refrain for the Midday Lessons
The LORD loves those who hate evil; he preserves the lives of his saints* and delivers
    them from the hand of the wicked.
                                                    Psalm 97:10

A Reading
After this, I shall pour out my spirit on all humanity. Your sons and daughters
    shall prophesy, your old people shall dream dreams, and your young people
    see visions.
                                                    Joel 3:1

The Refrain
The LORD loves those who hate evil; he preserves the lives of his saints* and delivers
    them from the hand of the wicked.

The Midday Psalm   *How Excellent Is His Greatness*
Bless the LORD, O my soul;* O LORD my God, how excellent is your greatness! you
    are clothed with majesty and splendor.
You wrap yourself with light as with a cloak* and spread out the heavens like a
    curtain.

You lay the beams of your chambers in the waters above;* you make the clouds
your chariot; you ride on the wings of the wind.

You make the winds your messengers* and flames of fire your servants.

You have set the earth upon its foundations,* so that it never shall move at any
time.

You covered it with the Deep as with a mantle;* the waters stood higher than the
mountains.

At your rebuke they fled;* at the voice of your thunder they hastened away.

Psalm 104:1–7

The Refrain

The LORD loves those who hate evil; he preserves the lives of his saints* and delivers
them from the hand of the wicked.

The Cry of the Church

O God, come to my assistance! O Lord, make haste to help me!

The Lord's Prayer

The Prayer Appointed for the Week

Grant, O Lord, that the course of this world may be peaceably governed by your
providence; and that your Church may joyfully serve you in confidence and
serenity; through Jesus Christ our Lord who lives and reigns with you and the
Holy Spirit, one God, for ever and ever. *Amen.* †

The Concluding Prayer of the Church

Almighty God, you opened the way of eternal life to every race and nation by the
promised gift of your Holy Spirit: Shed abroad this gift throughout the world
by the preaching of the Gospel, that it may reach to the ends of the earth;
through Jesus Christ my Lord, who lives and reigns with you, in the unity of
the Holy Spirit, one God, for ever and ever. *Amen.* †

The Vespers Office

**To Be Observed on the Hour or Half Hour
Between 5 and 8 p.m.**

The Call to Prayer

Bless God in the congregation;* bless the LORD, you that are of the fountain of
Israel.

Psalm 68:26

The Request for Presence

O LORD, watch over us* and save us from this generation for ever.

Psalm 12:7

The Greeting

One generation shall praise your works to another* and shall declare your power.

Psalm 145:4

The Hymn   *Benedictus Es Domini*
   Glory to you, Lord God of our fathers;* you are worthy of praise; glory to you.
   Glory to you for the radiance of your holy Name;* we will praise you and
   highly exalt you for ever.

   Glory to you in the splendor of your temple;* on the throne of your majesty,
   glory to you.
   Glory to you, seated between the Cherubim;* we will praise you and highly
   exalt you for ever.

   Glory to you, beholding the depths;* in the high vault of heaven, glory to you.
   Glory to you, Father, Son, and Holy Spirit;* we will praise you and highly exalt
   you for ever.

                                         Song of the Three Young Men 29–34

The Refrain for the Vespers Lessons
The heaven of heavens is the LORD's,* but he entrusted the earth to its peoples.
                                                          Psalm 115:16

The Vespers Psalm   *The LORD Is My Strength*
I love you, O LORD my strength,* O LORD my stronghold, my crag, and my haven.
My God, my rock in whom I put my trust,* my shield, the horn of my salvation,
    and my refuge; you are worthy of praise.
I will call upon the LORD,* and so shall I be saved from my enemies.
The breakers of death rolled over me,* and the torrents of oblivion made me
    afraid.
The cords of hell entangled me,* and the snares of death were set for me.
I called upon the LORD in my distress* and cried out to my God for help.
He heard my voice from his heavenly dwelling;* my cry of anguish came to his
    ears.
                                                          Psalm 18:1–7

The Refrain
The heaven of heavens is the LORD's,* but he entrusted the earth to its peoples.

The Cry of the Church
Even so come, Lord Jesus!

The Lord's Prayer

The Prayer Appointed for the Week
Grant, O Lord, that the course of this world may be peaceably governed by your
    providence; and that your Church may joyfully serve you in confidence and
    serenity; through Jesus Christ our Lord who lives and reigns with you and the
    Holy Spirit, one God, for ever and ever. *Amen.* †

The Concluding Prayer of the Church
Grant me, I beseech thee, O merciful God, prudently to study, rightly to understand and perfectly to fulfill that which is pleasing to thee, to the praise and
glory of thy name. Amen.

St. Thomas Aquinas

The Morning Office   To Be Observed on the Hour or Half Hour
                                                      Between 6 and 9 a.m.

The Call to Prayer
Hallelujah! Praise the Name of the LORD;* give praise, you servants of the LORD,
You who stand in the house of the LORD,* in the courts of the house of our God.
Praise the LORD, for the LORD is good;* sing praises to his Name, for it is lovely.

Psalm 136:1–3

The Request for Presence
I have said to the LORD, "You are my God;* listen, O LORD, to my supplication.

Psalm 140:6

The Greeting
You are the LORD, most high over all the earth;* you are exalted far above all gods.

Psalm 97:9

The Refrain for the Morning Lessons
Everyone will stand in awe and declare God's deeds;* they will recognize his
works.

Psalm 64:9

A Reading
In the evening of that same day, the first day of the week, the doors were closed in
the room where the disciples were, for fear of the Jews. Jesus came and stood
among them. He said to them, 'Peace be with you,' and, after saying this, he
showed them his hands and his side. The disciples were filled with joy at seeing the Lord, and he said to them again, 'Peace be with you. As the Father sent
me, so am I sending you.' After this he breathed on them and said: 'Receive the
Holy Spirit. If you forgive anyone's sins, they are forgiven; if you retain anyone's sins, they are retained.'

John 20:19–23

The Refrain
Everyone will stand in awe and declare God's deeds;* they will recognize his
works.

The Morning Psalm   The LORD Has Pleasure in Those Who Await His Gracious Favor
Hallelujah! How good it is to sing praises to our God!* how pleasant it is to honor
him with praise!
The LORD rebuilds Jerusalem;* he gathers the exiles of Israel.

He heals the brokenhearted* and binds up their wounds.
He counts the number of the stars* and calls them all by their names.
Great is our LORD and mighty in power;* there is no limit to his wisdom.
The LORD lifts up the lowly,* but casts the wicked to the ground.
Sing to the LORD with thanksgiving;* make music to our God upon the harp.
He covers the heavens with clouds* and prepares rain for the earth;
He makes grass to grow upon the mountains* and green plants to serve mankind.
He provides food for flocks and herds* and for the young ravens when they cry.
He is not impressed by the might of a horse;* he has no pleasure in the strength of
a man;
But the LORD has pleasure in those who fear him,* in those who await his gracious
favor.

Psalm 147:1–12

The Refrain

Everyone will stand in awe and declare God's deeds;* they will recognize his
works.

The Cry of the Church

O God, come to my assistance! O Lord, make haste to help me!

The Lord's Prayer

The Prayer Appointed for the Week

Grant, O Lord, that the course of this world may be peaceably governed by your
providence; and that your Church may joyfully serve you in confidence and
serenity; through Jesus Christ our Lord who lives and reigns with you and the
Holy Spirit, one God, for ever and ever. *Amen.* †

The Concluding Prayer of the Church

Lord God, almighty and everlasting Father, you have brought me in safety to this
new day: Preserve me with your mighty power, that I may not fall into sin, nor
be overcome by adversity; and in all I do direct me to the fulfilling of your purpose; through Jesus Christ my Lord. *Amen.* †

The Midday Office	To Be Observed on the Hour or Half Hour
	Between 11 a.m. and 2 p.m.

The Call to Prayer

Ascribe to the LORD the honor due his Name;* bring offerings and come into his
courts.

Psalm 96:8

The Request for Presence

Let your countenance shine upon your servant* and teach me your statutes.

Psalm 119:135

The Greeting
I will give thanks to you, O LORD, with my whole heart;* I will tell of all your marvelous works.

Psalm 9:1

The Refrain for the Midday Lessons
Among the gods there is none like you, O LORD,* nor anything like your works.

Psalm 86:8

A Reading
I shall give them a single heart and I shall put a new spirit in them; I shall remove the heart of stone from their bodies and give them a heart of flesh, so that they can keep my laws and respect my judgements and put them into practice. Then they will be my people and I shall be their God. But those whose hearts are set on their horrors and loathsome practices I shall repay for their conduct— declares the Lord YAHWEH.

Ezekiel 11:19–21

The Refrain
Among the gods there is none like you, O LORD,* nor anything like your works.

The Midday Psalm   *You, O LORD, Will Bless the Righteous*
Lead me, O LORD, in your righteousness, because of those who lie in wait for me;* make your way straight before me.
For there is no truth in their mouth;* there is destruction in their heart;
Their throat is an open grave;* they flatter with their tongue.
Declare them guilty, O God;* let them fall, because of their schemes.
Because of their many transgressions cast them out,* for they have rebelled against you.
But all who take refuge in you will be glad;* they will sing out their joy for ever.
You will shelter them,* so that those who love your Name may exult in you.
For you, O LORD, will bless the righteous;* you will defend them with your favor as with a shield.

Psalm 5:8–15

The Refrain
Among the gods there is none like you, O LORD,* nor anything like your works.

The Cry of the Church
Even so come, Lord Jesus!

The Lord's Prayer

The Prayer Appointed for the Week
Grant, O Lord, that the course of this world may be peaceably governed by your providence; and that your Church may joyfully serve you in confidence and

serenity; through Jesus Christ our Lord who lives and reigns with you and the Holy Spirit, one God, for ever and ever. *Amen.* †

The Concluding Prayer of the Church

O God, who on the day of Pentecost taught the hearts of your faithful people by sending to them the light of your Holy Spirit: Grant us by the same Spirit to have a right judgement in all things, and evermore to rejoice in his holy comfort; through Jesus Christ your Son our Lord, who lives and reigns with you, in the unity of the Holy Spirit, one God, for ever and ever. *Amen.* †

The Vespers Office   **To Be Observed on the Hour or Half Hour**
Between 5 and 8 p.m.

The Call to Prayer

Behold now, bless the LORD, all you servants of the LORD,* you that stand by night in the house of the LORD.

Lift up your hands in the holy place and bless the LORD;* the LORD who made heaven and earth bless you out of Zion.

Psalm 134

The Request for Presence

Look upon me and answer me, O LORD my God;* give light to my eyes, lest I sleep in death.

The Greeting

O LORD, I am not proud;* I have no haughty looks.

I do not occupy myself with great matters,* or with things that are too hard for me.

But I still my soul and make it quiet, like a child upon its mother's breast;* my soul is quieted within me.

Psalm 131:1–3

The Hymn   *Hail, O Festival Day!*

Lo, in the likeness of fire,
On those who await his appearing
He whom the Lord foretold
Suddenly, swiftly descends.

Forth from the Father he comes
With seven-fold mystical offering,
Pouring on all human souls
Infinite riches of God.

Hark! For in myriad tongues
Christ's own, his chosen apostles,
Preach to the ends of the earth
Christ and his wonderful works.

Praise to the Spirit of Life,
All praise to the fount of our being,
Light that enlightens us all,
Life that in all does abide:
Hail, O festival day! Blessed day that is hallowed for ever,
Day when the Holy Ghost shone in the world with God's grace.

Venantius Honorius Fortunatus

The Refrain for the Vespers Lessons

Those who are planted in the house of the Lord* shall flourish in the courts of our God;

Psalm 92:12

The Vespers Psalm   Be Merciful to Me, O Lord

You only are my portion, O Lord;* I have promised to keep your words.
I entreat you with all my heart,* be merciful to me according to your promise.
I have considered my ways* and turned my feet toward your decrees.
I hasten and do not tarry* to keep your commandments.
Though the cords of the wicked entangle me,* I do not forget your law.
At midnight I will rise to give you thanks,* because of your righteous judgments.
I am a companion of all who fear you;* and of those who keep your
    commandments.
The earth, O Lord, is full of your love;* instruct me in your statutes.

Psalm 119:57–64

The Refrain

Those who are planted in the house of the Lord* shall flourish in the courts of our God;

The Small Verse

The Lord is my shepherd and nothing is wanting to me. In green pastures He has settled me.

THE SHORT BREVIARY

The Lord's Prayer

The Prayer Appointed for the Week

Grant, O Lord, that the course of this world may be peaceably governed by your
    providence; and that your Church may joyfully serve you in confidence and
    serenity; through Jesus Christ our Lord who lives and reigns with you and the
    Holy Spirit, one God, for ever and ever. *Amen.* †

The Concluding Prayer of the Church

Almighty God, who has promised to hear the petitions of those who ask in your
    Son's Name: I beseech you mercifully to incline your ear to me who have made
    my prayers and supplications to you; and grant that those things which I have
    faithfully asked according to your will, I may effectually obtain, to the relief of
    my necessity, and to the setting forth of your glory; through Jesus Christ my
    Lord. *Amen.* †

The Morning Office
To Be Observed on the Hour or Half Hour
Between 6 and 9 a.m.

The Call to Prayer
Come now and look upon the works of the LORD,* what awesome things he has
   done on earth.
Psalm 46:9

The Request for Presence
O LORD . . . answer us when we call.
Psalm 20:9

The Greeting
My eyes are fixed on you, O my Strength;* for you, O God, are my stronghold.
Psalm 59:10

The Refrain for the Morning Lessons
The LORD's will stands fast for ever,* and the designs of his heart from age to age.
Psalm 33:11

A Reading
Jesus said: "Anyone who loves me will keep my word, and my Father will love
   him, and we shall come to him, and make a home in him. Anyone who does
   not love me does not keep my words. And the word that you hear is not my
   own: it is the word of the Father who sent me. I have said these things to you
   while still with you; but the Paraclete, the Holy Spirit, whom the Father will
   send in my name, will teach you everything and remind you of all I have said
   to you."
John 14:23–26

The Refrain
The LORD's will stands fast for ever,* and the designs of his heart from age to age.

The Morning Psalm   *My Merciful God Comes to Meet Me*
Rouse yourself, come to my side, and see;* for you, LORD God of hosts, are Israel's
   God.
Awake, and punish all the ungodly;* show no mercy to those who are faithless
   and evil.
They go to and fro in the evening;* they snarl like dogs and run about the city.
Behold, they boast with their mouths, and taunts are on their lips;* "For who,"
   they say, "will hear us?"
But you, O LORD, you laugh at them;* you laugh all the ungodly to scorn.
My eyes are fixed on you, O my Strength;* for you, O God, are my stronghold.
Psalm 59:5–11

The Refrain
The LORD's will stands fast for ever,* and the designs of his heart from age to age.

The Cry of the Church
Lord, have mercy on us. Christ, have mercy on us. Lord, have mercy on us.

The Lord's Prayer

The Prayer Appointed for the Week
Grant, O Lord, that the course of this world may be peaceably governed by your providence; and that your Church may joyfully serve you in confidence and serenity; through Jesus Christ our Lord who lives and reigns with you and the Holy Spirit, one God, for ever and ever. *Amen.* †

The Concluding Prayer of the Church
Lord God, almighty and everlasting Father, you have brought me in safety to this new day: Preserve me with your mighty power, that I may not fall into sin, nor be overcome by adversity; and in all I do direct me to the fulfilling of your purpose; through Jesus Christ my Lord. *Amen.* †

The Midday Office   To Be Observed on the Hour or Half Hour
                                       Between 11 a.m. and 2 p.m.

The Call to Prayer
Come, let us bow down, and bend the knee,* and kneel before the LORD our Maker.
For he is our God, and we are the people of his pasture and the sheep of his hand.*
   Oh, that today you would hearken to his voice!

Psalm 95:6–7

The Request for Presence
My merciful God comes to meet me.
         Psalm 59:11

The Greeting
I will give you thanks for what you have done* and declare the goodness of your Name in the presence of the godly.

Psalm 52:9

The Refrain for the Midday Lessons
Let me announce the decree of the LORD:* he said to me, "You are my Son; this day have I begotten you."

Psalm 2:7

A Reading
There are many different gifts, but it is always the same Spirit; there are many different ways of serving, but it is always the same Lord. There are many different forms of activity, but in everybody it is the same God who is at work in them all. The particular manifestation of the Spirit granted to each one is to be used for the general good. To one is given from the Spirit the gift of utterance expressing wisdom; to another the gift of utterance expressing knowledge, in accordance with the same Spirit; to another, faith, from the same Spirit; and to

another, the gifts of healing, through this one Spirit; to another, the working of miracles; to another, prophecy; to another, the power of distinguishing spirits; to one, the gift of different tongues and to another, the interpretation of tongues. But at work in all these is one and the same Spirit, distributing them at will to each individual.

1 Corinthians 12:4–11

The Refrain

Let me announce the decree of the LORD:* he said to me, "You are my Son; this day have I begotten you.

The Midday Psalm
Righteousness and Peace Have Kissed Each Other

I will listen to what the LORD God is saying,* for he is speaking peace to his faithful people and to those who turn their hearts to him.

Truly, his salvation is very near to those who fear him,* that his glory may dwell in our land.

Mercy and truth have met together;* righteousness and peace have kissed each other.

Truth shall spring up from the earth,* and righteousness shall look down from heaven.

The LORD will indeed grant prosperity,* and our land will yield its increase.

Righteousness shall go before him,* and peace shall be a pathway for his feet.

Psalm 85:8–13

The Refrain

Let me announce the decree of the LORD:* he said to me, "You are my Son; this day have I begotten you.

The Gloria

The Lord's Prayer

The Prayer Appointed for the Week

Grant, O Lord, that the course of this world may be peaceably governed by your providence; and that your Church may joyfully serve you in confidence and serenity; through Jesus Christ our Lord who lives and reigns with you and the Holy Spirit, one God, for ever and ever. *Amen.* †

The Concluding Prayer of the Church

Almighty and everlasting God, You have given to us grace, by the confession of a true faith, to acknowledge the glory of the eternal Trinity, and in the power of your divine Majesty to worship the Unity: Keep me steadfast in this faith and worship, and bring me at last to see you in your one and eternal glory, O Father; who with the Son and the Holy Spirit live and reign, one God, for ever and ever. *Amen.* †

The Vespers Office   To Be Observed on the Hour or Half Hour
                                           Between 5 and 8 p.m.

The Call to Prayer
The LORD is my strength and my shield;* my heart trusts him, and I have been
   helped;
Therefore my heart dances for joy,* and in my song I will praise him.

Psalm 28:8–9

The Request for Presence
Hear, O LORD, and have mercy upon me;* O LORD, be my helper.

Psalm 30:11

The Greeting
Your righteousness, O God, reaches to the heavens;* you have done great things;
   who is like you, O God?

Psalm 71:19

The Hymn   *More Holiness Give Me*
   More holiness give me, more striving within;
   More patience in suffering, more sorrow for sin;
   More faith in my Savior, more sense of his care;
   More joy in his service, more purpose in prayer.

   More gratitude give me, more trust in the Lord;
   More pride in his glory, more hope in his word;
   More tears for his sorrows, more pain at his grief;
   More meekness in trial, more praise for relief.

   More purity give me, more strength to overcome;
   More freedom from earth-stains, more longings for home;
   More fit for the kingdom, more used would I be;
   More blessed and holy, more, Savior, like Thee.

Philip Bliss

The Refrain for the Vespers Lessons
Remember me, O LORD, with the favor you have for your people,* and visit me
   with your saving help.

Psalm 106:4

The Vespers Psalm   *Who Can Ascend the Hill of the LORD?*
The earth is the LORD's and all that is in it,* the world and all who dwell therein.
For it is he who founded it upon the seas* and made it firm upon the rivers of the
   deep.
"Who can ascend the hill of the LORD?* and who can stand in his holy place?"
"Those who have clean hands and a pure heart,* who have not pledged themselves
   to falsehood, nor sworn by what is a fraud.
They shall receive a blessing from the LORD* and a just reward from the God of
   their salvation."

Such is the generation of those who seek him,* of those who seek your face, O God of Jacob.

Psalm 24:1–6

The Refrain

Remember me, O LORD, with the favor you have for your people,* and visit me with your saving help.

The Gloria

The Lord's Prayer

The Prayer Appointed for the Week

Grant, O Lord, that the course of this world may be peaceably governed by your providence; and that your Church may joyfully serve you in confidence and serenity; through Jesus Christ our Lord who lives and reigns with you and the Holy Spirit, one God, for ever and ever. *Amen.* †

The Concluding Prayer of the Church

O God, you have caused the holy night to shine with the brightness of the true Light: Grant that I, who have known the mystery of that Light on earth, may also enjoy him perfectly in heaven; where with you and the Holy Spirit he lives and reigns, one God, in glory everlasting. *Amen.* †

May Compline

Sunday
The Night Office   To Be Observed Before Retiring

The Call to Prayer
May the Lord Almighty grant me and those I love a peaceful night and a perfect
   end. *Amen.* †

The Request for Presence
Our help is in the Name of the Lord; the maker of heaven and earth.

The Greeting
Almighty God, my heavenly Father: I have sinned against you, through my own
   fault, in thought, and word, and deed, in what I have done and in what I have
   left undone. For the sake of your Son our Lord Jesus Christ, forgive me all my
   offenses; and grant that I may serve you in newness of life, to the glory of your
   Name. *Amen.* †

The Reading
I bind unto myself today
The strong name of the Trinity
By invocation of the same,
The Three in One and One in Three.

I bind this day to me forever,
By power of faith, Christ's incarnation,
His baptism in the Jordan River,
His cross of death for my salvation,
His bursting from the spiced tomb,
His riding up the heavenly way,
His coming at the day of doom,
I bind unto myself today.

I bind unto myself today
The virtues of the starlit heaven,
The glorious sun's life-giving ray,
The whiteness of the moon at even,
The flashing of the lightning free,
The whirling wind's tempestuous shocks,
The stable earth, the deep salt sea,
Around the old eternal rock.

I bind unto myself today
The power of God to hold and lead,
His eye to watch, his might to stay,
His ear to hearken to my need,
The wisdom of my God to teach,
His hand to guide, his shield to ward,
The Word of God to give me speech,
His heavenly host to be my guard.

Christ be with me, Christ within me,
Christ behind me, Christ before me,
Christ beside me, Christ to win me,
Christ to comfort and restore me,
Christ beneath me, Christ above me,
Christ in quiet, Christ in danger,
Christ in all the hearts that love me,
Christ in mouth of friend and stranger.

I bind unto myself today
The strong name of the Trinity
By invocation of the same,
The Three in One and One in Three.
Of whom all nature has creation,
Eternal Father, Spirit, Word,
Praise to the Lord of my Salvation,
Salvation is of Christ the Lord.

St. Patrick

The Gloria

The Psalm   *The Lord Himself Is God*

Be joyful in the Lord, all you lands;* serve the Lord with gladness and come
before his presence with a song.
Know this: The Lord himself is God;* he himself has made us, and we are his; we
are his people and the sheep of his pasture.
Enter his gates with thanksgiving; go into his courts with praise;* give thanks to
him and call upon his Name.
For the Lord is good; his mercy is everlasting;* and his faithfulness endures from
age to age.

Psalm 100

The Gloria

The Small Verse

Into your hands, O Lord, I commend my spirit; for you have redeemed me, O
Lord, O God of truth. Keep me, O Lord, as the apple of your eye; hide me
under the shadow of your wings. †

The Lord's Prayer

The Petition

Keep watch, dear Lord, with those who work, or watch, or weep this night, and
give your angels charge over those who sleep. Tend the sick, Lord Christ; give
rest to the weary, bless the dying, soothe the suffering, pity the afflicted, shield
the joyous; and all for your love's sake. *Amen.* †

The Final Thanksgiving

Lord, you now have set your servant free to go in peace as you have promised; for these eyes of mine have seen the Savior, whom you have prepared for all the world to see: a Light to enlighten the nations, and the glory of your people Israel. Glory to the Father, and to the Son, and to the Holy Spirit: as it was in the beginning, is now, and will be for ever. *Amen.*

🙠❧🙡

Monday
The Night Office   **To Be Observed Before Retiring**

The Call to Prayer

May the Lord Almighty grant me and those I love a peaceful night and a perfect end. *Amen.* †

The Request for Presence

Our help is in the Name of the Lord; the maker of heaven and earth.

The Greeting

Almighty God, my heavenly Father: I have sinned against you, through my own fault, in thought, and word, and deed, in what I have done and in what I have left undone. For the sake of your Son our Lord Jesus Christ, forgive me all my offenses; and grant that I may serve you in newness of life, to the glory of your Name. *Amen.* †

The Reading

Beginners must realize that in order to give delight to the Lord they are starting to cultivate a garden on very barren soil, full of abominable weeds. His majesty pulls up the weeds and plants good seed. Now let us keep in mind that all of this is already done by the time a soul is determined to practice prayer and has begun to make use of it. And with the help of God we must strive like good gardeners to get these plants to grow and take pains to water them so that they don't wither but come to provide refreshment for this Lord of ours.

St. Teresa of Avila

The Gloria

The Psalm   *I Call Upon the Name of the* LORD

I love the LORD, because he has heard the voice of my supplication,* because he has inclined his ear to me whenever I called upon him.

The cords of death entangled me; the grip of the grave took hold of me;* I came to grief and sorrow.

Then I called upon the Name of the LORD:* "O LORD, I pray you, save my life."

Gracious is the LORD and righteous;* our God is full of compassion.

The LORD watches over the innocent;* I was brought very low, and he helped me.

Turn again to your rest, O my soul,* for the LORD has treated you well.

For you have rescued my life from death,* my eyes from tears, and my feet from stumbling.

I will walk in the presence of the LORD* in the land of the living.

I believed, even when I said, "I have been brought very low."* In my distress I said, "No one can be trusted."

How shall I repay the LORD* for all the good things he has done for me?

I will lift up the cup of salvation* and call upon the Name of the LORD.

I will fulfill my vows to the LORD* in the presence of all his people.

Psalm 116:1–2

The Gloria

The Small Verse

Into your hands, O Lord, I commend my spirit; For you have redeemed me, O Lord, O God of truth. Keep me, O Lord, as the apple of your eye; Hide me under the shadow of your wings. †

The Lord's Prayer

The Petition

Keep watch, dear Lord, with those who work, or watch, or weep this night, and give your angels charge over those who sleep. Tend the sick, Lord Christ; give rest to the weary, bless the dying, soothe the suffering, pity the afflicted, shield the joyous; and all for your love's sake. *Amen.* †

The Final Thanksgiving

Lord, you now have set your servant free to go in peace as you have promised; for these eyes of mine have seen the Savior, whom you have prepared for all the world to see: a Light to enlighten the nations, and the glory of your people Israel. Glory to the Father, and to the Son, and to the Holy Spirit: as it was in the beginning, is now, and will be for ever. *Amen.*

Tuesday
The Night Office   **To Be Observed Before Retiring**

The Call to Prayer

May the Lord Almighty grant me and those I love a peaceful night and a perfect end. *Amen.* †

The Request for Presence

Our help is in the Name of the Lord; the maker of heaven and earth.

The Greeting

Almighty God, my heavenly Father: I have sinned against you, through my own
fault, in thought, and word, and deed, in what I have done and in what I have
left undone. For the sake of your Son our Lord Jesus Christ, forgive me all my
offenses; and grant that I may serve you in newness of life, to the glory of your
Name. *Amen.* †

The Reading

I asked my God for strength,
That I might achieve . . .

I was made weak,
That I might humbly learn to obey.

I asked for health,
That I might do greater things . . .

I was given infirmity,
That I might do better things.

I asked for riches,
That I might be happy . . .

I was given poverty,
That I might be wise.

I asked for power,
That I might have the praise of men . . .

Unspoken Prayers

I was given weakness,
That I might feel the need of God.

I asked for all things,
That I might enjoy life . . .

I was given life,
That I might enjoy all things.

I got nothing that I asked for,
But every thing I had hoped for.

Almost despite myself,
My unspoken prayers were answered.

I am among all men, most richly blessed!
Anonymous

The Gloria

The Psalm   *The LORD Will Save Those Whose Spirits Are Crushed*

Fear the LORD, you that are his saints,* for those who fear him lack nothing.
The young lions lack and suffer hunger,* but those who seek the LORD lack
nothing that is good.
Come, children, and listen to me;* I will teach you the fear of the LORD.
Who among you loves life* and desires long life to enjoy prosperity?
Keep your tongue from evil-speaking* and your lips from lying words.
Turn from evil and do good;* seek peace and pursue it.
The eyes of the LORD are upon the righteous,* and his ears are open to their cry.
The face of the LORD is against those who do evil,* to root out the remembrance of
them from the earth.
The righteous cry, and the LORD hears them* and delivers them from all their
troubles.
The LORD is near to the brokenhearted* and will save those whose spirits are
crushed.
Many are the troubles of the righteous,* but the LORD will deliver him out of
them all.

Psalm 34:9–19

The Gloria

The Small Verse

Into your hands, O Lord, I commend my spirit; For you have redeemed me, O
Lord, O God of truth. Keep me, O Lord, as the apple of your eye; Hide me
under the shadow of your wings. †

The Lord's Prayer

The Petition

Keep watch, dear Lord, with those who work, or watch, or weep this night, and
give your angels charge over those who sleep. Tend the sick, Lord Christ; give
rest to the weary, bless the dying, soothe the suffering, pity the afflicted, shield
the joyous; and all for your love's sake. *Amen.* †

The Final Thanksgiving

Lord, you now have set your servant free to go in peace as you have promised; for
these eyes of mine have seen the Savior, whom you have prepared for all the
world to see: a Light to enlighten the nations, and the glory of your people
Israel. Glory to the Father, and to the Son, and to the Holy Spirit: as it was in the
beginning, is now, and will be for ever. *Amen.*

Wednesday
The Night Office   To Be Observed Before Retiring

The Call to Prayer

May the Lord Almighty grant me and those I love a peaceful night and a perfect
end. *Amen.* †

The Request for Presence

Our help is in the Name of the Lord; the maker of heaven and earth.

The Greeting

Almighty God, my heavenly Father: I have sinned against you, through my own
fault, in thought, and word, and deed, in what I have done and in what I have
left undone. For the sake of your Son our Lord Jesus Christ, forgive me all my
offenses; and grant that I may serve you in newness of life, to the glory of your
Name. *Amen.* †

The Reading

There is no matter of life in the world more sweet or more delicious than continual
conversation with God. They alone can understand it who practice it and savor
it. I do not advise you, however, to practice it for this motive. The desire for

spiritual consolation must not be our purpose in carrying on this practice. Instead, let us do it out of love for God and because it is His will.

Brother Lawrence

The Gloria

The Psalm   *Exalted Is the Name of the Lord*

O Lord our Governor,* how exalted is your Name in all the world!

Out of the mouths of infants and children* your majesty is praised above the heavens.

You have set up a stronghold against your adversaries,* to quell the enemy and the avenger.

When I consider your heavens, the work of your fingers,* the moon and the stars you have set in their courses,

What is man that you should be mindful of him?* the son of man that you should seek him out?

You have made him but little lower than the angels;* you adorn him with glory and honor;

You give him mastery over the works of your hands;* you put all things under his feet:

All sheep and oxen,* even the wild beasts of the field,

The birds of the air, the fish of the sea,* and whatsoever walks in the paths of the sea.

O Lord our Governor,* how exalted is your Name in all the world!

Psalm 8

The Gloria

The Small Verse

Into your hands, O Lord, I commend my spirit; For you have redeemed me, O Lord, O God of truth. Keep me, O Lord, as the apple of your eye; Hide me under the shadow of your wings. †

The Lord's Prayer

The Petition

Keep watch, dear Lord, with those who work, or watch, or weep this night, and give your angels charge over those who sleep. Tend the sick, Lord Christ; give rest to the weary, bless the dying, soothe the suffering, pity the afflicted, shield the joyous; and all for your love's sake. *Amen.* †

The Final Thanksgiving

Lord, you now have set your servant free to go in peace as you have promised; for these eyes of mine have seen the Savior, whom you have prepared for all the world to see: a Light to enlighten the nations, and the glory of your people Israel. Glory to the Father, and to the Son, and to the Holy Spirit: as it was in the beginning, is now, and will be for ever. *Amen.*

~❧~

Thursday
The Night Office   To Be Observed Before Retiring

The Call to Prayer
May the Lord Almighty grant me and those I love a peaceful night and a perfect
   end. *Amen.* †

The Request for Presence
Our help is in the Name of the Lord; the maker of heaven and earth.

The Greeting
Almighty God, my heavenly Father: I have sinned against you, through my own
   fault, in thought, and word, and deed, in what I have done and in what I have
   left undone. For the sake of your Son our Lord Jesus Christ, forgive me all my
   offenses; and grant that I may serve you in newness of life, to the glory of your
   Name. *Amen.* †

The Reading   *Brigid's Feast*
I should like a lake of finest ale
For the King of kings.
I should like a table of the choicest food
For the family of heaven.
Let the ale be made from the fruits of faith.
And the food be forgiving love.

I should welcome the poor at my feast,
For they are God's children.
I should welcome the sick at my feast,
For they are God's joy.
Let the poor sit with Jesus at the highest place,
And the sick dance with the angels.

God bless the poor,
God bless the sick,
And bless our human race.

God bless our food,
God bless our drink,
All homes, O God, embrace.
                         from CELTIC PRAYER

The Gloria

The Psalm   *Come and Listen, All You Who Fear the* Lord

I will enter your house with burnt-offerings and will pay you my vows,* which I
    promised with my lips and spoke with my mouth when I was in trouble.
I will offer you sacrifices of fat beasts with the smoke of rams;* I will give you oxen
    and goats.
Come and listen, all you who fear God,* and I will tell you what he has done
    for me.
I called out to him with my mouth,* and his praise was on my tongue.
If I had found evil in my heart,* the Lord would not have heard me;
But in truth God has heard me;* he has attended to the voice of my prayer.
Blessed be God, who has not rejected my prayer,* nor withheld his love from me.

Psalm 66:12–18

The Gloria

The Small Verse

Into your hands, O Lord, I commend my spirit; For you have redeemed me, O
    Lord, O God of truth. Keep me, O Lord, as the apple of your eye; Hide me
    under the shadow of your wings. †

The Lord's Prayer

The Petition

Keep watch, dear Lord, with those who work, or watch, or weep this night, and
    give your angels charge over those who sleep. Tend the sick, Lord Christ; give
    rest to the weary, bless the dying, soothe the suffering, pity the afflicted, shield
    the joyous; and all for your love's sake. *Amen.* †

The Final Thanksgiving

Lord, you now have set your servant free to go in peace as you have promised; for
    these eyes of mine have seen the Savior, whom you have prepared for all the
    world to see: a Light to enlighten the nations, and the glory of your people
    Israel. Glory to the Father, and to the Son, and to the Holy Spirit: as it was in the
    beginning, is now, and will be for ever. *Amen.*

Friday
The Night Office   **To Be Observed Before Retiring**

The Call to Prayer

May the Lord Almighty grant me and those I love a peaceful night and a perfect
    end. *Amen.* †

The Request for Presence
Our help is in the Name of the Lord; the maker of heaven and earth.

The Greeting
Almighty God, my heavenly Father: I have sinned against you, through my own
fault, in thought, and word, and deed, in what I have done and in what I have
left undone. For the sake of your Son our Lord Jesus Christ, forgive me all my
offenses; and grant that I may serve you in newness of life, to the glory of your
Name. *Amen.* †

A Reading   *Litany of Penitence*
Most holy and merciful Father:
I confess to you and to the whole communion of saints
in heaven and on earth,
that I have sinned by my own fault
in thought, word, and deed;
by what I have done, and by what I have left undone.

I have not loved you with my whole heart, and mind, and strength. I have not
    loved my neighbors
as myself. I have not forgiven others, as I have been forgiven.
Have mercy on me, Lord.

I have been deaf to your call to serve, as Christ served us. I have not been true to
    the mind of
Christ. I have grieved your Holy Spirit.
Have mercy on me, Lord.

I confess to you, Lord, all my past unfaithfulness: the pride, hypocrisy, and impa-
    tience of my life.
I confess to you, Lord.

My self-indulgent appetites and ways, and my exploitation of other people,
I confess to you, Lord.

My anger at my own frustration, and my envy of those more fortunate than I,
I confess to you, Lord.

My intemperate love of worldly goods and comforts, and my dishonesty in daily
    life and work,
I confess to you, Lord.

My negligence in prayer and worship, and my failure to commend the faith that is
    in me,
I confess to you, Lord.

Accept my repentance, Lord, for the wrongs I have done: for my blindness to
    human need and
suffering, and my indifference to injustice and cruelty,
Accept my repentance, Lord.

For all false judgments, for uncharitable thoughts toward my neighbors, and for
my prejudice and
contempt toward those who differ from me,
Accept my repentance, Lord.

For my waste and pollution of your creation, and my lack of concern for those
who come after us,
Accept my repentance, Lord.
Restore me, good Lord, and let your anger depart from me,
Favorably hear me for your mercy is great.

Accomplish in me and all of your church the work of your salvation,
That I may show forth your glory in the world.

By the cross and passion of your Son our Lord,
Bring me with all your saints to the joy of his resurrection. †

The Gloria

The Psalm   *Whoever Does These Things Shall Never Be Overthrown*
Lord, who may dwell in your tabernacle?* who may abide upon your holy hill?
Whoever leads a blameless life and does what is right,* who speaks the truth from
his heart.
There is no guile upon his tongue; he does no evil to his friend;* he does not heap
contempt upon his neighbor.
In his sight the wicked is rejected,* but he honors those who fear the Lord.
He has sworn to do no wrong* and does not take back his word.
He does not give his money in hope of gain,* nor does he take a bribe against the
innocent.
Whoever does these things* shall never be overthrown.

Psalm 15

The Gloria

The Small Verse
Into your hands, O Lord, I commend my spirit; for you have redeemed me, O
Lord, O God of truth. Keep me, O Lord, as the apple of your eye; hide me
under the shadow of your wings. †

The Lord's Prayer

The Petition
Keep watch, dear Lord, with those who work, or watch, or weep this night, and
give your angels charge over those who sleep. Tend the sick, Lord Christ; give
rest to the weary, bless the dying, soothe the suffering, pity the afflicted, shield
the joyous; and all for your love's sake. *Amen.* †

The Final Thanksgiving
Lord, you now have set your servant free to go in peace as you have promised; for
these eyes of mine have seen the Savior, whom you have prepared for all the

world to see: a Light to enlighten the nations, and the glory of your people Israel. Glory to the Father, and to the Son, and to the Holy Spirit: as it was in the beginning, is now, and will be for ever. *Amen.*

∂❊ᕱ

Saturday
The Night Office   **To Be Observed Before Retiring**

The Call to Prayer
May the Lord Almighty grant me and those I love a peaceful night and a perfect
   end. *Amen.* †

The Request for Presence
Our help is in the Name of the Lord; the maker of heaven and earth.

The Greeting
Almighty God, my heavenly Father: I have sinned against you, through my own
   fault, in thought, and word, and deed, in what I have done and in what I have
   left undone. For the sake of your Son our Lord Jesus Christ, forgive me all my
   offenses; and grant that I may serve you in newness of life, to the glory of your
   Name. *Amen.* †

The Reading   *Hail to the Mother of God*
Hail to the Mother of God,
Hail to the Spouse of God Almighty,
Hail to the Flower of Grace Divine!
Hail to the heir of David's line!
Hail to the world's greatest heroine!
Hail to the Virgin pre-elect!
Hail to the Work without defect
Of the Supernal Architect!
Hail to the Maid ordained of old,
Deep in eternities untold,
Ere the blue waves of ocean unrolled!
Ere the perennial founts had sprung,
Ere in either globe was hung,
Ere the morning stars had sung.
Welcome the beatific morn
When the Mother of Life was born—
Only hope of ecstatic mirth
Danced along through Heaven and Earth
At the tidings of Mary's birth!

Happy, happy the angel band
Chosen by Mary's side to stand,
As her defense on either hand!
Safe beneath our viewless wings,
Mother elect of the King of kings,
Fear no harm from hurtful things.
What though Eden vanished be,
More than Eden we find in thee!
Thou our joy and jubilee!

Edward Caswell

The Gloria

The Psalm   *Zion Rejoices and the Cities of Judah Are Glad*

Zion hears and is glad, and the cities of Judah rejoice,* because of your judgments, O LORD.

For you are the LORD, most high over all the earth;* you are exalted far above all gods.

The LORD loves those who hate evil;* he preserves the lives of his saints and delivers them from the hand of the wicked.

Light has sprung up for the righteous,* and joyful gladness for those who are truehearted.

Psalm 97:8–12

The Gloria

The Small Verse

Into your hands, O Lord, I commend my spirit; For you have redeemed me, O Lord, O God of truth. Keep me, O Lord, as the apple of your eye; Hide me under the shadow of your wings. †

The Lord's Prayer

The Petition

Keep watch, dear Lord, with those who work, or watch, or weep this night, and give your angels charge over those who sleep. Tend the sick, Lord Christ; give rest to the weary, bless the dying, soothe the suffering, pity the afflicted, shield the joyous; and all for your love's sake. *Amen.* †

The Final Thanksgiving

Lord, you now have set your servant free to go in peace as you have promised; for these eyes of mine have seen the Savior, whom you have prepared for all the world to see: a Light to enlighten the nations, and the glory of your people Israel. Glory to the Father, and to the Son, and to the Holy Spirit: as it was in the beginning, is now, and will be for ever. *Amen.*

Index of Authors

Acknowledgments

"Brigid's Feast" from *Celtic Prayers* by Robert Van De Weyer. Copyright 1997 by Hunt and Thorpe. Used by permission.

"For We Are the Rind and the Leaf" from *Rilke's Book of Hours: Love Poems to God* by Ranier Maria Rilke, translated by Anita Barrows and Joanna Macy, Translation copyright © 1996 by Anita Barrows and Joanna Macy. Used by permission of Putnam Berkley, a division of Penguin Putnam, Inc.

"God, You Have Prepared in Peace the Path" from *An African Prayer Book* by Desmond Tutu. Copyright 1997 by Doubleday. Used by permission.

"Help Each One of Us, Gracious Father" Prayer from China, from *Another Day: Prayers of the Human Family* compiled by John Carden. Copyright 1986 by Church Missionary Society.

"How Majestic Is Your Name" from *Awake My Heart* by Fred Bassett. Copyright 1998 by Paraclete Press. Used by permission.

"I Would Not Live Forever" from *Awake My Heart* by Fred Bassett. Copyright 1998 by Paraclete Press. Used by permission.

"Morning Prayer" from *Celtic Prayers* by Robert Van De Weyer. Copyright 1997 by Hunt and Thorpe. Used by permission.

Excerpts from *A Short Breviary* edited by The Monks of St. John's Abbey. Copyright 1949 by St. John's Abbey. Used by permission of The Liturgical Press.

All verses, other than Psalms, are excerpted from *The New Jerusalem Bible* unless otherwise noted.

All verses from Psalms are excerpted from *The Book of Common Prayer* unless otherwise noted.

KJV refers to verses excerpted from the King James Version of the Bible.